CARING FOR CHILDREN
Revised

A
BENNETT
CAREER
BOOK

CARING FOR CHILDREN
Revised

By Mary Wanda Draper and Henry E. Draper

ABOUT THE AUTHORS: Mary Wanda Draper is an associate professor in the Department of Psychiatry and Behavioral Sciences, University of Oklahoma Health Sciences Center, College of Medicine. She has worked extensively in the field of early childhood development and parent education. Formerly the founder and director of the Oklahoma Child and Family Institute in Oklahoma City, she has been instrumental in the development of several parenting and child development projects in the state. She taught junior and senior high school prior to entering academic and administrative posts at the University of Wisconsin-Stout in Menomonie, Wisconsin, and Central State University in Edmond, Oklahoma. She served as a child development consultant for the Oklahoma State Department of Health. Her doctorate was earned at Texas Woman's University with post doctoral study at Harvard University. She often lectures to student, parent, and professional groups, appears on television, and serves as a consultant to early childhood, kindergarten, day care, and Head Start programs. She has authored numerous articles and is coauthor of other Bennett books, STEPS IN CLOTHING SKILLS and STUDYING CHILDREN.

Henry E. Draper is Director of child development programs in the Oklahoma State Department of Health and former director of the Institute of Child Development and professor of child development at the University of Oklahoma. He has held academic and administrative positions at the University of Wisconsin-Stout, Menomonie; University of Missouri, Columbia; Texas Technological University, Lubbock; and Brigham Young University, Provo, Utah. He continues to serve as a consultant to Head Start and early childhood programs across the U.S. He holds a bachelor's degree from Brigham Young University with a master's and doctorate from Oregon State University, a graduate fellowship at Merrill-Palmer Institute, and post doctoral study at Harvard University. Dr. Draper has directed a number of research studies and is currently working on a series of textbooks in early childhood development and parenting.

CHAS. A. BENNETT CO., INC., Peoria, Illinois 61614

Copyright 1979, 1975

**By Mary Wanda Draper
and Henry E. Draper**

All rights reserved

80 81 82 83 VH 5 4 3 2

*Library of Congress Catalog No. 78-52494
Printed in the United States of America*

ISBN 87002-281-4

The following copyright pertains to material on pages 57–60.

© **Meredith Corporation, 1969.**

All rights reserved

PREFACE

The demand for child care facilities is an ever-growing one. Each day more and more children are placed in the care of people outside the home. Naturally, we all want the best for these children. After all, children are the world's greatest resource. The future depends on them. What better reason could there be for devoting yourself to making life better for children?

This is why CARING FOR CHILDREN is important. Here is a book that will help you understand children and interact with them in a meaningful way. If you are thinking about a career in the child care field, this book has been written just for you. Each chapter is designed to help you develop the competencies needed for work with children.

What if you aren't planning a career in child care? Such a question need only be answered by another question. How many of us go through life without contacting children? CARING FOR CHILDREN is of use to almost everyone. It will help all people who spend time with children, whether baby-sitters, relatives, parents, or friends. Doesn't that include you?

In order to work with children successfully, you must have knowledge, skills, and a feeling of confidence. With this combination you will facilitate each child's learning and development naturally and spontaneously. Your broad goal should be to provide appropriate opportunities to develop each child's potential to the fullest extent. This is done in an environment which encourages children to explore actively, experiment, and discover the world about them. The environment should also enable children to interact with each other and with adults as happy, productive, and self-confident individuals. Experiences and activities should allow for each child's uniqueness, dignity, and worth as a person. The task is not an easy one for those who work with children, but it is a rewarding one.

As you read CARING FOR CHILDREN, keep in mind the underlying premise of the text: All children develop in a step-by-step process according to similar and predictable patterns, but each progresses at an individual rate. We must often speak and write in generalities, but when the actual child is concerned, generalities can only serve as a guide.

In this text a warm and realistic approach is taken to the tasks of caring for children. Examples of child and adult interactions and experiences are taken from actual everyday situations. For coping with and solving problems that concern children, alternatives that really work are provided.

The text itself is divided into six parts that contain a total of twenty-five chapters. Each chapter is introduced with a set of objectives. Any reader who can deal successfully with the objectives set forth will experience increased competency in working with children. At the end of all chapters except the last you will find "Chapter Highlights," to help review ideas, "Things To Do," which suggests activities that will make the chapter content more vivid, and "Thinking It Over," questions designed to provoke thought as well as recall. A list of references at the end of each chapter assists the learner in further study on specific topics of interest.

Another important feature of this text is the Appendices. The Appendices include a wealth of practical information. The reader who really wants to put CARING FOR CHILDREN into action will find many ideas. Included is information such as: an annotated bibliography of children's books, menus for children's snacks and meals, directions for making equipment and supplies, sketches of floor plans for children's activity centers, steps in securing and renewing a license to operate children's programs, an inventory of equipment and supplies needed to set up a children's program, and a list of distributors of children's equipment and supplies.

Part I (Chapters 1 and 2) of CARING FOR CHILDREN encourages the reader to think about the value of children, the quality of life, and the need for education on child rearing. Careers in child care are described.

Part II (Chapters 3-8) is about the development of children in all areas—physical, motor, intellectual, social, and emotional. The reader discovers how children learn important living skills like self-feeding.

In Part III (Chapters 9-14) the child's environment is considered. Among the important topics discussed are health, safety, food, clothing, and infant care. Emergency procedures are also described.

Behavior is the subject of Part IV (Chapters 15-17). A positive approach is taken to dealing with behavior. Many examples are provided on how to guide children to responsible behavior. The emphasis is on consistency and providing children with alternatives.

Part V (Chapters 18-20) is concerned with working in a center. The reader examines his or her own qualifications and learns how to seek a job in child care. Information is provided about the kinds of centers and their management.

Lastly, Part VI (Chapters 21-25) enables the reader to plan a children's program. Models, goals, objectives, and teaching strategies are discussed. Practical information comes in the form of many suggested activities for children. For example, the reader learns how to read or tell a story to children effectively. Chapter 25 provides many sample developmental units that could actually be used in a program.

In CARING FOR CHILDREN the authors emphasize that parents are the single most significant factor influencing the lives of young children. Therefore the text aims at assisting child care workers in supplementing, not supplanting, parents and families in the important tasks and roles of caring for children. Hopefully, this text will bring adults and children into closer and more meaningful relationships, reflecting the dignity and worth of each unique person and leading to fulfillment in daily living today and in the future.

ACKNOWLEDGMENTS

The authors are indebted to the following persons for their assistance with and contributions to the manuscript:

Catherine Matthews
Eva Lea Pearson
Sue Williams
Linda Holliman
Jill Fears
Lauranell Lasseter
Lou Wharton
Dr. Wesley Whittlesey, M.D.
Ron Wilkerson
Jane Fleisher Moss
Marge Morley
Bonnie Hire

Linda Helm
Kaye Sears
Prim Polk
Institute of Child Development
 University of Oklahoma
Oklahoma Department of Vocational
 and Technical Education
Oklahoma Child and Family
 Resource Project
Oklahoma State Department of
 Health

Special acknowledgement is given to Lenorah Polk for assisting with the development of the manuscript and appendix. Appreciation is extended to Paul Van Winkle and Kay Huffman for consultation and editorial assistance and especially for the encouragement and inspiration.

DEDICATION
To those who demonstrated the greatest expression of caring by being our parents, Mary and Emil—Mae and Harry.

Cover Illustration:
Immaculate Conception Pre-School
Peoria, Illinois

Photography by Ted Downes

TABLE OF CONTENTS

PREFACE 5

ACKNOWLEDGMENTS 7

PART I. CHILDREN—A CHALLENGE FOR THOSE WHO CARE 11
    Chapter 1. Getting Involved with Children 12
    Chapter 2. The Quality of Life 25

PART II. CHILDREN LEARN AS THEY LIVE 41
    Chapter 3. Talking About Development 42
    Chapter 4. Physical and Motor Development 54
    Chapter 5. Intellectual Development 74
    Chapter 6. Socialization 94
    Chapter 7. Emotional Development 104
    Chapter 8. Developmental Tasks and Skills 114

PART III. A WHOLESOME ENVIRONMENT 149
    Chapter 9. Promoting Children's Health 150
    Chapter 10. Insuring Safety 170
    Chapter 11. Handling Emergencies 194
    Chapter 12. Food For Children 206
    Chapter 13. Children's Clothing 220
    Chapter 14. Special Care for Infants 230

PART IV. GUIDING CHILDREN'S BEHAVIOR 249
    Chapter 15. Learning about Behavior 250
    Chapter 16. Promoting Responsible Behavior 266
    Chapter 17. Discipline 280

PART V. WORKING IN CHILDREN'S CENTERS 301
    Chapter 18. You and the Child Care Profession 302
    Chapter 19. Centers For Children 324
    Chapter 20. Managing Center Operations 336

PART VI. PLANNING A CHILDREN'S PROGRAM 367
    Chapter 21. Program Models 368
    Chapter 22. Goals and Objectives 384
    Chapter 23. Teaching and Learning Strategies 392
    Chapter 24. Activities for Children 416
    Chapter 25. Developmental Units 440

Contents

APPENDICES

Appendix A.	Meal Planning and Food Services	483
Appendix B.	Schedules and Routines for Children's Activities	493
Appendix C.	Sample Room Arrangements for Children's Activities	496
Appendix D.	Suggested Equipment, Materials, and Supplies for a Children's Program	500
Appendix E.	Suggested Resources for Equipment, Materials, and Supplies for a Children's Program	505
Appendix F.	Recipes for Art and Manipulative Supplies	507
Appendix G.	Songs, Action Rhymes, and Finger Plays	510
Appendix H.	Sample Recipes for Children's Food Experiences	516
Appendix I.	Annotated Bibliography of Books for Children	521
Appendix J.	Suggested Pamphlets for Child Care Workers and Parents	533
Appendix K.	Themes for Young Children's Activities and Samples of Ways to Develop Them	535
Appendix L.	Steps for Licensing	539
Appendix M.	Sample Children's Records	543
Appendix N.	Interview Sheet	552

PART I
Children—A Challenge For Those Who Care

Chapter 1.
Getting Involved with Children

Chapter 2.
The Quality of Life

Chapter 1.

Getting Involved with Children

Your Challenge

This chapter will enable you to . . . .

- Explain the importance of adequate child care.
- Tell how the needs for child care have changed over the years.
- State what career opportunities exist in the field of child care.
- Describe the kind of person who is best suited for working with children.

THE IMPORTANCE OF CHILD CARE

The value of children exceeds all other resources. Children will be tomorrow's citizens and leaders. They will operate the schools, industries, businesses, farms, and homes of the future. Children are an important part of the family. They carry on the cultural heritage and preserve societal and religious traditions for future generations. Children are essential for the continuance of families, the future of nations—and the existence of mankind.

The strongest bonds between people are often the relationships between parents and children and among the children themselves. Many families sacrifice a great deal for their children. You have heard and seen examples. A widow works long, hard hours on two different jobs to provide money to educate her son. A father gives part of his own body for a kidney transplant to save the life of his child. An older brother risks his life by entering a burning building to save his younger brothers and sisters. There is a saying, "Blood is thicker than water," meaning that family members often have commitments to each other which are greater than all other relationships.

Most parents are, by nature, proud of their children. They delight in their achievements. Have you noticed the pride shown by parents when their baby displays a big smile, the pleasure that comes with the baby's first tooth, and the excitement felt when a child takes that first step?

Wouldn't you agree that child care is an important responsibility which is best assumed by mothers, fathers, and other adults who are interested in their children and willing to devote time and effort to them? Caring for children requires affection, concern, knowledge, time, and energy. The complexity of understanding human

Ch. 1: Getting Involved with Children

Sharing time and fun brings father and son closer together.

Relationships between parents and children begin at infancy.

development leaves many parents poorly prepared to assume the role of parenthood. Many adults have little understanding of growth and development or alternative child rearing practices. Although adults often realize certain child rearing methods are not effective, they continue to use them for lack of better knowledge. For example, it is not appropriate to beat and abuse children or threaten them with cruel forms of punishment to achieve a change in the child's behavior. Some adults, however, continue to use these and other methods learned from their parents, which were in turn learned from the generation of parents before them under circumstances different from ours.

In nearly every culture, child care has been the responsibility of the mother. In some societies women are still expected to work in fields, herd flocks, or perform tasks away from the home, while child care is left to older women—or children. Nevertheless, the ultimate responsibility for the welfare of the child generally rests with the mother.

In our culture, society has assumed a greater role in the rearing of children through compulsory education. Even so, isn't it ironic that the first five or six years of a child's life, when the greatest acceleration of growth and learning occurs and when much of the child's personality is formed, is also the time when children receive informal and often unplanned guidance from adults?

Who can question how important it is for adults to understand child care when "well-meaning" parents feed children soda pop, doughnuts, and potato chips as a major portion of the diet? How can education for parenthood be ignored when "overly concerned" parents think rearing children is like training an animal? How can the need for education in child rearing be overlooked when "conscientious" adults think the use of fear and harsh punishment is the best way to deal with children? Every year, untold millions of children are stilted in their ability to develop and function fully because of inadequate care by adults, because of child rearing

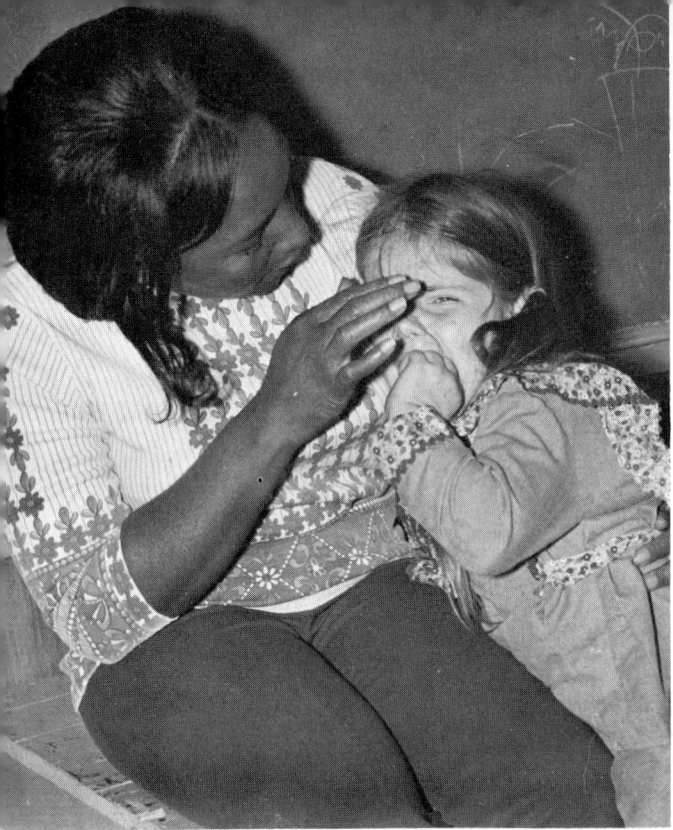

Child care requires understanding and gentle comforting in moments of stress.

ignorance, or because of personal problems which make them unable to relate to children in a wholesome way.

Unfortunately, much misery and unhappiness result from the lack of child rearing knowledge and skills. The inability of children to live happy and healthy lives is often preceded by a breakdown in their relationships with adults. Such situations not only suggest concern for the young child but also point out the need for child rearing education. With this learning, adults can provide the guidance children need for the best possible development. Perhaps an even more compelling reason for gaining a better understanding of children is to add to their enjoyment of living.

Parents who reject or abuse their children need professional help to resolve serious personal problems which may otherwise harm the mental health of their children. Parents who cannot, or will not, care for their children may be required to place them in a safer, healthier environment away from the home until the parents can be rehabilitated.

Children need to experience joy, pleasure, and support during the difficult moments of growing up. Helping children become happy, healthy individuals is a tremendous challenge for adults.

CHANGING NEEDS FOR CHILD CARE

Beginning in the seventeenth century, the industrial revolution brought about changes in the economy and affected the pattern of family life in this country. It ultimately influenced the trends in child care. As technology and industry flourished, more people were required to produce greater quantities of food, equipment, services, machinery, transportation, and materials in factories and fields away from their homes. Employment opportunities caused many families to move from rural areas to densely populated urban centers. As families became more mobile, the large, expanded family, which often included mothers, fathers, children, grandparents, uncles, aunts, and cousins, became a smaller primary unit usually consisting of a mother, a father, and their children.

Economic change included the trading of goods and services for money, which in turn was exchanged for food, clothing, and shelter. In the cities it was not practical for families to have gardens, farm animals, and orchards to supplement living requirements.

As industry and technology flourished, the demands for labor became greater and women entered the labor market. The number of working mothers with young children increased. Another contributor to the increase of working mothers was the need for manpower resulting from large-scale wars. (This was especially true during World War II when women made up a sizeable percentage of the labor pool for assembly-line jobs in shipyards, ammunition plants, and aircraft factories.) Working mothers needed care for their children on a much larger scale. Care had been provided by other members of the family, but this source was no longer adequate.

As more and more women joined the labor force, there was a greater need for suitable child care services. With women taking active roles in the working world today, the need for child care services is even greater. The Department of Labor, Bureau of Labor Statistics, reports that from 1940 to 1970 the labor force participation rate of mothers rose almost five times, from nine to forty-two percent. One-half of the mothers with children ages six to seventeen and one-third of those with children under age six were in the labor force in 1974. The Department of Labor projections for 1985 indicate that over six million mothers, ages twenty to forty-four with children under age five, will be working.

Why do mothers of young children work? In many single-parent families the mother *must* work to support the children. Widowhood, divorce, and desertion are some of the reasons. Even in families with both parents, mothers sometimes work. A mother may work because she likes to, she wants or needs extra income, it provides her with an interest outside the home, or the husband is ill or disabled and cannot work. You may also know of families in which the mother works and the father takes care of responsibilities at home. This is a reversal of the traditional roles and can

Oklahoma Child and Family Resource Program

The need for child care services and workers has expanded rapidly with the increase in working mothers.

be quite satisfactory if both husband and wife agree. Many women prefer a dual role as mother and career woman. The increase in the number of mothers pursuing professional careers in the past two decades shows this. If a mother is free to make the decision of whether or not to work, she may be influenced by the availability of a part-time or full-time job which is suitable to her training and interests and the availability of adequate child care arrangements.

Recent emphasis on family planning and population control is an attempt to balance the amount of resources and services available with the number of people who need them. Aside from the controversies surrounding family planning, contraception, abortion, and the population explosion, most people agree that every child has the right to assistance in growing, developing, and becoming a productive member of society. Even the militant revolutionist, the ardent pacifist, the rich in-

Part I: Children—A Challenge For Those Who Care

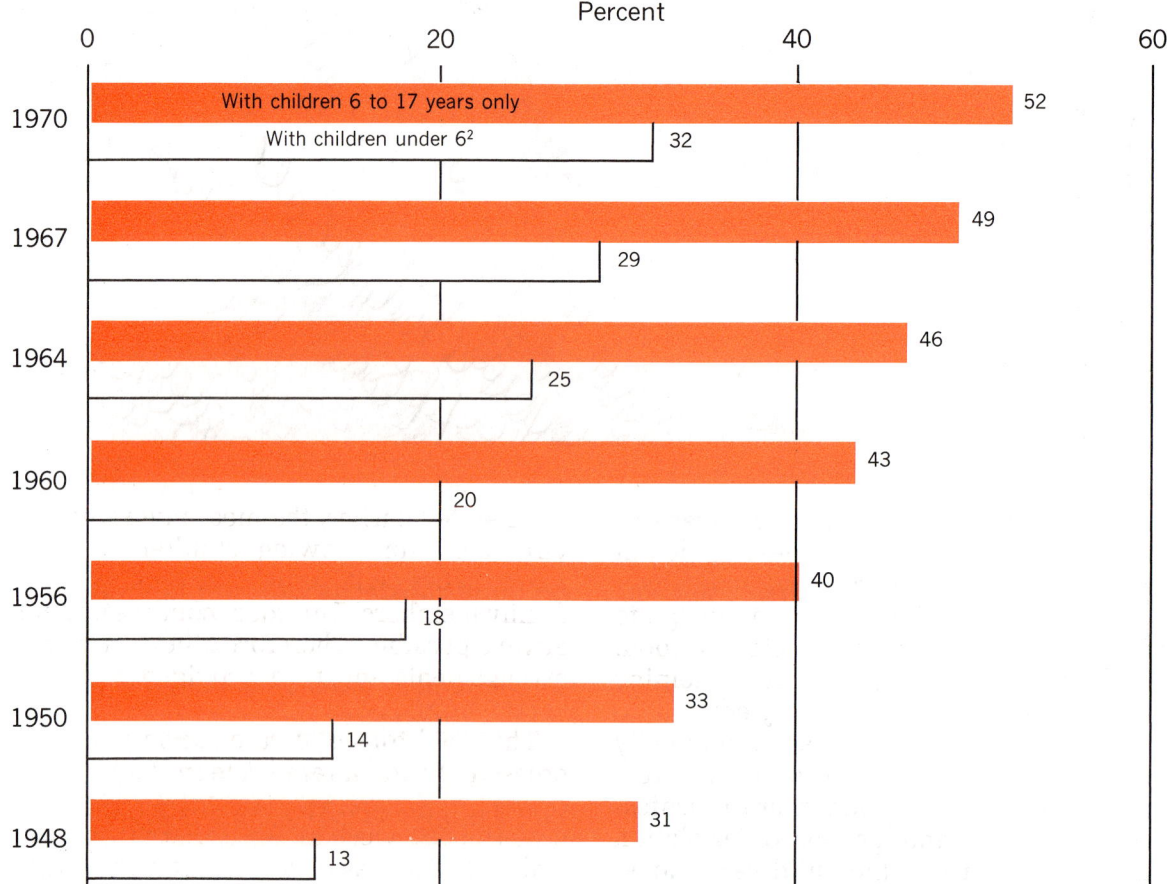

MOTHERS ARE MORE LIKELY TO WORK TODAY THAN EVER BEFORE
Labor Force Participation Rates of Mothers, by Age of Children, Selected Years, 1948–70[1]

[1] Includes women 16 years of age and over in 1967 and 1970 but 14 years and over in earlier years. Data are for March of each year, except 1948 when data are for April.
[2] May also have older children.
Source: U.S. Department of Labor, Bureau of Labor Statistics; U.S. Department of Commerce, Bureau of the Census.

dustrialist, and the low-paid wage earner support the idea that children need adequate care. Few people think children should be reared in a "helter-skelter" fashion. Without aid from adults, children cannot learn what they need to know in order to live successfully in society.

CHILD CARE SERVICES

Great emphasis on child care emerged when the federal government introduced and promoted the "war on poverty" in the 1960's. The Head Start movement was founded to help the disadvantaged child

Ch. 1: Getting Involved with Children

Oklahoma VoTech (Stillwater Head Start)
Children's programs, such as Head Start, provide meaningful activities for children while they are away from home.

and family make up for such handicaps as inadequate nutrition, poor health, dental problems, language deficiencies, lack of social stimulation, and less than adequate facilities in the home and neighborhood. Head Start made a real impact by helping the public see the need for early education, not only for children in the economically disadvantaged families but for all children.

A recent surge of public interest, professional concern, and proposed legislation indicates a thrust in the child care movement for the years ahead. Most states have already provided public kindergartens, and several states have proposed legislation for state-supported programs for children under age five. Private and parochial child care programs, as well as day care centers for young children, are becoming more numerous. Legislation has been proposed for federally supported child care as part of the welfare reform. Business and industry are assuming major roles in care by organizing child care centers for their employees.

As stated earlier, the most favorable environment for growing children is in a family setting with enlightened parents and family members. This ideal condition is not always possible. Therefore other child care arrangements must be provided to serve some young children.

The need for child care services has increased at such a rapid rate in the last few years that in many areas the demand exceeds the services available. Nonprofit social service agencies, religious organizations, commercial day care programs, and industrial day care services have attempted to fill this gap. Many children need child care services because of:

- Parents who work.
- Illness or death of one or both parents.
- Mental or physical handicaps of the mother or father.
- Emotional disturbances of the mother or father.
- Poor family relationships.
- Slum living conditions.

Part I: Children—A Challenge For Those Who Care

Oklahoma VoTech

Services to children may be found in residential areas in private dwellings which have been converted into nurseries and children's centers.

Many families seek the services of children's programs not because mothers work outside of the home, not because of poverty, and not because of crises. Their interest is simply to add enriching experiences to their children's daily living.

CAREER OPPORTUNITIES IN CHILD CARE

Qualified personnel are needed in the field of child care. The role of the child care worker, along with people in medical, educational, and social services, is equally important if we are to have a team committed to quality child care for all children. Numerous career opportunities exist for interested individuals who are willing to prepare for the responsibilities and tasks of caring for children. The job possibilities depend on training and qualifications.

Job titles vary to suit the needs and philosophy of a program. For example, some children's centers refer to teachers as *leaders* or *care givers*. Some centers make no distinction between an assistant teacher and an aide. Your greatest concern will not be the title of a position but its description and the expectations it holds for you as a potential employee.

As an individual interested in working with children, you may wish to pursue one of the following positions. Samples are listed to give you a view of the types of jobs available.

Director—Manages the overall operation of the program; gives leadership and works with teachers and other staff members to plan, implement, and evaluate children's programs; plans and initiates staff training; plans and initiates staff meetings; hires and releases personnel; coordinates center activities with community efforts; represents the center at the community level; interprets and describes the program to parents and other persons. A director may work with the children part of the time, but most of the time is usually spent on administrative duties.

Teacher—Plans and implements daily activities for children; arranges indoor and outdoor space and facilities; keeps records of children's development and progress; plans use of equipment, materials, and supplies; initiates staff meetings for personnel who work with children; assists with staff improvement; guides assistants, aides, and volunteers in working with children; assists with parent programs. A teacher works directly with the children. Some centers may require that a teacher have a college degree. Others may not.

Assistant Teacher—Helps carry out activities for the children; assists teacher with the above duties; assumes the responsibilities of the teacher when the teacher is unable to be present. The assistant works directly with the children.

Aide—Assists teacher or assistant teacher; helps with children's activities;

helps in keeping facilities ready for use with children. The aide works directly with the children most of the time.

Cook—Plans, prepares, and may serve nutritious and attractive food for children; assists teacher and assistants; aids with food experiences for children as part of daily activities; receives and stores food; maintains a clean kitchen and eating environment. The cook may work with the children part of the time.

Cook Aide—Assists cook with the above duties. The cook aide may work with the children part of the time.

There are other positions related to work with children's programs. For example, Head Start programs often use *child development specialists* as consultants for developing and improving programs and for training staff. A large industrial child care center may employ a *nutritionist* or *dietitian* to provide consultation or assistance in planning meals and snacks for children and for training cooks and cook aides. Other specialized positions may include such part- or full-time persons as *nurses, early childhood education specialists, educational coordinators, parent coordinators, parent educators,* and *social service workers.* These positions require advanced training such as a college degree.

Locations for employment include:

- Private homes.
- Child care centers.
- Family day care homes.
- Nursery schools.
- Kindergartens.
- Head Start programs.
- Child development programs.
- Hospitals for children.
- Special homes for children without families.

University of Oklahoma Institute of Child Development

Interaction with each child is an important part of the child care worker's responsibilities.

- Community, park, and recreation programs.
- After-school programs for school-age children.
- Service organizations such as VISTA and the Peace Corps.
- Public and private schools.

There is evidence of need across the country for professionally trained personnel to participate in these children's programs. A strong demand is projected for para- or pre-professionals such as aides and assistants to work as helpers with program activities, food services, transportation, social services, family visitation, custodial routines, and clerical tasks. A high school diploma is usually needed for this level of work. Some pre-professionals have post high school training.

After gaining experience as an aide or assistant, some people decide to continue

Part I: Children—A Challenge For Those Who Care

their training in a vocational school or college program. Others even go on to universities to become early childhood specialists, a position that requires a college degree. There are many opportunities.

The Office of Child Development in the U.S. Department of Health, Education, and Welfare in 1973 designated a credential called the *child development associate* (CDA). You will be hearing more about this role as you become involved in child care work. People who already work in children's programs, as well as those entering the field of early childhood, will have opportunities to qualify for the credential of a child development associate. The requirements for this credential are based on how successfully you can work with children and not necessarily on the amount of formal training you have had. The aim, as you can see, is that the child care worker be able to provide adequate and appropriate care of children by applying knowledge and skills in a meaningful way. A person interested in earning a credential as a child development associate must be able to demonstrate a level of competency which insures quality work with children.

It is really up to you to decide which area and at what levels of interest you want to become involved with children. The positions are all challenging.

The increasing public interest and the activity of business and industry in the child care field are bringing higher wages for trained, competent child care personnel. In the past, wages for work in child care have been minimal. Many states, however, are revising the licensing and certification standards for children's centers in an effort to require adequate services. This should increase the wage level for trained personnel. The aide or assistant often works for the minimum wage. Depending upon the amount of training and experience and the place of work, of course, wages will differ for each worker.

Some high school students take advantage of opportunities to work as *volunteers* in such programs as community child care programs and Head Start. This experience often qualifies them for better beginning salaries on a part- or full-time job. Volunteering for a few hours or a few days a week gives the potential child care worker the experience of involvement with children and with other child care workers. Volunteer work is an excellent way to develop confidence for becoming a full-time employee in a children's program.

Beyond formal training and experience, the child care worker can increase knowledge and skills by studying about children, observing them, and conferring with others who work with children.

IS CHILD CARE FOR YOU?

What kind of person is suited for work with children? Naturally, the first requirement is that you have a real concern—a love—for children regardless of race, religion, background, appearance, or ability. After all, you may be more of a parent to some children than anyone else is. Given this feeling for children, other necessary qualifications, like patience and a sense of humor, should come naturally.

Besides having an ability to handle children, you will also need skill in dealing with parents. Developing a friendly atmosphere between child care worker and parents, founded on mutual respect, will usually be helpful in getting the cooperation of parents. Most parents share concern for doing what is best for their children, which makes the child care worker's job somewhat simpler. Still, the worker must be

Ch. 1: Getting Involved with Children

Oklahoma VoTech
Volunteers learn about children as they work in community centers.

alert to ways of helping parents with child rearing tasks. Most parents are eager to accept suggestions if they are discussed in a pleasing yet professional manner. Remember, for some parents child care may be a sensitive area, thus the child care worker may need patience, diplomacy, and some skill in counseling.

When parents do not accept an idea for improving conditions which affect the child, generally their reluctance is not due to a lack of interest in the child or a misunderstanding, but often they are simply not convinced the suggestion is significant or accurate. One important rule for all child care workers is to help preserve the dignity and worth of all children and their families. Even if the child care worker and the parents hold different values or beliefs about children and how they should be cared for, the child and the family must be treated with respect and integrity.

Both men and women are needed in children's programs. Some children come from homes where there is no father. Some come from families without older brothers. These children benefit from having an opportunity to interact with men in their daily lives. High school boys find working with young children both challenging and rewarding. Some men have continued their studies at the college level, becoming child development specialists, and others have entered training for some area of social service.

Caring for children can be one of the most exciting and challenging jobs in the world—with never a dull moment! Most children are eager for new experiences and enjoy discovering new dimensions in the world around them. The simplest objects—a bird, a whirling fan, a shoe box, a tin can, a rock—become sources of amazement for children. By nature, chil-

More men are becoming interested in opportunities for work with young children.

dren are eager learners. They are curious, with strong desires to explore the world surrounding them. Along with happiness and enjoyment, children also bring inconveniences which require much work, time, and understanding. Young children need constant care, and not all child care tasks are easy or fun. Messiness, irritability, misbehavior, and illness are all a part of the growing up process.

Those who work with children must have an understanding of development and behavior in order to cope with special problems that arise daily. Each day the infant must be fed, provided with fresh diapers, bathed, cleaned, and continually cared for by persons who are concerned about the child's well-being. As the child becomes older, new needs arise, such as greater food variety, clothes that can be manipulated, special comfort in times of stress and strain, and tolerance while learning to become a more independent person. The child's high level of energy and eagerness for vigorous activity during the early years requires constant attention and never-ending patience. Child care can be boring and tiresome for the person who is not interested or who does not understand children, but for those who are committed to quality child care, working with children will be rewarding at every stage of development.

Nothing quite matches the challenge of caring for youngsters who are open and ready for new experiences. One man worked twelve years as a used car salesman and then turned his attention to working with children. In his own words: "It's a thrill to experience something new with a child." He studied at Syracuse University and went to work in the area of child care. Perhaps you would like to share the enthusiasm of this man. If so, caring for children may be the answer for you. The following chapters offer first steps in training for child care, as an employee and as a parent.

Ch. 1: Getting Involved with Children

Chapter Highlights

- The value of children exceeds all other resources.
- The ultimate responsibility for the welfare of the child *generally* rests with the mother in our society.
- Much misery and unhappiness for both adults and children result from a lack of child rearing knowledge and skills.
- As more and more women join the labor force, there is a greater need for suitable child care services.
- Mothers of young children work for different reasons: to support the children; as a result of widowhood, divorce, illness, or desertion; to engage in part-time work requiring the mother to be away from home only a part of the day or week; to pursue a professional career; to assume a preferred dual role as mother and career woman.
- The Head Start movement was introduced in the United States to assist the disadvantaged child and family to make up for environmental handicaps.
- Many career opportunities exist in the field of child care.
- A credential called the *child development associate* has been designated by the Office of Child Development in the United States Department of Health, Education, and Welfare to promote a competency-based qualification for child care workers.
- An important principle for all child care workers is to preserve the dignity and worth of all children and their families.
- An understanding of the development and behavior of children must be a concern of those who work with children in order to enhance development and cope with problems that arise daily.

Thinking It Over

1. What makes children such a valuable resource?
2. Explain the parents' responsibility in caring for children in our society.
3. What is meant by the saying, "Blood is thicker than water"?
4. Do you agree that many parents are poorly prepared to assume the important role of parenthood? Explain.
5. How did the industrial revolution affect family life?
6. Discuss some major reasons why mothers of young children work.
7. What was the purpose for organizing Head Start programs in the United States?
8. Why are adequate child care services needed?
9. Describe four positions a person trained in the area of child care can hold.
10. Distinguish between para- or pre-professional child care workers and child development specialists.
11. Name six child care facilities which employ child care workers.
12. What must you be able to do in order to receive the child development associate credential?
13. In what specific ways can child care workers increase knowledge and skills in the area of caring for children?
14. Discuss this statement: There's never a dull moment when caring for children.

Part I: Children—A Challenge For Those Who Care

Things To Do

1. In five minutes, list what mothers do for their children daily. Combine lists and discuss.
2. Make picture collages of a mother's day and of a father's day as each pertains to children.
3. Write a short story entitled "A Day in the Life of a Mom (Dad)."
4. Discuss family roles as portrayed in popular TV shows.
5. Role play a scene in which the father is returning home from work and the mother has had a very trying day with the children and vice versa. Discuss alternatives for solving this dilemma.
6. Play the record, "Saturday Morning Confusion," and discuss. List the problems portrayed in parent-child relationships.
7. Make a survey among working mothers you know concerning problems they have encountered with care of children while they work. Compile a list from surveys done by class members. Keep the list for future reference in studying about child care.
8. Interview a child care worker. (Use an interview sheet like the one in the Appendix.) Compare information with classmates. What do the interviews tell you?
9. Survey the community's child care services. Locate these centers on a city or community map. Are they clustered in certain areas? Are some areas in need of more centers? Are centers located in residential areas, on main traffic arteries, or in commercial centers? Does your community have any industrial day care centers?
10. Invite a group of mothers of young children to class to present a panel discussion on "Problems I've had with Baby Sitters."

Recommended Reading

Braun, Samuel J., and Edwards, Esther P. *History and Theory of Early Childhood Education.* Worthington, Ohio: Charles A. Jones Publishing Co., 1972.

Your Child From One to Six. Children's Bureau Publication No. 30-1962, Washington, D.C.: U.S. Department of Health, Education, and Welfare, 1962.

LaCross, Robert E. *Day Care for America's Children.* Public Affairs Pamphlet, #470, 381 Park Avenue South, New York, 1973.

Margolin, Edythe. *Sociocultural Elements in Early Childhood Education.* 833 Third Avenue, New York: Macmillan Publishing Co., Inc., 1974.

Neisser, Walter, and Neisser, Edith. *Making the Grade as a Dad.* Public Affairs Pamphlet, #157, 381 Park Avenue South, New York, 1971.

Parker, Ronald K. *The Preschool in Action: Exploring Early Childhood Programs.* 470 Atlantic Avenue, Boston, Massachusetts: Allyn and Bacon, Inc., 1972.

Weber, Evelyn. *Early Childhood Education: Perspectives on Change.* Worthington, Ohio: Charles A. Jones Publishing Co., 1970.

White House Conference on Children. *Report to the President: White House Conference on Children.* Washington, D.C., 1970.

Chapter 2.

The Quality of Life

Your Challenge

This chapter will enable you to . . . .

- *Define genetic counseling and identify the advantages of this service to parents.*
- *Explain how the prenatal environment, the health of parents, and the mother's age affect the quality of life.*
- *Name and describe the three stages of prenatal development.*
- *Describe how parents, brothers and sisters, family size, the family's social and economic status, and crises in the home influence the child's development.*
- *Relate the role of the center to that of the parents in caring for children.*

WHERE DOES IT BEGIN?

The quality of life begins long before birth. It begins before a child is conceived. The quality of your life was partially determined with the birth of your parents—both father and mother. Some people would trace the quality of life back several generations. The quality of egg and sperm that unite to form new life is fixed long before a child is conceived. Much of the potential for new life is decided years before that life begins.

All children are not born equal. All children do not have equal abilities even if they have equal educational and economic opportunities. Why? Because of *human biological defects*—inborn handicaps. Research reports that about one baby in every fourteen is born with a physical or neurological (dealing with the nervous system) handicap which will limit the quality

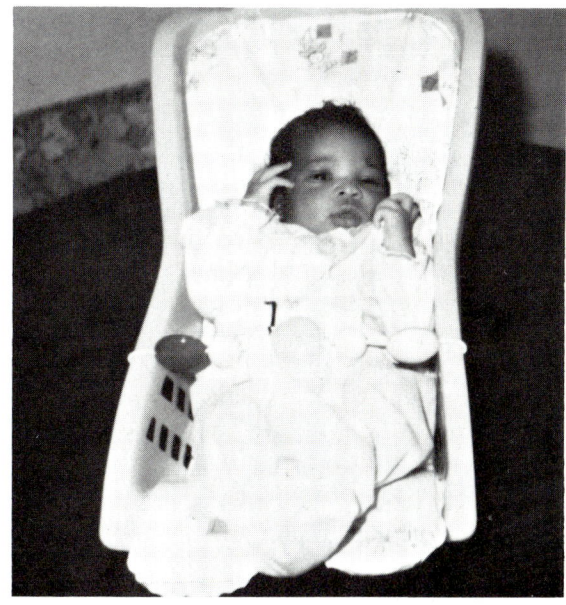

The quality of a child's life is greatly determined before birth by the health of both the mother and father.

25

Part I: Children—A Challenge For Those Who Care

of his or her life. Even with medical and educational help, these handicaps may not be completely overcome. Another ten to fifteen percent of all infants are reported to be born with hidden handicaps which may not show up until they have learning difficulties in school.

This basic problem of human biological defects serves as a stumbling block to political, medical, educational, and economic efforts toward improving the quality of life. These inborn handicaps make it difficult, and sometimes impossible, for people to overcome them even though money and schools may be provided. When a child is born with a biological handicap, efforts to overcome it or make up for it may come too late.

Handicapped children are born into families of all income levels. The challenge is this: What can be done to improve the inborn quality of human life and prevent serious handicaps even before children are born? Medical authorities estimate that if the knowledge now available about genetics (the study of heredity) and pregnancy could be used all over the world, half of all the inborn handicaps could be prevented. The task, however, is not an easy one because, as already stated, the quality of a baby's life begins with the birth of the baby's parents, if not earlier. To a great degree, young people and parents-to-be are determining the quality of life for their unborn children right now. As a youth, parent, or child care worker, you can improve the quality of life for yourself, your family, the children around you, and ultimately the generations to come.

SETTING THE STAGE FOR NEW LIFE

Even though the quality of life begins much earlier than conception, most people do not think about their contribution to a child's life until faced with parenthood. This, of course, is a time when concern is also very crucial. Parents, however, must think about the growth and development of the unborn child and prepare for it ahead of time.

Genetic Counseling

Part of the preparation for new life involves a concern for what the child will inherit from the parents. Technology and scientific research in the fields of medicine and human development have made it possible, to a certain extent, for parents to choose when a child is conceived, if they so desire. Perhaps in the future, couples will also be able to decide whether they want a boy or girl, the color of eyes and hair, the type of body build, and personality. Right now, however, parents have little control over the routine hereditary factors they pass on to their children. Still, assistance is needed to help parents recognize potential problems and ways to deal with them. Genetic counseling offers an answer.

Genetic counseling provides professional help to couples who suspect or know of possible hereditary defects that may affect their children. The science of genetics offers prospective parents some protection against having babies with inherited disorders. Almost 2,000 disorders caused by basic hereditary defects have now been identified and their patterns of inheritance determined. Already, the carriers of some genetic diseases—like sickle cell anemia, hemophilia, Tay-Sachs disease, and cystic fibrosis—can be detected by laboratory tests.

Simply knowing that a problem could occur helps parents be prepared if symptoms appear in the child. Sometimes early steps can be taken to help the child.

Ch. 2: The Quality of Life

Prenatal Influences

To improve the quality of life, we must recognize and deal with problems that interfere with a healthy pregnancy in addition to the genetic concerns. Many factors can affect the prenatal development of a child in the intrauterine (inside the uterus) environment. The problem, however, cannot be solved merely by immunizations and screening programs. Each person must understand what influences the prenatal (before birth) life of a child and assume a share of the responsibility in combating the problems that arise. Every time a child is born with a defect from causes which could have been prevented, the potential for healthy growth and development is hampered.

Are you familiar with what can affect the prenatal life of a child? If not, the following information should be of interest to you.

The Prenatal Environment

Medical counsel about pregnancy is advisable for all couples who plan to have children. A physical examination of the mother early in pregnancy is essential. The physician will recommend a proper diet, exercise, rest, and possible medical treatment needed to contribute to a healthy prenatal environment for the unborn child and to the continuing health of the mother. The size and structure of the pelvic region, the position and shape of the mother's uterus, and other physical conditions of the mother are checked by the physician. Special treatment or counsel can then be provided if necessary.

Healthy Parents

Prior to conception, the condition of both the father and the mother is important to the health of the female ovum and the male sperm. Healthy genetic material should be a concern of individuals long before they decide to marry or have children. Possible damage to an adult's genetic material can be caused by poor health habits, drugs, radiation, disease, and poor nutrition.

The quality of the parent's genetic material influences the health of the child.

After conception, the main influence upon the unborn child occurs through the mother. The condition of the mother's body, her general health, her emotional stability, her activity level, the nutritional value and amount of food she eats, and the medication she consumes are all important.

One of the greatest areas of potential for insuring the quality of life is in promoting sound nutrition. Greater progress can often be made in assuring the pregnant woman's nutritional status if the husband also understands nutrition. Through his encouragement, the mother-to-be can give greater attention to proper nutrition.

Research indicates that a woman who is malnourished may give birth to a child whose lifetime intellectual achievement and learning potential will be lower than the child of a properly nourished woman.

Part I: Children—A Challenge For Those Who Care

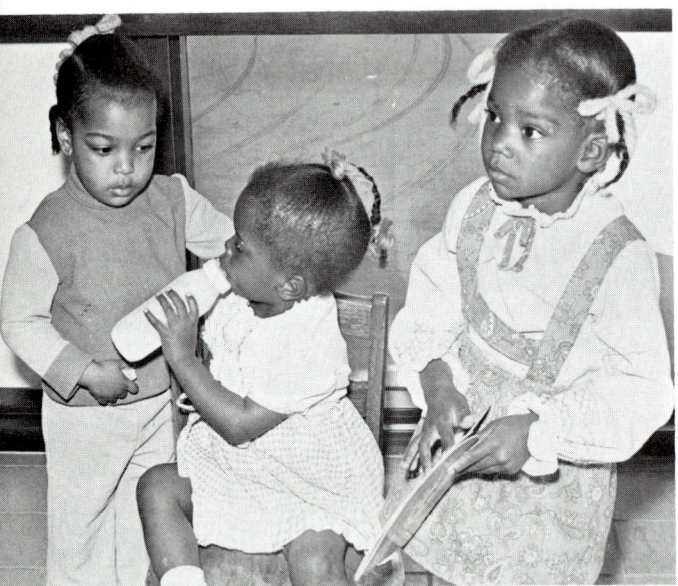

Proper nutrition and sound health during the prenatal period help insure the development of healthy and intelligent children. What signs do you see that these children are healthy?

Low birth weight is considered undesirable because brain cell growth may be less than normal. Evidence shows that what the expectant mother eats not only affects the growth of the fetus in general but also leads either to normal or inadequate brain structure. Even though the brain continues to grow rapidly after birth, the infant, if malnourished as a fetus, may remain below normal intelligence level the rest of his life. Fetal brain malnourishment cannot be reversed. If both fetal and post-natal malnourishment are severe, a forty- to fifty-percent deficit in brain cells can result. There is also evidence that when a fetus receives inadequate nutrition in the uterus, the infant is born small and future growth is often affected. The food eaten by the mother must be shared by her own body and by the fetus. Nutrients do not automatically go to the fetus first.

Infectious diseases that invade the mother's body can also affect the unborn child. Although the mother may recover in a short time, the unborn baby may develop chronic infection, malformation, blindness, or brain damage. Unfortunately, some infants die. Some of the greatest infectious hazards to the unborn infant in the uterus are those least harmful to the mother, such as German measles and toxoplasmosis.

As the unborn infant develops, cells grow and divide in order to serve different functions. This is called cell differentiation. At certain stages this process is sensitive to some substances. For instance, smoking during pregnancy or taking drugs such as alcohol may affect the unborn infant. Some drugs may damage the baby severely or even cause death.

Age

Along with health, the mother's age may have an effect on the baby. A girl under

PRENATAL DEVELOPMENT

Stage of prenatal development	Zygote	Embryonic	Fetal
Approximate age in weeks	0	2 8	40

age seventeen who becomes pregnant faces many more risks than a young woman between eighteen and the early thirties. This is because the maturing young person is developing another human being before the growth of her own body is complete. Likewise, women who are older than thirty-five are more subject to difficulties with pregnancy. For example, Down's Syndrome, also called Mongolism, is not uncommon among infants born to older women. Mongolism is the cause of approximately 12.5 percent of the mentally defective infants. Mongolism is also common in children of mothers who have had many pregnancies as well as mothers who are older.

Stages of Prenatal Development

In thinking about the quality of a new life, it helps to know a little about the prenatal development of that life. Each stage of prenatal development is crucial in the process of the child's total development. Nature has miraculously provided a developmental sequence (step-by-step process) in which each part of the organism grows and matures at the right time and in a way that contributes to the development of the next part.

The prenatal period averages about 280 days (counted from the beginning of the last menstrual period). This time period may be referred to as 10 lunar months of 28 days each or slightly over 9 calendar months. The average time from conception is 288 days. This is the amount of time required from fertilization to birth for most infants to mature and develop sufficiently for survival after birth and yet remain small enough in size to pass through the mother's birth canal for delivery. The prenatal period has been known to extend beyond the 9 calendar months to 10 or more months.

Premature birth occurs when the pregnancy does not extend over the full time period. The premature infant has not had ample time to grow and develop and may require special medical assistance for survival. If birth occurs before the thirty-sixth week, or about 250 days (based on 280 days), when the infant is not yet amply developed, a threat is posed not only to the quality of life but to survival as well. Modern technology, however, now makes it possible to save the lives of many premature infants.

Zygote Stage

Prior to conception, the male sperm, which was deposited in the female vagina during copulation, travels from the vagina through the cervix and into the uterus.* Some of the sperm move from the uterus into the lower regions of the Fallopian tubes and work their way toward the female egg, or ovum. The ripe ovum, which breaks out of one of the ovaries, falls into a Fallopian tube where it is carried by maternal fluids toward the uterus.

To survive, the egg must be fertilized and activated by a male cell on the first or second day after it arrives in the tube. When a sperm cell encounters an egg and penetrates its thin membrane, moving into its nucleus, the egg becomes fertilized. In its first stage of prenatal development, the fertilized egg is called a *zygote*. Some authorities refer to this stage as the period of the ovum.

---

*It should be noted here that as a result of scientific research, it is possible for male sperm to be deposited in the vagina by medical laboratory procedures. This can be done when a father cannot supply fertile sperm or when the mother and father have incompatible reproductive materials. The process, called *artificial insemination*, is rarely used at the present time.

Part I: Children—A Challenge For Those Who Care

Following fertilization, the remaining sperm in the vagina are killed by toxic, acid fluids contained in the vagina. The fertilized ovum continues to move down the Fallopian tube and into the uterus where it lodges against the wall, or lining, of the uterus. The uterus, through natural biological processes, has been especially prepared for nurturing the zygote. Tiny rootlike tissues which attach the zygote to the uterus wall provide for the transfer of nutrients from the mother to the zygote. This is the point at which the unborn child enters the second stage of development.

Embryonic Stage

The word *embryo,* from a Greek word meaning "to swell" or "teem within," is used to refer to the organism in the second prenatal stage. This is one of the most significant periods in the individual's development because cell specialization begins to occur. The organism starts to develop identifiable human characteristics. During the embryonic stage, the organism is not only growing by gigantic strides, but highly specialized cell differentiation is also occurring. Cells cluster and begin to form muscle, bone, organs, hair, and body parts.

Possible malformation, resulting from defective genetic material or environmental influences, often appears during the embryonic period. If the defect is serious enough, a *miscarriage* may result. This is the natural expulsion, or abortion, of the embryo. Miscarriage usually occurs during the first weeks of pregnancy and often before the pregnancy is even recognized.

Fetal Stage

Near the end of the second month after conception, the major characteristics of the prenatal organism have formed. The embryo passes into the next stage of development and is now called the *fetus,* from a Latin term meaning "young one" or "offspring." The fetal stage continues from about the eighth week until birth. During the fetal period, development is primarily a process of growth and maturation. From a small embryo about the size of a walnut, the fetus increases fifty times in size during the remaining seven months. The body, head, and limbs grow considerably, while the circulatory, respiratory, nervous, musculatory, and digestive systems undergo rapid development in preparation for the infant to function independently of the mother.

It is awesome to think about the complexity of such development. The heart, eventually about the size of a large orange pumps life-giving blood through a lengthy network of veins and arteries. The brain is more intricate than the most expensive and elaborate piece of man-made equipment. The eyes, ears, nose, and taste buds are fascinating organs which contribute to

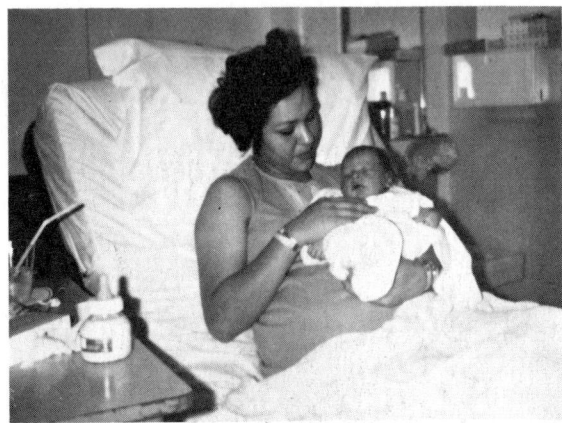

This baby is only a few days old. However, it took the tiny embryo nine months to develop into a complex human being.

a person's ability to live in a complex world. In a matter of only nine months, a fertilized ovum is capable of growing from a unit smaller than a dot into a living human being—one of the greatest wonders known to man.

THE CHILD IN THE FAMILY

After the child's birth, his environment expands considerably. At first the family unit makes up the child's world. Many believe the family setting is the most important part of a child's life in spite of trends toward radical changes in some family life patterns.

The home is a place where social experiences are sifted, evaluated, appreciated or twisted, magnified, and sometimes ignored. Home is the place to which the child returns, bringing new experiences and seeking recognition as a significant person. The home provides a stage for expressing the glory of achievement as well as a refuge for brooding over ill treatment—real or fancied. Some homes, as you know, do not provide a comfortable setting for family members. Some are scenes of continuing crises, lending to frustration and confusion.

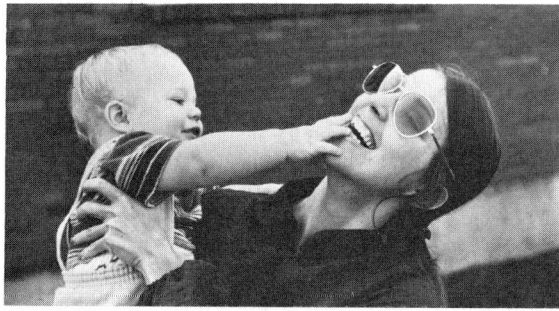
The close relationship between mother and child builds trust and security.

The home, because it is the child's first environment, establishes a foundation for attitudes toward people, things, and life in general. Children imitate patterns of behavior found in the home because they readily identify with members of their own family. Although patterns of life found in the home will change somewhat as each child matures, the early patterns will never be completely erased.

Many areas of home and family life influence the child's development. The parents, of course, are the primary influence. Brothers and sisters, family size, socioeconomic status, and crises in the home are other influences. Let's take a closer look at each of these.

Parental Influence

Numerous studies stress the impact of early home experiences upon the later development of the child. Consistent support is given to the importance of a child's relationship with parents, especially the mother, during the early years. The very closeness of mother and child during the prenatal period and immediately following birth places the mother as the most significant person in the child's early life. Even the child who spends a large portion of the day in a care center continues to respond to his mother as the single most important person he knows. The mother is usually responsible for helping the child build a sense of trust and security during the period of early infant care. She has the task of helping the child extend this trust to other family members. The quality of care a child receives from the mother during infancy has a significant effect upon the child's adjustment, behavior, and mental performance. Authorities suggest that extended periods of play between the mother and child are important because thought

Part I: Children—A Challenge For Those Who Care

The father has an important role in the care of his child.

processes, even the simplest ones, are stimulated.

Dr. Urie Bronfenbrenner, child psychologist, says the mother-child relationship should be like a ping-pong game. The mother motivates the child and the child motivates the mother. It is a back-and-forth relationship. Each supports the other.

The father's role is very important. Fathers have a definite influence in their children. Their influence can begin as early as infancy. Nowadays, when traditional roles are often abandoned, it is not uncommon for a father to adopt much or all of the role formerly reserved only for the mother. Sometimes circumstances force this situation. Other times, it is simply a matter of choice. Whatever the situation, the father is important to the child and needs to take an active part in caring for the child.

Research suggests that as children develop trust, cooperativeness, self-sufficiency, and emotional warmth through early relationships with parents, their school achievement from the first to the third grade increases. The success of children in intelligence-related tasks has also been attributed to positive, warm relationships and to success experiences at home.

Family situations can stimulate the child's natural curiosity, which contributes to cognitive (thinking) development. Parent-child communication is the beginning of the child's language development and cognitive processes. The child does not merely imitate the behavior of the parent and other family members, but learns from their behavior that which is meaningful to him. Successful early learning experiences often occur because parents are eager to supply information which is interesting to the child. The mother's and father's involvement with the child's learning and their warm interpersonal relationships provide a favorable climate for the child's progress.

Although the issue of predicting children's personality development from parental behavior remains controversial, most authorities agree that parental behavior and attitudes have a greater bearing on the child's personality formation than factors outside the home. In fact, the relationship of parents to children during early personality development is not likely to be overshadowed—even by later peer group influences.

Positive parental attitudes are founded on understanding, love, concern, and respect for each child as an individual. Children who are reared by adults who express a genuine love generally have fewer personal difficulties. They are more likely to gain a sense of security with less tension.

If parents have good feelings about their own roles, they will probably affect their children in positive ways. A mother who

Ch. 2: The Quality of Life

understands and accepts her marital role is less likely to have behavior problems with her child than the mother who is poorly prepared to cope with the daily responsibilities of marriage and parenthood. Likewise, the father who accepts the responsibilities of parenthood naturally gives more time and energy to rearing his children than one who refuses or hesitates to take a major role in parenting.

Parents who do all they can to extend positive influences on their children will see the results of their efforts. Their children develop more wholesome attitudes, self-concepts, and behavior. Although promoting a positive climate is not a simple task for parents—or child care workers—it is a worthwhile goal.

Children need guidance and discipline. *Negative* parental influences on children, however, are cause for concern. Rejection, abusive criticism, hostility, insincere care and affection, favoritism toward a sibling (brother or sister), a high or low degree of behavioral control, and a lack of emotional warmth are all negative attitudes that can be conveyed to children. A few negative incidents are not likely to harm a child. In excess, however, they can be very damaging. Negative influences can be felt by children in many ways. Children are likely to be highly emotional and experience frequent outbursts of temper when reared in homes where parents are overly harsh with their children. Parents who are dominating, possessive, inconsistent with discipline, disturbed with worry, and lacking in sense of humor add to children's difficulties.

Children from broken homes and homes in which parents are emotionally divorced may develop social problems. Repeated absence of one or both parents from the home, whether prolonged or not, may also add to the young child's difficulty in developing a positive self-image.

Even though children do not always understand the parental behavior just described, they are able to sense the psychological atmosphere of the home—whether or not all is well and how their parents feel about them and about each other. This, in itself, is enough to cause negative reactions in children. Just what are these reactions? Emotional problems, nervous habits, shyness and withdrawal, temper tantrums, abuse toward other children, stuttering, and ticks are characteristically found among children from family situations which involve consistent patterns of personal conflict.

Numerous studies have pointed out that in homes where parents—especially mothers—were not supportive and concerned, children became hostile, dependent, pessimistic, less self-confident, and more likely to fail. Children are more apt to become delinquent or develop personality problems if family relationships are seriously disturbed. Research indicates delinquency frequently stems from the children's inability to cope with life's tasks because their parents do not devote enough time to them and their developmental needs during early childhood.

Although troubled children often have maladjusted parents, it cannot be assumed that the parents are always the cause of problems. Remember that parents, even though a major influence, are still only one of many factors affecting a child's development.

The effect of the home environment on the child will depend to a certain extent upon the child himself. A child with tendencies to be insecure, nervous, or tense will more likely become upset by special attention given to a new baby than a child

Personality formation is influenced by brothers and sisters. Here a brother and sister learn about sharing.

who is secure and settled. A healthy and stable child usually reacts in positive ways to the attention and pampering received as the "baby" of the family, yet an insecure child may learn to depend on this kind of attention. This is readily seen by observing children from similar backgrounds where the parental influence is quite negative. Some of these children have a natural ability to pull through and maintain a wholesome outlook on life. Others are not so lucky. More easily affected by their environment, they develop hostilities, deep-rooted complexes, or any of the other difficulties already mentioned.

Can you see the need to provide education for parenting? Would you agree that parent education should begin during the teen years for those who are potential parents and for other adults who will care for children? Even if some do not become parents, they are better prepared to relate effectively with others. Through understanding children, adults often gain greater understanding of themselves.

Sibling Influence

The relationship between siblings (brothers and sisters) is thought by some authorities to have a great impact on children's personality formation. You have probably known a child who idolized an older brother or sister. Such feelings lead the child to imitate the older sibling and follow his example. Thus, the older brother or sister plays an important role in helping the young child form healthy or unhealthy behavior patterns and attitudes.

Not all children, of course, have older sisters or brothers. Some have younger brothers and sisters and must share in the responsibilities of caring for them. This, too, can affect a relationship, depending on the situation. Have you ever had this kind of responsibility? If so, what kind of influence were you on the child in your care?

Family Size

Family size may also influence the child. You can see that it is possible for an only child or one from a small family to develop different behavior patterns than one from a large family. A small family often emphasizes adult images and examples of adult behavior, whereas the large family often provides more sibling interaction. Either case can be supportive of the child or can detract, depending on how situations are handled.

Socioeconomic Factor

In our culture, the family's status in the community affects the child's ability to get along with others (socialization) both directly and indirectly. Directly, the family's social position and financial status determine social standards and expectations which influence the parents' methods of rearing children. Indirectly, this status will likely determine where the family lives, their level of living, and their style of life.

Even though there are often more children to play with in poor neighborhoods, this does not always compensate for the lack of quality in the child's surroundings. The physical environment of the home—size of neighborhood, condition of furnishings—sometimes has an indirect influence on the child's development. These factors may also influence parental attitudes and thus affect the child. Also, poor sanitary conditions, crowded rooms, and few furnishings may detract from the child's environment. Adequacy in these areas, however, may possibly increase the child's opportunities for development. Do you think this means that the more money a family has and the higher their social position, the better chance the children have to develop properly? Perhaps you would like to exchange ideas on this with others in the class.

Crises

No doubt all of the influences discussed so far contribute to the general atmosphere of the home. Still, there are factors which influence the home life of a child but which are beyond the control of parents, siblings, or economics. War, social disorder, occupational mobility, natural disasters, illness, accidents, and death are among these influences. Although parents or guardians cannot always prevent a serious illness or job mobility, they can do their best to make the atmosphere of the home as friction-free as possible. This wholesome climate can and does exist in many homes, even though there may be serious problems such as illness and accidents—but these parents make special efforts to foster positive development of their children in spite of the difficulties.

THE CHILD IN THE CENTER

You have read about the importance of a family setting for children. Still, many children spend a large portion of their time in child care centers. Can you now see why child care centers and young children's programs should promote parent education? Adults need to work together for the greatest benefit of the child. A center should not attempt to take the place of the parents or the family. A center should aim to cooperate with and support families in caring for children. Parents who join with center personnel as a cooperative team can provide a home environment that complements the center's goals, and centers can complement the home. It is a two-way street.

University of Oklahoma Institute of Child Development

Parents and child care workers join together to talk about child development.

Chapter Highlights

- The quality of life begins long before birth; some might trace the quality of life back several generations.
- Healthy genetic material should be a concern of individuals long before they decide to marry or have children.
- All children are not born equal; they do not have equal abilities even if they have equal educational and economic opportunities.
- The science of genetics offers prospective parents some protection against having babies with inherited disorders.
- To improve the quality of life, we must recognize and deal with problems that interfere with a healthy pregnancy in addition to the genetic concerns.
- One important way to help insure the quality of life is to promote sound nutrition.
- Each stage of prenatal development—zygote, embryonic, and fetal—is crucial to the child's total development.
- The home, because it is the child's first environment, establishes a foundation for attitudes toward people, values, and life in general.
- The quality of care a child receives from the parents, especially the mother, during infancy has a significant effect upon the child's adjustment, behavior, and mental performance.
- Mother-child communication is the beginning of the child's language development and cognitive processes.
- If parents have positive feelings about their own roles, they will probably affect their children in positive ways.
- Education for parenthood should begin during the teen years.
- Through understanding children a person often gains a greater understanding of himself.
- The relationship between siblings and the family size are thought by some authorities to have a great impact on children's personality formation.
- These factors influence the home life of a child but are beyond the control of parents, schools, or economics: war, social disorder, occupational mobility, disasters, illness, accidents, and death.
- A child care center should not attempt to take the place of the parents or the family; it should aim to cooperate with and support families in caring for children.

Ch. 2: The Quality of Life

Thinking It Over

1. Are all children born equal?
2. Have you ever heard your grandparents or other adults discuss the conditions of children born with handicaps many years ago? Compare their impressions to the situation as it is today.
3. How can genetic counseling be helpful?
4. Name four genetic diseases which can be detected in prospective parents by laboratory tests.
5. What are five possible causes of damage to a person's genetic material other than hereditary factors?
6. What are some of the influences on the prenatal growth and development of a child?
7. Explain what the following statement means to you: The quality of life begins before birth.
8. List five points of information which are gained from a physical examination and medical counsel during early pregnancy.
9. What precautionary measures can be taken by couples in preparation for pregnancy?
10. When should preparation for parenthood begin?
11. What is the relationship of a mother's diet to the size of a baby at birth and to brain cell growth of the unborn child?
12. State the major reason girls under seventeen face many more risks during pregnancy than young women between eighteen and the early thirties.
13. Name and describe the three stages of prenatal development.
14. How important is the mother's care of the young child to his or her future personality development?
15. How may the size of a family affect a child?
16. Interpret the following statement: The home establishes a foundation for attitudes toward people, things, and life in general.
17. What is the role of a child care center in the life of a family?

Things To Do

1. Have a discussion on genealogy and why it has become such an interesting hobby. If there is a genealogist in the community, this person can precede the discussion with a presentation on interesting discoveries and unusual findings of some who have researched their family trees.
2. Relate examples of children who resemble or act like a grandparent or great grandparent. Discuss why this happens.
3. Do independent study to learn about the transfer from parent to child of such traits and defects as color blindness, color of eyes, hemophilia, color of skin, sickle cell anemia, cystic fibrosis, Tay-Sachs disease, and others.
4. Invite a doctor, nurse, or other medical person to class to discuss the importance of sound health during pregnancy, including early physical examination, diet, and freedom from certain infectious diseases.

(Continued on page 38)

Part I: Children—A Challenge For Those Who Care

Things To Do Continued

5. Prepare a day's menu for a pregnant woman which meets nutritional needs within a determined budget and at a determined caloric level. Make a booklet which can be recommended for use during pregnancy, using all of the menus made by class members.

6. View a film which portrays the three stages of pregnancy. (*The Child,* Barnet, 48 min., International Film Bureau, Inc., 332 South Michigan Avenue, Chicago, Illinois 60614.)

7. Invite a pediatric nurse or nursery worker from a local hospital to discuss differences in babies at birth.

8. Invite a panel of mothers and fathers of young children to present a panel discussion on "Things I Wish I Had Known," concerning problems since the births of their children.

9. Invite a kindergarten teacher to speak to the class on individual physical differences as well as differences in intelligence, personality, and motor development of five-year-olds.

10. Prepare a bulletin board with a small child as the focal point; show the influences on the child's life.

11. Take a tour through the maternity division of a hospital. Follow with a discussion by hospital representatives.

Recommended Reading

Bernard, Harold H. *Human Development in Western Culture.* (Third Edition), Boston: Allyn and Bacon, Inc., 1970.

Briggs, Dorothy Corkille. *Your Child's Self Esteem: The Key to His Life.* New York: Doubleday and Co., Inc., 1970.

Dinkmeyer, Don C. *Child Development—The Emerging Self.* New York: Prentice-Hall, Inc., 1965.

Ehrlich, Paul R., Ehrlich, Anne H., and Holdren, John P. *Human Ecology.* San Francisco: W. H. Freeman and Co., 1973.

Hoff, John E., and Janick, Jules. *Introductions to Food.* Readings from *Scientific American.* San Francisco: W. H. Freeman and Co., 1973.

Journal of Nutrition Education. (Quarterly Journal). Berkeley, California: Society for Nutrition Education, 1973.

Mental Health Digest. National Clearinghouse for Mental Health Information, Vol. 4, No. 2, February, 1972. Washington, D.C.: Superintendent of Documents, Government Printing Office.

Neisser, Walter, and Neisser, Edith. *Making the Grade as a Dad.* Public Affairs Pamphlet, #157, 381 Park Avenue South, New York, 1971.

Nutrition Today. (Bimonthly Journal). Annapolis, Maryland: Nutrition Today, Inc., 1973.

Stanley, Julian C. (Edited by). *Preschool Program for the Disadvantaged.* Baltimore: The Johns Hopkins University Press, 1972.

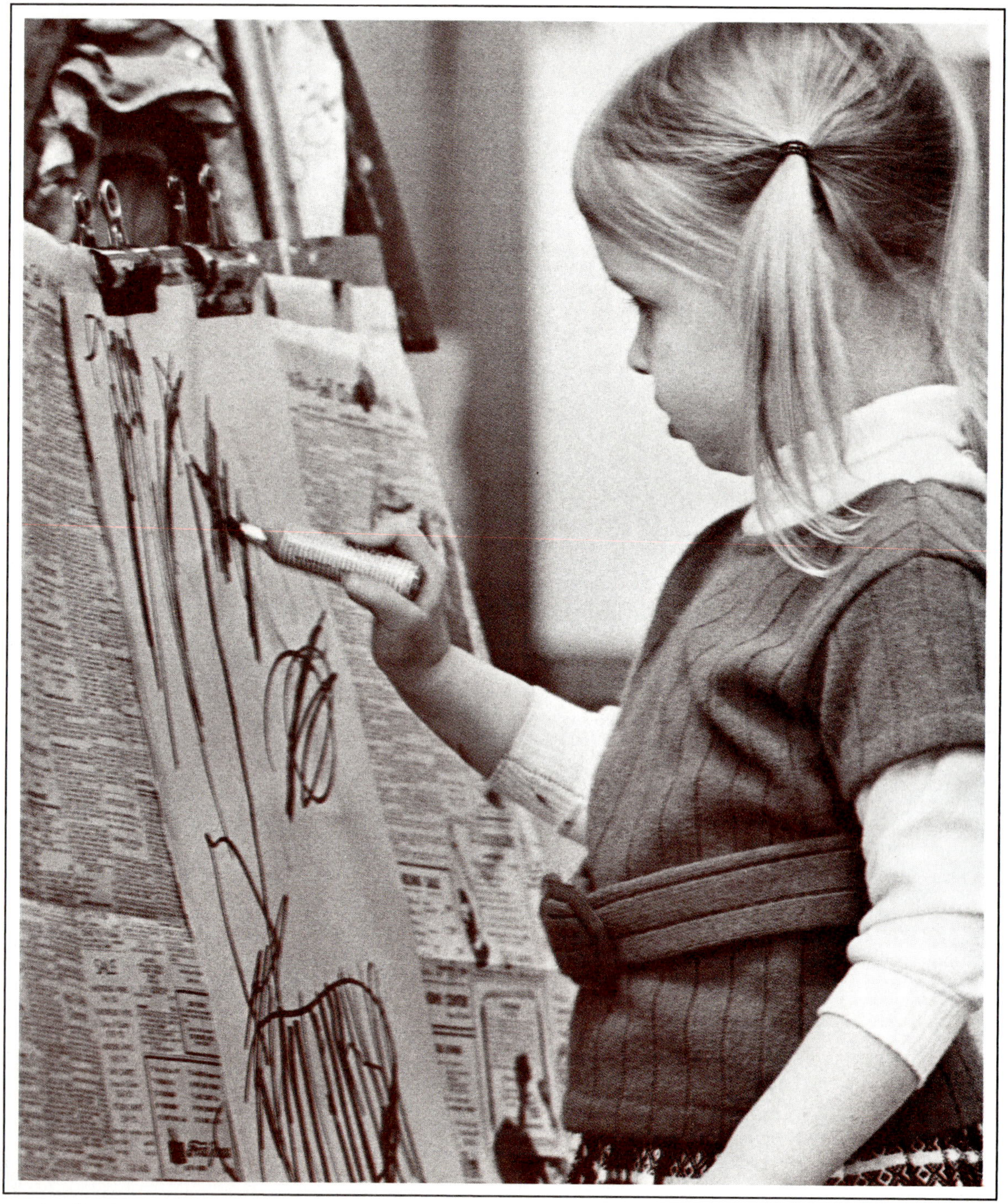

PART II
Children Learn As They Live

Chapter 3.
Talking About Development

Chapter 4.
Physical and Motor Development

Chapter 5.
Intellectual Development

Chapter 6.
Socialization

Chapter 7.
Emotional Development

Chapter 8.
Developmental Tasks and Skills

Chapter 3.

Talking About Development

Your Challenge

This chapter will enable you to . . . .

- Give reasons why some parents are not prepared to help their children develop adequately.
- Define the following terms as they relate to people: (1) development; (2) growth; (3) maturation; (4) behavior; (5) learning.
- Tell why there are similarities as well as differences in the development of children.
- Explain the meaning of this statement: There is no exact division in the stages and ages of child development.
- Identify and discuss influences on development.

YOU AND THE CHILD

The best way to prepare for parenthood or work in a children's center is to become knowledgeable about children—to learn how development takes place. You will soon discover that your understanding becomes a foundation which makes it possible to enhance the lives of children while enjoying activities with them. The conditions you establish will be stimulating, the activities you provide will promote healthy behavior, and you will be able to motivate children more effectively. As you acquire and use skills and competencies in child development, your satisfaction will increase and each child's life will be a little richer for having known you.

Certain concepts apply to each child's physical, intellectual, social, and emotional development. When you use these concepts as tools in making decisions, problems can be faced with confidence. Keep in mind that principles of development can also be applied to adults and will be especially useful when you deal with parents and other child care workers. Perhaps you will even be able to apply them to yourself. After all, wouldn't you agree that the better you understand yourself, the more effective you will be in working with children and other adults?

CHILD REARING

Many parents, even though they love their children, are not prepared to care for them in ways that provide the greatest opportunities for wholesome development. There is no single reason why this is true.

Ch. 3: Talking About Development

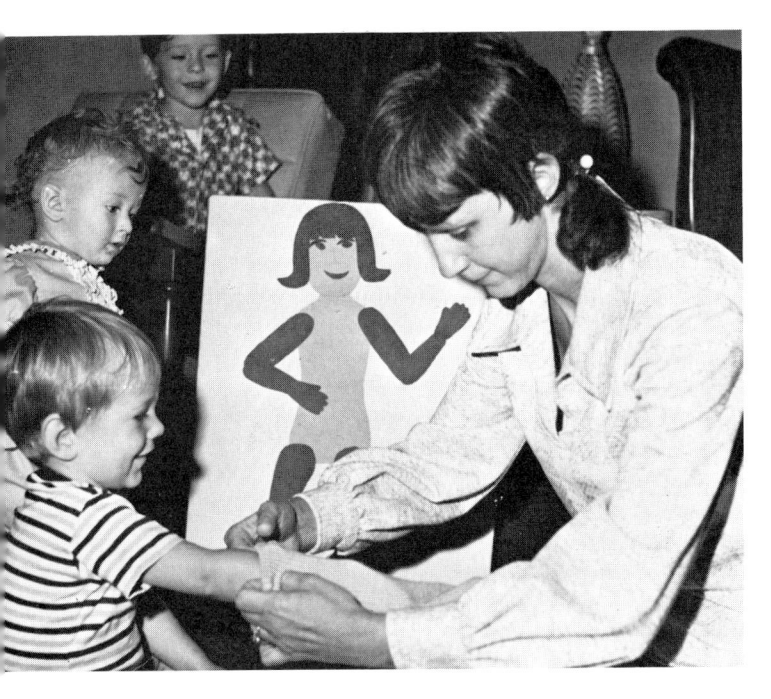

University of Oklahoma Institute of Child Development
Knowledge about child development is more meaningful for adults who plan and enjoy activities with children.

Oklahoma VoTech (Stillwater Head Start)
Adults can help children develop their minds and bodies by providing interesting experiences.

43

Part II: Children Learn As They Live

Kickapoo Head Start Center
Children need opportunities to develop their potentials while enjoying everyday experiences.

Parental attitudes, emotional problems, and lack of knowledge are probably major factors.

The *attitudes* of parents can greatly affect their children. You have probably heard expressions similar to these: "Our kids get by just fine." "What was good enough for me is good enough for my kids." "Kids grow best if you leave them alone." Although these attitudes, individually, are not likely to cause tragic consequences, not one is satisfactory either. Parents who have feelings like these about child rearing may be doing little to help their children develop. Education is needed to change those parental attitudes that do harm to children.

Far too often adults become overly *emotional* with child rearing. Unconsciously adults sometimes use children to satisfy personal motives—a desire to gain power, prestige, love, and even hostility or revenge. A continual re-examination of adult behavior will help avoid such exploitation of children. Shouting and harsh scolding, for example, seldom help children and they are often damaging to the self-concept. When working with children, personal disappointments and troubles should be put aside in order to devote one's energies and abilities to providing for wholesome child development. Adult self-control is so important when emotions, rather than good judgment, have a tendency to direct actions. Thinking before acting should be the rule.

Lack of knowledge about child rearing skills is the unfortunate situation of many adults. Conception, pregnancy, and birth require little brain power. Women with little understanding about development, maturation, growth, language, learning, and nutrition continue to have babies. Many fathers as well as mothers have little understanding of the development and behavior of children. Thus, their children are reared without parental understanding of developmental principles or the ability to make adequate parental judgments about child care. These inadequacies, however, do not justify parental ignorance.

Each child is special and deserves the highest quality of care. Even though the child rearing techniques of the past may have been "good enough" and children managed to "get by," efforts must be made to do better for the children of today. Concern must be directed at providing every child with an opportunity to develop fully, to be healthy and productive, and to experience joy in living. Ways must be found to help children achieve their fullest potentials. Understanding is the first step. Whether as a parent or child care worker, you can help.

UNDERSTANDING TERMS

To work successfully with children, you must understand the basic principles related to child care and development. Keep in mind that some of the concepts used in this text may not be used the same way in other references. This difference may be accounted for because authorities have different points of view or emphasize different aspects of development. You will, no doubt, wish to draw some conclusions of your own after your study of children.

Development

The word *development* is used as a broad term referring to any gradual physical or behavioral change in a person. This term can include a combination of such concepts as growth, maturation, learning, and behavior.

Growth

The word *growth* is used in numerous ways. You have probably heard phrases referring to how smart the child has grown—*intellectual growth;* the child growing in anger—*emotional growth;* and how the child grows older—*chronological growth.* In this text, however, the term growth means an increase in size or weight—the multiplication of cells and tissues, which causes the body to become larger and weigh more. For example, the child grew four inches and gained ten pounds last year. Other terms will be used to describe changes in the child's intellectual, social, emotional, and age levels.

Maturation

This word is often used in a broad sense and is sometimes substituted for terms like growth and development. Haven't you heard statements like these: "Leon certainly has matured in the last year. Look how much taller he is." "Jennie is more mature since she started school. She has learned to write her name and address and she gets along with other children very well." Actually, the speakers were referring to Leon's physical growth and Jennie's increase in academic and social skills, not maturation. Sometimes the term *emotional maturity* is used to describe a child like Jennie simply because she is acting her age.

Maturation is a more useful term when it is limited to a change in the *quality* of a characteristic even though a physical increase in size may not have occurred. If the tissues of the body change, such as the ossification, or hardening, of the bones, maturation is occurring; there is no reference to an increase in size or weight of the bones. If some mental process has increased in efficiency, such as the ability to distinguish between "more" and "less," even though additional knowledge has not been acquired, maturation has occurred. If children have better control over their emotions, they have attained more emotional maturity. In other words, maturation will be used here to refer to a *qualitative change*—a difference that improves the physical structure of the body; the intellectual functioning; or the ability to control emotions. Maturation will not refer to a quantitative, or amount of, change.

Behavior

The term *behavior* refers to any activity, whether a single act or response or a series. Good behavior means the child's actions are appropriate. Misbehavior, on the other hand, means the child's actions are inappropriate. Behavior is a useful term in explaining *how* children act and *what* they do.

Part II: Children Learn As They Live

Kickapoo Head Start Center
Children learn through play.

Learning

This term is often defined as a change in behavior which increases the individual's ability to deal more effectively with the environment. However, children also learn undesirable behavior. Thus, a more precise definition of learning is needed. Learning is any change in behavior. It is the attainment of knowledge, skills, and behavior patterns, whether positive or negative. A child who has learned to walk has increased ability in moving from place to place. A child who has learned to count can use simple forms of money or divide toys with playmates. A child is also learning when he gains attention by being destructive even though he decreases his ability to get along with others.

Understanding how learning takes place is important. Although today you are simply reading about learning, in the days ahead you will put your knowledge to good use. Just think, eventually you will be responsible for assisting children in the learning process. All you can do now to prepare for that responsibility will be time well spent.

Even though such concepts as development, growth, maturation, behavior, and learning may be studied separately, it is important to know how these concepts are interrelated. Understanding each concept helps you understand the developmental process and will expand your ability to work with children. This knowledge will help you determine more accurately the child's developmental level during each stage of life.

SIMILARITIES IN DEVELOPMENT

The similarities among people are numerous. Just as each person requires air, food, and water in order to survive, each requires nurture and security for normal development. People experience common patterns of development in the same sequence and at approximately the same stages. Although the rate of development may vary among individuals, the similarity of the sequence and the pattern makes it possible to anticipate approximately when certain developmental characteristics will occur. These predictable periods enable adults to plan activities which are appropriate for the developmental level of each child. For example, predictable developmental tasks exist for such areas as motor coordination, emotional behavior, social interaction, language acquisition, and concept formation.

Normal growth proceeds in a similar fashion for all persons regardless of sex, race, or ethnic group. Many similarities in development are shared in spite of irregularities resulting from birth, accidents, diseases, or environmental circumstances. As you work with children and as you study this text, you will become familiar with many common elements of child development.

INDIVIDUAL DIFFERENCES

Development is usually studied and discussed in general terms. Not all children, however, follow the general pattern of development. You must be alert to individual differences. For instance, it is helpful to know that all children do not like the same foods. In spite of the nutritional value of milk, some children may be allergic to it and become ill if forced to drink it. Some children like to be snuggled and cuddled, yet others feel smothered by this. Some children have accelerated motor development and show good rhythmic abilities; others at the same age are clumsy and poorly coordinated.

From the time children are born, there are observable differences in their general physical features. No two individuals are exactly alike, not even identical twins. Not only do infants have different features of the face, hair, and skin, but they are also unlike in their abilities and potentials. From the beginning of life, infants reflect differences in the ways they respond to the world about them. Contrasts in temperament can be seen in the child's level of activity, manner of withdrawal or attraction to something, amount of stimulation required to cause a response, and ability to change behavior. Of course, there are other differences, such as in learning patterns and attitudes.

Individuals feel, think, and act differently. Although developmental rates are similar, they vary from one individual to another. Each person is unique even though, in general, all are somewhat alike in stature and share the same needs for survival.

Just as children are not alike in appearance, abilities, and growth rates, they also respond differently to child rearing methods related to eating, sleeping, affection, and play. A method that works with one child may not work with another. One child may be easily stimulated to experiment with play dough or finger paint simply by having these materials available. Another child may need encouragement and help in getting involved with the same activity. Some children are more interested in playing with other children, whereas some are shy, preferring to spend more time playing alone. To force a child into social relationships may create greater

Even twins have individual characteristics although their physical appearances are very similar.

Part II: Children Learn As They Live

Physical growth accelerates during the early years. What physical changes will this little lady undergo in the next two or three years?

Platt

As mental abilities increase, the child's interests and curiosity expand.

problems and retard his development rather than enhance it.

The fact that children of the same age do not respond the same way to a given situation cannot be overemphasized. Can you see, then, that children's activities should provide a variety of experiences as well as equipment and materials?

STAGES AND AGES

Development overlaps from one chronological age to another; therefore it is practical to study development by stages, rather than by precise ages. A stage is a period of time during which certain developmental characteristics are most apparent. Stages extend from "womb to tomb." As you know, some of the most significant development occurs before birth—inside the mother's uterus. The focus in this text began with development from conception and will continue through about six years.

These are important years in the child's development, for this is the time when physical growth and mental abilities are accelerating. During these years children go through common stages of development. The stages and ages of children, shown in the chart, will be used to identify developmental levels.

As you probably know, the *chronological age* is the number of months or years since a child's birth. It is not unusual for children to be chronologically old enough for one stage of development when their behavior is at an earlier or later stage. In addition to chronological age other ages are used in the study of children. *Mental age* is one of these. Even though Gene is chronologically four years old, his intellectual level has been accelerated so that he actually functions at the mental age of a five-year-old. Thus, his mental age is higher than his chronological age. At times,

Ch. 3: Talking About Development

STAGES AND AGES OF DEVELOPMENT

Stage	Approximate Age
Prenatal	Conception to birth
Infancy	Birth to 18 months
Toddler	18 months to 3 years
Romper	3- and 4-year-olds
Kindergarten	5-year-olds
Primary	6 through 8 years
Preadolescence	9 through 12 years
Adolescence	13 through 19 years

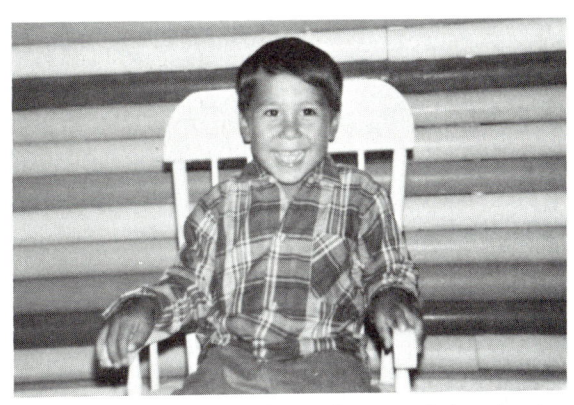

Proper nutrition during the early years helps develop happy and healthy individuals. Good health is reflected in this boy's bright eyes, happy smile, and clear skin.

the *weight age, reading age,* and *social age* are used. Keep in mind that a child's status in these areas may or may not be at the same level with his or her chronological age.

As you do additional reading, you will notice authors using other terms to identify the stages of development. You may even find differences in the range of ages assigned to a developmental stage. This will not be discouraging or confusing to you if you understand one thing: There is no absolute and uniform division of the stages and ages. The important thing for you now is to use the concept of stages as a tool to help you learn and apply principles of child development.

INFLUENCES ON DEVELOPMENT

Internal and external factors influence the rates and patterns of development in individuals either favorably or unfavorably. As you are aware, many children experience handicaps stemming from such physical defects as brain damage, blindness, deafness, or crippled limbs. Some children are faced with disabilities from learning or emotional disorders. The following factors affect the development of children, causing them to be normal, disturbed, disabled, accelerated, or retarded children.

Nutrition

The quantity and nutritional value of food consumed affects the child's development throughout life. As you know, the nutritional status of the mother during prenatal development is vital to the health of the developing child. The child's nutritional intake is also especially important during the early years while rapid growth is occurring and while bones and muscles are maturing.

Environment

The environment plays a powerful role in determining to what extent the child's potential can be reached. Nutrition, exercise, daily activities, health and safety, education, and relationships with family and friends, are all important environmental influences.

Glandular Functioning

Development throughout all stages of growth, including the prenatal period, is affected by the functioning of glands.

Part II: Children Learn As They Live

Oklahoma VoTech (Stillwater Head Start)

Each child comes into the world as a unique individual.

Physical and mental growth depend on thyroxin from the thyroid glands. Calcium in the blood is regulated by the parathyroid glands. Adequate functioning of the sex glands influences physical features as well as sex development of the individual. You may be interested in doing further study on the importance of the endocrine system.

Developmental Disorders

A single or multiple defect resulting from accidents, illness, or disease which damages the body in one way or another may disturb or delay normal development.

Other external influences can also affect development. Certain circumstances, such as parents who cannot read or who do not talk frequently with their children, may retard the learning opportunitites of a child or warp the child's ability to relate with others. Cultural factors influence child rearing practices which, in turn, have their effects on development. The position of the child in the family is considered by numerous authorities to have an effect on development. An example is the second or third child who develops at either a faster rate because of opportunitites to learn from older siblings or at a slower rate because of overprotection and pampering.

Genetics and Heredity

Development occurs partially as a result of the child's genetic endowment—his physical and temperamental characteristics which are inherited at the time of conception. As you have read, the influence of heredity exists before the child is conceived. The ovum of the mother and the sperm of the father carry the genetic materials (genes and chromosomes) which combine to form a unique newborn child. Whether the child is female or male, of course, is the most obvious result of this genetic influence. Hundreds of other characteristics are also determined through hereditary factors. Not all of them, however, are favorable. A defect existing in the genetic material from either the father or mother is called a genotype disorder and may be inherited by the offspring (newborn). For example, a defect in the genes of a parent might result in a physical defect such as weak eyes or a cleft lip in the newborn infant. Hereditary factors may place certain limitations on a child, but by the same token, they may also provide him with great capabilities.

Chapter Highlights

- The best way to prepare for parenthood or work with children is to become knowledgeable about them—to learn how development takes place.
- Knowledge of principles of development can help you better understand yourself.
- Even though parents love their children, many times their attitudes, emotional problems, and lack of knowledge about child development hinder them in providing appropriate situations for wholesome child development.
- The word *development* is used in this text as a broad term referring to any physical or behavioral change in a person.
- The term *growth* is used to indicate an increase in size or weight.
- The term *maturation* is used here to refer to a *qualitative change* in a characteristic, be it physical, intellectual, or emotional.
- The term *behavior* refers to any activity of the child—how he acts and what he does.
- The term *learning* refers to any change in behavior, either positive or negative.
- Such concepts as growth, maturation, behavior, and learning are interrelated in a child's development.
- Development is predictable because people experience many common patterns of development in the same sequence and at approximately the same stages.
- The rate of development varies from one individual to another.
- The quantity and nutritional value of food consumed affects the child's development throughout life.
- The environment plays a powerful role in determining to what extent the child's potential can be reached.
- Hereditary factors sometimes place certain limitations on a child, but by the same token, heredity may also provide the child with priceless capabilities.

Part II: Children Learn As They Live

Thinking It Over

1. What preparation can most men and women make for one of the most important tasks of a lifetime—that of rearing a child?
2. How will understanding yourself help you be more effective in working with children and other adults?
3. Why is it more practical to study child development by stages rather than by precise ages?
4. Distinguish between the terms *growth* and *maturation*?
5. How do you think children learn negative behavior?
6. Give three similarities in growth and development shared by all persons regardless of sex, race, or ethnic group.
7. What are four irregularities in development resulting from birth, accidents, diseases, or environmental circumstances.
8. Name four individual differences, other than physical, which may be observed in any group of children.
9. Why is it important to study normal development patterns even though there are individual differences in children?
10. What impact does nutrition have on the child's development throughout life?
11. How important is heredity to the development of an individual?
12. Describe two influences on development other than nutrition and heredity.

Things To Do

1. Invite a teacher of children with learning disabilities or mental retardation to speak to the class about types and causes of these handicaps.
2. Take field trips to observe three types of children's programs: one with children without special problems; one with mentally and/or physically handicapped children; and one with socioeconomically disadvantaged children. What activities enhance children's development? Why?
3. Clip newspaper articles about people who have either become assets or liabilities to society and discuss why you think this happened. Include your thoughts on what influences development, including the role of parents.
4. Have a panel of mothers and/or fathers who have more than one child discuss individual differences (physical characteristics, temperaments, social adjustment) in their children.
5. Bring a picture of your grandparents to class. Make a bulletin board display, using all the photos brought by class members. Then try to match class members with grandparents.
6. Write short descriptions, including physical and personality characteristics, of your parents. Read anonymous descriptions to the class. See how many class members can be matched with parents. Discuss heredity and environment.
7. Discuss this statement: Your success in whatever else you do in life means little if you fail in rearing your children. Follow with a discussion concerning successful personalities who have been unsuccessful in rearing their children.

Recommended Reading

Bernard, Harold H. *Human Development in Western Culture.* Boston: Allyn and Bacon, Inc., 1970.
Developmental Psychology Today. Del Mar, California: Communications Research Machines, Inc., 1971.
Dinkmeyer, Don C. *Child Development—The Emerging Self.* New York: Prentice-Hall, Inc., 1965.
Gardner, D. Bruce. *Development in Early Childhood.* New York: Harper and Row, 1964.
Hurlock, Elizabeth B. *Child Development.* New York: McGraw-Hill Book Co., 1972.
Ilg, Frances, and Ames, Louise. *Child Behavior.* New York: Harper and Bros., 1955.
Stott, Leland H. *The Psychology of Human Development.* New York: Holt, Rinehart, and Winston, Inc., 1974.

Chapter 4.

Physical and Motor Development

Your Challenge

This chapter will enable you to . . . .

- *Explain the importance of physical appearance and the meaning of physical growth patterns.*
- *Describe how growth can be measured.*
- *Define motor development and relate the term to physical fitness.*
- *Describe the pattern and directions of motor development.*
- *Name some of the motor tasks performed by young children at the different stages of development.*

PHYSICAL DEVELOPMENT

Helping children become healthy and happy individuals is simpler when you understand certain principles of physical development. Physical growth does not occur in isolation. Rather, it is one of many changes which occur in the total development of a human organism. As you learn more about physical, intellectual, emotional, and social development, you will begin to see how these areas are interwoven. They cannot be separated from each other. As an example, think for a moment of the way physical growth affects intellectual, social, and emotional development.

At an early age, Johnny gained weight far beyond the average child his age. Over the years, he was never able to lose this extra weight. Gradually, Johnny became self-conscious about his size and often ate more to compensate for his unhappiness. Quite dissatisfied with himself, Johnny compounded his problems with moodiness and by avoiding others as much as possible. Can you see why Johnny's physical development affected his feelings about himself and, in turn, his social and emotional development?

Johnny's developmental problems, of course, are some that many children—and adults—encounter. Even some of Johnny's classmates have developmental difficulties. Loren is shorter than other boys his age; Bonnie is the tallest student in her class; Darla is unusually thin; and Bryan is too frail to compete athletically with his classmates. Without careful consideration and help from the adults who look out for them, children like these could suffer social and emotional setbacks.

Although the importance of physical appearance is often given more attention than necessary, physical development is, nevertheless, worthy of great concern. As a parent or child care worker interested in physical development, you can help a child place appearance in its proper perspective. You may also be able to spot a physical problem and initiate a remedy. Moreover, you can guide a child toward a healthier and happier life. Wouldn't any of these be reason enough for you to learn more about physical development?

Physical Growth Patterns

The more familiar you become with growth patterns, the easier it will be to help children attain their growth potentials with less difficulty. If you know what to expect of children at various stages, you can plan daily activities designed to support each child's fullest development.

During infancy, the head, brain, spinal cord, and eyes grow rapidly. This growth becomes slower during early childhood. Infancy is also a stage in which a slight increase in growth of reproductive organs and sexual characteristics of the body occurs. Between late infancy and late childhood there is very little change of this type. Before and during puberty, a great increase in growth occurs with both primary (reproductive organs) and secondary (breasts and body and facial hair) sex characteristics. These areas of growth slow down and level during adolescence.

The term *somatic* comes from the word *soma* meaning body. The somatic growth pattern involves an increase in the number of cells. Rapid growth during infancy can

What could be more rewarding than helping children become happy, healthy individuals! Here Pam enjoys the pool, an experience that will help her physical and motor development.

be seen by the changes in weight and height, length of arms and legs, size of chest and abdomen, and width of shoulders and hips. This early growth spurt tapers off, however, and is slower during early childhood, followed by a faster growth rate around pubescence. A slow steady rate of body growth occurs in late adolescence.

Measurements of Growth

As you know, growth alters the size of the body, including its parts and organs. Shapes also change—like the young child's potbelly, which recedes during adolescence, and the round face that becomes oval. Not all growth changes, however, occur at the same rate. One child may become taller and heavier while another

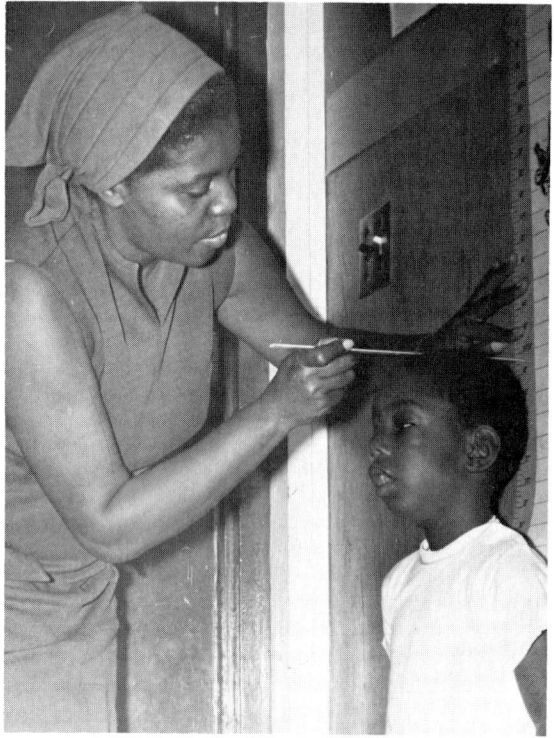

Part II: Children Learn As They Live

Height is one of the most practical indexes for measuring growth.

Oklahoma VoTech (Stillwater Head Start)

child's growth stays about the same. In one group of seventh graders, for example, the littlest boy in the group is small enough to be patted on the head by his teacher, while the biggest boy in the class looks developed enough to play football with the high schoolers. Although these two boys will probably never be the same size, the extreme difference at this age is likely due to different growth rates.

Any height, weight, length, or circumference changes in a child are measurable. The most practical indexes used for measuring growth are units of height and weight, expressed in terms of feet, inches, pounds, and ounces, or in metric units.

Height

Records of height are commonly shown with *growth curves*. The body length from head to toe is plotted on a graph for the child's age. The amount of increase in height from one year to the next can also be plotted. The charts shown here are growth curves of the average height for boys and girls.

These graphs point out two periods of accelerated growth during normal development. A *growth spurt* occurs during infancy, the stage of development between birth and about eighteen months of age. By the age of four, the growth rate becomes fairly constant for the remainder of childhood. The second growth spurt begins between ten and fifteen years of age. Again, this growth rate gradually levels off until the individual attains full height at about sixteen to nineteen.

The growth patterns for boys and girls are similar except for the time when the growth spurts occur. For girls, the growth spurt is approximately two years earlier than for boys, beginning between the ages of about ten and twelve. Girls reach maximum height at about sixteen. Boys start their second growth spurt at about twelve and continue to grow at a rapid rate until about age fifteen or sixteen, followed by a gradual increase until they reach maximum height at about eighteen. In early adolescence, just before the second growth spurt, the average girl surpasses the average boy in height. Following the growth spurts, however, the average final height for boys is greater than for girls.

Remember, *average* is simply the result of adding up all the heights and dividing by the total number of people measured. (Often, the term *mean* is used to indicate average.) This term is useful for referring to a height that represents a group of indi-

BABY GIRLS BIRTH TO ONE YEAR

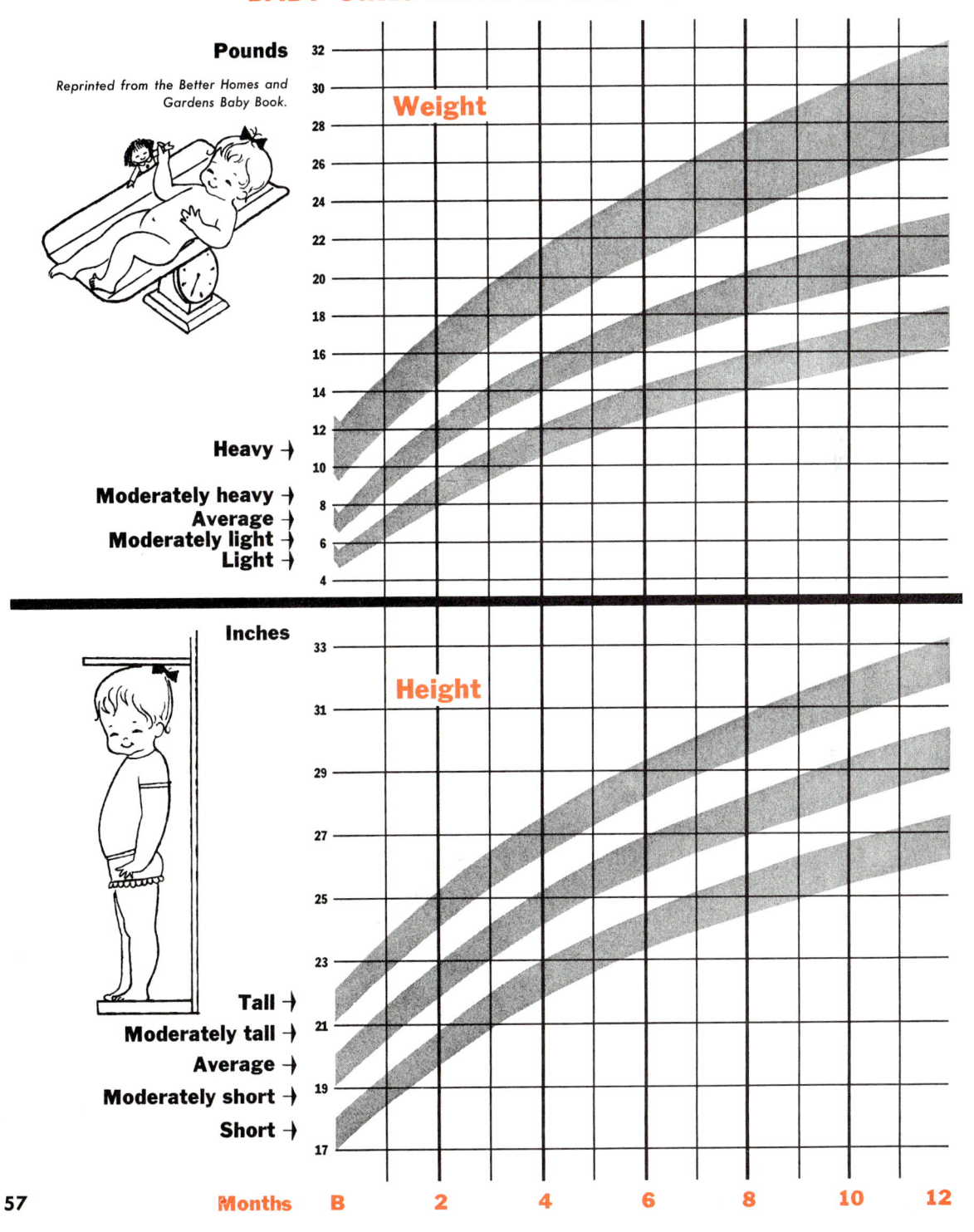

Reprinted from the Better Homes and Gardens Baby Book.

Pounds

Weight

Heavy →
Moderately heavy →
Average →
Moderately light →
Light →

Inches

Height

Tall →
Moderately tall →
Average →
Moderately short →
Short →

Months B 2 4 6 8 10 12

BABY BOYS BIRTH TO ONE YEAR

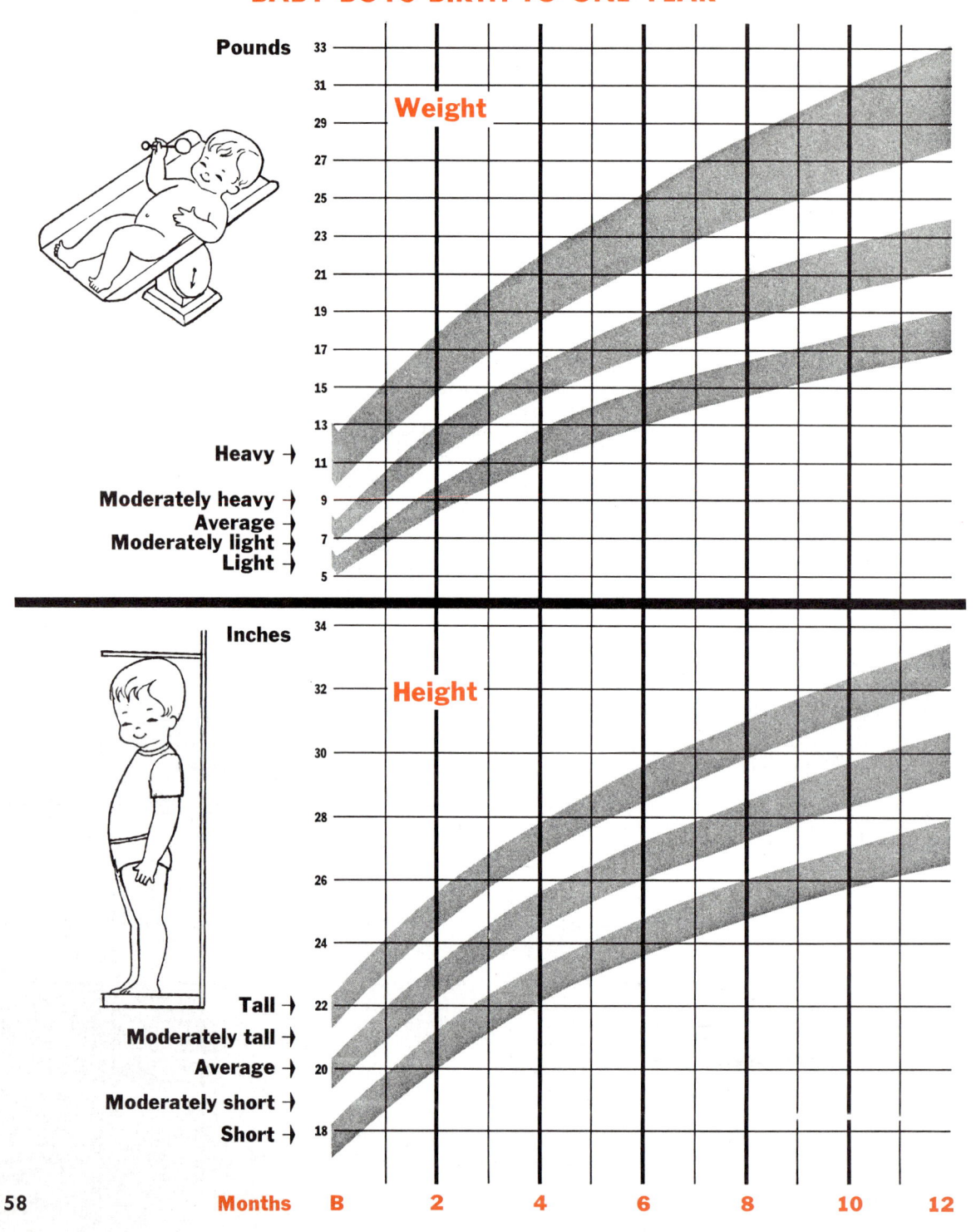

Weight (Pounds)

Heavy →
Moderately heavy →
Average →
Moderately light →
Light →

Height (Inches)

Tall →
Moderately tall →
Average →
Moderately short →
Short →

Months: B, 2, 4, 6, 8, 10, 12

58

GIRLS ONE TO SIX YEARS

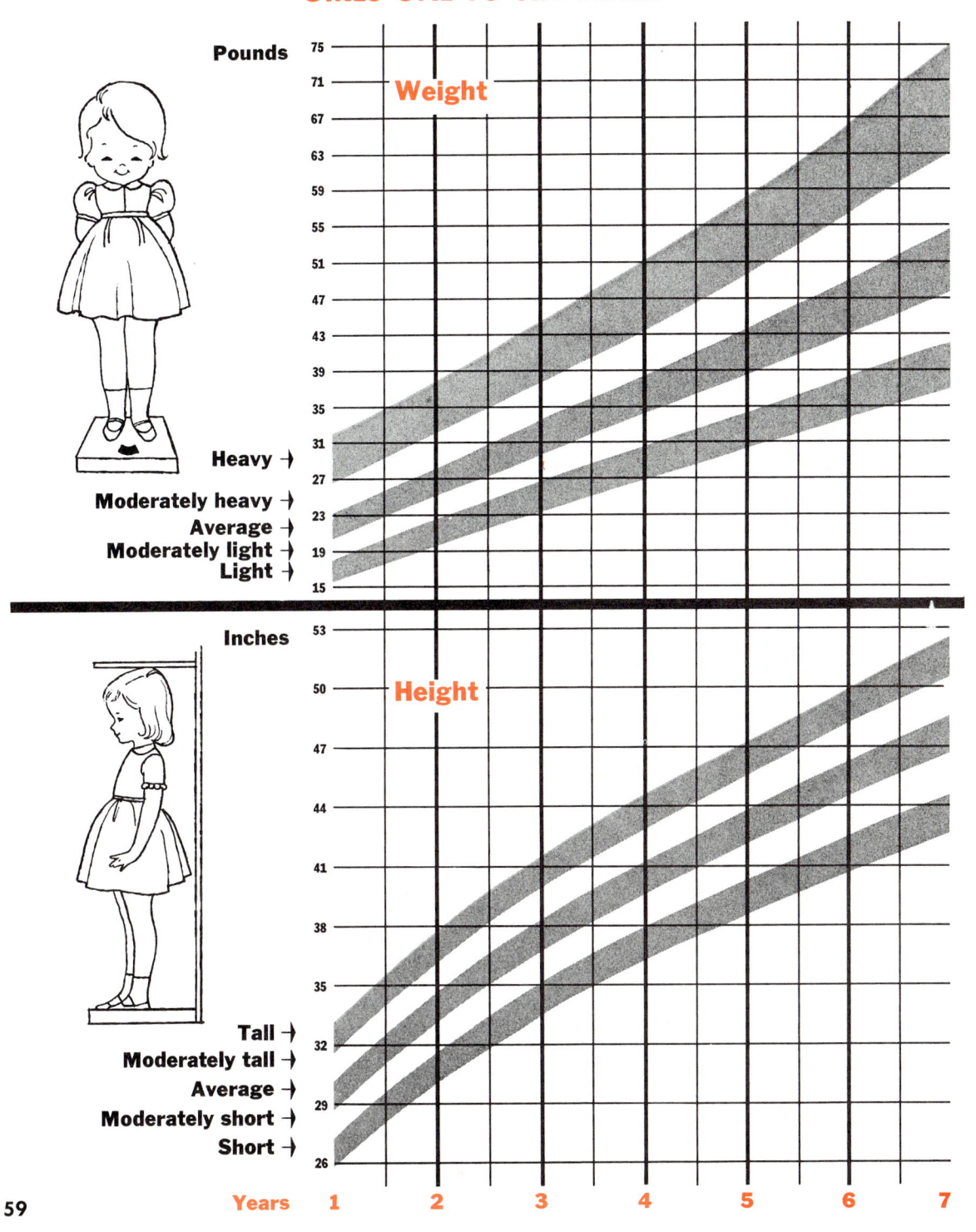

Pounds — Weight

75, 71, 67, 63, 59, 55, 51, 47, 43, 39, 35, 31, 27, 23, 19, 15

Heavy →
Moderately heavy →
Average →
Moderately light →
Light →

Inches — Height

53, 50, 47, 44, 41, 38, 35, 32, 29, 26

Tall →
Moderately tall →
Average →
Moderately short →
Short →

Years 1 2 3 4 5 6 7

BOYS ONE TO SIX YEARS

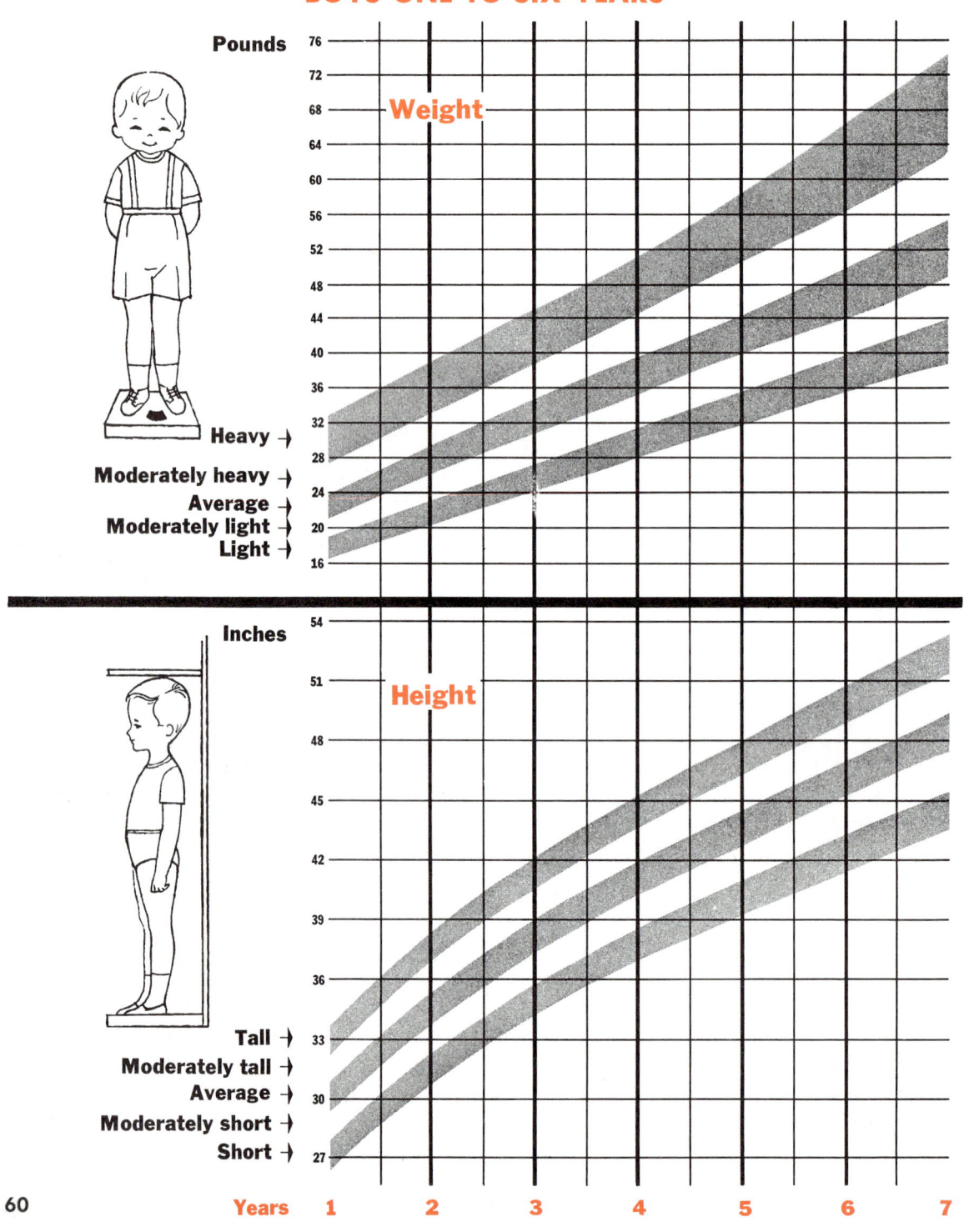

Weight

Pounds

Heavy →
Moderately heavy →
Average →
Moderately light →
Light →

Height

Inches

Tall →
Moderately tall →
Average →
Moderately short →
Short →

Years 1 2 3 4 5 6 7

viduals in a general way. In any group there may be just as many short and tall children as there are children of average height.

Because most children are not an average height, child development specialists have set up a range of inches typical for each age group. Serving as a kind of yardstick, this system provides a *standard range*. This simply means that 34 out of every 100 children of a certain age are of the average height or a little taller and another 34 percent are of the average height or a little shorter. All 68 percent (34 + 34) are within the normal range and are considered to be of average height. If a child is beyond the normal range in height, his growth may be labeled accelerated (taller) or retarded (shorter), whichever the case may be.

Slight variations from average height are generally not serious. Still, they can alert us to the possible need for medical attention. A pediatrician, for example, may recommend a certain diet, medication, or special treatment for a child whose growth rate is way out of line with the normal range.

Is there any way to insure the child's complete growth? The most practical answer to this often-asked question is that a suitable environment provides the best chances for good growth. Fresh air, sunlight, exercise, sufficient sleep and rest, and nutritious foods, including those from the basic food groups—milk and dairy products; meats, poultry and fish; fruits and vegetables; and bread and whole grain cereals—are required. Pleasant surroundings and a relaxed atmosphere also add to the child's well-being, thus making it more likely that physical growth will proceed adequately. Naturally, there can be no guarantee that even by following the best procedures, proper growth will be insured for all children. Other factors like physical defects may be involved.

Weight

Another good index for determining the child's health status is weight. A child seldom loses stature (height) but can, and often does, lose weight, either for a short or long period of time. Weight has the disadvantage of not being stable, even under ordinary circumstances. Height, on the other hand is nonreversible—once tall, always tall. Height, combined with weight, serves as a valuable aid in determining the general health of the child.

Metric Measurement

In most nations measurement is done by the metric system. Use of metrics in the United States is also increasing. Therefore some knowledge of the system is helpful.

The metric units most commonly used for body measurement are the centimetre (cm) for length and the kilogram (kg) for weight.

A centimetre is a little more than $\frac{3}{8}$-inch. Specifically, 1 inch equals 2.54 cm. An even smaller unit, the millimetre (mm), is preferred for fine scientific measurements. An inch equals 25.4 mm, so 1 mm is about as thick as a dime.

A kilogram is more than two pounds. More accurately, 1 kg equals 2.2 pounds. A smaller unit, the gram (g), is used for finer measurements. A gram has about the same weight as a paper clip.

If you consult references that use the metric system, you may find the term "mass" used instead of "weight." This is more precise scientifically, but for most purposes the terms are interchangeable.

Children develop motor coordination through play.

MOTOR DEVELOPMENT

Motor development is the attainment and use of control over the movement of different parts of the body. Motor development occurs rapidly during the early years of childhood.

The expectant mother can usually feel movements of the unborn child after three or four months of pregnancy. Early movements generally involve the whole body of the fetus. Nearer the time of birth, the activities of the fetus may involve the movement of limbs or specific parts of the body. These movements begin the pattern of motor activity necessary for later motor development.

Motor ability is the voluntary body movement which results as nerves and muscles work together. Daily activities, such as dressing, eating, and walking, require highly refined motor skills. Often, however, we take these body movements for granted.

Throughout history different motor skills have been perfected to satisfy the needs of the time. Great strength and muscle coordination were necessary for the primitive man to defend himself from wild animals and to engage in hand-to-hand combat for survival. Today, such motor skills as writing, typing, operating mechanical devices, driving vehicles, and playing musical instruments require greater use of fine muscles.

Motor coordination is the controlled and balanced movement of the body parts and is important to the total development of the child. The complex movements of sitting, standing, walking, running, jumping, and manipulating objects are gradually mastered during early childhood and serve the individual throughout life.

As children succeed in coordinating movements of the trunk, shoulders, arms, legs, and fingers, the development of other motor skills follows. Some motor skills are required for children to work and play successfully in the everyday world. When children feel confident about performing these skills, they are usually able to get along better with others. Success helps children think more positively about themselves and at the same time makes it possible for them to become independent and cooperative. On the other hand, failure to achieve certain motor skills may cause the child to be dissatisfied with himself, especially when too many tasks are attempted without success.

Three-year-old Tim is an example of a child with motor difficulties. Tim's mother first realized there was a problem when Tim continually spilled food during mealtime and often concluded each meal with a tantrum. He also appeared frustrated when playing with manipulative toys (those which require skillfull use of the hands) and when trying to button and zip his clothing. A doctor finally diagnosed Tim's problem as poor eye-to-hand coordination. These failures made it difficult for Tim to gain the independence he sought. With special help and encouragement from those who cared for him, Tim was soon on

Richard enjoys the challenge of running activities.

Some activities, such as swimming, require refined motor skills.

his way toward enjoying a happy, self-confident, and independent childhood.

Physical Fitness

Keeping the body in good condition has become a national concern in this country. One way of studying the physical fitness of a child is to measure the development of motor skills in relation to the child's height, weight, skeletal structure, speed and accuracy of movements, strength, and overall coordination. These measurements will point out those children who may need help in improving motor development.

To keep physically fit children, of course, need many activities and lots of room for vigorous action—room to turn, twist, stretch, pull, hop, skip, run, roll, climb, and jump. Unfortunately, many children grow up in situations which allow little opportunity for developing their natural movements. Examples are crowded apartments and busy streets, homes too small for large families, and little or no outdoor space for play around the house. Homes with fragile and delicate furnishings cause some parents to limit and restrict children's exploration and movements.

Children need practice in controlling movements of large sections of the body, such as the trunk and hip region, shoulders, arms, and legs, as well as the small muscles of hands and fingers. They need large boxes, ladders, walking boards, tunnels, large blocks, dolls, housekeeping materials, picture books, balls, rhythm instruments, digging areas, and space to move about while using these. As children crawl through tunnels, over boxes, and up inclined planes, they learn such concepts as space, distance, size, gravity, and the limitations of these for their body movements and abilities. They need help in learning patterns of movements—clapping, hopping, stamping, jumping, and skipping. These activities will help them develop their senses of rhythm and timing as well as improve motor control. Children need opportunities to experiment with maintaining balance while running around corners or curves, for example.

As children enter school programs, most encounter highly structured and group-oriented activities; they learn to stand in lines, circles, and game positions. Posture and exercise are important so that children maintain healthy bodies while developing comfortable work and play habits. Sitting

Central State University Child Study Center

Children need practice in controlling their fine muscles and in eye-to-hand coordination. Placing pegs in holes, as this boy is doing, will help with these skills.

for long periods of time requires control of body movements. Motor activities provide ways for children to learn important living skills plus cooperation with others while, at the same time, developing greater physical agility and body control.

Motor movements may be divided into three categories: (1) *primary movements,* such as walking, running, jumping, dancing, and skating; (2) *secondary movements,* such as buttoning, eating, lacing, cutting, painting, writing, and using tools; and (3) *integrated movements,* which combine both primary and secondary movements, such as playing rhythm instruments while dancing, operating the signals and horn while riding a bicycle, and catching a ball while running.

Sensory Abilities

The child's sensory abilities must function in order to perform even the simplest motor skill. For example, your ability to see where you are going, to feel the floor with your feet, or to keep your balance through use of the inner ear are all sensory-motor operations. Picking up a spoon requires seeing the spoon (sensory) as well as muscle control in reaching for the spoon with the arm and hand. Manipulating the fingers makes it possible to grasp and hold the spoon. In addition, the eyes must be coordinated with these body movements for successful completion of the eating task. Getting the food on the spoon, placing the spoon in the mouth, and returning it back to the plate require control of motor movements and use of the senses at the same time.

Direction Of Motor Development

There are two basic directions in which motor development takes place. The first is motor control from the head downward. Control of body movements starts at the head area and continues downward. For example, Christie, as a baby, was able to move her head with greater control than other parts of the body. Gradually, control of her shoulder and arm region was achieved. Following that came control of her trunk and hips and finally thigh and leg control.

The second direction is motor control from the center of the body outward. The muscles nearest the center of the body develop earlier than those extending outward. In the beginning, Christie moved by rolling over with control of her chest and trunk areas. Later her shoulders and arms were used in attempts to reach out. Finally

Ch. 4: Physical and Motor Development

Laura feels confident as she achieves control of motor skills.

Leah feels confident as she achieves control over large muscles for standing and walking.

arms and legs were controlled as Christie attempted to move about by crawling or creeping. By the end of the first year, Christie could manipulate blocks and other simple toys with wrist movements and then with the thumb and fingers. During this early period, Christie's eyes and head developed coordination with her hands. As you can see, the control of body movements requires several body parts working together in a coordinated way.

Pattern Of Motor Development

The pattern of motor development begins with large muscle, or *gross*, control and progresses to small muscle, or *fine*, control. This pattern can be seen as the child begins to use large muscles for moving about and playing. In the early stages, movements are not well coordinated, and children use their whole bodies in such activities as walking, running, climbing, pushing, pulling, and playing with large toys, blocks, boxes, and tunnels.

When first learning to move about, Chip stumbled, fell, and bumped into things. His gross movements were crude and clumsy. Gradually, with increased muscle control, movement and balance became easier. Chip learned to push and pull wheel toys and climb play equipment.

Eventually, fine control begins. For Chip this meant learning to eat with a spoon, manipulate objects with fingers and wrist, and use eye-to-hand coordination to place pegs in slots, put puzzles together, scribble, and hammer nails into boards.

As children develop, they need many opportunities to practice motor activities and motor control. They gradually achieve smooth and well coordinated movements. As the body matures, the process of motor

Oklahoma VoTech (Stillwater Head Start)

Children need many opportunities to develop fine motor control. These children are pounding nails into wood, a skill that some adults find difficult.

coordination becomes even more effective because the body is prepared for doing motor tasks. For example, at eighteen months, Carey walked everywhere—simply for the pleasure of walking. Now at age two, she is walking for a purpose—to get to a certain place. The walking is not only more automatic but is also better coordinated. Steps are balanced and ordered.

Rates of motor development will not be the same for every child. In the first place, maturation of the muscles and nerves used for motor coordination does not proceed according to a set schedule. Since some children mature earlier than others, some will make faster progress with motor tasks than the rest. Differences also arise from variations in the amount of practice and self-confidence, motivation and encouragement, learning opportunities, and assistance from others.

Motor development tasks are achieved in a sequence, or order, that can be easily observed. Rollo, for example, learned to

University of Oklahoma Institute of Child Development

Bill exercises eye-to-hand coordination as he places shapes into slots. The child care worker is close by, ready to offer help, encouragement, and praise.

roll over before sitting; sit up before standing alone; stand before walking; and walk before running. The charts shown here outline many of the motor tasks performed by young children at the stages of development. Remember, these will vary with each child. Still, the list provides a general indication of when children accomplish certain skills. The list seems long and is of little value if memorized, but when you work with children, you will see these motor tasks achieved. The charts also serve as a guide in planning daily activities for children. (Note that developmental tasks are listed on the charts. These are tasks to be learned at specified stages in order for the child to move successfully to the next stage of development. Developmental tasks are discussed in more detail in Chapter 8.)

Understanding motor development makes it possible to help each child proceed at his own rate and according to his own level of development. Imagine for a moment that you are a child care worker

Part II: Children Learn As They Live

MOTOR DEVELOPMENT—INFANCY

Developmental tasks: Reaches with hands, grasps, and manipulates objects; upright locomotion; coordination of eyes and body movements; takes in solid foods.

Birth to 3 months
Smiles spontaneously
Lifts head when supported at shoulders
Holds head steady without support
Responds to bell or rattle
Reaches

6 to 12 months
Pulls up to sitting position without help
Stands by holding on to something
Crawls or moves on stomach or in a sitting position without walking
Uses thumb and finger for grasping
Self-feeds with food items such as crackers
Pulls and pushes toys and objects
Imitates speech sounds

12 to 18 months
Turns pages of a book
Can say about three words
Builds tower of two cubes
Scribbles spontaneously

3 to 5 months
Smiles in response to others
Smiles at mirror image
Laughs
Rolls over
Holds head steady and erect when in a sitting position
Uses arms and hands in reaching
Uses both hands to grasp object offered
Crawling movements begin

9 to 15 months
Stands alone
Walks while holding on to something
Looks at pictures in baby picture book
Plays with blocks

14 to 17 months
Runs
Throws ball overhand without control of direction
Uses spoon; spills easily
Points to parts of face—nose, ear, eye, mouth, chin
Points to parts of doll—hair, mouth, hands, feet
Uses words to make wants known

5 to 9 months
Squeals with joy or pleasure
Transfers an object from one hand to the other
Reaches and grasps toy
Sits without support
Holds two toys or cubes
Creeps and crawls
Can self-feed with finger foods
Stands with support

11 to 15 months
Walks alone in a toddling fashion
Climbs on furniture
Grasps small objects with thumb and finger
Imitates words
Holds cup and bottle alone
Drinks from a cup
Shows right or left handedness

15 to 22 months
Walks up steps with help
Walks backwards
Removes simple items of clothing
Eats with a spoon
Builds tower of three cubes
Carries and hugs doll or stuffed animal
First tooth with biting and chewing replaces mouthing and gumming

Ch. 4: Physical and Motor Development

MOTOR DEVELOPMENT—EARLY CHILDHOOD

Developmental tasks: Independence and autonomy; toilet training; acquisition of language; self-feeding and dressing; cooperating and relating with others; formulating concepts of social and physical reality.	
18 to 30 months	**3 to 4 years**
Walks up steps alone Recognizes and points to pictures Makes sentences of two or three words Manipulates push and pull toys easily Stacks and lines up blocks Turns pages with ease Tears paper Puts finger into holes Waves "by-by" Begins taking things apart Can undress self	Runs, jumps, hops, skips, gallops Climbs and descends stairs Slides in skating and dancing motions Can march to rhythm Rolls and crawls on floor Balances self on one foot Kicks balls Jumps over a rope Pedals wheel toys Touches toes Can do sit-ups, chin-ups, and push-ups Throws and bounces a ball Catches a ball or a bean bag Pulls and pushes objects Strings beads Stands on one foot for a short time Builds with blocks Cuts with scissors Uses large crayons and pencils Rolls wrists and closes fists Cuts out assorted shapes with scissors Can fold paper Screws and unscrews objects Draws directed lines and scribbling Manipulates puzzles with few to several pieces Manipulates simple objects by putting parts which require little skill together Draws a circle—usually from a model Builds a tower of eight cubes—usually from a model Manipulates spoon and fork for self-feeding Dresses with success except for tying shoes, bows, and manipulating some fasteners
2 to 3 years	**4 to 5 years**
Runs Climbs on various objects such as furniture and stairs Kicks ball forward Throws ball overhand but without aiming Unwraps and removes covers from candy or other items, such as peeling banana	Climbs play equipment—jungle gym, towers, slides, and ladders Balances on one foot Catches and throws 3-, 5-, and 12-inch balls Bounces and catches balls Hops on both feet Hops on one foot—four steps

(Continued on page 70)

69

Part II: Children Learn As They Live

MOTOR DEVELOPMENT—EARLY CHILDHOOD (Continued)

2 to 3 years	4 to 5 years
Takes simple objects apart with little difficulty	Skips in unison to music
Unfastens clothing	Skips rope
Runs, jumps, tumbles, hops	Participates vigorously in outdoor play
Jumps and hops with one foot leading	Rides wheel toys with speed and skill
Climbs stairs with two feet on each step	Balances on beam or board
Throws balls of various sizes	Manipulates buttons, zippers, and may tie bows
Turns pages with ease	Threads beads or spools on string
Puts fingers in openings and holes	Plays jacks
Turns knobs by rotating wrist	Pounds and rolls clay
Constructs towers by stacking several blocks	Forms crude and some recognizable objects with clay
Scribbles up and down and across	Places blocks horizontally on floor
Holds cup and glass with control	Stacks blocks vertically
Eats with a spoon	Creates recognizable structures with blocks
Begins self-dressing with independence	Participates in finger plays
Can undress with ease	Controls crayons, pencils, paint brushes, chalk
	Understands and uses scissors
	Can follow line when cutting with scissors
	Cuts and pastes according to directions
	Maintains rhythmic beat with rhythm band and instruments
	Joins in games requiring group movement such as circles and dancing
	Places pegs in pegboard
	Builds structures with tinker toys
	Uses real hammer and saw in simple woodworking activity
	Can pour from a small pitcher into a glass
	Can hold and eat with spoon or fork correctly
	Can use knife to cut food
	Turns corners and about-face
	Self-dresses with ease
	Enjoys large-muscle activity—running, tumbling, climbing, fast-moving activities involving the whole body

responsibile for five-year-old Mary. After watching her daily activities for some time, you notice that Mary cannot do the same things other five-year-olds do. She has difficulty using wheel toys and climbing the jungle gym. Moreover, she cannot use scissors or dress herself. How would you go about helping Mary?

In the first place, if her problem is severe, you may need to encourage consultation with a physician. If, however, the problem is the result of a slow rate of development or lack of activity opportunities pursued in a step-by-step manner, there are ways you can help. It is likely that frustration will hinder Mary if she is faced

Ch. 4: Physical and Motor Development

with typical tasks of five-year-olds. Therefore, why not encourage Mary to perform simpler tasks that exercise her large muscles? After all, since these are the muscles that develop first, Mary may need extra practice using them before she goes on to develop her small muscles. Perhaps outdoor activity with plenty of running and jumping—simple games, using large balls—would be good for Mary. Puzzles with large pieces and clothing with simple fasteners could be used to help Mary gain confidence through successful efforts rather than repeated failures. Can you think of other activities which might help Mary with motor development?

Eye-to-hand coordination activities help children develop fine motor skills. Would this be a good activity for Mary, the five-year-old described in the text? Explain your answer.

Chapter Highlights

- Physical growth does not occur in isolation, but is one of many changes which occur in the total development of a human organism.
- An understanding of growth patterns enables one to help children attain their physical growth potentials.
- Knowledge of expected growth at various stages allows you to plan daily activities designed to support each child's fullest development.
- Growth spurts occur during infancy and again during the teen years.
- Growth patterns for boys and girls are similar except for the time when the growth spurts occur.
- A suitable environment, including fresh air, sunlight, exercise, sufficient sleep, rest, and nutritious foods, along with pleasant surroundings and a relaxed atmosphere, provides for a child's complete growth.
- *Motor ability* is the voluntary body movement which results as nerves and muscles work together.

Part II: Children Learn As They Live

- *Motor coordination* is the controlled and balanced movement of body parts.
- As children succeed in coordinating movements of the trunk, shoulders, arms, legs, and fingers, the development of other motor skills will follow.
- Children think more positively about themselves if they experience success with motor skills.
- To keep physically fit, children need many activities and lots of room for vigorous action—room to turn, twist, stretch, pull, hop, skip, run, climb, and jump.
- The child's sensory abilities must function in order to perform even the simplest motor skill.
- Children need help in learning patterns of movements—clapping, hopping, stamping, jumping, and skipping.
- Motor movements may be divided into three categories: (1) primary movements; (2) secondary movements; and (3) integrated movements combining both primary and secondary movements.
- There are two directions in which motor development takes place: (1) motor control from the head downward and (2) motor control from the center of the body outward.
- The pattern of motor development begins with the large muscle, or *gross,* control and progresses to small muscle, or *fine,* control.
- Rates of motor development will not be the same for every child.
- Tasks in motor development are achieved in a sequence, or order, which can be easily observed.

Thinking It Over

1. How important is physical appearance to a child? Explain your answer.
2. Describe how growth can be measured.
3. When can growth spurts be expected in children?
4. Interpret the term *standard range* in relation to a child's expected height at a particular age.
5. Discuss how a child's optimal growth can best be insured.
6. Define motor development.
7. How does motor development affect a child's opinion of himself?
8. How is motor development predicted?
9. What would you do to help a child who is below average in motor ability?
10. Name four conditions which may limit the physical activity of a child.
11. Explain what kind of physical activity children need for proper motor development.
12. What type of motor skills are generally expected of young children between the ages of about two and five years?
13. Give an example of a sensory-motor operation.
14. What is the difference between *gross* and *fine* motor control?
15. Are the senses important to motor development? Explain your answer.
16. Explain the two directions in which motor development takes place.
17. Discuss what is meant by the sequence, or order, of motor development.

Ch. 4: Physical and Motor Development

Things To Do

1. Invite a child development specialist or a physical education teacher to speak to the class on sequences in throwing and catching a ball, walking a balance beam, and other motor skills.
2. Invite a teacher of the upper level elementary grades to discuss the relationship between motor development and popularity.
3. Visit a kindergarten class or child care center and observe differences in ability to perform simple motor skills. Ask the teacher to demonstrate the steps that lead to the ability to skip, jump, and perform other gross motor skills.
4. Visit a physical education class in an elementary school and compare the difference in performance of motor skills to what you have observed in a high school class.
5. Invite a physical therapist to explain to the class how motor tasks help children improve brain function. As an alternative, invite a teacher of children with physical handicaps to discuss the relationship of motor functions to learning abilities.
6. Obtain a copy of the national physical fitness tests used in public schools and have class members test their motor performance.

Recommended Reading

Behrens, Herman D., and Maynard, Glenn. *The Changing Child: Readings in Child Development.* Glenview, Illinois: Scott, Foresman and Co., 1972.

Bernard, Harold H. *Human Development in Western Culture.* Boston: Allyn and Bacon, Inc., 1970.

Britton, Edward C., and Winans, J. Merritt. *Growing from Infancy to Adulthood.* New York: Appleton-Century-Crofts, Inc., 1958.

Developmental Psychology Today. Del Mar, California: Communications Research Machines, Inc., 1971.

Dinkmeyer, Don C. *Child Development—The Emerging Self.* New York: Prentice-Hall, Inc., 1965.

Espenschade, Anna S., and Eckert, Helen M. *Motor Development.* Columbus, Ohio: Charles E. Merrill Books, Inc., 1967.

Flanagan, Geraldine Lux. *The First Nine Months of Life.* New York: Simon and Schuster, 1962.

Gardner, D. Bruce. *Development in Early Childhood.* New York: Harper and Row, 1964.

Ilg, Frances, and Ames, Louis. *Child Behavior.* New York: Harper and Bros., 1955.

Muller, Philippe. *The Tasks of Childhood.* New York: McGraw-Hill Book Co., 1971.

Stott, Leland H. *The Psychology of Human Development.* New York: Holt, Rinehart, and Winston, Inc., 1974.

Chapter 5.

Intellectual Development

> ### Your Challenge
>
> This chapter will enable you to . . . .
> - Describe how intellectual ability is measured.
> - Explain how the five senses help a child learn.
> - Explain some of Jerome S. Bruner's ideas on early intelligence.
> - Describe some of Jean Piaget's theories on children's thinking.

AREAS OF INTELLECTUAL ACTIVITY

To understand the development of intelligence you should be familiar with three areas of intellectual activity:

- *The ability to use the senses*—to take in, identify, interpret, remember, and use sensory experiences through seeing, hearing, feeling, tasting, and smelling. (You smell the lovely fragrance of a flower.)
- *The ability to use verbal symbols*—to communicate and express thoughts and feelings through the use of spoken language, written letters, and other representation. (You write to a friend, telling about the sweet fragrance of the flowers in the greenhouse.)
- *The ability to perceive, think, reason, and form concepts or ideas*—to use the imagination, evaluate information, solve problems, and formulate new relationships of thought. (You wonder why flowers have nice fragrances, so you read a book on flowers to look for an answer.)

Learning disabilities may result when one or more of these areas of intellectual activity are impaired. Defective sensory organs can result in the inability to see, hear, feel, taste, or smell adequately. A damaged nervous system may account for an inability to send and receive stimulation through the body. Difficulties are also caused from emotional problems involving anxiety, insecurity, inferiority, anger, or hostility. The lack of such basic needs as security, safety, recognition, acceptance, and affection hinders mental health. Unmet needs, such as adequate food and rest, proper body elimination, and controlled body temperature, also handicap mental development. A hungry, tired, or insecure child will not be as enthusiastic about exploring the world about him as one who is healthy and happy.

INTELLECTUAL FUNCTIONING

Intellectual ability cannot be observed directly. It can be measured, however, by examining the level of the child's perform-

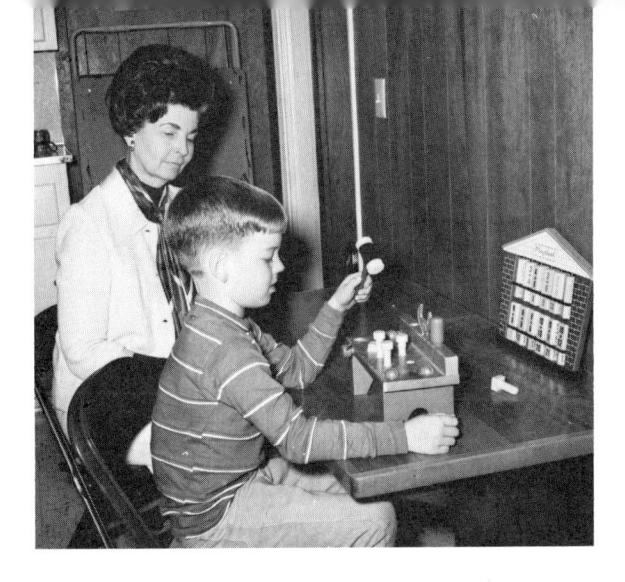

When appropriate, standardized intelligence tests may be administered by experienced professionals under controlled circumstances.

ance in certain activities. Even though this approach is indirect, a better understanding of the intelligence level may be determined. Of course, tests of this type must only be conducted and interpreted by trained professional people.

One way the level of intellectual performance is determined is to measure the intelligence quotient, or IQ. A system was devised by Alfred Binet, a French psychologist, for creating a ratio of mental age divided by chronological age. This ratio is multiplied by 100 to give the quotient—the child's IQ. The IQ represents the child's performance level in relation to other children who were tested under the same conditions. Binet's device has been revised and is now called the Stanford-Binet intelligence scale. An example of tasks five-year-olds are expected to do on this test include:

- Compare two weights.
- Name four colors.
- Compare three pairs of faces; choose the "prettiest" in each set.
- Define four ideas out of six.
- Assemble two out of three puzzles satisfactorily in one minute.
- Perform three tasks such as placing dolls, representing family members, in areas of a playhouse.

The average IQ, by definition, is 100. This does not mean that every child with an average IQ must have an exact score of 100 on the test. Most children have IQ's ranging between 80 and 110 points, all of which are considered average. A small percentage of children are considered gifted when IQ scores range extremely high; some are considered retarded if IQ scores fall far below average.

About 20 percent of the children in the United States experience a change in IQ of 15 points between ages six and ten years; some children change as much as 50 points. Environmental influences during the examination can affect the child's performance—attitudes of the child and the examiner; the emotional and physical state of

Part II: Children Learn As They Live

the child; and the atmosphere of the surroundings where the test is given.

The *level* of intellectual functioning is determined first by examining the child's ability to use the senses, to use verbal symbols, and to think. Tasks and questions are presented which range in levels of difficulty and abstractness. Abstract questions deal with the less obvious. For example, a simple question is: What colors are in the American flag? An abstract question is: What does the flag stand for? As the problems become more difficult and abstract, greater ability is required by the child. A second factor in determining the child's level of intellectual functioning is by the speed in performance. Still another factor is the child's use of imagination and creativity in arriving at solutions to problems.

Most tests for intelligence measure skills or knowledge the child already has rather than ability to learn a new concept or rule. Even a valid assessment may not be entirely accurate if the test is written. A child who knows a great deal about electricity, but has reading difficulties often cannot relay his knowledge adequately through a written test. For the most part, however, IQ tests are the best measures we have of what a child knows how to do and of what he has taken from his culture. The most appropriate use of IQ tests is to predict the child's success in school subjects. IQ tests do not measure general intelligence. IQ tests would probably have caused less confusion and controversy had they been labeled "academic" devices rather than measures of intellectual potential.

Psychologists are now developing new tests designed to measure learning ability. The child is first tested to determine what he knows; then he is given a learning task to do, followed by another test to determine how fast he has learned. There are unresolved questions about the effectiveness of this device, but it is another step toward discovering more about the child's learning ability.

THE FIVE SENSES

During the early years, the child learns primarily through his sensory system. This is called *sensory perception*. The infant is influenced by many kinds of stimulation—by his sensory contacts with objects around him. During infancy children accept or reject stimulation which is nearby or which is presented to them directly. If they like what they receive, they may coo, gurgle, smile, or laugh; if they dislike it, they may cry, kick, squirm, or make other rejecting responses. As infants gain motor ability to move about, they may seek or withdraw from certain stimuli. As children become older, they increase their ability to control the way they handle stimuli.

Your task in working with children is to provide activities and materials that aid the development of sensory and motor skills. Through proper health and enriched surroundings, you can provide such experiences. Just as the body requires activity and exercise for proper development of muscles and motor coordination, likewise, the senses need activities which stimulate their fullest development. Although normal growth and maturation is responsible for much of the increased ability of the child, learning also results from opportunities provided for the child through planned daily activities. Under normal conditions, however, sensory stimulation through planned activities is not a major problem because most children have an urge to explore and discover their environment on their own. They like to engage in vigorous bodily activities, and they have a natural

Kickapoo Head Start Center

Children learn through their senses. Which of the five senses are these children using?

University of Oklahoma Institute of Child Development

Sand play promotes small muscle development, sensitivity to texture, and social skills.

Part II: Children Learn As They Live

Children depend on sight as they participate in activities requiring visual skills.

desire to enjoy sights and sounds. This is called *self-motivation*.

Now let's take a closer look at the traditional five senses—seeing, hearing, feeling, tasting, and smelling. Four essential steps are needed for a child to perceive, or become aware of, a sensation:

- *Stimulation.* First, a stimulus is supplied—some object, activity, or movement takes place. (A bell rings.)
- *Activity.* The stimulus causes the receptor cells (receiver) in the sensory organ of the child to act. In the eye the visual receptor receives light waves; in the ear the hearing receptor receives sound waves; and in the mouth the taste receptor is stirred by chemical substances. (The sound of a ringing bell reaches the ear.)
- *Nerve impulses.* Nerve impulses travel from the receptor cells of the sensory organ through the nervous system to the brain. (The impulse triggered by the sound of the bell's ring is registered by the brain.)
- *Sensation.* When the impulses reach the brain, they cause sensations which cause the individual to become aware of the stimulus. (The ring is heard.)

The sensory organs are so much a natural part of our daily living that we seldom think about how or why we see or hear. We are seldom aware of how many daily activities are dependent upon the full use of the senses.

Seeing

Being able to see is important to survival even though some people, because of blindness, must learn to live without it. The eye is a marvelous organ which has the ability to adapt to bright light and dim light or even darkness. When the light is bright, the eye adjusts its mechanism to shut out part of the light; likewise, when it is dark, the eye adapts to receive more light. The visual system also has the ability to focus and permits clear and sharp vision of images near or far without conscious adjustment or blurring. For example, the eye can detect a tiny particle a few inches from the face and in a split second adjust its focus to a mountain or river many miles away. And what is more, the eye can achieve this task with more efficiency than the most expensive camera and in color, no less.

Through the ability to *visually discriminate*—when one is able to see and recognize differences—the child can compare and distinguish colors, sizes, shapes, numbers, distances, positions, and other characteristics of objects or sensations. This visual function is so natural that one is

Ch. 5: Intellectual Development

hardly conscious of it. Still, there are many people whose visual abilities have not developed adequately. As a result of this, what they see may be distorted or incorrect. For example, Jerry fell down because he could not accurately perceive the distance between where he was standing on the steps and the landing below.

Hearing

Hearing, or auditory skill, like sight, is highly significant in the learning process. Sound is created by vibrations which disturb the surrounding air and create pressure waves which travel through the air. These vibrations alternate between high and low pressure waves in the air and produce *sound*. The vibrations travel at high speed away from the object making the sound. Sound has three dimensions: *pitch,* the highness or lowness of the sound; *volume,* the strength or weakness of the tone; and *timbre,* the quality of the tone. For example, the autoharp can produce tones with varying pitch—from high to low; voices, depending on the volume of sound produced by the singers, can be strong or weak; and one voice can be distinguished from another by the quality of sound.

Sound waves pass through three principal parts of the ear: the *external ear,* the part we can see; then through the eardrum into the *middle ear;* and then to the "oval window" in the *inner ear* where the nerve impulses are stimulated to send messages to the brain.

Feeling

Another sensory channel is feeling, or the tactile sense. It is really made up of three separate senses: *cutaneous,* senses of pressure, pain, and temperature; *kinesthetic,* the skin's amount of resistance to

Children increase the keenness of their senses through such activities as listening to favorite stories and songs on a record player.

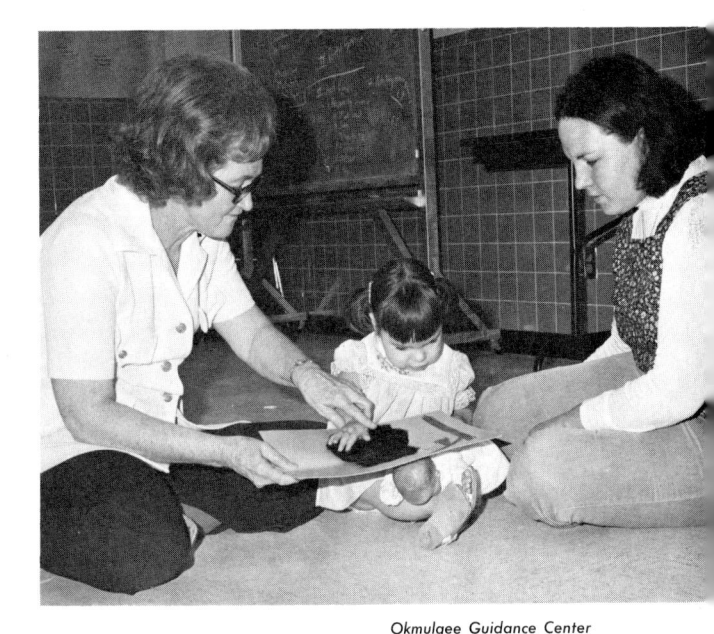

Okmulgee Guidance Center

Children need to experience how things feel. Here the child care worker helps a little girl feel a piece of soft fur attached to a sheet of paper.

79

Exploring through the sense of smell adds to the child's understanding of his world.

Infants explore the world about them through their senses and their body movements.

the movement over its surface; and the *labyrinthine* receptors, senses located in the inner ear which allow awareness of such positions in space as standing still and moving up or down, right or left, and backward or forward.

Smelling

Another sense which plays a relatively small but important role in the learning process is the sense of smell, provided by the *olfactory* nerve. Although it is indispensable to the survival of many animals, this sense primarily adds to a human's enjoyment or discomfort. Of course, it also alerts one to dangers which produce particular odors, such as fire and some poisonous gases. The olfactory nerves are located in the upper passages of the nose and are stimulated when vapor substances are inhaled.

Tasting

The *gustatory* receptor cells for the sense of taste are located in the mouth. A full quota of taste buds are present in a newborn baby's tongue. There are four main qualities of taste—sweet, sour, bitter, and salty. The taste buds for sweetness are mainly on the tip of the tongue; those for sourness are located along the sides of the tongue; buds for bitterness are at the back or base of the tongue; and the taste buds for saltiness are located primarily along the tip and sides of the tongue.

Can you see that even though most sensory input is visual and auditory, other senses are important for the enrichment of children's lives? Child care workers, as well as parents, can help stimulate the sensory perception ability of children through exciting activities such as feeling games, which help children learn to identify the texture of certain fabrics and materials by touching them. Smell and taste sensations can be stimulated by doing experiments with nutritious foods. Flowers can be smelled, music heard, and thousands of sights observed. The activities for children presented in Part VI provide suggestions for enriching children's experiences through sensory activities.

COGNITIVE DEVELOPMENT

The word *cognition* comes from the Latin word *cognoscere* which means *to know*. Cognition here means knowing about the world and objects in it, including the self.

Cognitive development (learning to think) begins early during infancy. Babies develop tools for thinking as they interact with the environment. They use sensory and motor resources as they explore the world about them, making changes in themselves as well as in others and in objects. They first learn to communicate through their senses and body movements and then through language. During early infancy, children do not distinguish between themselves and others, but with more experience and contact with the world about them they gradually begin to see themselves as separate.

EARLY INTELLIGENCE—BRUNER

Jerome S. Bruner, American psychologist and director of the Harvard Center for Cognitive Studies, describes infant's behavior from the beginning of life as intelligent, adaptive, and flexible. Through basic acts such as sucking, looking, reaching, and grasping, the infant develops four abilities important to human functioning:

- Voluntary control of his behavior.
- Internal control of his attention.

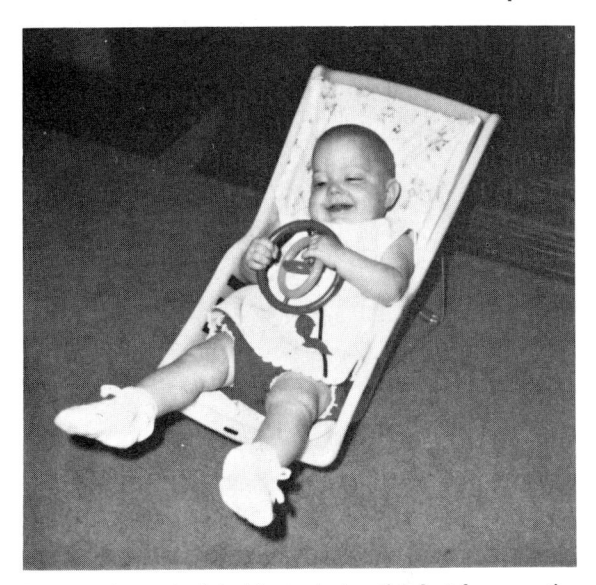

By grasping colorful objects during the first few months of life, this infant is developing abilities which will be used throughout life.

- The power to carry out several lines of action at the same time.
- Use of codes that make way for speech and communications.

Bruner's theory includes the notion that any complex idea can be reduced into simpler ideas. This makes it possible for a child to learn the foundation of any subject which is presented in a meaningful form at any stage of development.

Bruner tells us that regardless of how stimulating and enriching the environment may be, the child must be motivated to do something on his own about that environment. A child does not necessarily learn because he or she is exposed to information or material. The child, in order to learn, must initiate his own action. He must generate action within his own sys-

Part II: Children Learn As They Live

Play with colorful objects provides information about the world, which becomes a part of the infant's mental life.

tem and operate by his own power rather than simply react to what is happening.

Children give meaning and order to objects and relationships according to their own needs, abilities, and purposes. In this context, learning is viewed as goal-centered. A child is motivated by a tension—a special kind of eagerness—to accomplish a certain goal. The better a child perceives his goal, the stronger his motivation to act toward achieving it. Of course, a child requires help in formulating, clarifying, evaluating, and solving problems. Motivation may be thought of as a way to activate interest or direct interest that is already present in a child.

Field theorists, such as Bruner, believe children should be provided with situations which permit them to use their own capacities to pursue self-interests. Children must see the meaning for themselves in order to learn.

CHILDREN'S THINKING—PIAGET

One of the best known theories on the development of children's thinking is that of the well-known Swiss psychologist, Jean Piaget. According to his theory, cognitive development occurs in stages. Each stage prepares the child for the next stage; that is, every new experience is understood by a child on the basis of previous meaningful experiences. These meaningful experiences help the child progress from one stage of cognitive development to the next.

A significant term used by Piaget is *operation*—the mental activity which occurs as the individual adapts to the environment. Keep in mind the previous discussions on intellectual development and cognition as you study the following. According to Piaget, you must also remember that individual variation occurs among children and there will be exceptions to the age ranges at which some children fit into Piaget's stages of development.

Piaget's Stages of Development

Sensory-Motor Intelligence
(Birth to About 18–24 Months)

Although the infant has not yet acquired language skills, intelligence appears through actions. The infant's actions are governed by sensations causing simple learning to occur. The child responds to both the inner world of the self and the external world around him. Every response—every activity—is registered in the mental structure. Each new experience—*sensory-motor reaction*—makes a connection with similar experiences already registered. For example, what Alison sees is registered in her brain—the feelings of her body movements; the sounds she hears; and the touch of objects she manipulates. All of this information becomes a part of Alison's mental life.

Exploring with the senses becomes integrated with behavior patterns which assist the child in gaining knowledge about the world. An infant uses the information he already has in developing new patterns of action. For example, Andrew's thumb-sucking and grasping are integrated; grasping and looking at his hand are integrated. This results in a new behavior pattern for Andrew—exploring an object by grasping it, looking at it, putting it in his mouth, and playing with it.

During the early stages of infancy, the child does not realize that *objects are permanent*. The child demonstrates this when an object such as a rattle or baby bottle disappears from sight. The child does not look for it because he does not know it still exists. If part of the object is visible or if it is removed from sight very slowly so the child can follow it with his eyes, the object begins to take on some permanence. On the other hand, if the object is moved quickly out of sight, the infant does not realize it still exists. Infants gradually learn that objects are permanent by exploration, over and over, with everyday objects such as baby bottles, toys, and clothing.

The child's *curiosity* increases toward the latter part of the sensory-motor stage. Interest in objects and what is happening helps the infant achieve object permanence. The child begins to look for a vanished object at first by looking where he last saw it; he will gradually begin to look for it in the place where it disappeared. For example, Tammy began her search for the ball by first looking under the box where she found it while playing with her big brother. Eventually, Tammy looked under the corner of her blanket, the place where her brother had been moving the ball out of Tammy's sight.

Throwing and dropping toys at this stage are common ways for the infant to explore disappearance and reappearance. This provides a way for the child to study movements of objects and to gain an understanding leading to the concept of object permanence.

When the infant learns that particular actions cause a change in the environment, he will probably repeat these actions. For example, Tina, reaching for a toy suspended by a spring above her crib, hit it and caused the toy to move; she hit it again and again.

Moving from one place to another—*locomotor behavior*—helps the infant learn about the space he or she lives in. He learns that he is also an object in that space. As the infant successfully interacts with the environment, enjoying the materials and relationships he encounters, his development is stimulated and he continues to be interested. However, if the infant continually feels inadequate in dealing with these experiences, he may become frightened and inhibited or refuse to continue explorations.

Near the end of the sensory-motor stage, the child begins to find mental solutions to problems rather than going through a series of trial and error experiences. Finding mental solutions usually starts with acting out the situation. Piaget illustrated this process of combining thought with actions to solve a problem by reporting his daughter Lucienne's behavior when she attempted to get a small chain out of a match box. She looked at the small opening of the box but did not know how to open it wider. She began to open and shut her mouth, each time wider and wider. The opening of her mouth was Lucienne's sym-

Part II: Children Learn As They Live

JoAnne Michels

Robert understands the adult world better as he takes on an adult role through play.

Von enjoys pretending as a way of rediscovering reality for himself.

bolic way of representing the opening of the box. This example shows the cognitive stage between trying out a solution by actions and thinking it out.

Preoperational Stage
(About Age Two to Seven)

By the end of the sensory-motor stage, the child can solve problems by *imitation*, *pretending*, and *insight*. When the child has formed a mental image of what has happened, he can represent it by imitating the past action. Pretending is the ability to use a mental image of a behavior pattern to act out the pattern in a new situation. Kim demonstrated this ability when he pretended to be a mother feeding the baby. The mental image of his mother's behavior was used as he acted out the situation.

By this stage, the child has language abilities which begin to dominate his mental life. The child progresses from the sensory-motor stage toward more complex thinking. This second stage is a period of preparation for organized mental actions and for later abstract thinking.

The preoperational stage is also called the phase of *egocentricity*, which simply means the child thinks mostly from his own point of view. He finds difficulty in mentally putting himself in the place of another person. The child at this stage realizes his body is separate and different from other objects, including people, but he does not realize his experiences are his very own. He does not understand that his own thoughts and actions make up a part of the situation in which he participates. The child can play the role of another person by imitating and pretending, but when he does, he loses sight of himself. He cannot see himself from someone else's point of view. He uses fantasy to do what he cannot do by controlled thinking.

Children's knowledge, in the preoperational stage, is not yet systematized. Although the child may count objects or recognize that some objects are similar, he does not have the ability to arrange and rearrange objects in an organized and logical manner. Although a young child at about age three uses symbols, his thought is not organized into concepts and rules.

During the preoperational stage the child is primarily influenced by what is seen and heard or experienced at the moment. The child is guided by concrete *perceptions*. He believes what he sees without paying attention to changes which may be occurring from one form to another. Piaget demonstrated this by pouring beads from one short, wide container into a tall, thin container while a child watched. Then he asked the child if there were more or less beads in the second container. The child answered that there were more because the level has risen in the tall, slender container. To the child, the full container looked as though it contained more.

At this stage the child is not able to take both height and width into consideration at the same time. The child does not yet understand conservation—the unchanging quantity, or amount, of a liquid or solid substance regardless of its shape or form. In other words, conservation means the shape or form of an object can be changed, but as long as nothing is added or taken away, its amount stays the same. Let's take another example.

Two balls of play dough, which are both the same size, were placed in front of five-year-old Hans. He was asked to make a long sausage or a wide, flat cake out of one ball. Each time, he was asked if the two objects of play dough were still the same or if one was bigger or smaller. Most four-, five-, and six-year-old children have a tendency to think that things which change in shape also change in quantity. Like these children, Hans answered that the play dough was not the same in amount during these changes in form, but that they either became bigger or smaller according to their visual appearance.

A long period of preparation is required for the child to grasp the principle of conservation. Some authorities conclude that if the child has enough experience, such as manipulating the play dough ball and transforming it himself into a sausage and then into a ball again, he will eventually grasp the idea of conservation. The extent to which children begin to grasp this concept through experience during the preoperational stage is still undetermined.

The preoperational child is not able to think through a series of actions. For example, Jennie has learned to walk from her home to kindergarten, which is three blocks away. She cannot, however, draw a sketch or map of the route with pencil and paper. She does not have an overview of the route she travels, even though she can get to school and back by making the correct turns at the proper places.

In summarizing this stage, it can be said that the child at the preoperational stage solves problems by imitation, pretending, and insight; thinks only from his point of view; and is guided by perception and believes what he experiences at the moment.

Concrete Operational Stage (Seven to About Eleven or Twelve)

During this stage, the child's thinking operations are concrete. His thinking is bound to direct experience. Thoughts of objects are limited to direct experience.

The child, during this stage, grasps the concept of conservation. He understands that reverse operations will restore the substance to its original shape or form. An example of a reverse operation happened

Part II: Children Learn As They Live

Children see examples of classification in the grocery store.

Some toys and play materials are designed to provide classification experiences.

when seven-year-old Maria was shown two identical containers of water. She recognized that these contained the same amount of water. One glass of water was then poured into a tall, thin cylinder and she was asked if the two had the same amount. Maria responded correctly by explaining they were the same because the water from the cylinder can be poured back into the glass and the water level will again be the same in both glasses.

Formal Operations Stage (About Eleven to Fifteen)

This stage will not be discussed except to identify it as the fourth stage in which the child is able to deal with the mastery of a widening variety of problems. *Abstract thinking* occurs during this stage. This process involves the ability to deal with what is possible without reference to what is actual or concrete.

Relational Concepts

Piaget identifies four *relational concepts* in cognitive development that have roots in early childhood. These concepts are basic ideas needed for logical thinking and for understanding physical properties of the environment. Children develop these concepts through play. The four relational concepts are *classification, seriation, spacial (space) relationships,* and *temporal (time) relationships.*

Classification

Classification is putting things together or matching objects that are alike in such properties as color, shape, or size. Children learn to classify objects by actually putting things together that are alike and separating things that are different. For example, Rick, Dee, and Monty—all four-year-olds—were playing with empty grocery containers provided for them in the day care center store area. Concepts of classification were evident as they grouped the tomato cans together in one place, the milk cartons together in another place, and the cereal boxes in a third group. They even subdivided the cereal boxes because the labels were different. While Dee played in the house area, she separated the dishes into classes by color and by shape.

Prior to three or four years of age, most children are only able to handle one concept at a time. They should not be expected to separate objects by more than one property simultaneously—color and shape, for example. They usually start with shapes. Even if they cannot name them, they will generally know the differences in shapes. Later they grasp the idea of color. Gradually, children begin to place like objects, such as cups, nails, or buttons, into groups.

Seriation

Seriation is putting things in order or lining up objects in graduated fashion according to such properties as size, shape, or amount. You see seriation as the child begins to recognize the graduation in sizes of objects. Rick showed this skill while playing with empty cans. He carefully placed the largest in front of him and then began to insert cans one at a time according to size until he had nested five cans from the largest to the smallest.

During play the very young child manipulates objects, such as the cans, by trial and error until he succeeds in getting one to fit inside another, nesting all possible combinations. From about eighteen months of age, the more experienced child can "manipulate" the cans *mentally* and begins to make correct choices in placing the smallest can inside a larger one and so on until all the cans are nested.

Central State University Child Study Center
This carpentry board helps children develop skills in classification, seriation, and spatial relationships.

Spatial Relationships

Spatial (space) relationships include the idea of how objects fit into space; how objects relate to each other; and how a person as an object relates to other objects and to the space around him. The child is especially interested in his body and how it fits into space and how it relates to other objects. An excellent example of the child's desire for such an experience was demonstrated by Craig's use of his toy box. He ran to his toy box, dumped all the toys on the floor, and climbed in the box. He knew what to do with the box. Who wants all

Part II: Children Learn As They Live

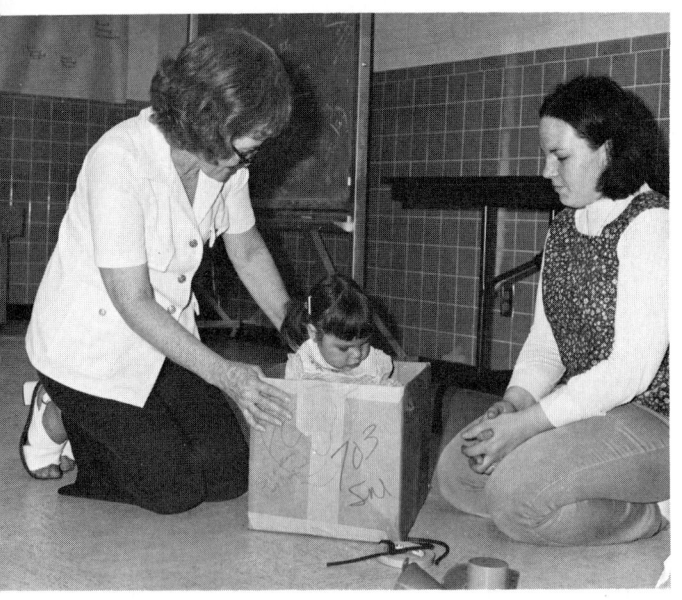

Okmulgee Guidance Center

Spatial relationships are experienced as a child sits inside a cardboard box.

Central State University Child Study Center

Playing with blocks and building constructions helps children grasp concepts about the relationship of one object to another.

Like most children, this girl enjoys crawling into empty spaces—a natural way to experience spatial relationships.

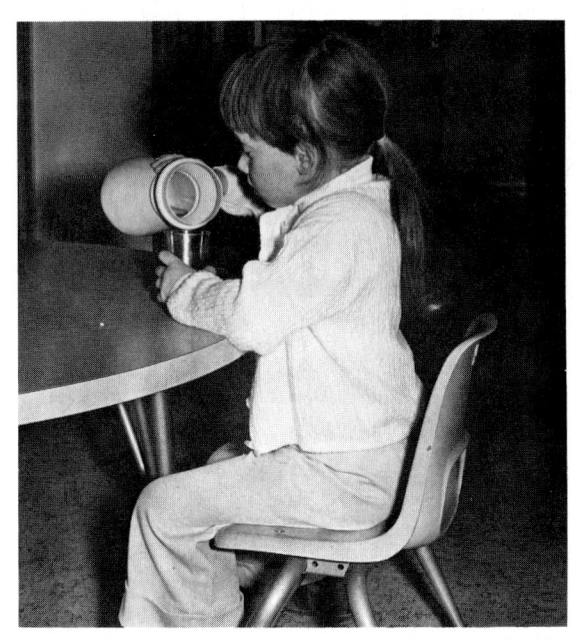

Pouring juice helps children experience spatial relationships concepts.

those toys crammed in a box, anyway? After all, the *empty* box served a much more exciting and meaningful purpose for Craig as he discovered the relationship of his body (one object) to the box (another object). Spatial relationships are important as children develop body awareness—the understanding of one's body shape, how it fits into space, and how it relates to other objects.

Temporal Relationships

Temporal (time) relationships connect the passage of time with what is going on in the environment. The concept of *time* is one of the more difficult ones for children to grasp and for parents and adults to provide appropriate opportunities to learn. Even though three- and four-year-olds often learn to memorize the numbers on the face of a clock and learn a system that indicates the time of day, they probably do not understand the idea of *the passage of time.* Eating and bed times are two times children are vitally concerned about, and they probably learn to judge the passage of time in these areas first. Routines for daily activities also provide experience in developing time relationships. Most young children can tell without a clock when it is time for certain TV shows. This has meaning for them; it is exciting.

Levels of Representation

Further understanding of how children learn is provided by Piaget's four levels of representation—steps by which children progress from concrete to abstract thinking. These levels are:

- *Object*—a real object such as a doll, telephone, ball, banana, or a drum.
- *Index*—a part of the real object or an extension of it, such as the ring of a telephone, the honking of a car horn, the voice of a mother, the tracks of a bird, the smell of bananas, or the light from a bulb.
- *Symbol*—a representation in the likeness of the real object, such as a picture of a banana, a plastic shape of a horse, or a photograph of a child.
- *Sign*—the object represented in an abstract way, such as by word, letter, or number. The object, a child, is represented by the word which is her name, Susie; the groups of objects—oranges, pears, and apples—are represented by the word *fruit*.

Kickapoo Head Start Center
These children grasp ideas about the passage of time as they observe the growth of plants which were only seeds when planted several days ago.

Study the chart shown here of the four levels of representation applied to the telephone.

As children's thinking develops, they gradually progress from one level to the next. The more experience they have with real objects, the easier it is to move to the next level of representation. For instance, young Trisha became familiar with the properties of a banana by exploring the

Part II: Children Learn As They Live

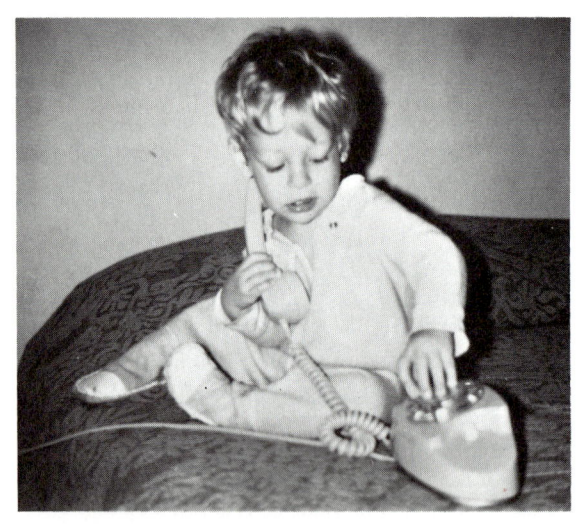

Experience with the real object will help this child develop concepts about the properties and use of a telephone.

Of course, many children operate on several levels at the same time. Take the case of four-year-old Pedro. All levels were in operation when it came to representation of his mother. He interacted with her daily (object level), heard her voice calling even though he could not see her (index level), could recognize her photograph (symbol level), and could recognize her name, Maria, when he saw it in print (sign level). Incidentally, even though children cannot spell or read, as such, they often learn to recognize the *sign level* of familiar objects, especially their own names.

Do you see why children begin to learn by playing with real objects and by firsthand experiences? A real doll means more to a child than the picture of a doll. Playing house means more than listening to a story about mother, father, brothers, and sisters. Handling a set of nesting-type plastic mixing bowls is more meaningful than watching a TV show explaining the concept of seriation. Hammering pegs into slots or gluing pieces of wood scraps together provide real experiences in grasping spatial relationships. Pouring sand through

real thing. Later, she was able to operate on the index (the smell or the peeling) and symbol (a picture of a banana) levels with little or no difficulty. However, Trisha may need to be older and able to read before she is ready for the sign level—the word "banana."

LEVELS OF REPRESENTATION

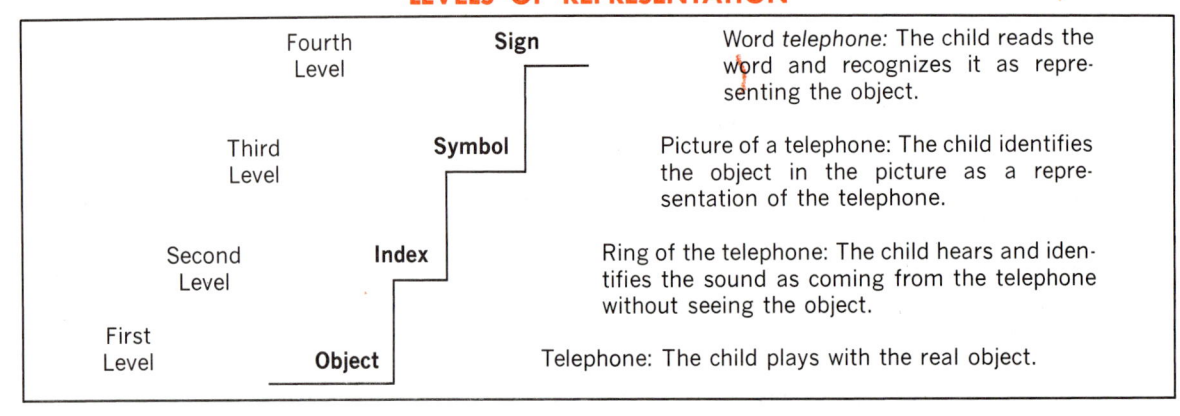

Fourth Level	**Sign**	Word *telephone*: The child reads the word and recognizes it as representing the object.
Third Level	**Symbol**	Picture of a telephone: The child identifies the object in the picture as a representation of the telephone.
Second Level	**Index**	Ring of the telephone: The child hears and identifies the sound as coming from the telephone without seeing the object.
First Level	**Object**	Telephone: The child plays with the real object.

Ch. 5: Intellectual Development

a funnel provides problem solving exploration—what happens if a thumb is placed over the narrow end of the funnel?

With the use of real objects, children eventually begin to use index and symbol levels leading to more abstract ways of dealing with their environment. Sounds, pictures, numbers, letters, and stories begin to take on meaning only after children develop the basic tools for thinking.

University of Oklahoma Institute of Child Development
Firsthand experiences mean more to this four-year-old child than looking at a television or hearing a story about mother and baby.

Chapter Highlights

- The three areas of intellectual activity are the ability to use the senses, the ability to use verbal symbols, and the ability to perceive, think, reason, and form concepts or ideas.
- One way the level of intellectual performance is measured is with the intelligence quotient, or IQ.
- The most appropriate use of IQ tests is to predict the child's success in school subjects.
- Most of the questions on an intelligence test measure a skill or knowledge the child already possesses rather than his ability to learn a new concept.
- The impact of the environment upon the child's learning is made primarily through his senses during the early years. This is called *sensory perception*.
- The five traditional senses—seeing, hearing, feeling, tasting, and smelling—are so much a natural part of our daily living that we are seldom aware of how many daily activities are dependent upon the full use of them.
- Cognitive development (learning to think) begins early during infancy through play.
- Jerome Bruner, American psychologist, views learning as *goal-centered*. (The better the child perceives his goal, the stronger the motivation is to act toward achieving it. The child must see the meaning for himself in order to be learning.)
- According to Jean Piaget, Swiss psychologist, cognitive development takes place in stages. Each stage prepares the child for the next stage.
- A significant term used by Piaget is *operation*—the mental activity which goes on as the individual adapts to the environment.
- Piaget identifies four relational concepts of cognitive development that have roots in early childhood:
  Classification—matching objects that are alike in such properties as color, shape, or size.

91

Part II: Children Learn As They Live

Seriation—lining up objects in graduated fashion according to such properties as size, shape, or amount.
Spatial—the idea of how objects fit into space; how objects relate to each other.
Temporal—the idea of the passage of time.
- Object, index, symbol, and sign are four levels of representation provided by Piaget. These are steps by which children progress from concrete to abstract thinking.

Thinking It Over

1. Have you ever taken an IQ test? What does the term IQ mean? What do IQ tests measure?
2. Why do you think most schools give their students some form of an IQ test at least one time during their high school years?
3. What was Alfred Binet's contribution to the field of intelligence testing?
4. Do you think a child care worker should know the IQ scores of the children he or she works with? Explain your answer.
5. What does the term *sensory perception* mean?
6. Define the term *self-motivation* and give two examples.
7. What is the relationship between the five senses—seeing, hearing, feeling, tasting, and smelling—and a child's intellectual development?
8. Identify one major principle of Jerome Bruner's theory of learning.
9. What is Jean Piaget's contribution to the study of child development?
10. Describe Jean Piaget's stages of development, giving examples with your explanation.
11. What is meant by cognitive development in a child?
12. According to Jean Piaget, what are the four relational concepts needed to enhance intellectual functioning?
13. What materials found around the house could be used to help a child develop the four relational concepts? Try to think of items not named in the text.

Things To Do

1. Invite a psychologist or psychometrist, trained in administering the Stanford-Binet test, to class to give a demonstration on intelligence testing. Either a child or a class member can be used in the demonstration. The test need not be completed, but the psychologist can discuss with the class the administration of the test and the use of results.
2. Make a sensory stimulation box. Each side of the box on the inside can be covered with a different material that has an interesting feel, such as burlap, vinyl, corduroy, satin, sandpaper, or fur-like fabric. Children can then put their hands through the hole in the top of the box, feel the sides, and describe what they feel, thus demonstrating the

(Continued on next page)

Ch. 5: Intellectual Development

Things To Do Continued

development of their sense of touch. Use the box with a young child and report results to the class.

3. A smell board can be made by dipping cotton balls into liquids with different odors, such as lemon juice, alcohol, vanilla, vinegar, and perfume. These can be glued onto a piece of cardboard or each placed in a vial. Students try to guess the smells on other boards or in the vials. When the smells vanish, the cotton can be saturated again. It's fun to make two boards using the same smells, but with the cotton placed at different spots on the board. The game is to try to match smells. Students can discuss ways to use this activity with children.
4. Blindfold a panel of class members and offer them one at a time such foods as chocolate chips, miniature marshmallows, small pieces of spaghetti, small banana chunks, raisins, and small pieces of pickles. (Students will think of other tasty foods.) See how many they can guess immediately. Discuss ways to use this activity with children. Try this experience with children and report findings to class.
5. Have class members go outside, close their eyes, and listen for sounds. Appoint a few students to make some sounds, such as crumpling leaves, breaking sticks, and dropping rocks. Class discussion can follow concerning the identification of sound when eyes are closed. This same activity can be carried out with indoor sounds. Discuss how to use this activity with children.

Recommended Reading

Behrens, Herman D., and Maynard, Glenn. *The Changing Child: Readings in Child Development.* Glenview, Illinois: Scott, Foresman and Co., 1972.

Bernard, Harold H. *Human Development in Western Culture.* Boston: Allyn and Bacon, Inc., 1970.

Developmental Psychology Today. Del Mar, California: Communications Research Machines, Inc., 1971.

Dinkmeyer, Don C. *Child Development—The Emerging Self.* New York: Prentice-Hall, Inc., 1965.

Karnes, Merle. *Helping Young Children Develop Language Skills.* Arlington, Virginia: The Council for Exceptional Children.

Lichtenberg, Phillip, and Norton, Dolores. *Cognitive and Mental Development in the First Five Years of Life.* Rockville, Maryland: National Institute of Mental Health.

Muller, Philippe. *The Tasks of Childhood.* New York: McGraw-Hill Book Co., 1971.

Phillips, John L., Jr. *The Origins of Intellect: Piaget's Theory.* San Francisco: W. H. Freeman and Co., 1969.

Pitcher, Evelyn Goodenough; Lasher, Miriam G.; Feinburg, Sylvia; and Hammond, Nancy C. *Helping Young Children Learn.* Columbus, Ohio: Charles E. Merrill Publishing Co., 1966.

Schwebel, Milton, and Ralph, Jane. *Piaget in the Classroom.* New York: Basic Books, Inc., 1973.

Chapter 6.

Socialization

Your Challenge

This chapter will enable you to . . . .
- Describe the socialization process.
- Explain what is meant by self-concept.
- Define life style.
- Explain how contacts outside the home affect the socialization process.

THE SOCIALIZATION PROCESS

Socialization is a developmental process children experience in learning to adapt to the world around them. How they get along with each other, how they function in society, and how they see themselves as individuals in the midst of others are important parts of this area of development. Through effective socialization children achieve recognition as cooperating, contributing, and responsible members of groups.

Each child learns the ways of his people by watching, listening, and imitating those around him. The socialization process is influenced by the people who pass down and interpret the culture to their children. Society teaches children to form attitudes, develop skills, gain knowledge, and perform roles that are suitable for daily living in the culture. These may be called goals of socialization. Independence, getting along with others, contributing to the welfare of self and others, and communicating are all part of these major goals. Of course, the socialization goals within a community are not always the same. For example, some groups in our society place great importance on individual achievement during the child's early years and through the teens, yet other groups emphasize the importance of sharing the responsibility of making a living for the family. Some groups require children to wait long periods of time to receive the rewards of their efforts, yet other groups grant immediate gratification.

Everyone the child contacts has an impact upon his or her social development—parents, teachers, friends, other children, and community members. A child's learning may be influenced and reinforced because parents and other adults think achievement is a basis for success in life; sometimes learning is inhibited because it is not promoted in the child's home. Much depends on how great a value the adults place on learning. Can you see

Ch. 6: Socialization

Outdoor play generates social interaction among playmates.

Josh learns through imitation.

that the goals of the people in society who promote the culture are important? An understanding of the goals of society—what is important to the people—helps us understand the influences of the family and community on the socialization of children.

SELF-CONCEPT

The child's *self-concept* means how the child views himself; how he sees the *I* (or the *me*); how the child evaluates himself in relation to the world. Another term used to refer to the self-concept is *self-image*.

Dr. Don Dinkmeyer, an educator and authority in child development, refers to the self-concept as a kind of map one uses to guide behavior. This map leads the individual into certain situations according to his understanding of himself.

Self-concept plays an important role in the socialization process. Children who

Dick feels good about himself.

95

Part II: Children Learn As They Live

develop healthy self-concepts are able to relate to other children and adults in positive ways. They feel good about themselves. They are able to act with self-confidence.

Children are curious about the world and enjoy exploring their environment and discovering relationships with people as well as with things. If a child sees himself as inferior, he or she may refuse to explore new areas of interest or to engage in challenging activities for fear of failure. If a child is struggling to learn "who am I," much time and energy is used in testing the limits of getting along with peers and adults. On the other hand, the child who feels confident will enjoy reaching out for new experiences.

The child's concept of himself is formed by the impression he thinks others have of him and by how others treat him. In effect, a child's perception of himself formulates as though he were looking at himself through the eyes of others—as if in a mirror. Fortunately, or unfortunately—whichever the case may be—adults and peers provide a mirror in the way they respond to a child. Because of their child rearing practices, parents and other close adults exert one of the greatest influences on the child's development of a self-concept. Gradually, the child learns what he is like as he understands how others feel about him, what they think about him, and how they respond to him.

You can probably think of examples that show how children see themselves according to the way others respond to them. Here is just one example. Four-year-old Terry thought he was unable to perform such simple tasks as assisting with serving snacks in nursery school because his teacher never asked him to help. Of course, one or two instances such as this one do not shape a child's total concept of himself, but because Terry was never asked to help and the other children were asked, he began to draw conclusions about his value or ability as a helper. In this case, Terry's teacher became aware of his disappointment and began to encourage him to help with a variety of simple tasks. Soon Terry gained confidence and his self-concept improved.

Upholding the Image

The child often accepts evaluations of himself by others as good or bad and then strives to live up to this image. For example, Laura's mother and father repeatedly told her she was doing good work at school, and her playmates reinforced the idea that she was very bright. Laura's behavior in school resulted in many successful accomplishments. She eventually saw a picture of herself as a smart girl. On the other hand, Marlin was continually told he was bad and was punished severely. Soon Marlin believed that he was bad and then did what he felt people expect bad children to do. Would the child feel differently about himself if he were shown a better way to behave or if limits were established which enabled him to respond with more positive behavior? We can communicate to a child, "You're okay; I still like you, but you can do better next time." Compare that statement with another: "There, you've done it again. You are a bad boy." Or, "Mother is going to have to spank you. Mother doesn't love bad boys. Why can't you be good like your sister?" How will this child see himself through the mirror of his mother's responses?

Once a child has an understanding about what is good and bad behavior, he usually becomes the best judge of himself. Haim Ginott, an authority on children's behavior, suggests that when a child intentionally behaves in a way that represents being good, he will decide that he was a good child at that time, but if he is in a bad mood or thinking bad thoughts at the time of his good act, and someone tells him he is a good child, he has a conflict with which to deal. For example, six-year-old Ramon was vigorously raking leaves in the front yard. When he finished, his stepmother said to him, "Ramon, you're such a good boy; I'm so proud of you." In a short while, Ramon scattered the leaves all over the yard. What happened? While Ramon was working, he was feeling angry because he did not get to go to the park with his older brother, Leo. Ramon was thinking bad thoughts about Leo and his stepmother while raking leaves. When his stepmother told him he was a good boy, Ramon had a conflict about his image, so he decided to maintain the image he had of himself at that time by behaving badly. What could Ramon's stepmother have said to him that would allow Ramon to draw his own conclusions about himself? Consider this: "Ramon, you did such a good job on the yard work; it was not easy but you managed it well." Ramon could then draw his own opinion as to whether he was a good or bad boy while doing a good job.

A threat to the child's worth, competency, or adequacy is a threat to the development of his self-concept. As a result, a child may put into operation a set of defense mechanisms designed to protect himself from insult or inferiority. The child may even attempt to enhance negative qualities, interpreting them as virtues for his own purposes. Take the case of Lorent. The image he had of himself was as a rude and impolite child. This was mirrored by his parents' remarks. They continually told Lorent that he was not courteous and had no manners. Lorent began to think that others expected him to be discourteous. He soon began to live up to this image by behaving rudely and disregarding courtesies.

Handicaps Influence the Self-Concept

Unfortunately, some children have undetected handicaps or disabilities which may cause them to be less than adequate in daily tasks. A child with poor eyesight, for example, often bumps into things. He appears clumsy and is unable to read well. Can you see how visual defects may contribute to a damaged self-concept? Other difficulties which may contribute to the child's negative self-image include poor health, poor motor coordination, language disabilities, and lack of experiences with the outside world—beyond the child's own home and neighborhood.

Encouragement is Needed

As you can see, the self-concept receives its nourishment from people. If the child has care, encouragement, security, love, and guidance, he or she will likely develop a positive self-image. The child who is rejected, discouraged, and frequently punished, however, will likely develop a negative picture of himself. Parents and other adults can help children develop positive images of themselves by encouraging them when they experience failure and by recognition of their work when success is accomplished. The child who feels good about himself—who sees a positive image of himself through treatment from others—will be happier, more productive, and self-motivated. Robbie's language skills, for example, probably developed with greater success because he felt confident about speaking freely, even though his words and

Part II: Children Learn As They Live

Every child needs encouragement from those who care.

Kris collected a variety of wood chips and received praise for a task well done. Now she displays a positive self-image.

sentences still lacked refinement. Jane was encouraged to develop her muscle coordination because she felt good about herself while playing with other children in activities which required control of body movements. A child's self-concept is also enhanced as he experiences success with living skills, such as buttoning his own coat, zipping boots, lacing shoes, self-feeding, and toileting.

Parents and child care workers can help children develop positive self-concepts by enabling them to feel adequate, secure, successful, and worthy. This is primarily a task of helping children like themselves, of helping them know they are significant persons of worth, and of treating them with respect and dignity.

LIFE STYLE

Closely related to the self-concept is the child's *life style*. This term refers to the individual's *unique or special way of behaving* based on how he sees the situation around him and how he feels about it. The child's interpretation of himself, his world, the people around him, his place in the world, and how he interacts or responds is his life style.

According to Alfred Adler, a psychologist concerned with the study of individual behavior, there is basic unity to all behavior. This means that the child's environment, heredity, and the child's view of himself and the surroundings are all contributing factors to the development of the whole child. The interaction between the environment and how the child interprets what is happening to him makes up the style of life. From this point of view, can you see that behavior can best be understood by learning about the child's life style?

When a child behaves a certain way, he has a reason for doing so. His behavior has purpose and is directed toward a goal. Understanding the child's life style helps you recognize the child's purpose or goal, and, thus, his behavior can be more easily understood. One must try to understand the child's interpretation of a situation. What does Hilda want? How does she see herself? How does she feel about what is happening to her? How does she see society? When we view children through an awareness of their individual life styles—from each child's perception of himself and the circumstances, we see the reason for the child's behavior rather than what may appear to be the situation from the adult's point of view. In applying this concept to working with children, you must look at a child's actions as a series of related events. Where is the behavior leading? This approach helps you become aware of each child's pattern of responses, his attitudes, values, and the basic assumptions (what is taken for granted).

Children must have help from adults as they work and play. Each child must have the freedom to be himself and experience life within the framework of his own life style. However, each child must learn limits of appropriate behavior and how to be a contributing member in society. The task of parents and child care workers is to help children meet the challenges of their everyday world with courage and confidence.

THE CHILD IN THE LARGER COMMUNITY

There is no magic formula or standard procedure in the home that can guarantee a child's success in life. You have read about how positive attitudes and behavior from adults in a family do much to help a child cope with situations. This influence extends to situations outside the home as well.

Joe sees the world through his own eyes, even though he may want to be like dad.

Early Social Experiences

Encounters with playmates, neighbors, and relatives are among the first social experiences a child has outside the home. For most individuals, these encounters will continue throughout life.

The influence of home and family can be observed as the child relates to others, using what he has already learned. Is the child extremely aloof? Perhaps he has been too sheltered at home, never learning how to approach others. Is the child unusually aggressive? Perhaps he is starved for affection and seeks attention this way. There are many possibilities.

As you know, members of the family guide the child's behavior. If they are optimistic, he probably will be too. If they have prejudices, he probably will share them. (Sometimes a child's viewpoint changes in later life, but this is not the

Kickapoo Head Start Center
Children who play together learn to get along with one another.

usual pattern.) Think about the following example and how racial prejudice, like many other attitudes, is easily passed on to children.

Julio's family moved into a predominantly white neighborhood when he was seven years old. Julio is Puerto Rican but exemplifies what can happen to a child of any minority race. At the time Julio's family moved, he was shy but eager to make friends. Within a very short time, however, Julio learned a harsh lesson about some people. Matt, a white child in the neighborhood, started the lesson by taunting the young Puerto Rican boy with name-calling. Matt understood little about what he said. He only knew he had heard his father's comments about Julio's family and he recognized the tone of these comments. It wasn't long before other children joined with Matt in jeering the boy who was "different." Julio would never forget.

What do you think is ahead for Julio if this experience is continually reinforced? Does Matt deserve the blame? Are children sometimes excluded from a group for reasons other than race—like appearance or popularity?

Children's Centers

Children have many social contacts which are more formal than those with playmates, neighbors, and relatives. Nursery schools, day care centers, child development programs, and other types of children's centers are examples of such social settings. Although philosophies, goals, and activities vary with each center, a common element of *group interaction* is found in all of them. Children coming together soon begin to adapt to their new social environment, different as it may be from their home settings. They may experience countless contacts with peers and adults. Often, for the first time, they learn to conform to group standards, make contributions, appreciate traditions, and cooperate with others. Even though children may need help in developing skills for getting along with others, where children are found together, they learn much through trial and error. Of course, the more the adults in children's centers know about child development, the more they can help children limit these errors.

As a child care worker in a children's center, you will have an ideal opportunity to observe children and help guide their development. Such a setting provides many opportunities for children to display all sorts of attitudes and behavior. Interesting observations can be made by watching children during dramatic play. This happened with Karen in nursery school. Assuming the role of mother, Karen scolded the children (played by classmates) vigorously. She constantly complained about how bad the older brothers and sisters were. Not one child received a kind word from little Karen. Why do you suppose Karen acted out the mother's role this way? Observing children can be informative. The children's center is an excellent place for watching—and helping—if your eyes and ears are open and your heart is willing.

School Life

The next major social situation a child encounters is school. Healthy relationships in school with peers and adults are difficult to establish when home experiences have been limited.

When Kirk started kindergarten, he was unable to share and cooperate. For several years, his divorced mother had worked during the day while his grandmother cared for him. She was kind and loving but allowed Kirk to have his way with toys and play. With no other children around, Kirk was never challenged or motivated to develop social behaviors, including sharing and cooperating.

Children's relationships with their parents often determine how they feel about their teachers. Consider these extremes—overprotection and rejection. Each produces handicaps for the child. Link, overly protected at home, became so dependent on his mother that he expected the same kind of support from his teacher. Viola, who was rejected at home, developed deep feelings of insecurity. Her weak self-concept carried over into the school setting where she had difficulty forming friendships and meeting academic expectations.

For the child, home and family life carries over to school life. Any major upset in the family is likely to have a serious effect on school work. Feelings of insecurity will often lead to poor adjustments. Low regard for education by some parents often results in a negative influence on their children's progress in school. The child receives little help and encouragement at home, and there is often a lack of communication between the parents and school personnel. You can probably think of many other ways a child in school is influenced by his home and family.

Children's relationships with their parents often determine how they feel about their teachers.

Later Life

The influence of home life and family relationships on the child's later life is, of course, similar to the influence on school experiences. Adult life, however, presents a much more complex set of decisions to make in new situations. As an adult, will the individual be equipped to achieve his standards of success? This is a key question for all parents, teachers, and child care workers.

There are so many parts of adulthood that can be influenced in early life. For example, the vocational goals of an individual may be greatly affected by the attitudes toward work in the home. Marital happiness—or unhappiness—of parents influences children's attitudes toward marriage, often affecting later abilities to cope with their own marriage situation. The way a mother and father care for their children may reflect the way they were reared or a rejection of their own parents' child rearing methods. By this time, you can surely see how important the early years are to a child.

Part II: Children Learn As They Live

Chapter Highlights

- *Socialization* is the process by which children adapt and learn to live in the world around them.
- The socialization process is influenced by the people who pass and interpret the culture to their children.
- Society teaches children to form attitudes, develop skills, gain knowledge, and perform roles that are suitable for daily living in the culture. These are called *goals of socialization*.
- The goals within a culture, or even within a community, are not always the same.
- Children who develop healthy self-concepts are able to relate to other children and adults in positive ways.
- One of the greatest influences on the development of self-concept is the child rearing practices of parents and other close adults.
- The child who receives care, encouragement, security, love, and guidance will likely develop a positive self-image, but the child who is rejected, discouraged, or harshly punished will likely develop a negative self-image.
- Parents and child care workers have the task of assisting children in developing positive self-concepts by helping them experience feelings of adequacy, security, success, and worth.
- Encounters with playmates, neighbors, and relatives are among the first social experiences a child has outside the home.

Thinking It Over

1. Define the term *socialization*.
2. List four major goals of socialization.
3. Why is it important that children develop adequate social skills?
4. What problems do you think might arise when the goals of socialization differ within a culture?
5. What is the relationship between a positive self-concept and the ability to adapt to one's environment?
6. Distinguish between telling a child he did a task well and telling him he's a good child.
7. Why do the child rearing practices of parents and other close adults have such an impact on the self-concept of a child?
8. List three ways adults can aid a child in developing a positive self-image.
9. Other than the parents, who influences the development of the child's self-concept during the early years?
10. Describe three living skills which, if appropriately developed, will enhance a young child's self-concept.
11. What could you do to help improve a child's self-concept?
12. How are relationships in school affected by home experiences?

Things To Do

1. Observe a group of young children at play. Find a leader, a follower, a loner, a bully, a crybaby, a hitter, and a teaser. If possible, get family background, such

(Continued on page 103.)

as the number of family members and their ages. Do not discuss children by name but discuss behavior and why children react in certain ways. (Caution: One observation is not sufficient to label an individual as a certain type.)

2. Observe a group of teenagers in a social situation. Find a leader, a follower, a loner, a bully, a crybaby, a hitter, and a teaser. These types are harder to identify at this age, for they have learned to be more socially acceptable. Discuss the indicators of these types (without names) and ways they have learned to adapt to social situations. (Example, the crybaby no longer cries, but whines instead; the hitter no longer hits physically, but hits verbally.)

3. Observe a child or children in make believe play. Record the social situations acted out and discuss these.

4. Observe a master teacher at both the early childhood and high school levels. Record examples of how he or she enhances the self-concepts of students. Are the techniques used at the different levels similar? Discuss.

5. Interview parents of small children. Ask them two questions:

- How important is your role as a parent in helping develop the self-concept of your child? (Be prepared to define the term *self-concept*.)
- Give examples of how you help build a positive self-concept in your child.

Recommended Reading

Behrens, Herman D., and Maynard, Glenn. *The Changing Child: Readings in Child Development.* Glenview, Illinois: Scott, Foresman and Co., 1972.

Bernard, Harold H. *Human Development in Western Culture.* Boston: Allyn and Bacon, Inc., 1970.

Briggs, Dorothy Corkille. *Your Child's Self Esteem: The Key to His Life.* New York: Doubleday and Co., Inc., 1970.

Coller, Alan. *Assessment of Self-Concept in Early Childhood Education.* ERIC Clearinghouse in Early Childhood Education. Urbana, Illinois: University of Illinois, Curriculum Lab, 1971.

Developmental Psychology Today. Del Mar, California: Communications Research Machines, Inc., 1971.

Dinkmeyer, Don C. *Child Development—The Emerging Self.* New York: Prentice-Hall, Inc., 1965.

Fraiberg, Selma H. *The Magic Years.* New York: Charles Scribner's Sons, 1959.

Jones, Eva. *Raising Your Child in a Fatherless Home.* London: Free Press of Glencoe, Collier-Macmillan, Ltd., 1963.

Lichtenberg, Phillip, and Norton, Dolores. *Cognitive and Mental Development in the First Five Years of Life.* Rockville, Maryland: National Institute of Mental Health.

Margolin, Edythe. *Sociocultural Elements in Early Childhood Education.* New York: Macmillan Publishing Co., Inc., 1974.

Mental Health Digest. National Clearinghouse for Mental Health Information, Vol. 4, No. 2, February, 1972, Washington, D.C.: Superintendent of Documents.

Neisser, Walter, and Neisser, Edith. *Making the Grade as a Dad.* Public Affairs Pamphlet, #157, 381 Park Avenue South, New York, 1971.

Young, Leontine. *Life Among the Giants.* New York: McGraw-Hill Book Co., 1956.

Chapter 7.

Emotional Development

Your Challenge

This chapter will enable you to . . . .

- Tell how children display <u>emotions</u>.
- Define emotions.
- Define and discuss the term <u>affection</u>.
- Define and discuss the term <u>love</u>.
- Explain what negative emotions are and how they should be handled.

WHAT ARE EMOTIONS?

Most authorities agree that <u>emotion</u> is a mental state or condition of excitement or disturbance that causes an individual to act in certain ways. Emotions are often accompanied by physical changes in breathing, the pulse rate, and glandular secretions. Occurring in different degrees, emotions can be sudden responses of feelings caused by stress and pressure or subtle feelings which develop over a period of time. Some emotions have pleasant associations—love, affection, happiness; some have unpleasant associations—anger, fear, hatred. Can you add to these associations?

An infant will show emotional excitement when experiencing extreme pleasure or discomfort. For instance, when Johnny is hungry or if he is uncomfortable because of a wet diaper, he immediately expresses feelings of discomfort. He lets these needs for help be known by crying, screaming, or some other emotional expression. When Johnny is excited by the tinkling of a bell over his crib, he gurgles or squeals with excitement and joy. Some infants are less responsive and rarely show their emotions; others get excited easily and express feelings openly.

The development and expression of emotions are important to children. Without them, they would never experience and express wholesome feelings. Because affection and love are two of the most important emotions to a child, they will be discussed here.

AFFECTION

Affection brings feelings which express concern, warmth, regard, caring, sympathy, and helpfulness. Affection is an emotional response of one person toward another person, thing, or animal. Emotional responses appear to be spontaneous in young children and can often be stimulated by a small amount of social contact. Learn-

Some emotions are expressed openly, yet others are more subtle.

Dee shows affection for her pet dog, Ward.

ing to be affectionate plays an important role as children become attached to certain objects or people. Children are more likely to develop affection for those who like them and who are friendly toward them. For a very young child, affection is conditioned by pleasant experiences. For example, those who care for baby Eilene's needs, play with her, and bring her pleasure and satisfaction provide opportunities for Eilene to return warm, gentle feelings toward them.

Young children are especially open about their feelings toward others. This is obvious when you observe children during daily activities. They make little distinction between sexes when it comes to choosing friends. Within his peer group, four-year-old Raul selected as friends those children who liked him and who showed affection for him, regardless of whether they were boys or girls. During the latter part of childhood, however, preadolescents usually show little physical affection for those of the opposite sex. They often engage in activities in peer groups of the same sex.

Children often show affection for their brothers and sisters in relation to how these family members treat them. Naturally, children show greater affection for siblings who show affection for them. They respond positively to those who do not tease, ignore, or criticize them.

Strong affection may develop between two siblings if an older child in the family adopts one of the younger children as a favorite. Likewise, two children in a family who are near the same age tend to enjoy common interests and may develop strong affection for each other. Girls frequently admire or idolize an older brother who

Affection generally develops between brothers and sisters of a similar age.

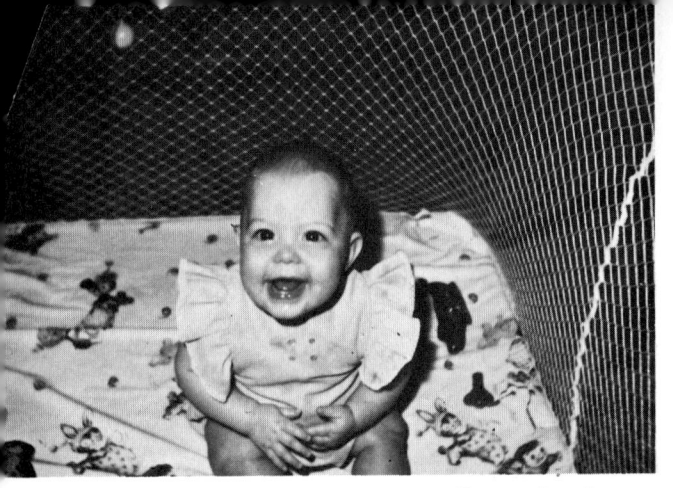

This infant is eager to express affection for the approaching person.

pays attention to them and treats them kindly. This often results in expressions of affection.

People outside the family who bring care and pleasure to children are often regarded with affection. A teacher who shows sincere interest and a willingness to help them will soon experience the children's affection for him or her. A lonely child may develop a strong attachment to an adult or teenager who shows an interest in him. This sometimes happens even when the older person is regarded as less than desirable. Young children are generally not concerned about the character of those for whom they develop affectionate feelings.

Although affection is important, too much can be a problem. Children who are smothered with affection are not usually given opportunities to express their own affections. This is sometimes referred to as "smother love." Unfortunately, overly affectionate behavior on the part of parents and other adults tends to be self-serving. Such affection satisfies the desires and wishes of the adult rather than contributing to the wholesome development of the child.

Research reports that children from lower socioeconomic environments often show more affection than children from the middle and upper classes. The reason for this has never been completely explained. Some think that social and achievement pressures in the middle and upper socioeconomic classes require control of affectionate behavior, while less pressure is present in lower socioeconomic groups.

Patterns of Affection

Some studies of infants and young children indicate a predictable pattern of affectionate responses. First signs of affection are usually in the form of an outgoing and warm manner. An infant under five months old, for example, expresses affection for anyone who approaches him in a friendly way, fixing a gaze on the observer's face while kicking, waving arms, smiling, and turning his body. As early as six months, the same child may limit affection to one or more specific persons—usually people within the family. At this age the infant also begins to respond to cuddling by reaching for the loved one's face or mouth.

During the latter half of the first year, the child will show affection toward familiar people and sometimes fear toward strangers. In the second year the child will usually show affection for others by such emotional behavior as hugs, pats, strokes, and kisses. By this time affectionate responses are directed toward toys and other possessions in addition to people. To the child, there is little difference between objects and people. That is, the affection a young child has for a pet or stuffed toy may be just as great as the affection shown for a member of the family.

Toddlers show affection by wanting to be with their favorite people constantly and by trying to help in whatever they are doing. These young children follow much the same pattern of affection with pets and toys. Favorite toys are hugged, sometimes even loved to pieces. Typically, wherever they go, toddlers will take the toys they like best. They may also want to play with a pet constantly. If children at this stage are not watched closely, they may hug and stroke a pet too hard and cause injury to the animal.

During the third and fourth years, emotional dependence on the family is usually replaced in part by emotional dependence on other children and on adults outside the family. For instance, at age four, Felicia expresses affection toward those who recognize her, who show personal interest in her, and who express affection for her. Felicia is emotionally stimulated by those who make her life pleasant. She sometimes shows affection by physical contact such as hugging, by saying "I love you," or by simply showing a feeling of contentment and pleasure.

By the time children are about six years old, they generally have the attitude that showing affection is childish. If this happens, they often become embarrassed by displays of affectionate behavior. Kissing, hugging, and affectionate names like honey and precious can be quite embarrassing and distasteful to children.

Spontaneous expressions of affection still occur from time to time among older children. Such expressions usually happen in spurts and at unexpected times. For example, eight-year-old Ken suddenly gave his mother a big hug. Why? Because she gave him permission to go to the baseball game with a friend and his father.

As children reach school age, affection for special friends is often shown by wanting to be with them, by confiding in them, and by keeping in touch with them through

Children enjoy being near one another.

personal contacts, telephone calls, or letters. This affection is not usually expressed physically or with words, but it does exist.

Adults sometimes impose forms of kissing which children are too young to understand. Kissing on the lips is primarily an adult expression which can be sexually stimulating. Children do not derive these pleasurable sensations from kissing. Children usually enjoy a hug, a big squeeze, or a pat on the shoulder more than a kiss. Some children try to push adults away who kiss them or who demand a kiss. Some children, on the other hand, learn to adjust to kissing as an expression of affection.

During the early years, it is important for children to receive feelings of sincere love from adults and others who care for them.

LOVE

Love is a much stronger and more complex emotion than affection. It is a feeling of deep personal attachment and commitment. Sometimes love is openly expressed; sometimes it is not. Love between a brother and sister, for example, may not always be shown even though it exists. The healthy emotional development of a child, however, hinges upon adequate expressions of love. The child who is loved but is never given signs of this love has little advantage over the unloved child.

Marla Hawkins had two young children, a divorce, and no job, all by the age of twenty-two. After finding a job as a waitress, she arranged to leave her children with a neighbor during the day. The neighbor lady had children of her own and did little other than feed Marla's children. After long hours of being on her feet, Marla was too tired to give attention to her children. Her patience had worn thin. Her temperament suffered. After a time, the children, who had almost no adult influence, became behavior problems—whiny, argumentative, and destructive. Marla's problems were now complex.

Think about this situation. Can you say that Marla did *not* love her children? Is it possible that she made mistakes which compounded her problems? What were they? What can Marla do now to help herself and her children?

A climate of love in the home helps children develop positive attitudes and behavior toward themselves, society, and the world. Most authorities in human development conclude that a child must feel loved in order to have adequate emotional development. A positive, supportive, and trusting relationship with the parent is needed in early infancy—in fact, throughout the child's life.

During the first year, it is important for the infant to receive feelings of sincere love and concern from parents and other adults who care for him. During this stage of development the child is more concerned about himself than about the love of others.

In the second year, children may turn their love outward or inward, largely depending upon how they are treated. For example, if Ertha's mother or another close family member neglects her, she may turn her attention inward to herself. If she experiences neglect very often, her withdrawal and concern for herself may become fixed. She may have difficulty maturing to the point at which she can think of others. Studies have indicated that children who show little love and affection for others tend to be self-devaluating, dependent, anxious, and disagreeable. Furthermore, children who experience severe lack of love from others have tendencies to become suspicious, fearful, and overly aggressive. These characteristics interfere with positive emotional responses in relationships with others.

Adults who give love when children do the right thing but withhold it when they do something wrong are asking for trouble. This condition causes children to develop feelings of guilt and anxiety. They tend to be self-centered in response to this adult pattern. On the other hand, children who receive consistent love and affection usually show positive feelings for others and express little dependency, anxiety, or conflict. They are able to form close and intimate relationships more successfully.

What effects do love and affection have upon the child's development as he becomes older? The following list will help you answer this question.

Expressions of love and affection:

- Give the child a sense of security.
- Contribute toward feelings of acceptance and value as an individual.
- Make it easier for a child to accept himself and others.
- Reassure the child of his worth.
- Cultivate his social interest and feelings for others.
- Help the child identify with parents, siblings, peers, and others.
- Produce a desire to please others by sharing love and affection.

Child care workers, as well as parents, show their feelings for children by what they do. The message of love must be one that children can easily understand. One easy way is to give them a warm and friendly smile. Simple words also carry the message of how adults feel about children. For example, a short statement from an adult to a child: "That was a big help, Terry." This statement effectively conveys the meaning to the child about his behavior. Gestures often give the child a message of love such as a pat on the child's head, a hand on the shoulder, a clap of hands as the child approaches, a hug, cuddling the child, and rocking the child. Other ways to show love and affection are by giving children attention, such as reading to them, playing with them, and just listening to them talk or tell their stories.

Adults often force children to do things which are supposed to reflect love but which the children do not always understand. Such things as feeding children the right foods, putting them to bed at an early hour, or making them wear coats and boots in winter weather are all done in the interest of children. Children, however, do not usually recognize these as gestures of love, affection, and concern. Listen to parents and other adults as they talk with children;

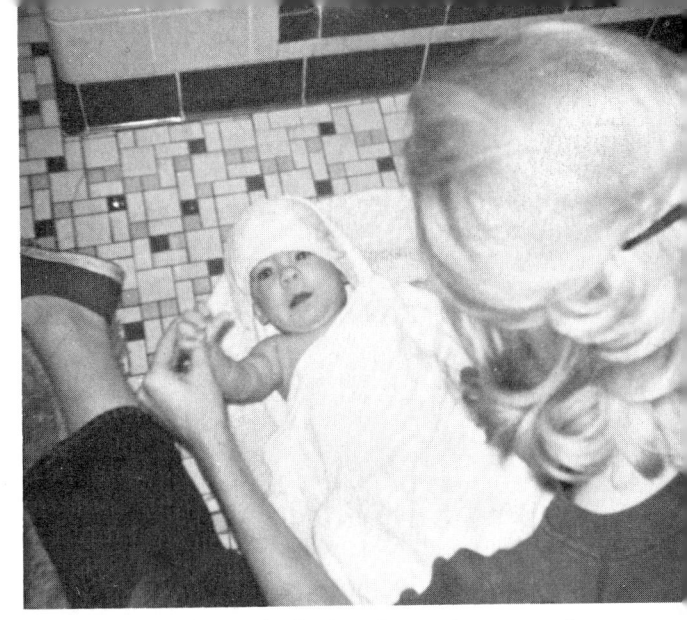

Playing with baby at bath time is another way of showing love and affection.

Part II: Children Learn As They Live

listen for messages of love and affection that children can understand.

NEGATIVE EMOTIONS

Many hours after five-year-old Craig had been in bed, he could still hear his parents arguing in the living room. He could hear his mother crying—sometimes in pain. This was nothing new for Craig, for it had gone on all of his young life. However, it still frightened him and would probably continue to do so.

Craig's anxiety, like many negative emotions, was first experienced at home. It is likely that anxiety will not be the only negative emotion Craig will feel. Eventually, he may resent and even fear his parents because of their behavior.

As you know, children learn from what is going on around them and from what is taught by parents and others. Adults and older brothers and sisters set examples for younger children. If they respond to children with impatience, anger, nervousness, and rudeness, how will children know what it's like to be patient, even-tempered, calm, and polite? Obviously, children who are exposed to negative emotions will likely develop into adults who express the same negative feelings.

Since no two children are exactly alike, emotional development is an individual matter. How a child reacts to a situation depends greatly on his past experiences and his self-concept.

Some children are shy and withdrawn because they feel inferior and lack self-confidence. When children believe they are inadequate, they usually avoid contact with others. They find things to do alone. Some children may express negative feelings in a passive, or quiet, manner if they are not the aggressive type. They may withdraw from others to be alone and silent with their inner feelings.

Negative emotions are usually expressed, however, by aggressive behavior or open hostility. A child may show negative feelings by being rude, loud, bossy, boisterous, or hostile. Inwardly, the child may be insecure and afraid; he may feel he is not accepted or wanted.

Some common problems of children who do not have satisfactory emotional development include speech problems, day dreaming, extreme dependence on others, temper tantrums, overaggressive actions, dishonesty, crying, nervous habits, and withdrawal. Of course, some of these same problems may result for other reasons.

Children with emotional problems often become discouraged easily. Negative feelings may contribute to other behavior problems such as thumb-sucking, stuttering, nail chewing, depressed feelings, fear, inferiority, and thoughts of rejection by peers or family members.

The emphasis in this discussion on emotional development has been on positive rather than negative feelings. Certainly this contributes to the quality of life. That is not to say that negative emotions should never be expressed. There are times when the expression of negative emotions is needed. Crying for the loss of a loved one sometimes helps to ease the sorrow. Dissatisfaction with a theme you write may stir you to write a better one. Fear of having an accident on icy roads may influence you to drive at a slower speed. Can you think of others?

Notice that strong, aggressive emotions are helpful only if controlled. Sorrows, dissatisfactions, and fears which persist

Ch. 7: Emotional Development

and enlarge can cause considerable torment. Those who care for children have the difficult job of showing them, by example, how to express positive emotions and control strong emotions, using them all to the best advantage.

University of Oklahoma Institute of Child Development
Emotions may be expressed by some children through play.

Chapter Highlights

- Emotion is a mental state or condition of excitement or disturbance that causes individuals to act a certain way.
- Emotions have pleasant associations—love, affection, happiness—and unpleasant associations—anger, fear, and hatred.
- Infants show emotional excitement when they experience extreme pleasure or discomfort.
- Affection of one person toward another person is more likely directed toward those who are friendly, kind, and affectionate.
- Too much affection as well as too little can cause problems.
- Studies of infants and young children indicate there is a predictable pattern of affectionate responses.
- The healthy emotional development of a child hinges upon adequate expressions of love.
- An adult's message of love must be one that children can easily understand, such as a warm and friendly smile; a few simple words; gestures in the form of a pat on the child's head, a hand on the shoulder, a clap of hands as the child approaches; reading to them; and playing with them.
- Negative feelings may bring about behavior such as hostility, thumb-sucking, stuttering, nail chewing, depressed feelings, fear, dissatisfaction, and thought of rejection by peers or family members.
- The expression of negative feelings is sometimes needed but is most helpful if controlled.
- Those who care for children have the challenging task of showing them, by example, ways to express emotions effectively.

Part II: Children Learn As They Live

Thinking It Over

1. List three pleasant and three unpleasant emotions.
2. As you grew up, how did your parents express love and affection for you?
3. How do sisters and brothers express emotional feelings for each other?
4. What was the last thing that happened to you that caused you to believe you were liked and appreciated? Explain. What was the last thing you did to make someone else feel liked and appreciated?
5. Discuss problems which can be brought about by giving a child too much affection.
6. Outline the predictable pattern of affectionate responses in infants and young children.
7. Do you know a family in which there seems to be love among the family members, but there are no visible signs of this love? How has this affected the children in the family?
8. Explain, with examples, the importance of sincere love and concern in the lives of infants and young children.
9. Describe what can happen when adults give love to children for doing the right thing but withhold it when children do something wrong.
10. List four ways adults may show love to children in a manner they can understand.
11. Can you remember some things that used to frighten you as a child? How have you learned to handle feelings of fear as you have become older?
12. What are typical ways children behave when they become angry?
13. Give three examples of ways a child may express negative feelings.
14. Describe three possible problems in children's behavior which may reflect unsatisfactory emotional development.
15. Describe a situation in which the expression of negative feelings can be helpful.

Things To Do

1. Collect cartoons which portray emotional feelings in children and adults. Make a bulletin board with these illustrations. Discuss these in class.
2. Observe a group of young children under the direction of a teacher. Record ways by which the teacher shows them they are liked and cared for.
3. Bring to class poems that express love, affection, happiness, anger, fear, and hatred. Discuss these in class. (Students may write their own poems.)
4. Bring to class newspaper or magazine articles that relate expressions of positive feelings of parents toward their children. Discuss.
5. Collect newspaper articles describing incidents of child abuse. Discuss these in class. Discuss the problems that occur when people do not learn to control negative feelings. Describe the emotions which were probably in operation in each case of child abuse.
6. Observe children in a play situation. Record the ways they express both positive and negative feelings.
7. Record for one week the ways people express their emotions to you. Add approximate ages of people involved. Discuss any relationships you find between types of emotional responses and age.

Ch. 7: Emotional Development

Recommended Reading

Arnstein, Helene S. *What to Tell Your Child.* New York: Bobbs-Merrill, 1962.

Behrens, Herman D., and Maynard, Glenn. *The Changing Child: Readings in Child Development.* Glenview, Illinois: Scott, Foresman and Co., 1972.

Bernard, Harold H. *Human Development in Western Culture.* Boston: Allyn and Bacon, Inc., 1970.

Bettelheim, Bruno. *Love Is Not Enough.* Glencoe, Illinois: The Free Press, 1950.

Briggs, Dorothy Corkille. *Your Child's Self Esteem: The Key to His Life.* New York: Doubleday and Co., Inc., 1970.

Coller, Alan. *Assessment of Self-Concept in Early Child Education.* Urbana, Illinois: University of Illinois, Curriculum Lab.

Developmental Psychology Today. Del Mar, California: Communications Research Machines, Inc., 1971.

Fraiberg, Selma H. *The Magic Years.* New York: Charles Scribner's Sons, 1959.

Lichtenberg, Phillip, and Norton, Dolores. *Cognitive and Mental Development in the First Five Years of Life.* Rockville, Maryland: National Institute of Mental Health.

Mental Health Digest. National Clearinghouse for Mental Health Information, Vol. 4, No. 2, February, 1972, Washington, D.C.: Superintendent of Documents.

Wolf, Anna W. M. *Your Child's Emotional Health.* Public Affairs Pamphlet, #264, 381 Park Avenue South, New York, 1973.

Chapter 8.

Developmental Tasks and Skills

Your Challenge

This chapter will enable you to . . . .

- Define the term <u>developmental task</u>.
- Name three authorities on child development and psychology and describe their theories on the stages of development.
- Define the term <u>critical period</u> as related to learning.
- Name and describe the developmental tasks and skills.
- Tell how children master developmental tasks and skills.
- Explain the purpose for sequencing activities.

LEARNING DEVELOPMENTAL TASKS AND SKILLS

In exploring children's learning, we are faced with questions like these: What should be learned? When and where should learning take place? To answer these questions, we must think about the needs and goals of children. We must decide what it is that will help children enjoy life more fully and what it is that will help them be productive members of society now and in the future. We need to know what will help them develop their fullest potentials.

Whether we intend it or not, children never stop learning. The *when* of learning depends not only on the level of the child's development but also on the degree of the child's interest. Learning is a continual process; the child is learning something all the time. Even when a child loafs during an activity or refuses to do a given task, he is learning a mode of operation. A carefully planned children's program enables child care workers to enhance learning by introducing activities which support the goals for the children and which encourage self-motivation.

Ideally, every childhood experience will contribute to the child's development. One of the goals for adults who work with children is to provide a setting which approaches this ideal. In the process of learning developmental tasks and skills, children need adult understanding and guidance. You can help children as they learn by being sensitive to their special needs. You can:

- Respond to the child's need for attention.
- Expect children to regress at times to babyish ways of behaving.
- Be sensitive and alert to clues which indicate a child's interest.
- Recognize a child's intentions.
- Encourage children to explore and pursue their curiosity.

Children need help in learning developmental tasks and skills. Here are some reasons why:

- Children need broadening experiences for building language skills—words, sentences, and verbal symbols.
- Confusion occurs easily by apparent changes in sizes and shapes of objects.
- Making choices and taking turns are needed to play simple games.
- Distinguishing between fantasy and reality is not easily achieved with limited experiences.
- A child's strong feelings toward his parents often result in anxiety when separated from them.
- Children sometimes have great concern about being little and supposedly unimportant. They may compensate by attempts to control.
- Concepts about the beginning and the end are difficult, such as with birth and death.
- Children need to develop an awareness of time and other intangible concepts.
- Unseen things are often of great interest—God, heaven, warmth, roots.
- Children sometimes fear the possibility of losing parts of their bodies. This may cause frustration over cutting hair or fingernails.
- The concept of self develops slowly and gradually.

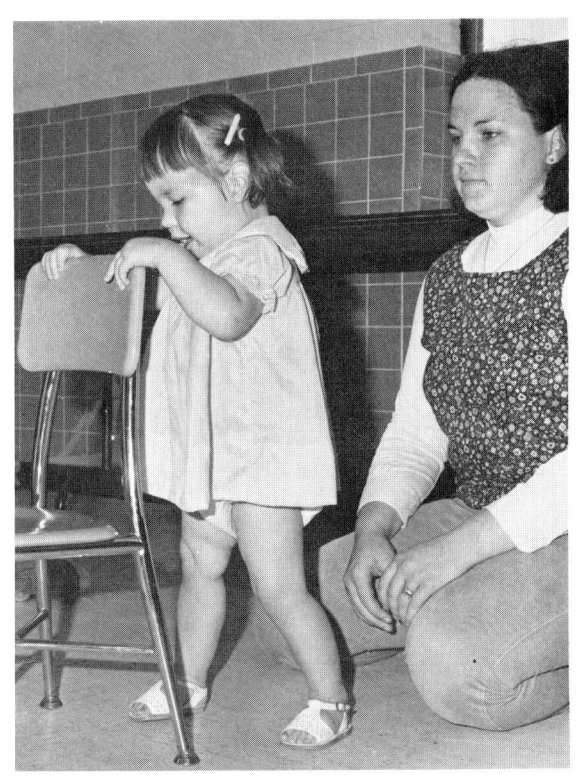

As children progress from one stage of development to the next, they need to experience success with tasks required for everyday living.

WHAT ARE DEVELOPMENTAL TASKS?

Children learn as they live—walking, talking, reading, playing, and getting along with others. As children move from one phase, or stage of development, to the next, they need to experience success in *achieving the tasks* required for meaningful and happy living. These are called *developmental tasks*, and they occur in all areas of development.

There is a continuous relationship between individual needs, the maturation process, and the demands of the culture which influence development. The increasing of physical powers and the broadening

Part II: Children Learn As They Live

of intellectual capacities help each child meet new demands and expectations.

Robert J. Havighurst, psychologist, educator, and author, identifies developmental tasks as the result of individual needs generated by social demands. Basic to children's mental health are security, belonging, recognition, approval, status, and independence. Certain tasks must be mastered if a child is to maintain a normal course of development in meeting these needs. In other words, a developmental task is a skill, a responsibility, or an attribute to be achieved or acquired for effective daily living.

Although authorities use different terms and categories to describe the developmental tasks, the stages and tasks are similar. Three approaches are presented here to help you grasp the developmental task concept. The significance of helping children learn, however, does not lie in memorizing the particular task division. It is important, though, for you to be familiar with the concept of developmental tasks in order to provide appropriate experiences for children as they grow and learn. Compare the tasks identified by the following authorities.

Dr. Havighurst has made a significant contribution to child development by showing how influences combine to make it necessary for people to achieve tasks for living together as individuals within a society and culture. These influencing factors are biological, cultural, and psychological. Havighurst's idea of developmental tasks has implications for all who work with children. The following definition is found in most references which include a discussion of developmental tasks:

"A developmental task is a task which arises at or about a certain period in the life of the individual, successful achievement of which leads to his happiness and to success with later tasks, while failure leads to unhappiness in the individual, disapproval by society, and difficulty with later tasks."*

Havighurst developed a framework for explaining developmental tasks. He divided the stages of development into the following categories and identified the developmental tasks for each: Infancy and early childhood, middle childhood, adolescence, early adulthood, middle age, and later maturity. The first two categories are presented here to help you become acquainted with his concept.

Developmental tasks of infancy and early childhood:

- Learning to take solid food.
- Learning to walk.
- Learning to talk.
- Learning control for eliminating body wastes.
- Learning sex differences and sexual modesty.
- Formulating concepts of social and physical reality.
- Achieving physiological stability.
- Learning to relate emotionally to others.
- Learning to distinguish right and wrong and developing a conscience.

Developmental tasks of middle childhood:

- Learning physical skills.
- Building wholesome attitudes toward oneself.
- Learning to get along with others of the same age.

---

*Robert J. Havighurst, *Developmental Tasks and Education,* Third Edition, New York: David McKay Company, Inc., 1972.

Ch. 8: Developmental Tasks and Skills

- Learning an appropriate masculine or feminine social role.
- Developing fundamental skills in reading, writing, and calculating.
- Developing conscience, morality, and a scale of values.
- Achieving personal independence.
- Developing attitudes toward social groups and institutions.

According to Philippe Muller, authority in child development and psychology, each

STAGES OF DEVELOPMENT ACCORDING TO MULLER*

Stage	Task
Infancy	
Newborn	• Entirely physiological.
Young baby	• Coordination of eye and body movements—the first "action." • Injection of solid food.
Early language	• Acquisition of language. • Toilet training.
School age	
Early childhood	• Growth of self-awareness. • Attainment of physiological stability. • Formation of simple concepts related to physical and social reality. • Concepts of good and evil and appearance of a conscience
Childhood realism	• Social communications with peers. • Appropriate sex role. • Healthy attitude about own development. • Mastery of physical skills for games. • Reading, writing, arithmetic. • Concepts for daily living.
Ages of first choices	• The change of logic.
Adolescence	
Puberty	• Recognition of limitations. • New human relationships.
Age of enlightenment	• Achievement of emotional independence. • Choice of the life partner.
Age of vital choices	• Choice of career. • Formation of a personal philosophy.

*Muller, Philippe. *The Tasks of Childhood.* New York: McGraw-Hill Book Co., 1969, pp. 136, 147, 184, 197.

Part II: Children Learn As They Live

Only when the child is ready physically and socially will he feel the need to try a new task.

phase of development has a *central task* which must be learned by the child. The achievement of these central tasks leads to other tasks which are part of the total developing process. He presents central tasks in three stages of development for young children, as shown in the chart.

Erik Erikson, a neoanalyst and recognized authority on personality development, formulated a model of significant tasks in eight areas of personality development. He identified these as the "eight stages of man." Each stage requires the accomplishment of a certain attribute before the next stage can be managed successfully. These stages are shown in the chart.

As you can see, the idea of the developmental task concept is that a child who successfully accomplishes a certain task at about the right time will be able to cope with expectations of society and will have success with later tasks. Success with a task contributes to the child's stability and happiness in daily living as an individual and family or group member. Success brings courage to face the next task. When a task is not mastered, the child suffers from inabilities which handicap progress with future tasks. Frustration and unhappiness often accompany problems when failure is frequent.

The developmental task concept is a valuable tool for understanding children because it specifies the important developmental achievements necessary for children at each stage of life. It is also important for planning instructional, or teaching, efforts—for helping children learn. Finding the best time for teaching a child certain things is easier if you understand when the child is most ready to learn. As you saw in the charts, the developmental task concept includes the idea that some tasks must be accomplished to set the stage, or build the necessary foundation, for the development of tasks to follow.

THE CRITICAL PERIOD

From the previous discussion, you know there is an appropriate time for tasks to be accomplished. We call this time the critical period. It is a time when certain conditions are present—the body is ready, societal pressures arise, and the individual feels the need to achieve a certain task. The child has reached a *state of readiness*. He learns the required task and is then prepared for the next step in the developmental process. Having accomplished the tasks of one stage, the child seeks or yearns for the next stage.

Before the critical period, a child is not ready to accomplish a given task. Efforts

STAGES OF PERSONALITY DEVELOPMENT
ACCORDING TO ERIKSON

Developmental Stage	Task of Personality Development
Infancy—first one or two years	Basic trust, security, optimism.
Early childhood—eighteen months to four years	Autonomy, independence, learning control, making decisions, developing new motor skills and mental powers.
Play age—three and one-half years to school age	Initiative, imagination, cooperation, relationships with parents, conscience development, exploration of the world through the senses.
School age—elementary and some junior high	Industry, life skills—relating with peers, teamwork, mastering studies, self-discipline.
Adolescence—thirteen to twenty years	Identity, self-certainty, role experimentation, sexual identity, development of set of ideals, concept of self and society.
Young adult	Intimacy, romantic love, understanding of self and allowing oneself to be understood by others.
Adulthood	Generativity—involvement in the development and well-being of others of the next generation, working productively and creatively, marriage, parenthood.
Mature adulthood	Integrity—peak of adjustment, proud of accomplishments, satisfaction with one's life cycle and its place in time and space through meaningful actions, relationships, and values.

Erikson, Erik H. "The Problem of Ego Identity". *Journal of American Psychoanalytical Association*, April 4, 1956, pp. 56-121.
  Smart, Mollie S. and Smart, Russell C. *Children: Development and Relationships*. New York: The Macmillan Co., 1972, pp. 649-650.

to push the child to master a task may cause frustration, often resulting in a waste of time and effort for both the adult and the child. If the task is attempted too early, it may be achieved only temporarily or partially. If the task is too difficult, the child may become discouraged and fail. For example, if parents try to force a child to achieve bowel control with strict toilet training before the child's muscles and nerves have developed sufficiently, the child will likely experience frustration and increased difficulty. On the other hand, if training is delayed beyond the critical period, the child may become frustrated and his development impaired; the following developmental task is likely to be more difficult, causing the child to be even less competent. Repeated failures may result in feelings of inadequacy which discourage the child from attempting other tasks such as self-dressing and grooming.

LAYING THE FOUNDATION

Authorities tell us that the satisfactory accomplishment of developmental tasks

Part II: Children Learn As They Live

What might happen if this infant is pushed to walk too soon?

during infancy lays a wholesome foundation for growth and development in later developmental periods. During infancy, a pattern of adjustment is generally established for all the later periods of life.

Some developmental tasks, such as crawling and walking, result primarily from physical maturation, while other tasks, such as learning to read and write, arise from cultural pressures. Notice this as you read about Matt's development in the following paragraphs. Also, think about what success means to children as they move from one stage of development to the next.

In the early months of Matt's life, he made his needs known by crying and squirming. As he grew physically and developed socially, he became aware of his environment and those around him. Gradually, Matt took more interest in others, enjoying social interactions with family members and those close to him. As his development progressed, Matt was able to communicate by words and more meaningful gestures, bringing him recognition as an individual. As a baby, Matt's digestive system developed. He learned to chew and eagerly changed from liquid to solid foods. Between the ages of about nine and fifteen months, Matt's muscles, bones, and nerve tissues developed enough for him to take his first steps. As physical maturation continued, he learned to run, jump, and skip.

By age two, Matt could play successfully with older children but had not learned to play with children his own age. He enjoyed parallel play—being around others but playing by himself with his own toys. From this stage, Matt began to play with one child at a time and then in groups for short periods.

Between the ages of one and four, Matt faced the task of developing a sense of independence. Even though he was able to view himself as an individual apart from his parents and other close adults, he was still dependent on them for certain needs. By about age six, Matt's nervous system had matured enough for him to learn simple writing skills. His eye and muscle coordination, however, did not develop enough to master the skills until later. Fortunately for Matt, failure to develop certain tasks was not a problem. With plenty of timely encouragement and some trial and error, Matt learned the tasks at the appropriate stages of development.

Some developmental tasks are the result of personal values and individual intentions. Deciding on the type of work you would like to do is one of these. This task comes later in life after many basic tasks leading to adulthood have been accomplished.

Can you now see the usefulness of the developmental task concept in helping identify important activities for children at different stages? Although we must always recognize the individual differences that make each child unique, development follows a predictable pattern which makes it possible for us to know what to expect of children at each stage of development.

A CLOSER LOOK AT THE DEVELOPMENTAL TASKS AND SKILLS

A simple awareness that there are such things as developmental tasks and skills is not enough if you are going to work with children. You also need to be familiar with the specific tasks so you can help children achieve success. As you read more about developmental tasks, think about what you might do to help a child who is having difficulty with each of them.

Weaning

Weaning, the changeover from bottle or breast milk to cup feeding and solid foods, usually occurs within the first year. The length of time needed to change from milk to baby food varies with different children.

Successful weaning is greatly affected by the behavior of parents or other adults who care for the child. For example, the infant, accustomed to a liquid diet, may push away from solid food. Forcing the child to take the solid nourishment often results in increased refusal rather than success. The child will eventually accept solid food if it is offered repeatedly in a relaxed and pleasant atmosphere. Whether bottle-, cup-, or breast-fed, children will eat more solid foods as they attain more teeth and as their teeth harden.

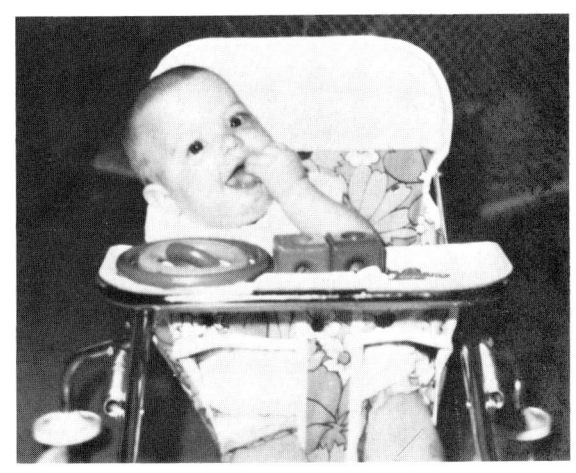

Infants attempt to feed themselves by hand before using a spoon.

Self-Feeding

Infants show interest in self-feeding during the latter part of the first year as they attempt to feed themselves with a spoon. Let's look at a typical case.

By the age of eight months, Hilary could hold her bottle after it was placed in her mouth. A month later she could remove the bottle as well as put it back into her mouth. At ten months, Hilary began to reach for the spoon used to feed her. This showed she was ready to face the task of self-feeding.

While trying to use a spoon, Hilary also learned to hold a cup. At the age of twelve months, she could only hold a cup momentarily. She used both hands. Gradually, she was able to use one hand for this task.

During her second year, Hilary learned to manipulate a fork in addition to a spoon. Moreover, she spilled less food. During the third year, spreading butter and jam on

Part II: Children Learn As They Live

bread with a knife was a great accomplishment. Hilary did not learn to use the knife for cutting, however, until she was about four.

All of the tasks that Hilary faced required effort, concentration, and practice. The same is true for all children. Children should be expected to dawdle and tire during the early stages of self-feeding experiences. Between the third and fourth year, however, dawdling usually reaches its peak. Eating skills then become more automatic and less tiring. By the age of five, most children who have had opportunities to learn can manage self-feeding with success and independence.

As self-feeding skills improve, children can coordinate eating and talking. By the age of ten, children have usually mastered control of eating utensils. By this age, most children have developed self-feeding skills, social graces, and appropriate table behavior.

In children's centers it is not unusual to have some four- and five-year-olds who have not mastered the expected self-feeding skills. These children need encouragement and assistance as they catch up. Children with poor eye-to-hand coordination have difficulty in developing eating skills. As they succeed in eye-to-hand skills, they will be likely to succeed with eating skills. We help children most by starting at their present level of skill and working step-by-step until they have accomplished the desired task.

Some children have limited opportunities at home to develop self-feeding skills. Extreme poverty may limit the experiences of some to eating foods with fingers from a common bowl shared by family members. Some children from affluent homes may be overprotected, possibly even fed by an adult to prevent soiling clothes or disarranging table appointments.

A word of caution: We must be careful not to communicate to a child that family eating habits at home are wrong because they differ from those in the center. We must always maintain the child's concept of worth and dignity for himself and his family. Children are quite flexible and usually adapt readily to patterns of behavior in the center even if they are somewhat different from those in the home. Children learn there are more ways than one to do something.

Walking

Early motor activity becomes apparent as a child's natural desire to pull into an upright position is satisfied. Between three and four months, the infant can sit for about a minute, and by about seven or eight months, sitting occurs without support. By nine months, most babies can sit independently for about ten minutes.

Although crawling (the body is close to the floor) and creeping (the body is raised from the floor) are not necessary to achieve the task of walking, many infants go through these stages of development. *Crawling* usually occurs between twenty-eight and thirty-four weeks. The trunk muscles, arms, and legs are not strong enough to support the body weight for a walking position. As the child attains additional coordination and equilibrium, by about forty weeks, *creeping* on hands, knees, and feet is usually accomplished.

Standing and walking result as the child learns to use the legs for movement. Through this exercise, the child gains experience in self-reliance. Allowing the child to walk without adult help, as much as possible, enhances the development of

Ch. 8: Developmental Tasks and Skills

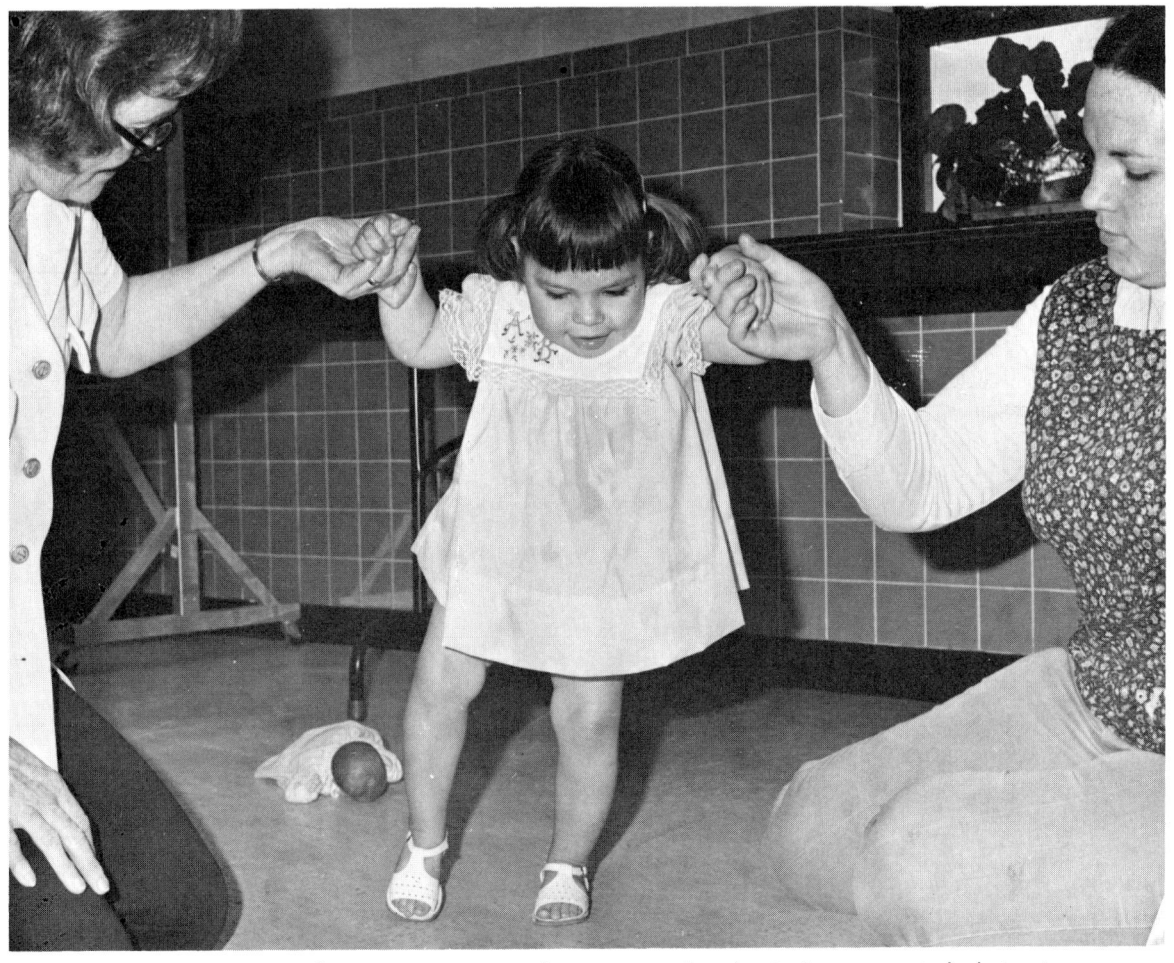

Children may need some assistance and assurance when beginning a new task, but not so much that independence is stifled.

self-assurance as well as locomotion. A safe environment with freedom for the child to wander in secure space, attended by an adult, promotes development of this task.

Children will, no doubt, fall many times in the process of learning to walk. They should not be helped so much that independence is stifled, nor should adults console them every time they fall. As children begin to walk, steps will be short and of unequal distance. As they become older, they will lift their legs higher than necessary in the stepping process. By the second and third year, a leveling will occur as they begin to move efficiently and smoothly.

A child will acquire the skill of walking when the muscular system is sufficiently

Part II: Children Learn As They Live

developed and after control of body balance and body movement has been successfully accomplished. Shoes that are too tight, bulky, or heavy; excessive fear of falling; and too much pressure from adults to walk are all factors which can inhibit a child and prevent him from mastering the skill of walking.

Toilet Training

During late infancy, toilet control becomes a major developmental task. Toilet training is generally started toward the end of infancy at about fifteen to nineteen months. By this time the child is usually able to exercise control over the basic skeletal muscles. Development of the nerves that control urination is completed sometime between two and four years of age. *Bladder control* (control of urination) is achieved by some children as early as eighteen months. Complete *sphincter control* (bowel movement regulation) is usually attained during the fourth year.

Two conditions are necessary for the child's accomplishment of adequate toilet training. One is *readiness* of the neuromuscular system (nerves and muscles working together) and the other is *emotional stability* between the child and adult. Children's ability to *understand* has increased by this age, enabling them to respond directly and with positive attitudes to simple requests of others.

The muscles in the trunk region which regulate the organs of elimination are the last to be controlled. There is great variation in the time when children begin control over their organs of elimination. It is unwise to form expectations by comparing one child with another, as some develop this muscle control much sooner than others. By the time a child is two or two and one-half years old, the dry habit during the

Robert Michels

Toilet training must take place in a relaxed and comfortable atmosphere.

day is usually well developed. By about three to three and one-half, the dry habit during the night is usually progressing successfully. By the age of about two years, bowel control is underway, followed in a few months by the child's ability to use toilet facilities independently. Children are considered to be toilet trained when they are able to recognize and control the need to urinate or defecate and when they can be responsible for keeping themselves dry and clean.

Adults who work with children will be wise to accept toileting accidents as part of the routine with young children. A few mishaps will, no doubt, occur and should be handled without scolding. A firm, kind attitude helps build the child's understanding of toileting habits while increasing self-confidence. Maintaining a calm, casual, and objective attitude about toileting will help children face toileting experiences with less anxiety. Young children are very proud of their toileting progress and respond positively to adult recognition of this accomplishment.

By the fourth year, children are usually quite comfortable about toileting routines and can manipulate simple clothing with ease and confidence. Care should be taken to provide children with simple, easy-to-manipulate clothing in an effort to help them develop independence and success in toileting tasks.

Communication Skills

Babbling and other vocal sounds occur naturally during infancy, especially for the first six months. Infants usually leave the meaningless crying and babbling stage at about six weeks and move to cooing, crying, or other sounds that eventually become part of meaningful speech.

Infants, as well as young children, need an environment which encourages verbal experiences. They need many opportunities for vocalization—making sounds.

Infants develop a number of sounds to which adults attach meanings without having to learn them. Later, infants learn new sounds by imitating others. Intelligible sounds usually occur between twelve and eighteen months as the child begins to use specific sounds that have been taken from adult language. At about eighteen months, single-word sentences are often used to convey messages. By this time, the child knows that a word stands for something. Meaningful single words are commonly used to convey a thought or message. For example, "milk" may mean "I want milk" when a child points to the bottle. Other single words often used at this early stage include go, here, mama, and no. Meaningful speech and short sentences typically occur between eighteen and twenty-eight months. From about eighteen months until the fourth or fifth year, the period of baby talk occurs.

Infants enjoy communicating. They are delighted when their requests are understood and satisfied. An example is "mama cwaker"—"Mother, I want a cracker." Baby talk gives way to accurate pronunciation as children hear and understand words of others. Children are easily motivated to go beyond baby talk to advanced speech. Parents and adults can help children enjoy the task of communicating by providing experiences that encourage speech development in a natural way. Sound games, musical activities, and story time are only a few activities which offer ways for children to master language skills.

Overcorrective, anxious, and demanding adults may hinder a child's speech development. Children need to practice speaking without pressure or ridicule. Mimicking or treating baby talk as cute or entertaining only prolongs it by bringing attention and recognition to the infant's performance.

Many authorities agree that a period of speech readiness occurs between twelve and eighteen months. This is a critical period for spoken language to be acquired. If speech is not learned during this period, the parents may need to seek counsel from their doctor or a speech specialist. Speech is a means of expressing feelings, and children with delayed or inadequate means of expressing their feelings may face difficulties.

Between three and four years of age, most children increase their speaking ability rapidly. By this time, speech becomes the primary means of expression. Person-

Communications skills develop through play.

ality development, associations with others, and understanding of the environment are affected greatly by a child's ability to communicate.

In studying the speech development of young children, authorities have listed several tasks concerned with increasing communication skills during the preschool age:
- Understanding the speech of others.
- Building a vocabulary.
- Combining words into sentences to express thoughts.
- Expressing needs and relating experiences.
- Increasing conversational skill to gain attention.
- Improving pronunciation and diction (saying words clearly).
- Using all the parts of speech.

Some children have little opportunity at home to practice language skills or hear good examples. A lack of communication interchange means a lack of models for children. Children in some homes hear mainly commands and short phrases of direction or correction—"stop it," "go play," "no," "shut up," "hush." Such communications do little to promote adequate speech patterns.

Communication skills are accomplished in a gradual step-by-step fashion. Children should not be forced to speak correctly or punished for speaking incorrectly. We must be patient and work with each child at his or her level of language development. Encouragement and recognition of children's efforts will help. As the child experiences success, a positive self-concept develops. Children who express themselves adequately usually feel good about themselves.

Formulating Ideas

By the end of infancy, young children begin to view with curiosity what is going on in the world about them. They generalize first about people, things, sounds, and images. Gradually, they begin to use such symbols as numbers and letters with meaning. They begin by grasping the idea of grouping things into such categories as human; animal; plantlife; things that are large, small, round, and square; and concepts of hot and cold, old and young, and near and far. When a child's neurological (nervous) system is ready, experiences are needed to help form many concepts that will be helpful throughout life.

Relating to Self and Others

Children share their experiences with those who care for them mainly through verbal communications. They say what they think and how they feel. They may imitate others by playing roles—nurse, fireman, mother, father, teacher. Children develop habits of speech and ways of behaving by copying the actions of others. As you know from previous discussions, developing a positive self-image or self-concept is a significant task for all children. They learn to identify themselves as separate individuals through experiences with those around them. From early infancy throughout childhood, they must achieve the task of self-identification. They are eager to have others recognize them as individuals with worth and importance.

Developing a Conscience

As children leave infancy, they begin to develop an understanding of what is good and what is bad, according to the standards of those around them. Children learn from others to place value on approved behavior. They learn to avoid punishment by understanding acceptable and unacceptable behavior. They learn responsibility for their behavior by the responses they receive from others—punishment, affection, recognition, and expectations. With proper guidance they develop a conscience which urges them to do what they have learned is right.

Learning About Sex

Sex is an important part of life, and the foundations for healthy attitudes are established in early childhood. In learning about sex, children relate best with adults who remain calm and open. Children need help in acquiring a wholesome outlook concerning sexuality.

Children begin to gather information about sex during the years prior to school age. This is the time when they learn *anatomical* (body) *differences* between the male and female. By the age of three, most children recognize gender—whether male or female. They are curious and interested in sex differences. Naturally, children observe each other and often attempt to see these differences. You will probably see children following their curiosity by observing one another during toileting as well as other activities. Adults should feel comfortable in naming the genital organs by the proper terminology, such as penis or vagina.

Between the ages of three and five, children begin to raise questions about sex. They give cues on how much information is wanted. As you may know, many adults are reluctant to respond to a young child's inquiries in this area. Children, however, do need relaxed and comfortable situations

Part II: Children Learn As They Live

in which to learn about themselves. Following short, simple, and factual answers, a child will either be satisfied or will ask another question. Children should feel free to ask questions or make statements regarding sex. If they do not get positive responses from adults, they will probably look for information elsewhere, or they will experience frustration and feelings of guilt about their curiosity.

In addition to the physical functions of the body, children are curious about social differences between males and females. First, children learn to distinguish between boys and girls by such features as their clothes, hair, stature (body build), skin, and voice. Gradually, they recognize differences in expected *sex roles*—what males are expected to be like and what females are expected to be like.

Boys and girls, until about age three or four, are very much alike in the things with which they play, what they like to do, and how they see themselves. Both boys and girls may be found playing with dolls and animals, wearing dress-up clothes, playing with blocks, sand, and water, or playing cowboy. Little concern is given to the role characteristics of either sex. As children approach the age of three, they begin to view themselves and their environment from a different perspective. They are beginning to recognize themselves as girls or boys.

Many children have difficulty in identifying with a male or female, such as the father or mother, when one or the other is absent from home either permanently or a great amount of the time. Research indicates that most children spend more time during the early years with women than with men. Men and boys working in children's centers offer a much-needed male

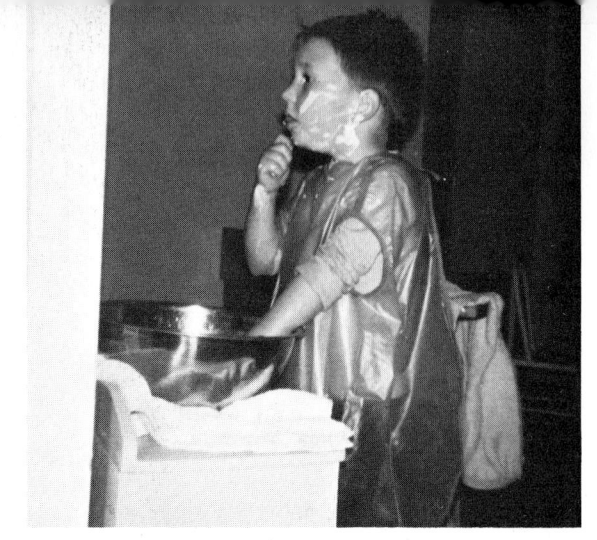

Children develop ideas about sex differences through role playing.

model with whom children, especially boys, can identify.

During the early years, young children need to see where both men and women work and what types of work they do. They can learn that many occupations may be pursued by both men and women. Field trips are especially good for providing this experience. Having people come to the center and talk with children about their jobs also helps boys and girls learn about adult roles—nurse, policeman, social worker, dentist, secretary, clerk, and so on.

Dramatic play with dress-up clothes helps boys and girls identify sex differences. Keep in mind that children gradually identify sex differences themselves. They will ask questions when they are ready. There is no need to force this information on children, but it is important to provide a climate which helps each child learn comfortably and without restraint.

Of course, we do not want to establish rigid male and female roles for children. Three- and four-year-old boys may enjoy playing house and working in the kitchen; likewise, girls may thoroughly enjoy dig-

Dramatic play helps Michelle identify with a mother role.

The predominate use of one hand over the other generally becomes evident between the ages of three and five.

ging in the dirt, playing with trucks and trains, and feeding animals—and why not? We want children to grow up to be creative and productive in whatever they do. The importance of early experiences is to provide ways for children to become acquainted with roles and feelings of boys and girls and men and women in very natural ways.

The *how* of helping children learn about sex differences and sex roles has not only been controversial in the past few decades but has also been misused in many respects. For instance, on the one hand, parents and adults who care for children may attempt to stifle curiosity and withhold information about their sexuality. On the other hand, they may go into too much detail for the child's level of understanding. Research and clinical evidence suggests that both restrictive sex training and overly permissive training, including overexposure to sexual information, may leave children frustrated and sexually unstable.

The greatest help comes from adults who demonstrate healthy sexual attitudes. Children learn more effectively when they receive information about sex from adults who are capable of being objective, who are comfortable in discussing sex, and who are free from notions or superstitions about sex. How well prepared are you for helping children in this area?

Handedness

As you are well aware, daily living skills require the use of hands and arms. Skills used in performing everyday manual tasks usually require the major use of one hand with assistance from the other. For example, one hand holds the paint brush or chalk while the other hand helps steady the paper.

Handedness, the predominate use of one hand over the other, generally becomes evident between the third and fifth years. A person is considered *right-handed* if the right hand is dominant most of the time or *left-handed* if the left hand is dominant most of the time. Children may shift from one hand to the other until about the third year. A person who uses both hands with equal skill and time is said to be *ambidex-*

Left-handed children must learn to cope with a primarily right-handed society.

trous. Few people, however, are ambidextrous. For example, few are able to throw or bat a ball equally as well with both hands or write successfully with either hand.

As you know, there are more right-handed than left-handed people in our society. The culture we live in provides most equipment and furniture for use by right-handed people. Think about how the following activities are related to handedness: cutting, sawing, hammering, painting, drawing, writing, throwing, catching, playing musical instruments, sewing, measuring, dialing, eating, and manipulating toys and other objects. Do you see what problems left-handed children could have when learning these skills? Even methods of teaching are directed toward right-handedness. Imagine the problems a right-handed person would have teaching a left-handed person to knit or crochet. (Some have used mirrors to overcome this problem.) Unless it is impossible or difficult, it is usually an advantage for a child to be right-handed.

The child with left-handed tendencies who tries to imitate the right-handed model in writing or performing any manual task (like tying a bow) will probably face some difficulties. Movements may be awkward and inefficient. Frustrations are likely to occur when a child faces too many learning and social situations which are complicated by the conflict between left- and right-handedness.

Child development specialists do not agree on whether or not an attempt should be made to change a child's handedness. Parents and other adults faced with this question must consider the child involved. In a mild way, right-handedness may be encouraged. One way to do this is by handing things to a child so that he will be more likely to take them with the right hand. If he persists in left-handedness, it is probably best to avoid trying to force the child to change. Every effort should be made to form a cooperative and consistant pattern between the home and the center. Handedness is a concern which parents and child care workers should talk about together. Pressure, ridicule, and scolding should all be avoided. Even though children who are left-handed face some difficulties in skill development, they can usually function comfortably if undue strain is not added to the situation.

Self-Dressing

It is easier for young children to pull off their shoes and socks than to put them on. Greater motor coordination is needed for putting on clothing. Some clothes, of course, are more difficult to put on than others because of complicated fastenings and adjustments which require greater motor skill. Children show the most rapid improvement in dressing skills between one and one-half and three and one-half years.

Girls usually dress themselves earlier and more efficiently than boys. This is primarily because girl's wrists are more flexible, they are better coordinated, and their clothes are usually simpler. By age five, children should be able to dress themselves, except for such details as tying shoelaces. The task of tying shoelaces is usually mastered by age six. Naturally, it takes some children a little longer.

Eye-to-hand coordination is necessary until dressing becomes so automatic that children can manipulate the clothing without having to see exactly what they are doing. During the learning stage, a child must be able to see a zipper or a button and hole in order to manipulate them. By three or four years of age, most children can cope with fasteners even in difficult positions by looking into a mirror. Around age six, skills for self-dressing are developed well enough to enable children to manipulate fasteners and make adjustments without using their eyes to guide hand movements.

Grooming Skills

Along with the tasks of self-dressing, children gradually develop grooming skills. Even before she was able to walk, Katy represented the typical young child's ability with grooming skills. She attempted to brush her *hair,* but not until she was two or three could she actually brush without doing more harm than good. Most children are able to brush and comb their hair by kindergarten age but still need help with parting it. Some hairstyles for girls or boys may require adult help. An example is braiding. Using bows and headbands may also require help.

Most early attempts at *bathing* are limited to splashing and playing with toys and bath articles. For example, during a bath, Timothy, age one and one-half, tried to bathe himself, using the soap and washcloth to run down the center of his face and body. He was more interested, however, in watching the soapsuds splatter as he hit the water with both hands. Toward the end of his second year, Timothy began

Gradually and with practice, children develop grooming skills.

to settle down and could cover most of the front of his body with soap. By the time Timothy was six years old, he could wash his back.

For most young children, *brushing teeth* is a game, especially when they like the taste of the toothpaste. By the time a child has all his baby teeth, about age three and one-half, he will be able to brush his teeth successfully with little or no help. Children should be provided with a toothbrush and encouraged to develop a pattern of brushing daily. Not only is this a health practice, but it also contributes to a feeling of inde-

Between the ages of three and four, children can usually brush their teeth successfully with little or no help.

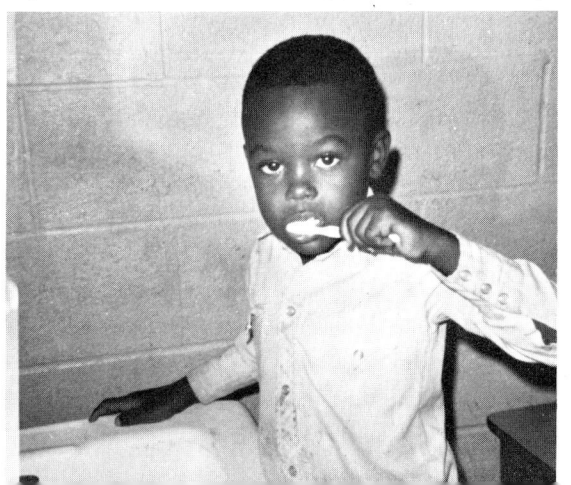

Children enjoy dot-to-dot experiences after they have had opportunities to scribble and practice, using crayons and marking pens.

Using a large paint brush is helpful in gaining control over eye-to-hand movements.

pendence on the child's part. Children enjoy praise for their efforts and often repeat a behavior such as brushing teeth if complimented.

Scribbling, Drawing, and Writing

Up to one year of age, children play and scribble with pencils. By eighteen months, they scribble in the middle of a page and by age three, they attempt to make symbols—though scarcely recognized as letters. According to numerous authorities, the body is not biologically ready for handwriting until about six. Until this time, the nerves and muscles of the fingers, hands, and wrists—in addition to eye-to-hand coordination—are not developed sufficiently for the fine control required in writing. Follow the sequence of Kim's progress in developing writing readiness skills.

- Kim began her scribbling experience by using a large, thick piece of chalk or a large thick crayon which was easy to grasp and hold with her hand and fingers. After several weeks of playing with the chalk or crayon, Kim successfully achieved the task of manipulating the markers with one hand.
- Following many opportunities to scribble, Kim gained control of arm, hand, and finger movements.
- She was finally ready to start drawing simple straight lines. Kim's mother helped her begin at the left side of the paper or chalkboard and proceed to the right side. She enjoyed dot-to-dot exercises which helped her remember to go in a left-to-right direction.
- In addition to crayons and large sheets of newsprint, Kim used chalk on a chalkboard because she could erase and practice many times.
- When the above task was mastered, Kim was ready to draw lines from left to right without dots to follow. She began by connecting cutouts of different shapes.
- Drawing circles was another step in Kim's writing readiness activities. She began at the left and moved in a clockwise motion to achieve the drawing of a complete circle. This required lots of practice.

- Kim's next achievement was the completion of the figure eight.
- Finally, Kim was on her way to drawing pictures.

Can you see how appropriate activities and materials enhanced Kim's skill development in scribbling and drawing? Can you also see that she could easily become discouraged if she had been expected to print her name or draw pictures before she was developmentally ready?

As Kim increased awareness of her body and learned positions of laterality (left and right directions) through large muscle activities, she also developed concepts of spatial relationships. Early experiences helped build the foundation for future tasks such as learning to read and write.

As you know, in our culture we learn to read from left to right. We begin at the top of the left side of a printed page and proceed across to the right side of the page. This pattern continues downward to the next line until the page is completed. Again, as Kim developed control of her arm muscles and coordination of eye-to-hand movements—first by scribbling and later by drawing—she was preparing for reading and writing as well as other manual skills.

The following developmental sequence is helpful in understanding the tasks which lead to developing writing skills:

Following the use of large brushes on a large surface area, a child can generally succeed with smaller brushes on a smaller surface area.

Three and one-half to four years	Prints some large, single manuscript (capital) letters randomly on a page.
Five years	Prints first name in large, irregularly shaped letters which get larger toward the middle or the end of the name. Letters are often reversed, such as the misuse of the letter s.
Six years	The entire alphabet is printed in large, irregular letters with many reversals. Words are copied, using all capitals with some reversal and transposition-switching of letters. Numbers one through twenty are printed with frequent reversals in the numbers three, seven, and nine.
Seven years	Some children continue to print; however, most children can write by this age. Writing is large, strained, and irregular in size and shape. Numbers are smaller with many errors.
Eight years	Most children are able to write in large, dark, square-like letters by now. Capitals and looped letters are very tall. Numbers are small but there are fewer errors than in the past.
Nine years	Children no longer are limited to printing. Writing becomes smaller, neater, more evenly spaced, and slanted. Individual writing style shows at this stage. Letters are in good proportion.

Part II: Children Learn As They Live

Physical Activities

Even though motor development was discussed earlier, two common activities are discussed here to represent children's use of motor skills in daily activities.

Ball Throwing and Catching

Arnold Gesell, M.D., a prominent author in child development, indicates that skill in throwing a ball requires a sense of balance, timing in letting the ball go, and appropriate control of muscles of the fingers, arms, trunk, head, and legs in order to control the ball's direction. As you can see, the ability to throw and catch requires well-coordinated movements of the entire body, not just the hands and arms.

Some children roll balls and try throwing them before age two but are not able to do this well. By four, most children are still not able to throw and catch skillfully. By six, most children have accomplished this task with consistent success. Keep in mind that marked variations in skill development occur at every age; thus, exceptions to these norms exist.

In the beginning, both hands are used and there is great body movement as children try to throw and catch. Gradually their movements become refined and only one hand is needed to accomplish this task.

Catching is just as difficult as throwing. You may have watched a child like Suzan learn this skill. In the beginning, she used her entire body to catch and hold the ball. Then she used only her arms with less movement of the body. Later she perfected a coordinated movement with her hands and was able to catch the ball between her palms. By age five, Suzan could catch a five-inch-diameter ball with success, and by age six, she could catch a twelve-inch ball as well.

Table blocks provide skill development as children build constructions.

Block Building

During toddlerhood, the first stage of block building begins with the child carrying large blocks from place to place and moving them about in irregular groupings. For example, by age three, the child places blocks in equal stacks or rows to make simple constructions. Gradually these structures take on more complex arrangements for dramatic play; they represent something specific like a house, tower, bridge, or tunnel. The child will be more likely to build the difficult structures at the edge of a table when using table-size blocks, but more familiar construction goes on in the center of the table.

MASTERING DEVELOPMENTAL TASKS AND SKILLS

There are several ways children learn to develop tasks and skills. You should be familiar with these and use them to the

Ch. 8: Developmental Tasks and Skills

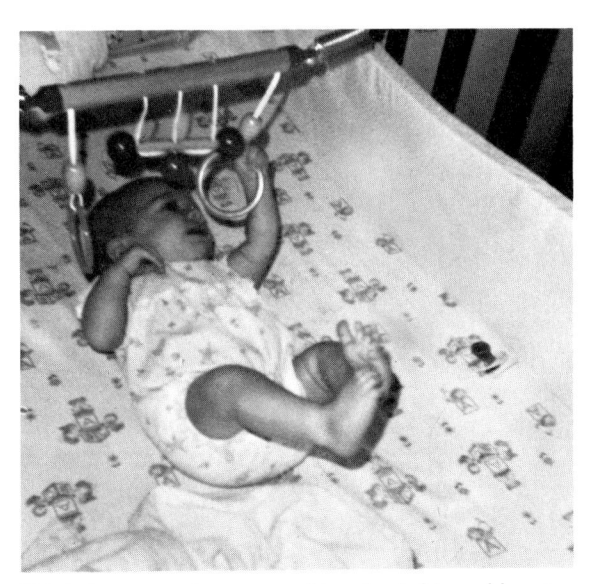

This infant uses the senses of touch, sight, and hearing to explore colorful objects.

best advantage. Mastery comes for the most part through the *senses, play,* and *other experiences.*

Senses

As you know, the sensory experiences—touching, tasting, seeing, hearing, and smelling—are basic to helping children build foundations for thinking, learning, and communicating. Adults can encourage children to explore their surroundings by fully using their senses. This means providing opportunities which invite and encourage children to expand their *sensory perception* and *acuity*. Sensory perception is awareness, knowledge, and insight gained through the senses; acuity is the keenness or sharpening of the senses.

Early in life infants begin exploring by using their mouths—not only for sucking and eating but also for releasing tension and experiencing pleasurable sensations. Sucking a thumb or a toy reflects an infant's sense of pleasure while learning about the surroundings through touch, texture, and taste. As Mike sucked his finger, he discovered there were feelings in both hands and mouth at the same time. He was learning to use more than one sense at a time—touch and taste.

By the age of three months, Mike could hold his hands in front of him and study them as playthings. Of course, he quickly directed his hands into his mouth. Coordination skills began when Mike used hands and eyes together in play activities. Reaching for a toy and grasping it was mastered at five months, followed by banging the object on a hard surface to achieve a noise; thus, the senses of touch, sight, and hearing came into action to help Mike learn.

Hearing, like vision, is quite well developed at birth. Both of these senses become more discriminating as the child has daily opportunities to recognize objects and react to sounds. When Mike turned toward a sound, a coordinated skill was developing—he directed body movements, hearing concentration, and eye focus toward the source of the sound.

When Mike learned that he could actually produce a sound, his own voice became a part of play. He learned that sounds could be repeated time and time again.

Eyes are used for exploring as well as for seeing toys and enjoying play. Even as a tiny infant, Mike showed interest in patterns and soon followed objects with his eyes. A colorful mobile on his crib and a sunny shadow on a wall served as learning experiences while enhancing the physical development of muscles and nerves needed to improve his sight.

As you can see in reading about Mike, the senses are vital to development. Chil-

Part II: Children Learn As They Live

dren need many firsthand experiences in using their senses. Doing things themselves helps children solve problems and form concepts while enjoying the use of materials. Active participation generates new ideas and offers ways for children to express their feelings and thoughts. Consider the following ways of helping children use and improve their senses:

- Encouraging the touching and feeling of things; developing an awareness of texture.
- Listening to sounds; developing ability to distinguish between high and low pitch, soft and shrill noises, loud and quiet sounds.
- Looking at and seeing things; developing appreciation for beauty; recognizing shapes, colors, and sizes of objects; becoming aware of differences and similarities.
- Tasting foods; identifying differences, such as sweet, sour, salty, smooth, coarse, grainy, crunchy, cold, and hot.
- Developing a keen sense of smell—for delicious aromas, burning food, staleness of garbage, sweet scents, burning paper, the fragrances of flowers, and the freshness of the air and rain.

Play

Through play children learn much that helps them master the developmental tasks and skills. In fact, research indicates that developmental tasks and skills are likely to be mastered more quickly with challenging and stimulating play during infancy and the early years. Play serves as media for mental, physical, and social development as children increase their basic sensory abilities and motor skills.

Play changes as children progress from cuddling and singing during early infancy to more involved activities like peek-a-boo. Early play experiences begin with the child's own curiosity. A mustache, necklace, and earring are all cause for investigation. As the child develops his self-concept, he participates more in individual and group play. In all stages of play, stimulation by others who interact with the child and provide tools for learning is important.

Every child needs tools for learning. Exploring with toys and other materials through play helps children express ideas and thoughts of their own. The selection of toys, equipment, and materials should be made on the basis of each child's maturing skills. Simple and inexpensive items are plentiful and often preferable to elaborate, expensive items. Some materials allow the child to be creative. Self-expression with paints and paper, for example, enables the child to turn an original idea into a concrete representation. Certain play activities stimulate children to use and develop their senses. Finger painting, shaping play dough and clay, building with blocks, housekeeping, and dramatic play are examples.

Aside from sleeping, playing is perhaps the biggest time consumer for children. This is how they learn. An adult who works with children should appreciate the value of playtime by providing the guidance and materials needed to help children make the most of this time.

Play is not just a way to pass the time or to keep children busy. Play in the lives of children helps them:
- Enjoy life.
- Learn about their environment.
- Enhance their self-concepts.
- Get along with others.
- Develop the keenness of their senses.
- Develop their muscles and use their bodies.

Ch. 8: Developmental Tasks and Skills

- Develop their minds, solve problems, and think about new ideas.

Children's play should be suitable to their stage of growth and development. The following characteristics for the play of young children are helpful in planning activities and in expanding your knowledge about child development.

Toddlers
- Generally play best with one child rather than a group. They like to be with other children but prefer to have their own playthings.
- Enjoy a large amount of space and freedom to play indoors and outdoors.
- Muscles do not work too well, but they like to run, climb, and walk.

Rompers
- Enjoy birthdays, holidays, and special events such as Halloween.
- Have greater muscle development and control over their bodies.
- Enjoy playing around the house and around others.
- Eager to do things when asked and like to be complimented.
- Enjoy playing with other children but get tired after about twenty minutes.
- Are capable of doing simple tasks such as setting the table, stacking magazines, and pouring juice.

Kindergartners
- Enjoy playing with other children.
- Learn to share things with others.
- Enjoy playing with large equipment such as swings, boxes, and slides.
- Like to play in dirt or sandboxes.
- Are very active—running, jumping, and skipping.

Learning to use household objects properly helps children express ideas and thoughts of their own.

- Muscles work much better and they have fewer accidents.
- Are still interested in the self but are learning to be part of a group.
- Like to act out home situations and pretend.
- Delight in playing dress-up.

Other Experiences
You have read that children learn developmental tasks and skills through their sensory experiences and play. Certainly there are still other ways.

One of these is through *interaction with others*. From others, children learn by observation. For example, one of the developmental tasks—talking—begins by mimicking others. Without verbal exchanges, the child would find speech a difficult task to conquer. The same is true of other tasks.

Part II: Children Learn As They Live

This planned excursion to the fire station will help the children in several ways. Can you name them?

Educational experiences also broaden a child's ability to learn developmental tasks and skills. Planned excursions to places like the zoo, park, fire station, airport, tortilla factory, bus depot, clothing factory, museum, bakery, car wash, bank, or theatre can be both fun and instructional. Reading stories and poetry, viewing movies and filmstrips, playing records and tapes, and using tape recorders and typewriters also help activate children's imaginations and stimulate questions which increase their understandings of the world about them.

The home is not, of course, the only environment for learning. The center should also provide ways to help each child master the expected tasks of early childhood development. Children are prepared for dealing with the tools for thinking and activities at a young age. Are you prepared to help them learn as they live?

SEQUENCING ACTIVITIES

A developmental approach to child care includes a continuous reminder of the following principles: Development follows a pattern; development proceeds by stages and is sequential in nature; and development is blended with individual variation and uniqueness. Remember, every child is different and each will progress at a little different rate. Even though children's development follows a general pattern, there will be variations in the speed and manner by which each child proceeds.

From this point of view, preparation for meaningful activities requires an understanding of what can generally be expected of children at given stages of development and a knowledge of how children progress from one level of competency to the next.

What happens to a child when we expect too much too soon? If your answer includes frustration, lowering of the self-concept, and perhaps future problems with skill development, you are quite right. No matter how hard you coax and how many beautiful and exciting materials you provide, the child will not be able to respond beyond his readiness level. Usually a step-by-step process is followed toward development of a certain task. Appropriate activities and materials must be provided along the way. Mastery of a single step at a time eventually results in mastery of the desired task.

There is no easy way to establish a sequential program of activities based on principles of development. However, this may be your most important task if you are to help each child grow at his individual rate and according to his unique abilities.

Ch. 8: Developmental Tasks and Skills

The two examples that follow will help you see what is involved.

Mastering the Use of Scissors

Consider the following situation in light of sequential development. Can you identify the source of Jake's frustration?

Six children, ages three and four years, were seated around a table with scissors, magazines, paste, and cardboard. They were to cut pictures from magazines and paste them on cardboard squares to form collages. Three-year-old Jake was very upset because he could not cut out the pictures. The teacher tried to help by showing him how to tear out the pictures instead of cutting them. This resulted in even more frustration.

How could you make this a pleasant and rewarding experience for Jake and the other children? First, you must understand the developmental level related to eye-to-hand coordination and muscle control of three- and four-year-olds. What are they generally capable of doing? Then you must look at Jake's level of developmental skill in using scissors. You must also know the sequence of developmental skills necessary for learning to cut with scissors. Here is an order of tasks Jake should eventually accomplish. The question to be answered is: Where is he now?

- Manual dexterity—control of hand and finger muscles.
- Hold the scissors correctly and securely.
- Manipulate the blades by controlling the handles with thumb and fingers.
- Hold the scissors in one hand and the material to be cut in the other hand at the same time.
- Manipulate the scissors to achieve a cutting action through the material.

Manipulating play dough helps develop finger and hand muscles as well as eye-to-hand coordination.

- Cut out the desired product.

How could you help Jake, now that you know the sequence for cutting with scissors? You would have to plan scissor-cutting activities within Jake's range of abilities which will lead to success with future tasks.

Study the following example of a sequence of activities for learning to use scissors. Keep in mind that it may take weeks or months for children to master some of the steps—and years to master the art of cutting.

Developing Muscle Control (Sequence No. 1)

Give children play dough to manipulate with both hands. Let them punch it, pull it apart, and make balls and other shapes with it. Let them work with the play dough

The child may punch the play dough before control of the scissors is achieved.

Gradually, the child achieves success in cutting the sausage.

until good control with their hands and fingers is obvious. (Notice that scissors have not been introduced yet.)

Manual Dexterity for Manipulating Scissors (Sequence No. 2)

Have the children make a sausage with the play dough. Then give them scissors and let them cut the playdough sausage into many pieces. You may have to demonstrate how to hold the scissors. The play dough will be soft and pliable and the children will have success in manipulating the scissors to cut the sausage.

Cutting Action with Straws (Sequence No. 3)

Give the children paper drinking straws or thin strips of construction paper about $\frac{1}{2}$ inch wide and 6 to 8 inches long. They

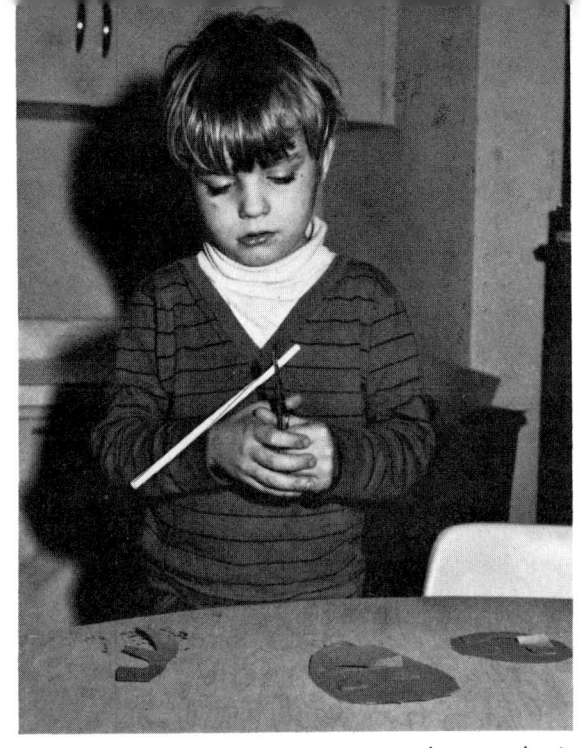

Paper drinking straws are easy to cut—but not plastic straws like this one!

Children need practice in holding the scissors and manipulating the blades successfully. Here the boy cuts paper.

can practice cutting the straws or paper strips with one snip of the scissors.

Cutting Action with Paper Strips (Sequence No. 4)

Give the children strips of paper 4 or 5 inches wide. They can practice cutting into the paper around all the edges.

Cutting Action with Paper Scraps (Sequence No. 5)

Provide scrap paper to cut any way the children wish. Practice is needed to achieve success in manipulating the scissors for more than one snip at a time.

Cutting Simple Designs (Sequence No. 6)

When the children appear to have sufficient control for manipulating the scissors correctly, they are ready to try cutting a given design. A simple geometric shape such as a circle or an oval about 4 or 5 inches in diameter drawn on paper is simple and easy to see. The width of the line

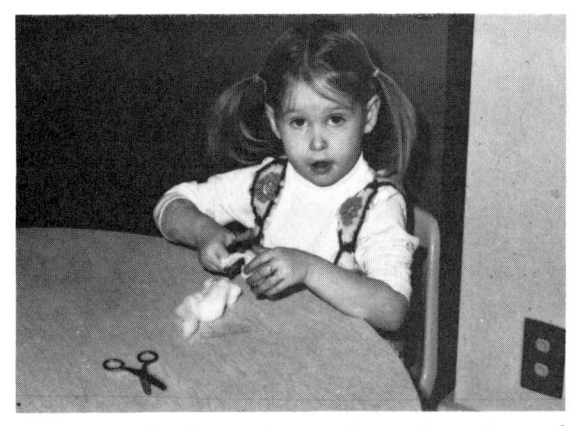

Cotton may also be used to practice cutting action and scissor control.

Part II: Children Learn As They Live

should be about ¼ of an inch wide in order to allow gross scissor action. The paper should be about 5 by 7 inches because the children can easily hold this size in one hand. If the paper is too large it will be difficult to manage. It will flop around. If it is too small, the outline of the shape will be difficult to follow. Help the children practice holding the scissors in one hand while rotating the paper with the other hand. In the beginning stages, any attempt should be regarded as a success. Reinforce the confidence of the children with encouragement and praise.

Cutting Shapes
(Sequence No. 7)

When the children have succeeded with the last step, they are ready to try cutting more complex patterns—squares, diamonds, and simple shapes such as outlines of apples, leaves, and boxes.

Cutting Pictures from Magazines
(Sequence No. 8)

After the children have successfully proceeded through all previous steps and have mastered each task in using the scissors, they will be ready to cut pictures from magazines.

Mastering the Balance Beam

The balance beam is a board approximately 2 inches thick and 4 or 6 inches wide. Would you expect all children from ages two to five years to be able to walk forward on the beam, one foot in front of the other, from one end of the board to the other without losing their balance if the board were placed 4 inches off the floor? Some children would no doubt succeed, but others would fail. The following sequence is needed to succeed on the balance beam:

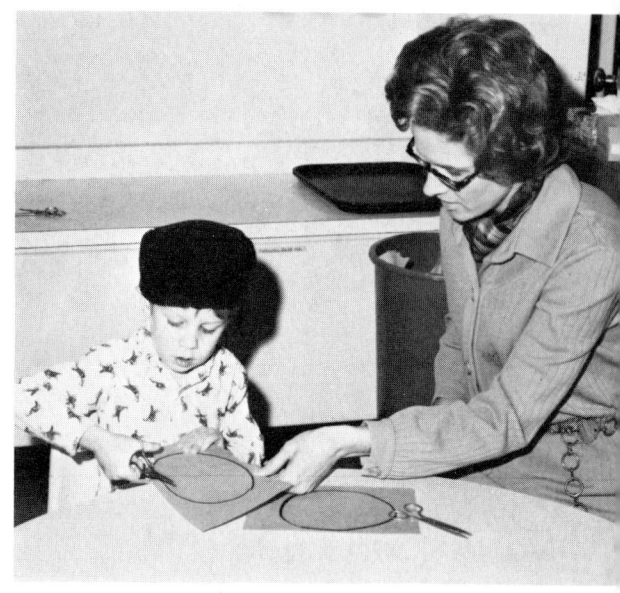

This child is cutting out a simple design. A little adult assistance is alright, but allow the child to work as independently as possible.

- Walk, one foot in front of the other, on a wide straight line (about 6 inches wide) flat on the floor. This line may be made with chalk, strips of tape, or painted on the floor.
- Walk on a narrower line (2 inches wide), one foot in front of the other.
- Walk on a balance beam placed flat on the floor. Because it is 2 inches thick, some young children may have difficulty with balance. They will need lots of practice—probably daily for several weeks. Perhaps they will begin by moving sideways with one foot leading. Gradually, they will learn to face forward and place one foot in front of the other.
- Walk on the balance beam 2 inches off the floor. You may have to hold a child's hand in the beginning. This gives him

Ch. 8: Developmental Tasks and Skills

Success in cutting simple shapes leads to confidence in trying more complex tasks.

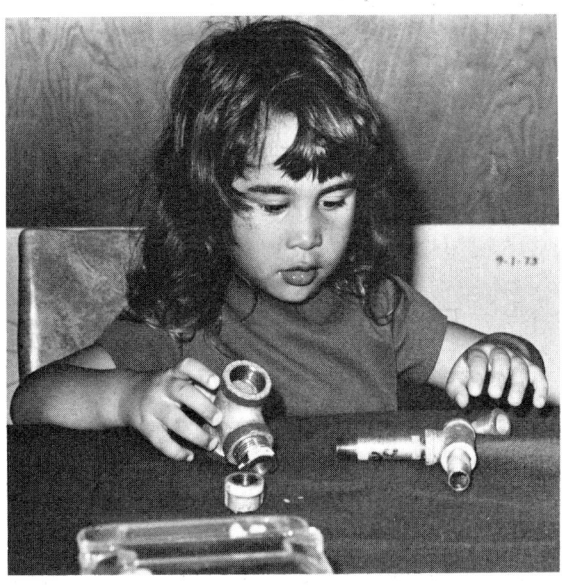

Children have a natural desire to pursue problem-solving tasks.

confidence that you are with him in his task. Gradually, he will gain his balance.
• Walk on the beam when it is 4 inches above the floor's surface.

As children master the balance of the right and left sides of their bodies, they are developing concepts of right and left positions which are a part of learning to read and write.

We don't usually study calculus before mastering general mathematics and algebra. Do you get the idea? Learn to observe children's progress to see what help each child needs for successful experiences leading to continuous and smooth development. Remember, each experience must be regarded by the child as a success. Encourage and support him. Working with small groups of children makes it much easier for you to see where each child is in his development.

Can you see the reason for careful planning? Even though children may have many choices in their daily activities, you must plan ahead in order to make appropriate choices possible. Children have a built-in tendency to be logical and to proceed in a problem-solving manner. However, when we place obstacles in their way—unrealistic expectations and inappropriate activities—they can be stifled. Help children enjoy their development with meaningful and interesting activities.

143

Part II: Children Learn As They Live

Chapter Highlights

- Developmental tasks are those tasks that must be mastered at each stage of development in order for children to live meaningful and happy lives.
- Whether we intend it or not, learning never stops.
- Although they use different terms and categories, Robert J. Havighurst, Philippe Muller, and Erik Erikson are recognized authorities who have dealt with the developmental task concept.
- The developmental task concept is a valuable tool for understanding children because it specifies important developmental achievements necessary for children at each stage of life.
- The child has reached a state of readiness, also known as the *critical period,* when certain conditions are present—the body is ready, societal pressures arise, and the individual feels the need to achieve a certain task.
- If a task is too difficult or attempted too early, the child may become discouraged and fail; on the other hand, if accomplishing a task is delayed beyond the state of readiness, the child may become frustrated and his development impaired.
- Successful accomplishment of developmental tasks during infancy lays a wholesome foundation for growth and development in later developmental periods.
- A child will acquire skill in walking when the muscular system is sufficiently developed and after control of body balance and body movement has been successfully accomplished.
- During late infancy, toilet control becomes a major developmental task. Two conditions, *readiness* of the neuromuscular system (nerves and muscles working together) and *emotional stability* between the child and adult promote successful toilet control.
- Parents and adults can help children enjoy learning to communicate by providing experiences that promote speech development in a natural way. Overcorrective, anxious, and demanding adults may hinder a child's speech development.
- Children develop many habits of speech and ways of behaving by copying the actions of others.
- From early infancy throughout childhood, children face the task of self-identification.
- As children leave infancy, they begin to develop concepts of what is good and what is bad, as indicated by those around them.
- Children learn more effectively about sex when they receive information from adults who are capable of being objective, who are comfortable in discussing sex, and who are free from notions of superstitions about sex.
- Developmental tasks and skills are mastered more readily with challenging and stimulating play during infancy and the early years.
- Play serves as media for mental, physical, and social development as children increase their basic sensory abilities and motor skills.
- Children also learn developmental tasks and skills through interaction with others and through educational experiences.
- Children master developmental tasks through a step-by-step process.

Thinking It Over

1. Define *developmental task*.
2. What is meant by the term *critical period*?
3. Compare Havighurst's and Muller's explanations of developmental tasks.
4. Relate the statement, "You have to walk before you can run," to developmental tasks in early childhood.
5. How happy and excited did you feel when you learned to drive a car (if you have)? Relate your feelings to those of a child who has accomplished a developmental task or skill. What effect does this have on the self-concept?
6. What are some advantages in knowing when infants and young children can be expected to accomplish certain developmental tasks and skills? How can this information be misused when dealing with children?
7. Give three ways parents can help their children develop self-feeding skills at home.
8. Explain two conditions necessary for a child to accomplish adequate toilet training.
9. What are some of the first words babies say? How do they learn these words?
10. Describe a situation which may hinder a child's language development.
11. List four tasks young children must accomplish in order to make speech progress during the years before they enter school.
12. Describe how a child develops a conscience.
13. State the conditions necessary for a child to be able to dress and undress himself.
14. Describe the steps by which a child develops the motor skill required to throw a ball.
15. Can you remember being exceptionally fast or slow in learning certain motor skills, such as skipping, jumping rope, playing jacks, or throwing and catching a ball? How did this make you feel?
16. Do you think there is a relationship between popularity and the ability to perform motor skills? Explain your answer.
17. Have you known about a baby who refused to give up the bottle even after establishing a routine of eating regular meals with solid foods? What suggestions do you have for weaning a child without creating additional problems for him?
18. Can you remember when you first learned that lying and stealing were wrong? How do children develop concepts of right and wrong?
19. Do you think some parents connect good parenting with early toilet training? Discuss the problems with this notion.
20. What is the difference between a child's acquiring a healthy outlook on sexuality and a child's sex education?
21. What are the advantages and disadvantages of left-handedness? What problems can occur when trying to change a child's handedness?
22. Why are a child's toys called his tools for learning? Give examples.
23. Name four educational experiences (such as field trips or excursions) and tell how they would be helpful to children in learning developmental tasks and skills.

Part II: Children Learn As They Live

Things To Do

1. Make tape recordings of conversations with children of the following ages: one, eighteen months, two, two and one-half, three, four, and five. Compare the language development skills as children progress in age.
2. Based on your knowledge about developmental tasks and skills, establish criteria for selecting materials and toys for infants, toddlers, and rompers.
3. Take a trip to a toy department or a toy store and choose a toy which can promote learning and a toy which does little to foster development in children. Use these toys as the basis for a class discussion on challenging and stimulating play during infancy and the early years.
4. Working in groups of about four or five students, identify materials and toys which provide sensory and motor experiences for each of the following age groups: infants, toddlers, and rompers. Match the toys with the appropriate developmental tasks as presented in this chapter. Discuss the main features of each item as it relates to development at a given stage.
5. Have a panel of mothers discuss their experiences in toilet training their children. Those with more than one child can discuss differences in their own children. From the discussion and from child development references, develop some guidelines which can help parents in toilet training.
6. Develop a display of play materials (according to stages of development) which enhance children's development.
7. Observe young children at different age levels doing the following: finger painting; cutting with scissors; playing with large blocks and boxes; playing with dress-up clothes; doing finger plays and rhythmic activities; and playing on outdoor equipment. Compare differences and similarities of how children at different stages of development play with materials and toys.
8. While observing the activities in the above situations, identify which children are right-handed and which are left-handed. Are there differences in their performance levels? Should there be differences in the way materials and activities are presented? Why?
9. Identify a developmental task at which some children fail. Write a short story, from your point of view, about the child's feeling of failure. Read stories in class and discuss what a child development worker can do to help children accomplish these tasks with success and to reinforce the child's self-concept.
10. Prepare a book or group of pictures illustrating types of work which employ men and women. How can you use these pictures with young children for experiences about career development? Try using these pictures with a young child and report the results to the class.
11. Compare the way boys and girls are portrayed in children's texts and storybooks which you find at home or in the library. Write a report on what you find. Consider traditional versus modern roles, stereotypes, the activities of boys and girls in fiction and reality, and the way adults are portrayed (their careers and duties).

Recommended Reading

Behrens, Herman D., and Maynard, Glenn. *The Changing Child: Readings in Child Development.* Glenview, Illinois: Scott, Foresman and Co., 1972.

Bernard, Harold H. *Human Development in Western Culture.* Boston: Allyn and Bacon, Inc., 1970.

Developmental Psychology Today. Del Mar, California: Communications Research Machines, Inc., 1971.

Dinkmeyer, Don C. *Child Development—The Emerging Self.* New York: Prentice-Hall, Inc., 1965.

Havighurst, Robert J. *Developmental Tasks and Education,* Third Edition. New York: David McKay Co., Inc., 1972.

Hurlock, Elizabeth B. *Child Development.* New York: McGraw-Hill Book Co., 1972.

Muller, Philippe. *The Tasks of Childhood.* New York: McGraw-Hill Book Co., 1971.

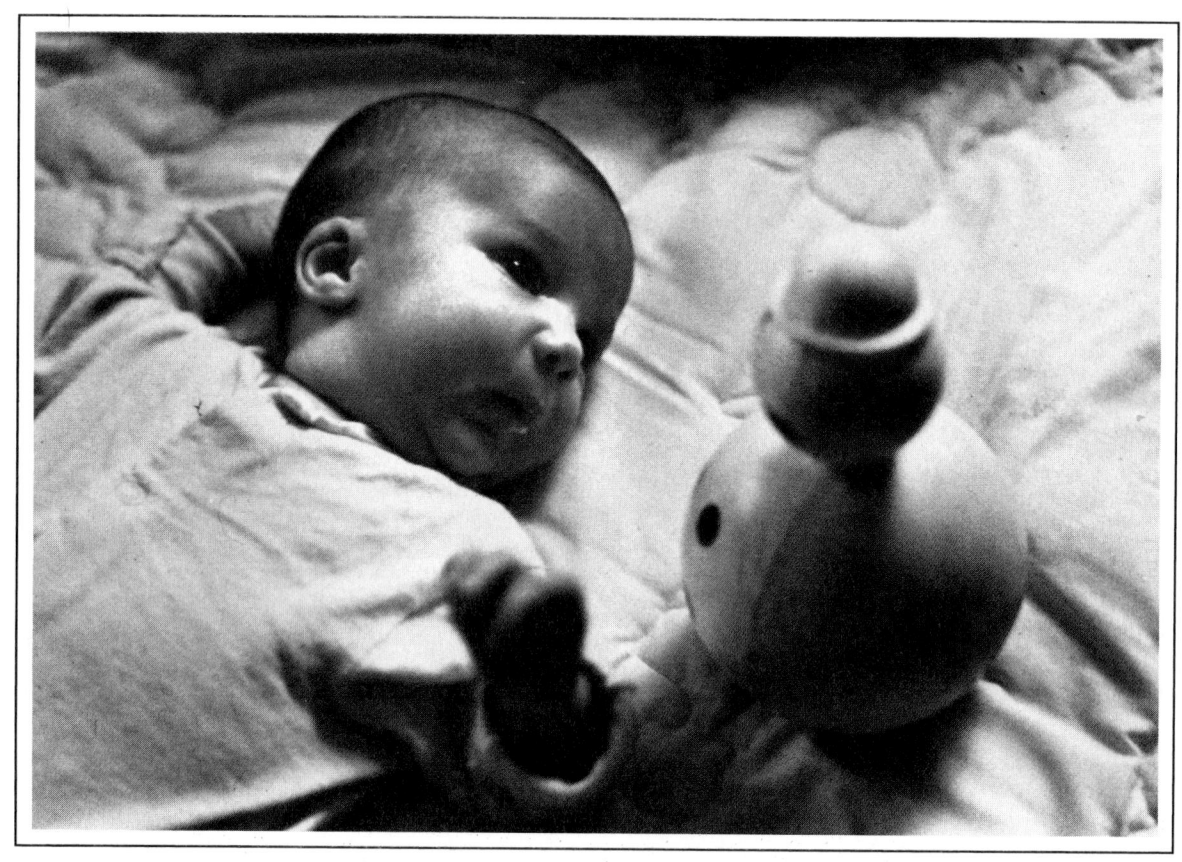

Farrell

PART III
A Wholesome Environment

Chapter 9.
Promoting Children's Health

Chapter 10.
Insuring Safety

Chapter 11.
Handling Emergencies

Chapter 12.
Food for Children

Chapter 13.
Children's Clothing

Chapter 14.
Special Care for Infants

Chapter 9.

Promoting Children's Health

Your Challenge

This chapter will enable you to . . . .

- List the signs of a healthy child.
- Tell what immunization children need against disease.
- Describe children's diseases.
- Tell what must be done in the center to protect children's health.
- Describe how to care for a child who is ill.
- Explain how to prepare a child for hospitalization.

THE HEALTHY CHILD

Healthy children are active, alert, and interested in new experiences. They excite easily, reflecting happy and cheerful feelings while engaging in vigorous activities like creeping, running, climbing, jumping, hopping, and tumbling. Healthy children are often noisy. They may be found talking, singing, chattering, and banging toys. Sometimes they play alone and sometimes with others. Healthy children also enjoy quiet activities which require concentration, effort, and skill. Are you familiar with these signs of a healthy child?

- Sleeps soundly.
- Eats without much coaxing.
- Gains steadily in height and weight over the months.
- Teeth in good condition.
- Few aches and pains.
- Enjoys both individual and group activities.

PLANNING FOR HEALTH CARE

Everyday care promotes good health when children are in clean, safe surroundings with nourishing foods, plenty of fresh air, exercise, rest, proper clothing, and support from adults and positive relationships with other children. Still, even the healthiest child is subject to illness and disease.

Medical science has made great strides in protecting children's health. In the past, many diseases contributed to a high infant mortality rate. Now such diseases can often be prevented or easily cured.

In the U.S.A. most children do not suffer from such vitamin deficiency diseases as

Williams
Healthy children are active children.

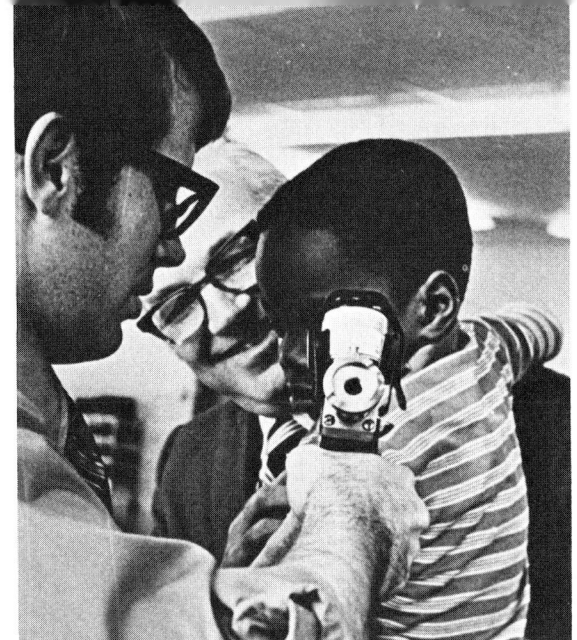

Oklahoma Journal
A youngster takes his vaccination against rubeola (hard, red measles).

scurvy, pellegra, or beriberi. Medical and professional advice is readily available on *what* and *how* to feed children to avoid illness and defects which may result from poorly selected foods. With proper food storage, preparation, and sanitation, many illnesses of the digestive system can be avoided. Respiratory diseases like pneumonia and bronchitis can now be treated medically for effective results.

Immunization

Immunization against diseases should be provided for every child by the family, local health clinic, welfare agency, or children's center. Parents should be encouraged to provide these immunizations for their children during the preschool age. Major diseases which children need protection against through immunization are:

- Whooping cough (pertussis).
- Tetanus.
- Polio (infantile paralysis).
- Diphtheria.
- Measles.

One injection often includes immunization to combat more than one disease, thus requiring fewer injections. Two common multiple injections are: DPT (diphtheria, pertussis, and tetanus); red measles and rubella. Immunization for polio is given orally.

Repeated immunizations for protection from these diseases, other than measles, should be continued with carefully kept records of the type of injection and the date given. This information may be needed in the future if a child becomes ill, moves to another community, changes doctors or clinics, transfers to another children's center, or when the child enters school.

When children have the *DPT* injections, some mild reactions can be expected, such as a low fever, fussiness, or soreness around the area of the injection. These

Part III: A Wholesome Environment

immunizations do not cause coughs or colds. If such symptoms appear, children should be checked for infection.

In some areas smallpox vaccinations are administered. The reaction to a *smallpox* vaccination appears about one week later when the vaccine begins to take. A blister usually forms and should be left uncovered unless the child tends to scratch it. A small gauze dressing can be placed on the area if regular clothing does not prevent scratching. Sponge baths are recommended, but tub baths or showers can be carefully taken from the time the blister appears until the scab falls off.

Red measles (rubeola) can cause such serious complications as encephalitis and bacterial infections of the respiratory tract in the ears, sinuses, or lungs. Encephalitis involves the brain and can be very serious. A measles vaccine is administered by an injection and is best given after the child is one year of age. The baby may have received antibodies from the mother before birth. These antibodies can prevent a successful take of the vaccine until the child is about twelve months old. People cannot catch measles from contact with a vaccinated child.

Rubella (German measles) is caused by a different virus than that which causes red measles. Even though rubella is a mild illness and is not serious for the patient, it carries a great risk to other people. Vaccine is recommended at any age for susceptible women under certain conditions. Rubella carries a great risk for a pregnant woman. Rubella, during the first three months of pregnancy, can cause severe damage to the unborn baby.

Children who are exposed to either type of measles should be checked by a doctor immediately. They may be given an inoculation for protection against current exposure or to make the case milder, if measles are contracted. If a child contracts a mild form of rubeola (red measles), immunity will occur. An individual can have rubella, however, more than once.

If a child is exposed to any of the above diseases before immunization is given or shortly thereafter, the doctor or clinic should be notified immediately. The body does not develop immunity immediately, and medical attention may be needed.

Preventive steps may also be taken to protect children against such diseases as tuberculosis and typhoid fever.

Tuberculosis (TB) is contagious (spreads from one person to another). Young children usually have less resistance to tuberculosis than older children or adults. Until the child reaches the age of eighteen, regular physical examinations should include a skin test for tuberculosis. This is done by injecting a small amount of a harmless fluid called tuberculin into the skin of the forearm. In two or three days a doctor can tell by measuring the spot on the arm whether the reaction is positive or not.

The sooner this disease is detected, the better the chances are for a cure. Children who have been exposed to tuberculosis should be tested immediately. If exposed, children need repeated testing. This disease attacks the skin, glands or lymph nodes, body joints, bones, lining and membranes covering parts of the body, and the lungs. Common symptoms for all types of tuberculosis include loss of weight, failure to gain weight, enlarged neck glands, paleness, chronic fatigue, and unexplained fever. Children rarely cough as a symptom, whereas adults usually do.

Recognizing Diseases

The chart of children's diseases on pages 154–157 will help you learn about the symptoms, spreading, and prevention of some communicable diseases. This information does not take the place of a medical diagnosis. The brief descriptions of what to do are general. When signs of serious illness prevail, professional help from a clinic, doctor, or nurse should be secured as soon as possible.

HEALTH CONCERNS

Any time a number of children are brought together in a group, the spread of illness and disease can become a problem. For this reason, health concerns in a children's center are extremely important. Attention must be given not only to the children but also to the staff, to health records, and to the conditions of the center itself.

Daily Checks

An informal inspection of the children entering the center should be conducted each day by one of the staff members. Look for the following signs of ill health and poor health habits. These signs can be found during the daily check and throughout the day while children are present:

- Dirty hands and face.
- Sore throat, redness, or itching of the mouth and throat area.
- Discharge from the eyes, ears, or nose.
- Rash on face, neck, chest, or stomach.
- Dirty hair and scalp (lice are prevalent in some areas where children are not kept clean).
- Sneezing and coughing.
- Drowsiness when the child is usually wide awake.
- Watery or glassy eyes.
- Fever, flushed face, and hot dry skin or exceptional paleness and coldness.
- Unexpected profuse perspiring.

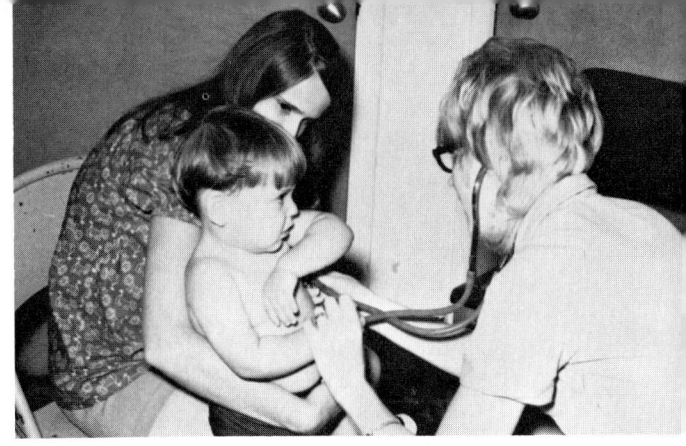

Some centers have professional medical personnel available to deal with health problems.

- Hoarse voice and swollen glands.
- Pain in ear, head, chest, stomach, abdomen, or joints.
- Stiff back or neck.
- Nausea, vomiting, diarrhea.

Some child care centers have facilities and staff to care for sick children until they can be released to their families or admitted to a clinic or hospital. Many, however, are not prepared for this type of service. Therefore a policy must be established for quick action in getting children home or into a physician's hands when a cause arises.

Before working in the center, each staff member should have a TB skin test and secure a health certificate from a city or county health clinic or local physician. Staff members are in continuous contact with children and must maintain good health. When staff members become ill, they should not remain in the center. Not only is there the possibility of spreading illness but also efficiency is below normal.

Some states require centers to have professional medical personnel available before a license to operate is granted. Having a nurse as one of the staff members, or available for consultation, is an excellent arrangement for safeguarding the health of children, especially infants.

Part III: A Wholesome Environment

COMMUNICABLE CHILDHOOD DISEASES

Disease	I.P.*	Symptoms	Source of Contact	Period of Communicability	What To Do
Chicken Pox	13–17 days.	Slight fever, mild constitutional symptoms; rashlike, small blisters on body, chest, back, 14–21 days after exposure.	Contact with diseased case; droplets from nose and throat; or airborne spread of secretions of respiratory tract of infected person.	As long as 5 days before the eruption of chickenpox; not more than 6 days after the first crop of blisters.	Confine for 6 days following first symptoms; apply baking soda and water paste. Trim fingernails to prevent breaking blisters.
Common Cold	12–72 hours.	Runny nose; sneezing; overly tired; usually no fever, or sudden high fever for a short duration.	Contact with infected person; discharge from nose and mouth; sneezing and coughing.	Nasal washings taken 24 hours before onset and 5 days after onset have produced symptoms in experimentally infected volunteers.	Keep comfortable; plenty of rest and liquids; confine until symptoms disappear and child feels well.
Diphtheria (Serious Disease)	2–5 days.	Sore throat and fever; symptoms become severe rapidly. Occasionally affects other mucous membranes or skin; lesions marked by patch or patches of grayish membrane with surrounding dull red inflammatory zone.	Contact with a diseased person or a carrier of the disease; discharge from nose and throat; or lesions.	Usually 2 weeks or less; seldom more than 4 weeks.	Contact doctor; confine until released by doctor or health department.
Dysentery (Bacillary)	1–7 days.	Diarrhea; malaise; toxemia; fever; cramps.	Bowel discharge of infected person or carrier; contaminated food or drinks; flies.	During acute infection and until infectious agent no longer present in feces; usually within a few weeks.	Sanitary conditions necessary. Consult with doctor or nurse.
(Infectious) Hepatitis	Variable 10–50 days.	Onset is usually abrupt, with fever, malaise, nausea and abdominal discomfort, followed within a few days by jaundice.	Person-to-person contact between infected individuals; water contaminated with human excretions. Contagious for duration of illness. Spreading is primarily through infected feces, urine, and/or diapers.	During latter half of incubation period continuing through a few days after onset of jaundice.	Isolation during first 2 weeks of illness and at least 1 week after onset of jaundice. Sanitary disposal of feces and urine; controlled handwashing before and after meals and toileting. Gamma globulin** for family contacts but not for contacts at day care center.

154

Ch. 9: Promoting Children's Health

Disease	I.P.*	Symptoms	Source	Period of Communicability	Control
Impetigo	4–10 days.	Vesicular (blistering) and crusting skin lesions, commonly on the face and often on the hands.	From skin lesions of infected persons; from carriers' nasal secretions.	As long as purulent (containing pus) lesions continue to drain.	Avoid common use of toilet articles; avoid contact with infants and debilitated (weak) persons.
Influenza	24–72 hours.	Fever; chilliness or chills; discomfort; aches or pains; general malaise; sore throat; cough.	Discharge of nose and throat from infected persons, possibly airborne.	Probably limited to 3 days from clinical onset.	Consult with doctor or nurse.
Red Measles (Rubeola)	10–15 days.	Fever, cold symptoms; sneezing and inflamed eyes; hard and dry cough; runny nose 3 to 4 days prior to rash, beginning on the face, becoming generalized; blotchy, dusky red color.	Contact with someone who has rubeola; discharge from nose and throat early in illness before symptoms appear.	From beginning of the prodromal period (warning symptoms) to 4 days after appearance of rash.	Confine for 7 days after appearance of rash; follow doctor's advice for care. Vaccination; gamma globulin must be given within 2–3 days after exposure for effectiveness.
Meningitis (Epidemic)	2–10 days.	Sudden fever; intense headache; nausea, often vomiting; stiff neck.	Direct contact with diseased person; nose and throat droplets of person carrying disease but not sick.	Until meningococci are no longer present in discharge from nose and mouth; usually disappear within 23 hours after start of treatment.	Isolate until 24 hours after start of doctor's medication. Confine until released by doctor or health department.
Mumps	12–26 days; ordinarily 18.	Fever; vomiting; aching glands near ears and jaw line; painful swelling of salivary glands. May affect testes or ovaries.	Contact with someone who has mumps; droplets from nose and mouth of infected person.	48 hours before swelling commences. Urine positive as long as 14 days after onset of illness.	Confine to bed until fever and swelling subside; remain indoors unless weather is warm.

* I.P.—Incubation period, the amount of time from exposure to symptoms.
** Gamma globulin is a fraction of blood plasma rich in antibodies and used against measles, hepatitis, etc.

Part III: A Wholesome Environment

COMMUNICABLE CHILDHOOD DISEASES (Continued)

Disease	I.P.*	Symptoms	Source of Contact	Period of Communicability	What To Do
Pediculosis (Lice)	Eggs hatch in 1 week; maturity in 2 weeks.	Infestation of the scalp, hairy parts of the body, or of clothing, especially along the seams of inner surfaces, with adult lice, larvae, or nits (eggs). Crab lice usually infest the pubic area. They may infest the eyelashes.	Direct contact with infected persons or with clothing containing lice.	While lice remain alive on the infected person and until eggs in hair and clothing have been destroyed.	Follow doctor's orders.
Pinkeye (Conjunctivitis)	24–72 hours.	White of eyes redden and are runny with matter; swollen eyelids; develops about 48 to 72 hours.	Contact with items used by infected person—fingers, towels, handkerchiefs, etc.	During course of active infection.	Remain away from others until recovered. Local application of prescribed medical treatment.
Poliomyelitis	3–21 days; commonly with 7–12 day range.	Headache; stiffness of neck or back; slight fever; gastrointestinal disturbance.	Throat secretions and stool of infected people and carriers; no known way to prevent spreading; contagious as long as fever persists.	7 to 10 days before and after onset of symptoms.	Preventive measure is vaccine. Confine until released by doctor or health department.
Ringworm (Skin Infection)	10–14 days.	Dry, circular splotches on skin and bare spots on scalp.	Direct contact with others who have the disease; contact with clothing and items of infected persons; lesions of animals.	As long as lesions are present.	Thorough bathing—soap and water; application of prescribed medicine. Remain under medical treatment until cured.
Rubella (German Measles) (3-day)	14–21 days; usually 18.	Mild fever; headache; sore throat; symptoms similar to a cold; rose rash; (conjunctivitis) inflamed eyelids and eyes.	Contact with someone who has rubella; droplets from nose and throat, especially before rash appears.	About 1 week before and 4 days after onset of rash.	Contact doctor and follow instructions.

156

Ch. 9: Promoting Children's Health

Disease	I.P.*	Symptoms	Spread by	Period of Communicability	Control
Scabies (Itch)	3–4 days or longer.	Severe itching and scratching; mite burrowed under skin between fingers, bends of body, and in folds of skin; small lesions like pinholes in a line.	Direct contact with infected person or clothing items of person, particularly undergarments and soiled bedclothes.	Until mites and eggs are destroyed by medical treatment.	Application of prescribed medical treatment by doctor. Confine until symptoms are no longer present.
Sore Throat (Simple)	2–5 days.	Scratchy throat, sore, swallowing difficult; may have fever.	Upper respiratory discharges from infected persons.	As long as fever (if present) persists.	Consult doctor or nurse.
Streptococcal Infections (Including Scarlet Fever and Strep Throat)	1–3 days.	Sudden infection; nausea; vomiting; headache; fever; sore throat; glands of neck swollen; rash within 24 hours with fine, "grainy" touch—neck, chest, folds of elbow, and groin.	Contact with case of carrier of disease; discharge from nose and throat; may be spread through mild and unrecognized case.	During clinical illness; 7 to 10 days or until nasal, eye, and throat discharge ceases.	Confine until symptoms disappear, but at least 7 days. Penicillin is normally used for treatment.
Tuberculosis	4–6 weeks; variable 6–12 weeks.	Listlessness; poor appetite; weight loss; low fever; identified by skin test.	Droplets from coughing or sneezing of persons with disease during infectious stage.	As long as infectious tubercle bacilli are being discharged—coughing, sneezing, singing, etc.	If noninfectious and with medically approved conditions, child may attend school; otherwise, follow medical advice.
Whooping Cough (Pertussis)	Within 10 days, not exceeding 21 days.	Low fever; cough gradually becomes paroxysmal (sudden attack) usually in 1 to 2 weeks, lasting 1–2 months. Series of coughs which limit inhalation, ending with whoop.	Contact with case; discharge of nose and throat; articles freshly soiled with discharge.	7 days after exposure to 3 weeks after onset of typical paroxysms.	(Immunization before age 5.) Confine for at least 21 days after beginning of whoop; follow medical advice.

*I.P.—Incubation period, the amount of time from exposure to symptoms.

Part III: A Wholesome Environment

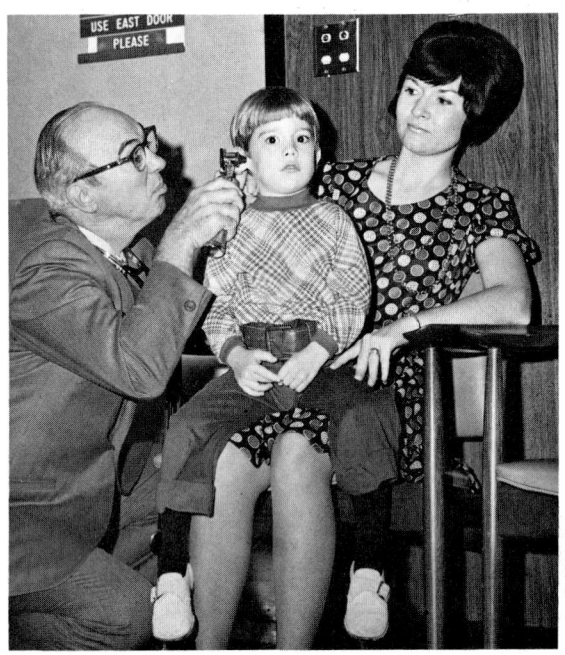

Okmulgee County Health Department
A periodic medical examination helps insure children's health.

Maintaining Records

The children's center should have provisions for emergency medical services at all times. Each staff member should know exactly what to do in order to secure the services needed. The following information should be posted at each telephone:

- Telephone number of family and center-related doctors and other medical personnel.
- Emergency telephone numbers of all hospitals in the area.
- Telephone numbers of local poison center if available.
- Procedures for securing ambulance services.
- Telephone numbers of police and fire stations.
- Telephone numbers and names of each child's parents, guardians, relatives, or friends to be contacted in case of emergency.

Each child should have a medical examination with health records available to the parents and the center staff. Following the examination, some children may need special assistance such as dental work or vision and hearing corrections. The center staff can be helpful to parents in treatment referrals by cooperating with public health and local welfare officials.

A periodic medical examination helps insure children's health—at least once every six months for infants and toddlers and once every year for three- and four-year-olds, kindergartners, and school-age children. Records in the center should be updated each time a child has an examination. A center clinic or a community clinic may be used when parents are unable to afford examinations for their children. Local health officials and physicians will often cooperate with a center staff if plans are made in advance. Parents can often assist as adult volunteers in getting children to and from the clinic. In some communities, local health services are provided, whereby physicians and nurses rotate volunteer services for a certain amount of time. Federal funds are available for certain health services to children and families who qualify. Check with the local or state health and/or welfare agencies to get current information about services available and ways to pay for the services.

In addition to emergency and medical records, the center should maintain other records which aid the staff. A bulletin board is helpful for informing the center staff members of the latest information. It will also provide guidelines for each person's role and responsibility. The board should be located in an easy-to-view area and may include these items:

- Daily schedule of children's activities.
- Daily schedule of staff responsibilities.
- Special events—vaccinations, health clinics, dental and physical checkups, and safety meetings.
- Attendance sheet for each group of children.
- Plan for fire drill, including evacuation routes.
- Plan for emergencies such as storms and severe weather.
- Announcements—inservice training, future meetings, and children's birthdays.

Check Points in the Center

A well-lighted and properly ventilated area, with the temperature controlled at a constant level, is needed for *children's activities*. Small children are affected more than adults by rapid changes in temperature. Drafts should be located and stopped. Equipment—blocks, puzzles, pegs, and all furniture should have washable, nontoxic finishes. Balls, spools, and push-and-pull, fill-and-empty, and carry-and-drop toys should have smooth edges and be easy to handle by infants and toddlers. All materials and equipment should be in good, safe working condition.

Children need clean facilities for toileting, washing, and brushing teeth. The *washroom area* should be well ventilated and equipped with child-size furnishings in excellent operating condition. The washing and toileting facilities should be scrubbed and disinfected daily. Staff members also need clean facilities to be used for washing hands while caring for children and while preparing and serving food. Drying racks or hangers for items such as washcloths, towels, linens, and clothing should be in an easily accessible area of the utility room or possibly the washroom or bathroom.

The *crib area* must be clean with washable floor coverings. Mobiles and other objects should be well constructed and safely situated. All equipment and furniture including cribs should be washable. These should be finished with nontoxic, scratch-resistant paint or coverings. Soiled diapers for laundry or for disposal should be placed in special closed containers. Paper and plastic bags, labeled with names, for diapers to be taken home should be kept in designated places.

The *kitchen or food preparation area* and its equipment should be cleaned daily. Bottles and feeding equipment may be kept in soapy water until washing is completed. The best sanitary cleaning methods and equipment should be used for all eating and drinking utensils.

Can you see there are many things to think about as you plan a healthy environment for children in a center? Many of these requirements are established by law or licensing standards. Each state has minimal health and safety standards which must be met before a center is legally allowed to operate. Local health departments and welfare agencies expect centers to maintain certain standards which may differ from state to state. Most states, however, will require:

- An inspection of the center, facilities, and staff.
- Health certificates for each staff member.
- A permit or license before the center begins to operate.

Part III: A Wholesome Environment

Part V explains licensing standards in greater detail, but these requirements should alert you to the responsibilities involved in insuring the children's health. Unfortunately, many centers operate without a license and many licensed centers operate below standards. These hazards can only be eliminated by adults, including you and other workers, who are concerned about the well-being of children.

WHEN CHILDREN ARE ILL

Even if every precaution is taken in the home and center to protect children's health, illness will still occur. You read about the signs of ill health earlier in this chapter. Be alert for these signs. Should a child appear to be even slightly ill, take no chances. Keep him quiet and still, lying on a bed or cot until medical help is available or until his parents can take him home.

Many children's illnesses are contagious in their early stages. Therefore a sick child should be kept away from others. Watch the child closely to see if his appetite has dropped from the usual, although this is not always uncommon. Feed the child liquids such as fruit juices, broth, and milk or water frequently.

The Sick Room

Under normal circumstances, children who are ill are better off at home than any other place. Of course, some children have no provisions at home for care. Thus, a special place in the center is needed to care for sick children until they can either go home or be admitted to a clinic or hospital if the illness is serious.

The size of the center will probably determine what kind of space is available for a sick room. If a separate room is handy, it can be equipped for one or more sick children. If not, perhaps a small area of a large room could be set off with permanent or portable partitions.

The sick room should be near a bathroom. If possible, a window near the bed will provide some diversion for the child when not asleep, but drafts should be prevented. A small bell or buzzer which the child can use when help is needed is not only important but is also interesting to the child. A bedside table to hold tissue, cotton, thermometer, water, paper bags, and other items will save many steps for the busy child care worker.

Caring for the Sick Child

Serious after-effects of children's illnesses can often be avoided if the child is kept quiet and in bed for twenty-four hours after his temperature has returned to normal following an illness. A sick child needs attention and care throughout the day and night. The best place for the sick child is at home with a parent who can provide lots of attention. Some child care centers, however, do care for children until they can be taken home. Knowing what to do will help you ease the child's discomfort, whether at home or in a center.

Medication

Under certain circumstances, some children may be on special medication. Information about such cases should be included in the child's health records in the center, and each staff member should understand the directions for use of the medication.

Do not give a child medicine unless by doctor's instructions. In the stores you will find aspirin especially made for children in flavors they often like. If the doctor prescribes aspirin for a child, be careful how

Ch. 9: Promoting Children's Health

you give it. *Follow the doctor's orders.* A child should not be told that medication is candy. This can lead to trouble if the child ever gets his hands on the so-called candy when an adult is not close by.

The same principle applies to vitamin supplements. Many are produced in the shapes of animals or other figures that appeal to children. Concern has been expressed over making such items too appealing to children. Indeed, the concern goes much deeper.

Over the years the drug problem has become quite serious. Some say that young people who experiment with drugs have been exposed to extensive drug use all their lives. Examine your medicine cabinet. What do you find—leftover prescription drugs, aspirin, pain relievers, cough and cold remedies, medicine for stomach troubles, tranquilizers, stay-awake pills? Many cabinets have all of these and more. Is it any wonder that so many turn to drugs with so little concern? As you care for children, remember this. You have an opportunity and responsibility to help children learn about the health and safety of their bodies.

Food

Liquids, especially water, should be given to a child who is ill about every hour, particularly when he has a fever. Sweetened weak tea or cracked ice may be substituted for water. If the child has diarrhea or is vomiting, no food should be given. Liquids should also be withheld if vomiting persists.

Bowel Movement

The child may need assistance with elimination. A casual and relaxed atmosphere will usually add to the child's general well-being and to success with this need. Plenty of liquids, especially fruit juices, often aid the process of elimination. If a child has no bowel movement for forty-eight hours or has pain in the abdomen, a nurse or doctor should be consulted. Laxatives or enemas should not be given without medical advice.

Bathing

Whether at home or in the center, the child will need a daily sponge bath. A washcloth, with warm water and mild soap, will be sufficient to cleanse each part of the child's body. Rinse and dry one area completely before sponging the next. Care should be taken to prevent chilling during and after the bath.

Taking the Child's Temperature

A fever may be detected by a child's listlessness, drowsiness, face and neck heat, flushed face, and especially bright and glassy eyes. The temperature should be taken with a thermometer and recorded on the child's record along with the method used and the hour of the day taken. The normal temperature is 98.6°F., the same as for adults. Usually, a morning and evening temperature recording is sufficient. This record should be kept for parents and for medical purposes.

A child's temperature can be taken by one of three methods. Temperature is usually taken by *mouth* when the child is three or four years old. For a younger child or one who is very sick, the temperature can be taken by *rectum*. The temperature can also be taken by *armpit*. To take a child's temperature, follow this procedure:

In SI metric Units, normal body temperature is 37 degrees Celsius. An increase of 1 °Celsius is equal to nearly 2° F.

Part III: A Wholesome Environment

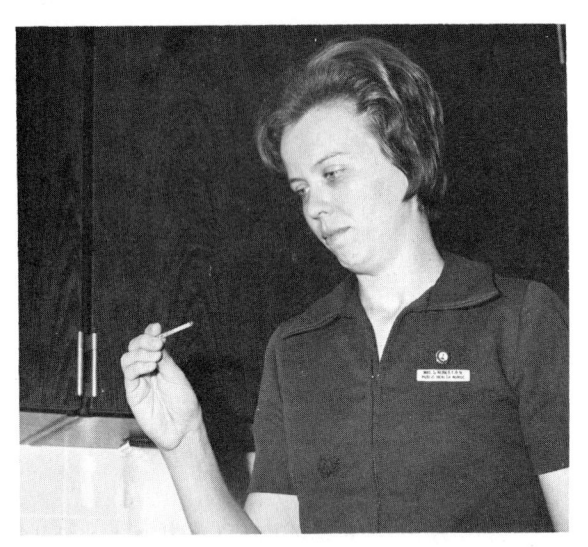

Okmulgee County Health Department
When taking a child's temperature, grasp the thermometer by the end opposite the bulb.

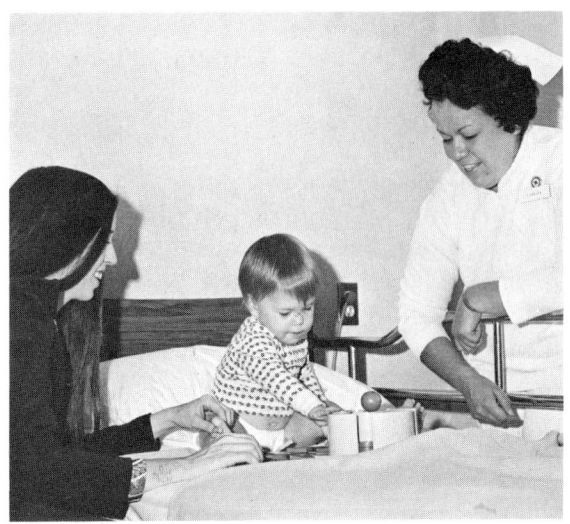

Okmulgee Hospital
Children need amusing things to do while confined to bed or close quarters.

- Grasp the thermometer by the end opposite the bulb.
- Rotate the shaft until the mercury comes into view.
- Holding the thermometer firmly, shake it briskly with sharp wrist action until the mercury drops to about 96°F. or to the level specified on the thermometer instructions.
- Take the temperature, using one of the following methods:

By mouth. Explain the procedure beforehand to help the child relax and to keep him from biting the thermometer or spitting. Place the thermometer under the tongue with the mouth closed. Hold it in place for three minutes.

By rectum. Lubricate the bulb of the thermometer with petroleum jelly. Hold the child on your lap or place him on a bed face down or on his side. Gently insert the thermometer for one inch into the rectum and hold in for three minutes. Be alert for sudden body movements to avoid injury. Rectal temperature, normally, is one degree higher than by mouth (oral).

By armpit. Slip the thermometer into the armpit, holding the child close to you. Press the child's arm against the side of his body and keep the thermometer in place four or five minutes. Temperature by this method may be slightly lower than with other methods. This method is suggested only when the other two methods are not possible—when the child is too young for oral temperature or too ill or overly active for rectal temperature.

Children have high temperatures more often than adults. If a child's temperature exceeds 104°F., sponging with cold water may be necessary, but take care to guard against chilling. The amount of fever does not necessarily indicate the seriousness of an illness. Some serious conditions do not cause more than a one- or two-degree rise in temperature, yet a simple cold may cause a sudden high temperature.

Convulsions

Convulsions are generally characterized by jerky body movements, quivering spells, or spasms. A child with high fever or a sick child should be watched closely to detect the possible onset of convulsions. Should convulsions occur, seek medical help immediately. The convulsions cannot be stopped, but you can prevent the child from injury. Until medical assistance takes over, you should:

- Remain calm. Convulsions usually last only a few minutes.
- Place the child on his abdomen on a bed, rug, or floor away from furniture or objects to prevent injury. This position also helps prevent drawing saliva into the lungs or swallowing the tongue and allows for easier breathing.

Convulsions may indicate the beginning of infection or a disease. If the convulsions occur at repeated intervals and without fever, epilepsy may be the problem. Medical supervision is required to prevent epileptic seizures.

Keeping the Sick Child Occupied

Very sick children usually remain in bed with little difficulty, but as children begin to recover or if they are not severely ill, they are eager to get out of bed. Children need amusing things to do while confined to bed or other close quarters. It may be wiser to allow a child to get out of bed if he or she is well enough. Rest in a comfortable chair or on a sofa may be easier than staying in bed. A change in surroundings, with more activity in the room and a different position for sitting or lying down, may help the child recover faster. As he feels better, however, he is more likely to become bored. This is when the ingenious adult can help by providing ideas for things a child can do. Here are a few suggestions. Can you think of others?

- Provide cuddly animals or dolls, especially the child's favorite—but remember to remove these from a small child's crib when he is asleep to avoid smothering accidents.
- Crayons and paper; stringing beads; toys such as telephones, tape recorders, and listening devices; pegboards; puzzles with easy-to-handle pieces; and other simple manipulative toys.
- A nearby aquarium with fish or a gerbil in a cage is fun to watch.
- If not too ill, the child may be able to make a mobile. Hang it where the child can watch it move when blown by a current of air—or a paper fan made and used by the child.
- Old magazines and catalogs can be cut, using the pictures to decorate a shoebox or other container. If the product is finished, it can be used to hold small toys, crayons, paper, tissues, or other items the child might want to keep beside the bed.
- Sheets of paper or paper sacks decorated with pictures or greeting cards make interesting scrapbooks or tote bags.
- Water colors and an improvised easel are excellent for art activities.
- Clay, play dough, and finger paints—although messy—will keep a child amused as well as quiet.

Simple activities are best for sick children since their levels of energy, motivation, and strength are lower than usual. Special adult attention is needed to keep the child secure, content, and under control.

Part III: A Wholesome Environment

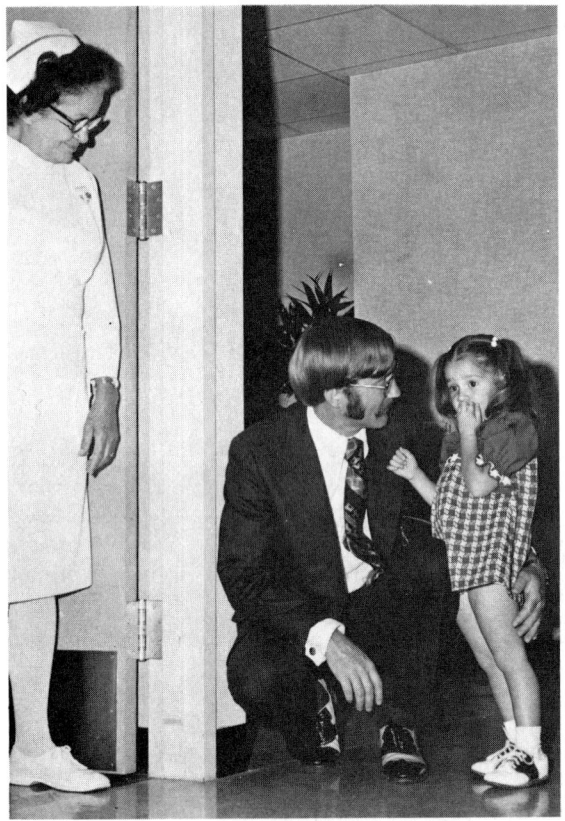

Okmulgee County Health Department

Parents can give children assurance and help in overcoming anxiety about hospitalization.

Preparing Children for Hospitalization

Research has shown that children, including infants, who are hospitalized show some reactions to the hospital situation. Disruptions in the routine and the nature of care to which children are generally accustomed may bring about changes in behavior. Such changes may last up to several weeks after returning home. Changes in patterns of sleeping, eating, and elimination are common problems.

Separation from the child's everyday environment, parents, and close friends may cause anxiety and frustration. This is called separation anxiety.

Children from ages one to three have difficulty understanding what is real. They may think the separation will be permanent. They are not able to judge the passage of time and this makes it difficult to understand that *later* they can go home. Separation from close family members, especially the parents or adults who care for the child daily, may even cause the child to interpret the disappearance of this person as punishment for being bad. Authorities tell us that two- or three-year-old children with separation anxiety may resort to thumb or finger sucking, feeding difficulties, a desire to return to using the bottle, and loss of bladder or bowel control. A child this age may seek ways to gain control by getting into power struggles with close adults. This is a method of getting into a conflict with an adult in order to get attention and keep the adult near. For example, the child may insist by words or actions that the parent stay near every minute. The parent tries to explain or leave and the struggle begins.

Children who are hospitalized very long and who do not have warm and parentlike relationships during this time may experience more serious effects. Depression, delayed development, reluctance to form deep relationships, and impulsive behavior can occur.

Children from ages four to six experience less separation anxiety but encounter other difficulties. Hospitalization during this stage can be positive or negative depending on how well the child is prepared for the experience. For example, when hospital procedures are not well understood, the child may develop fears of being punished. The child's limited ability to recognize reality combined with his capacity for fantasy can cause confusion and frustration. A misunderstanding about the purpose of certain medical procedures, especially those which bring pain, can cause what authorities call *mutilation anxiety*. The child becomes very fearful of bodily harm.

Preparing a child for a hospital experience should begin several days prior to the date for entering. Depending on the age and level of development, more or less time may be needed to help a child understand why hospitalization is necessary and to accept the reasons for going. Compare the following cases.

Nancy, age three, went into the hospital to have her tonsils taken out. Not having been prepared, she was terrified each time the doctor or nurse came into her room. She screamed when the nurse tried to take her temperature, and it was a struggle to secure a blood sample. When the nurses and orderly appeared to take Nancy to the operating room, she became hysterical. No doubt, the white uniforms and face masks were frightening to Nancy. She was so upset that the operation had to be postponed until the doctor could calm her down.

Von, age four, was well prepared for his tonsillectomy. Although he was somewhat apprehensive about having part of his body taken out, he felt confident about staying in the hospital. His parents had prepared him in advance for what was ahead. They read several stories to him about children who went to the hospital, one about another boy who had his tonsils removed.

They explained beforehand why the nurses and doctors wear uniforms and how the face masks worn during surgery are to prevent bacteria from spreading and to protect each person. A new word—surgery—was introduced to Von and explained with stories. His questions were answered with simple but factual explanations.

Von was expecting some new experiences and was not frightened about facing them. Pictures of hospital rooms, nurses, doctors, and patients were available to Von for a couple of weeks prior to his hospital trip. He was told that his throat would hurt for a few days after surgery. He knew he would be unable to talk much for a day or two after coming home. He also learned he would be able to eat plenty of ice cream and gelatin for dessert, a pleasant thought to a four-year-old.

When Von's mother took him into the children's ward of the hospital, she and a nurse gave him a tour of the entire floor. First, they went to the reception area and desk to meet the ward nurses, then to the nursery to see where the newborn babies stay. From there they went to see the oper-

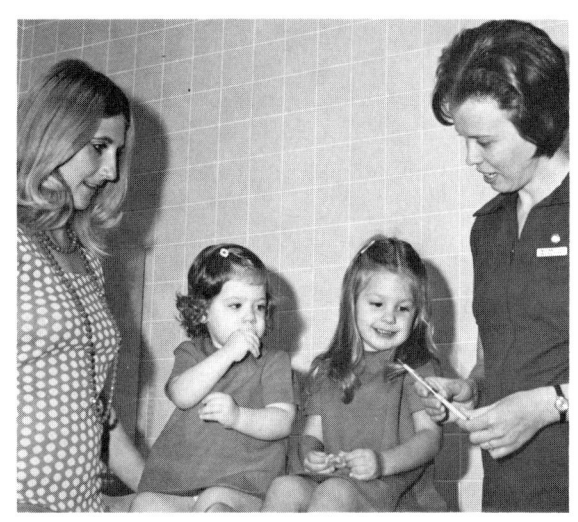

Okmulgee County Health Department

Preparing children for hospitalization should begin several days before entering.

Part III: A Wholesome Environment

ating room and the rolling bed which Von would ride. Finally, after seeing the patients' rooms along the hallway, the elevators, and the water fountains, Von arrived at his room. He met his seven-year-old roommate who was also going to have a tonsillectomy.

Knowing beforehand that he would have some freedom to move about and play with some of his own toys which he brought along gave Von a feeling of security. He enjoyed pretending that his bed, with the protective bars, was a cage. For a while, he was a monkey, then a camel, and finally a rhino. He greeted the nurses who came in from time to time and asked many questions about what was going to happen to him next.

Von was not surprised or frightened, although a little anxious, when the intern came in to take the first blood sample. He had played doctor and nurse with his sister and mother at home the week before, so he had some idea of what to expect. Von was very brave—and he said so—when he was wheeled off the next morning to the operating room.

Do you see how important it is to prepare children for a hospital stay? This can be an enlightening childhood experience, and many fears and anxieties can be eliminated or lessened with careful planning. Review these suggestions for helping children get ready to go to the hospital:

- Give the child the reason for going to the hospital.
- Explain, in simple terms, what will take place—for example, a tonsillectomy, ear surgery, or diagnostic tests for further help.
- Describe the appearance of the hospital and personnel, using as many pictures as possible.

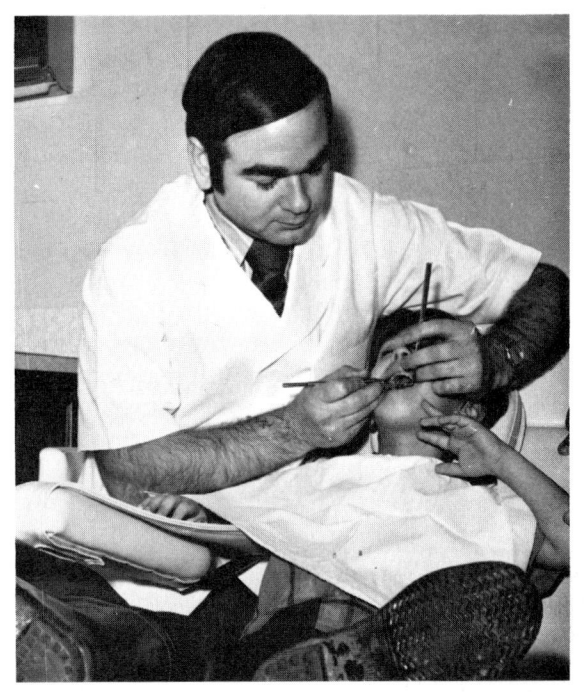

Oklahoma State Department of Health

Children should also be prepared for a visit to the dentist.

- Explain the reasons for uniforms and face masks.
- Talk about the procedures which can be expected, such as blood samples, urine specimens, injections, pills, and temperature recordings.
- Explain why the parents cannot always go with the child into the operating room.
- Describe possible outcomes of surgery or medication such as nausea; vomiting; pain; temporary loss of hearing, sight, or speech; inability to move one or more limbs; or having to lie still for a long time.
- Answer the child's questions with frankness and honesty, making the responses as simple and short as possible.

- Use well-illustrated pictures and stories to help the child become familiar with hospital routines and experiences for patients.
- Encourage the child to prepare a tote bag or suitcase containing personal items, especially some favorite toys, to take to the hospital.
- Take the child on a tour of the hospital and help acquaint him with the new environment.

As you can see, many of these same principles can be applied when preparing children for a visit to the doctor, dentist, or clinic. Children's centers which conduct clinics periodically can take advantage of opportunities to familiarize children with medical procedures. Special activities can also be conducted in the center from time to time in order to introduce hospitalization and medical services to children. This is an appropriate and interesting theme for activities during one or two days of a children's program.

Chapter Highlights

- Signs of a healthy child are: sleeps soundly; eats without much coaxing; gains steadily in height and weight over the months; teeth are in good condition; few aches and pains; enjoys both individual and group activities.
- Five major diseases which children need protection against through immunization are: whooping cough (pertussis); tetanus; polio (infantile paralysis); diphtheria; measles.
- Careful immunization records concerning type of injection and date given should be kept on all children for future reference in case the child becomes ill; moves to another community; changes doctors or clinics; transfers to another children's center; or enters school.
- Red measles (rubeola) can cause such serious complications as encephalitis and infections of the respiratory tract, ears, sinuses, or lungs.
- Rubella (German measles) is a rather mild illness caused by an entirely different virus than that which causes red measles.
- Maintenance of healthy children and staff is vital in a children's center.
- Both children and adults should have regular physical examinations. Health certificates and TB skin tests are required of staff members who work in children's centers.
- Some signs of possible ill health among children are: sore throat; redness, or itching of the mouth and throat area; discharge from eyes, ears, or nose; rash on face, neck, chest or stomach; dirty hair and scalp; sneezing and coughing; drowsiness when the child is usually wide awake; watery or glassy eyes; fever, flushed face, and hot dry skin or exceptional paleness and coldness; unexpected, profuse perspiring; hoarse voice and swollen glands; pain in ear, head, chest, stomach, abdomen, or joints; stiff back or neck; nausea; vomiting; diarrhea.
- Areas in the children's center which require special attention for safeguarding health of children and staff are: children's activities area; washroom and toilet area; crib area; kitchen or food preparation area.
- Signs which might indicate fever in a child are: listlessness; drowsiness; hot face and neck; flushed face; especially bright and glassy eyes.
- The three methods of taking temperature are: *by mouth; by rectum* (the most accurate measurement); *by armpit* (the least accurate measurement).

Part III: A Wholesome Environment

- The procedure to follow in case a convulsion occurs is: place child on abdomen on a bed, rug, or floor away from furniture or objects; seek medical help immediately; remain calm until help arrives.
- When ill, children need amusing things to do while confined to bed or other close quarters.
- Preparing a child for a hospital experience as a patient should begin several days prior to entering.

Thinking It Over

1. What are the signs of a healthy child?
2. Name five major diseases against which children need protection through immunization.
3. Can you remember what immunizations you were given when you were a young child? Are there others available today? Why do you think immunization is important?
4. Describe the difference between red measles (rubeola) and rubella (German measles).
5. What are some common ways communicable diseases are spread? What could you do in a children's center to help control the spread of diseases?
6. What type of health check should be conducted daily in a child care center?
7. What health precautions regarding the child care center staff should be taken in order to insure the safety of the children?
8. What information is needed on each child in a child care center for use in case of a health emergency?
9. What information should the bulletin board in the child care center contain in order to help insure the health and safety of children?
10. State specific precautions to take when a child becomes ill at a children's center.
11. How can you tell that a child has a fever?
12. Describe the three methods of taking a child's temperature.
13. What should you do if a child has a convulsion?
14. Name four suggestions for children's activities when they are recovering from an illness but are not yet able to resume their usual routine.
15. Which areas in a child care center need special care to provide healthful and safe conditions for children?
16. What precautions should child care workers take concerning medication for children?
17. What attitude toward medication would you like to instill in the children under your care?
18. Why is it important to prepare a child for hospitalization?
19. Explain what can be done to help a child get ready to enter the hospital as a patient.

Things To Do

1. Invite a doctor or nurse to talk about:
   - Characteristics of healthy children.
   - Signs of approaching illness.
   - When to call the doctor.
   - A good immunization program for children from birth to first grade.
   - The dangers of both kinds of measles.
2. Invite a children's center director or coordinator to discuss the importance of children's health records in a children's center (including anecdotes concerning times when they were very necessary) or the advantages of a healthy staff.
3. Work in small groups of three or four students and write, with illustrations, a children's book on "The Travels of Herm-the-Germ in the Nursery School."
4. Develop a sample health record file for individual children in a children's center.
5. Make a bulletin board which might be seen in a children's center. (It should be attractive for the children as well as useful for the staff.)
6. Make a collage portraying signs of ill health and poor health habits in children.
7. Compile a notebook of suggestions called, "Fun and Games to Recover By."
8. Write a short story entitled, "I'm OK—You're OK—Physically." (As an alternative, write a practical guide to handling illnesses in the children's center.)
9. Role play scenes showing adequate and inadequate preparation of children for hospitalization.
10. Observe a group of young children in a child care center playing and interacting. Identify characteristics of those who appear healthy and those who appear unhealthy. Check the accuracy of your choices with the center manager. Report your findings to class and discuss.
11. Make posters with photographs or drawings depicting signs of a healthy child and of an unhealthy child. List the signs of each.

Recommended Reading

Benenson, Abram, Editor. *Control of Communicable Diseases in Man.* Washington, D.C.: The American Public Health Association, 1970.

The American Red Cross. *Standard First Aid and Personal Safety.* Garden City, New York: Doubleday and Co., Inc., 1973.

Your Child From One to Six. Washington, D.C.: U.S. Department of Health, Education, and Welfare, Office of Child Development, 1962.

Chapter 10.

Insuring Safety

Your Challenge

This chapter will enable you to . . . .

- Distinguish between protecting children and overprotecting them.
- Demonstrate how actions can be combined with words to help children learn about safety.
- Explain what safety precautions must be taken at each stage of development.
- Explain why many accidents happen during childhood.
- State the guidelines that should be followed to prevent accidents outdoors; with equipment, toys, matches, poisons, animals, and hazardous objects; on streets; in vehicles; and to the eyes.
- List the safety rules that should be followed in the center.

THINKING ABOUT SAFETY

Four-year-old Autumn and her parents were at a large shopping center with a beautiful fountain and pond in the center of the mall. Autumn was fascinated by the sight and sound of the splashing water. Cautiously she moved closer and reached out, hoping to feel just a little of the spray from the fountain and maybe even touch the water. She reached a little farther, then still a little farther, and suddenly splashed into the pond. While Autumn screamed with fear (or was it glee?), her father quickly plucked her from the water, bringing a happy ending to an embarrassing moment.

Autumn's fall into the pond will probably be remembered as a humorous experience. The incident does, however, have a serious lesson. Children are curious and not aware of all the hazards that may go along with experimentation. Autumn's father rescued her, but what about the children who experiment when adults are not close by? Who will rescue them? One answer, of course, involves prevention. Only by providing a safe environment can we protect children from unnecessary harm.

Safeguards Without Overprotection

How safe are the children you care for? How free of hazards are their surroundings? During the critical early years children must be protected from accidents while they learn to protect themselves.

Protection, however, can be carried to an extreme.

Judy is a sad example of what can happen to a child who is overly protected. Judy, at six, is handicapped by severe shyness and fears. An only and long-awaited child, she has been subject to constant supervision by her mother from birth. Her six years have been filled with maternal warnings: "Judy, watch out for the dog; dogs will bite. Judy, don't you dare go near the water. Stay close to mother. Judy, stay off the sliding board; you might fall." In moderation, these warnings might have little effect, but for Judy, nearly every move, every potential adventure, is a reason for fear. A shy and fearful child, she will probably carry these traits into adulthood. Can you see that providing a safe environment for a child does not mean total restraint?

Every child must be protected, but not overprotected. Children must have opportunities to explore and move about, but they must also learn to become aware of dangers. Gradually, they will learn to function safely and protect themselves if they are guided carefully rather than instilled with fear.

Helping Children Learn the Safe Way

Adults are responsible for helping children learn how to satisfy normal and healthy needs in the safest ways possible. They must provide opportunities for children to become aware of what they *can* do as well as what they *cannot* do. Consider this example. Mrs. Holmes grasped Johnny's hand firmly as they crossed the street. When they were safe in the play area, she let him go, saying, "Do you see that it's safe to run and play here? Go on now and have fun." Johnny will soon learn that although it is safe to run in the play area, it is not safe to run across the street. Experiences like these guide children in developing ideas about safety in their environment. Remember, however, young children also learn by copying the behavior of others and absorbing adult attitudes. Young children will try nearly anything they see others do—strike matches, stand on chairs, and drink liquids, to mention only a few. This makes your job doubly challenging, for you must watch for the child's mistakes as an imitator (car wax may look like food to a child). You must also set a good example. (Have you ever jaywalked with a child on a busy downtown street?) Think about your habits for a moment. Are your actions safe and correct examples for children who watch you?

When at the height of activity, children are too busy having fun and exploring their surroundings to worry or think seriously about dangers and unsafe places to play. They often invite danger by taking risks. For example, a child may jump right into a stream or puddle of water on a hot day with little thought about the depth or cleanliness of the water. Children like to

Children, fascinated by the sight and sound of splashing water, are rarely aware of the dangers awaiting them.

A child may be too busy exploring to think about dangerous or unsafe places to play.

A child may be surrounded by danger and not even be aware of the hazards.

climb on excavations and construction sites; play in puddles; and hide in weeds, discarded refrigerators, between boxes, around fences, and in and around garbage cans. They like to walk on railroad tracks, narrow boards, and ridges. Children get a thrill from climbing trees, even though the limbs may hang over spiked fences or other dangerous objects. Can you remember as a child how important it was to have help on certain occasions when you were in danger? Growing and learning to be responsible for your own health and safety often required help from adults, with some limits, to give you a feeling of protection in your freedom.

As children grow older, they become more active and cover more territory indoors and outdoors. If children are provided with safety experiences, they often learn to make many safe judgments by the time they are four or five years old. Children need freedom to practice safety in the presence of adults. With simple suggestions from adults, children gain a sense of security in their actions. Children often gain insight from simple explanations by adults. An explanation is more meaningful, however, if combined with action involving the children. For example, if the child can understand a simple explanation of why the kitchen range can be dangerous, this approach will likely be more helpful than forbidding the child to go near the range. The explanation becomes more meaningful by allowing the child, under close supervision, to place his hands near enough to the burners to feel the warmth. Remember, however, that some children's memories are short, causing them to forget quickly any danger. Often they simply do not realize the meaning of danger. Sometimes the explanation is weak even though the adult feels otherwise. So, be patient. A simple explanation may need to be followed by several gentle reminders before

Ch. 10: Insuring Safety

the child really understands. Since accidents involving young children are seldom prevented by harsh warnings or punishment, such measures should be used only if absolutely necessary. For example, a sharp warning might stop a child who is about to touch a hot range but is out of your reach at that instant.

Action and words are usually more meaningful than words alone. Children should be shown ways to accomplish tasks safely—holding on to handrails while walking up and down stairs, walking instead of running indoors, and holding an adult's hand while walking in traffic or on busy sidewalks. You can help children develop courage and confidence by helping them succeed safely.

Planning ahead for safety is a responsibility of the child care staff in a center. Community members, and especially parents, expect children's centers to operate safely. One serious, avoidable accident can cause the public to lose confidence in a center's program and in the people working with the children, besides suffering and grief.

RELATING SAFETY TO DEVELOPMENT

Studies indicate that certain accidents occur more frequently at one stage of a child's development than at others. The more you know about how children grow and develop, the better able you will be to provide a safe and healthy environment. You will be able to foresee and prevent potential accident situations. Understanding that children learn by touching, tasting, and smelling, as well as seeing and hearing, should help you in providing patient and sympathetic, yet careful, supervision. Children depend on adults for help in learning limits for safety at all stages of development. On the following pages you will find some practical ideas on safety for children at different developmental stages.

INFANTS

Infants up to six-months of age need complete protection and constant supervision.

Babies are constantly shifting positions as they roll from side to side, wiggle, turn, and gradually move themselves within their cribs.	Cribs must have sides for protection, with crib bars spaced close enough to prevent baby's head from catching between them. Firm mattresses, properly fitted, help prevent legs, arms, or head from lodging at edges. Pads can be purchased to fit around the inside edge of a crib to keep the infant's head from slipping through the bars.
Sucking on toys, crib slats, or other objects is common during this stage.	Lead-free, nontoxic paints and finishes must be used for all furniture, toys, and baby equipment. Small objects that may get into baby's mouth must be kept away.
Babies are helpless in water.	An adult *must* remain with the baby while bathing—*regardless* of phone calls or doorbells.

Part III: A Wholesome Environment

From six to eighteen months infants become very curious and eager to examine their world.

Practically everything within sight is exciting and interesting to growing infants.	They need lots of freedom but in protected areas with close supervision. Gates at doorways and stairways help prevent them from falling or wandering into unsafe places.
Their index fingers are used constantly as a probe to find out about things.	Unused light sockets and electrical outlets should be taped or neutralized with dummy plugs. Drawers and cabinets should be locked if they contain any hazardous items. Breakable items should be out of reach.
Curiosity about objects above the eye level offers challenges for the exploring infant.	Lift the infant occasionally to satisfy curiosity.
Roaming all over, making no distinctions about boundaries, they enjoy discovering their world. They pull themselves up or grasp for balance without thought of dangers which may be at hand.	Containers of hot foods and liquids should never be left with handles extending over the edge of the range or counter tops. Dishes of hot foods should be placed in the center of the table to avoid burning exploring hands. Use of tablecloths which hang over table edges should be avoided to prevent pulling hot food or objects off or onto the child.

TODDLERS

From eighteen months to three years, toddlers are adventurous, requiring the watchfulness of adults.

Since they can now rotate their forearms, toddlers turn doorknobs, open cabinets and storage areas, and find their way into closets and pantries.	Dangerous items should be stored on upper shelves. These include paint, paint thinner, turpentine, cleaning fluids, and all drugs and medicines. Danger areas should have locked doors to keep children from suddenly dashing through or falling, such as from second-story landings or openings leading to construction sites or traffic. Closets, cabinets, and old refrigerators large enough for children to crawl into should be locked or have the doors completely removed.

Ch. 10: Insuring Safety

Open windows without screens are hazardous for young children.
National Safety Council

Toddlers are experimenters. They like to take things apart and fit them together; they try to use all types of objects as playthings.	Sharp, pointed scissors, knives, heavy tools, and electrical appliances should be kept out of reach. They can play with pots and pans, blunt scissors, wooden hammers, empty cardboard boxes, and large spoons which are large enough to handle safely.
Climbing onto objects is a major activity, but at this stage children cannot judge the safety of heights.	Adults must offer protection from falls. Windows should be checked for screen fastenings or window guards to protect children from falling out. Vehicle doors should be locked and secured with safety latches. Safety belts are needed to prevent crawling back and forth over seats as well as to prevent injury from quick stops or turns in traffic. Buses without safety belts require close adult supervision with quiet activities and materials for children to work with in their seats while riding.
They enjoy waterplay.	Ponds, pools, and basins of water must have constant adult supervision. These areas should be emptied, fenced, or covered securely when not in use. Children need help in learning to respect water and its depth.

Part III: A Wholesome Environment

ROMPERS

Three- and four-year-olds are busy making discoveries about themselves and finding their place in the world while learning by doing.

They can take verbal directions with a great amount of success. They are beginning to understand the reasons for safety measures, such as keeping floor areas clear of toys and play equipment that could cause tripping. However, they get excited about their activities and easily forget about safety.	Reminders are needed—but they usually don't resent it because they are eager to please.
Attention spans are getting longer; and they can sit for ten to twenty minutes doing interesting manual tasks. By four, many children enjoy building simple things and using tools.	This is an ideal stage for focusing on safety habits, both by example and explanation.
They feel important as group members, and enjoy having simple tasks to do within their ability. They like to be helpers.	Hazardous tasks should be avoided, such as carrying glass containers and sharp or heavy objects. Adults will need to be patient during this stage as children are gaining eye-to-hand coordination. Spills and mishaps, which will occur from time to time, require understanding and encouragement to try again.
At this stage, children begin to exhibit greater self-control. They are surefooted and enjoy running and doing things with their entire bodies. By age four, they can cover large areas of space, going in every direction.	All traffic lanes should be clear of objects or loose coverings on which children can trip while playing. Supervision is needed in play areas, on sidewalks, and in other areas where children run and play.
They hurry up and down stairs, in and out of doorways, through halls, and along sidewalks.	Stairs should have strong rails for support, and children should be encouraged to use them.
Riding wheel toys is fun because children are becoming competent with motor skills.	They should learn to ride in the designated areas. They understand the meaning of limits and are eager to please adults—another advantage in teaching safety.
They enjoy playing with others. They often take turns pushing and pulling each other, getting into rocking boats in pairs, and climbing and tumbling together.	Wheel and large toys should be strong enough to bear the weight of two children.

Ch. 10: Insuring Safety

Climbing trees and going over fences are favorite activities. At this age, reaching the first fork in a very low-forked tree is climbing.	They need protection from falls by learning how to get a sure footing and proper handhold. Their clothes need to give them freedom of action and shoes need to be safe for running as well as for climbing low bannister railings, jungle gym bars, trees, and other objects.
Throwing and catching balls and bean bags become tasks within their ability range.	They need supervision to protect them from running out into unsafe areas such as driveways or streets to retrieve balls or other objects.
They especially enjoy outdoor play.	They need guidance in learning limits of play.

KINDERGARTNERS

Five-year-olds are discovering their importance as individuals while continuing to explore the world about them.

They are becoming independent and seeking ways of entertaining themselves. Although they enjoy being around others, they like to engage in individual activities. Interest spans are expanding; some can enjoy a simple activity for a half-hour or more.	Watchfulness is needed to safeguard them without restricting their independence.
Motor coordination is improving. Eye-to-hand activities such as pegs in slots, hammering, and puzzles are favorites.	Manipulative activities such as table games still require adult guidance in helping them develop respect for safety, work habits, and routines.
Exploring the world directly about them can be accomplished with greater success, but they still have strong urges to test and experiment through their senses.	Guidance to help children learn about danger and hazards is meaningful at this stage. Swings, shelves, windows, and other objects are often given a full test.

ACCIDENTS ARE CAUSED

The United States Department of Health, Education, and Welfare reports that more children are crippled by accidents than by diseases. More children die from accidents than from the combination of cancer, congenital malformations, and pneumonia, according to the Children's Hospital Medical Center in Boston. Common causes of accidental deaths among children between the ages of one and five are motor vehicles, fires, drowning, poisons, and falls.

Part III: A Wholesome Environment

Curiosity often leads children to unsafe places.

A medical research team studied every child entering the Children's Hospital Medical Center at Boston to investigate facts surrounding each accident, such as the child's relationship to his parents and family member, the daily routine, and the physical environment. The results indicated that accidents are most often influenced by family, home, environmental, and/or emotional conditions. Examples are fatigue, hunger, and family illness. Even such situations as a mother's worry or a child's uncertainty were sometimes contributing factors. Consider the following conditions which may cause accidents when several occur at the same time.

Accidents are more likely to happen when:

- Staff members and parents do not understand what to expect at particular stages of a child's development.
- A child is in the care of persons not familiar with the routines and activities of children.
- A child is hungry, tired, angry, or confused.
- Few safe areas are available for play.
- Hazards are present—sharp knives, busy streets, bottles of medicine, slippery sidewalks, open heaters, open electrical outlets.
- Adults have little concern for close supervision of children's activities and freedom of movement.
- Hazards are attractive to a child. (Small children may not be able to resist experimenting with a flame in an open heater, sharp objects, matches, electrical cords, and other hazardous objects or situations.)
- A child's environment has considerably changed by moving or vacations.
- Members of the staff are not prepared to cope with or manage the activities of young children because of lack of knowledge of rules and safety procedures.
- The space and equipment are not safely planned for children's activities.
- Routines are not established consistently so that children know what is expected of them and what they can expect.
- Staff members are unhappy with their work or have conflicts with each other.
- Staff members are at work but should be at home because they are not feeling well.
- Staff members bring personal problems to work. This often causes them to be preoccupied instead of alert to the children's needs and moods.
- Unsatisfactory transportation arrangements exist to and from the center and for field trips.
- A parent is ill, pregnant, or despondent over marital or family problems.
- The relationship between parents is continually tense.

Ch. 10: Insuring Safety

- Grandparents or relatives living in a child's home require extensive attention because of illness or disability.
- Family members are ill and require the major attention of the parent.
- A family is economically and/or socially unstable.

PLAN FOR PREVENTION OF ACCIDENTS

Tired after a busy morning with the children at the day care center, Mrs. Potter, a child care assistant, was not as alert as usual. Fridays were always tiring, but this one was especially so since Mrs. Potter had awakened early in the morning to do laundry before coming to work. Without the usually watchful eye of Mrs. Potter, three-year-old Deena, an active child, managed to wander off unnoticed. Finding a tricycle on the porch of the center, Deena began to ride. While riding, Deena came too close to the edge of the porch and the back wheel slipped over the side, sending Deena and the tricycle tumbling to the ground. Deena suffered a broken collar bone, and Mrs. Potter felt much anguish over her negligence. Can you analyze this incident and list factors which may have combined to cause the accident? Refer to the list you just read.

If you are alert and safety conscious, you probably thought of several ways Deena's accident might have been prevented. Learn to think ahead. Some accidents are bound to happen, but why take chances? As you work inside or outside the home or center, imagine what you might do if you were a child. Be conscious of the little things around you that sometimes lead to trouble. When you are under pressure, slow down and take extra precautions. Finally, review the guidelines on the next few pages and then be reasonably assured that after you have done all you can, the children you care for will be safe.

Outdoor Safety

Providing a safe outdoor area for children is a basic requirement. Although sunlight is an aid to health, shaded areas provide protection from the sun while adding to the general comfort of the children during hot weather. Drainage should be adequate to eliminate standing water from rain or melted snow. Persistent damp areas should be eliminated both for safety in the activities of children and to prevent bacteria and insect growth. Activity areas should provide ample space for children to move about and play without restriction, even though such areas must be fenced for safety purposes. The play yard must be checked daily and kept free of broken glass, nails, sharp sticks, and other harmful objects.

Supervising outdoor play consists of watching children, yet allowing each to set an individual pace in learning to use play equipment. Children need to move about freely within safe surroundings as they become actively involved in play, whether independently, in small groups, or in organized games.

Digging areas should be carefully checked each day for sharp or dangerous objects. Equipment, such as shovels, buckets, and scoops, should have smooth edges, with handles, hinges, or working parts in safe condition for use by the children.

Water play may be provided in shallow basins, pools, or portable equipment. These require daily cleaning. Swimming instructors, certified as lifeguards, are employed by some centers to teach children how to swim. Wading and swimming pools

Part III: A Wholesome Environment

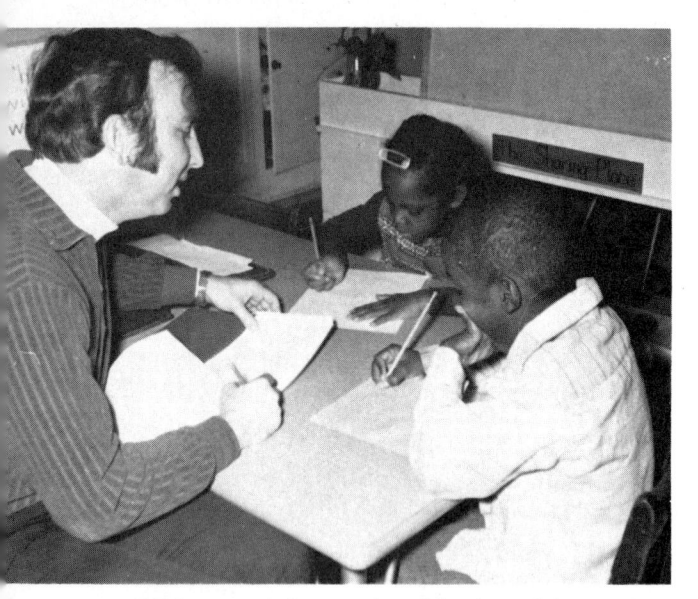

Children need the security of having adults nearby.

University of Oklahoma Institute of Child Development
Safe equipment must be sturdy and kept in good repair.

must have close and constant supervision, with well-qualified adults watching children at all times.

Safe Equipment

Enriching children's surroundings with safe and appropriate equipment is an excellent way to widen their learning opportunities. Research indicates however, that many centers for children are far from safe, and many have only minimal facilities which are not designed to enhance the children's environment.

Even in small centers, equipment for outdoor activities serves two major purposes. It enables children to exercise and move about freely, and it provides opportunities for developing physical and motor skills, formulating concepts, improving sensory abilities, and enjoying relationships with peers. Children learn safety through well-planned experiences during which they can learn to make judgments and decisions. Children gain strength, coordination, and agility while developing physical abilities.

All equipment must be sturdy, well constructed, and kept in good repair. Wheel toys and equipment with movable parts should be constructed to avoid pinched fingers and frustration because of hard-to-operate parts. Equipment, of course, is safer for children if selected with their particular developmental levels in mind.

Low climbing, crawling, and walking equipment should be located where the surface is soft or padded for protection from possible falls. Grass, sand, or mats are recommended. Hard surface areas are needed for most wheel toys.

The Food and Drug Administration's Bureau of Product Safety continually investigates the hazards of toys and playground equipment. According to the bureau, a 1970 estimate stated that close to a million injuries result yearly from outside

Ch. 10: Insuring Safety

playground equipment. Some changes that may be made in the future on playground equipment and some things you should look for when you purchase or use present equipment are:

- Nonremovable caps for all hollow metal tubing, so a child's finger cannot be caught.
- Adequate instructions for adults on how to assemble playground equipment so that it will not fall apart or tip over.
- Lock washers or self-locking nuts on all bolts, to prevent bolts from loosening and protruding dangerously or allowing equipment to collapse.
- Closed hooks instead of open-ended hooks, such as on swing chains, that can pull loose and allow the child to fall from the swing.
- Removal of V-sections and other dangerous openings where a child can catch his head.

To report an accident related to playground equipment, write to Playground Equipment, Bureau of Product Safety, Food and Drug Administration, 5401 Westbard Avenue, Bethesda, Maryland 20016.

Storage for outdoor equipment and supplies should be near the area of use. Well-organized storage for equipment will not only make getting things in and out easier but will also help keep the equipment in good condition. Scratches, paint chips, and broken parts can often be avoided by proper storage. A sturdy door with a lock will add protection to the property and safety for the children. Otherwise, children might be tempted to play in the storage area where safety hazards exist.

Eliminate Hazardous Toys

In a recent one-year period, the Food and Drug Administration's Bureau of Product Safety banned about 200 hazardous toys. In most cases, manufacturers stopped making these toys or modified them to make them safe. When you buy toys for children, check them carefully. Although much is being done to insure toy safety, certain harmful products may still be found. What makes a toy hazardous? Here are just a few examples:

- Squeeze toy with removable squeaker.
- Stuffed animal with sharp wire in the ears.
- Spinning top with a spike in the base.
- Xylophone with sharp keys.
- Doll with straight pins in bows.

Some general hazards to be avoided in toys are: sharp wires, prongs, pins, and edges; material that shatters into sharp slivers when dropped; excessive heat production; objects that are small enough to put in ears, nose, or mouth of small children; toxic paint; highly flammable items; and electrical and mechanical hazards.

The Child Protection and Toy Safety Act provides that if a toy is considered to be unsafe, the manufacturer must either correct the hazard or stop production of the toy.

If you believe a toy is hazardous and should not be on the market, you may want to notify FDA's Toy Review Committee, describing the toy, its name (if any), model number (if any), and the name and address of the manufacturer (or distributor). Also give the name of the store stocking the toy. Again, send your comments to Toy Review Committee, Bureau of Product Safety, Food and Drug Administration, 5401 Westbard Avenue, Bethesda, Maryland 20016.

Playing With Matches

One exciting but dangerous adventure for children is striking matches. Tommy

One exciting but dangerous adventure for children is striking matches.

and Karen, ages four and six, with their three young friends, were playing in the bedroom when they decided to light a candle and place it in the center of the bed. Before they knew it, the candle had tumbled over and the bed was on fire. Although the children were uninjured, their home was heavily damaged. At times, children find ways to experiment even when their parents have taken precautions to provide a safe environment.

Keeping matches out of the hands of children is not easy because matches are used for so many purposes around the home. However, by making an effort to store them in safe locations, by teaching children that matches are not toys, and by keeping a watchful eye on children at play indoors and out, the chances of tragedy by fire are greatly reduced. This is extremely important in the children's center where so many children are gathered together under one roof.

If matches are needed in the center for some reason, find a safe shelf or cupboard for them. Purses should be stored on shelves, hooks, or in closets where children cannot reach them. (Purses often contain matches as well as other objects that could be harmful to children—pills, nail files, lighters, and others.) Also consider developing the habit of keeping your pockets free of matches and other harmful objects. On some days, making these efforts may seem like an inconvenience, but a moment's inconvenience is a small price to pay for safety.

Poisons

As you know, certain chemicals can be fatal or cause serious illness when swallowed, breathed, or absorbed through the skin. Some of the common poisons are found in cleaning fluids, bug killers, nail polish, paint thinner and remover, insect spray, soldering fluids, metal polishes, disinfectants, and medicinal products in liquid and pill form.

The body reacts to these in different ways. For example, cyanides are almost immediately fatal, whereas lead and DDT work slowly; only after months of exposure does the destructive evidence begin to appear. Carbon tetrachloride may cause reactions that are difficult, even impossible, to determine and treat. The American Medical Association reports that overdoses of aspirin are the most common cause of accidental fatal poisonings by mouth and the leading cause of poisoning for children under five.

Precautions will help you prevent accidents from poisons. Are you familiar with these?

- Label all drugs and household products.
- Read labels carefully before using the

Oklahoma State Department of Health

Common household cleaners, personal grooming products, and medicines should not be accessible to young children.

product. Most products are dangerous only when misused.
- Store medicines—pills, capsules, and liquids—in original containers. Never change these from one container to another. Throw old medicine away in covered garbage containers or disposals. Never leave medicines within reach or sight of children.
- Use cleaning fluids, furniture polish, fumigants, paint thinners, and paint removers in a well-ventilated room when children are not present. Keep containers closed securely and locked or stored out of reach when not in use.
- Use insecticides sparingly so as to avoid inhaling mist or fumes. Keep away from skin. Do not use around food, bed coverings, or toys. Use when children are not present.
- Wash fresh fruits and vegetables thoroughly before serving. Follow directions carefully when using tenderizers or food preservatives.

To help prevent accidental poisoning of children, the Food and Drug Administration now requires special *child-resistant packaging* for some products. Originally for products containing aspirin, this law now applies to other possibly hazardous items as well. Manufacturers and packers must select and use specially designed packages—box, bottle, or other container—that a sample of 200 children under five years old cannot open 85 percent of the time, but that a panel of adults can open 90 percent of the time. Manufacturers who do not comply with this requirement must so state on the package. This, however, is only one extra safety precaution. You should still do your best to keep drug products stored where they are out of children's reach.

Poisoning can also occur from plants and trees. As a parent or child care worker, you will want to become acquainted with the poisonous plants and trees in order to help protect children as they explore and learn through their senses. Children must learn to refrain from putting plants and leaves in their mouths. The chart on pages 184-186 identifies poisonous plants and trees found in vegetable and flower gardens and in other areas near homes.

183

COMMON POISONOUS PLANTS/TREES

Plant	Toxic Part	Results if Eaten
Autumn Crocus	Bulbs	Vomiting and nervous excitement.
*Azaleas	All parts	Fatal. Produces nausea and vomiting, depression, difficult breathing, prostration, and coma.
*Bittersweet	Berry, leaves	Abdominal pain, vomiting, diarrhea, and depression.
Black Locust	Bark, sprouts, foliage	Children have suffered nausea, weakness, and depression after chewing the bark and seeds.
Bleeding Heart (Dutchman's Breeches)	Foliage, roots	May be poisonous in large amounts. Has proven fatal to cattle.
*Burning Bush	Fruit, leaves	Nausea, vomiting, diarrhea, weakness, chills, coma, and convulsions.
Buttercup	All parts	Irritant juices may severely injure the digestive system.
*Castor Bean	Seeds	Fatal. One or two castor bean seeds are near the lethal dose for adults.
*Cherries (wild and cultivated)	Twigs, foliage	Fatal. Contains a compound that releases cyanide when eaten. Gasping, excitement, and prostration are common symptoms that often appear within minutes.
*Cyclamen (Sowbread)	Underground stems	Vomiting and diarrhea. May be fatal.
Daffodil	Bulbs	Nausea, vomiting, diarrhea. May be fatal.
*Daphne	Berries	Fatal. A few berries can kill a child.
*Dieffenbachia (Dumb Cane)	All parts	Intense burning and irritation of the mouth and tongue. Death can occur if base of the tongue swells enough to block the air passage of the throat.
Elderberry	Shoots, leaves, bark	Children have been poisoned by using pieces of the pithy stems for blowguns. Nausea and digestive upset.
*Elephant Ear	All parts	Intense burning and irritation of the mouth and tongue. Death can occur if base of the tongue swells enough to block the air passage of the throat.
*Four-o'clock	Root, seed	Acute stomach pain, vomiting and diarrhea in children. May be fatal.
*Foxglove	Leaves	One of the sources of the drug digitalis, used to stimulate the heart. In large amounts, the active principles cause dangerously irregular heartbeat and pulse, usually digestive upset and mental confusion. May be fatal.
Golden Chain	Beanlike capsules in which the seeds are suspended	Severe poisoning. Excitement, staggering, convulsions, and coma. May be fatal.
Hyacinth	Bulbs	Nausea, vomiting, diarrhea. May be fatal.
Iris	Underground stems	Severe, but not usually serious, digestive upset.
*Ivy	Leaves	Excitement, difficult breathing, and coma. May be fatal.

COMMON POISONOUS PLANTS/TREES (Continued)

Plant	Toxic Part	Results if Eaten
Jack-in-the-Pulpit	All parts, especially roots	Like dumb cane, contains small needle-like crystals of calcium oxalate that cause intense irritation and burning of the mouth and tongue.
*Jessamine	Berries	Fatal. Digestive disturbance and nervous symptoms.
*Jimson Weed (Thorn Apple)	All parts	Abnormal thirst, distorted sight, delirium, incoherence, and coma. Common cause of poisoning. Has proved fatal.
*Larkspur	Young plant, seeds	Digestive upset, nervous excitement, depression. May be fatal.
*Laurels	All parts	Fatal. Produces nausea and vomiting, depression, difficult breathing, prostration, and coma.
Lily of the Valley	Leaves, flowers	Irregular heart beat and pulse, usually accompanied by digestive upset and mental confusion.
Mayapple	Apple, foliage, roots	Contains at least 16 active toxic principles, primarily in the roots. Children often eat the apple with no ill effects, but several apples may cause diarrhea.
*Mistletoe	Berries	Fatal. Both children and adults have died from eating the berries.
*Mountain Laurel	All parts	Watering of the mouth, eyes, and nose, loss of energy, slow pulse, vomiting, low blood pressure, lack of coordination, convulsions, and progressive paralysis of arms and legs until death.
*Narcissus	Bulbs	Nausea, vomiting, diarrhea. May be fatal.
*Nightshade	All parts, especially the unripe berry	Fatal. Intense digestive disturbances and nervous symptoms.
Oaks	Foliage, acorns	Affects kidneys gradually. Symptoms appear only after several days or weeks. Takes a large amount for poisoning. Children should not be allowed to chew on acorns.
*Oleander	Green or dry leaves, twigs, flowers	Extremely poisonous. Nausea, severe vomiting, stomach pain, dizziness, slowed pulse, irregular heartbeat, marked dilation of pupils, bloody diarrhea, drowsiness, unconsciousness, paralysis of the lungs, and death. (A single leaf is said to be sufficient to kill a child.) Deaths have been reported from eating weiners roasted on the branches.
Poinsettia	Leaves	Fatal. One leaf can kill a child.
Poison Hemlock	All parts	Fatal. Resembles a large wild carrot. Used in ancient Greece to kill condemned prisoners.
Potato	Seeds, sprouts	Abdominal pain, vomiting, diarrhea, and depression. May be fatal.
(Red Sage) Lantan Ramara	Green berries	Fatal. Affects lungs, kidneys, heart, and nervous system. Grows in the southern U.S. and in moderate climates.
Rhododendron	All parts	Fatal. Produces nausea and vomiting, depression, difficult breathing, prostration, and coma.

Part III: A Wholesome Environment

COMMON POISONOUS PLANTS/TREES (Continued)

Plant	Toxic Part	Results if Eaten
Rhubarb	Leaf blade	Fatal. Large amounts of raw or cooked leaves can cause convulsions, coma, followed rapidly by death.
Rosary Pea	Seeds	Fatal. A single rosary pea seed has caused death.
Star-of-Bethlehem	Bulbs	Vomiting and nervous excitement.
*Tulip	Bulb	Nausea, vomiting, abdominal pain. One bulb has been known to kill an adult.
*Water Hemlock	All parts	Fatal. Violent and painful convulsions. A number of people have died from hemlock.
Wisteria	Seeds, pods	Mild to severe digestive upset. Many children are poisoned by this plant.
*Yew	Berries, foliage	Fatal. Foliage more toxic than berries. Death is usually sudden without warning symptoms.

*Can be fatal if taken in quantities which a child might eat. Fatality may be averted by prompt medical attention.
Courtesy of Oklahoma Poison Information Center, Oklahoma State Department of Health.

Fireworks

Never use fireworks which are forbidden by law in your community. Fireworks, even if legal, need to be handled with caution. Young children should never have fireworks without close adult supervision. Children are intrigued by fireworks and should have safe opportunities to use them only when they are old enough to understand the dangers involved as well as how to handle them. Until they reach this stage, children should not be allowed to have fireworks in their possession or to be with older children who are using them.

Playing with Pets

Children must be taught how to play with pets to avoid harming the pet or themselves. Animals have instinctive responses and cannot be treated like toys. Adults should demonstrate how to handle pets, encouraging the children to pet animals gently without teasing or abusing them. Animals, especially dogs, should not be petted or touched while they are eating. Children should avoid all strange or unknown animals. They should stay away from any animal exhibiting unusual behavior—excessive growling or barking, muscle spasms, and frothy mouth.

Children under three years of age are seldom ready to assume the responsibility for having a kitten, puppy, or other pet. Unless especially prepared, they do not have the ability at this age to cope with animals.

A child care center is an ideal place to have pets in cages or bowls. Children not only enjoy this but also learn how to feed and care for the animals properly. Suggested pets for centers are gerbils, hamsters, birds, rabbits, and fish. All pets in children's centers should be chosen with care. Birds, for instance, should be only domestic-born to avoid spreading diseases. Turtles are not fit pets for centers. They are known carriers of diarrheal disease and have been responsible for many outbreaks of Salmonella infections. It has been esti-

Ch. 10: Insuring Safety

Children need help in learning how to handle pets safely.

Children under age three are seldom ready to have pets.

mated that 28,000 cases of Salmonella from turtles occur each year in this country.

Streets and Vehicles

How often have you heard or read about a child who was injured after darting into the street? Concern about the danger of streets and vehicles should be shared by all parents and child care workers. Crossing streets and getting in and out of cars and buses require careful supervision. In dealing with this potential danger, think first about the location of the center. Is it situated on a busy downtown street, at an intersection, or on a quiet side street? Are there alleys, sidewalks, or driveways? After the specific features of the center have been considered, the second step is to set up a routine for handling the coming and going of children. Each center will need to devise a suitable routine of its own.

Riding together can be an exciting experience when children have adults to assist with good safety habits.
Kickapoo Head Start Center

Part III: A Wholesome Environment

Keep these ideas in mind for the day when you help with the planning:

- If children know they must follow a certain procedure, they will feel secure and safe. Establish a routine and stick to it, particularly when large numbers of children are boarding and exiting from vehicles. For example, if several children leave together on a bus, help them learn to gather their things at the appropriate time and wait by the window or door of the building in readiness. This enables the child care worker to tell at a glance if all the children are ready and accounted for. In addition, the children can be more easily supervised from door to bus.
- If possible, use the center's driveway when transporting children to and from the center. If there is no driveway, park as close to the entrance as possible so that children will not have to cross the street. This also applies when returning children to their homes if the center provides such a service. Watch each child, making sure each is a safe distance from the vehicle before starting up again and that each child reaches his or her door safely.
- When children are taken for outings, be sure that enough adults go along to supervise. Instruct the children ahead of time on how they will walk and cross the streets. (Perhaps they would like to walk with partners.) In crossing streets, an adult should be at the head of the line and at the end when there are many children. Some children's centers use a rope to walk children safely from one area to another, such as on field trips and when crossing streets to go from a building to a play area. A soft textured, durable, fiber rope about one-half inch in diameter should be selected. The rope is about ten to fifteen feet long depending on the number of children. The rope forms a chain with a loop for each child to hold onto with one hand. The teacher takes the lead end of the rope in front of the children, and an aide or parent holds the end of the rope behind the children. This method enables the adults to keep the children in a group between the adults. The rope is suggested as a safety device when there are not enough adults to hold each child's hand personally.
- Help children learn the safety rules for crossing streets: (1) Always cross at corners; (2) Obey the lights; (3) Walk, don't run; (4) Stop and look both ways before crossing; (5) Never walk between two parked cars; (6) Don't chase balls, other toys, or animals into the street; (7) When getting out of a car or bus and crossing a street, always walk in front of the vehicle so the driver can see where you are.
- When using special services for transporting children, such as taxis or buses, be sure the drivers understand all the rules for safety of the children. Some centers contract taxi service. The drivers are given special training about the center's policies and procedures for transporting children. The drivers also become acquainted with each child to be transported. At the time of arrival, the driver must go into the center with the children to be sure each is accounted for by the staff. The same procedure must be followed at departure time. The driver goes into the center to get those children assigned to the taxi, and each must be released by a staff member.

When transporting a child in a car, think about his safety. A car seat designed for

Ch. 10: Insuring Safety

children is a wise investment. The National Highway Traffic Safety Administration has set up a standard for manufacturers of children's car seats. All child-seating systems manufactured since April of 1971 should meet this standard. All systems, however, are not equally effective. Keep these points in mind when purchasing new, or evaluating old, restraint systems:

- Any seat that hooks over the back of the car seat is unsafe.
- The seat must give protection from front and rear-end crashes, cushioning the child and preventing him from being thrown free.
- The seat must have an adequate head restraint as protection against whiplash injury.
- The seat's restraint belts must be at least 1½ inches wide.
- The child's upper body should be restrained by belts or impact pad.
- Any seat constructed of easily bent, flimsy, bare metal strapping, or padded only with thin sponge rubber is unsafe.
- There must be no sharp or pointed hardware.
- Do not use the wrong type of restraint system for the size of the child; the chart shown here will give you this information.

Eye Safety

The National Society for the Prevention of Blindness, Inc., lists the following causes of eye injuries:

- *Falls*—nearly 20 percent of all eye injuries are caused by falls.
- *Cinders*—in over 7 percent of all eye accidents, damage is caused by specks of dust or small particles of metal or wood.
- *Blows*—four out of ten eye injuries are caused by blows on or near the eye.
- *Sharp objects*—more than 20 percent of all eye injuries are caused by pointed objects.
- *Weapons*—"BB" guns, slingshots, bows and arrows, cause over 17 percent of the more serious eye injuries.

AUTOMOBILE RESTRAINT SYSTEMS FOR CHILDREN

Type of Restraint	The Child To Be Protected			
	Infants up to 9 months	Children 8 or 9 mos. up to 4 yrs.	Children 4 to 5 years	Children at least 55 in. in height
Infant Car Bed	Yes			
Infant Carrier	Yes			
Child Car Seat	No	Yes		
Child Harness	No	Yes		
Vehicle Lap Belt	No	No	Yes	Yes
Vehicle Shoulder Belt (worn with lap belt)	No	No	Yes*	Yes

*If child is at least 55 inches in height.

Consumer News

Part III: A Wholesome Environment

A safe environment is vital for protecting children's eyesight. Take steps to make the surroundings safer:

- Keep sharp instruments away from youngsters.
- Make sure that toys are suitable for the child's stage of development.
- Supervise play as much as possible; the child needs freedom but also the security of adult protection.
- Teach children not to rub their eyes with their hands and fingers. Dirty hands can cause irritation and infection.
- If a young child wears glasses, hardened lenses are available and are safer than regular lenses. (Hardened lenses are now required in prescription glasses.)
- Infants need to be in the sunshine, but eyes must be protected by turning the face away from the direct rays of the sun.

Watch for Hazards

Infants are often easier to protect than young children because as tiny babies, they are kept near adults. Supervision is routine because of the infant's helplessness. However, as they begin to move about alone, they require more attention from adults. As toddlers, children do not understand risk and danger or the need for safety.

As soon as children begin to crawl and walk, their surroundings must be made as safe as possible. All nooks and crevices should be kept free of hazards since toddlers are curious and continuously exploring. Since they also discover their environment by tasting and testing, any substance the child might consume, from glue to shoe polish, should be kept out of reach except when in use with an adult present. Plastic bags, silk undergarments, and other smooth enveloping fabrics should be kept in safe places away from cribs or play areas. These items may smother a child if they are accidentally slipped over the head.

All interesting objects, especially those that are valuable, breakable, or have sharp edges or points, should be removed from the reach of a child's exploring fingers. In the home, many parents like to teach their children to avoid touching and handling objects on tables and shelves, making visits to other homes and buildings less difficult. This can be done as long as the parents realize that accidents do happen. If objects are left within reach, they should be as hazard-free as possible.

There is no way an adult can remove every potential hazard from the home or children's center. Children are ingenious at finding exciting things to do. Eighteen-month-old Matt removed and swallowed a pin from a door hinge. Another child about the same age, managed to open and consume the contents of a brand new can of car wax. Two brothers, ages three and four, drank a bottle of insect spray. Never underestimate the abilities of children you care for. Don't leave them unattended at home or at the children's center. Both indoor and outdoor supervision is necessary to increase and insure children's safety.

RULES OF SAFETY

Safety rules in the children's center are necessary to help prevent accidents. Consider these in review:

- An adult should be alert and present with children at all times. Children must not be left alone, unsupervised.
- Children must remain in the center until the parents or responsible persons come for them. Children are not to return to their homes alone or be released to unauthorized persons.

Ch. 10: Insuring Safety

- Transportation for children's excursions and trips should be in the center's approved transportation vehicles or planned within walking distance.
- Private cars should not be used to transport children for center excursions and field trips. (A center's insurance usually does not cover private transportation.)
- Children should be prevented from wading or playing in stagnant bodies of water or street drainage. These are often contaminated.
- Outdoor play areas must be fenced.
- All areas should be checked daily for harmful objects such as bottles, cans, waste paper, or other litter.
- Garbage should be stored in closed containers out of the reach of children.
- Free-standing heaters or radiators should have ventilated, cabinet-type covers or fences around them to safeguard children from burns.
- Each staff member should be familiar with the fire escape routes and routines for evacuating the building. Fire drills should be held regularly. Each staff member should also know the locations and operation of all fire extinguishers in the center.
- Children must play inside the center's fenced yard area. They should be prevented from entering street and public sidewalk areas during activity periods unless supervised.
- Stairs should have low handrails for children, and stairways should be well-lighted.
- Rugs should be secured to floors by safety tacking or stripping with skid-proof tape to prevent tripping and stumbling.
- Floor areas must be kept free of litter and scattered toys which block or obstruct traffic lanes and play areas.
- Hot water faucets should be identified for the children—perhaps by painting them with a strip of red waterproof paint—to prevent scalding and burning.
- Spilled water, other liquids, and food should be wiped up immediately to prevent slippery spots on the floor.
- Harmful supplies, such as medicines, cleaning agents, and insecticides, should be locked in cabinets or stored in containers out of the children's reach.
- Electrical outlets must be covered with safety latches or dummy plugs.
- Tempting goodies such as cookies, popcorn, and snacks, should be stored in safe places, not above stoves, ovens, or other hazardous areas. (Children have ways of getting to these items.)

Chapter Highlights

- During the early years, children must be protected from accidents while they learn to protect themselves.
- Providing a safe environment for a child does not mean total restraint or overprotection.
- Adults are responsible for helping children learn how to satisfy normal and healthy needs in the safest ways possible.
- Actions along with words are usually more meaningful than words alone; children should be shown ways to accomplish tasks safely.
- Planning ahead for safety is a responsibility of the child care staff in any children's center.

Part III: A Wholesome Environment

- The more you know about how children grow and develop, the better able you will be to provide a safe and healthy environment.
- Some of the common causes of accidental deaths among children between the ages of one and five are motor vehicles, fires, drowning, poisons, and falls.
- Some studies indicate that accidents are often influenced by such conditions as: fatigue, hunger, family illness, or even a mother's worry.
- Enriching children's surroundings with safe and appropriate equipment is an excellent way to broaden their learning opportunities.
- Before buying toys for children, you should check them carefully for safety.
- By teaching children that matches are not toys and by keeping a watchful eye on children at play indoors and out, the chances of tragedy from fire are greatly reduced.
- There are certain precautions which help prevent accidents from poisoning; most important is to keep poisonous items stored where they are out of children's reach and sight.
- Children must be taught how to play with pets to avoid harming the pet or themselves; animals have instinctive responses and cannot be treated like toys.
- Crossing streets and getting in and out of cars and buses requires careful supervision.
- Children should be taught safety rules for crossing streets.
- Steps should be taken to make surroundings safe for protection of children's eyesight.
- Hazardous objects should be placed beyond the reach of young children.
- Safety rules in the children's center are necessary for the prevention of accidents.

Thinking It Over

1. Can you remember certain frustrating safety restrictions placed on you as a child? As a young adult, do you think they were necessary? Why?
2. Is there such a thing as overprotecting or overrestraining a child? Explain.
3. How can you demonstrate safety rules to a child?
4. Nearly all children experience accidents while growing up. Can you remember an accident that happened to you? How could it have been prevented?
5. Name five conditions which may contribute to accidents during childhood.
6. Why is it harder to protect toddlers from accidents than it is to protect infants?
7. List two safety precautions and the reasons for them for each of the following: infants; toddlers; rompers; and kindergartners.
8. How can an increased knowledge of how children grow and develop increase your ability to provide a safe and healthy environment for them?
9. List safety precautions that should be taken concerning the following: outdoor areas, play equipment, toys, matches, poisons, fireworks, animals, streets and vehicles, eyes, and indoor hazards.
10. What is a child care worker's responsibility in helping the child learn safety rules for crossing streets?
11. Why is it necessary for a children's center to have certain safety rules?
12. Name five safety rules that should be followed in the center.

Things To Do

1. Invite a doctor or nurse who serves in the emergency room of a hospital to discuss with the class a day in the life of the emergency squad, with special emphasis on children and accidents.
2. Using pictures from magazines or drawings, illustrate and discuss how toddlers explore and investigate the world about them. Discuss several examples of accident situations and ways adults can help insure children's safety.
3. Invite a policeman or insurance representative to talk with the class about vehicle and street safety for children.
4. Develop guidelines for insuring the safety of young children as they cross streets and travel to and from a children's center. Present this information to a kindergarten or nursery school group of children.
5. Invite a fireman to speak on fire hazards and emergency measures to take when fire occurs in a home or children's center.
6. Inspect and rate your home for safety conditions. Make a checklist for this purpose.
7. Using pictures, illustrate safety rules for children to follow in their center.
8. Have a panel of parents discuss accidents their children have had, how they happened, and how they might have been prevented.
9. Have class members develop slogans for bumper stickers to communicate safety for children.
10. Using a scale from 1 to 5—least safe to most safe, rate the safety of toys and play equipment in a child care center. (If you cannot visit a center, bring toys from home for class members to rate.) Discuss how the rating indicates which areas will require closer supervision during children's activities.
11. Make a list of daily activities for children that require safety precautions. Suggest ways to help children develop safety habits in these activities.

Recommended Reading

Benenson, Abram, Editor. *Control of Communicable Diseases in Man.* Washington, D.C.: The American Public Health Association, 1970.

The American Red Cross. *Standard First Aid and Personal Safety.* Garden City, New York: Doubleday and Co., Inc., 1973.

Chapter 11.

Handling Emergencies

Your Challenge

This chapter will enable you to . . . .

- *State what to do in an emergency.*
- *Give the first aid procedures that must be followed for different emergency situations.*
- *List the items needed in a first aid kit.*

BE PREPARED FOR EMERGENCIES

Have you given much thought to what a responsibility it is to care for a child? One high school girl did—after a near tragedy. Carmen was seventeen at the time and living in a large Chicago apartment building. During the summer, she made a little spending money by caring for the two small children of a working mother on the second floor.

It was a hot afternoon in July when Carmen decided to bathe two-year-old Ramon before his mother's return. She had just placed Ramon in the tub when a crashing sound came from the living room. Carmen hurried out to find Ramon's five-year-old brother, Paolo, staring wide-eyed at a table lamp that had fallen (with his help) to the floor. Carmen placed the lamp back on the table and turned toward the bathroom, dragging Paolo behind her.

As she stepped into the room, a tremor of fear gripped her. Ramon was lying face down in the tub of water. Quickly, Carmen reached down and grabbed him from the water. She ran with him through the living room, out the apartment door, and down the hall, screaming for help. A neighbor lady, Mrs. Ramirez, peered out to see what was wrong.

"Mrs. Ramirez," Carmen cried, "Ramon fell into the water! Help me—please!"

Within seconds Mrs. Ramirez had her strong and capable hands on the child, forcing his chin forward and his head back. Methodically, she began to breathe into the boy's mouth, covering his mouth and nose with her lips. Carmen waited breathlessly, until, after some of the longest moments in her seventeen years, Ramon was breathing on his own again.

It is an unfortunate commentary on life that we often learn too many lessons the hard way. Carmen and Ramon were lucky. Carmen learned that her own lack of knowledge about emergency procedures could have cost Ramon his life if Mrs. Ramirez had not been close by. Would you

194

Ch. 11: Handling Emergencies

have had the knowledge to handle such a situation?

Whether you are a babysitter like Carmen, a parent caring for your own children, or a child care worker at the center, you must be prepared to meet emergency situations by knowing what to do in case of an accident. Accidents do occur from time to time, and children are dependent upon adults for help.

In the center, someone who is familiar with first aid procedures should be present at all times. In many communities, the Red Cross chapter provides training sessions for center staff members if requested. As a staff member responsible for the safety of children, you should enroll in a first aid class if you have not already completed this training. Handbooks are also provided by certified first aid courses; these should be studied and reviewed periodically.

WHAT TO DO IN AN EMERGENCY

If you are present when an accident occurs, follow these steps in handling the situation:

- Remain calm. Do not panic. You are in charge until competent help is available. Remember that excited or hysterical behavior only alarms the victim and can lead to rash actions.
- Before taking action, observe the situation quickly but carefully. Remember, the child is your greatest concern.
- If you observe that the child must have immediate attention, give only the necessary help according to prescribed first aid procedures.
- When another competent adult is present, give him or her instructions to call an ambulance or doctor if needed. Often the center director will make necessary transportation arrangements to the child's home, doctor, clinic, or hospital. If no one else is readily available, call for help yourself after you have administered emergency first aid. You should seek professional help for all serious cases. Also request professional help when in doubt about a child's condition.
- Stay close to the child until help arrives. Depending on the situation, you may need to calm other children or excited adults. You must prevent others from following incorrect first aid procedures. Sometimes co-workers need to be encouraged to carry on with the day's routine. A well-trained staff should handle these problems with relative ease. Make the child as comfortable as possible while waiting for the doctor, nurse, or parents. Children need a feeling of security and a sense of assurance at this time. Having an adult nearby to give encouragement and register calm concern is comforting and helps children relax.
- As soon as the child is in good hands and you or another worker can place the call, notify the child's parents or guardians. A minor accident, such as a cut, bruise, or splinter, may not require this. Parents should, however, be informed of any accident before the child goes home.
- Local regulations may require the staff members to file a report on all accidents and illnesses. If there are no such regulations, staff members should be encouraged to file an informal report with the center director or teacher in charge of the center. The report should include the circumstances of the accident or illness. It should be made out as soon as possible in order to include the details which may be forgotten if the report is delayed. Even when there are no regulations requiring a report, the center may wish to keep its own written reports. These may

SAMPLE ACCIDENT REPORT

Name of center _____ Date _____

Name of child _____ Home address _____

Place (location) of accident _____ Time of accident _____

Brief description of situation:
What was the child doing? _____
How did accident happen? _____
_____

Equipment or materials involved. _____
Hazardous conditions present. _____
Degree of injury: ____ ____ ____ ____
                Minor Temporary Permanent Death
                          Disability Disability

Adults in charge: Name of adult in charge: _____
Present at site of accident? ____ ____ Was parent notified? ____ ____
                          Yes No   (guardian)   Yes No
How was parent notified? _____ ; _____
    (guardian)   Phone   Other (identify)

                                                    Name of person who notified parent

Procedure:
First aid administered?   ____ ____   By whom? _____
                           Yes No
Referred to physician?   ____ ____   By whom? _____
                           Yes No
Referred to nurse?   ____ ____   By whom? _____
                     Yes No
Referred to clinic?   ____ ____   By whom? _____
                   Yes No
Referred to hospital?   ____ ____   By whom? _____
                      Yes No
Parent refused treatment?   Yes _____   No _____
What procedure was followed before child was placed in hands of parent or physician?
Describe: _____
_____

Other information: **Other adults present:** _____
                                                          (list)
Remarks: _____ _____
_____ _____
_____ _____
_____ _____

_____   _____
Signature of teacher/nurse in program   Signature of Director

_____
Date child returned to program

Ch. 11: Handling Emergencies

Adults receive training in order to learn about safety features and hazards of toys and play equipment.

be helpful in case legal or medical questions arise in the future.

FIRST AID PROCEDURES

It is important that you be familiar with first aid procedures, but it is also important that you understand what you can do with your knowledge. Since your specialty as a child care worker will be working with children, not medicine, you cannot expect to take the place of a doctor or nurse. Many injuries have been aggravated by incorrect emergency treatment. Therefore administer first aid cautiously but confidently when necessary. The following guides will help you become more familiar with the correct procedures.

Broken Bones and Dislocations

Know these signs: swelling; tenderness or pressure over the injury; discomfort or pain when the victim tries to move the part; discoloration of the skin; body part out of shape.

When in doubt about a fracture, treat the injured part as though it is broken. Remember that simple fractures (the wound has not broken through the skin) sometimes occur with little immediate pain. If you suspect a broken bone, do not move the victim, especially the injured part of the body. Unless you are trained in the transporting of injured people, only authorized people should move the child onto a stretcher to be taken to a hospital, clinic, or doctor's office. If for some reason you must move the child, take great care when moving the injured part. Keep in mind that some fractures, such as those of the spine, may cause permanent disability of the victim if untrained hands are involved. (This

197

Part III: A Wholesome Environment

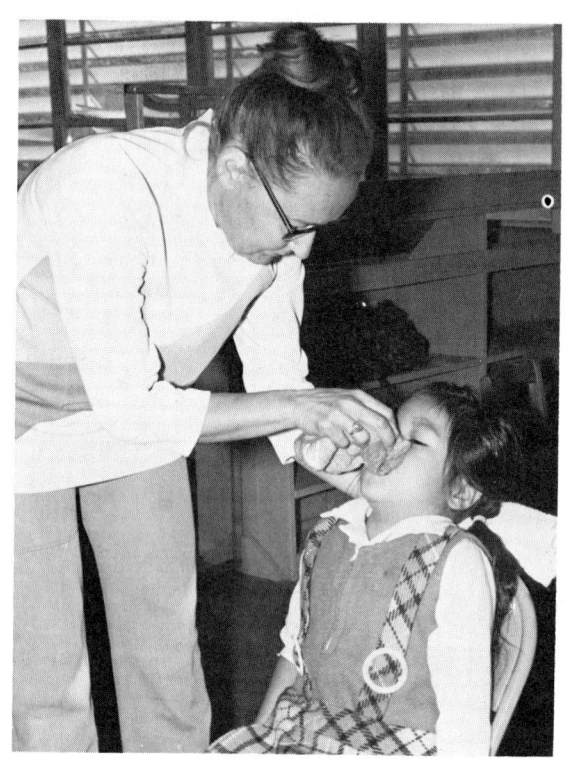

Oklahoma VoTech (Stillwater Head Start)

In case of a nosebleed, keep the child in a sitting position with the head tilted back. Press gently against the side of the nostril for several minutes.

is why victims of diving accidents should not be removed from the water except by trained people. The face should be held above water until help arrives. This may prevent further injury to the spine.)

When a portion of the bone protrudes through the skin, cover the area lightly with a loose bandage or clean cloth to protect it. Splints and bandages should be applied only by trained people.

Burns

Immediately dipping the burned area in cold, but not running, water helps remove the heat. Minor burns (including sunburns) may be treated with soda and water paste, petroleum jelly, or burn ointment. Bandage the area. Do not break blisters. Deep burns need medical attention at once. Keep the child warm and cover the burned area with a sterile cloth or a clean sheet until medical help is available. Do not let the child touch or pick at the burned area.

Cuts and Bleeding

Cleanse small cuts and scrapes well with soap and water. Direct pressure over the wound should stop bleeding. The wound may then be treated with an antiseptic from the first aid supplies. Read the directions carefully before applying any medication. Bandage the area if necessary.

Cover large or deep cuts with gauze and press firmly over the wound to stop the bleeding. Continue to add bandages if needed without removing the first ones. Call for medical help immediately.

Bruises

To take care of a bruise, a towel or cloth which has been wrung out in cold (or ice) water can be applied. This may be held over the bruised area for a half hour or longer, depending on the child's degree of discomfort. A limb may be elevated to help ease pain.

Nosebleed

Keep the child calm and in a sitting position. Have the child breathe through the mouth. Press gently against the side of the nostril for several minutes. If the bleeding continues, apply ice packs against the back of the neck or a cold, wet cloth over the nose. If heavy bleeding occurs, contact the nurse or doctor. Do not attempt to remove objects from the nose; this is a task for the doctor, unless, of course, it is protruding and obviously easy to remove.

Insect or Object in the Ear

For insects, buzzing sounds may be stopped by dropping lukewarm olive or mineral oil into the ear with an eye dropper or by squeezing the oil from a sterile piece of cotton or sponge. Avoid removing any object; leave this to a doctor. Temporary relief from an earache may be attained by using hot or cold treatment with a water bag, towel, or heating pad.

Eye Injury or Object in the Eye

In case of an accident such as a hard blow or cut, seek medical help immediately. Try to keep the child from rubbing his eyes. Dirt rubbed in the eye can cause infection that may scar the cornea and cause partial loss of sight. With clean hands, dislodge an object with the corner of a clean handkerchief, sterile gauze, or tissue, or lift the upper lid and pull it down over the lower lid to allow tears to form and wash out the speck.

The eye may need washing out with a medicine dropper or eye cup, using a very mild salt water solution (boiled water cooled to room temperature: one-fourth teaspoon of salt to one cup of water). If the speck still does not come out, bandage the eye lightly to prevent the child from rubbing it, and call for medical assistance.

Splinters

Clean the area with soap and water. Use sterilized (boiled five to ten minutes) tweezers or a needle to remove the object. If the child is four years old or older and wants to try, allow the child to remove the object if possible. If the child is unable to accomplish this task alone, he will be more likely to allow you to try. Allow the area to bleed a little after the removal by applying pressure around it. Apply a mild antiseptic from the first aid supplies according to directions. A bandage may be necessary depending on the size of the break in the skin. A deeply imbedded splinter or other object may require medical service.

Poison

The center receptionist or director should look up the phone number of the local *poison control center* and post it with other emergency numbers such as fire and police. Call a doctor or the closest poison control center immediately in case of poisoning. Be prepared to call an ambulance if ordered by the doctor. Have the container of "poison" ready so you can give the doctor information from the label, either over the telephone or in person. If the child must be taken to the hospital or doctor's office, carry the container with you. Some lables on containers of substances give directions for what to do in case of poisoning.

The important point to remember is that the poison should be diluted or removed from the body before the body absorbs it. Although many poisons can be treated by causing the victim to vomit, there are some caustics which can cause additional injury by burning the throat again as they come up.

Learn the difference:

- Caustics, such as lye and many drain cleaners, eat away skin and other body tissue. You can usually tell if someone has swallowed a caustic because there will be burns on the lips and in the mouth. The victim should be rushed to a hospital.

Part III: A Wholesome Environment

- If the poison is not a caustic, vomiting will greatly reduce the danger of the poisoning. *Noncaustics* include such substances as aspirin, sleeping pills, drugs of any kind, cough syrups, ink, and paint. Several glasses of salty or soapy lukewarm water may be used to cause vomiting. Many glasses of warm milk may also be used. If the child does not vomit immediately, slip a clean finger down the back of the throat or touch the back of the throat with a spoon. Call for medical assistance.

Some medical doctors advocate using a commercial charcoal mixture, "Universal Antidote," such as Syrup of Ipecac. Do not make your own charcoal mix. The main use of the mixture is for the first phase of treatment—to help inactivate the poison before it is absorbed. Follow this treatment immediately with medical assistance.

Animal Bites

A child bitten by any animal must see a doctor. Wash the wound with soap and water and get the child to a doctor as soon as possible. Even if the bite does not appear serious, the saliva of the animal may contain bacteria, including rabies (hydrophobia). A booster shot for tetanus is necessary in most cases even if rabies treatment is not. The animal should be captured if at all possible and placed under medical observation for ten days to detect whether it has rabies. This is very important, for if the animal is not rabid, the child may be spared the painful rabies treatment. If the animal cannot be found, however, the child may have to undergo the treatment whether the animal was sick or not.

Insect Bites

Wash the area and apply antiseptic for minor bites from insects such as mosquitoes, ants, and spiders. For stings from bees, wasps, hornets, yellow jackets, and sometimes ants and mosquitoes, the stinger may need to be removed with tweezers if it remains in the skin. Apply diluted ammonia, a paste of baking soda and water, or vinegar to the area. If the child shows unusual reactions, such as nausea or convulsions, call for medical help. (Some people are highly sensitive to certain insect bites and stings.) Calamine or a similar lotion often helps stop the itching. Cold compresses help prevent swelling.

Tick bites may be treated as the above insect bites but be sure to remove the head, which often becomes imbedded in the skin. An ointment or petroleum jelly over a tick will often cause it to dislodge. Special procedures by a physician are sometimes required to remove the head if it breaks off under the skin. Kill the tick by burning or by flushing it down the toilet. Cleanse the bitten area with soap and water and use a mild antiseptic. In areas where ticks are prevalent, children should be checked two times each day by looking in hair and folds of the skin. Some ticks carry Colorado tick fever or Rocky Mountain spotted fever, and children can be inoculated for protection. A doctor is required for children with fever from these tick bites.

Snake Bites

Take the child immediately to a doctor or hospital if the doctor cannot come to the child. While waiting for the doctor or ambulance, tie a band made of a strip of cloth or a handkerchief firmly but not too tight just above the bite to slow the flow of venom into the body. Do not allow the band to become too tight if swelling occurs. Keep the child quiet with the bitten limb or area in a downward position. Do not try to use a snake bite kit unless you have had instructions. You could harm the child rather than help him.

Human Bites

Call the doctor if the skin is broken. A human bite can be very serious. Wash the area thoroughly with soap and water.

Frostbite

Do not soak in warm water or apply heat. Apply an ointment prepared for frostbites or apply petroleum jelly. If the area remains extremely red and does not begin to improve within several hours, contact the doctor.

Choking

If a child gets an object caught in the throat and does not expel it by coughing, hold the child upside down by the feet. When the child is too heavy to hold by the feet, place him in a jackknife position over your shoulder or over a chair back. If the object does not come out, take the child to a doctor or hospital immediately or summon medical assistance. *Do not attempt to reach down the throat for the object.*

Swallowed Objects

A doctor should be called immediately if the child swallows a sharp object such as a needle, pin, or tack. Items such as fruit seeds, buttons, small coins, or other non-sharp objects are often passed in a bowel movement. Watch the child's bowel movements for a few days to be sure it has passed; if it has not, notify the doctor.

Lice

Head lice (pediculosis) usually causes itching of the child's scalp. (Children with lice should be at home until lice are eliminated.) The back of the neck may become swollen and sores on the scalp may result. Scars are sometimes caused by scratching. A 90 percent inert talc of DDT powder should be dusted into the hair and scalp. Topocide, an emulsion of 12.5 percent benzyl benzoate, 1 percent DDT, and 2 percent benzocaine, is an agent readily available for the treatment of lice. Keep powder out of eyes. Wrap the head in a clean towel or cloth for four or five hours. Use a fine tooth comb to remove nits and dead lice. Do not wash the hair for at least twenty-four hours. Then shampoo and dry the hair and repeat this treatment. Persons can become reinfected; thus, all children should be checked periodically. Check with a local doctor or nurse for new treatments which may be available.

Fleas

Itching and reddening usually occur on the skin area where fleas have attacked. After cleansing with soap and water, apply an antiseptic or water and soda paste. Try to locate the area where the child contacted the fleas and apply a safe insecticide. Check pets which may have been in the area.

Abdominal pain

For mild pain associated with food or drink, keep the child quiet and as comfortable as possible until relief is achieved. If relief is not obtained shortly, request medical help. Abdominal pain in children is a frequent symptom of serious illnesses or diseases as well as possible appendicitis. Do not give a laxative or medicine by mouth unless by doctor's instructions.

Electrical Shock

To prevent shocking yourself, never touch the child until contact with the source of the shock has been broken. If you can, turn off the electric power. Using rope,

Part III: A Wholesome Environment

a wooden pole or stick, or a piece of dry cloth looped around the child, pull him away from the source. Do not use anything metal because it will conduct electricity to you. If breathing has stopped, apply artificial respiration. Seek medical help.

Unconsciousness

If the child can be moved, turn him on his side or abdomen so that secretions may drain from the mouth. Do not try to give an unconscious child food or liquids. Seek medical help, keeping the child warm in the meantime. Artificial respiration should be applied if breathing stops.

Fainting

Faintness may be detected by unusual pale skin tone and dizziness. Have the child sit with head lowered to the knees. Make sure plenty of fresh air is available and that clothing is loose. Follow the guidelines under unconsciousness if necessary.

Artificial Respiration

Artificial respiration is used whenever breathing has stopped or been hampered. Smoke and water inhalation, electrical shock, and choking due to a foreign object in the throat or windpipe can cause stoppage of breath. The following steps should be followed when administering artificial respiration to infants or small children.

1. Clear the child's mouth of any objects or substance by using your middle finger of one hand. With the same finger, press the child's tongue forward.
2. Place the child in a face-down position and head-down inclined position and pat him firmly on the back to help dislodge any foreign object in the air passage.
3. Place the child on his back and use your middle fingers of both hands to lift the lower jaw until it is outward.
4. Hold the jaw in the above position using only one hand.
5. Place your mouth over the child's mouth and nose. Make a relatively leakproof seal. Breathe into the child with a smooth, steady action until you notice the child's chest rise. As you begin this action, move your free hand to the child's abdomen, between his navel and ribs, and apply moderate pressure to prevent his stomach from becoming filled with air.
6. When the child's lungs have been inflated, remove your lips from his mouth and nose and allow the lungs to empty. Repeat this cycle, keeping one hand pressing on the stomach and the other beneath the child's jaw. You should continue at the rate of about twenty cycles per minute. After every twenty cycles, you should rest long enough to take one deep breath. If you feel resistance to your breathing into the child and if the chest does not rise, repeat, starting with the second step.

Shock

A child in your charge may experience shock as a result of injury, fracture, bleeding, poisoning, or fright. Shock is characterized by paleness in color of the face, restlessness, coldness, sweating, thirst, and sometimes coma. Place the child in bed with the head lower than the feet. Keep the child quiet and warm. Conserve the child's heat by covering with a blanket rather than applying additional heat. Contact the nurse, clinic, or doctor as soon as you have taken these precautions with the child.

Ch. 11: Handling Emergencies

EQUIPPING A FIRST AID KIT

Place the following items in a sturdy box with a tightly closed lid. Keep the kit and first aid book in a convenient place. It should be easy for adults to get and yet out of the reach and sight of children.

Items	Amount
Compressors	1 dozen
Gauze Roll—1"	3
Gauze Roll—2"	2
Adhesive Tape—½"	2 rolls
Bandage Scissors	1 pair
Bandaids	2 boxes
Cotton Roll	1
Needles	1 package
Tweezers	1
Tongue Blades	12
Splints for Legs	1
Triangle Bandage	1
Safety Pins	1 package
Tourniquet	1
Paper Cups	2 dozen
Wash Cloths	2
Towels	2
Basin	1
Sanitary Napkins	1 box
Thermometer	1 oral
Aromatic Ammonia	1
Hand Soap	1 bar
Baking Soda	1 box
Peroxide	1 pint
First Aid Book	1

Chapter Highlights

- A person who cares for children must be prepared to meet emergency situations by knowing what to do in case of an accident.
- The following are steps to be observed in handling emergencies:

  - Remain calm; do not panic.
  - Before taking action, observe the situation quickly but carefully.
  - If a child needs immediate attention, give only necessary help according to prescribed methods.
  - Call an ambulance or doctor if necessary.
  - Stay close to the child until help arrives.
  - As soon as the child is attended, notify the child's parents or guardian.
  - File a report (formal or informal—as required) of accident or illness.

- Many injuries are aggravated by incorrect emergency treatment; therefore first aid should be administered cautiously.
- If there is some doubt about a fracture, treat the injury as though it were a fracture.
- With some fractures, like those of the spine, only persons trained in the transportation of injured people should be allowed to move a child.
- Minor burns may be treated with soda and water paste, a petroleum jelly, or a burn ointment; deep burns need medical attention at once.
- Cleanse small cuts and scrapes with soap and water; large or deep cuts should be covered with gauze and have direct pressure applied to stop the bleeding. Medical help should be attained immediately if bleeding continues.
- Do not attempt to remove any object from a child's nose or ears unless it is protruding and obviously easy to remove; generally speaking, this should be left to the doctor or nurse.

Part III: A Wholesome Environment

- Using sterile methods, try to remove or wash from the eye any foreign particle. Keep the child from rubbing the eyes. Seek medical assistance.
- An important point to remember is that poison should be diluted or removed from the body before it becomes absorbed.
- A child bitten by any animal must have medical attention.
- If a child shows unusual reactions, such as nausea or convulsions, when bitten or stung by an insect, medical help should be secured immediately.
- Abdominal pain in children is frequently a symptom of serious illness or disease; therefore medicine should not be given unless it is done so by a doctor's instructions.
- As soon as certain precautionary measures have been taken with a person in shock, a clinic, nurse, or doctor should be contacted immediately.

Thinking It Over

1. What steps should be taken when an accident occurs?
2. Do you have any scars which are reminders of accidents you had as a child? Explain how these emergencies were handled.
3. What suggestions do you have for child care workers or parents in handling emergencies with young children?
4. Give examples of situations which call for artificial respiration.
5. Describe what you would do in the following situations:

   - Five-year-old Brandon is riding his tricycle in the driveway when he is hit by a car. He is conscious, crying, and one leg is bent at an unnatural angle and bleeding from an open wound.
   - You find a child lying across an electrical wire that has come down from a utility pole. The hysterical mother arrives at the same time you do.
   - After a bee sting, Rachael's foot swells excessively. Shortly, you notice that her arms and legs are jerking uncontrollably.
   - You discover a toddler with an open can of cleaning fluid. Half of the fluid is gone.
   - During lunch in the center, the children call to you and point out that something is wrong with Sean. He is gagging but not coughing.

6. What is Syrup of Ipecac used for?
7. What would you do if a young child under your care were burned? Give reasons for your actions.
8. Explain how to administer artificial respiration.
9. List the symptoms of shock and give the procedures for handling this emergency.
10. Explain the difference between emergency treatment for small cuts and scrapes and the treatment for large or deep wounds.
11. What should you do if a child receives a hard blow or cut on the eye?
12. List the items found in a first aid kit that you might need when treating a large cut.
13. Is there a poison control center in your community? What is their phone number and address?

Ch. 11: Handling Emergencies

Things To Do

1. Develop a form to record telephone numbers to be used in emergencies. It should be posted or placed by the telephone in the children's center. Include such numbers as: fire department, police department, ambulance, nearest hospital, poison control center, every child's parents or guardian and doctor.
2. Contact the nearest Red Cross center and request a demonstration of artificial resuscitation. Ask them to bring their doll "Resusci-anne" which can be used by students to learn and practice the administering of artificial respiration.
3. Describe briefly on paper an emergency situation which may arise in a child care center. Collect each class member's description and place them in a box. Each student is to draw one (not his own) and explain and/or demonstrate emergency measures to be taken.
4. Make posters of labels on common poisons, giving instructions for emergency treatment in case of internal consumption. Post these in the classroom to help students become familiar with them.
5. Make a first aid kit and equip it properly. Display the kit in an appropriate place in the school for all students to see.
6. Make a flip chart which lists steps to take in case of the following emergencies: broken bone; burns; object in eye; poisoning; insect bites or stings; object caught in throat; abdominal pain; shock; animal bite; and bleeding. Place the flip chart in a child care center where it can be readily referred to by staff members.
7. Look through newspapers and find accounts of emergency situations which could happen in a child care center. Make posters with these and give a positive title to each such as: "It's Not The Emergency But How It's Handled That's Important," "Make Stepping Stones Out of Stumbling Blocks," or "Make Lemonade Out of a Lemon."

Recommended Reading

Benenson, Abram, Editor. *Control of Communicable Diseases in Man.* Washington, D.C.: The American Public Health Association, 1970.

The American Red Cross. *Standard First Aid and Personal Safety.* Garden City, New York: Doubleday and Co., Inc., 1973.

Chapter 12.

Food for Children

Your Challenge

This chapter will enable you to . . . .

- *Name different eating patterns and habits of children and tell how to handle each.*
- *State guidelines for handling children at mealtime.*
- *Explain the importance of good nutrition.*
- *Name and describe the four basic food groups.*
- *Explain how to make meals and snacks nutritional.*

EATING PATTERNS AND HABITS

Most children enjoy eating and will eat wholesome foods if they are provided. They like to smell and touch foods before putting them into their mouths. Some authorities think that children have better appetites when they are introduced to tantalizing aromas during the cooking process.

Children are curious about what they eat. The tastes, textures, and shapes of foods are intriguing to children because they are eager to explore the world about them, and food is a major part of their world. Mashing, squeezing, and playing with foods is not uncommon but is a natural phase of learning for children.

Children will usually let you know when they are hungry or when they have had enough to eat. Of course, they must be introduced to new foods from time to time. Children need help as they take each step in learning to feed themselves—from breast to bottle or bottle to cup, from liquids to solid foods, and from eating with fingers to using forks and spoons.

The need for food that builds a sturdy body in which a mind can develop is a continuous concern. Every child's development depends greatly upon the foods eaten.

As a child progresses through the stages of development, it is not unusual for his or her eating patterns and habits to change. This shows up by changes in appetite, sudden likes and dislikes for foods, and other ways. This is a normal process for many children. The adults who understand such behavior will find working with these situations fairly easy.

Obviously, all children do not have similar *appetites*. Even the same child's appetite may differ from one meal to the next as well as from one day to the next. Chil-

Children need nutritious food served attractively and in child-size portions.

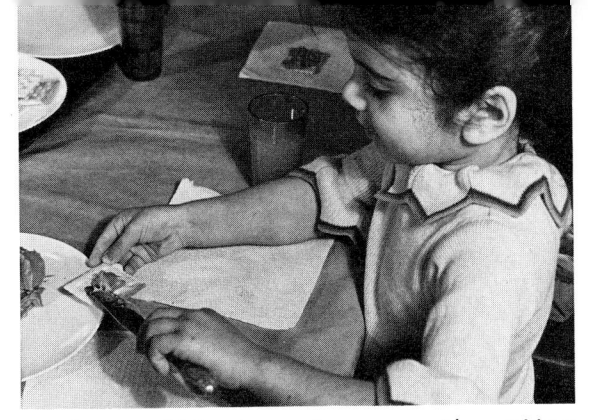

Snacks, in addition to meals, can provide nutritious foods as well as learning experiences and social interaction.

dren go through similar stages, yet each has a unique growth pattern accompanied by variations in food tastes and eating habits. Appetites may also change with stages of development so that during the slower growth periods the child may not want as much food as during rapid growth periods.

This often happens when a child reaches the latter half of the first year and may continue until near the age of three. When the rate of body growth in height and weight slows down, so does the appetite. This is normal and smaller portions should be served to the child during this time. The child will let you know when more is wanted.

An overtired or excited child who is in a strange setting or a child whose regular routine is interrupted may also experience a change in appetite. Even the amount of muscle or body fat can affect appetite. Adults sometimes worry when children eat less than usual or not as much as other children. This should not be a cause for alarm unless symptoms of illness accompany the loss of appetite. For example, listlessness, unusual fatigue, or a prolonged loss of appetite may require medical attention. A concerned adult can usually remedy the less severe situation, however, by following simple guidelines.

First of all, do not make an issue over the child's appetite. Children often rebel if forced to eat. Compelling them to eat may only make things worse and could lead to further problems. Children usually have ways of letting adults know when they want more or when they have had enough. Secondly, provide meals that are nutritionally balanced. With meals that contain a variety of nutritious foods, children will usually eat what they need.

Dawdling at mealtime is another childhood eating pattern which frustrates many adults. Sally is a dawdler. She eats rapidly at the beginning and as soon as her hunger is satisfied, she dawdles through the remainder of the meal, picking and playing with the food until the meal is finished. Urging Sally to speed up the eating process, however, may spoil her pleasure in eating. Here again the adult is probably wiser to avoid making an issue of it. If Sally plays with her food too long, it can be removed without threats or comment.

It is not unusual for children to have food "jags," asking for the same food day after day and then suddenly refusing to eat it. If the menu is not too impractical and if adults can be casual about the "jag," the child will probably end it soon. For instance, Tim's hearty appetite for peanut butter sandwiches will probably run its course sooner if he isn't nagged about it. Can you think of foods you particularly liked for a time as a child?

Sometimes children are troublesome during mealtime. This may simply be a child's attempt to discover himself, an attempt to *express independence* by displaying likes and dislikes in his own way. With a limited vocabulary, children may tell adults what is wanted or not wanted by a simple "no" or "I won't." When Jill closes her mouth and refuses food, this is her way of saying she does not like the food or has had enough of it. Accepting this type of communication prevents children from getting the idea that refusing food is a way to get attention at the table.

Have you ever known a child who wanted to stand rather than sit while eating? This phase usually passes, so allowing the child to stand during the meal is often the best solution if this becomes a problem. The idea of *standing while eating* will usually run its course, and in a short time the child will be ready to sit as others do. Also, keep in mind that while children are growing and developing, they need many safe opportunities to run, jump, climb, and explore. Then they will be more willing to sit still long enough to eat a meal.

Although there are no perfect schedules for all children, trying to follow fairly *regular eating routines* is good for them. It gives them a sense of order and security. Hunger and digestion are natural and regular aspects of daily living. Even a baby will establish feeding schedules if allowed to do so. Children under three often go through a period of insisting on rigid routines. This may include demands that table and chair, as well as dishes and foods, be placed in definite spots. Satisfaction of children's demands in this area helps them grow through this period of rigidity and often makes way for flexibility later. Preschool children have their own regular body needs. An orderly pattern for meals, snacks, play, naps, bathing, and bedtime is often essential for a child's well-being emotionally and physically.

In thinking about the eating patterns and habits of children, you may be able to think of others besides the ones mentioned here. Have you ever known a child, for example, who would eat only one food at a time, completing each serving of food before going on to the next? This, like so many children's habits, can be irritating to some adults, yet it can be viewed with patient amusement. Now, analyze yourself. How will you handle situations like those described when you are in charge?

HANDLING CHILDREN AT MEALTIME

To help you in dealing with children at mealtime, consider the following suggestions:

- Watch for the amount of food a child seems to want and need. Children often need either more or less food than adults expect them to eat. A child may not always want the same amount of food every day. If chosen from a well-planned meal, the amount the child takes is usually adequate in the long run. You may not need to insist that children have perfectly clean plates before dessert if small portions are given. Children will probably complete the foods served if they are in small amounts.
- Some children get along better if they eat less at a time but eat more often. If a

Ch. 12: Food for Children

child does not want milk with lunch, perhaps it can be served with a cookie in the afternoon.
- Adults will find greater success with children's mealtime if a few simple rules are initiated early. Decide what these rules will be and stick to them. Children need to know what to expect from adults in order to feel secure.
- Just like adults, children dislike some foods, especially the first time they are tasted. If a child won't eat spinach, for example, some other green vegetable may be substituted. If a child will not eat vegetables, use them in soups and serve plenty of fruits. Children will usually feel different about these foods later on, so after a time, try them again.
- Children learn by imitating others; thus, group feeding often helps children learn from peers and adults when good examples are set daily.
- Foods which are chosen or refused often reflect the choices and attitudes of someone admired or watched closely. Too much praise for eating spinach may communicate an adult's anxiety to have a child eat this food. Seeing others eat spinach without comment may work better.
- Some children may want to eat certain foods they really like and leave out all the others. If this happens, encourage new foods from time to time even if it is only to take a taste.
- Between three and six years of age, children enjoy helping in the kitchen and at the table. They like to set the table, beat eggs, shell peas, pass simple-to-handle foods, hand bread slices, and even fold napkins.
- As mentioned before, avoid nagging or forcing children to eat. In most instances, continuous coaxing is not only useless but can turn mealtime into a battleground. If a child is too slow in finishing, end the meal quietly without comments about the child's eating habits. The next meal will probably make up for it. A healthy child won't go hungry very long.
- As children grow from toddlers to preschoolers, they like to make choices about foods they eat—another aspect of developing independence. Letting a child choose between two vegetables may encourage him to eat a vegetable that he might not otherwise try.
- Give children plenty of attention and companionship at other times during the day so they will not feel they have to make a fuss to keep you close at mealtimes.
- Even if messy, let children begin to feed themselves when they are first interested. Grabbing for the spoon indicates readiness. If you discourage them they may give up trying, and you will have a much harder time getting them to do things for themselves. Children may still need a helping hand, however, especially when tired or sick or just plain bored with the task of eating.
- A casual and relaxed atmosphere helps children develop good eating habits with less frustration.
- Adult interest in the foods served and general conversation about them offers children opportunities to learn about the foods they eat.

NUTRITION, CHILDREN, AND YOU

As you have read, the child goes through several stages of physical development during the early years of his life. Some of the changes that occur are seen easily; others are hidden. It is normal for the rate of growth in height and weight to be slower during the latter half of the infant's

Part III: A Wholesome Environment

Kickapoo Head Start Center
Eating in a relaxed setting encourages children to establish sound eating patterns. Would you say that this little girl enjoys mealtime?

first year. From ages one to three, energy needs are at the lowest level of childhood, but the pattern changes in both muscle and skeletal growth. At this stage, growth of muscles and bones, which is not always obvious, occurs more rapidly than the rest of the body. The muscles and bones must receive adequate nourishment as young children develop strength and coordination for standing and walking and then for running, jumping, and other body movements. The child's legs and arms grow at a faster rate than the trunk. This is especially noticeable as the child loses baby fat and outgrows clothes quickly.

When a child is about eighteen months old, there is a growth spurt in skeletal and muscle structure if the child has had sufficient protein. The large back muscles, buttocks, and thighs need to be developed to support added activity. Minerals also need to be deposited in the skeleton to insure that it becomes stronger and can support the greater weight, even though the skeleton itself is growing more slowly.

If the child does not receive proper nourishment, physical development may be impaired. Perhaps you have seen news photos of malnourished children around the world—even in the United States. Physical evidence of improper diets takes many forms, depending on the deficiencies. Sometimes only a lack of energy is apparent. Such signs as low resistance to colds and infection, poor muscle tone, unhealthy skin, overweight or underweight, stunted growth, softened bones, poor teeth and gums, easily bruised skin, and sensitivity of eyes to light may appear. In extreme cases, severe bone diseases can develop.

Mental performance can also be affected by a poor diet. A hungry child (or adult) cannot concentrate well, and if hunger persists, negative personality traits may appear. Tension, depression, and even apathy often accompany malnutrition.

It is easy to take nutrition for granted. So many people, even without the right nutrients, continue to function, shrugging off the little signs of trouble, assuming that as long as hunger is satisfied, nutrition is no problem. However, stop and think. An automobile continues to run even without regular tune-ups. The appliances around your home keep going even when you don't oil and clean them, but will they last longer and run more smoothly and efficiently if you maintain them better all along? No doubt they will and the same is true of the human body. Supply your body with its nutritional needs and you increase your chances for a longer, healthier life.

Surprising though it may seem, malnutrition is a problem for many people in the United States, particularly for those with low incomes. Lack of money prevents people from buying the proper variety of foods

Ch. 12: Food for Children

needed for a good diet. The problem, however, does not end there. Many Americans have the money but do not spend it on a balanced diet. Instead, too many dollars go for high-calorie foods that provide few of the nutrients needed for good health. An example is snack foods—potato chips, soft drinks, candy, fried pies, and the like.

Do you see that nutrition can be just as great a problem in your neighborhood or in the child care center where you work as it is elsewhere? You may even need to re-evaluate your own diet. After all, a child care worker should also practice good eating habits. The following pages will sharpen your sensitivity to nutritional needs.

A Closer Look at Nutrition

Each day your body uses nutrients from the food you eat. *Proteins* are used for growth and repair of the body. *Vitamins* and *minerals* are needed for growth and to keep the body functioning properly. *Fats* and *carbohydrates* are energy sources.

Most foods contain more than one nutrient, but no single food contains all the nutrients in the amounts needed. What effect could this have on a very finicky eater?

To get the nutrients needed, food must be chosen wisely from a variety of *everyday foods*. These foods fall into four basic groups. When choosing the foods you will eat and planning menus for others, think about these groups. Plan to include at least the minimum number of servings in each group. Note that serving sizes may differ. Young children usually need smaller servings than adults and teenagers, partly because children require smaller amounts of nutrients. (See the chart on page 214.) Now read about the four basic food groups—milk, fruit-vegetable, meat, and grain. Use this information to increase your nutrition awareness.

Milk Group

Milk is the leading source of calcium, which is needed for bones and teeth. It also provides high-quality protein, riboflavin, vitamins A, C, and D, and many other nutrients.

Regardless of age, everyone needs some milk each day. The following amounts of whole fluid milk are recommended daily:

8-ounce cups*

Children under nine	2 to 3
Children nine to twelve	3 or more
Teenagers	4 or more
Adults	2 or more
Pregnant women	3 or more
Nursing mothers	4 or more

Part or all the milk may be skim, evaporated, dry, or buttermilk. Cheese and ice cream may replace part of the milk. The amount of other dairy products it will take to replace a given amount of milk is figured on the basis of calcium content. Portions of various kinds of cheese and ice cream and their milk equivalents in calcium are:

1-inch cube cheddar cheese = ½ cup milk
½ cup cottage cheese = ⅓ cup milk
2 tablespoons cream cheese = 1 tablespoon milk
½ cup ice cream = ¼ cup milk

Fruit-Vegetable Group

Vegetables and fruits are valuable chiefly because of the vitamins and minerals they contain. Count on them to supply nearly all the vitamin C and over half of the vitamin A needed. Vitamin C is required for healthy gums and body tissues. Vitamin A is needed for growth, vision, and healthy condition of the skin and other body surfaces.

---
*See metric information, page 215.

Part III: A Wholesome Environment

The following foods are *good* sources of vitamin C: grapefruit or grapefruit juice, orange or orange juice, cantaloupe, guava, mango, papaya, raw strawberries, broccoli, brussels sprouts, green pepper, and sweet red pepper.

Fair sources of vitamin C are: honeydew melon, lemon, tangerine or tangerine juice, watermelon, asparagus tips, raw cabbage, collards, garden cress, kale, kohlrabi, mustard greens, potatoes and sweet potatoes cooked in the jacket, spinach, tomatoes or tomato juice, and turnip greens.

The following are *good* sources of vitamin A: dark-green and deep-yellow vegetables and a few fruits—broccoli, carrots, chard, collards, cress, kale, pumpkin, spinach, sweet potatoes, turnip greens, winter squash, apricots, cantaloupe, and persimmons.

From the fruit-vegetable group, *choose four or more servings every day,* including:

- One serving of a good source of vitamin C or two servings of a fair source.
- One serving, at least every other day, of a good source of vitamin A. If the food chosen for vitamin C is also a good source of vitamin A, the additional serving of a vitamin A food may be omitted.

The remaining one to three or more servings may be of any vegetable or fruit, including those that are valuable for vitamins C and A. Count $\frac{1}{2}$ cup of vegetable or fruit as one serving. Foods which are ordinarily served whole or halved, such as a medium apple, banana, orange, or potato, half a medium grapefruit or cantaloupe, or the juice of one lemon, may also be counted as one serving.

Meat Group

Foods in this group are valued for their protein, which is needed for growth and repair of body tissues, muscle, organs, blood, skin, and hair. They also provide iron, thiamine, riboflavin, and niacin.

Included in the meat group are beef, veal, lamb, pork, variety meats (liver, heart, kidney), poultry, fish, and shellfish. Eggs are also an excellent source of protein. Dry beans, dry peas, lentils, nuts, peanuts, and peanut butter can be used as alternates.

Two or more servings should be chosen each day. Count the following as a serving:

- 2 to 3 ounces of lean cooked meat, poultry, or fish (without bone)
- 2 eggs
- 1 cup of cooked dry beans, dry peas, or lentils
- 4 tablespoons of peanut butter

Grain Group

Protein, iron, several of the B-vitamins, and food energy are provided by foods in this group. All breads and cereals that are whole grain, enriched, or restored are included in this group. Read the labels carefully for this information. Some specific foods included are: breads, cooked cereals, ready-to-eat cereals, rice, cornmeal, crackers, flour, grits, macaroni, spaghetti, noodles, rolled oats, quick breads, and other baked goods if made with whole-grain or enriched flour.

Choose four or more servings daily. If no cereals are chosen, have an extra serving of breads or baked goods, making at least five servings per day. The following will count as one serving:

- 1 slice of bread
- 1 ounce ready-to-eat cereal
- $\frac{1}{2}$ to $\frac{3}{4}$ cup cooked cereal, rice, cornmeal, grits, macaroni, noodles, or spaghetti

Ch. 12: Food for Children

Other Foods

Many other foods supply calories and can add to the total nutrients in meals. Butter, margarine, other fats, oils, sugars, and unenriched refined grain products often round out meals and help satisfy the appetite. Such foods may be used in baked goods, mixed dishes, during preparation, or at the table.

Specific Nutritional Needs

According to research findings, there seems to be no difference in the nutritional needs of boys as compared to girls during the preschool years. The nutritional requirements of both sexes do become different, however, when children reach the age of about ten to twelve. You can see this in the chart on page 214. Children need different amounts of vitamins from infancy through the preschool years.

As you look at the chart, note the nutritional requirements for preschool children. How much vitamin C (ascorbic acid) is required by a three-year-old each day? How much vitamin A? Do the required amounts of B-vitamins (thiamine, riboflavin, and niacin) change during the preschool years? Refer back to the four basic food groups to see what foods supply the proper amounts of these particular vitamins.

Vitamin D, the sunshine vitamin, is essential for maintaining sound health. It helps the body use calcium and phosphorus in bone development. This is particularly important to the growing child. Since the body contains a substance that can be converted to vitamin D by the sun, sunshine is one means of getting this vitamin. Most children, however, cannot be in the sun long enough to get an adequate amount of vitamin D. As shown in the chart, every child needs at least 400 units of vitamin D each day. If a child drinks a quart of milk daily, this requirement should be filled since milk is fortified with vitamin D. To be on the safe side, however, consult a doctor before giving the child any extra amounts of the vitamin. If necessary, the doctor may suggest the use of capsules, tablets, or liquid drops as an additional source. Remember, the child should not be led to believe that such supplements are candy.

There are numerous minerals required by the body in both large and small amounts. All are important, but some are obtained more easily than others. As the bones are developing throughout the preschool years, there is a need for sufficient calcium and phosphorus. Milk is an excellent source of these minerals for children and adults. The need for iron is especially significant. Some studies indicate that the requirements for iron increase steadily during the preschool years. These studies of nutrition with preschool children have frequently shown low blood levels of iron, indicating that many children lack an adequate supply of this mineral. Iodine, obtained by using iodized table salt, and fluorine, which is often added to drinking water in many communities, are two other important minerals. The body requires many additional minerals besides these, most of which are consumed by eating a variety of foods.

At an age when children are doing much growing, proteins are essential. Without sufficient protein, children's bodies will not adequately take care of cell growth and repairs. As a result of protein deficiency, a child may be underdeveloped.

Carbohydrates and fats, of course, are needed as sources of energy. Carbohydrates are obtained from grain products, beans and peas, potatoes, lima beans, corn,

Part III: A Wholesome Environment

Food and Nutrition Board, National Academy of Sciences—National Research Council
Recommended Daily Dietary Allowances[1], Revised 1973

Designed for the maintenance of good nutrition of practically all healthy people in the U.S.A.

	Age (years) From Up to	Weight (kg)	Weight (lbs)	Height (cm)	Height (in)	Energy (kcal)[2]	Protein (g)	Vitamin A Activity (RE)[3]	Vitamin A Activity (IU)	Vitamin D (IU)	Vitamin E Activity[5] (IU)	Ascorbic Acid (mg)	Folacin[5] (µg)	Niacin[7] (mg)	Riboflavin (mg)	Thiamin (mg)	Vitamin B$_6$ (mg)	Vitamin B$_{12}$ (µg)	Calcium (mg)	Phosphorus (mg)	Iodine (µg)	Iron (mg)	Magnesium (mg)	Zinc (mg)
Infants	0.0–0.5	6	14	60	24	kg×117	kg×2.2	420[4]	1400	400	4	35	50	5	0.4	0.3	0.3	0.3	360	240	35	10	60	3
	0.5–1.0	9	20	71	28	kg×108	kg×2.0	400	2000	400	5	35	50	8	0.6	0.5	0.4	0.3	540	400	45	15	70	5
Children	1–3	13	28	86	34	1300	23	400	2000	400	7	40	100	9	0.8	0.7	0.6	1.0	800	800	60	15	150	10
	4–6	20	44	110	44	1800	30	500	2500	400	9	40	200	12	1.1	0.9	0.9	1.5	800	800	80	10	200	10
	7–10	30	66	135	54	2400	36	700	3300	400	10	40	300	16	1.2	1.2	1.2	2.0	800	800	110	10	250	10
Males	11–14	44	97	158	63	2800	44	1000	5000	400	12	45	400	18	1.5	1.4	1.6	3.0	1200	1200	130	18	350	15
	15–18	61	134	172	69	3000	54	1000	5000	400	15	45	400	20	1.8	1.5	2.0	3.0	1200	1200	150	18	400	15
	19–22	67	147	172	69	3000	54	1000	5000	400	15	45	400	20	1.8	1.5	2.0	3.0	800	800	140	10	350	15
	23–50	70	154	172	69	2700	56	1000	5000	—	15	45	400	18	1.6	1.4	2.0	3.0	800	800	130	10	350	15
	51+	70	154	172	69	2400	56	1000	5000	—	15	45	400	16	1.5	1.2	2.0	3.0	800	800	110	10	350	15
Females	11–14	44	97	155	62	2400	44	800	4000	400	12	45	400	16	1.3	1.2	1.6	3.0	1200	1200	115	18	300	15
	15–18	54	119	162	65	2100	48	800	4000	400	12	45	400	14	1.4	1.1	2.0	3.0	1200	1200	115	18	300	15
	19–22	58	128	162	65	2100	46	800	4000	400	12	45	400	14	1.4	1.1	2.0	3.0	800	800	100	18	300	15
	23–50	58	128	162	65	2000	46	800	4000	—	12	45	400	13	1.2	1.0	2.0	3.0	800	800	100	18	300	15
	51+	58	128	162	65	1800	46	800	4000	—	12	45	400	12	1.1	1.0	2.0	3.0	800	800	80	10	300	15
Pregnant						+300	+30	1000	5000	400	15	60	800	+2	+0.3	+0.3	2.5	4.0	1200	1200	125	18+[8]	450	20
Lactating						+500	+20	1200	6000	400	15	60	600	+4	+0.5	+0.3	2.5	4.0	1200	1200	150	18	450	25

FOOTNOTES TO TABLES OF RECOMMENDED DAILY DIETARY ALLOWANCES

[1] The allowances are intended to provide for individual variations among most normal persons as they live in the United States under usual environmental stresses. Diets should be based on a variety of common foods in order to provide other nutrients for which human requirements have been less well defined. See text for more-detailed discussion of allowances and of nutrients not tabulated.

[2] Kilojoules (KJ) = 4.2 × kcal

[3] Retinol equivalents

[4] Assumed to be all as retinol in milk during the first six months of life. All subsequent intakes are assumed to be one-half as retinol and one-half as β-carotene when calculated from international units. As retinol equivalents, three-fourths are as retinol and one-fourth as β-carotene.

[5] Total vitamin E activity, estimated to be 80 percent as α-tocopherol and 20 percent other tocopherols. See text for variation in allowances.

[6] The folacin allowances refer to dietary sources as determined by Lactobacillus casei assay. Pure forms of folacin may be effective in doses less than one-fourth of the RDA.

[7] Although allowances are expressed as niacin, it is recognized that on the average 1 mg of niacin is derived from each 60 mg of dietary tryptophan.

[8] This increased requirement cannot be met by ordinary diets; therefore, the use of supplemental iron is recommended.

Growing children need nutritious meals. Here's an interesting way for children to enjoy an outdoor meal.

dried and sweetened fruits, sugars, syrup, jelly, jam, honey, fruits, and vegetables. Fats are found in butter, margarine, salad oils, cooking fats and oils, meat, cheese, eggs, whole milk, cream, and nuts.

Carbohydrates, fats, and proteins give heat and energy to the body. This heat and energy is measured in terms of *calories*. The differences in calories needed are usually due to normal individual differences. Changing levels of physical activity cause some children to deviate from established patterns. Even so, you should be familiar with the following recommendations. The average need for infants up to one year of age is about 1,000 calories per day; at one to three years of age about 1,300 calories; and at three to six years of age about 1,600 calories. It is important that children receive adequate amounts of calories for their activities and for growth. If there are not enough calories in their diet, the proteins are used for energy instead of for tissue building and repair.

Some foods contain few nutrients even though they are loaded with calories. These are not good foods for children—or adults. For example, children should not be given an opportunity to develop a preference for such empty calorie foods as cakes, cookies, candy, soft drinks, and artificially sweetened beverages. These foods cannot replace essential nutritious foods in a child's diet. Such practices can also lead to weight problems which are difficult for children to overcome. Moreover, the food preference patterns may be established and carry over into adulthood. As long as the child is active and not overweight, however, extra calories should be no problem.

Metrics in Food and Nutrition

Metric units have long been used for precise measurements in scientific nutrition. The chart on page 214 shows examples.

Converting common kitchen measurements to metric units is difficult. Precise conversion often results in amounts that are not convenient. For example, an 8-oz. cup equals 236.5 millilitres (ml). Eventually, convenient metric standards will probably be adopted. Possible new standards include: 1 cup equals 250 ml; 1 tablespoon equals 15 ml; 1 teaspoon equals 5 ml. Until new standards are determined and new measuring utensils are widely available, the customary measurements now used in food preparation are likely to remain in common use.

PLANNING MEALS AND SNACKS FOR CHILDREN

Making arrangements to serve children nutritional foods during their stay in a children's center is a big responsibility. Will you know which children have urgent needs for nourishing foods? What can you do to help?

Meals

With very little adjustment, each day's meal pattern can be used by all, including

Kickapoo Head Start Center
Milk is a major source of protein, calcium, and vitamin D, nutrients needed by all children. Note that the child care workers in this center provided each child with a glass of milk to go with lunch.

young children. Look at the following meals for one day. By making minor changes in the amounts served to each person, these patterns will fit the needs of adults as well as children.

Breakfast

Citrus juice or fruit
Whole grain cereal with milk
Toast
Butter or margarine
Milk

Lunch

Main dish of meat, eggs, fish, poultry, dried beans or peas, or cheese
Vegetable or salad
Bread
Butter or margarine
Simple dessert or fresh or cooked fruit
Milk

Dinner

Meat, poultry, or fish
Vegetable
Relish or salad
Bread
Butter or margarine
Fruit or dessert
Milk

Your help is needed to meet the challenge of providing nutritious foods and to encourage sound eating habits during children's early years of growth and development. Serving meals in a children's center is discussed in Chapter 20. You may also be interested in trying out some of the recipes in the Appendix.

Snacks

Planning food for the children's center usually includes snack times as well as mealtimes. Although some children may have eaten a hearty breakfast, others may have had little or no breakfast before coming to the center. You will need to find out as soon as possible if there are children in your center with poor eating patterns at home. It may be necessary to have breakfast or a healthy snack for some children soon after they arrive at the center.

Children can easily form habits of eating and nibbling all day long. This contributes to tooth decay and reduces appetites for regular meals. Nibbling on crackers, bread, or cookies will become a habit unless adults plan adequately for children's regular meal and snack times at home and in the center.

Snacks are usually best at mid-morning and mid-afternoon. Some children sleep better if they have a light snack just before bedtime.

Snacks should be a part of the total day's food plan, including foods which contribute to the child's nourishment and health.

Ch. 12: Food for Children

Kentucky Youth Research Center, Inc.
On an outing to a supermarket, children show interest in the bananas, a nutritious food that will make a tasty snack when they return to the center.

The following foods are appropriate for snacks:

  Milk
  Raw vegetables
  Vegetable juices
  Fresh, dried, or canned fruit
  Fruit juices
  Fruit drinks with milk
  Cheese wedges
  Ice cream or sherbet
  Crackers or simple cookies (without nuts and chocolate)
  Toast
  Cereal products

Chapter Highlights

- It is a normal process for a child to develop changing eating patterns as he or she grows and becomes more independent.
- All children do not have similar appetites. Even the same child's appetite may differ from one meal to the next as well as from one day to the next.
- Most appetite variations and changes in young children can be handled with ease if adults, first, do not make an issue over the child's appetite, and second, provide meals that are nutritionally balanced.
- Children will usually let you know when they are hungry and when they have had enough to eat.
- Although there are no perfect schedules for all children, trying to follow fairly regular eating routines is good for them.
- Every child's development depends greatly upon the foods eaten.
- To get the nutrients needed by the body, menus must be planned to include a variety of *everyday* foods. These foods fall into four basic groups—milk, fruit-vegetable, meat, grain. Children need about the same foods as adults, but the servings usually need to be smaller.
- Planning and serving nutritious foods during a child's stay in a children's center usually includes snacks as well as meals.
- Snacks should be a part of the total day's food plan, including foods which contribute to the child's nourishment and health.

Part III: A Wholesome Environment

Thinking It Over

1. How does the rate of body growth affect appetites in young children?
2. What, other than body growth, causes appetite variations in healthy young children?
3. Do you think it is a good practice to make a child clean his plate? Explain your answer.
4. Name some foods you did not like as a child but that you like now. How do you explain your change in attitude?
5. How would you handle children who behave in each of the following ways at mealtime: dawdles; on a food "jag"; negative toward food; stands while eating?
6. How does a regular schedule and routine affect the eating habits of young children?
7. Give suggestions for handling the following mealtime situations with young children:
    - Tracy will not eat the food offered by her mother. Mother knows that the child needs this food for proper nutrition.
    - Steve dislikes many of the vegetables which are enjoyed by others in the family.
    - Laura always seems to get in the way when a meal is prepared. She puts her fingers in the food and fusses because mother won't give her enough attention.
    - While eating in his highchair, Jason reaches often for the spoon held by his mother. His mother prefers to hang onto spoon and dish, however, because food goes all over child, chair, and floor if she doesn't.
8. Do you think children should eat meals with the family? Explain your answer.
9. Give three suggestions for making mealtime a pleasant experience for children.
10. What is meant by the term *empty calories*? Make a list of foods which may be classified by this term.
11. Name the four basic food groups and give the number of daily servings the body needs from each group.
12. Is there any relationship between overweight children and overweight adults? Give reasons for your answer.
13. Are the nutritional requirements for a child different from an adult's? What are the main differences other than calorie intake?
14. Explain the major functions of the following nutrients as they affect the human body: proteins; carbohydrates; fats; vitamins; and minerals.

Things To Do

1. Invite a group of four or five young children to class for a snack. Plan a cooperative (children and students) food preparation period to make nutritious snacks for children. Prepare such foods as kabobs (vegetables, canned meat, wieners, fruit); milk shakes with different flavors; toast cut in different shapes with cookie cutters. Record children's responses.
2. Report and discuss results of the above experience. How did the children re-

(Continued on page 219)

Things To Do Continued

spond? What value is evident from the snack experience? What indications of curiosity did you see?

3. Give a food demonstration to kindergarten children, including such preparation as cereal cookies, milk products, and meat dishes. Emphasize simple nutrition facts throughout the demonstration.
4. Plan menus for several days in a child care center. Share these with a center in the community.
5. Working in groups of four or five students, develop games such as Bingo and Concentration, using food and nutrition facts which four- and five-year-old children can use to develop knowledge in this area.
6. Write an Ann-Landers-type response to the following letter:

Dear Ann:

My three-year-old daughter has always been a healthy, happy child with no apparent physical or emotional hangups. Now, all of a sudden, she won't eat the foods offered to her at mealtime. Ann, these are not new or strange foods; these are her favorite meals. This is causing a real family problem. I do not think she should be given any food between meals if she does not eat at mealtime, but her father thinks some snacks are better than no food at all.

Please rush your answer to us before our daughter becomes ill physically, before her father becomes ill emotionally from aggravated anger, and before I run away from home.

Read and discuss answers written by class members.

7. Working in groups, develop puppet shows for young children in which you present facts about the four basic food groups. Present the shows to a local center or invite the children to your school for the shows.
8. Prepare "mini" bulletin boards illustrating possible solutions for changing such mealtime behavior as dawdling, negativism toward food, and standing while eating. Post these on a large bulletin board.
9. Put different foods in a "feely" bag one at a time. Take turns reaching into the bag to feel the food and describe it, giving nutrition facts about it. Children will enjoy doing this too.

Recommended Reading

Hoff, Johan E., and Junick, Jules. *Food* (Introductions), Readings from *Scientific American*. W. H. Freeman and Co., 1973.

Foods for Baby and Mealtime Psychology. Freemont, Michigan: Gerber Products Co., 1963.

Journal of Nutrition Education, (Quarterly Journal). Berkeley, California: Society for Nutrition Education, 1973.

Nutrition Today (Bimonthly Journal). Annapolis, Maryland: Nutrition Today, Inc., 1973.

Chapter 13.

Children's Clothing

Your Challenge

This chapter will enable you to . . . .

- Describe the features to look for when choosing clothing for children.
- Tell how children learn from their clothing.
- Name products designed to help children learn through clothing.
- List clothing guidelines to be used in the center.

THE SIGNIFICANCE OF CLOTHING

To a child, clothing may be the key to an imaginative land of adventure. With the right hat and a pair of boots, the child shifts easily into the role of a cowboy or a cowgirl in the Wild West. Mother's old dress and high heels or Dad's old hat and tie create a temporary adult world for children. A towel across the shoulders becomes a cape, thus, an instant Superman. Manufacturers are designing dress-up clothes to fit all sorts of character roles, such as a fireman, cowboy, nurse, astronaut, and even an animal. Obviously, clothing is important and useful to children. For many, clothing is very important throughout life.

Whether it's diamonds and furs or shirts and jeans, each person says something about himself through his clothing. Color, style, attention to fads, cleanliness, and fit are all considered in the selection and wearing of clothing. Children soon learn that clothing provides warmth and protection as well as enchanting experiences. As the child becomes older, clothing may serve other purposes—as status symbols or social expressions.

Have you ever had an experience like this? On Friday you wear a dress that no longer fits or a shirt you outgrew last year. All day you feel moody and uncomfortable. On Monday you wear an outfit that fits and looks great. Now you feel at ease, cheerful, and much more sociable than you did on Friday. Many of you have probably experienced these moods, prompted by your feelings about the way you look. Even though it may not be wise to place so much value on personal appearance, it is a common occurrence to do so.

Clothing does much to boost or deflate the morale. Often it is not an issue of cost but an issue of liking or disliking a garment. People generally prefer clothing similar to what their friends wear. Why else would you ask three friends what they are wearing to a party before you make the

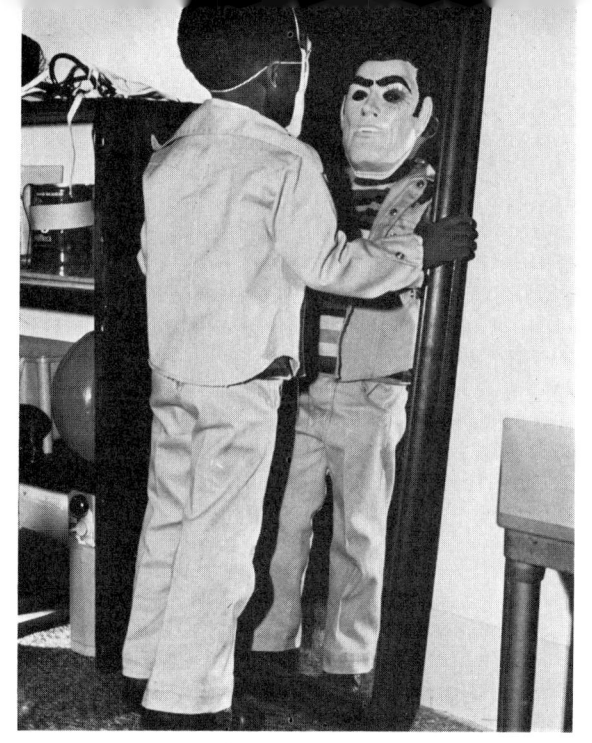

University of Oklahoma Health Sciences Center
Shawn enjoys the freedom of imaginative play which allows him to explore and pretend through dress-up activities.

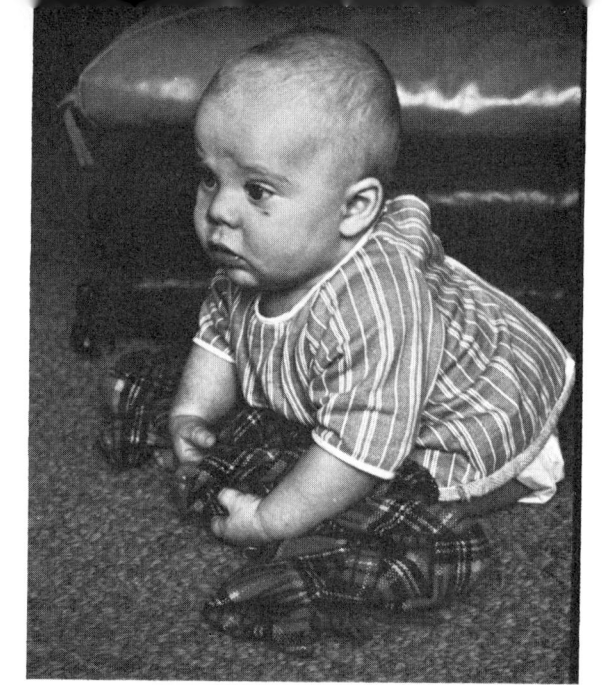

The infant's clothes should be comfortable, with lots of ease for reaching, crawling, and creeping.

decision yourself? Each person strives to fulfill the image he has of himself and the closer he comes to achieving this, the more comfortable he is with his appearance. By this, you can see how important clothes can be to people, children included. How children will feel about clothing as they become older is influenced by their family and friends. As a parent or child care worker, you will influence the value system about clothing.

Imagine for a moment a room full of young children from different backgrounds. One little girl, in particular, catches your eye. She stands alone, her dress rumpled and nearly two sizes too large for her. Her shoes are worn and the cuffs of her grayish white socks are stretched and sagging around the two thin ankles. Her hair hangs straight, with straggling wisps falling in all directions to her shoulders. She stares at the floor, looking as though she needs a friend.

Do you feel something for this child as you watch? You are the child care worker. What will you do?

CHOOSING CLOTHING FOR CHILDREN

As children grow and develop through the stages of early childhood, their needs for clothing change. The infant's clothes should include snap crotches for easy and quick dressing by adults. These will also be less frustrating for children—especially before they are toilet trained. Easy on-and-off styles are especially helpful at this early stage. With extended movements, including exploration, reaching for objects, trying to walk, and lots of crawling and creeping, the infant needs comfortable clothes with freedom for action. Reinforced areas on the clothing are important where there is strain on the knees of pants or elbows of jackets.

Part III: A Wholesome Environment

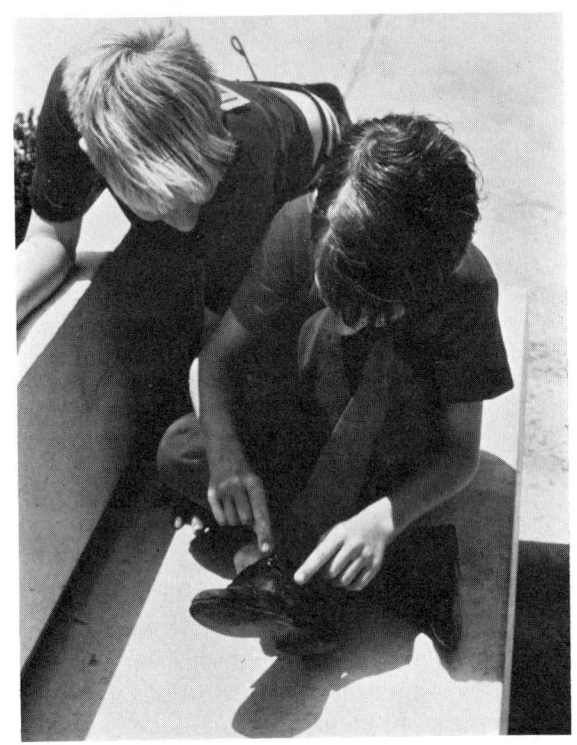

Self-dressing skills contribute to every child's feeling of independence.

At about fifteen to eighteen months of age, children begin to indicate interest in dressing themselves. They can take off clothes more easily than they can put them on. During these early periods of interest, a child may want to dress himself one day but not the next. Clothes are often put on backwards or inside-out while learning is taking place.

Self-dressing skills should be encouraged and developed, using the child's clothing as a tool. When children show interest in dressing themselves, they need opportunities to practice these skills.

Garments which are difficult to handle are frustrating for the child. If Janie's one-piece jumpsuit buttons at the shoulders slightly to the back and just beyond her reach, she may tug at the shoulders and try to pull the garment down without unbuttoning, or she may tear the buttons loose with harsh tugging. This type of restriction requires adult assistance which often detracts from Janie's sense of independence and mastery of her environment.

To help a child feel self-sufficient, look for clothes with these features:

- Easy-to-recognize fronts and backs of garments.
- Front, rather than back, openings.
- Large neck openings for slipovers.
- Pants and shorts with elastic at the waist.
- Easy-to-reach pockets and buttons.
- Attached belts which fasten in the front.
- Large, easy-to-operate zippers.
- Smooth buttons of substantial size.
- Snaps that are easy to handle—not too tight.

As toddlers attempt self-dressing, they get impatient with clothes which are not easy to get on and off. Clothes must fit properly to meet changes in development. Clothes need self-help features, freedom for movement, and durable construction in washable fabrics.

Preschool rompers are very active, with interest in self-dressing and clothing selection. Rompers enjoy dressing like others and playing dress-up. Clothing styled for comfort and action, with self-help features, is important at this age also.

What to Look For in Clothing

Regardless of age, young children should have clothing which is chosen with several points in mind. Proper health, safety, growth, and development of the child may be enhanced if thought is given to these considerations.

Ch. 13: Children's Clothing

Sturdy, easy-to-care-for clothes help children feel comfortable as they explore and play outdoors.

Clothing Safety

The safety of a child should always be a primary concern of adults. Follow these tips for safety with clothing:

- Outer clothing of bright colors helps the child to be more easily visible to motorists.
- Details of garments, such as buttons, snaps, and belts, should be secure to prevent children from pulling them off and putting them into their mouths, noses, and ears. Belts, ties, sashes, and drawstrings should be attached to the garment. Children like to experiment, and these items can choke, trip, or cut off circulation if children misuse them.
- Clothes should be fire-resistant and made of nonflammable fabrics. Read the labels to help find such information. (A strict standard for protecting children from burning sleepwear went into effect in July of 1972. A mandate issued by the Commerce Department requires that all children's pajamas, nightgowns, and robes in sizes 0 through 6X either pass a strict flame test or be permanently and conspicuously labeled flammable. This standard was based on the fact that one out of nine clothing-fire accidents involves preschool children in sleepwear.)

Fabrics

Washable and easy-care fabrics are most appropriate for children's clothes. Flammability is also a factor, as just mentioned. Since children give clothing much hard use, choose fabrics that will wear well. Children often refer to their clothes by color, so choosing colors they like may increase their enjoyment in wearing the clothes. Children are also intrigued with details, such as buttons, zippers, pockets, bows, borders, and fabric designs, another thought to keep in mind when you buy for children.

Fit

As you have read, clothes should be comfortable and fitted for action. A proper fit will allow the child freedom of movement, yet prevent him from tripping and falling. Clothes that are too tight or too loose can be as hazardous as objects lying on the floor where a child walks.

Even though children outgrow their clothes rapidly during the early years, it is not wise to fit them with clothes that are too large. Such clothing not only looks cumbersome but is also a problem for the

Part III: A Wholesome Environment

A proper fit in clothing will allow freedom of movement. What problems might this child have with clothes that are either too baggy or too tight?

child to wear. It is far better to choose clothes like these, which are especially designed for growing children:

- Outfits made of stretch fabrics.
- One-piece dresses without definite waistlines.
- Pants with elastic waistbands.
- Clothing with adjustable waistbands and shoulder straps.
- Two-piece outfits.
- Items with deep hems.
- Clothes with large seams, pleats, and tucks which can be let out inconspicuously.

If possible, clothes should be tried on for the proper fit before purchasing. Features to consider for a proper fit are:

- Lightweight and absorbent fabrics with stretch or ease qualities.
- Smooth fit all over.
- Adequate fullness in pant legs and skirts for easy knee-bending but not full enough to get in the child's way.
- Ease through the body of the garment, permitting free body movements.
- Collars and sleeves that fit smoothly without binding or rubbing.
- One-piece outfits with sufficient length from neck to crotch to enable the child to bend and stoop with ease.
- Coats, jackets, and sweaters which fit smoothly over other clothes without binding.
- Underwear that fits snugly enough to be comfortable but not binding and not too loose. These should be of soft, absorbent fabrics.

Shoes

Properly fitted shoes are necessary to help children develop motor skills while providing stability for balance and comfort in moving about.

For crawling, soft shoes and socks should be used. Hard shoes are needed for walking. Shoes should be $\frac{1}{4}$ inch wider than the foot and $\frac{1}{4}$ to $\frac{1}{2}$ inch longer. Socks should be $\frac{1}{2}$ inch longer.

Choosing the right shoe size is important to a growing child, since proper development of the feet is at stake. If corrective help is needed, a doctor's advice should be sought in selecting special shoes. A reputable dealer in children's shoes can help fit most children correctly. Costs may be a little higher for good shoes but worth the investment in order to avoid possible developmental damage. In selecting shoes,

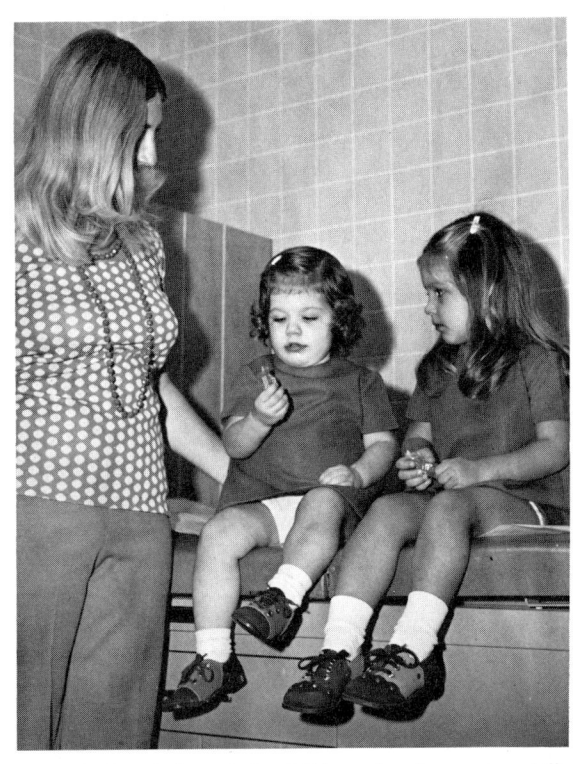

Ch. 13: Children's Clothing

Properly fitted shoes help children develop motor skills while providing stability for balance and comfort in moving about.

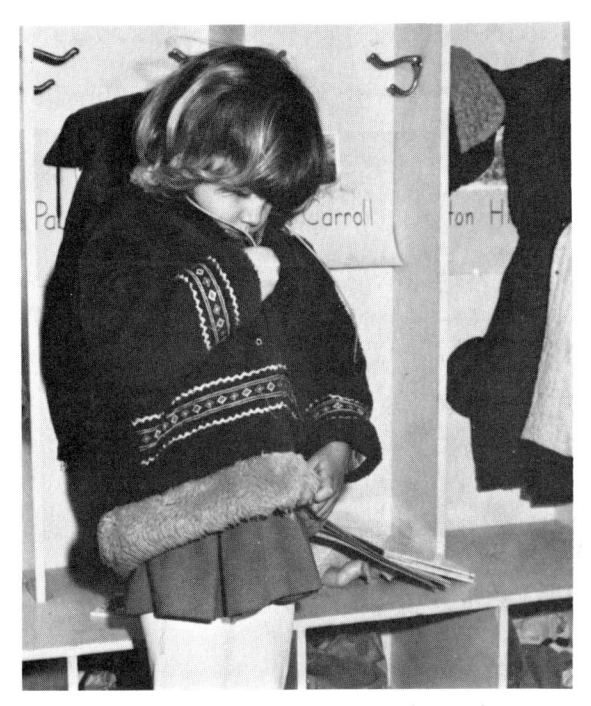

A child may be as interested in manipulating the zipper on a jacket as in putting a puzzle together.

look for built-in support. If sneakers or tennis shoes do not provide adequate support, guard against excessive use. Because the child grows so rapidly during the first nine years, shoe size and proper fit should be checked about every three or four months. After this, shoes can be kept for six months if they do not wear out first.

Inspect shoes carefully before buying. In addition to built-in support, look for outside support, tough materials, sturdy construction, and soles that are thick enough to last a reasonable length of time. When buying inexpensive shoes, be especially watchful for the above features.

CHILDREN LEARN FROM THEIR CLOTHES

At first thought, who would think that many concepts and skills are learned by children as they handle and wear their clothes? Yet this is quite true.

In the first place, the child's *sense of touch* is stimulated early by the fabric in clothing. Children enjoy the texture, or *hand,* of a fabric. Notice how they feel and stroke their garments to stimulate their sense of touch. Corduroy, velveteen, suede, flannel, and other soft fabrics are favorites.

Secondly, *manipulation, dexterity,* and *coordination skills* are encouraged when children have clothes designed with features that promote such skills. Fastening garments with the use of buttons, zippers,

225

snaps, and hooks offers as much interest to many children as actually putting on the garments. Even two-year-olds enjoy manipulating buttons and zippers. By age three, most children can handle a variety of fasteners if they are located conveniently on the garment. Don't be surprised if you find a child who likes to take his shoes off and put them on again for the sheer pleasure of handling the laces and buckles.

Some clothes are designed with specific learning features—big zippers, buckles, buttons, laces, snaps, and hooks. Others even have colorful button-on patches of different shapes, such as triangles, circles, squares, and rectangles. All of these provide learning experiences for children.

Finally, the child learns many *concepts* with clothing. You can easily see how the learning features just described will do more than simply teach manipulative skills. A zipper may help a child learn the meaning of up and down. The patches teach colors and shapes. Many clothes are made purposely of bright primary and secondary colors to help children develop color concepts. Two-piece sets help children learn to mix and match appropriate colors and patterns in tops and bottoms when making the big decision on what to wear.

Special Learning Products

To help children learn through clothing, manufacturers have designed products which serve this purpose.

Educational units, consisting of a child's garment packaged with a record and a book, are a relatively new idea. The record tells the story in the book while the child looks at the book and listens to the record. The garment has an appliqué or cutout of an animal, object, or person in the story stitched on it. The idea behind this type of product is that a child will eventually recognize the words and learn to "read" the book. The manufacturer's feeling is that the child will be intrigued with the outfit and enjoy the coordinated materials—clothes, record, and book.

The effectiveness of such products has not been fully determined. You should, however, be aware of these items. Sometimes such an investment may be worthwhile.

Designers of children's clothing have introduced a number of lines of educational clothes for boys and girls. They feature these learning designs:

- Word and letter associations—a pair of pants with a large letter *C* and the picture of a cat. Letters of the alphabet are upside down on the garment so children can look down at them.
- Manipulation—large, easy-to-reach zippers, buttons, buckles, and snaps which help children learn to dress themselves.
- Concepts—stop-and-go signals are in red and green on clothing for learning concepts of traffic safety; right and left and up and down have directional arrows for the children to follow.

Commercial patterns are available for making clothes which help children learn how to button, zip, lace, and snap. If you don't want to make the whole garment, you might take some bright scraps of material and make patches that button or snap to dress up a simple purchased outfit. If you are quite imaginative, you could create something of your own—a bib apron, for example, with pockets that zip, button, and snap for carrying crayons, paper, or other small items. Can you think of others?

Patterns for manipulative toys are also available. A doll with zippers, buttons,

Smocks protect children's clothes while painting and working with other messy materials such as play dough, finger paints, and planting soil.

snaps, and laces is one example. These toys are designed with the idea that play is a way of learning and that the right kind of toy can help children learn to solve problems, develop coordination, and formulate concepts.

Many fabrics are now available which have prints of objects to identify and words to match. These are appropriate for children's clothes as well as the clothing of adults who work with children. Such fabrics can also be used in making wall hangings, curtains, and furniture covers for children's activity areas.

CLOTHING IN THE CENTER

In the children's center, an extra set of clothes is needed for each child in case of emergencies. Children sometimes have accidents with paints or other materials. Rain or snow may require a change of clothes to keep a child dry and comfortable while wet clothes are drying. Toileting mishaps and illnesses also require a change of clothes. Label the extra set and place it with the child's personal belongings.

Using smocks or painting bibs is a handy way to protect children's clothes while painting, working in the science area, or with other messy materials like play dough and finger paints. Discarded men's shirts can be used to make smocks for this purpose.

Smocks or aprons can also be designed as learning clothes, with colorful cutouts or appliqués of fruits, vegetables, animals, and children. Some may have large zippers or buttons in front for easy manipulation. Volunteers or parents may want to make plastic or washable aprons or smocks for the children's art activities.

Children's activities should not be restricted in order to prevent clothing from being soiled. Sometimes a discussion with parents and staff members about children's clothes and center activities is very helpful. Parents often overlook some of the center's problems but take them for granted at home. For example, at home Mike wears his oldest jeans while finger painting, but in the center he sports a new outfit which mother expects will stay clean.

Part III: A Wholesome Environment

Children should feel good about their activities and uninhibited by thoughts of punishment which may occur if clothes are soiled. Parental cooperation in making each child's world an interesting and comfortable environment is a must.

Learn to communicate not only with the children but with the parents as well. Achieving an understanding with parents on something as simple as clothing may open the line of communication to even more important issues.

Chapter Highlights

- Children soon learn that clothing provides warmth and protection as well as sensory experiences.
- As children pass through the stages of development, their clothing needs change.
- Infants require clothes which are easy to put on and take off, with freedom for action, reinforced areas where there is strain, and soft, smooth, easy-to-care-for fabrics.
- During late infancy, about fifteen to eighteen months, children begin to indicate interest in dressing themselves.
- The child's clothing can be used as a tool for encouraging self-dressing skills.
- The safety of a child, a primary concern, can be fostered through the use of safe fabrics and safety features in clothing construction.
- Clothes that are too tight or too loose can be as hazardous as objects lying on the floor where children walk and run.
- Properly fitted shoes are necessary to provide stability for balance and comfort in moving about while children develop motor skills.
- The child's sense of touch is stimulated early by the feel of fabric in clothing.
- Manipulative and coordination skills are encouraged when children have clothes designed with features that promote such tasks as buttoning, zipping, snapping, and hooking.
- Some clothes are designed to help the child learn such concepts as direction (up and down), colors, shapes, and word or letter associations, such as stop and go and right and left.
- A children's center should keep an extra set of clothes for each child in case of emergencies.
- Children's activities should not be restricted in order to prevent clothing from being soiled; neither should the design of clothing restrict children's activities.

Thinking It Over

1. What are three major functions of young children's clothing?
2. How do the clothes you wear affect your mood and outlook? Do you think children are affected by the clothing they wear? How and why?
3. Does the clothing worn by your friends affect your selection of clothes? Do you think young children are affected in a similar way? Explain?
4. How can clothing worn by young children assist in the development of their senses? Development of a positive self-concept?
5. Why is comfort in clothing important to young children?
6. List the safety features which should be considered when buying children's clothes.

(Continued on page 229)

Ch. 13: Children's Clothing

Thinking It Over Continued

7. What features in clothing help the child develop manipulative and coordination skills?
8. Identify at least five simple concepts which may be formed through clothing especially designed with learning in mind.
9. How much emphasis should be placed on keeping children neat and clean during every day activities? Explain your answer.
10. When children are learning to dress themselves, what features should their clothing have?
11. What should you keep in mind when selecting shoes for children?
12. How important is safe and nonrestricting clothing for children?

Things To Do

1. Make a check sheet to use in evaluating garments for children. Consider such features as self-help, sensory development, concept formation, and development of a positive self-concept.
2. Take a field trip to a children's clothing store or department. Examine garments, using the check sheet above. Discuss your findings when you return to class.
3. Obtain some pattern leaflets or pattern books containing children's clothing from a fabric store. Select patterns that have self-help features. Draw alterations on other patterns to improve the appropriateness of children's clothing.
4. Construct manipulative dolls, boards, or books, which include zippers, buttons and buttonholes, hooks and eyes, snaps, and lacings. Use these with children. Report results of their experiences.
5. Conduct experiments with garments which are flame resistant and those which are not to observe the effects of excessive laundering on the fire-resistant qualities. Discuss cost of upkeep and special handling of garments which have been treated to be flame resistant.
6. Observe children in child care centers and record their attitudes toward clothing. Do children who are overly concerned with cleanliness behave any differently than those who seem unconcerned with soil and dirt on their clothes? Explain.
7. Make posters which point out the value of self-help garments for young children. Display these in a child care center where parents can see them when they bring and pick up their children.
8. Working in teams of two to four students, borrow children's clothes from family, friends, or a local store. Identify the favorable and less favorable clothing features. Make a short presentation to the class, showing the garments and your assessments. (With several teams it will be possible to cover the various stages of development such as infants, toddlers, rompers, and kindergartners.)

Recommended Reading

Draper, Mary Wanda and Bailey, Annetta. *Steps in Clothing Skills*. Peoria, Illinois: Chas. A. Bennett Co., Inc., 1978.

Chapter 14.

Special Care for Infants

Your Challenge

This chapter will enable you to . . . .

- Describe the special concerns connected with feeding infants.
- Demonstrate the correct procedure for bathing a baby.
- Tell what clothing an infant needs.
- Explain how to handle the diapering of an infant.
- Describe how a child care worker can provide safe and loving care for infants.

YOUR ROLE

Caring for infants requires some very special considerations. Stop and think about what a responsibility this is. Development during infancy affects a person's entire life. When you care for a baby on a regular basis, your role in his or her life becomes very important. In fact, as a child care worker, sometimes you serve the role of a mother or father to a child. Don't you agree that if you can help provide a good, healthy start in life for a child, you have accomplished a very worthwhile goal?

When you take the parents' place for a portion of each day, you must know how to provide for the baby's needs. To be truly effective you must be cautious but confident as you learn the correct techniques. Caution will cause you to stop and think before making mistakes. Confidence will enable you to assume responsibility with the assurance that you know what to do, a feeling that children can usually sense.

SCHEDULES

When an infant is first brought to the center, you will not be familiar with his particular schedule. Ask the parents to provide this information so that you can follow a similar pattern if possible. This will help the baby, since he will have enough adapting to do without changing his whole routine. If necessary, keep a record of the infant's schedule for easy referral, particularly if the center accommodates several infants.

In planning for the infant's comfort, schedules need to include times for feeding, naps, bathing, exercise, play, and affection. With personal attention and individual treatment, the baby will sense your concern and find comfort in it. The schedule need not be elaborate and rigid. Actually, many people feel that a newborn will soon display an eating and sleeping pattern which becomes the basis for a schedule that can be changed to meet the

Ch. 14: Special Care for Infants

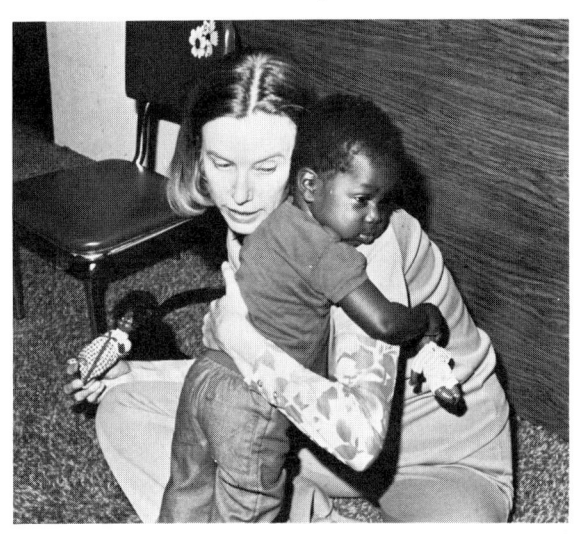

Infants depend on adults to meet many needs during the first two years of life.

Healthy infants receive tender, loving care.

baby's needs. Some guidelines on schedules are mentioned on the pages that follow, but they will not apply exactly to every infant because of individual differences. It's like one young mother said: "Every time I tried to follow the books, my baby let me know that she hadn't read them!"

FEEDING INFANTS

During the first year of life, the infant experiences the most rapid growth and development. The birth weight is more than tripled and nine to ten inches are added to the birth length. This rapid growth period requires sufficient food and nutrition. Hunger is exhibited by crying, and the infant expresses the search for food by turning the head to the side when stroked on the cheek. The infant also displays a satiety reflex—closing the mouth and/or turning the head away—which indicates that enough food has been consumed. Some babies simply resist further feeding, yet others will vomit if they cannot handle more food.

Supplying the Right Foods

Knowing what kind of food to supply is vitally significant during the first year. The digestive system of the infant is not able to digest starches and solid fat because the digestive tract enzymes have not been fully developed. Bones contain mostly cartilage and are quite soft because the bones have not yet ossified (hardened). There is little subcutaneous fat, and muscles are poorly developed. You can readily see why the infant needs just the right diet in order to develop properly.

Milk, of course, is the major food supply for the infant. The question often arises as to which type of milk to feed the young infant—cow's milk or human milk? Both

Part III: A Wholesome Environment

NUTRITIONAL VALUE OF COW'S MILK AND HUMAN MILK*

Content	Cow's Milk (Whole, 3.7% fat)	Human Milk
Water	87.4 %	85.2 %
Calories	65 cal.	77 cal.
Protein	3.5 g	1.1 g
Fat	3.5 g	4.0 g
Carbohydrates	4.9 g	9.5 g
Calcium	118 mg	33 mg
Phosphorus	93 mg	14 mg
Iron	Trace	.1 mg
Sodium	50 mg	16 mg
Potassium	144 mg	51 mg
Vitamin A value	140 I.U.	240 I.U.
Thiamine (Vitamin B_1)	.03 mg	.01 mg
Riboflavin (Vitamin B_2)	.17 mg	.04 mg
Niacin	.1 mg	.2 mg
Ascorbic Acid (Vitamin C)	1 mg	5 mg

USDA
*Based on 100 grams of milk (1 cup = 244 grams)

are suitable foods for infants. Study the chart shown here which compares the nutritional value of both cow's milk and human milk.

Other foods, such as strained fruits and vegetables, cereals, and meat, are usually added to the infant's diet within a few months after birth. Orange juice is often added within two weeks. This food supplies the additional ascorbic acid that the baby needs. Babies may also require vitamin supplements. Vitamins A and D and the B vitamins, in addition to ascorbic acid, should be included in food supplements, according to the doctor's recommendations.

In some cases, the doctor may prescribe these supplements in pill or liquid form. Breast-fed babies, for example, require additional vitamin D, whereas cow's milk is fortified with vitamin D. Remember, however, very large amounts of vitamin D can be harmful to a child, so follow the doctor's orders.

The Feeding Schedule

Generally, a mother chooses from two types of feeding schedules for her child. One is more traditional and rigid. Called a *set schedule*, it includes specified times for feeding, usually every three or four hours. Several decades ago mothers were advised to employ a rigid schedule, assuming the baby would soon get used to it. Sometimes, however, enforcing a very rigid schedule will upset the infant, especially if his hunger pattern doesn't fit the schedule.

Thoughts about types of feeding have changed in our society over the years. Thus, a more recent type of feeding schedule, called *self-demand,* has come into use, providing the mother with an alternative to the set schedule. This approach to feeding is based on the belief that the child should be fed only when hunger is shown by crying or agitation.

Since babies are unstable while very young, they seem to respond quite well to a self-demand approach. It is generally recommended that new mothers be encouraged to initiate self-demand feeding according to the infant's requirements. At first the baby may want small but frequent feedings. These will usually increase in frequency to three- or four-hour feeding intervals. As you can see, the time intervals between feedings are likely to be similar to those used with a set schedule. The primary difference will be in who sets the times—mother or baby.

Studies show that early experiences with feeding affect the child's later life. With either feeding schedule, you may be sure

Ch. 14: Special Care for Infants

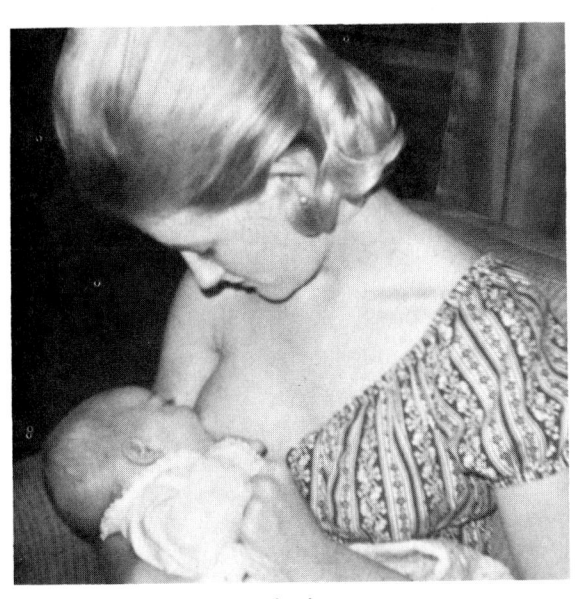

Some mothers decide early during pregnancy, or even before, to breast feed their babies.

Bottle feeding allows the father to help.

about achieving the same immediate effect—satisfaction of hunger and nutritional needs. Many mothers like to think about the long-range effect. Even during the first few months an infant develops feelings and associations connected with what goes on around him. It is quite possible that negative feelings could be experienced by a baby who cannot adapt to a set feeding schedule. These feelings usually show up in the child's disposition. Self-demand feeding considers the individuality of the child. This type of scheduling, if handled properly, usually helps promote the development of a happy, comfortable baby—without spoiling him.

Feeding Methods

A mother decides early during pregnancy, or even before, whether or not to breast feed her baby. Numerous studies indicate the majority of mothers who breast feed do so for less than three months, although many mothers do so for much longer.

People have long debated the issue of *breast feeding* versus *bottle feeding*. Some mothers have a preference for bottle feeding. (Occasionally, circumstances will not enable a mother to breast feed.) The use of the bottle makes it possible for someone other than the mother to feed the baby more often. Bottle formulas can also be individually suited to each baby.

Others feel that breast feeding is better for the mother and child. It encourages a closeness that contributes to the emotional well-being of both. Breast feeding is also convenient and helps the mother's uterus contract to a normal size. Even when a baby is breast fed, a supplemental bottle can be given on occasion. Above all, breast milk is believed by many to be better for the baby, helping digestion, possibly re-

Part III: A Wholesome Environment

ducing allergies and rashes, and offering certain protection against disease. A mother's milk is especially suited to her child, giving him a good start in life.

An alternative to breast or bottle feeding is *cup feeding*. Some mothers choose to cup feed their babies from the time they are born. This method is sometimes chosen instead of the bottle by mothers who believe that an opportunity for greater physical closensss occurs with cup feeding than with bottle feeding because the infant *must* be held in the adult's arms. The cup method is also frequently used with babies that have disorders, such as cleft palate or cleft lip. Studies indicate that babies fed by the cup method have fewer ear disorders which are sometimes aggravated by sucking.

Preparing To Feed The Infant

All equipment—bottles, caps, nipples, spoons, and dishes—must be clean. The preparation area and materials, including counter tops, sinks, and dish towels, must also be clean. In addition, be sure your hands are washed thoroughly before preparing the formula and other foods.

Several kinds of bottles are available—glass, plastic, and disposable. The disposable type can usually be purchased in sets containing a lightweight liner in which a plastic bag is inserted. Expanders, available with most sets, fit inside the liner to collapse the bottle as the infant drinks the milk. This prevents air from passing through the nipple into the baby's stomach. The plastic bag, which serves as the bottle, is thrown away at the end of the feeding. This avoids all of the usual bottle washing but is a convenience which does cost a little extra. The nipples and plastic liner should be washed in soapy water and rinsed thoroughly in clean water.

The formulas prescribed for infants are not all alike. If there is no specified formula given, a *standard formula* of equal parts of water and evaporated milk is usually prepared. In a measuring cup or pitcher, measure water from the tap and pour into a saucepan or pitcher. After scrubbing and rinsing the top of the evaporated milk can, open it and measure out an equal amount of milk. Pour this into the mixing container and stir well. As you can see, these steps can be combined and one measuring pitcher used simply by adding the milk to the desired level after the water is measured.

After preparing the formula, pour it into the bottles. A funnel may be helpful in speeding the process and avoiding spills. Some bottles need to be filled with milk or formula; others are needed for drinking water and fruit juice.

To sterilize, place formula bottles in a sterilizing container and add two or three inches of water. Cover the sterilizing container with a lid and boil. Follow the directions on all appliances designed for this purpose. Boil for exactly 25 minutes unless otherwise specified by appliance instructions; then remove the sterilizer from the heat until it is cool enough to hold your hands against the sides. Remove the sterilizer lid, and cover each bottle with an unused paper cup by placing it tightly over each nipple. Place the bottles in a cool place or refrigerate until ready for use.

Premixed, or *instant,* formulas are slightly more expensive than standard formulas but are time and energy savers and usually offer more nutritional value than evaporated milk. Vitamins and minerals are added to most premixes.

Follow the directions on the containers for instant formulas. Some are in powder form to be mixed with water and poured into bottles. Others are concentrated liquids in cans and usually need to be diluted with water. Some formulas are completely premixed and ready to be poured into bottles, and some are even available in the feeding bottle ready to have the screw-on nipple attached.

Immediately after use, bottles and nipples should be rinsed thoroughly and filled with clean, cold water until they can be washed thoroughly. When washing, bottles should be scrubbed inside and out with a brush and soapy water and then rinsed with plenty of hot water. Nipples should have wash and rinse water squeezed through the holes to eliminate all traces of formula. Both should be allowed to dry in a clean place.

The Feeding Process

For best results, the adult who is feeding the baby, whether mother, nurse, or child care worker, should be relaxed, comfortable, and interested in caring for the child. How well the infant eats is often affected by the adult's or mother's tension or relaxation during the feeding process.

Different children respond in different ways to what appears to be the same, or very similar, situations. Therefore child care workers need a number of approaches for working with and handling children during feeding times. When one way does not work, other ways may have to be tried until a successful method is discovered.

Holding an infant in the arms while bottle feeding offers the comfort of close cuddling. This warmth is as significant as the food itself because it provides the infant with a relaxed and secure feeling. Even a tiny baby needs continuous reassurance from adults in order to feel secure and confident. They need to feel that others care about them.

Whether parent, nurse, or child care worker, the adult should be relaxed, comfortable, and interested in caring for the child.

The average baby takes two to four ounces of breast milk or formula by the time he is released from the hospital. Some may wait only three hours between feedings; others wait as long as five or six hours. This time lapse is usually determined by the baby's stomach size and development of the digestive system. A baby's irregular hunger intervals are usually caused by uneven functions in digestion. An infant's size may affect the appetite, but often small babies have just as great a capacity for consuming milk as larger babies. As already indicated, with self-demand feeding the eating pattern is set by each individual baby and will vary from one child to another—even in the same family.

Some babies will give up one night feeding in the first months, yet others will not be satisfied unless fed about every four or five hours during the night. Babies usually make up for feeding times they miss by

Part III: A Wholesome Environment

taking more at other feeding times or by requiring an extra daytime feeding. Even on self-demand schedules it is best to feed infants in the evening hours to avoid hunger in the night or early morning hours. A fussy period during the day may indicate hunger. Juice, water, or simply attention may suffice. If not, an extra serving of formula may be needed. Babies who do not settle down after feeding may need formula changes or solid foods.

Some Common Feeding Problems

A new baby may be too weak or too sleepy to get the formula through the bottle if the *nipple* is too hard. Changing to a softer nipple with larger openings will usually solve this problem. However, nipples with holes that are too large may cause the infant to gulp or choke easily. A constant flow of liquid should be maintained. Firmer nipples with ordinary openings will be needed as the baby's sucking ability improves.

Weighing the infant once or twice weekly will help indicate normal *weight* gain. After the initial weight loss immediately after birth, if the baby continues to lose weight, something may be wrong. If this happens, the nurse or doctor should be consulted. Babies should not be fed too often—usually not more than six times daily—or the appetite will not develop normally. Each feeding should last about fifteen to twenty minutes but not longer than thirty. If feeding takes too long, the infant may be unable to get the milk through the nipple—or a loss of appetite may be the cause. If the bottle of milk is taken in less than ten minutes, a nipple with smaller openings should be used. Extra sucking while feeding at the breast may be alright, but extra sucking should not be allowed with the bottle.

During the first two or three months, *burping* is part of the feeding process. Feeding the baby in a semi-sitting position will allow swallowed air to rise to the top of the baby's stomach, which will assist in the elimination of air when the baby is burped. Some babies are not easily burped and require finding a special position, such as over an adult's shoulder, lying on the stomach on an adult's lap, or even in a sitting position. If the baby fusses when put to bed following a feeding, it may indicate inadequate burping. Placing the baby on his stomach is best after feeding to allow for additional burping. In this position the baby is less likely to choke if spitting up occurs.

Babies naturally *hiccup,* some more so than others. If the hiccups do not disappear quickly, giving the child a little water which has been boiled and cooled will usually work. Persistent hiccups should be reported to a doctor.

Many infants *spit* often. As long as they gain weight adequately, this should be no cause for worry. Some spitting can be eliminated by burping adequately after eating and preventing the baby from gulping the formula too rapidly.

Infants *dehydrate* easily; thus, if a baby *vomits* half or more of each feeding, this may be an indication of an allergy or illness. The doctor should be contacted if vomiting occurs for more than two feedings in succession.

A great proportion of children suck their *thumbs* at one time or another between birth and up to age seven or eight. Thumb sucking pressure and length of sucking time is not the same with each child. No clear evidence shows that thumb sucking is related to the style or length of feeding (breast verses bottle or set schedules verses self-demand schedules).

Ch. 14: Special Care for Infants

Thumb sucking seems to be a frequent and normal part of development. Research evidence suggests this behavior is not a neurotic symptom. It may even provide real relaxation and peace to a baby or young child. There is also no convincing evidence that moderate thumb sucking affects permanent structure of teeth or jaw formation. Probably the only harmful effect of thumb sucking occurs when adults express undue concern if the child sucks his thumb. Adult anxiety can be easily transferred to the child in such situations.

The infant must do a great deal of adjusting and adapting during the first few weeks of life. *Crying* is about the only way to communicate hunger and other needs. After you have cared for a baby for a time, you will begin to recognize the differences in the messages the baby is attempting to convey.

Learning to Eat

Babies discover new ways of eating food as they are fed. Giving an infant fruit juice with a spoon and then from a cup teaches the baby new feeding patterns. Infants do not often like to drink from a cup when first introduced to this new way, but they soon begin to accept it.

When beginning a new way of feeding, adults must be patient and offer attention to help children develop additional trust and confidence as they face different tasks. Each new step means giving up a comfortable way for something the baby is not sure about; thus, all infants need encouragement and approval as each new step is introduced.

During the eating process, infants also learn to manipulate the tongue, swallow, and become accustomed to various foods and their textures, flavors, and aromas.

Spoons and forks with short, broad handles are recommended for early learning experiences.

Children are usually unpredictable about eating habits. Give them time to learn. The infant will eat when ready, and this is the key thought for adults to remember.

One of the first clues to a child's desire for independence with eating occurs when the child tries to hold the cup or spoon even though the parent or adult is holding it. This usually takes place for the first time when the child is about eight to ten months old. Soon the adult's hand is pushed away and the child attempts to take control.

One way to help this become a comfortable task is to provide the correct eating equipment. The best spoons and forks are short and straight with broad handles. The child can grasp this type easily. The mouth of the spoon should be wide and shallow. Plastic dishes and cups give adults peace of mind with less anxiety about breakage. However, as you know, these should be selected with care because some plastic items are porous, crack easily, and may

Part III: A Wholesome Environment

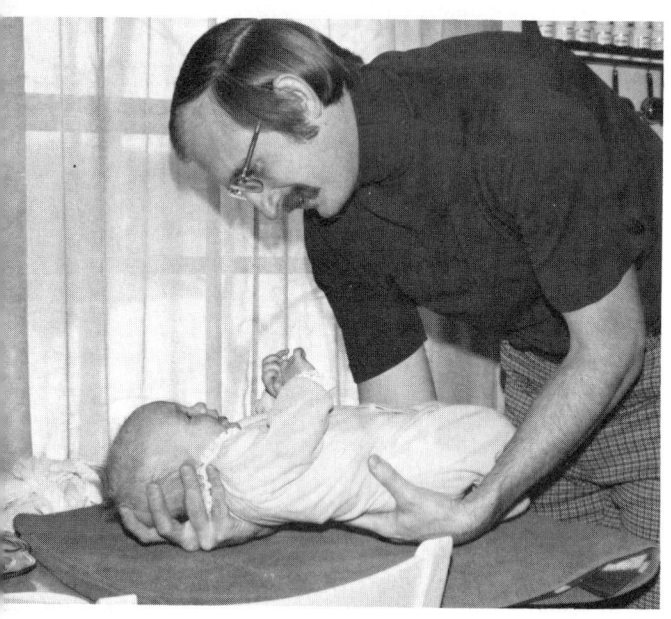

The adults voice, the touch of his hands, and his attention provide an enriching adult-child experience.

absorb bacteria. Divided plates will keep foods from running together, and the ridges give the child something to push the food against when trying to get it on the spoon or fork. Because children like to identify the various foods on their plates, they often try to keep them separate while eating. To help control the mess a baby makes when learning to eat, a rimless bowl may come in handy. Baby can't get a grip on this type of bowl so it is more likely to stay on the table rather than suddenly appear upside down on baby's head!

BATHING THE BABY

Bathing is an excellent time to exercise tender loving care for infants. The touch of your hands, your voice, and your attention are all part of enriching this experience. Although infants do not understand the reasons for a bath, this is a time when they begin to respond with positive feelings to your gentle care.

The baby can never be left alone while bathing. Phones and door bells will have to ring if others are not available to answer them. Otherwise, carry the baby with you. You must remain with the infant throughout the entire bathing process.

Babies are slippery and wiggly; they need careful but confident handling to keep them secure. Fright can be greatly eliminated by avoiding quick or sudden movements.

Preparing The Room

Avoid drafts or breezes by closing doors and windows where necessary. Keep the room temperature between 75 and 80°F. Cover the floor area with newspaper or an absorbent, washable rug or large towel. A table or cabinet top is needed for bathing equipment and caring for the baby when taken out of the bath water. Cover the table or surface with a heavy terry cloth towel or pad. A toilet tray (flat dish with soap or baby cleanser, lotion, oil, powder, extra diaper pins, and soft washcloth) is most useful at the left of the tub if you are right-handed or vice versa. A wastebasket and diaper container should be close by.

An infant's bathtub, large clean dishpan, or small tub, two-thirds full of water at 100 to 105°F., should be to your right (or left if left-handed). Place a folded diaper or towel under the tub to prevent sliding. Test the water temperature with your elbow until it feels pleasantly warm but not hot. A pitcher of warm water should be kept close to the tub.

Baby's clean clothes should be nearby on the table, cabinet top, or on a chair.

Steps in Bathing the Baby

The following steps should be taken when giving a tub bath and will help you

Ch. 14: Special Care for Infants

develop safety and efficiency while giving the infant a pleasant bathing experience. These steps should become a natural part of your child care skills.

- Lift the baby onto a large towel, supporting the back and neck continuously.
- Use a towel to keep the baby warm after removing clothes.
- Wash the face, eyes, and ears with water from the pitcher, using a squeezed-out washcloth. Use gentle motions. Cleanse the nose with a cotton swab and follow with baby oil if needed to prevent drying skin. Eyes may be wiped gently with fresh cotton or a soft corner of the washcloth. In wiping mucus from the eyes, stroke from the inner corner toward the nose. Using a gentle soap, wash the baby's head and rinse with the washcloth. Except in the diaper area, soap is not usually necessary when the baby is very young because the skin is quite sensitive.
- Place the baby in the tub, holding him with one hand under the back and buttocks while supporting the head with your arm. Soap the baby with your free hand and rinse. Another method can also be used to hold the infant: Carefully slip one arm under the baby's neck and clasp your hand around his shoulder with thumb on top and fingers under his armpit. With your other hand under his buttocks, lift slowly and place him gently in the water. Keeping the shoulder hold, use your other hand to wash his body.
- Safely lift the baby out of the tub, supporting his head and back, and place him on a towel. Blot the baby dry (do not rub him dry) and then gently massage with small amounts of baby lotion or powder. Always sprinkle powder on your hand, not directly on the baby; this will pre-

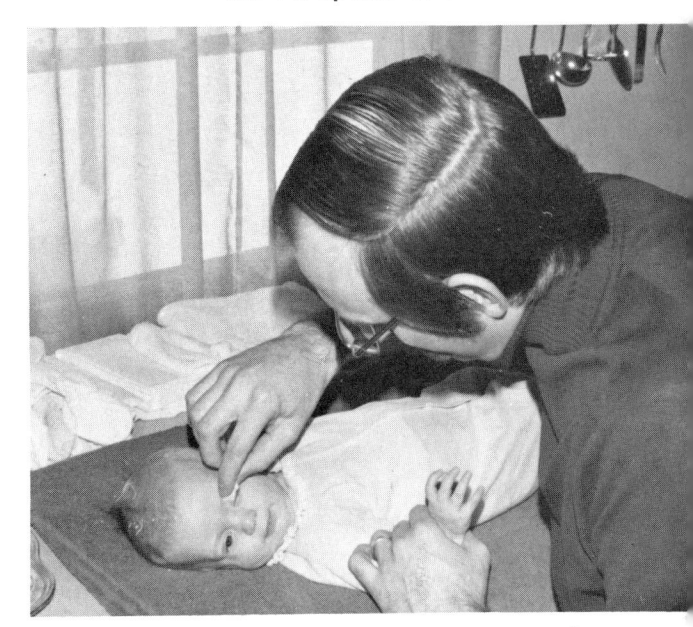

Wipe baby's eyes gently with fresh cotton or a soft cloth.

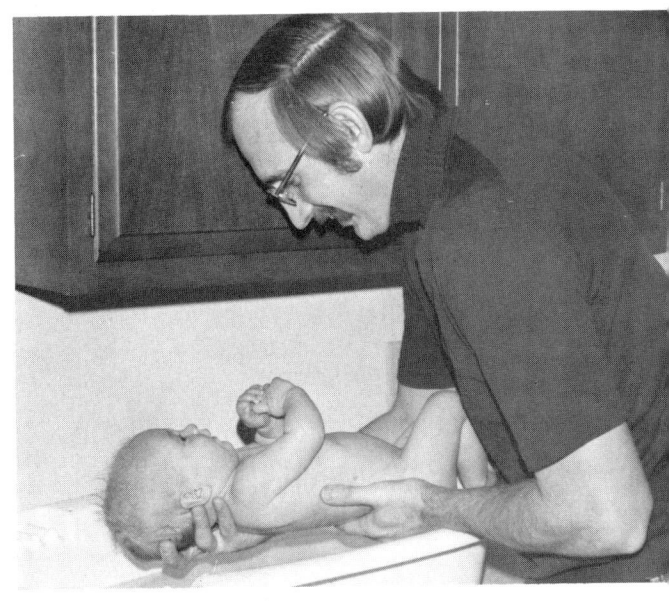

Hold the baby with one hand under the back and buttocks while supporting the baby's head with the other arm.

Part III: A Wholesome Environment

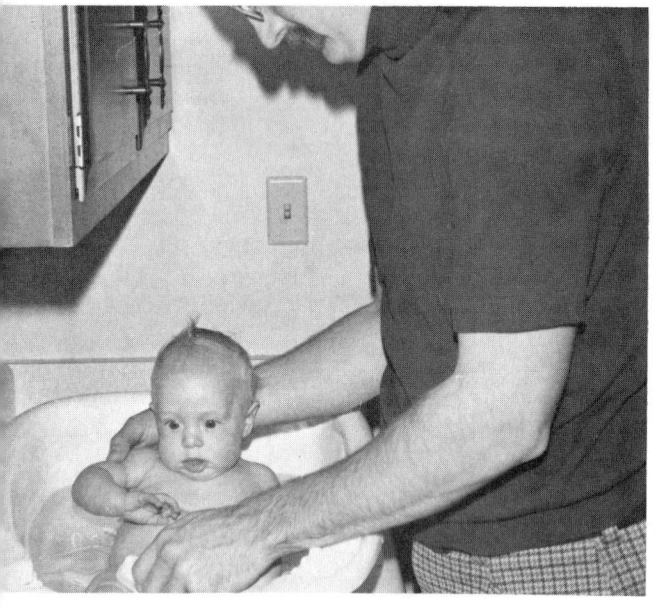

Support the head and shoulders with one arm while washing with the other hand.

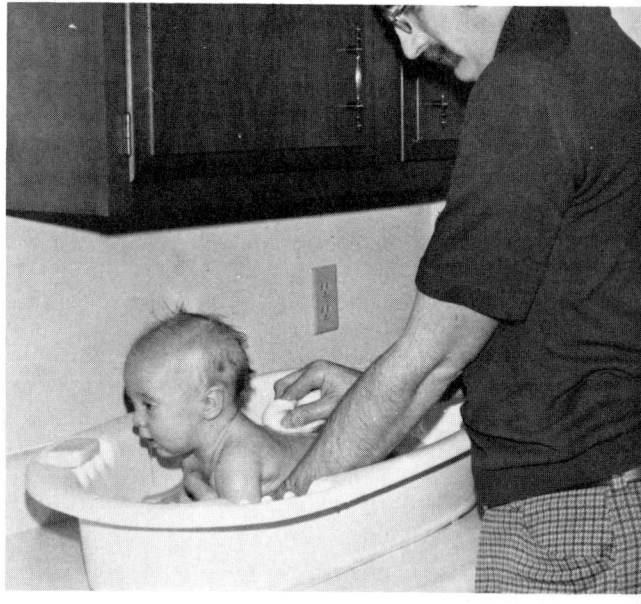

Use one hand for support and the other for washing.

Gently and safely lift baby out of the tub.

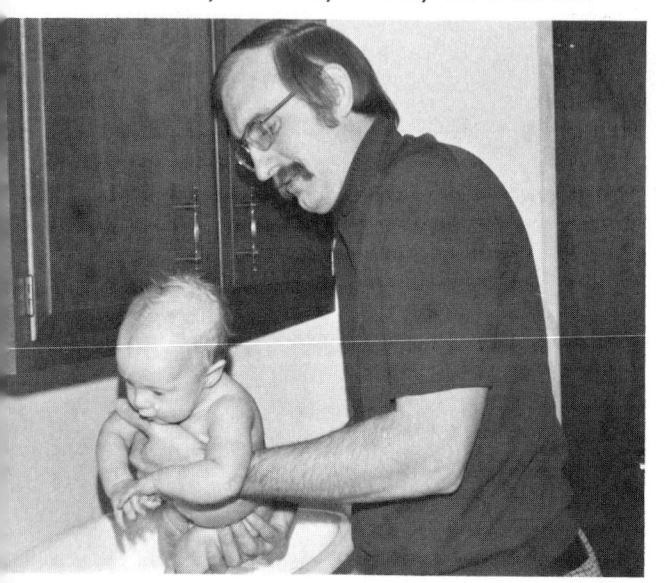

A bath seat helps control the active infant, yet lets her enjoy the fun of floating toys and splashing water.

vent him from inhaling it. Fold the towel over the baby to keep him warm.
- To cleanse the genitals of a male child use small swabs of cotton moistened in oil. Wipe off the excess oil. For a female, gently wipe the genital area with a washcloth. Cleanse from front to back to avoid bringing feces from the anal area into the vagina. Clean the folds of the vulva.
- Now that baby is refreshed from head to toe, dress him in clean clothes and—give him a big hug!

For the very young infant, a sponge bath will be adequate until the naval and/or circumcision is healed completely. The sponge bath is less startling for the baby, and you will feel more confident too if bathing children is a new experience for you. Expose only one area of the baby's body at a time when sponge bathing. Wash and dry each area before proceeding to the next. Start with the face and end with the diaper area.

As babies become familiar with the bathing process, they will feel more secure, enjoying their freedom from cumbersome clothes. Physical activity will turn the bath into play. Splattering and slapping the water and playing with floating toys are part of learning and exploring—and they are fun too. If baby gets too carried away, a bath seat securely attached by suction to the bottom of the tub will help control activity. Taking enough time to play with the baby and enjoy bath time will make this part of the day a pleasure for baby—and for you.

Shampooing

Infants need only one or two hair shampoos weekly. Use a baby shampoo. Hold the baby's face up and tuck him under your arm, holding him snugly against your body. Support the back with your forearm. Placing the baby's head in your hand will give a safe and secure hold. There are devices on the market which may help secure the baby while shampooing.

Lather the hair and rinse with baby's head tilted downward to prevent water from running into the eyes. Talking gently to the baby during this process adds reassurance. You may wish to tell stories and nursery rhymes or sing songs.

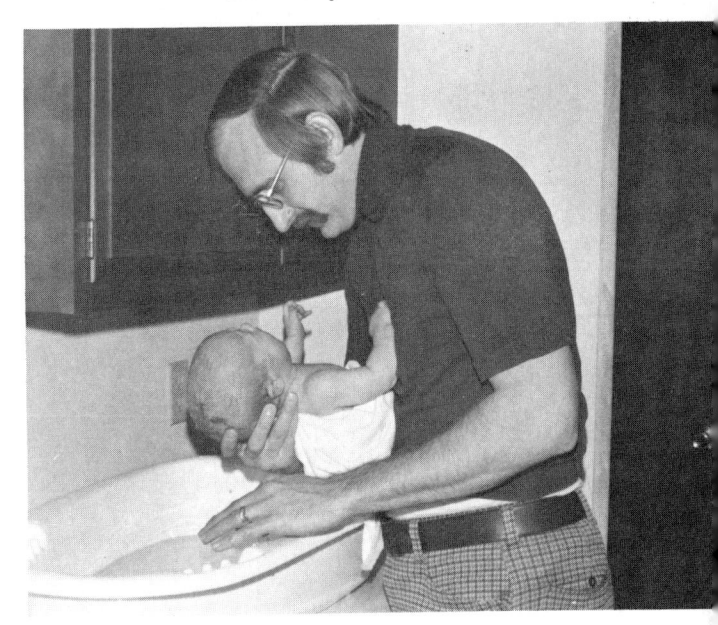

Use a football hold while rinsing after the shampoo.

CLOTHING FOR THE INFANT

Diapers

With a baby around, diapers are a big part of the daily routine. As you care for a baby, you will spend many hours putting on and taking off diapers, often as many as ten changes in a day. Even though the infant can't say so, he is grateful for the

Part III: A Wholesome Environment

Woops! Time out for sunshine between diapers.

comfort he feels when you attend to this chore.

An ample diaper supply is a must. Baby sometimes seems as though he makes sure to dirty diapers nearly as fast as you wash them. Flannel and bird's-eye diapers are often used. To keep them soft, laundry products are available in the stores, but watch how you use them. One young mother in a laundromat was doing the family wash with a friend. Suddenly, the two began to laugh as they peered into the washer. Others around them soon learned why they were so amused. The young mother had accidentally poured fabric softener in the load with her husband's shirts and starch in with the diapers!

A convenient alternative to cloth diapers is the disposable diaper. These are handy for trips and especially busy times. Some mothers use them all the time, even though they are more expensive and add to the ever-increasing quantity of waste produced each day.

Diaper inserts can be purchased to take care of the worst soiling. Mattress pads are also handy in the crib to protect in case the diaper isn't always adequate.

Another type of convenience is the professional diaper service. For a fee, they will pick up, clean, and deliver the diapers. This service could be particularly useful to the child care center that has a number of infants in its charge each day—or to busy mothers with full-time jobs and many home responsibilities.

Changing Diapers

Changing should be done in the baby's crib, if possible, or on a bed with secure sides. You may want to put down a pad of some type for protection. A wash basin or container of clean water should be nearby.

After removing the diaper soiled from urine, cleanse baby with balls of cotton moistened with baby oil. Place cotton in a covered container for disposal. When changing diapers after a bowel movement, cleanse the soiled area of the baby with a soft tissue or toilet paper. Flush the waste down the toilet. Cleanse the diaper area with a soft wet washcloth and follow with baby oil. When diarrhea occurs, special caution must be taken to avoid skin irritation. After careful cleansing, a mild baby lotion may be used on the diaper area.

One way to fold the yard-square diaper is to first fold it lengthwise to three thicknesses. Then fold one end over as needed to fit the baby. Holding the baby's ankles securely, lift his buttocks enough to slip the diaper under. (For girls, the extra thickness will probably be most useful in the back; for boys, use it in front.) Bring the other end of the diaper between the legs and up to the waist. Place the back corners of the diaper over the front corners and pin in place, catching the undershirt at the same time. Use medium-sized pins and place

Ch. 14: Special Care for Infants

Buy only what is needed because babies outgrow their clothes quickly.

Washable, no-iron dresses make laundry time easier for Christie's family.

them perpendicular to baby's body. The infant will not be stuck by the pin if you hold two fingers under the diaper where you are placing the pin. Talking to the infant while you change his diaper adds to his feelings of trust and security while promoting language development.

Wet diapers should be stored in a covered pail until wash time. Fill the pail with a mixture of water and a small amount of borax or vinegar. Before placing soiled diapers in the pail, rinse them in a flushing toilet, always holding tightly to one end. Diapers which are flushed down the toilet can cause expensive plumbing repairs.

Diaper Rash

Diaper rash is a problem for many babies. Several precautionary measures can be taken: boil the diapers, add antiseptic to the rinse water, use extra rinses, or dry diapers in the sun. Regular sun drying is helpful if possible. These procedures will help prevent bacteria that cause the rash. (Some diaper service agencies advertise that procedures they use destroy germs more effectively than home laundering.) Rubber or plastic pants can also aggravate a diaper rash because they hold in moisture. The limitation of their use may help. If the rash is quite troublesome, a medication may be needed. A doctor's assistance should be sought if a serious rash develops in the diaper area or elsewhere.

Other Clothing

When buying clothing for infants, think twice about sizes. Tags and labels generally give recommendations for the appropriate age, but the baby may not fit these at all. Guidelines according to weight are often more helpful. It is wise to buy only a minimum number of items in the small sizes, particularly for newborns. Moreover, do not buy many impractical items. A tiny baby will not need many fancy clothes, and he will outgrow them quickly anyway. Many darling clothing outfits have been wasted because they were too small for a rapidly growing infant.

Part III: A Wholesome Environment

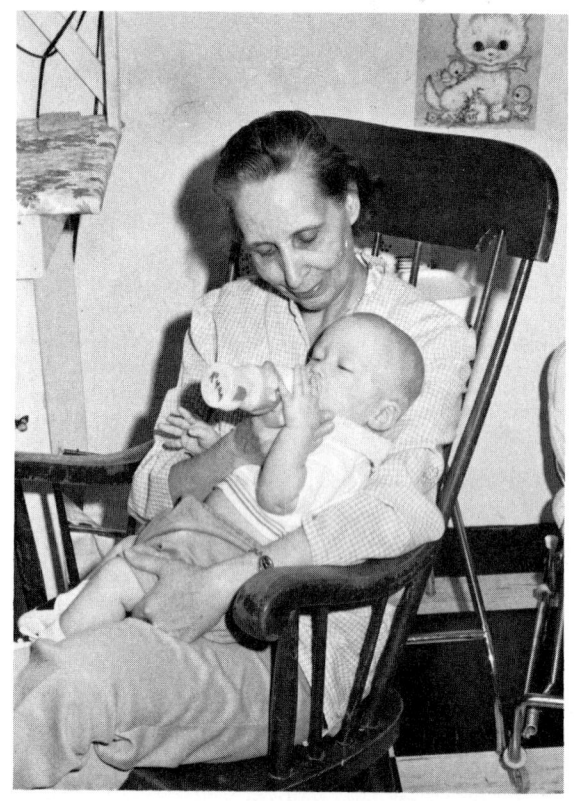

A baby learns the meaning of love through special attention—cuddling, gentle play, and soft words from caring adults.

Booties may be used, but they are often more inconvenient then useful. In trying to keep them on the child, a mother is likely to tie them too tight. Many garments made for infants today have feet in them, eliminating the need for booties.

Other helpful hints on buying clothes for babies can be found in Chapter 13.

SAFE AND LOVING CARE

Safety For Infants

You have read about safety precautions that concern children. Check Chapter 10 for those precautions that apply especially to infants.

In addition, keep these thoughts in mind:

- Protect babies from falling—at tops of stairs, from highchairs and cribs, off of couches and chairs. Use guard rails or remain in the child's presence.
- Check a sleeping baby regularly to be sure the cover is not over his head. If the room temperature is comfortable, only one cover is needed. With several covers in the crib, a baby is more likely to become tangled or completely covered. The blanket can be pinned in place if desired.
- Refrain from placing stuffed animals or other objects in the crib when baby sleeps. These too can block an infant's breathing.

Give Them Love

Regardless of how many precautions you take or how adept you are at feeding, bathing, and diapering the infant, these acts have little meaning without love. A baby knows love through the special attention—cuddling, gentle play, soft words—given by adults.

Obviously, a mother who brings an infant to a child care center each day will not be able to spend a great deal of time giving her baby that special attention. This should seldom be cause for criticism. As you have read, many circumstances often demand that the mother work. Some mothers simply find that they are more effective mothers if they have a self-satisfying outside interest during the day. The reason why the infant is in the center should not affect your attitude. Since more and more mothers are turning to day care centers, it is fast becoming an acceptable practice to people in all walks of life. This, however, puts a heavy responsibility on

Ch. 14: Special Care for Infants

the shoulders of the child care worker. Not only must you know the procedures to follow, but you must also take time to give love. The days may often seem too hectic for this, but it is important. The infant who experiences little or no love through the early years may suffer serious emotional problems in later life. Our world needs happy, healthy people. Will you do what you can to help?

Chapter Highlights

- The treatment an infant receives from others will influence the development of his self-concept which, in turn, affects his entire life.
- In planning for the infant's comfort, include times for feeding, naps, bathing, exercise, play, and affection.
- During the first year of life, the infant experiences the most rapid growth and development.
- Milk is the major food supply for infants, but other foods such as fruits and vegetables, cereals, and meat are usually added to the infant's diet within a few months after birth.
- Some infants may require vitamins which should be given under the direction of a physician.
- A mother generally chooses from two types of feeding schedules: a rigid or *set schedule,* which includes specified times for feeding usually every three or four hours, and the more recent type called *self-demand,* which means feeding the child when hunger is shown by crying or some other form of agitation.
- Breast feeding versus bottle feeding has been a long-debated issue. The use of the bottle makes it possible for someone other than the mother to feed the baby, and bottle formulas can be individually suited to each infant; breast feeding is convenient, good for the baby, and promotes the contraction of the mother's uterus to normal size. Both can provide the infant with a warm and satisfying contact with the mother.
- The adult who is feeding the baby should be relaxed, comfortable, and interested in caring for the child.
- Holding an infant in the arms while feeding offers the comfort of close cuddling, which can be as significant as the food itself.
- When beginning a new way of feeding, adults must be patient and offer attention to help children develop additional trust and confidence in trying something different. One way to help make this a more confortable experience is to provide the correct eating utensils.
- Bathing is an excellent time to exercise tender loving care for infants.
- The baby can never be left alone while bathing.
- When buying clothing for infants, it is wise to buy only a minimum number of items in the small sizes. A tiny baby does not need fancy clothes and will outgrow them quickly. An ample diaper supply is a must with a baby around.
- Some safety precautions that apply especially to infants are: protect babies from falling; check a sleeping baby regularly; and keep stuffed animals or other objects out of the crib when the baby sleeps.
- Regardless of the precautions taken or the effective schedule provided, the infant's care has little meaning without affection—cuddling, gentle play, soft words, and attention to all needs.

Part III: A Wholesome Environment

Thinking It Over

1. What should be included when planning an infant's schedule?
2. What happens to the infant's weight and length during the first year?
3. Do infants require more or less of the adult's time than the toddler? Explain.
4. Which is best for the baby: breast feeding or bottle feeding? Give the reasons for your answer.
5. What does human milk contain in greater amounts than cow's milk?
6. Why are other foods added early in life to the baby's milk diet?
7. How can very young babies be fed other than by bottle or breast?
8. Why are vitamin supplements sometimes added to a baby's diet?
9. What type of feeding schedule did your mother use with the children in your family? Is this schedule similar to any used today? Compare a set schedule with a self-demand schedule.
10. How important is cleanliness in preparing an infant's food? Explain.
11. Do you think babies should be held while taking their bottles? Explain.
12. What are some problems in feeding infants?
13. Should young children be encouraged to feed themselves when they want to try even though they are quite awkward, messy, and inept? Why or why not?
14. What are some safety precautions which must be observed at bath time?
15. There are several ways to take care of diaper needs. Name them.
16. Describe how to diaper a baby.
17. What can be done to lessen the chance of diaper rash?
18. What are some special safety precautions to observe with infants because of their extreme dependence on adults?
19. Taking the role of the child's mother, what would you expect as quality care for infants of working mothers?

Things To Do

1. Make out a 24-hour schedule of all necessary activities for a six-week-old infant, including time for special attention and enrichment of his or her daily life.
2. Have a panel of young or new mothers discuss the feeding problems of infants.
3. Make posters which give step-by-step procedures for sterilizing bottles. Divide the steps among several class members and give a demonstration.
4. Debate the following issues:
   - *Set feeding* schedule versus *self-demand* for infants.
   - Breast versus bottle feeding.
5. Ask a pediatric nurse or a physician to talk with the class about different types of formulas for infants, including the addition of vitamin supplements and other foods in addition to milk.

(Continued on page 247)

Things To Do Continued

6. Using a doll, give a step-by-step demonstration of bathing a baby. As an alternative, make arrangements to visit an infant care center to observe this process. Report your observations to the class.
7. Practice diapering a baby by using a doll or take a trip to an infant care center where this can be observed.
8. Working in groups of three or four students, plan three types of layettes: minimum, adequate, and extravagant. Visit an infant's wear department or use catalogs to provide the costs of these layettes. Discuss the advantages and disadvantages of each of the three layettes.
9. Invite a child care worker to talk with the class about infant care in a center. Provide this person beforehand with a list of questions that have been composed by the class.

Recommended Reading

Can I Love This Place? Washington, D.C.: Educational Systems Corporation, 1969.

McEnery, E. T., M.D., and Syrdam, Margaret Jane. *Feeding Little Folks*. Chicago, Illinois: National Dairy Council, 1952.

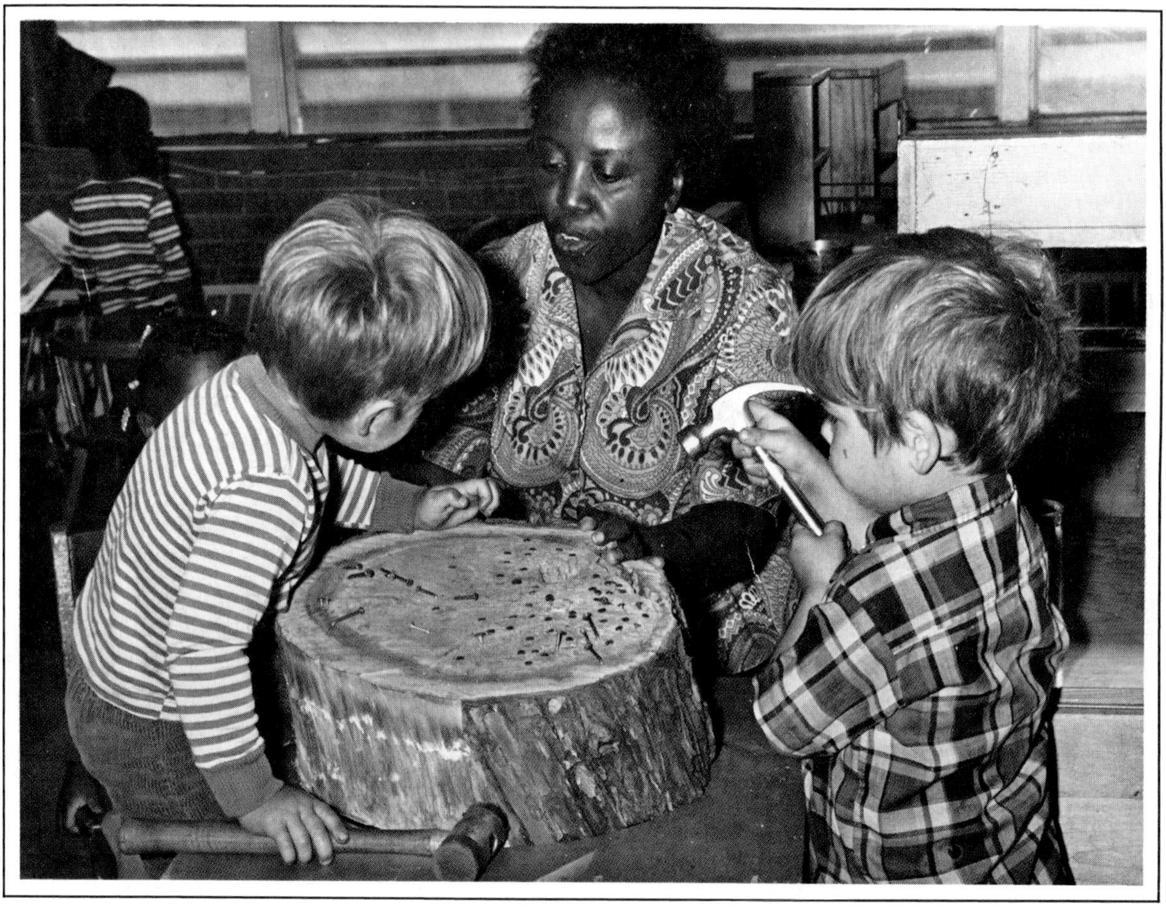

PART IV
Guiding Children's Behavior

Chapter 15.
Learning About Behavior

Chapter 16.
Promoting Responsible Behavior

Chapter 17.
Discipline

Chapter 15.

Learning About Behavior

Your Challenge

This chapter will enable you to . . . .

- *Define behavior.*
- *Describe three types of behavior.*
- *Tell what influences behavior.*
- *Explain some principles that help us understand behavior.*
- *Describe four goals of misbehavior.*
- *Describe some ways children learn behavior.*

WHAT IS BEHAVIOR?

Actions and reactions, prompted by a combination of thoughts and feelings, make up *behavior*. Someone observing the actions of a child would be seeing a *display* of thoughts and feelings through behavior. Here, action refers to what the child is doing. Running, shouting, or sitting quietly and looking at a picture book are all examples of behavior.

As you know, behavior may be *positive* or *negative*. The following definitions will help you understand and deal with children's behavior—as well as the behavior of adults, for that matter.

- *Positive behavior*—actions appropriate in a given time, place, and situation (also called acceptable or good behavior). For example, Lottie may roll and tumble, screeching and making loud noises while outdoors during the free play period. This is considered positive behavior because it is appropriate in time—during the free play period; place—outdoors; and situation—children are free to engage in the activities they choose.
- *Negative behavior*—actions inappropriate in a given time, place, and situation (also called unacceptable or bad behavior or misbehavior). Take the above example of Lottie. If she rolled and tumbled, screeching and making loud noises while indoors where others were having story time or during nap time, this would be considered negative behavior. Why?
- *Exceptional behavior*—actions which are not approved of but are tolerated for special reasons. The adult response may indicate that the behavior is tolerated only because of certain circumstances but that it is not usually appropriate. For instance, if two-year-old Marie is away from home and she becomes very hungry

and tired, she may begin to fuss or cry. Although the fussing is not considered positive behavior, it is tolerated because her parents know why she is crying. Marie has a good reason.

Of course, children make mistakes in judgment while they are learning self-discipline. Even though their behavior is inappropriate, it may be tolerated. This was the attitude toward Ignacio as he learned to feed himself. While eating, he spilled some milk because he had not gained full control of his hand muscles. His grandmother, who cared for him, understood that Ignacio must make mistakes before mastering the art of eating. Therefore she tolerated his behavior.

A child may misbehave because he is upset for special reasons such as an accident, illness, moving to a new neighborhood, or starting to school for the first time. Again, one must be willing and able to look at each situation from the child's viewpoint.

Some misbehavior cannot be allowed and must be stopped. This type of negative behavior may endanger the health or well-being of the child or someone else. It may even include behavior which is in conflict with the law or society. Can you think of some examples of this type of misbehavior?

In talking about behavior, we seldom refrain from making a judgment. For example, Christy is finger painting at the art table. You can describe her behavior, but can you say it is positive or negative? You probably cannot until you know how she is acting. Just the fact that she is doing something, finger painting in this case, does not necessarily constitute positive or negative behavior. Christy deliberately smears paint on Philip's storybook. Now describe the nature of Christy's behavior? Have you also judged her behavior? What if Philip pulled Christy's hair first?

Obviously the term behavior is subject to a number of qualifying words—good, bad, acceptable, unacceptable, and many others. It would be impossible, however, to divide behavior into specific categories like good and bad for all people.

Why is this true? Probably because not all people live by the same set of values or the same standards. For example, an old Japanese custom made it appropriate to belch following a good meal. This was a compliment to the cook. In America, however, most children are taught that this behavior is in poor taste. Even in the same community, behavioral standards may not be the same. Some men, for example, never open doors for women. Some women approve of this and others do not. You can see that standards for all behavior would be very difficult to establish. Nevertheless, we try to develop certain standards that promote the well-being of people and help maintain some social organization. We pass laws for the country, make rules in schools, set up policies in business, and enforce standards in the home, to name a few.

What does this have to do with you as a future parent or child care worker? It should give you an understanding about differences in behavior. It should help you see that children in child care centers come from all kinds of families and environments. Races and religions will be different; income levels will be different; and so will behavior. You cannot expect every child to conform to all of your standards. It is important that you appreciate and respect the differences. If you do, it will be much simpler to help children learn those expectations of behavior that must be enforced in the center.

Part IV: Guiding Children's Behavior

Children are influenced by the amount and kind of personal care they receive.

WHAT INFLUENCES BEHAVIOR?

As you know, behavior is a display of thoughts and feelings through action. Several forces, both external and internal, influence thoughts and feelings.

The *external forces* are the same ones you have read about before—people and the environment. We know from experience that what happens to us through our own lives affects the way we behave. Playmates, parents, and others may influence what children think about and how they feel. Behavior is often learned from others. Children learn to behave in certain ways by watching the people around them.

Every child encounters a unique range of experiences which combine to make him think, feel, and act the way he does. Each learns and feels what it is like to have someone help or ignore him. Every child is influenced by the impact of personal care or neglect. Depending on the home situation, a child may experience hunger, cruelty, love, sharing, poverty, prejudice, or wealth. The list seems endless.

You can readily see why behavior is so difficult to analyze. As a child care worker, you can only know a small portion of all the influence upon children. You can, however, communicate with children and get to know them.

Through daily interactions, you may discover some of the *internal forces* that influence each child. What goes on inside the child to make him behave as he does? This is a key question for every child care worker. In child guidance today, a well-recognized concept is that behavior has a *purpose,* or *goal.* Children have reasons for their actions, for the way they behave.

Todd, for example, would not cooperate at rest time. Even though the other children quietly lay down to rest, Todd would not. One key to understanding this situation is to look at it from the child's point of view. See it through the child's eyes and discover his goal. Remember, understanding anyone's goal helps understand his behavior. With Todd, a few thoughtful questions helped the teacher learn that Todd had spotted a new toy and wanted to play rather than rest. The teacher then assured Todd that playtime would follow nap time and asked him to lie down and watch as she placed the toy on a shelf where it would be saved for him. This time, Todd cooperated. Not all situations, of course, will be so easy to handle, primarily because the purpose of one's behavior is strengthened by *motivation.*

Motivation is an underlying force which stimulates, or excites, a person to strive for some goal or to try to satisfy some need. **Motivation** leads behavior toward a purpose.

Note that Todd was uncooperative simply because he wanted to play with a new toy. What if he demanded to play with the toy (his behavior), but what he really wanted was attention (his goal)? Now the child care worker's job is doubly difficult. What is Todd's motivation? What is the driving force that leads him toward further misbehavior? The child care worker should consider the possibility that Todd's real problem concerns more than just the desire to play with a new toy.

To discover the purpose of a child's behavior look at the situation from his point of view, as was done with Todd. Ask yourself these questions:

- What is the child's goal?
- What is the motivation behind that goal?
- What are the child's true needs?

Also, look for clues that help reveal both goals and motivations—repetitious behavior, self-assertive behavior aimed at establishing identity, and the developmental stage of the child, to name a few.

UNDERSTANDING BEHAVIOR

Understanding and dealing with behavior is probably one of the most difficult tasks a parent or child care worker must face. Although you may not have the background qualifying you to be an expert on the subject, you can learn a few principles that will help increase your understanding.

You begin to understand why children behave certain ways as you see them relating to others—as you see them interacting in situations. Generally, your best insights into understanding behavior will be gained by considering the child in two roles:

- As an individual—the child's concept of self, signs of independence, special style of behaving, and unique mental and physical characteristics.
- As a participator—the child's interaction and relationships with peers, older children, parents, and others.

Every child's behavior has a purpose. What might be motivating the actions of these youngsters?

Observing children in light of these two roles gives us information useful for planning activities with them. As you understand each child's special ways of behaving, you can help them enjoy daily activities which support and build character as well as healthy bodies. Each child benefits from success experiences as an individual and as a member of a group.

It is not always easy, however, for a child to behave as a part of the group and at the same time maintain identity as an individual. On the one hand, the child tries to *break out* and be a separate person; on the other hand, the child strives to be a

253

Part IV: Guiding Children's Behavior

As you see children interact with each other, you begin to understand their behavior.

part of a group, conforming to expectations of others in order to *fit in*. Can you see why we sometimes have difficulty getting children to cooperate? Can you see why children may become frustrated at times? They do not always make good judgments about when to exercise independence and when to conform.

We live by some basic *assumptions*—or accepted ideas—about people. Consider these, too, when working with children. By accepting these assumptions, it may be easier to understand children and the reasons for their behavior:

- Every person has certain rights and privileges which are his own.
- Every person has worth and dignity.
- Every person wants to contribute to a group.
- Every person has responsibilities.
- Every person must, at times, face desirable or undesirable consequences of his or her behavior.

Just as every child is a unique person, each grows and learns in a unique way. Each develops a *pattern of behavior*, a manner of behaving which is repeated and therefore can be expected or anticipated. We can look forward to the child behaving in a similar way under similar circumstances.

As you explore ways of helping children develop healthy patterns of behavior, review some of their basic emotional needs:

- *Security.* Every child needs to develop thoughts and feelings of safety, security, and self-confidence.
- *Belonging.* Every child has a desire to feel the rapport, or harmony, of family, friends, and others.
- *Recognition.* Children seek approval for, or sympathy with, their efforts and accomplishments. More simply, they like to be noticed rather than ignored.
- *Affection.* Children want a warm re-

sponse from adults and other children; they need personal care and attention.
- *New experiences.* Children need new experiences, new ways of learning, growing, and discovering the world about them.

As children grow and learn, they try to fulfill these emotional needs. Through their behavior patterns, you will be able to see which children have the greatest needs in this area.

UNDERSTANDING MISBEHAVIOR

All behavior, even that which is negative, has its roots in a child's goal and motivation, as mentioned earlier. What does the child really want? What is his target? Why is he determined to act a certain way? What is the driving force that leads him to misbehave? When you learn the answers to these questions, you begin to understand why a child acts as he does. It becomes easier to help children redirect their misbehavior into desirable actions when you understand their purposes. You can also help children achieve their goals in appropriate ways if you understand what they are after. If a child wants attention, there are healthy ways to achieve this goal and to satisfy a basic need.

Goals of Misbehavior

Have you thought about children having goals of misbehavior? A child may act in a way which he thinks will enable him to get what he wants even if it does not meet with the approval of others or even if his behavior is harmful.

Let's review some desires which all children (and adults, too) experience. These give clues to why a child misbehaves; to the motivation which drives a child toward his goal:

Ch. 15: Learning About Behavior

Understanding the child's behavior requires patience and concern.

- The child wants to feel important in his own eyes.
- The child needs to receive attention and recognition from others.
- The child seeks ways to prove his abilities or to compensate for his weaknesses and failures.

Dr. Rudolph Dreikurs, a child psychiatrist, formulated *four goals of misbehavior*. These help illustrate why children misbehave.

Attention

The desire for attention is not only a goal for many young children but is one experienced by many adults. Also, like children, some adults misbehave in order to get attention—even though they are grown up. Do you get the idea? The motivation to feel

255

significant and to receive recognition from others is so strong that some people use whatever means they can to succeed, even if inappropriate. There are several ways a child may begin to compensate for feelings of inferiority. He may put into operation attention-getting devices, usually beginning with simple acts of misbehavior such as acting silly, showing off, nagging at others, and being a nuisance.

If a child does not achieve the goal of attention with simple acts, he may resort to less appropriate ways of behaving, such as temper tantrums, hitting, kicking, screaming, fighting, calling names, making loud and obnoxious noises, throwing things, and refusing to cooperate.

Providing wholesome ways for children to receive attention helps prevent much of the misbehavior related to this goal. Providing interesting and exciting things for children to do often helps them achieve their goals without misbehavior. For example, art activities bring attention to children's work through displays of pictures, crafts, and other items children create—even if they are never completed. Praise for a job well done or attention to efforts of a given task are positive ways to recognize children and give them attention. Greeting each by name as they arrive at the center as well as calling each by name in group activities gives attention and makes children feel important.

Of course, some children require more attention than others; some get little at home, yet others may get too much. Learn all you can about each child and find ways to satisfy the desire for attention without misbehavior.

Power

A child may have a desire for power. This is another common goal of misbehavior. Even young children experience a need to feel that they are in command or in charge from time to time. (Obviously, power is another goal which many adults strive for in everyday living.) Children benefit from activities which enable them to exercise leadership and gain recognition for responsible action—being in charge of snack time in a small group and having the task of handing out napkins; pouring juice; counting cookies; starting the record player when it is time to begin a new activity with music; leading a song; and telling about an exciting event.

How can you achieve successful results in dealing with the child whose goal of misbehavior is power? First, avoid a power struggle because no one will win. Children have almost endless energy, and the more intense the situation becomes, the more excited the child gets and the more powerful is the motivation to succeed. This excitement often gives the child greater energy to continue the fight. Adults often become angry or disgusted and force the child to cease his misbehavior. This may end the power struggle for the moment and may achieve immediate obedience, but it does little else. The adult may make the child conform to certain behavior; however, in most cases little has been taught, and the child will more than likely misbehave again if the opportunity arises. Sometimes strong measures of fear and negative punishment are used which may harm the child's self-esteem and/or relationship with adults. In any case, the adult loses the long-range goal for the child—that of helping him develop positive and rewarding behavior patterns.

Sometimes a child will feel successful in the struggle for power just by observing that the adult has lost self-control. If the child is punished as a result of a power struggle, he may experience quick relief from the guilt of misbehavior by paying the price for being bad. The child, in this situation, may consider the consequences not serious enough to prevent similar behavior in the future.

The following points for dealing with problems of a power struggle will be helpful as you work with children in a center or in your family:

- Maintain respect for the child and for yourself.
- Remain calm and keep a moderate but firm tone of voice.
- Avoid a conflict in the form of words or physical action.
- Direct comments to the child's actions rather than character.
- Use positive and simple statements. Say what is necessary and then stop talking—don't say too much.
- Get on the child's eye level in a dialogue.

When working with children, kneel or stoop down so the children do not have to always look up. Have you thought about what it feels like for children to always look up to adults? In some cases this may increase a child's desire to seek power.

Revenge

Children who think no one likes them or who feel mistreated may seek revenge. This is a serious problem of misbehavior. The child's goal is retaliation, usually against an adult. The child's misbehavior often leaves the adult feeling hurt and personally attacked. Children who are thwarted, or not allowed to explore and express themselves freely, may feel a desire to retaliate against the adult to whom they are responsible.

To work effectively with a child who is seeking revenge, you must understand some of the reasons why the child has moved to this level of misbehavior. Motivation to seek revenge may result from a power struggle, especially if the child was forced to be obedient. Revenge takes many forms, such as refusal to cooperate, running away, self-inflicted harm, disrespectful comments, and telling lies. An extreme case of revenge may result in suicide. The very young child may resort to such action as kicking, hitting, biting, tearing things apart, purposely marking walls and furniture, refusing to participate, and withdrawing love.

If a child feels successful in revengeful behavior, it will likely occur again. For some children revenge is a way to get recognition for being destructive or negative. An expression of their feelings might be something like this: "If I can't be good, I'll be bad and then you will be sorry." "At least, I can be horrible."

Disability

The fourth goal of misbehavior is a real or imagined disability. A child may try to fail when all else has been unsuccessful. The child who misbehaves but is unable to achieve recognition and power resorts to a display of inability. This behavior often impresses the adult with feelings of extreme sympathy for the child or utter despair, thus leaving the child in a position to do whatever he wants. The child deliberately resorts to failure as a way to achieve his goal. "I can be successful as a failure." "They cannot keep me from failing." The child still has a place in the world, even though as a failure. The child who assumes the role of being a failure but is still active, may become destructive and sometimes violent. As long as he is physically active, however, there is a chance he can be helped to redirect his actions into

Part IV: Guiding Children's Behavior

A child may learn by modeling another child's actions.

Oklahoma Vo Tech

appropriate or winning behavior. You will be wise to seek professional assistance in working with a child who has reached this stage of misbehavior.

The passive (inactive) child at this stage of misbehavior usually gives up and refuses to do anything. He withdraws from others, finding satisfaction in being unmovable and uncooperative. He does nothing and he says nothing. It is difficult to help a child at this level because he views his image as one of failure and he refuses all offers of help. Again, professional assistance is usually needed in working with a child who displays this behavior.

WAYS CHILDREN LEARN BEHAVIOR

The more we know about how children learn, the easier it will be to help them develop satisfying and appropriate patterns of behavior. Consider these ways in which children (and all of us for that matter) learn from others and from experiences in daily living.

Imitation and Identification

Children often learn by *imitating* or modeling someone else's behavior. They repeat or copy another's actions, either consciously or subconsciously. A child's behavior may change if he or she is motivated to imitate someone else.

Some children learn by *identifying* with another person whom they like and respect. Allegiance to, or acceptance of, the same values of the other person is shown. When a child chooses someone as ideal, he begins to acquire the same likes and dislikes, often striving to look and act just like the ideal person.

Imitation and identification are closely related since a child often imitates the person with whom he is identifying. Studies reveal, however, that just because imitative behavior is observed, this does not necessarily mean that identification has occurred. Children may imitate the actions of others even when they do not actually wish to be like them.

Imitation and identification are so common that we may not realize a child is using someone as a model. Therefore, children need many examples of positive behavior to serve effectively as guides.

Ch. 15: Learning About Behavior

Character symbols such as politeness and respectfulness are skills for social behavior which are sometimes learned through imitation or identification. Because children often learn these skills by watching others' behavior, adults should consistently set appropriate examples. Adults may undo previous teaching by their own inconsistencies. For example, when an adult scolds a child who was impolite and is rude himself, something is amiss. The do-as-I-say, not-as-I-do philosophy merits little respect. Many children notice such inconsistencies. Even if they do not notice, of course, our influence should still be the best possible.

Reinforcement

Children often behave in ways that bring them satisfaction and rewards. A child may be motivated to behave in a particular manner because of the pleasure enjoyed as the result of his actions. A complimentary statement, a gesture of affection, or recognition in some meaningful way is enjoyed by the child after certain performances. This method of learning is called *positive reinforcement.*

For example, one morning at a day care center, four-year-old Eddie took it upon himself to clean up the table after the morning snack. Upon noticing this, Miss Murray, the aide, praised Eddie highly for his efforts. Pleased with himself for receiving this recognition, Eddie continued to follow this routine each day. Occasionally, if Miss Murray did not happen to recognize Eddie's fine accomplishment, he would carefully point out to her how clean the table was. Eddie, of course, was motivated to behave in a way that pleased Miss Murray simply because she made him feel good about his actions. The recognition Eddie received is called a *stimulus.* The

By praising the boy, this child care worker has given him a feeling of satisfaction. Will he be likely to repeat the praiseworthy behavior another time?

stimulus brought pleasure and *reinforced* Eddie to repeat his behavior so he could receive the stimulus again.

It is a good idea here to note that sincere verbal responses are generally most useful. In addition to personal recognition, offering material reinforcers like tokens and toys can encourage and actually shape behavior—the child repeats certain behavior in order to receive a material stimulus. Using *only* material stimuli, of course, should neither be the ultimate goal of rein-

Part IV: Guiding Children's Behavior

forcement nor decrease or eliminate the all-important personal contacts that come with verbal exchanges.

This does not mean, however, that material reinforcement should not be used. Some people, especially those who work with disadvantaged children or children with learning problems, find that material reinforcers are quite useful if handled properly and accompanied by a few words of praise.

Consider the group of kindergarten children who took part in a "token economy" approach to learning. The teacher handed out small plastic animals when children put forth an effort or achieved a given task in such activities as art, music, story time, block play, and manipulative experiences. At the end of the morning, these could be exchanged for participation in a favorite activity. Some teachers used raisins as reinforcers; the children ate them immediately. Others used tokens that have exchange value; they were traded for extra milk or fruit or for special activities and equipment during free time. Other teachers have applied this same technique of reinforcement to suit their own situations.

Reinforcement can also be used to help children learn how *not* to behave, because they learn to expect unpleasant consequences or simply no stimulus at all. They learn to avoid doing things which cause negative reinforcement. For example, in some programs if a child misbehaves in a group setting he may receive *time out*. This means that for a certain time, such as two to three minutes, he cannot participate in any activities. Another example of unpleasant reinforcement is simply no recognition of the inappropriate behavior.

Studies have shown, however, that the most effective learning generally occurs through positive or pleasant experiences rather than through negative or painful experiences. With many positive reinforcers, children can enjoy the results of their good behavior. Negative experiences do not provide this opportunity. Relate this principle to yourself and you be the judge: Do you react better to a person who ignores your efforts or to one who offers praise?

Learning to behave may start with *extrinsic motivation*—something in the child's environment that causes him to want to behave a certain way. The basic idea behind using reinforcement is to help the child be able to control his behavior and motivate himself without special rewards. The goal is for the child eventually to achieve *intrinsic motivation,* or *self-motivation*—something inside the child causes him to want to behave in a certain way. This is shown in the diagram.

Eventually, most children begin to recognize their independence and will behave appropriately without continual guidance. As they develop self-confidence and skills for daily living, they gradually start behaving appropriately without looking for rewards, assuming, of course, that no other problems enter in. As children enjoy learn-

MOTIVATION

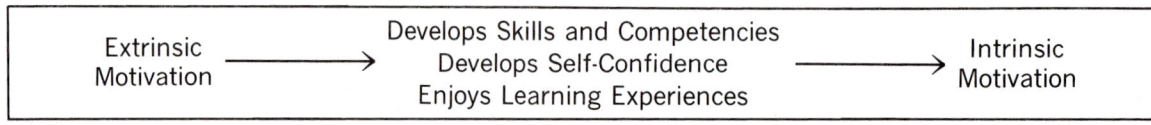

| Extrinsic Motivation | → | Develops Skills and Competencies
Develops Self-Confidence
Enjoys Learning Experiences | → | Intrinsic Motivation |

Ch. 15: Learning About Behavior

ing through meaningful activities, they are more likely to be self-motivated.

Insight

Children learn living skills and problem solving—ways to explore and deal with their environment—through insight. *Insight* means the ability to think and reason so as to learn the nature of things. Insight promotes understanding. Helping the child think about his behavior through explanation and illustration leads to understanding, or insight. Through many daily experiences with objects and the general surroundings, concepts are formed. The child begins to relate, or put together, ideas and information in such a way as to develop understandings. When an adult explains to the child what will happen if certain things are done, this provides information the child needs to develop the concepts on his own. Insight is especially useful to children as they develop intellectual and social maturity—as they interact with the environment and get along with others.

As children expand their experiences and as they mature, insight is gained. They continuously receive information about themselves and others. Even though they do not understand everything they come in contact with, they store up information and experiences that will eventually have meaning, thus bringing about insight.

Until age three, Nicoli had to be watched closely by his mother in order to prevent him from wandering into the street. Although she told him many times of the danger, he did not understand. It was natural that Nicoli would be eager to explore his surroundings, moving further and further away from familiar territory. Eventually, Nicoli became more aware of safety when he and his mother could talk together

Kickapoo Head Start Center

A child gains insight through everyday experiences.

about what can happen when a little boy goes into streets without holding an adult's hand. He gradually began to understand the reason for limits in this situation.

It is more practical to describe to children the possible results of some activity before it actually occurs than to let them always learn by trial and error. As you read the example that follows, note how Miss Santini, the child care worker, used not only insight but also imitation and reinforcement to help Jake.

In an effort to wash modeling clay off his hands, Jake stood at the sink conscientiously rubbing a bar of soap between his hands. Miss Santini noticed that the water was very near the top of the sink and still running. Knowing that she had to intervene to prevent a mishap, Miss Santini walked over and calmly turned off the water. After draining a little water from the sink, she showed Jake how to turn the water on and off (leading to imitation) and

Part IV: Guiding Children's Behavior

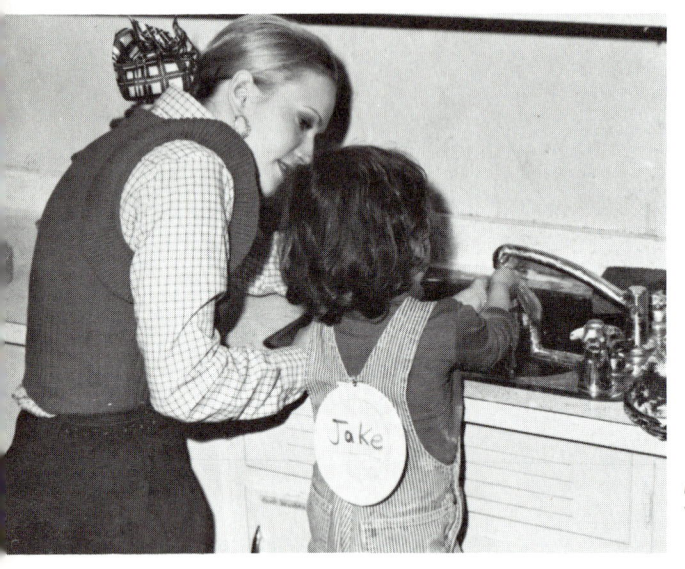

praised Jake's ability to do the same successfully (reinforcement). Miss Santini followed this intervention with a brief explanation of what happens when the water fills the sink and spills over, pointing out the amount of work that would be needed to clean up spilled water (insight). Consequently, what could have been an unpleasant situation for Jake became a learning experience instead. Do you see the value of using each of these approaches with young children?

University of Oklahoma Institute of Child Development
The child care worker helps Jake learn through modeling, insight, and reinforcement.

Chapter Highlights

- Actions and reactions, prompted by a combination of thoughts and feelings make up *behavior*.
- *Positive* behavior is action appropriate in a given time, place, and situation; it is also called acceptable or good behavior.
- *Negative* behavior is action inappropriate in a given time, place, and situation; it is also called unacceptable or bad behavior or misbehavior.
- *Exceptional* behavior is action not generally approved of but tolerated for special reasons.
- Some misbehavior cannot be allowed and must be stopped. It usually endangers the health or well-being of the child or someone else.
- Because community behavioral standards may not be the same, you cannot expect every child to conform to the same standards.
- Every child encounters a unique range of experiences which combine to make him think, feel, and act the way he does, making behavior very difficult to analyze.
- Children have reasons for their actions and for the way they behave; thus many child guidance authorities say behavior has a purpose, or goal.
- Your best insights into understanding behavior will usually be gained by considering the child in two roles: as an individual and as a participator.
- In helping children develop healthy patterns of behavior, basic emotional needs should be reviewed: security; belonging; recognition; affection; and new experiences.
- Dr. Rudolph Dreikurs, a child psychiatrist, formulated *four goals of misbehavior*: attention; power; revenge; and disability.

Ch. 15: Learning About Behavior

- The more we know about how children learn, the easier it will be to help them develop satisfying and appropriate patterns of behavior.
- *Imitation* and *identification* are such common ways children learn that we may not realize a child is using someone as a model.
- Children often behave in ways that bring them satisfaction and rewards—*positive reinforcement.*
- Reinforcement starts with *extrinsic motivation*—something in the child's environment that causes him to want to behave a certain way. The goal is for the child to achieve *intrinsic* or *self-motivation*—something inside the child that causes him to want to behave a certain way.
- Children learn living skills and problem solving—ways to explore and deal with their environment—through *insight.*
- It is usually more practical to describe to children the possible results of some activity before it actually occurs than to let them always learn by trial and error.

Thinking It Over

1. What does the word *behavior* mean?
2. What is meant by the terms *positive, negative,* and *exceptional behavior?*
3. Do time, place, and situation alter the appropriateness or inappropriateness of certain behavior? How?
4. Can behavior be categorized as good or bad for all people? Explain.
5. How can behavioral standards be established for the children in a child care center?
6. What is meant by external and internal influence on behavior?
7. What is meant by this statement: Behavior has a purpose or goal?
8. Can you always find the reason for a child's actions? Explain.
9. How important is the *motivational* aspect of behavior?
10. Is it ever difficult for you to decide whether to be an individual or to conform? How much harder is this decision for a young child? Give examples.
11. Name four basic emotional needs we all have? How do these affect a child's behavior?
12. Explain briefly Dr. Rudolph Dreikurs' *four goals* of *misbehavior.*
13. Which one of Dr. Dreikurs' goals of misbehavior is most serious? Why?
14. Have you ever had a power struggle with a child? Who really won? Why is it wise to avoid a power struggle? How can power struggles be prevented?
15. Describe three ways children learn behavior.
16. What is the difference in learning through imitation and learning through identification?
17. How does extrinsic motivation differ from intrinsic motivation?
18. How does *insight* promote appropriate behavior?

Part IV: Guiding Children's Behavior

Things To Do

1. Write an anecdote about an example of behavior which can be positive, negative, and exceptional, depending on the time, place, and situation.
2. Relate a recent episode of your own behavior, either positive or negative, and explain the reason for the behavior as you see it. Discuss the reasons with your class.
3. Observe children in child care centers to identify examples of Dr. Dreikurs' four goals of misbehavior.
4. List examples of your own behavior which resulted from insight and examples of inappropriate behavior resulting from not heeding insight.
5. Observe a young child for several sessions and list the types of behavior observed, giving explanations for each based on information in this chapter.
6. Discuss examples of misbehavior and suggest ways to help children redirect their actions to positive behavior.

Recommended Reading

Chess, Stella, and others. *Your Child Is a Person*. New York: Viking Press, 1965.
Dreikurs, Rudolf, M.D. *Children: The Challenge*. New York: Hawthorn Books, Inc., 1964.
Dreikurs, Rudolf, M.D. *The Challenge of Parenthood*. New York: Hawthorn Books, Inc., 1948.
Ginott, Haim G. *Between Parent and Child*. New York: Macmillan Publishing Co., Inc., 1965.
Hymes, James L., Jr. *Behavior and Discipline*. Englewood Cliffs, New Jersey: Prentice-Hall, Inc., 1965.
Hymes, James L., Jr. *The Child Under Six*. Englewood Cliffs, New Jersey: Prentice-Hall, Inc., 1963.
Osborne, Ernest. *Democracy Begins in the Home*. Public Affairs Pamphlet, #192, 381 Park Avenue South, New York, 1953.

Chapter 16.

Promoting Responsible Behavior

Your Challenge

This chapter will enable you to . . . .

- List ways to instill a sense of responsibility in children.
- Describe how to communicate effectively with children.
- Explain how your own attitude is important in dealing with behavior.
- Tell how an encouraging and positive response is helpful.
- Explain the use of imitation, reinforcement, and insight in dealing with behavior.
- Describe how removing the causes of misbehavior and providing a suitable environment are helpful.

A SENSE OF RESPONSIBILITY

Developing responsibility in children means preparing them to accept the results of their own behavior. All people need a sense of responsibility in order to get along with others and to be content with themselves. As children become more responsible, they are better able to accept and deal with the unpleasant parts of life. Of course, responsible behavior usually brings pleasant and satisfying results, too. Early promotion of responsible behavior, which is appropriate for the developmental level, gives the child a better start in life.

How can we instill a sense of responsibility in children? In this chapter you will discover many ways.

LEARN TO COMMUNICATE WITH CHILDREN

Effective communication is the real key to helping children learn responsible behavior. If you cannot communicate well with children, the principles you want them to learn may not be clear to them. Communication means the sending and receiving of messages in such a way that the messages have meaning and are understood. There are many ways to communicate with children—talking, gestures, facial expressions, and other actions. The most common, of course, is to communicate with words.

One of the best ways to be sure a child is getting the correct message is to keep the

Ch. 16: Promoting Responsible Behavior

communication simple and to keep the channels open and clear. For example, when children are very upset, they cannot concentrate on what someone is telling them. Until they are calm, the channel for receiving a message is probably closed.

You read earlier that much of what goes on inside each child is not readily detected by the child care worker. Communicating with the child will help you discover some of these innermost thoughts and feelings. As a guide to successful communications, try the suggestions that follow.

Get On The Child's Level

This suggestion has three meanings. You are already familiar with the first. *Look at the situation from the child's viewpoint.* Try to understand as though you were in the child's place.

It is surprising to think how many concepts adults take for granted but which are totally unknown to small children. In the last chapter, remember how Jake came close to letting the water in the sink run over? Miss Santini realized that Jake did not understand how water continues to fill the sink until it spills over the edge. Another adult, attributing his own level of knowledge to Jake, might have scolded the boy for letting the water run to the top. Do you see how easy it is to expect a child to understand more than he is capable of at the time? As further evidence, think of the refreshingly simple questions that children ask about things which adults take for granted—questions like: Where does the rain come from? Why does the moon keep moving? Where do hospitals get their babies? Is it any wonder that we must at least try to see the child's viewpoint before we can respond correctly?

Secondly, get on the child's level by kneeling or sitting on the floor to talk face-

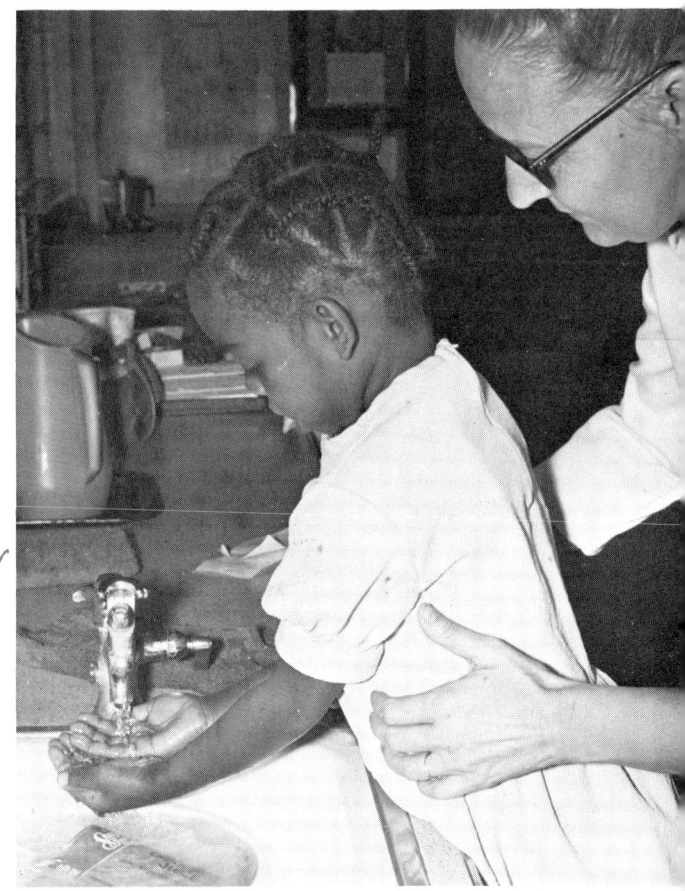

Oklahoma VoTech (Stillwater Head Start)
There are many ways to communicate with children—talking, facial expressions, and body gestures. Are words being used here?

to-face with the child. Some centers have short stools for this purpose.

Finally, get on the child's level by using vocabulary and terms the child will understand. You can relate this principle to yourself. What does the next sentence do for you? "Sedulously avoid polysyllabic profundity and pompous prolixity." Now imagine the child's dilemma with much simpler sentences.

Part IV: Guiding Children's Behavior

Maintain Respect

All behavior, including what is said or done, should be treated with respect for the child and yourself. Each person is entitled to dignity and the preservation of individual rights, even when disagreement or unpleasantness occurs. Differences in people's personalities and styles of living may cause conflicts. These differences may conflict with what is considered acceptable or appropriate. Nevertheless, respect must be granted. Ways to maintain respect include:

- Listening to the child's point of view.
- Treating the child as a worthwhile person.
- Avoiding sudden outbursts of your temper, such as shouting or hitting.

When an adult speaks too loudly to a child, the child usually becomes more anxious and upset. When children are upset, their emotional activity becomes so great that they often do not listen or think clearly. If the adult speaks calmly, it tends to settle the atmosphere for the children. Be patient. Give children an opportunity to get ready before communicating.

Sympathize With the Child

Before instructing or correcting a child, doesn't it seem appropriate to tell the child you understand how he or she must feel? A statement which shows understanding (before giving the main message) often helps a child know that you are sharing his feelings and that you do sympathize with his situation, even though you may not agree with his behavior. Such a statement usually helps clear the channel for the main message. Letting a child know that you understand that he is angry or frustrated, even though you cannot allow him to violate the limits, helps the child recognize that his feelings are acknowledged. This will sometimes allow him to rechannel his activities into acceptable directions. To tell a child, "Now that didn't hurt; you're a big boy, so don't cry," is to deny his legitimate feelings. If children know their thoughts and feelings are understood, they will be more likely to listen to what you have to say. Consider this example:

Situation: Tony, age three, begins to cry when Richard, age four, grabs a toy from him on the nursery playground.

Avoid This

"Richard, give the toy back to Tony. Good boys don't grab things like that. You mustn't make Tony cry; now give the toy back."

Try This

"I know you want to play with the toy, Richard. It's hard to wait when you're excited, but you will have to wait your turn. Sometimes you feel like grabbing toys and hanging on tightly so no one else can have them. Most people feel that way some of the time, Richard, but we still have to take turns. When it's your turn, you may play with the toy."

EXAMINE YOUR OWN ATTITUDE

Do you believe that:

- Children basically are not hostile or destructive?
- Each child has potential that can be developed?

Ch. 16: Promoting Responsible Behavior

Physically getting on the child's level helps open the way to effective communication.

- Children are worth the time and effort required to help them?

Without these beliefs, an adult may find it hard to help a child develop responsible behavior. Children draw many conclusions about themselves through the way adults treat them. Studies in human behavior indicate that children must develop good feelings about themselves in order to behave in responsible ways. Therefore, to help children build good feelings, we must first have a sincere relationship with them, based on the beliefs just mentioned.

In addition, adults must convey these and other attitudes to children. Edith Neisser, early childhood educator, suggests six adult attitudes which help give children feelings of self-confidence, security, and worth:

- Believe in the child. Have confidence that he or she is the kind of person who can succeed.
- Allow the child the right to try several times. Consider failure as an unsuccessful attempt but not as something bad.
- Provide plenty of opportunities for successful achievement. Don't set standards so high that children constantly fall short of expectations.
- Be pleased with a child's efforts and show confidence in his ability to become competent.
- Accept each person as an individual so each child can like himself.
- Guarantee the child certain rights and privileges.

As a parent or child care worker, your behavior counts so much toward promoting responsible behavior in children. Start now to make these attitudes a regular part of your own behavior if they aren't already. You may find that even if you never work with children, such attitudes will be

Part IV: Guiding Children's Behavior

Encouragement enables children to continue their efforts and to gain self-confidence.

just as helpful to you in your dealings with youth and adults.

BE ENCOURAGING

Children need lots of encouragement. Encouragement enables children to continue their efforts even in difficult situations. Children need encouragement to act in particular patterns until they become comfortable and feel natural with their behavior.

Our world is complicated, and children are often discouraged and have feelings of failure. Encouragement helps the child have faith in himself and the desire to try again. Encouragement lets children know that someone else has confidence in them. When children experience encouragement, they begin to develop self-confidence because they know someone cares about what they are doing and recognizes their efforts.

Many children also need to be encouraged to develop interest in what others are doing and to be a part of a group. Encouragement promotes the child's sense of responsibility and willingness to contribute to the welfare of others.

BE POSITIVE

Dr. Haim Ginott, a well-known child psychologist, says the child who hears the word *don't* before a command often detaches the *don't* and then acts. For example, an adult says, "Don't walk in the mud!" The child discards the word *don't* and then acts by walking in the mud. Some authorities call this behavior a *negative response*. Actually, it is a negative command. What would the positive and more appropriate statement be?

Try this: "Walk on the sidewalk or step on the dry area. Mud is not for stepping in."

If the child still insists on stepping in the mud, try: "I know you feel like stepping there, but mud is not for shoes, is it? Shoes are a mess when they get covered with mud and water."

Keep in mind that children enjoy exploring through their senses. They should be given opportunities to play with mud and water—in appropriate places, of course. There should be times when they may take their shoes off and feel the mud squish between their toes. They may enjoy making mud pies because they like to feel the texture of mud with their hands and fingers. They need to know why, when, and where to play. By giving children this information in a positive form, the adult is much more likely to see appropriate results.

Here are some other examples of speaking positively, rather than negatively:

Avoid This

"Don't throw the ball at the baby."
"Don't hit your brother."
"Don't ever let me catch you touching that vase again."
"Don't pinch the dog."
"Stop hitting the baby right now."

Try This

"Throw the ball at the box."
"Hit the punching bag."
"Vases are for flowers. Isn't this one pretty? If you take the vase from the table, it might fall and break."
"Pet the dog gently."
"Talk softly to the baby and pat her gently."

Situation: Tom spills his milk.

Avoid This

"How could you be so clumsy?"
"Why aren't you more careful?"
"Stop playing while you are eating."

Try This

"Accidents sometimes happen."
"The sponge (or dishcloth) is in the kitchen. You may help wipe up the spilled milk."
"Perhaps holding the glass with both hands will keep it from spilling next time."

A positive response to Tom's accident does three things:

- It offers understanding by getting the message to Tom that accidents can happen. He knows there is a sympathetic attitude toward his mistake.

Part IV: Guiding Children's Behavior

Jake is pleased with himself as he helps clean up after an art activity.

- He is given the opportunity to compensate for making the mistake and for his guilty feelings. He can work off the tension he feels while helping clean up the spill he caused. He can demonstrate his worth by doing a constructive task in helping clean up the mess.
- He is given some instruction for avoiding the same accident by changing his behavior the next time.

The adult may be able to help prevent the accident next time by using a glass that will not tip so easily—such as a short, squatty glass rather than a tall, thin one. The size and shape of the glass should be one which the child can grasp easily.

Can you think of other examples and ways to help children recognize their worth while learning to direct their own behavior?

Learning Principles

You read that children learn behavior through reinforcement, imitation or identification, and insight. All of these may be used to promote responsible behavior in children. You will need to try many ways of helping children until the best ones are found. What works with Johnny may not work with Kim. What works with Kim one time may not work the next. How can you help children develop self-motivation for responsible behavior? How can you assist children in developing an inward desire to behave in a responsible and acceptable way? Note how these questions are answered in the following situation, using the three ways a child learns behavior.

The aide wishes to encourage the children to pick up their materials and supplies and replace them where they belong. This is to be done at the end of each session of activities every day. Consider these three approaches.

Use of Imitation

The aide begins to put her materials away while giving instructions to the children to do the same. (Remember, use the guidelines for effective communications.) As she is *demonstrating through her actions,* which consist of putting things away, she might also say: "I know that some of you would still like to work with the play dough and lollipop sticks, but the rest want to go outdoors. Now, for you who are going outdoors, it's time to put your materials in place so they will be ready for use tomorrow." The aide helps put things away, encouraging children in a firm but kind manner to do the same.

The imitation approach, as you know, depends on the children following the example of the aide and other children.

Sometimes extra stimulation is needed. One way to arouse a child's interest in putting things away is to mark shelves with color-coded shapes which match the equipment or materials. This not only helps children learn where things belong but also adds interest to the putting-away activity. By doing this, children develop responsible habits for keeping things in order. They learn respect for property and for an orderly environment.

Sometimes your behavior may not be worthy of imitation. Remember, however, that the child may imitate you anyway. The child's action may be a reflection of your actions. If adults shout, hit, and are rude, children will think this is an acceptable way to act. Therefore, to promote responsible behavior, the adult must provide an example that displays responsible behavior.

Use of Reinforcement

A reinforcement approach can also be used. Using this method, the aide provides some type of reward for the children. For example, she might use a token reward that can be traded for a game or the privilege of participating in a special activity. With some children, a positive gesture such as a pat on the shoulder or a compliment—"My, what a good job you did!"—is enough to reinforce the behavior.

As you know, reinforcement offers children a type of reward or recognition for their efforts. A reward gives the child pleasure and encourages him to continue the responsible behavior. Often a combination of imitation and reinforcement is useful. If the child does well (or at least tries) when copying your example at clean-up time, tell him you appreciate his efforts. The child can learn responsible behavior with a combination of both methods—imitation and reinforcement.

Use of Insight

We know that with the insight approach, children must learn *why* the materials and supplies are to be replaced. They must be able to understand that replacing things is as much a part of the routine as using them. Each child needs to develop an awareness of individual responsibilities to the group in cooperating to keep things orderly. When children learn the reasons for respecting property and when they understand why things are kept in place when not in use, they will be more likely to want to put things in place.

As you can see, the use of all three approaches can and will be necessary to help children learn responsibility and independence. Why? Because some children will respond to one method more readily than others. Also, at different ages or in different situations, one method may work better than another. A combination of all three methods will give adults the best chance for success in helping children learn.

Some centers use one approach as the primary method in working with children. The other methods may be used to support and strengthen the learning process. Once again note: *Consistency* is the key to success in focusing on either a single approach or on a combination. Child care personnel should understand and be able to use all of these approaches in working with children. If a center uses one approach, such as a material reward for reinforcement of children's behavior, every worker must understand this system and be able to apply it. The same is true, of course, for any other method.

Part IV: Guiding Children's Behavior

Children do not have the maturity to make good judgments in all areas of behavior.

REMOVE THE CAUSES OF MISBEHAVIOR

If we know the reason for misbehavior, we can often prevent it from happening again by eliminating the cause. Naturally, responsible behavior is more likely to occur if potential causes of misbehavior are abolished. Think about this example. Children are seated and kicking each other under the table during a coloring activity. What would you do? One possible solution is to separate the children so their feet won't touch. Another is to remove one or more of the children from the table and initiate another activity until they think they can control their kicking.

You can also change the situation so the behavior changes. For example, children start fighting on the bus while going to the day care center. If time permits, stop the bus and allow a few moments for the children to settle their problems. Children can often solve their own problems without dictating or direct interference from adults.

If the children continue to fight, the adult may have to change the seating arrangement. Have you noticed that people like to sit in the same place in classrooms, on buses, and in other routine situations? Changing the children's seats may work if you tell them they may have their old places back next time. Giving children interesting things to do while traveling can change mischievous behavior into interesting exploration. Stringing wooden beads, lap books, string play, and other intriguing activities help children direct their attention in appropriate ways.

You may have to set the limits firmly. For example, you might tell the children, "Fighting is especially dangerous in the bus because it distracts the driver. Besides that, you could easily be injured if you lose your balance when shoving and hitting in a moving bus. Until you are willing to sit without fighting, you will sit apart from each other." (The children must then be separated.)

When the adult knows the fighting is done to get attention, another possibility might be to say to everyone: "Children, let's all look at Sara and Timmy because they need lots of attention. They are fighting in order to get us to look at them. Let's give them some attention so they can stop their fighting."

Often, very young children do not have the maturity to make good judgments; they need to keep from making mistakes. You may need to remove potential causes of misbehavior, as in the following example:

Situation: Trudy, age three, tears pages from a magazine.

Avoid This

Leaving important papers or magazines within reach of the child. (While learning, Trudy cannot distinguish between what is important and what is not.)

Try This

Keep a stack of older magazines available in a designated place, giving repeated explanation, when needed, that these are not taboo. She can either tear, cut with scissors, or mark on the paper with paints, crayons, or chalk. (This teaches the child responsibility. Be very careful in situations like this to make it clear that only the specified magazines are for the child's use. Otherwise, the child may reason that all magazines can be used this way.)

In addition to papers and magazines, other items may be potential causes of misbehavior. Place out of reach those fragile and precious items which children might break while playing. Such items can be replaced with unbreakable and yet interesting things to fulfill the child's desire to explore and develop curiosity.

PROVIDE A SUITABLE ENVIRONMENT

As you know, the environment has an important influence on behavior. If adults expect children to learn responsible behavior, then they must provide an environment which contributes to this goal. Let's consider some ways to provide an atmosphere for children which helps promote responsible behavior.

Allow children to be active and expressive. Most children become frustrated quickly if they do not have enough room to move about and play. Knowing this, adults can provide places and ways for children to be active. They can also develop a tolerance for children's frustrations when they must be in close quarters.

Consider this example: When riding in the back seat of a car, children may become restless because they have little space in which to move. They can usually tolerate confinement on short trips, but on long trips this closeness may lead to such problems as fighting, teasing, and complaining. Adults have several alternatives. If possible, stop the car periodically and allow children a short time to run and play. Place boxes or traveling bags between two children to keep them separated and to offer each some privacy. Provide children with items of interest, such as soft toys or picture books, which can be used in small spaces.

You can expect children to become impatient at times. If no alternative is possible, adults may have to tolerate children's restlessness and frustration. Remember, looking at the situation from the children's point of view will help adults understand why they become restless.

Give children opportunities to explore their environment. Knowing that children learn through their senses, you can provide experiences which help fulfill children's natural desires to explore their environment.

Part IV: Guiding Children's Behavior

Kickapoo Head Start Center
The child care worker can provide opportunities for children to explore their environment in constructive and wholesome ways.

Situation: Mike enjoys feeling and touching by exploring liquids.

Avoid This

Limiting activities which provide the child with liquids to explore. (The child may blow bubbles in his milk, put his hands in his cereal bowl, spill water on the floor, or play in the toilet bowl in order to have experiences with liquids.)

Try This

Give the child a pan of water to play with outside if weather permits or inside where it is okay to splash and spill the water. Provide for supervised play periods while the child is bathing.

Children enjoy taking things apart and attempting to put them together again. This can be an exciting learning adventure for children when adults have provided something each child can handle. However, be sure the object cannot be damaged. A child may be given acceptable things for play such as plastic jars with metal lids. This helps prevent the child from exploring such things as breakable jelly jars or electrical appliances.

When planning activities, keep in mind that the child must learn to function in a group as well as individually. Opportunities for both kinds of activities will be needed. Plan group activities so that each child can work confidently at an individual pace and level within the group. Specific activities will not be listed here, but in the following chapters, you will find many activities that will help children develop responsible behavior through a well-planned environment.

Ch. 16: Promoting Responsible Behavior

Chapter Highlights

- Developing responsibility in children means preparing them to accept the results of their own behavior.
- Promoting responsible behavior during the early years gives the child a better start in life.
- Effective communication is a major factor in helping children learn responsibility.
- There are many ways to communicate with children—talking, making gestures, facial expressions—but the most common way is with words.
- In talking with young children, keep the communications simple and the channels open and clear.
- The following principles serve as a guide to successful communications: (a) get on the child's level by kneeling or sitting on the floor, using vocabulary and terms the child will understand, and by looking at the situation from the child's point of view; (b) maintain respect for the child and yourself; and (c) sympathize with the child.
- An adult may find it hard to help a child develop responsible behavior unless he or she believes that children are basically good, each child has potential that can be developed, and children are worth the time and effort required to help them.
- Adult attitudes concerning children are conveyed by the adult to the child in both verbal and nonverbal communications.
- Children must develop good feelings about themselves in order to behave in responsible ways.
- Encouragement urges children to continue their efforts and promotes the child's sense of responsibility and willingness to contribute to the welfare of others.
- One way to promote responsible behavior in children is by providing an image that displays responsible behavior.
- Responsible behavior may be reinforced by a simple gesture such as a pat on the shoulder or by a word of praise or a smile.
- Children are more likely to gain insight and behave appropriately when they understand *why* certain behavior is necessary.
- If we know the reason for misbehavior, we can often prevent it from happening again by eliminating the cause.
- If adults expect children to learn responsible behavior, they must provide an environment which contributes to this goal.

Thinking It Over

1. What does developing responsibility in children mean to you?
2. List four ways to help instill a sense of responsibility in children.
3. How can we prevent misunderstandings in communications with children?
4. What are three examples of ways people communicate with each other? Are you ever misunderstood? Why?
5. How do we get on a child's level for effective communication?

(Continued on page 278)

Part IV: Guiding Children's Behavior

Thinking It Over Continued

6. How do children develop good feelings about themselves?
7. Why is your behavior so important when you work with children?
8. Why is encouragement important in the behavior of children?
9. Why are positive responses much more desirable than negative ones?
10. Can misbehavior ever be prevented? Explain your answer.
11. How does a suitable environment promote responsible behavior in children?

Things To Do

1. In groups develop skits that demonstrate appropriate and inappropriate ways of communicating with children. Present these to the class and ask members of the class to point out the good and bad communication techniques used in each skit.
2. Make posters illustrating six adult attitudes which give children feelings of self-confidence, security, and worth. Display these where parents can see them when they take children to a children's center.
3. Prepare a questionnaire which will show whether or not a person has the right attitudes for work with children. Ask the class to answer the questionnaire, and then report back on the results.
4. Observe what goes on in a children's center while the children play grocery store, laundromat, restaurant, or in other situations. Make notes of positive and negative comments. Write appropriate responses which might have been used in place of the negative comments. Discuss the value of the positive responses.
5. Interview a child care worker to find out what behavior problems are encountered in a center and how they are handled by the person interviewed. To help with your interview, compile a list of possible behavior problems to take with you. Make a written or oral report of your findings, including your own ideas on how the problems might be handled.
6. How did you imitate teenagers and adults when you were a child? Relate your memories to the class.
7. Visit a children's center and observe adult-child interactions. Record examples of positive reinforcement. Report your findings to class and compare notes.
8. Interview the mother and father of a young child. Ask them to indicate how they handle behavior problems with their child. In class make a list of common behavior problems of children derived from the interview.
9. In a group think of examples of misbehavior that could have been prevented. Write a short verbal exchange between children and adults to demonstrate each. Record these on tape. Play these for the class and ask for suggestions on how the misbehavior could have been prevented.

Ch. 16: Promoting Responsible Behavior

Recommended Reading

Baruch, Dorothy. *How To Discipline Your Children.* Public Affairs Pamphlet, #154, 381 Park Avenue South, New York, 1973.

Brown, Thomas E. *Concerns of Parents About Sex Education.* SEICUS, Study Guide No. 13, New York: Association Press, 1968.

Dreikurs, Rudolf, M.D. *Children: The Challenge.* New York: Hawthorn Books, Inc., 1964.

Ginott, Haim G. *Between Parent and Child.* New York: Macmillan Publishing Co., Inc., 1967.

Hymes, James L., Jr. *Behavior and Discipline.* Englewood Cliffs, New Jersey: Prentice-Hall, Inc., 1965.

Chapter 17.

Discipline

Your Challenge

This chapter will enable you to . . . .

- Define discipline.
- Explain the self-control approach to discipline.
- Tell how children can be allowed freedom of expression.
- Describe how to provide alternatives for children.
- Explain how to set limits for children.
- Describe some special behavior problems that adults face in working with children.

WHAT IS DISCIPLINE?

Much child abuse occurs every day. No doubt, many cases go unreported, and sometimes harsh forms of punishment are disguised by some parents as a form of discipline. You may know of people who have experienced discipline in its more severe forms—whippings, beatings, long-term isolation. Parents and teachers have spent long hours puzzling over which of numerous disciplinary methods are appropriate and effective for use in schools and homes. Some have tried prescribed techniques only to be dismayed at the results. Others have resorted to methods used on them during their childhood. Is it any wonder that discipline is a distasteful subject for so many people? Yet it need not be.

Unfortunately, the word discipline arouses unpleasant thoughts—partly because of a lack of understanding about what the term really means. How would you define discipline? Do you equate it with punishment? Many people think discipline is the same thing as punishment even though this is not necessarily so. With a proper understanding of discipline, adults will be better able to put this important subject in its proper perspective. With insight into the structure (makeup) and function (application) of discipline, many adults will find that caring for children need not involve harsh tactics.

A suitable definition of discipline forms the basis for its understanding. Think of discipline as guidance which corrects, molds, strengthens, improves, and ultimately helps the child learn to control his own actions. Discipline is a combination of support, encouragement, and limits. This definition can be divided into short-range and long-range goals. On a daily basis, the adult wishes to correct, mold, strengthen, or improve a child's behavior. For example, a mother corrects her child when he puts the spoon in his mouth upside down. At that moment she wants the child to perform a correct technique. This is her short-range goal. On a long-range basis, the adult should help the child learn self-discipline. For example, some day in the future, even when the mother is not close by, the child will want to use the table manners he has learned. When the child becomes *internally motivated*—has a desire inside himself—to apply the rules of society, striving to interact successfully by himself as well as with others, he is becoming a self-disciplined person. Wouldn't you agree that this is the major purpose of discipline?

Discipline has been the subject of much controversy for years. We have seen discipline in all forms—from one extreme of severe physical punishment to the other extreme of child indulgence. Most people would agree that the best approach is somewhere in between. The question is "where?" To help in your search for an answer, let's take a look at one possibility—the self-control approach.

THE SELF-CONTROL APPROACH TO DISCIPLINE

Self-control, as an approach to discipline, refers to helping children develop the ability to direct their own behavior in a responsible manner. In some ways, this approach is similar to permissiveness, a term which has become the subject of much controversy and many misconceptions. When the application of permissiveness first arrived on the scene, many parents jumped on the bandwagon, happy to find what they believed to be an effective alternative to physical punishment. For some, however, it was like jumping into deep water without the benefits of a swimming lesson. Thinking that permissiveness meant letting children have total freedom to do as they pleased, these people soon discovered that their children controlled nearly all situations. Instead of permissiveness, the parents were practicing indulgence. The children did not get the direction and control they really needed. Parents sacrificed respect for rebellion. Those who saw this became quite disenchanted with permissiveness. People started to say things like: "None of that permissiveness stuff for me; I believe in good old-fashioned discipline." What these people failed to see is that permissiveness is not all bad, if used correctly and if not carried to an extreme. The self-control approach, like permissiveness, does not mean a lack of limits. Rather, self-control discipline emphasizes freedom of expression and the providing of alternatives combined with direction and limits. Actually, correct use of self-control discipline will put this approach somewhere in between the two extremes of severe physical punishment and total lack of control. Isn't this, after all, what we want?

In the previous paragraph, four terms were mentioned in connection with the self-control approach. They are: *freedom of expression, providing alternatives, direction,* and *limits*. These are very important terms. As you read on, you will begin to see why.

Freedom of Expression

The self-control approach means allowing children the right to have all kinds of feelings and wishes and to express them freely. Remember that children often dream and play make-believe. These dreams and fantasies are sometimes

Part IV: Guiding Children's Behavior

Every child needs the freedom to express feelings.

expressed. Unrealistic as such dreams may be, to children they are quite important. Even though many of a child's wishes cannot be fulfilled, adults must show respect for them. Hostile feelings can also be created which may eventually erupt into misbehavior. If a child senses that his feelings and wishes are cause for ridicule or not worthy of concern, he may resort to denying himself the freedom of expression and keep his feelings inside. The child then loses confidence, no longer able to express himself freely.

While playing with blocks, two lively youngsters began to fight because a tower one had built was knocked down. The child care worker quickly intervened, explaining to the children that he understood their feelings about both wanting to play with the blocks but that hitting was not allowed. Someone could be hurt. Since both children had angry feelings inside, he asked them each to draw a picture to show how they felt. If appropriate and safe, an adult could also encourage children to hit a punching bag, saw wood, or hammer. They could make up songs or poems or even talk on a tape recorder in order to express feelings.

When children feel angry, they can be allowed to express their feelings *but not in a destructive way.* Adults can help children express their angry feelings without damage to things or people. This helps children know that adults understand and care how they feel. Here is a case in point:

Teacher: "You seem to be angry, Joe."
Joe: "I am!"
Teacher: "You feel like you would like to hurt someone."
(Joe nods his head sharply.)
Teacher: "You're angry at someone."
Joe: "Yeah, you!"
Teacher: "Tell me more about how you feel."
Joe: "You let Jack paint and I wanted to have a turn."
Teacher: "That made you angry. You said to yourself, something like: 'She likes Jack more than me.'"
(Joe nods again.)
Teacher: "I'll bet you feel that way other times, too, don't you?"
Joe: "I sure do."
Teacher: "I feel angry sometimes too, Joe. When you feel that way, come to me and we'll talk about it."

You have no doubt heard statements like these directed at adults by children: "I won't love you if you don't let me do it; I hate you." Children can sense an adult's need for love and they may take advantage of this weakness. By threatening an adult with taking away love, children often feel they can get their own way. Some adults succumb to this. As you can imagine, the situation continues to get worse until both adult and child are frustrated.

Adults should understand that children may not like them every minute of the day. Expressions of dislike are commonly made by children but are quickly forgotten. A calm acceptance of a child's anger by adults is a far better alternative to distress when such declarations are made.

Providing Alternatives

Giving children opportunities to make choices should begin early in their lives. Using the right method to provide choices is important. These three guidelines will help:

- *Offer the child a choice only when one is available.* For example, Ellen wants to go outdoors in the rain. Since you will not allow her to go out without boots and a coat, the choice about whether or not to wear them is not available. What could be done in this case?

Children need many opportunities to make choices. With interesting surroundings children can choose from different activities.

Avoid This

"Do you want to put on your coat and boots?" (Ellen might answer: "No, I don't need them.")

Try This

"Do you want to wear your red coat or green jacket?" (If such a choice is possible.)

or

"Ellen, do you want to play indoors or outdoors? If you choose to go out, you must wear your boots and coat."

Of course, no choice about wearing a coat and boots outdoors was available in this situation. Instead, Ellen was given the choice of staying in or going out. If she chooses to go out, she knows that she must wear the proper clothing, but at least the choice is hers—self-controlled discipline.

- *Be prepared to honor the child's decision.* If a child is given a choice, the adult should always accept the decision which the child makes, whether or not the adult thinks it is a good one. Thinking carefully before offering a choice will likely result in more reasonable alternatives. Adults must allow children to experience the results of their choices, whether

Part IV: Guiding Children's Behavior

Offer a choice only when one is available. Is there a choice about wearing coats and boots to play in the snow?

pleasant or unpleasant. As children experience disappointment when making poor judgments, they are likely to seek ways of improving.

With pleasant or positive consequences, they will likely be motivated and encouraged to repeat similar action. Of course, the more help we can give children in learning to make sound judgments on their choices, the less apt they are to make poor ones.

- *Be consistent about giving choices.* If you develop a pattern of interacting with the child which he understands and expects, the child will begin to respond in a consistent way too. You will both know what to expect from each other under certain circumstances. Consistency is very important, for neither of the other guidelines will be effective without it. For example, if Ellen is allowed to violate the conditions for going outside one time, she will assume that the conditions can be violated another time. When this happens, the whole purpose of allowing the child a choice is lost.

Examples on Providing Alternatives

At first, it may be difficult for you to decide just how to phrase words so that reasonable alternatives are provided. You may not be used to working with this approach. With practice, however, you can develop the habit of turning commands and unrealistic questions into choices that really promote responsibility in children. The examples that follow are similar but will help you begin to think along these lines.

Situation: Mealtime.

Avoid This

"Brad, do you want an egg for breakfast?" (He may say no. Because he was given the decision, it must be honored and he will not have to eat an egg.)

"Would you like some carrots with lunch today, Jeri?" (Why is this a poor question?)

"Do you want to come in for lunch, Suzie?" (If the child says no, then she should be allowed to continue what she is doing because she was given a choice which must be respected. Was there really a choice to give?)

Try This

"Brad, do you want your egg scrambled, boiled, or fried?" (Be prepared to cook the egg the way he chooses.)

Ch. 17: Discipline

"Would you like to have sliced raw carrots or chopped cooked carrots?" (When Jeri chooses, perhaps she can help prepare the simple dish. This gives her additional motivation to eat what she has chosen.)

"You may wash your hands and face now, Suzie. Do you want me to help you or do you want to do it by yourself? It will soon be time for lunch."

or

"Lunch is about ready; you may wash your hands now and come to the table, Suzie." Or, "You can wash your hands and come in the kitchen and help me."

Let's go a few steps further with Suzie's situation. If Suzie is reluctant to come for lunch, the adult needs to alert her to the consequences of not coming on time (providing she is old enough to understand). Since Suzie has a responsibility to the family or group to respect lunchtime, she will have to miss the meal if she comes in late. Once she knows this, Suzie must assume the responsibility for choosing to be on time or to be late. Perhaps inviting her to help in the kitchen with some simple task will encourage her to make the right decision.

If Suzie persists in not coming on time, then allowing her to experience the consequences of her decision may be the best way to prevent the problem from continuing. This means that if she comes to the table late and decides to eat, she must not be allowed to do so. The explanation should be given that since she was not on time, she must wait until the next meal. This may seem harsh, but children learn quickly. Suzie will not be harmed by missing one meal. The next time she is more likely to be on time because the consequence of being late—missing the meal—was not pleasant. If this approach is used in the center, it should be thoroughly discussed and understood by the parents beforehand.

What is the key to helping the child recognize the importance of making wise choices? Again, the answer is consistency. If Suzie is late for another meal, the same response must be carried out. Only in a rare case would a child be content to skip lunch continually and have just the evening meal. Should this happen to Suzie, the adult must work with the child to help her understand the reason for eating lunch. Ways to interest her or engage her in the meal must be pursued.

Situation: Snack time in the center.

Avoid This

"What kind of drink do you want?" (You may not have what each child chooses. You may not have the time or budget to allow different beverages at one snack time.)

Try This

"Would you prefer orange juice or lemonade? If you wish, you may help make the one you choose." (Why is this a wise approach? What must the adult be prepared to do?)

Whether it is for meals or snacks, children need food which is nutritious for meeting the needs of growth and development. Often, however, they can choose

Part IV: Guiding Children's Behavior

how they want the food prepared and perhaps decide between the kinds of food available. This *may* give clues to the types of foods most acceptable to children.

Situation: Bath time.

Avoid This

"Do you want to take your bath now?" (Why is this a poor approach?)

Try This

"It's time for your bath now. Would you like me to turn on the water for you or do you want to do it?" (Why is this a better approach?)

What are some other ways of approaching this situation? Remember, when the child is given a choice, the adult must honor that choice. Otherwise, the child cannot build trust and confidence in the adult's word. If the choice is honored only part of the time, the child may become confused and frustrated. How can any child be expected to behave consistently when adults do not?

Situation: Buying clothing.

Avoid This

"What kind of shirt do you want, Gary?" (He may choose a very expensive and impractical one.)

"Linda, which shoes do you like?" (What is the danger in this question?)

Try This

"Gary, you may choose from the shirts on this counter. Which one would you like to wear to school?" (The child must then be allowed to choose. If he wants a green one, then the green one should be purchased even if all of his other shirts are green. Why? Because he was given this choice.)

"You may choose from several pairs of these play shoes." (The child should then be shown choices only from play shoes and within the price range of the budget. Be prepared to honor her choice.)

Children can be given many opportunities for learning to make choices about the clothes they wear and even about buying clothes. If a child needs certain items of clothing, the adult, of course, must make the decision concerning how much money can be spent for the items. Perhaps the child can be given a choice on the color or style of clothing to be purchased. This opportunity for making choices will help the child develop independence and a sense of importance.

Situation: Indoor block play in the center.

Avoid This

"Do you want to play with the building blocks?" (The children may have different answers, some saying yes and some no; some may not be able to decide.)

Try This

"You may choose the blocks you wish to build with. Those choosing the large blocks may play in the yellow area; those choosing

Ch. 17: Discipline

the small blocks may play in the green area; and those choosing some of both may play in the blue area." (These choices provide opportunities for children to learn cooperation as well as responsibility and independence.)

When possible, children should have other opportunities to make decisions throughout the day. How could you provide children in the center with the choices in these situations?

- Self-selected play indoors or outdoors during cold weather.
- Story time with a variety of books available.
- Lunchtime with the children seated in small groups.
- Work period, using creative media like brush or finger painting.
- Dramatic play like house or store.

List some situations and approaches for giving young children opportunities to develop independence and responsibility by making choices related to money. Keep in mind the principles that were applied in the above examples. Do the same with toys.

Direction and Limits

As you have just read, children need opportunities for expression and choice. It is not always simple, however, to decide where to draw the line between allowing and stopping freedom. Too much freedom, in the form of indulgence or overpermissiveness, can be as bad for children as not enough. Children may demand privileges that are impossible or impractical, taking advantage of overindulging adults. They may become confused with too much freedom because they are not ready to make decisions on their own. According to numerous authorities, too much freedom may cause children to become anxious or tense.

To keep self-controlled discipline from getting out of hand, *limits must be set* to give children the proper direction. Limits help prevent dangerous acts. They also help children learn the difference between appropriate and inappropriate behavior. Children want to know how far they can go. They need help in learning what their limits are, as you can see in this example:

Situation: John is marking on the wall.

Avoid This

"How could you do such a terrible thing?"

A bowl full of Halloween treats cannot be eaten in one night. How might a limit be set in this situation?

287

Part IV: Guiding Children's Behavior

"What are you doing?"
"What's wrong with you?"
"You are a naughty child."
(Why are these poor responses?)

Try This

"No, John, walls are not for drawing. Here is the chalk and there is the chalkboard."
"Here are paper and crayons for drawing."

How to Set Limits

All children need limits to help them develop self-control and independence. Children (and adults!) have difficulty in dealing with their own desires and impulses—their sudden urges to do something, to act inappropriately. Children need help from adults to control these impulses. By setting limits, adults help children learn when to stop and when to continue their actions.

In telling children about the limits, an approach like this one is often effective:

- Put the child's wishes into words: "You wish you could play out in the rain."
- State the limits clearly: "But the rule is that we do not play outside in the rain."
- Help the child express unhappy feelings which may result because of the limit: "I can see you're unhappy about this rule. You would like it to say that anytime is outdoor playtime. Sometimes you even wish there were no rules at all."
- Tell the child what can be done to fulfill the wish in part if possible: "You may play inside at the water table if you wish, or you may play with the blocks, in the dress-up corner, or read a story."

Note how this approach is used in the following example.

Situation: Tina takes three books off the reading shelf to take home from the center.

Avoid This

"No, you cannot take the books home. Don't you know the books belong in the center?"

Try This

"I know you want to take the books home with you, Tina. You want to very much, but these are books for the children to use while in the center. You may look at the books while you are waiting to go home and then return them to their places before you leave. Which one do you want to read?"

Of course, if there are enough books available, it would be a splendid practice to allow each child who wishes to take one book home. There can be an understanding with both the child and parents that the book is to be returned the next day.

As you set limits for children, you must consider the answers to several questions:

- Is the limit necessary?
- How does the limit contribute to the child's well-being and safety?
- Is the limit needed for the well-being and safety of others?
- Will this limit allow the child to continue experimenting and learning through exploration?
- Is the limit for the child's benefit, for the convenience of adults, or for both?
- Can the limit be enforced? How?
- Is the limit still useful for the child's age level or has it been outgrown?

Ch. 17: Discipline

- Who should enforce the limit?
- How can the limit be explained to the child?
- Can the child help set the limit?

If you are not sure about the limit to set, wait until you have thought through the problem carefully. An unclear limit only invites trouble and confuses the child. For example, what is the problem with this teacher's statement to a child on the playground? "You may splash Jennie with a little water but do not soak her." Can you see that this only invites the beginning of trouble which may become impossible to control?

Not all limits need to be explained to a child, but there should always be a good reason for setting a limit. After hitting another child, Melinda was told by the aide: "Playmates are not for hitting. If you want to hit something, you may use the punching bag." Melinda then knew that hitting another person was inappropriate, but that hitting the punching bag was acceptable. The aide did not explain why Melinda could not hit another child, yet there was a good reason for setting this limit.

Children will usually cooperate when there are not too many limits and when they have some freedom to make decisions and choices within the boundaries of the limits. Arnie had been throwing paint. In response, the teacher said: "You may not throw the paints, Arnie. Paints are for painting and drawing. Balls are for throwing." The teacher gave Arnie a choice: Either use the paints to make a picture or give up the activity.

Children usually respond better to simple direct statements. Harsh tones and authoritative wording may achieve temporary obedience but they often set up barriers between the child and you. Consider the tone and wording in the following examples:

Situation: Joey's bedtime.

Avoid This

"You know it's bedtime and you're too young to stay up late. Go to bed!"
"You have watched TV long enough; you must go to bed now!"

Try This

"It's close to bedtime. You may put your things away and get ready to climb into bed."
"Time is up for watching TV today. It's time for bed."

Situation: Children are throwing toys—blocks.

Avoid This

"Stop throwing those toys this instant!"

Try This

"Toys are for play, not for throwing."
"Blocks are for building, not for throwing."
"I cannot allow you to throw the blocks because it's too dangerous."

Threatening children often invites them to repeat a forbidden task or act. "If you do it one more time. . . ." This warning serves as a challenge to the child. He sometimes commits the forbidden act because he must prove something to himself and to others, or sometimes he may want to test the limit. Also, after children hear threats

Part IV: Guiding Children's Behavior

again and again, they simply disregard them, confident they will not be carried out.

Situation: Children are shouting.

Avoid This

"You had better stop yelling right now!"

Try This

"Please stop shouting at one another." (Firmly, but not loudly, spoken.)

As you set limits, try not to lose touch with the child's point of view. Also think about his physical, psychological, and emotional maturity. For example, you have learned that children need exercise for their general health and well-being. They need many ways to use energy and express their feelings. Restricting running, jumping, climbing, and other physical activities not only prevents optimal physical development but can also result in emotional tensions and frustrations. Note how this applies to the next situation.

Situation: Ginny is running and jumping on the sofa and chairs.

Avoid This

"Don't run. Can't you walk like a good girl? Don't jump all over."

Try This

"You may play outdoors or in the playroom; those places are for running and jumping."
"This furniture is for sitting and this room is for walking, not for jumping. You may jump on the porch and run in the grass or on the sidewalk. Would you like to use the jump rope or foam jumping pad?"

Enforcing the Limits

Limits must be stated firmly but in a kind and respectful way. One message, however, should be quite clear: *This limit is real.* The child must realize that limits will be enforced. How to enforce them is a difficult question.

Your relationship with a child from the very beginning could be a trial period as far as self-controlled discipline is concerned. What you do at first may affect the pattern of the relationship. The skeptic may scoff at the thought of children respecting limits which are set as described on the previous pages. What the skeptic has forgotten is that the key to success hinges upon being consistent and honest with the child from the time of the first encounter. A child is not likely to respect the limits you set today if they are not consistent with the limits you set yesterday. Moreover, he or she will not respect the limits if you do not do as you say you will do. The better able you are to follow these guidelines from the start, the easier it will be to enforce limits later without resorting to punishment. Those who must continually use punishment as a means of control may have made early mistakes in consistency and honesty. Trying afterwards to make up for mistakes may not work.

Have you ever observed a parent who repeatedly tells a child *no*, only to see the child go right ahead and perform the forbidden act? This happens frequently with one couple and their two-year-old son. Another mother and father tell their two-year-

Ch. 17: Discipline

University of Alabama Center for Developmental and Learning Disorders

Limits must be stated firmly but in a kind and respectful way.

old daughter *no* and they never have to say another word. It is evident that the little girl has learned that her parents mean it when they say *no*. Early in her life she discovered that exceeding the limits meant facing the consequences. The little boy has not learned this. Which set of parents do you think will use the most physical punishment as a means of control in the years ahead?

In order to enforce a limit, you may have to provide or explain a *consequence*. Some consequences will be ones you create and carry out (like a lost privilege). Others will occur as a direct result of the child's actions (like a burned finger).

Sometimes children may be allowed to experience the natural consequences of their behavior—unless, of course, the consequences would be harmful. For example, Trina, while pounding a plastic dog with a hammer, was told: "If you pound on the toy, it may break. Then you won't be able to play with it anymore." Before long the toy dog did break. Trina's mother then took the broken pieces and threw them away. Unhappy about her broken toy, Trina experienced the consequences of her behavior. If the toy had been new or expensive, Trina's mother might have approached the situation differently. Can you suggest another method she might have used?

Often the adult will have to combine the limit with a suitable consequence which he devises. During story time, Raul caused considerable disturbance. The adult then told Raul: "Everyone must be quiet during story time. You may talk and play after the story is finished, but you will have to be quiet now, Raul, or leave the group." After a second disturbance, the adult took Raul's chair and placed it well outside the circle. Raul had been told what the acceptable behavior was. He chose not to follow it, so the adult, true to his word, made Raul leave the group.

Another example will help you see how the adult must add a consequence when necessary.

Part IV: Guiding Children's Behavior

Children develop a sense of satisfaction as they make decisions leading to self-controlled discipline. This child has decided to play in the safe tree within the limits of the playground.

Situation: The children can climb only certain trees.

Avoid This

"You can't climb those trees because I say so."
"Don't ask why—just stay out of those trees."
"Get out of those trees right now!"

Try This

"Some trees are stronger than others and will hold you safely when you climb. These trees are weak and dangerous, not for climbing. You may climb in that tree or play on the jungle gym."

By allowing the children to make a choice between the climbing tree and the jungle gym, you give them a sense of satisfaction in making the decision themselves—again, an opportunity for self-controlled discipline. If the children choose the inappropriate behavior—climbing the forbidden trees—it is time to let them know that there are consequences for going beyond the limits. The adult might say: "You children must decide whether you want to play in the climbing tree or in another area. Anyone who climbs the wrong trees will lose the privilege of playing outdoors for the rest of the day."

This statement alerts the children to the consequences of breaking the limit. If a child insists on breaking the limit and climbs the forbidden tree, he must suffer the consequences and lose the privilege of playing outdoors.

Children generally expect to be stopped when they go beyond the limits of appropriate conduct. If adults do not stop their actions, children may become more anxious and upset. For example, a child is hanging out of the bus window. If allowed to do this, the child may think the adult does not care about his welfare and safety. However, if he is not allowed to do this, he will learn that limits have reasons and that adults care about what happens to children. Establishing and enforcing reasonable limits gives this message to the child: You don't have to be afraid all the time that you will go too far with your actions, because I will help you. I will let you know when you must stop.

The adult must understand that the child will be unhappy and probably somewhat resentful about some restrictions. *The child should not be punished for not liking the limits.*

What do you do when children deliberately go beyond the limits?

Ch. 17: Discipline

- First, try to discover their goal or reason—Why did they go beyond? Was it for attention or for some other reason?
- Look at the situation from a child's viewpoint. Is the limit appropriate?
- When a child persists in misbehavior by violating a reasonable limit, the adult must take action. (Consultations may be needed with parents or professionals if the child is extremely difficult to handle.)

Opinions are varied on what kind of action should be taken when children deliberately misbehave. Understandably, adults have limits to their patience. There is a point when an adult's tolerance of children's actions must stop. Most would agree that once the adult is sure the limit was justified and that the child understood the limit and had no good reason for exceeding it, the adult may show disappointment and even anger.

It may be all right to express anger to a child if respect between the child and adult can be maintained. The worth of the child must not be sacrificed when an adult becomes angry. Statements to the child should be directed at the child's actions and misbehavior but never at his character or at the child as a person.

Situation: Child throws something in anger and breaks a mirror.

Avoid This

"You stupid idiot!"
"You are a mean little brat!"
"When will you learn to behave yourself?"
"You make me so mad."
"How could you do such a thing?"

Try This

"I know you feel angry, but throwing things at mirrors is not allowed. Now I'm very angry."
"You must learn that I have feelings too and that I become very angry when you misbehave this way."

Sarcasm is sometimes used by adults in attempting to discipline children. For example: "How many times must I repeat the same thing? Are you as stupid as people think?" Such responses often cause children to defend themselves or to make a counterattack. They may seek revenge or fantasy in order to deal with the sarcasm. A sarcastic response deflates the child's faith in himself—damages his self-concept—distorts the image that is developing, based on other's attitudes.

Excessive anger is seldom, if ever, warranted, mainly because it is usually accompanied by shouting and severe physical punishment. This does not mean that physical punishment is taboo. It does mean that an adult must use good judgment when considering the use of physical punishment. Of course, if you work in a children's center, it is usually against the law to use physical punishment. What is wrong with spanking or hitting a child? For one thing, physical punishment has a message for the child. It tells him: "When *you* are angry, hit!" Spanking seems to give children the right to imitate this action—the right to hit—when they become angry or frustrated. Since children learn by example, the adult who repeatedly uses physical punishment as a means of control may well expect the children in his care to resort to hitting.

Physical punishment is also undesirable because it may cause poor development of

Part IV: Guiding Children's Behavior

the child's conscience. Spanking or slapping relieves guilty feelings for some children and damages the self-esteem of others.

Sometimes children ask for physical punishment by deliberately misbehaving. Why? This may help relieve their guilt; or it may be the only way they can successfully get attention. Children believe they have paid for their misbehavior and feel free to repeat it if they experience relief of guilt by spanking. When children ask for punishment, they need help rather than a spanking to manage guilty, angry, or frustrated feelings. There are acceptable ways of helping children express anger and guilt. As children learn to direct their negative feelings into appropriate and acceptable actions, physical punishment will not be needed, even as a last resort.

Examining adult motives should help you further understand the problems associated with physical punishment. What are some of the reasons adults resort to this action? Anger, frustration, fatigue, and personal problems may result in impulsive actions by an adult. Often the adult does not consider the possible consequences for the child. You may be able to achieve immediate obedience from a child by physical punishment, but in the long run, self-discipline will probably be hindered.

SPECIAL PROBLEMS

Adults who work with children face many common problems in the area of behavior. Dr. Haim Ginott has written a great deal about discipline with young children. He provided some excellent suggestions for handling problems with children.

Promises

Dr. Ginott formulated what he called self-defeating patterns of discipline. These are ways of teaching which have little or no success. Threats and sarcasm are two which you read about earlier in the chapter. Making promises is a third.

A promise is not needed to help a child learn discipline. Children should not have to make promises to adults. Relationships are better built on trust rather than promises. Why? Because promises build up unrealistic expectations in children. Here is an example:

Molly, age five, had been looking forward to going to the zoo on Saturday. Her mother had promised to take Molly and one of her friends. Early Saturday morning it was discovered the car had motor trouble that could not be repaired until Monday. The excursion had to be cancelled. Molly, however, became very unhappy, repeatedly crying, "But, mother, you promised!"

Adults sometimes have a tendency to promise a child something to achieve immediate results. Later, they may be unable to follow through with the promise.

Promises concerning children's behavior should not be made, because this encourages dishonest behavior. Evaluate the following statements.

"Maria, if I take you to the store, you must promise not to touch anything."
"Hank, you must promise you will not whisper or talk during church."

Honesty

To promote honesty, one must be ready to listen to the truth from children even if it is unpleasant. To grow up honest, children must not be encouraged to lie about their feelings. Children learn whether or not "honesty is the best policy" from the reactions of others.

Why do children lie? Here are a few reasons to consider:

Ch. 17: Discipline

- Children may lie in self-defense to prevent punishment.
- Children may lie to get what they want through fantasy if they lack it in reality.
- Children may use lies to tell the truth about fears and hopes. A lie may reveal what the child would like to be or what he would like to do.

How should you respond to children when they lie? A mature reaction to a child's lie should show understanding of the meaning of the lie. The lie should not be condemned or denied. We can often prevent defensive lying by not asking questions which might cause the child to need to lie.

Children do not like to be questioned when they suspect answers to questions are already known. Children usually respond more positively to statements of understanding than to questioning about suspected lying.

Avoid making a big issue over tall stories or asking many questions for which you already have answers. You should not hesitate, however, to let a child know that what was said is recognized as a lie.

By communicating understanding and respect to a child before pursuing the problem, adults can usually avoid provoking a child into lying as a defense.

Situation: Karen, age four, tells the teacher she got a baby sister for her birthday. The teacher knows she did not.

Avoid This

"Karen, why do you say things like that?"
"Little girls shouldn't tell stories that are not true."
"Where did you get the baby?"
(This might provoke the child to tell additional lies.)

Try This

"You wish you had a baby sister."
"You would like to help care for a baby sister."
"You would like a baby sister to play with."
"What did you really get for your birthday?"

When a child lies, adult reactions should be realistic but not hysterical or moralistic. This is not the time to teach the child what is right or wrong. The purpose of the adult's response is to help the child realize there is no need to lie.

Situation: Kelly *accidentally* broke his fire truck and then hid it.

Avoid This

"Where is the fire truck? I saw you playing with it."
(Kelly might answer with a lie—"I don't know.")
"Find it. I want to see it."
(Kelly: "Maybe someone took it.")
"You are lying. You broke the truck. Now don't tell me you didn't. If there is one thing I can't stand, it's lying. Now you will have to be punished."

Try This

"I see that your fire truck is broken."
"Your fire truck didn't last very long. You had it only three days."
"That's too bad. It was too expensive to break so soon."

Part IV: Guiding Children's Behavior

(These statements indicate understanding and give the message that toys should be taken better care of by the owner.)

Stealing

Ginott offers two suggestions when you discover that a child has stolen something:

- Avoid sermons and dramatic reactions.
- Maintain a firm, calm response.

  Situation: Mark takes a marking pen from the shelf in the center and puts it in his pocket. The teacher notices this.

The teacher might say: "The pen belongs on the shelf. Please put it back;" or: "The pen belongs to the center. You may use it while you are here." If Mark says he does not have the pen, then what? Teacher: "The pen in your left pocket (teacher points to it) has to remain in the center. Put it on the shelf after you are through with it." If Mark refuses, the teacher may have to take the pen out of his pocket, saying, "The pen belongs to the center and must stay here."

This child may need special help if such behavior occurs frequently. The first step is to consult with the parents. Then perhaps a professional, such as a psychologist or social worker, can offer help or make a referral for further help.

When the adult knows the answer to a question concerning the child's behavior, no question should be asked of the children involved. It is usually better to make a simple statement about the situation. For example, when Jill, Marty, and Randy ate part of the crackers prepared for snack time in the family day care center, the adult said, "Children, I'm disappointed because you ate the crackers. I'm upset that you took the crackers without asking, because they were for snack time." Why is this a better response than becoming dramatic?

How would you handle the following situation? Glen, age six, takes money from your purse. Why is it better not to ask Glen why he did it? List statements which would help Glen understand that what he has done was not necessary, that he must be responsible for his misbehavior, and how such behavior can be prevented.

Chapter Highlights

- Discipline provides training which corrects, molds, strengthens, and improves development and ultimately helps the child learn to control his own actions.
- When a child becomes intrinsically-motivated, he exercises a desire inside himself to apply discipline. This helps him become an independent person, striving to function successfully by himself as well as with others.
- Self-controlled discipline emphasizes freedom of expression and choice combined with direction and reasonable limits.
- The self-controlled approach to discipline means allowing children the right to have all kinds of feelings and wishes and to express them freely.

Ch. 17: Discipline

- Three guidelines in providing children with opportunities to make choices are:
  1. Offer the child a choice only when one is available.
  2. Be prepared to honor the child's decision.
  3. Be consistent about giving choices.
- Too much freedom, in the form of indulgence of overpermissiveness, can be as harmful for children as not enough.
- Children may become anxious or tense when given no limits.
- By setting limits, adults help children learn when to stop and when to continue their actions.
- If you are not sure about the limits to set, wait until you have thought through the problem carefully. An unclear limit only invites trouble and confuses the child.
- Not all limits need to be explained to a child, but there should always be a good reason for setting a limit.
- Children will usually cooperate when there are not too many limits.
- The child must realize that limits will be enforced.
- In order to enforce a limit, you may have to provide or explain a consequence.
- The child should not be punished for not liking the limits. The adult must understand that the child will be unhappy and somewhat resentful about some restrictions.
- By communicating understanding and respect to a child before pursuing the problem, adults can usually avoid provoking a child into lying as a defense.
- Avoid making a big issue over tall stories or asking many questions for which you already have answers. However, let a child know that what is said is recognized as a lie.
- The purpose of the adult's response to a child's lie is to help the child realize there is no need to lie.

Thinking It Over

1. Give three examples of different types of discipline used by teachers you have had during your school years? Tell why or why not each was effective.
2. Define discipline.
3. Do discipline and punishment mean the same thing? Explain.
4. Why has permissiveness become a distasteful word to many?
5. What do you do when you feel angry? What do you think causes you to react in this manner?
6. Do you love everyone every minute of the day? How does this apply to children?
7. Name three guidelines to use in providing children with alternatives.
8. Do you think it is worth the time and effort it takes to provide children with opportunities for making choices throughout the day? Why?
9. Is an explanation of a limit always necessary? Should there always be a reason for a limit?

(Continued on page 298)

Part IV: Guiding Children's Behavior

Thinking It Over Continued

10. As you grew up, did your parents ever set limits for you? Did you always agree with these limits? How did you develop the ability to set limits for yourself?
11. What can happen if a limit is set in haste?
12. Explain why some parents must resort to physical punishment more often than others.
13. Should promises be made to children? Explain.
14. How would you deal with a child who tells you she is moving to another state when you know this is not true?
15. Do you think most children steal something at some time during their lives? What do you suggest as a way to help children learn they should not steal?

Things To Do

1. Find newspaper and/or magazine articles concerning child abuse. Make a report on this subject.
2. Observe in supermarkets and department stores how parents correct or direct their children. Discuss your observations.
3. Have a panel of elementary teachers discuss discipline in the classroom.
4. Interview friends or classmates concerning how they will discipline their children when they have their own. You might want to prepare ahead of time examples of behavior problems. Have those you interview react to these examples. Compare and evaluate the results.
5. Divide into groups and each group write a case study in which discipline is needed. Exchange case studies and each group write a solution to the situation. Then present these to the entire class and discuss. Rate the solutions according to how well they met the definition of discipline given at the beginning of this chapter.
6. Prepare a series of one-minute radio or television spots to inform parents of creative and effective ways to handle discipline problems—grocery shopping with a young child, toilet training, quarreling with playmates. Work individually or in groups and present to the class.

Recommended Reading

Baruch, Dorothy. *How To Discipline Your Children.* Public Affairs Pamphlet, #154, 381 Park Avenue South, New York, 1973.

Dreikurs, Rudolf, M.D. *Children: The Challenge.* New York: Hawthorn Books, Inc., 1964.

Ginott, Haim G. *Between Parent and Child.* New York: Macmillan Publishing Co., Inc., 1967.

Ch. 17: Discipline

Hymes, James L., Jr. *Behavior and Discipline.* Englewood Cliffs, New Jersey: Prentice-Hall, Inc., 1965.

Mental Health Digest. Washington, D.C.: National Clearinghouse for Mental Health, Superintendent of Documents.

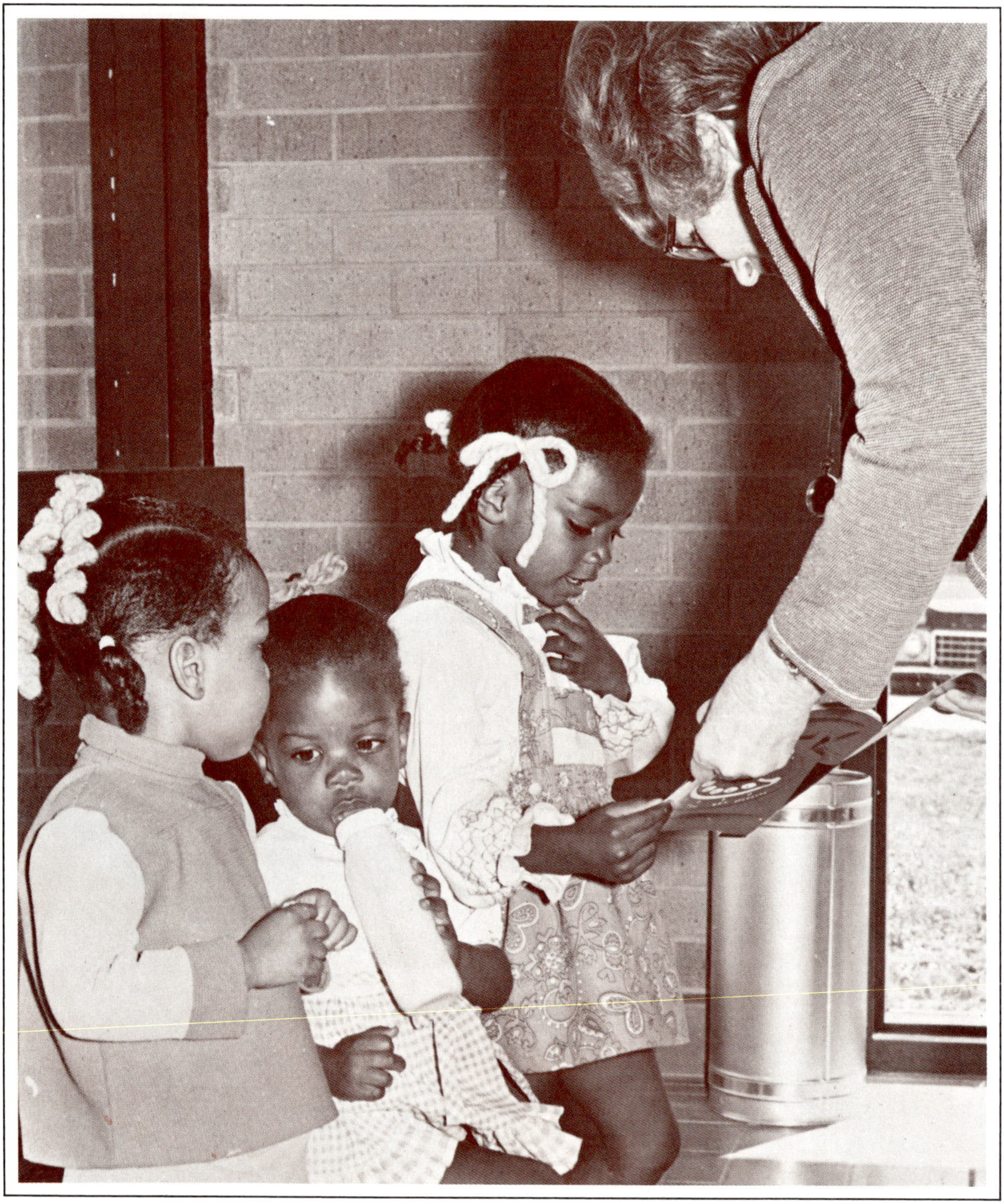

PART V
Working In Children's Centers

Chapter 18.
You and the Child Care Profession

Chapter 19.
Centers for Children

Chapter 20.
Managing Center Operations

Chapter 18.

You and the Child Care Profession

Your Challenge

This chapter will enable you to . . . .

- Decide whether or not you have the personal qualifications needed for working with children.
- List ways to prepare for a career in child care.
- Describe what to do when applying for a job.
- Distinguish between pre-service and in-service training.
- List what will be expected of you on the job.
- Describe how you can make your job easier.
- Tell how your work should be evaluated.
- Write your first philosophy of child care.

PERSONAL QUALIFICATIONS

Are you the kind of person who is suited for work in the child care field? Those who plan to enter any type of work are well advised to think about their personal qualifications for the job. If you want to work with children, your qualifications are especially important. After all, a child care worker's influence on a child can last a lifetime. Think about yourself for a moment. Do you have:

- A willingness to continue and broaden your understandings about children and their development?
- A sense of value for human dignity, worth, and especially a high regard for children as learning, growing beings?
- The ability to respond to children with a warm, relaxed, and friendly manner but not so casual as to be meaningless?
- A sense of organization and a willingness to share ideas and consider suggestions from others?
- Self-confidence and a sense of security which comes through being informed about children, their abilities and needs, and the developmental possibilities of a children's program?
- An interest in improving communication with both adults and children?

Ch. 18: You and the Child Care Profession

- A basic knowledge of child development, child rearing, and guidance?

If you feel that you are suited for a job in child care, the next question is what type of job would you most like? Your interests, qualifications, and abilities will influence your decision. Perhaps you will be interested in more than one job. You might be able to secure better positions as your skills improve through experience and training. For a review of the job opportunities in child care, take a second look at Chapter 1.

PREPARING FOR A CAREER IN CHILD CARE

Perhaps you have already begun preparing yourself for a career in child care. Baby-sitting with your sisters and brothers or with children in your neighborhood is one way to get acquainted with the characteristics and needs of children.

As a sitter, you are responsible for the safety and well-being of each child. You have opportunities to observe children as they play alone and as they interact with others, including yourself. Baby-sitting is one way to find out whether you enjoy young children. Of course, the more you know about them the more likely you are to appreciate their special ways.

Volunteering as a helper in a child care center or a Head Start program is another way of preparing for work with children. As a volunteer, you work with trained teachers and adults who are responsible for the care of children. You can see and become involved with children's activities in group settings. Volunteer work provides a way to become familiar with the routine and plan for children's daily experiences.

In addition to gaining experience in children's centers, you may enjoy volunteer

A child care worker must have the desire and the patience to work with children in all sorts of activities.

- A good physical condition and mental alertness?
- A willingness and ability to participate in children's activities; a real interest in exploring the child's world?
- An interest in learning, leading to a positive self-concept which promotes working with other adults and children without feeling threatened or inferior?
- Patience and tolerance with active, curious, and at times, noisy and difficult children?
- The ability to be objective and professional with the staff and parents above the level of letting personality conflicts hinder the program?
- The ability and willingness to cooperate and follow instructions?
- A sense of humor and a pleasant disposition?
- An appreciation for the efforts of children?

Part V: Working In Children's Centers

Volunteers provide services to children and families and learn about child care and development at the same time.

work in the children's section of a hospital. Again, each experience you encounter will add to your qualifications as a child care worker.

It will be to your advantage to learn as much as you can about children. High schools often provide courses in child development or care and guidance. Family life education and general home economics courses usually include a unit of study on the young child. Some high schools operate a preschool or nursery program to provide direct experience for students to observe and interact with children. Vocational programs may have child care occupational training in which high school students attend school part-time and work in a children's center part-time.

Continuing education and adult education programs often provide training in child development and parent education. Some of these programs are part of high school programs, and others are part of college and university programs. The over-all objectives are usually the same: to help adults continue to learn to function more effectively in their daily living with children.

Some one- and two-year college programs offer special courses in child development or child care. Others provide a full program of work in this area, which results in an associate degree.

Colleges and universities offer more advanced training for work with children. A bachelor's degree may be earned in many four-year programs of work in early childhood or child development. Some programs combine study about young children with family life education.

Find out what type of training is available to meet your interests and needs. A school counselor can usually provide information to help you become familiar with opportunities for training and for work.

APPLYING FOR WORK WITH CHILDREN

Applying for a job will not be a frightening experience if you know what to expect and are prepared. Many people, especially when applying for their first full-time position, feel insecure and convey this feeling to the potential employer. Since you will want to put your best foot forward, follow these guidelines and be confident that you have the situation well under control.

Locating the Jobs

In looking for a job, you may need to seek help from other sources in finding openings. Often school counselors have information that can help you. Other possibilities are newspaper advertisements, job placement through training programs, and employment agencies. Employment agencies charge a fee for their service but may know of opportunities that are not easily discovered by the average job seeker. Many cities have a youth employment service which helps teenagers find part-time and full-time work. There is no charge for this service.

If possible, apply for work at several centers. This may give you more than one alternative from which to choose. You can compare the types of centers, the working conditions, the neighborhoods, and other factors which may help you decide which center is most suitable for your abilities and interests.

You may want to apply for work at a particular center even though you know there are no job openings. Some centers keep your application on file in case an opening comes up. Other centers may not take the time to interview you if they have no openings. It is best to accept this graciously. You may want to come back again later when they do have an opening.

Your Appearance Counts

How important are first impressions? Think about your own experiences. Like most people, haven't you, at one time or another, judged a person by his appearance? Employers do this with potential employees.

In the child care field, an employer must consider the example you will set for children. Cleanliness and neatness will both be important. If you are sincere about wanting the job, one good way to show this is by presenting a good appearance.

What to Bring With You

An embarrassing moment can occur if you arrive for an interview or you are about to fill out an application blank and you do not have the information needed. Not only could this cause a delay, but it might also reflect on your efficiency. The applicant who comes prepared may beat you to the job.

One solution is this: Before you begin applying, get a clean folder or large envelope. Collect all the information you think you might need and place it in the folder or envelope. Take this with you wherever you apply, having everything ready at a moment's notice.

Several things should be included in your folder of information. Each person about to seek employment in a children's center should have:

- A social security number (carry the card with you or write down the number).
- A birth certificate or naturalization papers (if not born in the United States).
- A health certificate and a TB skin test.

Credentials are usually requested when you apply for a job. These include an official transcript of your high school credits, supplied by your high school, and additional post-high-school training. Credentials may also include a list of references the employer may call to inquire about you or letters of recommendation by previous employers, teachers, or other individuals who can convey information about your competencies and potential as an employee.

You would also be wise to have a typed *resumé*, or *vita*, which contains information about your personal background of work experience and special training. (See the sample resumé.) This is useful to employers when reviewing your credentials. Include starting and terminating dates for your schooling and job history. This information can be easily transferred to an application form if figured out in advance. If you write a letter of application for work, it is appropriate to include a resumé. It is also appropriate to leave a copy with a prospective employer when you have a personal interview.

When preparing a resumé, be sure you do not defeat the purpose. A sloppy resumé full of misspellings and self-serving statements can do more harm than good. It is far better to state the facts simply and honestly, checking carefully for errors and retyping if necessary.

If you are applying at several places, you may want to have photocopies or carbon copies made so that you can leave the information with the prospective employer. Many large libraries and banks have copy machines available for public use for a small fee.

Filling Out Application Forms

Application forms are not all alike. Most, however, require the same basic information—name, age, address, telephone number, social security number; parents' or guardian's name and address and telephone number; schools attended, job history, hobbies, interests, activities, honorary positions held, and references. Some applications may ask for more information and others, less.

When filling out application forms, *read over any instructions carefully* before entering information. Fill out all blanks honestly and clearly and where questions do not apply to you indicate with a note, "does not apply," or dashes. As references, list names and addresses of those who can give a report on your qualifications or performance abilities. (It is a good idea to include the names, addresses, and telephone numbers of references in your folder of information for quick referral. This may also be included in your resumé.)

The Interview

Few people can go into an interview without feeling nervous. Most actors and actresses admit to at least a few butterflies before a stage performance. This is perfectly normal. The tricky part is in not letting others know that you are nervous, whether on the stage, behind the podium, or across the desk.

How can you do this? First of all, follow the guidelines already mentioned so that you are prepared and confident that all is under control. Secondly, don't be afraid to show a pleasant smile and look the interviewer in the eyes. Be a good listener. The interviewer is probably experienced enough to know how to handle the situation, so let him lead the way. Sit quietly in a relaxed position. Fidgeting is the first clue to nervousness. Answer the interviewer's questions clearly and honestly and show your own interest by asking questions yourself. If the interviewer does not volunteer this information, you might ask questions like these:

- What is the role of this position in relation to the center program? (What are the specific duties of this position? How does this position fit into the working team or staff?)
- What is the organizational structure of the center? (What is the flow of responsibility to and from the director, lead teachers, assistants, volunteers, and others? To whom does each worker report and from whom does one seek help and information while working?)
- What is the salary range for this position—lowest to highest?
- What are the employee benefits (for full-time work)? (Insurance, retirement, social security, vacation, sick leave, other?)

Ch. 18: You and the Child Care Profession

SAMPLE RESUMÉ

ANITA BETH COBB

Permanent Address: 1511 W. Warner
                     Brownwood, Colorado 65711

Social Security Number: 448-56-3613

Date of Birth: April 2, 1959

Place of Birth: Brownwood, Colorado

Height: 5'6"   Weight: 120   Health: Excellent

Marital Status: Single

Education Background:

   1971 to 1974, Central Junior High, Brownwood, Colorado

   1974 to 1977, Brown High School, Brownwood, Colorado

Work Experience: Rae Dee's Dress Shop, Brownwood, Colorado, duties as a sales clerk.
                   Cobb's Day Center, Brownwood, Colorado, duties as a teacher's aide.

Present Position: Graduate of Brown High School, Brownwood, Colorado

Organizations: Child Development Club
                 National Science Club

Special Honors: Dean's Honor Roll, Senior Year at Brown High School

References:

Mrs. James Warner
289 Oak
Brownwood, Colorado
255-7677

Mrs. Ted Jackson
444 S. W. 29th
Denver, Colorado
289-7566

Mrs. Ronald Hefner
9196 Winnview
Brownwood, Colorado
455-2345

APPLICATION FOR EMPLOYMENT

PERSONAL INFORMATION

DATE _____ SOCIAL SECURITY NUMBER _____

NAME _____ AGE** _____ SEX** _____
         LAST   FIRST   MIDDLE

PRESENT ADDRESS _____
                    STREET   CITY   STATE

PERMANENT ADDRESS _____
                    STREET   CITY   STATE

PHONE NO _____ OWN HOME _____ RENT _____

DATE OF BIRTH** _____ HEIGHT _____ WEIGHT _____ COLOR OF HAIR _____ COLOR OF EYES _____

MARRIED _____ SINGLE _____ WIDOWED _____ DIVORCED _____ SEPARATED _____

NUMBER OF CHILDREN _____ DEPENDENTS OTHER THAN WIFE OR CHILDREN _____ *CITIZEN OF U.S.A. YES ○ NO ○

IF RELATED TO ANYONE IN OUR EMPLOY, STATE NAME AND DEPARTMENT _____ REFERRED BY _____

EMPLOYMENT DESIRED

POSITION _____ DATE YOU CAN START _____ SALARY DESIRED _____

ARE YOU EMPLOYED NOW? _____ IF SO MAY WE INQUIRE OF YOUR PRESENT EMPLOYER _____

EVER APPLIED TO THIS COMPANY BEFORE? _____ WHERE _____ WHEN _____

EDUCATION	NAME and LOCATION OF SCHOOL	YEARS ATTENDED	DATE GRADUATED	SUBJECTS STUDIED
GRAMMAR SCHOOL				
HIGH SCHOOL				
COLLEGE				
TRADE, BUSINESS OR CORRESPONDENCE SCHOOL				

SUBJECTS OF SPECIAL STUDY OR RESEARCH WORK _____

*WHAT FOREIGN LANGUAGES DO YOU SPEAK FLUENTLY? _____ READ _____ WRITE _____

U. S. MILITARY OR NAVAL SERVICE _____ RANK _____ PRESENT MEMBERSHIP IN NATIONAL GUARD OR RESERVES _____

ACTIVITIES OTHER THAN RELIGIOUS (CIVIC, ATHLETIC, FRATERNAL, ETC.) _____

EXCLUDE ORGANIZATIONS, THE NAME OR CHARACTER OF WHICH INDICATES THE RACE, CREED, COLOR OR NATIONAL ORIGIN OF ITS MEMBERS.

*THIS QUESTION MAY NOT BE ASKED IN STATES PROHIBITING SAME.   MADE IN U.S.A.

**NOTE: THIS INFORMATION MAY BE ASKED FOR BUT DISCRIMINATION BECAUSE OF SEX PROHIBITED BY FEDERAL LAW. ALSO DISCRIMINATION BY AGE PROHIBITED BY LAW IN STATES WITH FAIR EMPLOYMENT PRACTICES.

(CONTINUED ON NEXT PAGE)

FORMER EMPLOYERS (LIST BELOW LAST FOUR EMPLOYERS, STARTING WITH LAST ONE FIRST.)

DATE MONTH AND YEAR	NAME AND ADDRESS OF EMPLOYER	SALARY	POSITION	REASON FOR LEAVING
FROM				
TO				
FROM				
TO				
FROM				
TO				
FROM				
TO				

REFERENCES: GIVE BELOW THE NAMES OF THREE PERSONS NOT RELATED TO YOU, WHOM YOU HAVE KNOWN AT LEAST ONE YEAR.

	NAME	ADDRESS	BUSINESS	YEARS ACQUAINTED
1				
2				
3				

PHYSICAL RECORD:
LIST ANY PHYSICAL DEFECTS _____

WERE YOU EVER INJURED? _____ GIVE DETAILS _____

HAVE YOU ANY DEFECTS IN HEARING? _____ IN VISION? _____ IN SPEECH? _____

IN CASE OF
EMERGENCY NOTIFY _____
                  NAME   ADDRESS   PHONE NO.

I AUTHORIZE INVESTIGATION OF ALL STATEMENTS CONTAINED IN THIS APPLICATION. I UNDERSTAND THAT MISREPRESENTATION OR OMISSION OF FACTS CALLED FOR IS CAUSE FOR DISMISSAL. FURTHER, I UNDERSTAND AND AGREE THAT MY EMPLOYMENT IS FOR NO DEFINITE PERIOD AND MAY, REGARDLESS OF THE DATE OF PAYMENT OF MY WAGES AND SALARY, BE TERMINATED AT ANY TIME WITHOUT ANY PREVIOUS NOTICE.

DATE _____ SIGNATURE _____

DO NOT WRITE BELOW THIS LINE

INTERVIEWED BY _____ DATE _____

REMARKS: _____

NEATNESS		CHARACTER	
PERSONALITY		ABILITY	

HIRED _____ FOR DEPT. _____ POSITION _____ WILL REPORT _____ SALARY WAGES _____

APPROVED: 1. _____ 2. _____ 3. _____
           EMPLOYMENT MANAGER   DEPT. HEAD   GENERAL MANAGER

Boorum & Pease

Part V: Working In Children's Centers

In her pre-service training this young woman works with children for short periods in the center before the job begins.

In-service training provides opportunities for the staff and director to work together in learning sessions.

- What are the possibilities for advancement?
- What additional in-service training and education are provided and what is expected?

If possible, you should have a tour of the center to see the facilities and the program in operation. You need to meet the employees because these are the people you will work with if you are offered and accept a position.

At the completion of the interview, thank the interviewer for his or her time and consideration. If the interviewer has not told you already, you are justified in asking when a decision will be made concerning this position. If you do not hear from him by the time mentioned, you may call to see if the position has been filled.

PRE-SERVICE AND IN-SERVICE TRAINING

Some child care programs offer formal training to help prepare you for the job. Pre- and in-service training usually consists of a series of classes, workshops, or seminars which offer training and educational expansion in such areas as child development, child guidance, children's learning, center activities, center organization, and job expectations.

Pre-service training may consist of days or weeks of concentrated effort *before* a program opens or *before* you begin to work in the center on a full-time basis. Particular sessions provide opportunities for the trainees to work for short periods of time in a center or to observe children's activities while engaging in study and training. Pre-service training helps a person know what to expect in a program by being prepared realistically. Learning on the job then becomes easier.

In-service training has a more direct purpose than learning in general. The purpose of in-service training is to update and improve the knowledge and abilities of the staff in relation to working with children.

This may include a wide range of areas such as child development, guidance, health, social and psychological services, parent involvement, working with volunteers, nutrition and meal service, program planning, and record keeping. In-service training, combined with the experience you have on the job, can help you move up on the career ladder. For example, an assistant may have the opportunity to move up to the position of leader after in-service training and experience which helps develop the competencies required of a group leader.

In-service training usually consists of periodic training sessions in which employees meet together to discuss and study certain phases of child care. The sessions may be conducted by the center director, lead teacher, or by an outside specialist in early childhood development or related areas. In-service training, like pre-service training, includes workshops or seminars to provide opportunities for improving the staff's abilities to work with children and with each other. These may be one-, two-, or three-week sessions which include all-day study and participation, or they may be once-a-week or once-a-month sessions which continue for several months or throughout the year. There are many designs for scheduling this type of training. Some training is held after working hours. Other training may be conducted during periods of the day set aside for this purpose.

Many programs include special sessions to identify and re-identify the respective roles of each person, as a lead teacher, assistant, volunteer, cook, maintenance worker, or whatever the position may be.

In some centers, training may not be as formal as that just described. You are trained informally by those with whom you work. A very small center may not be able to manage extensive training programs. If custodial care is the main objective, little emphasis may be placed on training in special areas. Such situations demand that you take the initiative yourself. Should you find yourself in this type of program, do your best to become knowledgeable about children and their needs. Encourage others to do the same. This is your opportunity to upgrade the quality of the care administered, a fine contribution to the child care field.

WHAT THE JOB EXPECTS OF YOU

At last you are on the job. What will be expected of you? Here are a few things your employer might expect:

- Be on time for work or advise ahead of time that you will be late.
- Come a little early and stay a little late *when necessary.*
- Follow instructions and understand the reasons for them. Listen carefully when instructions are given.
- Accept reasonable suggestions and criticisms in order to increase your competencies.
- Admit your mistakes. You are not expected to be perfect, just responsible.
- Try to complete tasks which have been assigned to you and do so willingly.
- Demonstrate an interest and enthusiasm for your work and in the children's activities, especially with the children and parents.
- Ask if you can help when you see extra tasks which need attention.
- Learn to use resources outside the center for implementing the program.
- Continue learning about children and your job.
- Maintain a good physical condition.

Part V: Working In Children's Centers

- Demonstrate respect for yourself and your work; avoid catty, back-biting conversations about children and others who are not present.
- Honor confidential information.
- Set a good example for children and fellow workers.
- Cooperate as much as possible.
- Think continually of the children's well-being and safety. Is everybody in sight? Any child missing? Is rough or dangerous play developing?

Now let's take a closer look at a few of these expectations:

Good Health

As a child care worker, you should be physically prepared to carry out the work of the day. This calls for good health which is maintained primarily by an adequate diet and proper rest. Good health will also help you be mentally alert, an important part of working with children.

Knowledge

Continuous study about children and experience from working with them will not only increase your understanding but will also increase your efficiency and ability to relate with children. Intuition, using instinct to determine what might happen and what should be done, is a valuable tool. It is not, however, an adequate tool in itself. Simply having feelings and notions about children and what to do while working with them is not enough. Knowledge and understanding about children's behavior and development are needed to back up or clarify intuitive notions.

You have, no doubt, noticed that an application of knowledge is just as important as the knowledge itself. It is one thing to know the facts and have information about children and how they grow and learn, but it is something else to be able to apply that knowledge in a meaningful way. Your job will demand of you knowledge, plus the ability to use that knowledge.

Attention to Duties

Whether you work with children in a public or private setting, knowing the responsibilities of your job can make your work easier and more enjoyable. The following list summarizes some of the tasks which child care workers can expect:

- Helping children with activities.
- Preparing supplies, materials, and equipment for children's learning and play activities such as games, puzzles, music, art, science, story time, dress-up, housekeeping, store and shopping center, digging, sand and water play, large and small toy activities, and block play.
- Checking and repairing equipment for safety and adequate functioning; checking and preparing the outdoor and indoor areas for safety.
- Room arrangement and preparation of activity areas; cleaning, straightening, and preparing these areas periodically during the day and at closing.
- Changing books, pictures, and other materials used by the children.
- Displaying children's work.
- Cleaning science areas and caring for pets, plants, and other science media.
- Preparing food for children—snacks and meals.
- Serving food and cleaning the eating area and kitchen; guiding children as they help with preparation, service, and cleanup.
- Daily check of children and keeping records: health, attendance, developmental progress.

- Attending to parents and other adults who may visit the center.
- Communicating with parents and the public by telephone and at times by correspondence.
- Ordering, receiving, and storing equipment, materials, and supplies.
- Transportation of children to and from the center and on field trips and excursions.

Do some of the duties just mentioned sound more appealing to you than others? No doubt they do. This is typical of almost any job. Still, all jobs must be performed so everything runs smoothly. Even if you feel at times that the duties you are given are the least pleasant, try to do them willingly, without complaints and grumbling. In the long run, it is the agreeable employee who gets ahead.

Cooperation

A most important part of any job is the ability to work well with others. A center's purpose of caring for children adequately can only be accomplished when it functions smoothly, with all persons on the staff fulfilling their respective roles and cooperating in the process.

Employees can strengthen their own positions as well as the center program by supporting each other. An attitude of unity makes it possible to provide a healthy, happy, and improved environment for both children and adults. When the center or the personnel are represented in community or professional settings, employees should be prepared to support the program and staff members in positive ways. Strength is added to any center when the staff works as a team committed to the children and to the program.

When problems arise—and they will from time to time—an *objective approach* to solving them often brings positive results. This means taking a nonpersonal point of view in which each person respects the others involved. A professional atmosphere should prevail. The term *professional* means the ability and willingness to consider a problem or situation in the context of the program, excluding personal biases or personalities. Workers need not feel threatened or insecure because of questions or criticisms when such comments are objective and are directed at the efforts or performance rather than at the personality or character of the staff members.

If a problem arises between employees, a confrontation is usually healthy if held before or after working hours in a professional setting and in private. Talking it over objectively usually leads to a better understanding of each other's viewpoints. Arguments, disagreements, and other conflicting communications should be completely avoided in the presence of children or parents or while the program is in session.

When an employee wishes to suggest a change, there is an appropriate procedure to follow. This procedure is part of the organizational structure of the total program. For example, a child care assistant presents suggestions or problems to the group leader. After talking together about them, if the situation requires further attention, the leader either takes the suggestion to the director and represents the assistant or suggests that the assistant discuss the idea with the director. In some organizational structures, the assistant and the teacher present suggestions to the staff, team, or to a council or a committee comprised of various representatives of the program. Knowing to whom one should go with a problem, question, or suggestion can often eliminate staff conflicts and per-

Part V: Working In Children's Centers

Oklahoma VoTech (Beggs Project)
To work successfully in a center employees must be willing to share ideas and give support to one another.

sonal frustrations. The employer is not always the one to consult first. In some centers the child care worker does not come into direct contact with the employer except occasionally. In other centers the staff's employer may also be the supervisor, director, group leader, or lead teacher, in which cases the employee has direct contact with the employer.

Although disagreement may occur with the lead teacher, assistant, or volunteer, each staff member has a responsibility to respect the positions of those in authority and the procedure by which the administration operates. Obviously, well-thought-out suggestions presented in a reasonable manner are more likely to be given consideration than spontaneous ones or those which represent only personal opinion.

Working successfully in a center calls for willingness to share ideas and give support wherever possible. It cannot be overstated that quality child care requires a cooperative effort on the part of each staff member and respect for one another as contributors to the children's welfare.

Concern for the Community

The child care center represents the service and professional contribution of those individuals working in the program. Likewise, each worker is a representative of the center.

The challenge of providing a program for children is partially met through community resources. The center staff should become familiar with the community, its needs, its leaders in all fields, and its physical and institutional resources. Parks, libraries, churches, recreational centers, art centers, zoos, museums, airports, waterfronts, industries, colleges and schools, shopping centers, and many other community components provide excellent opportunities for field trips, excursions, and an inflow of ideas. Having a guest come for group discussions or a demonstration helps children appreciate the community in which they live while learning facts about it. A music house, for example, might show simple instruments to the children. Representatives of the local fire and police departments can demonstrate how their services benefit children, families, and communities. A dentist can help children understand the significance of dental health and help eliminate fears and anxieties associated with his or her services. Very simple industrial procedures involving wood, metal, and plastic forming can be introduced for children to observe or try themselves.

Members of a center staff should keep in mind that in addition to being on the job during working hours, they are often contributing to the image of the center while engaged in nonprofessional or off-the-job activities. As an individual, the staff member sets an example both in and out of the center.

HOW TO MAKE YOUR JOB EASIER

Naturally, an excellent way to make your job easier is to do what is expected of you on the job according to the guidelines just given. In addition, good *management* can help.

Management is the key to making you more successful on the job while increasing your enjoyment of work. Management refers to the organization of work in relation to what is expected. This involves making decisions about what tasks must be pursued, when events and activities must take place, and how effective these are when finished. You might compare management to a road map. It is a plan for knowing:

- What the goals and objectives are—why is the program operating?
- Where you are going—what tasks and activities will be included along the way?
- How you will get there—what will you do to accomplish the tasks and activities?
- When you have arrived—what activities actually occurred?
- Assessment—how successful was the activity and what changes are suggested for the future?

To understand clearly what is meant by management, it may help to think about management as it relates to a specific job in the center. Suppose you are the cook in a small center. Would it make sense to come in each morning and look in the cupboards to see what's on hand for lunch? You discover the ingredients for macaroni and cheese and a jello salad. Unfortunately, there's not enough time to jell a salad. That should have been done yesterday. Oh well, how about cottage cheese? Jello sounds better with macaroni and cheese, but it's too late. Now to boil the macaroni. Another problem—the large kettle didn't get washed yesterday. It will only take a little extra time to wash it now. At last lunch is served—fifteen minutes late, but that's the best you've ever done. Of course, foods from all four basic food groups weren't served, but you can't expect miracles when things don't go well. This (we hope) is an exaggeration of poor management. You can see, however, that good management could have made a great difference. Can you offer some suggestions? Do you see how the same principles would apply to any job in the center?

Management includes planning ahead and scheduling. Activities and tasks should be identified and listed. Priorities must be determined. What activities and tasks are best for accomplishing the program's goals and for doing your job well? Planning priorities with your fellow workers and the director or a group leader helps to establish continuity. Continuity is the even flow of activities, a logical order for how things happen. Once you achieve continuity through proper management, your job will be much easier.

EVALUATING YOUR WORK

Work evaluation goes hand in hand with proper management. Only through evaluation can you decide how to revise and improve your activities, tasks, and procedures. There are two kinds of personal evaluation—self-evaluation and employer evaluation. The first is how you judge your own performance. The second is your

Part V: Working In Children's Centers

Kickapoo Head Start Center
Here a child care worker assists children as they apply paint to wood. How might she evaluate the success of such an activity at day's end?

employer's judgment of your performance. Both should be based on the same criteria.

Goals establish the major priorities of what is to be achieved with children. Evaluation of your work should be made in light of these goals. Regardless of how hard you work, how sincere you are, and how much you enjoy caring for children, don't you agree that your real success must be measured according to how effectively you have achieved your own goals plus those of the program? Evaluation must be made on the basis of some criterion, or measuring device, which indicates the expected outcomes. For example, to determine how successful you have been in helping children with language development, you must know what the standard expectations are in this area. The following are a few sample criteria for measuring success with five-year-olds in language skills after working with them for at least eight months:

- Children can listen to stories and recall certain parts.
- Children express themselves with sentences, identifying positions and locations of objects.
- Children can recognize their own names in print.
- Children can listen to and carry out instructions.
- Children are beginning to understand and use symbols such as pictures, words, and numbers.
- Children can communicate their thoughts and feelings to others in a meaningful way.

Evaluation includes rating your performance in areas which have already been discussed, such as helping to plan children's activities; working with the children indoors and outdoors; assisting with meal and snack times; conducting field trips and other special events; helping with children's records and other administrative tasks assigned to you; and working with fellow employees.

An effective evaluation is objective; that is, it has minimal influence from personal bias or attitudes. An objective self-evaluation should be based on how well you were actually able to do what was expected whether you completely agreed with the assignment or not. To evaluate your own work as accurately as possible, you need the comments and assessment of your performance by your director, group leader, and fellow workers. Periodically, staff meetings should be held to discuss the success of the program and provide information needed for self-evaluation. Here again, comments, criticisms, and suggestions should not be interpreted in a personal way, involving your character and personality. These remarks should be professional, with direct and indirect reference to your efforts and accomplishments. Here are some questions you might ask yourself:

- Do I know the objectives of the total program? The goals for the children?
- Am I familiar with the expected developmental level of each child in my charge?
- Am I aware of the home circumstances of each child? Income level? Life style?
- Do I know each child's religious and ethnic background?
- Am I aware of outstanding qualities of my fellow workers, so that I can appreciate and promote the center more effectively?

As you and your co-workers share ideas and concerns about the program, you will begin to recognize your own strong and weak points. Only by recognizing a weakness with an open mind can one begin to overcome it. You will also benefit from recognizing your strong points in order to use them as effectively as possible.

Another approach to evaluating your involvement with children and your role in the program is to ask yourself at the end of each working day:

- What do I think about today's program? Was it good, not so good, excellent?
- What would I do differently if I could repeat today?
- Do I really feel good about my relationship with the children and the other adults? Why or why not?
- Even though I may be tired, do I leave at the end of the day with a certain enthusiasm prevailing?

These questions are suggested to help you see yourself better in relation to your job. You may have other ideas of your own on how to judge your effectiveness as a child care worker. Your primary concern in self-evaluation is with the performance of your tasks. Comparison with fellow employees is of no worth to you and usually leads to problems. It is not realistic to compare your work with another staff member unless you are performing the same task in the same way. This can help you improve if you are less competent.

Continuous evaluation helps to achieve greater quality in staff performance and in the program. No two staff members will have exactly the same abilities. One teacher may be able to tell stories very effectively, whereas another may be more successful with music and creative movements. Some may do well at leading outdoor activities and others at conducting science experiments. Thus, you generally do not evaluate your contribution and performance by how many things you can do but how well you do those for which you are responsible. From time to time the staff or administration may decide to reassign certain tasks so that each worker is functioning in an appropriate role. The director, supervisor, or group leader may change assignments and present a new role for which you seem more suitable. Often strengths are discovered as a result of new and different experiences which must be continuously evaluated.

PHILOSOPHY OF CHILD CARE

Before anyone starts a center or begins to work in one, he or she should first think about a philosophy. As most professional people start their careers, they try to formulate a philosophy concerning work. Teachers, for example, are sometimes

Part V: Working In Children's Centers

Oklahoma VoTech

The more you know about children, the easier it will be to establish a set of values to guide you in formulating a philosophy about working with them. What principles do you think should be a part of this child care worker's philosophy?

asked to state or write their philosophy of education. In so doing, they might consider questions like these: What kind of person must I be in order to motivate my students? How can I best help them learn? What values should be considered first in my classroom? What type of environment must I provide in order to accomplish the required goals? Similar questions will be considered by those who start child care centers and those who work in them.

Perhaps you are ready to begin formulating your own philosophy about working with children. Of course, the more you know about children the easier it will be to establish a set of values to guide your planning and activities either as a parent or child care worker. What principles concerning work with children are most important to you? If you can answer this question, you are well on your way to stating your personal philosophy on caring for children.

In addition to the personal philosophies of the staff members, every program also reflects a philosophy, whether written and published or simply implied by the nature of what goes on. The philosophy of a program refers to the underlying attitudes and goals. It is an expression of the ideals of the program.

Your personal philosophy may not always correspond exactly to the philosophy of the center. In order to be a good, supportive employee, however, you should work with the basic philosophy of the program. If you have firm convictions about how to work with children, ask about a program's philosophy before accepting a job. If you have a flexible outlook and your philosophy is based on general principles which any center would uphold, you may be able to adjust to the philosophy of most centers. If you cannot support the philosophy of the center, seek a position elsewhere. Your early experiences in child care may even help you formulate a philosophy, considering the principles of the center where you work.

Thinking about a personal philosophy may be a new experience for you. To help you explore your own thinking, decide how you feel about the topics that follow.

A Little Freedom for Children

Adults often expect children to be miniature adults. Since it is inconvenient to

Ch. 18: You and the Child Care Profession

Children need settings in which they can play happily and explore.

Being messy is often a part of children's daily learning experiences.

clean mud from both clothes and child, is the child expected to stay out of the mud? Children need settings in which they can play happily and explore. Even though some adults have difficulty coping with children's messiness (like playing in the mud), the ingenious adult can find ways to manage and satisfy the needs of the child.

One mother decided how her child could enjoy finger painting without getting paint all over the floor and table. She put Prim in the bathtub. What a delight! Not only did Prim enjoy the freedom to finger paint on her improvised easel made of a cardboard box, but she also had fun painting herself—arms and legs included. When she finished painting, she had fun washing the paint off, as she was already in the bathtub.

Another mother heard about this idea and tried it with her three- and five-year-old girls. After about twenty minutes, she decided to check on the experiment. Five-year-old Betsy looked up—with paint all over herself—saying, "Mother, this is the best you have ever been to us!"

Adult attitudes about children's play reflect their knowledge and understanding of how children grow and learn. There are times when children need freedom to be messy—making mud pies, finger painting, water playing, digging, and mixing cookie dough. Does your philosophy on caring for children allow room for a little inconvenience? Granted, a little freedom for children at times can be trying for the adult, but isn't something that means so much to a child worth that extra effort?

Each Child—A Special Person

The premise that every child is a unique and worthwhile individual should be a

319

part of the philosophy in every children's center, regardless of its size. You will recall earlier emphasis placed on the individual differences of children and the necessity for recognizing each child as a significant person. Every adult who works in a center, whether a teacher with a degree, a cook, or a volunteer, must consider each child as a person of great value, regardless of how different or difficult the child may be. Each child has a contribution to make and each has expectations from others. Will this attitude be part of your philosophy—even when a troubled child tries your patience?

A Team Approach

For a program to serve children, families, and the community effectively, each employed person and volunteer must be willing to combine efforts to meet common goals. Children do not know or care which adult has the highest degree or amount of formal training in early childhood. The children do know, however, which adults they can relate to and communicate with and which ones understand their needs and feelings. Adults should work together as a team interested in the well-being of each child, aiming toward the positive growth and development of the children in their charge. This should be part of the philosophy of any center.

A team provides strong leadership and support for a children's program. Even when each adult has separate responsibilities such as preparing materials and arranging the room for activities, *planning together* makes it possible for everyone to know what each person's responsibility is and what is expected of him. Together, team members can provide a setting in which children work and play as independent, yet secure and happy, individuals. A task of every program should be to help the children feel as confident and comfortable with one adult as with another. A key to success in this task is using a team approach in which roles are understood by each staff member and responsibilities are carried out according to a plan.

Small Groups

Children need individual attention and assistance which can be given in small groups. Working with five to eight children in a group enhances learning opportunities, while making it possible for the adult to observe each child's progress and special needs. Even within a small group, every child needs recognition by name. This helps develop a positive self-concept which, in turn, provides encouragement for further development. In small groups, each child has numerous opportunities for participating in both conversation and action. Each child needs to interact on a one-to-one basis with children and adults. A center's philosophy should take into consideration the individual attention needed by children.

A Developmental Center

A developmental center provides a setting in which children are able to progress gradually, step by step, and at an individual rate or pace from one task to another. Learning about an object, for example, begins by touching it, looking at it, and listening to it—and may continue by taking it apart and reassembling it. During this time, the child may talk about the object, ask questions, or simply murmur to himself. Concern for each child's individual development is a task for the staff and should be incorporated in the center's philosophy. Making use of materials and ideas to help each child progress at an individual

Ch. 18: You and the Child Care Profession

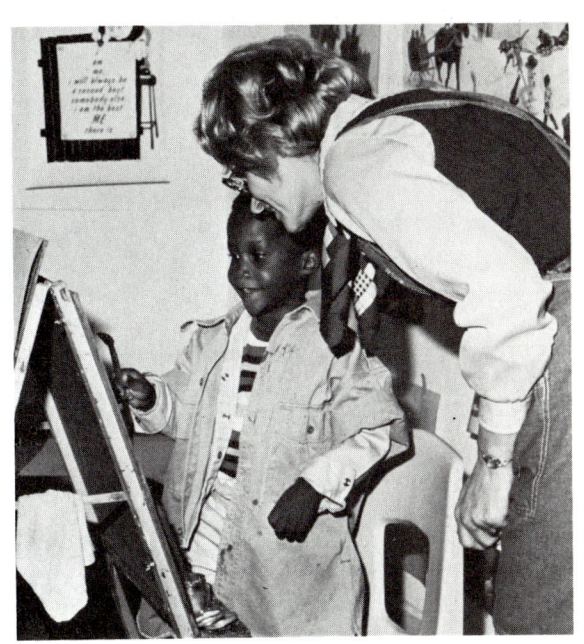

University of Oklahoma Health Sciences Center
Every child needs to be recognized individually.

Kickapoo Head Start Center
In a developmental center each child progresses at an individual pace. Here children put icing on vanilla wafers. Earlier the children talked about the project. Then they made the icing. Later they will have a delicious snack. Each child is able to help with such a project to the extent that his ability allows, and all enjoy the end result.

pace requires careful planning and organization, as well as an understanding of the child's development.

Other Concerns

By now you should have a more clear-cut idea about what can be included in a philosophy of child care. What you have just read, however, is certainly not the limit. Everything you have learned about children can be used to help you formulate your personal philosophy. As you learn more, your ideas may change. Many find that with experience new discoveries and attitudes are uncovered. Are you prepared to put your philosophy on caring for children into words? Why not try it?

Chapter Highlights

- Personal qualifications are a primary concern when hiring individuals to care for children.
- A child care worker's influence on a child may last a lifetime.
- Baby-sitting is one way to get acquainted with the characteristics and needs of children.

Part V: Working In Children's Centers

- Volunteering in a child care center or a Head Start program is another way of preparing for work with children.
- Training for child care work is available at many high schools, vocational schools, junior and senior colleges, and universities.
- Before applying for a job, one should collect all the information needed and place it in a folder in order to have everything ready at a moment's notice.
- Credentials, including an official transcript of high school and post-high-school training, and letters of recommendation, are usually requested when you apply for a job.
- When filling out application forms, read over the instructions carefully before entering any information. Fill out all blanks.
- As a child care worker, you should be physically prepared to carry out the work of the day. This calls for good general health, adequate diet, and proper rest.
- Working successfully in a center calls for willingness to share ideas and give support whenever possible.
- Ideal members of a center staff are constantly aware of their contribution to the image of the center while engaged in nonprofessional or off-the-job activities.
- Good management is the key to making you more successful on the job while increasing your enjoyment of work.
- Evaluation of your work should be made in light of goals which establish major priorities to be achieved with children.
- Continuous evaluation helps to achieve greater quality in staff performance and in the overall program.
- The philosophy of a program refers to its underlying attitudes and goals.

Thinking It Over

1. Do you think you are suited for work in the child care field? Why?
2. How much influence do you think a child care worker has on a child?
3. Where can you receive the education and training you need for the job you want to hold?
4. How would you proceed to get a job as a child care worker?
5. Have you ever been interviewed for a job? If so, what advice would you give someone going for an interview?
6. Assuming you are the director of a child care center, what would you expect from your employees?
7. Explain the difference between pre-service and in-service training.
8. What are some important considerations in maintaining good health?
9. Discuss the importance of cooperation among fellow employees as well as between employer and employee?
10. Discuss the relationship of management and evaluation of your work.
11. Describe your personal philosophy concerning the child care profession.

Things To Do

1. Invite the school guidance counselor to bring a *Dictionary of Occupational Titles* or *Occupational Outlook Handbook* to class and point out various jobs and job descriptions in the area of child care.
2. Have a panel of child care workers discuss advantages and disadvantages of their work.
3. Collect cartoons relating to employee problems. Post these and use them to launch a discussion on ways to prevent problems.
4. Prepare a bulletin board which portrays personal characteristics needed by a child care worker.
5. Obtain job applications from local businesses and practice filling these out in class.
6. Write a paper on "What I Have to Offer An Employer."
7. Develop a *Do* and *Don't Do* list in preparation for an interview.
8. Prepare an envelope with necessary information which may be needed for a job interview. Prepare a resumé.
9. Invite the principal or a teacher to conduct an interview with one of the students, or make arrangements to video tape an interview and play it back for class discussion.
10. Invite a nurse to talk with the class on how to maintain good health—an important requirement for any employee.
11. Invite an employer to talk to the class on what makes a good employee.
12. Write a personal philosophy concerning child care. Keep this for future reference to determine any changes in philosophy as a result of more knowledge, experience, and maturity.

Recommended Reading

Dunn, Lucile; Bailey, Annetta; and Draper, Mary Wanda. *Steps in Clothing Skills*. Peoria, Illinois: Chas. A. Bennett Co., Inc., 1970.

How to Operate Your Day Care Program. Wyomissing, Pennsylvania: Ryan Jones Associates, Inc., 1970.

Spodek, Bernard. *Teaching In The Early Years*. Englewood Cliffs, New Jersey: Prentice-Hall, Inc., 1962.

Young, Leontine. *Life Among the Giants*. New York: McGraw-Hill Book Co., 1966.

Chapter 19.

Centers For Children

Your Challenge

This chapter will enable you to . . . .

- Name and describe the three types of child care.
- Name and describe the different types of child care centers.
- Explain what services are now provided in child care.
- List what to look for in a good center.
- Explain what must be done to establish a children's center.

GETTING ACQUAINTED WITH CHILD CARE SERVICES

If you have a special interest in how children grow and develop and if you enjoy being around them, you are needed in the world of services for young children. The following information about children's centers, planning activities, and managing the operation of a center will help you become familiar with child care work. You will want to get acquainted with the role of a child care worker—what to expect on the job and ways to make your work with children enjoyable and successful.

In addition to study, one way to learn about what goes on in child care is to visit several children's centers in your neighborhood or community to observe the children in action and the program in progress. Directors and teachers are often eager to talk with you about their programs and help you become familiar with what they are doing with children.

TYPES OF CHILD CARE

There are basically three types of child care: custodial, developmental, and comprehensive.

Custodial care offers limited service, providing for the safe care of children with little or no attention to special efforts for enhancing each child's development. Incidental learning occurs as children play with one another. Minimal physical and motor development results from free play activities. As children interact with one another and with adults, social development occurs but in limited ways. A custodial program consists mainly of free play, rest and nap times, snacks and meals, and sometimes watching television. Of course, some custodial programs are housed in excellent facilities and do an outstanding job of caring for children. Nevertheless, the program is limited in scope and should be recognized for what it is.

Ch. 19: Centers For Children

Blocker Head Start Center
The field of child care needs people who are interested in children.

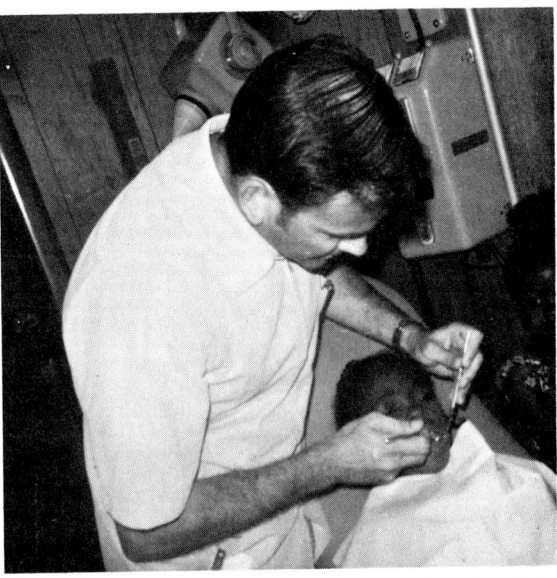

Kickapoo Head Start Center
Dental services are provided by comprehensive programs.

Developmental child care takes special efforts to enhance development through planned activities which offer stimulating and enriching experiences. The environment is organized to provide opportunities for physical, emotional, social, and intellectual development. Specific goals in such areas as sensory perception, motor coordination, concept formation, language skills, self-image, and living skills are set. Developmental care often includes parent involvement. Do you see how this type of care can supplement home care?

Comprehensive programs, in addition to providing developmental care, provide children and families with health, nutrition, psychological, and social services. This type of child care is, of course, the most desirable. As you can see, however, it is expensive and requires coordination of services among community agencies.

TYPES OF CENTERS

Child care centers are not all alike. In the first place, the kind of child care they provide will be different depending on each center's program and philosophy. Secondly, they are different in physical setup and in size. As you read about the kinds of child care centers, try to decide where you would prefer to work and where you would send your children if faced with this decision.

Day Care Centers

These facilities operate in fifty states and generally provide group care for children ranging in age from about eight weeks to fourteen years. A few centers offer twenty-four-hour care and some include infant care. The number of children in a day care center may vary from a small number like eight or ten children to over

Part V: Working In Children's Centers

Family day care is provided for five or fewer children in a private home.

a hundred, depending on the type of center facility, program design, and the staff available. Large centers are often divided into groups such as infants, toddlers, preschoolers, and school-age children. These centers are located in residential areas, commercial centers, industrial plants, hospitals, and other locations where children require care.

Day care centers are located in a variety of buildings—converted houses, churches, community centers, commercial buildings, or new buildings. These facilities are designed for the purpose of child care and are not used as regular living quarters by a family.

Family Day Care Homes

Family day care homes provide child care for a fee in the home of a family. Nearly all states require a license for those who charge a fee for child care in their homes. Social service agencies, such as child welfare departments, often assist in supervising or help in planning these programs.

Family day care homes are usually located in residential homes in the neighborhood of the children served. The children are often under three years of age and require much individual attention. Some children, however, are older, even through school age. School children sometimes go to day care homes before and/or after school hours; some may return for lunch if time permits. In most states a maximum of five children is permitted by law in a family day care home. This number also includes the children who are members of the family operating the center. A family with four children, for example, could only take in one additional child.

Group Day Care Homes

A number of states have a category of child care called group day care homes. The enrollment in these homes ranges from about one to fifteen children. Residential homes serve as the facility for this type of care. The program in group day care homes is similar to that of day care centers. The age range of children in these settings varies from infancy through school age.

Nursery Schools and Kindergartens

Nursery schools and kindergartens function during the day to offer enrichment programs in the form of instruction or special emphasis on the child's early development and learning. Nursery schools are usually part-day programs for two or three hours per session. Some nursery programs operate only morning or afternoon sessions; others have both. Some are open for only two or three days a week and some are open every day.

Ch. 19: Centers For Children

University of Oklahoma Institute of Child Development
Nursery schools located in many residential areas serve three- or four-year-old children with a two- or three-hour program.

Beggs Project
Parent involvement in Head Start programs helps parents learn about child development assistance. Here parents help prepare lunch for the children.

Kindergarten programs also vary in their offerings. Some are full-day sessions, and others are half-day programs operating in the morning for one group of children and in the afternoon for another group. For example, some kindergartens may be full-day for five days a week—open from 8:30 or 9:00 a.m. until 2:00 or 3:00 p.m. Others may be open for one group from 9:00 until 12:00 a.m. and for another group from 1:00 until 4:00 p.m. Many states now have included kindergarten as part of the public school program.

Child Development and Learning Centers

Child development and learning centers may be privately operated programs, special projects supported by federal and/or local funds, or part of a public school program. One example of this program has been the Child and Family Resource Project (CFRP). This is a federally funded program serving children and families in low-income areas of a given community. The number of families varies with the facilities and the funds or other resources available for operating them.

Head Start

As a program, Head Start came into being during the mid-1960's when a pediatrician, Dr. Robert Cooke, and his committee were appointed by the federal government to develop a program for young children of disadvantaged backgrounds. Head Start is now nationwide under the direction of the Office of Child Development in the United States Department of Health, Education, and Welfare.

327

Part V: Working In Children's Centers

Home Start emphasizes home-centered experiences in which parents provide activities for their children's development in an atmosphere of love and concern.

Head Start is a community program which includes the cooperation of educators, physicians, nurses, social workers, psychologists, parents, and teachers in an effort to improve the development of disadvantaged children from three to six years old. Emphasis is placed on health, nutrition, education, parent involvement, and social and psychological services.

One of Head Start's greatest contributions to early childhood has been the use of a *team approach* in working with children in daily activities. The team includes the teacher, aide, and volunteer. These adults work with small groups of children, which enables them to give more individual attention to children's special needs. Children also have greater opportunities for participation and interaction with one another in a small group setting with five to seven children participating in an activity with an adult. Depending on the nature of the activities, the adults may rotate among the groups or float from one group to another as needed. Other times, each adult works with groups of children according to the abilities he or she has.

A major goal of the Head Start program is to focus on developmental activities which help disadvantaged children improve physical development, motor coordination, sensory and perceptual skills, self-concept, living skills, and thinking and reasoning abilities. Ideally, children are helped to progress from one stage of development to the next according to each child's ability and uniqueness.

Some Head Start programs are organized in day care settings, and others operate like kindergartens or child development centers. The type of program organization depends greatly on other neighborhood facilities available and the needs of the children who participate. There are a number of experimental Head Start centers across the nation. The purpose of these is to develop programs which more appropriately meet the needs of the children served.

Home Start

One of the most recent programs to evolve out of the Head Start movement through the Office of Child Development in Washington is called Home Start. Emphasis is placed on working with children and families in the home. Ages of children range from infancy to school age. A major

Ch. 19: Centers For Children

focus of this program is on education for "parenting" to enable families to provide more appropriate home experiences for the optimal development of their children.

Parent and Child Centers

Parent and Child Centers were initiated in 1968 when Congress appropriated funds for a pilot project which had as its objective the prevention of developmental lags in young children by providing special services to the total family. These included such assistance as medical, nutritional, social, educational, legal, and psychological services. Local centers were established to teach parents techniques of child care and to provide opportunities for learning how to work with their children both in the center and in the home. Parent and Child Centers are similar to Head Start in organization but serve children of three years and under and include parents, especially mothers, in the center program.

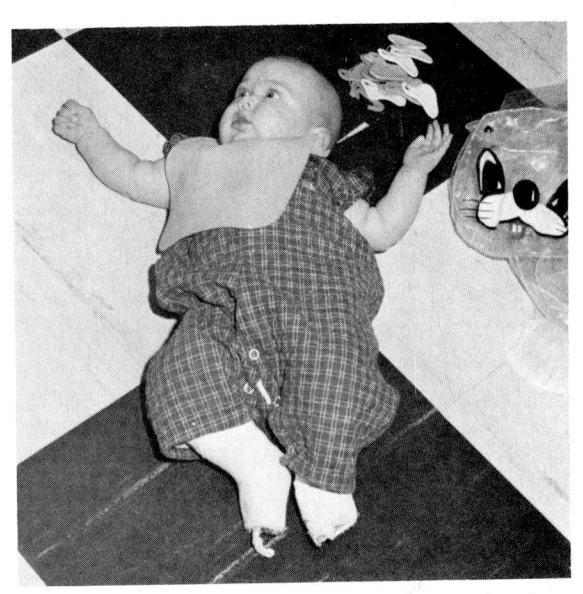

Oklahoma City Christian Day Care Center

Some handicapped children benefit greatly from child care programs that are prepared to include children with special needs. Although this infant wears casts on her legs, the special attention she receives in the center enables her to thrive.

EXPANDING SERVICES IN CHILD CARE

Day care, now more appropriately called *child care*, originated to provide custodial service for children ranging in age from infancy to eight or twelve years. As you recall, this service was provided primarily because mothers worked outside the home either all day or part of the day.

The amount of time child care centers are open varies from one center to another. Some open as early as 6:00 or 7:00 a.m. and do not close until 6:00 or 7:00 p.m.; others remain open for twenty-four hours. The twenty-four hour programs often serve hospitals or industries where parents are engaged in shift work. Children are usually in these centers for eight to twelve hours. Other child care centers provide service for school-age children only before and after school because parents are away from home and the children need care during these hours. Drop-in programs offer care for children while parents are attending college classes, shopping, or engaged in other activities for short periods of time.

Are you aware that some children attend more than one children's center each day? For example, a child may go to a child care center from 7:30 a.m. to 1:00 p.m., a nursery school from 1:30 until 3:30, and return to the child care center until the parents pick up the child. Another child may attend a morning Head Start or kindergarten program and then remain in a child care center for the afternoon.

Although specific directions are not included in this text for care of the disabled

Part V: Working In Children's Centers

In a good center both children and adults are relaxed as they enjoy the center activities.

or handicapped child, it is important to note that children who are blind, deaf, emotionally disturbed, learning disabled, mentally retarded, or otherwise physically or developmentally handicapped, may benefit greatly from child development, Head Start, and certain child care programs. There are some excellent centers which include a combination of handicapped and nonhandicapped children. Perhaps you will want to study more about working with disabled or handicapped children after you have completed this study of child care or, indeed, while you are proceeding with it.

Today, more emphasis is placed on expanding child care programs to include learning and stimulation experiences. Many centers are beginning to emphasize the child's physical, emotional, social, and intellectual development by planning and carrying out activities aimed at achieving certain goals for the children. Thus, the concept of child care is evolving toward the enrichment of the child's daily living beyond general care and safety. Unfortunately, however, many programs claim they are providing for the total development of each child but in reality they are only skimming the surface.

A variety of programs for preschool children are emerging and, consequently, families have greater choices in the selection of programs for their children. Parents also have opportunities to be involved in the planning and implementation of children's programs. You have probably read newspaper and magazine articles lately which report on some of the new and exciting programs for children. Many of these include parents and family members as a part of the program, both in community centers and in their own homes.

WHAT TO LOOK FOR IN A GOOD CENTER

The following list of questions identifies areas of concern for both parents and child care workers in evaluating a center. Do you have additional questions to include?

- Is the center licensed?
- Are conditions safe and sanitary (fire protection, adequate heating and ventilation, toilet and washrooms clean, kitchen and eating facilities clean and adequate)?
- Does it appear to provide a comfortable and pleasant atmosphere for the children—routines followed but without rigid or demanding procedures?
- Is each child's health protected and promoted (medical examinations, health records, first aid supplies, daily health checks, space for a sick child, regulated temperature)?

Ch. 19: Centers For Children

- Is the food nutritionally adequate, well-prepared, and attractively served?
- What are the age ranges of children?
- What are the group sizes? Are these groups small enough for individual attention and interaction?
- Are the workers pleasant and respectful toward each other and the children?
- Do the children seem relaxed, enjoying the center activities?
- Is there ample room indoors (35 square feet or more per child) and outdoors (75 square feet per child) for the children's play and work?
- Is the equipment sturdy, safe, and appropriate for various age ranges of children?
- Are materials and supplies well organized and arranged for convenient use?
- Are emergency numbers (hospital, fire, police, etc.) posted by the telephone?
- Are enough adults present to insure children's safety and to assist in all activities?
- Is an evacuation plan posted for all to observe?
- Is there a plan of activities and experiences to meet goals for children (language skills, concept formation, motor coordination, sensory perception, self-concept, living skills, general physical development)?
- Do children have opportunities for first-hand experiences?
- Are there ample opportunities for developing social skills—cooperating, respect for each other's feelings, responsibility, independence, self-assurance?
- Are parents involved in the program—observing, participating from time to time, making suggestions, knowing what the center's goals and objectives are for the children?
- Are records kept on each child's progress and development—attendance, health, special problems, strengths and weaknesses, areas of special need?
- Does the staff cooperate as a team to consider the well-being of each child?
- Does the center cooperate with other community groups and use available resources to improve and maintain a quality program?

Materials, like books, are well organized and arranged for convenient use in a good center.

ESTABLISHING A CHILDREN'S CENTER

Your interest in child care may inspire you to do more than apply for a job in an existing center. If circumstances permit, you may want to establish your own center. To give you an overview of the procedures for establishing a center, the general steps are outlined here. Of course, these will vary according to the community and state, but this list includes the minimal steps to follow:

- Locate a possible site for the center.

Part V: Working In Children's Centers

- Contact the city's Building Inspection Department and request that the site be checked to determine whether it is zoned for child care services.
- Apply for a permit of occupancy. This usually carries a fee ranging from about $5.00 to $100.00. The inspection department will have a representative inspect the building construction and safety features. If the facility meets the requirements, a permit will be granted. If it does not, the inspection department will issue a letter or list of recommendations for repairs, changes, and improvements needed. Another request will have to be made for a permit after alterations are completed.
- Follow local and state standards for meeting requirements necessary for a license to operate. When the center facility is ready for occupancy and the staff is ready for work, contact the licensing division of the welfare and/or health departments and request inspections.
- A license to operate will be issued if requirements and standards are met. Otherwise, recommendations for changes or improvements will be made and the previous step must be repeated.

Each step in this process may have to be repeated until approval is granted. (Steps for securing a license to operate family day care homes and day care centers are provided in the Appendix.)

Social security, tax regulation, insurance, and employee benefits should be investigated thoroughly. Adequate insurance coverage for children is of high priority when establishing a children's center. Several types of coverage should be considered:

- Liability, hospitalization, and accident for children.
- Same for adult employees.
- Social Security for employees.
- Liability, comprehensive, and collision for center vehicles and drivers.
- Property insurance.

Financing a business requires the expertise of both legal and financial professionals. Should you consider establishing a children's center, you will be wise to secure the services of an attorney and an accountant. The attorney can advise you about the aspects of setting up a business and suggest an accountant to provide financial counseling. Some concerns you will encounter in establishing a business include identifying the amount of money required to secure a loan and start a center and qualifying for financing and securing a loan.

The Small Business Association (SBA) in your community, at no charge, can provide basic information to help you become familiar with financing procedures. The local banks are usually eager to give you general information concerning requirements for securing a loan and establishing a business.

The Chamber of Commerce is another source of general information about establishing a business. They usually provide information about zoning and securing permits to build or convert an existing building into a center.

Bookkeeping and record procedures are necessary for conducting any business, including children's services. The director should secure professional and legal assistance in setting up adequate budgeting and bookkeeping systems. Tax laws require exact and accurate information to be filed annually. Books and records are subject to audit periodically and should be kept in order and up-to-date monthly. An operating budget will include many items. See

Chapter 20 for more information on budgeting.

A written statement summarizing the goals and objectives, philosophy, and activities of the program should be available to parents and community members. The names of the director and owner or sponsor, as well as a list of staff members, should be available with addresses and phone numbers.

Licensing Requirements and Minimum Standards

Most states offer legal protection for children who participate in public or private programs by requiring centers to secure a license to operate. The license is granted upon meeting certain minimum standards set by both state and local communities. Children's centers must meet the requirements in order to operate legally in a given locality. Federally supported programs have additional requirements. Although specific qualifications and standards vary from one geographical area to another, there are requirements common to all centers. These are concerned with:

- Personnel standards.
- General facility standards.
- Food preparation and service.
- Sanitation and health standards.
- Fire regulations.
- Construction codes.
- Electrical services.
- Ventilation.
- Plumbing and sewage disposal.
- Safety requirements.
- Water supply and drinking water facilities.
- Space per child (this varies from area to area): outdoors—75 to 100 square feet per child; indoors—35 to 50 square feet per child.

- Program: adult/child ratio; health and safety regulations; daily activities for the well-being and development of children; equipment and materials suitable for children; records and reports for business and legal purposes; children's records (health, dental, psychological, developmental, etc.).
- Social services.

Unfortunately, not all children's centers in operation abide by the regulations established in their state and local community. Such program violations neither insure the children's welfare nor present a positive image in the field of early childhood. For immediate security of children as well as for future gains, each center staff member and director has a responsibility to the children, their families, and the community to maintain the minimum standards and regulations while operating a program. Each center should strive toward the continuous improvement of both the physical facilities and the children's program. The most beautiful and modern facility with the latest equipment is of little value to the children unless it is used according to a well-planned and appropriate program, designed according to the needs of the children.

Bulletins containing licensing requirements are available in state and local welfare agency offices. Licensing alone, however, is not enough to insure adequate care, protection, guidance or supervision, and opportunities for children to develop favorably. A program with identified goals and objectives for the children and a well-thought-out plan for implementing activities has a greater potential for meeting children's needs and attracting qualified child care workers.

Part V: Working In Children's Centers

Chapter Highlights

- One way to learn about what goes on in child care is to visit several children's centers.
- There are basically three types of child care: custodial, developmental, and comprehensive.
- The kind of child care a center provides will vary depending on each center's program and philosophy.
- Nearly all states license family day care homes in which children are usually cared for during the day.
- Nursery schools and kindergartens function during the day to offer enrichment programs with special emphasis on the child's early development and learning.
- Head Start is a community program designed to improve the development of disadvantaged young children.
- One of the most recent programs to evolve out of the Head Start movement is *Home Start* which emphasizes working with children and families in the home.
- A license is granted to a center if it meets certain minimum standards set by state and local welfare and public health units.
- Bulletins containing licensing requirements are available in state and local welfare agency offices.

Thinking It Over

1. Describe three types of child care.
2. Why do you think so many people leave their children in centers which provide only custodial care?
3. What does developmental child care provide a child that custodial child care does not offer?
4. Why aren't all child care programs comprehensive since they offer children and their families much more than other types?
5. Why do child care centers differ so radically even in the same community?
6. What is the difference between a day care center and a family day care home?
7. How did the Head Start program begin in the United States?
8. How are families getting involved in child care programs in the United States?
9. What are some of the areas of concern for both parents and child care workers in child care centers?
10. If you were interested in establishing a day care center, what general steps would be necessary to get this operation started?
11. Are all child care centers today licensed to operate? Why or why not?
12. Where can a person obtain licensing requirements for child care centers?
13. Do you think all licensed children's centers provide adequate care, protection, guidance, and supervision as well as opportunities for children to develop favorably? Explain.

Ch. 19: Centers For Children

Things To Do

1. Make a survey of child care centers in your community. Talk to the directors and determine what type of child care program is carried out in each center.
2. Visit two or more kindergartens in your community. Check the similarities and differences in the programs.
3. Obtain a copy of requirements for licensing a children's center in your community.
4. Visit a family day care home and consult with the person providing child care. Explore the possibility of serving as a volunteer in the day care home.
5. Have a person from a local Head Start program describe the program.
6. Visit a local child care center and check each of the requirements listed for licensing.

Recommended Reading

Can I Love This Place? Washington, D.C.: Educational Systems Corporation, 1969.

Environmental Criteria, Preschool Day Care Facilities. College Station, Texas: College of Architecture and Environmental Design, Texas A&M University.

How to Operate Your Day Care Program. Wyomissing, Pennsylvania: Ryan Jones Associates, Inc., 1970.

Kritchevsky, Sybil; Prescott, Elizabeth; and Wailing, Lee. *Planning Environments for Young Children: Physical Space.* Washington, D.C. 20009: National Association for the Education of Young Children, Publications Department, 1969.

LaCross, Robert E. *Day Care for America's Children.* Public Affairs Pamphlet, #470, 381 Park Avenue South, New York, 1973.

Spodek, Bernard. *Teaching in the Early Years.* Englewood Cliffs, New Jersey: Prentice-Hall, Inc., 1972.

Stanley, Julian C. Edited by *Preschool Programs for the Disadvantaged.* Baltimore, Maryland: The Johns Hopkins University Press, 1972.

State and Local Day Care Licensing Requirements. Prepared by Social and Administrative Services and Systems Association in conjunction with Consulting Services Corporation, for the Office of Child Development, Washington, D.C.: Department of Health, Education, and Welfare, 1971.

Chapter 20.

Managing Center Operations

Your Challenge

This chapter will enable you to . . . .

- *Explain the responsibilities of management toward personnel.*
- *Give guidelines on setting up a budget for the center.*
- *Name and describe the types of records that must be kept in a center.*
- *Explain how purchasing should be handled.*
- *Give advantages and suggestions concerning storage and distribution.*
- *Explain management concerns on transportation.*
- *Describe how communications should be handled in the center.*
- *Name and describe the services required by child care centers.*

MANAGEMENT

Whether you aspire to become a center director or child care worker, knowledge about managing a center will make you a more valuable staff member. Efficient operation of a center depends upon the director's management skills and the cooperation and support of each employee. In this chapter you will read about these major concerns in managing a center: personnel, budgeting, records, purchasing, storage and distribution, transportation, communications, and services.

PERSONNEL

The most important task in operating a center is to secure and maintain quality personnel. The selection of an employee requires careful consideration of each applicant's qualifications in relation to the position on the staff. The quality of the center's service depends on the performance and contributions of all the center's personnel. The atmosphere of the center is determined by the staff and how they work together for the benefit of the children.

Regardless of how excellent the facilities are and how well the program is planned, success depends on the staff. Even though it may cost more to secure people who are well qualified for their roles, the long-range returns are usually worth the investment.

Staff Organization

A written job description should be on file for each position, explaining tasks and responsibilities of the employee. Some job descriptions also include qualifications required to secure the position as well as the range of pay.

An organizational chart of personnel will usually be posted in the center office and available to anyone who is interested. It shows the relationship of each position to others in the center. The lines of responsibility should be outlined clearly. In the organizational chart shown here, arrows illustrate the flow of responsibility.

Personnel Policies

The conditions under which each employee works must be identified. These policies are often developed by a personnel policy committee of the advisory or governing board in cooperation with the center director. If there is no board, the owner or director usually assumes this task with a staff committee. Policies should be reviewed at least once each year to be sure they meet legal requirements and current employment practices. Policies generally include:

- Length of work day, week, and year.
- Basis for wage and salary calculation.

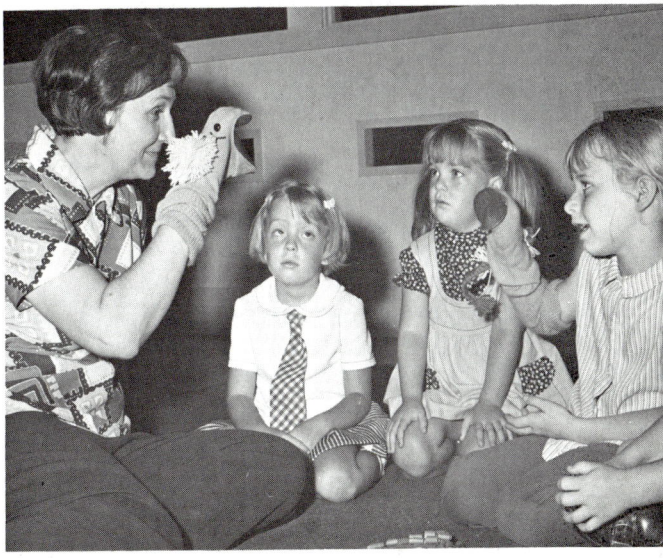

University of Oklahoma Institute of Child Development
Regardless of how excellent the facilities are, the success of a center depends primarily on the staff.

- Special training requirements and expectations.
- Allowable expenses and reimbursements.
- Medical and health requirements.
- Holidays, vacations, and leave of absence conditions.

ORGANIZATIONAL CHART SHOWING FLOW OF STAFF RESPONSIBILITY

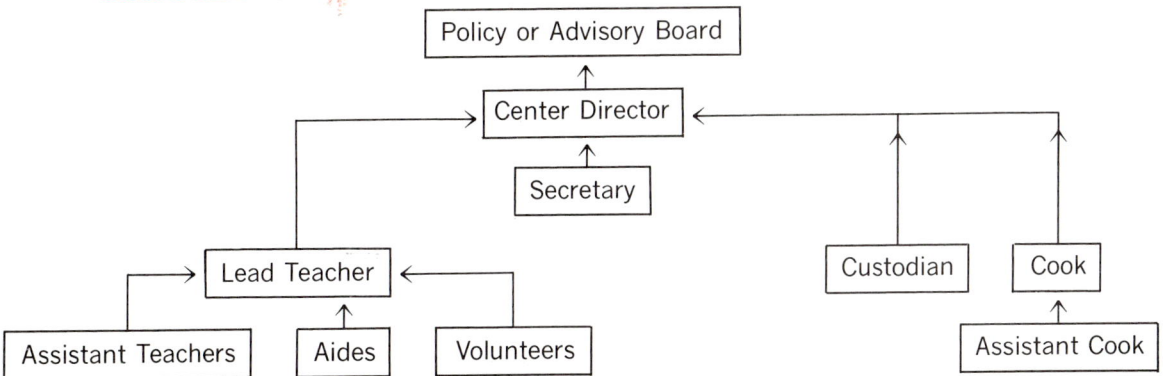

Policy or Advisory Board
↑
Center Director
↑
Secretary

Lead Teacher
↑
Assistant Teachers | Aides | Volunteers

Custodian | Cook
↑
Assistant Cook

337

- Sick leave conditions.
- Fringe benefits.
- Resignation procedures.

Hiring Personnel

Every potential employee should fill out an application form. The form should be simple and questions factual and clearly stated. Information should be related to the position for which the application is made.

Interviews should be complete enough to secure the necessary information about an applicant in order to make fair and sound decisions about employment. Depending on the position, applicants may be interviewed by more than one person. For example, an applicant for the position of lead teacher may be interviewed by the center director and by representatives of the governing board's personnel committee. An assistant teacher may be interviewed by the lead teacher and director or simply the lead teacher, who makes recommendations to the director. Again, this depends on the center policies and organizational structure.

References should be checked to secure information about the applicant's quality of performance. It is an advantage to know what a potential employee's strengths are in order to make appropriate assignments and receive the greatest returns for the investment.

The applicant should be given written information about personnel policies and the job description. When hired, withholding tax forms for income tax purposes should be filled out. The new employee should be placed on the payroll on the date that employment officially begins.

An orientation to the center facilities—restrooms, personal storage, work areas, lunch time, special meeting places, and conference rooms—helps the new employee get off to a good start. Remember to provide details about policies such as those concerning coffee breaks, snacking, and smoking.

Wages and Salaries

Wages (hourly pay) and salaries (monthly pay) are usually established by an individual center but in keeping with national and state trends. If possible, the wages and salaries should be competitive and generous enough to attract qualified personnel. At the same time, the wage and salary structure should remain in keeping with other community organizations providing similar services. For instance, if a child development learning center wants to attract a qualified teacher with certification for the four- and five-year-old group, a salary offer might be comparable to kindergarten teachers in the local school system.

Providing a range in wage or salary usually supports the employee who is more experienced and who does outstanding work. By having a range of pay instead of a single figure, an incentive is offered for the employee to provide the best possible service.

You will no doubt be interested in the difference between wages and salary as payment for services rendered. Those who work for wages work by the hour and when their required number of hours have been completed, their work day is complete. The regular work day usually consists of eight hours and the work week, forty hours. Some wage earners may have the option to work overtime, in excess of the specified number of hours per week. They are usually paid more per hour for overtime than the pay received per hour for the first forty hours of work in a week. The salaried person works on a monthly or yearly pay basis, with a specified mini-

Ch. 20: Managing Center Operations

mum number of hours per day (generally eight) and per week (generally forty). The idea behind a salaried position is that the person has specific duties and responsibilities for which he or she is qualified by education and specialized training. He should usually be able to complete tasks within an eight-hour day. A salaried employee accepts a position with an understanding about the required duties; thus, at times he may feel the responsibility to work until the tasks are completed, even if this takes him beyond the normal minimum of an eight-hour day, without the benefit of additional or overtime pay.

Salaries are usually paid to professional persons and are generally higher, by comparison, than wages. Salaried personnel do not usually punch time cards or fill out time sheets each day to indicate the number of hours worked, whereas wage earners do. It is interesting to note that some wage earners make as much per year, or more, because of overtime than salaried personnel, even though their base pay as wage earners is less.

Leadership and Supervision

Staff members should be given special assistance and leadership for updating and improving their effectiveness as employees.

Periodic meetings to discuss new trends, research findings, and possibilities for improving the children's program is a responsibility of the person in charge of the center's operation. In some centers this task is delegated to the lead teacher.

All staff members benefit from educational leadership. Perhaps one of the most effective means of supervision for achieving quality staff performance is when the staff and leaders sit down together and evaluate their effectiveness as a team in relation to the center's purposes.

Beggs Project

Staff members need special assistance and leadership for updating and improving their effectiveness as employees.

Individual conferences including the director and employee can be helpful in discussing an individual's strengths and areas related to work that need improvement. Sound guidance and help may be necessary for a new employee to feel secure and comfortable in learning a new role.

BUDGETING

Budgeting, the planned use of money to meet program needs, can make or break a children's center. Although you may not initially have the responsibility of planning and using a center budget, you will be wise

339

Part V: Working In Children's Centers

to learn as much as possible about this management task. You might think of a budget as a statement of a center's services expressed in dollars rather than words. As you can see, this means you must know what services are offered and the details about these in order to develop a budget.

A well-thought-out-budget is the key to operating a successful program. The activities of the children and the services to families would not be possible without adequate financial operations. An understanding of budgeting will help expand your competencies as a child care worker and will help you appreciate the role of a manager.

As you think about budgeting, keep in mind the priorities of the total program. What is most important? Consider these questions: Does the budget include a plan for maintaining overall quality? How is the money divided? Is there a guide for selecting and purchasing equipment, materials, and supplies? Are accurate records kept on all money received and money spent?

A budget must be practical and realistic. It must be appropriate for the program objectives. If there is not enough money to operate the program adequately, two considerations should be made: Is the program too broad and the number of children too great for the amount of money available? Is the budget plan accurate and appropriate in meeting the program needs?

Of course, it is better to have a smaller program which is adequate for the children than to try to stretch the budget. Remember, quality child care is a major goal.

Setting Up a Budget

The two major parts of any budget are *income* and *expenses*. When starting a center, a budget must be prepared. Income is estimated in order to determine how much money will be available for expenses. All assured sources and amounts of income should be listed. Then a general breakdown of expenses must be made, with a realistic cost figure allowed for each. Both categories should balance. That is, the total amount for expenses should not exceed the total amount of income. Obviously, the center will be in trouble if income will not cover expenses.

Once a budget is set up, careful records must be maintained to keep expenses in line. For example, if an annual figure of $600 is allowed for advertising ($50 per month) and $200 has been spent by the end of the first two months of the center's operation, then only $40 per month can be allowed for the remainder of the year. By totaling all expenditures in each expense category at any time during the year, you can readily see how much has been spent in relation to how much more can be spent.

The budget plan should be kept up-to-date whenever changes occur. After a budget plan has been made, some *flexibility* is needed. You should not exceed ten percent, however, when moving money from one category to another. For example, the budget plan calls for $300 per month for consumable supplies and $600 for rental equipment. The program needs more money for consumable supplies and you prefer to transfer some from equipment rental. You should not transfer more than $60, or ten percent of $600, from the equipment rental category. This keeps the budget in line with program objectives.

All budgets will not have exactly the same breakdown of income and expenses. The size of the center and the type of program will influence what is included. The list that follows, however, will give you a general idea of what many centers itemize under income and expenses.

Ch. 20: Managing Center Operations

INCOME

Fees for Children
Weekly or monthly fee for each child to participate in the program

Funds from Federal or State Sources
Welfare under Title XX of the Social Security Act

Funds from Other Organizations or Individuals
United Fund
Donations from service clubs and individuals

Milk Fund
U.S. Department of Agriculture reimbursement per one-half pint of milk

Other
Memorials
Cash gifts

EXPENSES

Personnel
Salaries and wages of all persons employed by the center
Salaries and wages for substitutes during vacations, in-service training, illness, and other staff absences

Employment Benefits
Social Security
Workmen's compensation
Accident and health insurance
Retirement
Unemployment insurance
Allowance for conferences, training, other

Insurance and Bonding
Liability for each child
Accident and health for each child
Fidelity bond
Vehicle liability
Owner's and tenant's insurance

Consumable Supplies
Program supplies—paper, art materials, clay, paper towels, napkins, etc.
Office supplies—paper, duplicating materials, pencils, forms, etc.
Maintenance supplies—mops, brooms, soap, light bulbs, toilet paper, etc.
Food—meals and snacks

Occupancy
Rent or lease of facility or purchase payments
Utilities
Maintenance and repairs
Renovation

Equipment Rental and Purchase
Program furniture
Office furniture
Office machines
Durable equipment for program, such as record players, blocks, games, autoharp, piano, and tape recorders
Durable equipment for operating and maintaining center, such as janitorial and kitchen equipment—vacuum cleaners, electrical appliances, etc.
Buses, automobiles, vans

Telephone and Telegraph
Cost of installation
Rental of equipment
Local service
Long distance service

Postage
Stamps
Other postal services

Services
Food (if not included under consumables) such as catering
Diaper
Laundry

Travel
Allowance for staff if not included above
Transportation of children

Consultant and Contract Services
Part-time physicians, nurses, child care specialists, nutritionists, others (may be included under personnel)

Part V: Working In Children's Centers

Health, social, and psychological services

Other

Publications—professional, newsletters, bulletins, etc.
Visual aides, exhibits, displays
Membership in professional organizations
Legal services
Annual audit
Advertising
Miscellaneous

A Sample Budget

A sample budget will enable you to see how one center's income and expenses balance. Neither the amounts nor the specific items in this example should be taken as a recommendation for setting up a center budget. In looking at each item you can see how costs will differ according to time, location, and need. Even though these figures are realistic and accurate for one center, they can only be used here to help you see how a budget is set up.

INCOME

Children's Fees ($125 per month per child × 12 months × 100 children)	$150,000
United Fund ($20 per month per child × 12 months × 100 children)	24,000
Community Service League ($4,000 per year donation)	4,000
Milk Fund (USDA reimbursement at 3¢ per one-half pint × 1 pint per child × 100 children × 300 days)	1,800
Private Donations	3,000
TOTAL INCOME	**$182,800**

EXPENSES
Personnel

Number of Persons	Position	Percent of Time	Number Months Employed	Cost
1	Director ($10,000 per year x 1 director)	50%	12	$ 5,000
1	Lead Teacher ($9,000 per year x 1 teacher)	100	12	9,000
3	Teachers ($8,500 per year x 3 teachers)	100	12	25,500
5	Assistant Teachers ($4.00 per hour at 30 hours per week for 50 weeks x 5 teachers)	100	12	30,000
1	Teacher's Aide ($7,500 per year)	50	12	3,750
1	Secretary/Bookkeeper ($8,000 per year)	100	12	8,000
1	Cook ($3.75 per hour at 20 hours per week for 50 weeks x 1 cook)	50	12	3,750
1	Custodian ($3.75 per hour at 20 hours per week for 50 weeks x 1 custodian)	50	12	3,750
1	Nurse ($9 per hour at 20 hours per month for 12 months x 1 nurse) (plus volunteer time)	12.5	12	2,160
1	Substitute Teacher ($25 per day x 30 days per year x 1 teacher equivalent)			$ 750
			Personnel Subtotal	**$91,660**

Ch. 20: Managing Center Operations

Employment Benefits

FICA/Social Security (6% of total cost of personnel) .... $ 5,500
Accident and Hospitalization
   ($15 per month × 12 months × 13 full-time equivalent employees) 2,340
Workmen's Compensation (30¢ per $100 of total cost of personnel) 275
Allowance—Training and Conferences (3% of total cost of personnel) 2,750
Increase in Salaries (6% of total cost of personnel) 5,500

                                                                         Benefits Subtotal $16,365

Insurance on Children (100 children at $6 per year each) .... $ 600

                                                                          Insurance Subtotal $ 600

Supplies

Program Activities ($6 per child per month × 12 months × 100 children) ...... $ 7,200
Food ($9 per child per month × 12 months × 100 children) 10,800
Office ($10 per employee per month × 12 months × 13 full-time
   equivalent employees) 1,560
General ($5 per week × 52 weeks) 260

                                                                          Supplies Subtotal $19,820

Occupancy

Lease ($1,250 per month × 12 months) $15,000
Utilities (Average $250 per month × 12 months) 3,000
Maintenance and Repairs ($20 per month × 12 months) 240
Renovation ($500 per year) 500

                                                                        Occupancy Subtotal $18,740

Equipment

Program—Purchased Equipment ($25 per child per year × 100 children) ...... $ 2,500
Office—Purchased Equipment ($110 per person × 4 employees) 440
Office—Rental Equipment ($80 per month × 2 offices × 12 months) 960

                                                                        Equipment Subtotal $ 3,900

Telephone and Telegraph ($25 per month × 3 telephones × 12 months) .... $ 900

                                   Telephone and Telegraph Subtotal $ 900

Postage ($15 per month × 12 months) .... $ 180

                                                                           Postage Subtotal $ 180

Services

Food—Milk. Only (10¢ per child per day × 300 days × 100 children) .... $ 3,000
Diaper ($3 per child per week × 52 weeks × 15 children) 2,340
Laundry (25¢ per child per month × 12 months × 100 children) 300

                                                                         Services Subtotal $ 5,640

Part V: Working In Children's Centers

Travel

Transportation of Children—Mileage
(100 miles per day × 15¢ per mile × 2 vehicles × 300 days)............... $ 9,000
Conferences and Training Meetings
(Average $25 per day × 8 persons × 4 days per year) 800
Travel Subtotal $ 9,800

Consultant and Contract Services

In-service Workshops ($75 per consultant × 6 days)......................... $ 450
Dental Care for Children ($20 per child × 100 children)..................... 2,000
Contractual Services for Children—Developmental, Social, Psychological
Testing, Referrals, Consultations ($25 per child per year × 100
children).. 2,500
Legal—Attorney and Audit ($600 per year) 600
Advertising (Average $50 per month × 12 months) 600
Consultant and Contract Services Subtotal $ 6,150

Other

Contingency Fund (For unexpected expenses)
(Approximately 5% of total budget—.05 × $173,755 = $8,688) .... $ 8,688
Other Subtotal $ 8,688
TOTAL EXPENSES $182,443

RECORDS

Record keeping is an important part of the operation of any business. It would be difficult, if not impossible, to list all of the reasons why records are needed. First of all, they are needed for systematic management of the center. In addition, they are needed for tax purposes, for inquiries on personnel and children, and for solving problems that may arise. Can you name other reasons?

A child care center's records will be primarily of three kinds: financial, personnel, and children's.

Financial Records

The operation of a center requires a system of financial procedures, including a set of records. Accurate financial records provide a continuous view of the center's financial status. Financial records include any dealings that involve the income and outgo of money in the business. This involves working with the budget, payroll, and other records that affect finances.

Most centers employ a bookkeeper or accountant who records all financial transactions. Although you do not have to understand the system unless you are in charge of the records, you should know enough to be able to talk with the accountant when necessary.

Whether you work in a large or small center, your general understanding of a system for keeping financial records will be to your advantage. Not only will you appreciate the necessity for accurate bookkeeping, but your knowledge about operating a center will be greater.

Forms for bookkeeping purposes should be standard. Simple forms are recommended for keeping most financial records. Some forms are printed on index cards. Others are kept on 8½ × 11 inch loose sheets, in notebooks, or in ledgers.

The bookkeeping system can be very simple or very elaborate and complex, depending on the director's management skills and philosophy. If this responsibility is delegated to a staff member, there may be specific guidelines established by the director and perhaps by a governing or advisory board. Should the center receive federal funds or financial support from outside sources, the necessity for accurate financial records is not only essential but may require specified forms and policies for bookkeeping and accounting purposes.

A familiarity with the different kinds of financial records will broaden your understanding of center operations. Perhaps you can arrange a visit to a local center in which the director is willing to show you a set of records and give a general explanation of how the financial system works.

You must realize, of course, that this discussion will not qualify you to keep records, but it will help acquaint you with some basic elements of a financial system. To really understand thoroughly how a financial system functions, you need to actually work with a person in charge of keeping the records for a center.

Personnel Records

Personnel records are closely related to the financial records of the business. Often the same person in charge of bookkeeping also handles the records of personnel. Some personnel records are needed to figure payroll and insurance benefits for employees. Naturally, personnel records will also serve other functions. For example, they are often used to provide other businesses with information on former employees when they seek other jobs.

Records concerning information about each employee are confidential and must always be protected in locked files. An employee's records should be kept on file for three to five years after the person leaves. Only a few persons, such as the director, bookkeeper, and secretary, should have access to these files. A folder is usually prepared to include the following information:

- Application forms.
- Vita or resumé, including references.
- Physical and health status.
- Employment date.
- Promotions, changes in position, wage or salary changes.
- Records of sick leave, vacation, leave of absence, and special leave for training.
- Reports of travel and other expense allowables.
- Evaluation reports.
- Other reports or records requested or administered by the director or person in charge of personnel.
- Termination date.

Several personnel records are linked directly with finances. You will see examples of these on the following pages.

Records of Staff Time

Keeping staff time may be efficiently achieved by using individual 5 × 7 inch index cards. These are easy to handle and may be filed in card holders or file card boxes.

A cumulative accounting of each staff member's time must be recorded. This is

Date _____

PERSONNEL INFORMATION RECORD

Name: _____ Center: _____
Address: _____
Telephone: _____
Date of Employment: _____ Starting Salary: _____
Position when Hired: _____
Hired by: _____
    Promotion: From: _____ To: _____
    Reason: _____
    _____ Date: _____
    Promotion: From: _____ To: _____
    Reason: _____
    _____ Date: _____
    Promotion: From: _____ To: _____
    Reason: _____
    _____ Date: _____
Date Terminated: _____ Reason: _____

	Date	From	To
Salary Increase:			
Salary Increase:			
Salary Increase:			
Salary Increase:			

Payroll Copy: _____ File Copy: _____ Employee Copy: _____

Forms on pages 346–352 adapted from Ryan Jones Assoc., Inc.

Ch. 20: Managing Center Operations

or form should be filed by the employee requesting absence from work. Approval by the director insures that information of anticipated absences has been approved and cleared.

Sick Leave

Although an employee cannot always anticipate illness or absence from work related to illness, a form should be filled out as soon as possible upon returning to work. The employee should give as much advance notice as possible. A telephone call the night before or early in the morning will often provide enough time to find a substitute worker if needed. In some cases, such as medical examinations and hospitalization, the employee can file a request for sick leave prior to the date of absence.

Children's Records

Accurate and up-to-date records for each child are needed to keep families, health officials, and the center administration informed of the child's health and developmental status. These records should be kept in a logical order, such as alphabetical, and available at all times. In the Appendix you will find examples of the types of records needed for children.

All records must be filed in the main office of the center. With daily notations, record keeping is easier to manage. These records also provide information for planning activities. These must be confidential.

Records can be handled in a number of ways. Some centers use a letter-size folder for each child with an information sheet for each section of the records.

Another method is to use 5 × 7 inch index cards for keeping children's records. These can be filed alphabetically in a card file and updated daily.

TIME SHEET

NAME: _____

Center: _____

Date: Month	Day	Hours		Reason*

Employee's Signature

* (SL—Sick Leave)   * (AL—Annual Leave)
* (CT—Compensatory Time)
* (OT—Overtime)

Director's Signature

---

usually done at the end of each month. Cards are also appropriate for this purpose.

Vacation, Leave, and Special Purpose Absence

Leave from the center should be scheduled in advance. This makes it possible to arrange for substitutes or assign responsibilities to co-workers. A 5 × 7 inch card

Part V: Working In Children's Centers

CUMULATIVE TIME RECORD

NAME_____ Center_____

Year_____

Time in Days	Earned / Used	Jan.	Feb.	Mar.	April	May	June	July	Aug.	Sept.	Oct.	Nov.	Dec.
Sick Leave (SL)	E / U												
Annual Leave (AL)	E / U												
Compensatory Time (CT)	E / U												
Overtime (OT)													

The following information is needed for children's records:

Background Information
- Child's full name, address, and birth date.
- Parents' names, home and business addresses, and telephone numbers.
- Name, address, and telephone number of person to contact in case of emergency (business and home telephone numbers).
- Names, addresses, and telephone numbers of physician and/or clinic to be contacted in cases of emergency.

Health Information
- Childhood diseases and other illnesses prior to entering the program.
- Information concerning accidents and illnesses of child while enrolled in the program.
- Particular symptoms or unusual observations regarding the child while in the center, such as nasal or ear drainage, headache, fever, or rash.
- Immunization records.

Attendance Information
- Date of enrollment.
- Daily attendance record.
- Notes concerning reasons for absences.
- Date of discharge or termination.

Developmental Information
- Notes of child's progress in specific areas of development.
- Notes of comparison with child's and parent's personal objectives.
- Checklist of competencies acquired by the child, with approximate date and age.
- Special problems or difficulties apparent with the child's daily experiences.

ABSENCE FROM WORK REQUEST

Name: _____ Date: _____

Center: _____

Type of Absence: (Check One)   Vacation _____

                                Personal Business _____

                                Illness _____

                                Compensatory Time _____

Dates to be Absent: _____

_____

Remarks: _____

_____   _____
                                                   Signature of Employee

_____

                                                   _____
_____   Approval by Director

_____   _____
                                                   Rejection by Director

PURCHASING

Buying equipment, materials, supplies, and services for a center is a major task in the management process. The person responsible for purchasing must have knowledge of the children's program as well as all other operations of the center. This is not a task that can simply be carried out from behind a desk in a business office. The purchaser must be well acquainted with everything that goes on which requires the use of goods or services—program activities, food services, maintenance and repairs, clerical and office needs, community services, and general supplies, to name a few.

Two keys to purchasing know-how are:

- Knowledge of each component of the center and what is required to carry out its function.

349

- Knowledge of suppliers of services and goods within the general vicinity.

The director of a small center often assumes the responsibility of purchasing. This includes consulting about purchase needs with staff members who work in each component. The director may choose to delegate the purchasing responsibility to a specific staff member—perhaps you.

Each major component of the center, such as the program, food service, office, and maintenance, has unique requirements. Each person in charge of a component should be consulted about the goods and services purchased for that component. If the center is very large, the person in charge of a component may request goods and services on special forms and then approve the purchase orders before they are processed.

When too many members of the staff make purchases, this can be expensive as well as confusing for bookkeeping. The time required to make purchases may be used more appropriately for carrying out other responsibilities. The cost to a center in staff time is usually one of the most expensive budget items; it should not be misused in such tasks as purchasing when one person can assume this role.

Standard forms for purchase orders are available at business supply dealers. Purchase orders should be required for most purchases. Of course, there will be times when a staff member may need to make a special purchase, but this should be an exception rather than a practice. For special purposes, a *petty cash fund* should be maintained to make it possible for the staff to purchase goods from time to time. The amount in this fund depends on the size of the center and usually ranges from $25 to $100. If a purchase amounts to less than $3 or $4, it is probably wise to forego the purchase order and use the petty cash funds. Why? A good reason is it will often cost about $2 or $3 per hour of staff time just to process the purchase order. For petty cash purchases of small items, a receipt with the date and list of items or services should be submitted to the person in charge of purchasing.

Accounts with Vendors

Look for a vendor (supplier of goods or services) who carries a variety of goods or services with the quality needed by the center. Prices should be competitive. Make comparisons with other vendors on the basis of quality and price to meet your needs.

Should the center require very large quantities of certain goods, the specifications for these should be submitted to selected vendors for bidding. *Specifications* include such information as amount, color, type, and quality of the product. Be sure the vendors who are bidding are willing to deliver goods at time intervals that allow adequate storage and distribution for all items. Once you have received the bids from several vendors, you can choose the company with whom you wish to do business.

After a center has been in operation long enough to have selected vendors and when business with them is satisfactory, *charge accounts* may be established. A charge account, as you know, makes it possible to purchase goods and services on credit and pay for them on a monthly basis. All accounts should be paid monthly by numbered checks after a statement has been received from the vendor. A careful accounting should be made to see that each purchase order corresponds with items on the monthly statement.

REQUISITION/PURCHASE ORDER

Date: _____ Requisition No. _____

Requested by: _____ Purchase Order No. _____

Authorized by: _____ Center: _____

Approved by: _____

QUANTITY	DESCRIPTION	SUPPLIER	UNIT COST	TOTAL COST

Shipping Instructions:

Received by: _____ Date: _____

Approved for Payment by: _____

The center account should maintain enough cash in the bank to pay bills within a ten-day period after receiving the statements. Many vendors give a small discount (about two percent) if bills are paid within ten days.

Purchasing Techniques

Good decision-making about what to purchase and from whom is a key to effective management. Consider these suggestions:

- Be sure products have been tested under operating conditions. Do not be swayed by impressive salesmanship.
- Purchase quality products which serve the center's purposes. The cost of products may be increased by attractive and

Part V: Working In Children's Centers

PETTY CASH RECORD

Center:_____ Date:_____

Name of Employee Using Petty Cash_____

Purpose:_____

_____

Amounts:_____

_____
Signature of Employee

_____
Approval of Director/or Bookkeeper

---

fancy packaging which does not affect quality.
- Do not pay tax unless required by law. Secure information from the center's attorney or the Internal Revenue Service about tax exemptions. File the tax-exemption stipulations with each vendor. Staff members should have copies of exemption status in order to make petty cash purchases.

STORAGE AND DISTRIBUTION

There are numerous advantages to storing equipment, materials, and supplies in a central place in the center:

- It is easy to keep a current inventory of items on hand. This makes it possible to see what items are used most.
- Portable equipment can be checked for safe and proper working condition.
- Prevention of any component of the center from ordering an oversupply of goods is possible.
- It is easy to identify items that are not being used by anyone. These can be sold or disposed of properly.
- Space does not have to be provided in several areas of the center for storing the same kind of goods.

Some items, of course, will need to be stored near the area of greatest use. For example, there should be space near the art activities area to store enough paper and supplies to last for several days.

Distributing equipment and supplies depends somewhat on the size of the center and the management procedures. Here are a few suggestions to make distribution a smooth operation:

- Procedures for requests from the central storage area should be realistic. The person in charge of storage should not be used as a runner for other staff members. Neither should staff members be spending much of their time going back and forth to the storage area.
- If the storeroom is not open during all the hours the center is in operation, some way must be provided for staff members to have access to the area. Perhaps one person could be responsible for a key and the records of items secured or re-

352

turned during the times when the storage manager is not present. If the center cannot assign one person to handle all distribution personally, other arrangements can be made. For example, a clipboard with an attached sheet could be kept in the storeroom. Whenever a worker removes supplies or checks out equipment, this information can be noted on the sheet. The date, supplies removed, amounts, and identification of the worker can be noted. Later the worker in charge of storage or purchasing can check this list to see what items need replenishing.
- An inventory of the items should be kept up-to-date.
- Equipment should be numbered with a system for checking items in and out. For example, if someone uses a tape recorder, the person in charge of storage should have a record of where it is and for how long it will be out.

TRANSPORTATION

Children travel to and from centers in different ways—by private cars, center buses, commercial vehicles, and by walking. Whatever method of travel is used, the children's safety is of primary importance. Although safety was discussed in an earlier chapter, it is emphasized again here. Competent adults must insure the safe travel of children whether riding or walking.

One accident could have serious results for either a child, the center's reputation, or both. Each staff member should be thoroughly familiar with traffic codes, regulations, and safety practices in the area where the center is located. Parents should know the rules and regulations and be asked to assist in providing for the safety and well-being of the children while traveling to and from the center. Parents can also help insure children's safe travel on field trips, excursions around the neighborhood, and during other activities which involve travel.

Suggestions for insuring children's safety should be provided for parents who are responsible for getting their own children to and from the center. Examples should also be set and explanations given to help children learn to travel safely. Only through consistent supervision and reinforcement by adults will children learn safe practices that become a routine part of their behavior.

Traveling in Vehicles

At least one adult in addition to the driver should accompany children in all types of vehicles which transport children. Each child should be provided with a seat in the car or bus and should remain seated during travel. Head, arms, and legs should be kept inside—never allowed to extend out the windows. Safety belts should be used in cars. Many buses are now equipped with safety belts. For their safety, it is very important for children to remain in their seats during travel.

Safety seats for small children are available for cars and buses. These prevent infants and toddlers from falling or bumping heads while traveling, especially in heavy traffic. Tests have found that some of these seats are safer than others. *Consumer Bulletin* or *Consumer Reports* may provide help in choosing the best safety seat for the money.

Doors of vehicles should be securely closed and locked during travel. Safety locks should be in working order on all doors for vehicles carrying children.

Each vehicle should be in excellent operating condition, displaying a safety sticker to indicate it has been inspected by

Part V: Working In Children's Centers

an authorized inspection station. Every driver must maintain an operator's license to drive the type of vehicle used to carry children. Many states require special licenses for those who drive vans or buses to transport children. Check your licensing bureau for the requirements in your area.

The length of time children are in travel should be less than one hour. Centers often serve children in the neighborhood; however, in some areas children must travel a long distance to reach the center. Quiet, interesting devices or toys should be provided for children who must travel more than a short distance. Activities may include lap games or a tote or travel bag of interesting items to manipulate such as easy-to-handle puzzles or "feely" objects. Children also enjoy question-and-answer games while traveling. For example: "What animals can you name?" "How many windows do passing cars have?" "How many green trucks can you see?"

Children must have adult supervision while traveling by commercial bus, train, or subway. Again, children must remain seated, never running or playing in aisles or corridors.

Children should be taught to respect both people and property while riding in automobiles, buses, and other types of vehicles. Respect for people means remaining quiet with no shouting or loud talking; no throwing things; and no fighting with playmates or brothers and sisters. If children misbehave, the vehicle should be stopped until they are settled.

Children must also learn respect for the driver—no talking to him or distractions while traveling. Respect for property means no marking on seats and handrails and no throwing paper or trash on floors of vehicles or out the windows. Lunch boxes and sacks should not be opened in the vehicle. Eating can be messy and hazardous, especially if food is spilled or dropped on the floor.

Entering and Leaving Vehicles

Getting children in and out of vehicles safely requires adult supervision. Children should remain seated until the vehicle is completely stopped and the adult indicates it is safe to leave.

A side street or special driveway area should be provided at the center away from the main flow of traffic. The entrance and exit driveways should be clear of any parked vehicles.

Children should be taught where the traffic lanes lead *in* and *out* of the center. Adults must hold very young children's hands to offer security and provide safety while crossing streets, getting in and out of vehicles, going up and down steps, and when walking along busy streets or pathways.

Legal Requirements

When transportation is provided by the center, adequate provisions must be made for meeting legal requirements. Appropriate liability and collision insurance, a licensed driver, and vehicle safety and operating inspections are major prerequisites for operating passenger vehicles. The specific regulations vary from one state to another. Each center director should investigate the legal requirements for transporting children and operating vehicles.

COMMUNICATIONS

Center staff members will have numerous occasions for communicating with parents, guardians, and others responsible for children who attend the center program. Staff members will also be in contact with health, psychological, and social services personnel; doctors; nurses; and others in the community from time to time regarding the center's activities and services. Each adult who works in the center as a paid employee or a volunteer should be familiar with the program, its goals, objectives, and organization. Inquiries often include the need for such information as:

- Center name, location in community, address, and telephone number.
- Size of centers.
- Number of children served.
- Adult-child ratio.
- Age ranges of children.
- Groupings of children—infants, toddlers, three- and four-year-olds, five-year-olds or preschoolers, school-age children, other groupings.
- Program design, philosophy, goals and objectives, types of activities, scheduling.
- Ethnic groups and socio-economic levels of families served.

The staff should have a clear understanding from the director or sponsor about what is confidential information and what is public information. The staff should give out neither type of information until the source requesting it is identified and considered appropriate to receive the data.

Telephone Contacts

Occasions will arise when staff members will need to communicate with parents and others by telephone. Each call, in or out, regarding information about a child or about center business should be logged on an index card or other specified form and filed in the receptionist's or director's office, or other designated place. A form like the one shown here can be used.

Since telephones in the center are business phones, they should be used only for that purpose. In answering calls, anything from a very short statement of the center's name to a longer statement including a greeting may be used. Here are some possibilities:

"Children's Day Care Center."
"Good afternoon, this is the Central Avenue Children's Center. May I help you?"
"This is the Sunny Side Day Care Center, Mrs. Roberts speaking."
"Centerville Nursery School, Miss Ramirez speaking."
"Good morning, this is Mr. Carson with the Smithville Kindergarten."

Although the director may not care for a set style of greeting, a blank "hello" puts the caller at a disadvantage. It is neither cordial nor informative. At least the name of the center should be given.

When receiving messages for the director or another staff member who cannot take the call, be certain to get the following information:

- Name of party calling and establishment represented, if any.
- Telephone number where party can be reached.
- Any message or other information.
- Time of day and date the call was received.

A log of all long distance calls is needed for business purposes. Information can be recorded on a form similar to the one used for routine phone messages.

Intercommunication Devices

Large centers may have intercommunications systems, or intercoms, which make it possible for the director to talk with staff

Part V: Working In Children's Centers

TELEPHONE MESSAGE

Date: *June 23, Wed.*   Time: *9:30 a.m.*

To: *Mrs. Johnson, Center Director*
(Name of Person Called)

From: *Mr. Sellers, Diaper Service, Inc.*
(Name and Source of Person Calling)

Subject of call: *Inquiry about delivery of diapers Tuesday morning.*

Information: *Four dozen too many diapers were delivered. Can these be picked up tomorrow a.m.? Call at your earliest convenience.*

June Stewart
(Signature of Staff Member Making or Receiving the Call)

---

members and for staff to talk with each other throughout the center. Main units may be connected with outside lines. Others in the system may not. Intercommunications should consist of:

- Identification of persons calling and receiving.
- Clear, concise statements giving and receiving information.

Correspondence

Items of correspondence such as business letters, newsletters to parents, and bulletins containing center information bring attention to the quality of a center's management. Each item should contain the following information in addition to the message it carries:

- Current date.
- Center's name, address, and telephone number.
- Contact-person for reply purposes.

Correspondence is generally handled by the secretary; however, in centers where other staff members assume this responsibility, there are usually policies governing procedures. For example, letterhead stationery should be used for all letters. Copies of each letter should be filed for future reference and as a record of communication. The number of bulletins and dates of dissemination should be recorded along with a list of persons receiving the bulletins. A list of parents should be checked each time newsletters are sent.

All incoming mail should be attended to promptly. Business correspondence and letters concerning specific information about a child or the center's operation

Ch. 20: Managing Center Operations

Educational services may include staff training and workshops.

Beggs Project

should be filed with a copy of the response made or action taken.

Services

Every center has need of some services. These will vary in relation to the size of center, amount of budget, program needs, and geographic location. The following services are usually concerns of every center. As you become acquainted with children's centers in your community, you will no doubt gain further insight into this area of management.

Professional Service

Some children's centers provide professional services from community sources. These may include one or more of the following:

- Health and medical services including consultation on nutrition, dental assistance, speech and hearing screening, general health screening, and immunization programs.
- Educational services such as testing, consulting, provision of learning materials, and training for staff.
- Guidance and counseling including psychological services such as testing, therapy, and group or individual counseling.
- Welfare and social services including case workers, home economists, and child development advisors.

As you know, some programs offer comprehensive care for children. Head Start is an example. A center usually has a contract with service agencies to provide services such as those mentioned above.

357

Part V: Working In Children's Centers

Emphasis is placed on securing nutrition, health, psychological, social, medical, and educational expertise to improve staff competencies and to provide sufficient services directly to children. Some programs include these services to all family members of children enrolled.

Some day care centers are partially supported by local and/or state welfare agencies. The federal government provides funds for certain programs through Social Security. These often include casework services carried out by qualified and experienced social workers. The center staff gains its own rewards by cooperating with the caseworker who has specific responsibilities for:

- Intake information on family needs—interviewing parents and collecting information related to the needs of families for individual child care service.
- Contact with parents—discussing a child's progress and work at the center and in the home.
- Referrals—the family may be referred to other agencies for their child care problems if day care is inappropriate.
- Work with center staff—conferences to evaluate center needs and services to children and families.
- Follow-up—casework service offered to a family after the child terminates the day care program experience.

Many public and private child care centers, nursery schools, and kindergartens do not receive federal, state, or local funding. You will find that many of these centers, however, strive to cooperate with community sources to help form a team to serve the children and their families. For example, local mental health centers may offer training for child care personnel; community councils may form to organize ways of improving child care programs through staff training and financial support; and school programs may collaborate with children's centers to provide training for students who are potential child care workers and who offer volunteer service to a center.

Food Service

Nutrition for children, meals, and snacks have been discussed in earlier chapters. This section is concerned with the management aspects of preparing and serving food for children while meeting nutritional requirements.

Food is an expensive budget item, yet meals and snacks must be carefully planned to meet the nutritional needs of children as efficiently as possible. The fact that children are developing eating habits and attitudes about food makes it necessary to serve attractive and high-quality foods.

Menus

Menus planned within the recognized nutritional standards are minimum requirements for any center. Often one-third to one-half or more of the child's daily food needs are met by child care centers. Some half-day programs may provide only snacks, some full-day programs provide two and even three meals. Many disadvantaged children depend on the center to provide their entire nutritional needs for the day.

As you have already discovered, there is a great amount of variation among children in appetites, tastes, eating patterns, and food attitudes. These considerations must be given serious thought when planning menus for children, especially when a wide range in ages and stages of development is present. In addition to staff members, there

Ch. 20: Managing Center Operations

Beggs Project

Food is an expensive budget item and requires careful planning and skill in preparation in order to meet the nutritional needs of children.

Oklahoma VoTech

Nutrition consultants provide assistance in planning menus and preparing foods for children's centers. Food can be served so that it is interesting and fun for children to eat. Wouldn't most youngsters enjoy a tasty tidbit served on a toothpick?

are usually nutrition consultants available from health departments, the dairy council, welfare, or public schools to help with planning meals for children.

Children enjoy attractively served foods prepared for their tastes. They like to be able to identify the foods they eat—so don't be surprised when they frown at casseroles and other combination dishes. Hot foods should be served hot and cold foods should remain chilled until ready to serve. Like adults, children enjoy well-seasoned, but not highly seasoned, foods which are well cooked but not overcooked.

Menus can be posted on the bulletin board or displayed to indicate to parents and visitors what the children will be eating each week or month. Parents will appreciate receiving copies of these in newsletters or handouts. Some centers have their menus published in the local newspapers. When parents know what the children have at the center, it is helpful in planning to meet daily food requirements

Kickapoo Head Start Center

Children are more interested in eating when they can manage the equipment. Note that the table is sized for the children, and the child care worker joins them at their table.

at home to round out the child's diet for the day. (The Appendix contains suggestions for menu planning.)

Planning menus by the month offers a long-range view of what the children will be eating, also providing information for market orders and the budget. Records of all foods served, along with records of the costs, are a part of the management's responsibility.

Preparing and Serving Meals and Snacks

The food preparation and eating areas must meet local health and sanitation standards. The center should expect periodic inspections without notice. Water and milk supplies must meet local and state health regulations. Cooks and other persons who work with the preparation and service of foods must maintain health certificates renewable in most states every six months. As a part of the health examination, a chest X ray for tuberculosis is required. All staff members, at one time or another, help with food service and should have a chest X ray and general physical examination as minimal health requirements.

Food should be served under sanitary conditions in a clean, bright atmosphere. Plastic glasses or plates which crack, scratch, or mar from repeated use and cleaning should not be used because they are unsightly and bacteria can be carried in the cracks.

Drinking water should be available to children in drinking fountains or from sanitary cups. These should be located both indoors and outdoors.

The size of dishes and eating utensils should fit the size of the child. Children naturally develop more interest in eating when they can manage the equipment. Sitting at a comfortable table and chair height with feet flat on the floor gives support and satisfaction to the children.

Managing food service for a very large number of children can be difficult, especially if help is limited. Careful planning is needed to organize the staff and center for adequate meal service. You have to keep reminding yourself that some children do not have regular mealtimes at home; thus, the center may be providing the only opportunity these children have for enjoying pleasant mealtime experiences while developing better eating habits.

Every effort should be made to arrange children in small groups for meals and snacks. This offers greater possibilities for close relationships to develop among children and with adults. The small group setting provides a homelike atmosphere, giving each child an opportunity to talk and contribute to the group. Each can pour juice or milk, pass food, carry a tray to or from the table, count out napkins, and set, clear, or wipe the table. Each child should have opportunities to interact and be recognized individually for participation

—whether a verbal contribution or overt action.

Parents and volunteers can be very helpful during mealtime. They can make it possible to seat children in small groups by providing the necessary guidance and supervision. These helpers need to know the daily schedule and the goals of the program. Some volunteers may be able to assist at the center only at mealtime, but this can be very beneficial with advance planning.

Types of Food Service

Food may be prepared by a cook in the kitchen of the children's center or it may be catered by a professional catering service. There are advantages and limitations to each of these plans.

Meal preparation in the center requires adequate kitchen facilities and equipment. One or more part-time or full-time cooks may be employed, depending on the size of the program and number of meals to be served. Menu planning and food purchasing are time-consuming tasks for either the cook, center manager, or other staff member assigned to this role.

The cook has an opportunity to observe the children, their eating habits, and food preferences. This information, in addition to suggestions from the center manager or teaching staff, helps in planning and preparing food. The cook should have a basic understanding of nutrition for young children as well as behavior patterns related to eating. The cook must also have knowledge of menu planning and appropriate ways to serve food to young children. This task may require in-service or special training.

Advantages for the children include opportunities for learning through helping with meal preparation, a variety of table service, and a variety of individual dishes for the children. Cleanup time is a meaningful experience for children—scraping plates, stacking, separating flatware, and wiping tables. Children also experience more of a homelike setting with kitchen-prepared food service—unless, of course, they are accustomed to TV dinners at home!

Catering simplifies the tasks of food preparation and service. The food arrives at the center ready for mealtime in pre-portioned servings. Little kitchen equipment is needed with the exception of a warming oven, sink, and refrigerator. A few serving utensils and dishes will be needed for snack times and special occasions. A limited amount of space is needed for handling foods prior to serving.

Catered food is usually planned on the basis of approved menus that meet nutri-

Oklahoma VoTech

Catering should be planned on the basis of approved menus to meet nutritional needs of children. Would the type of food these women are serving likely be part of a catered meal?

tional requirements for young children. It is served in containers which meet sanitation standards. Depending on the type of catering service, the eating utensils—forks, spoons, knives—may either be a part of the individualized packages or furnished by the center. If you consider the use of catered meals, be sure the service meets minimum standards for nutrition, quality of food, and quality of service.

Catered food service is generally a little more expensive per serving than kitchen-prepared meals. However, the savings in time, facilities, and utilities may offset the difference.

Of course, catered meals place some limitations on children's experiences during mealtime. There is little opportunity for children to be involved in helping prepare and serve meals with the exception of setting the table with placemats and beverage glasses. As you can see, cleanup activities with catered meals are also limited. There is less variety in service with catered meals. The individualized containers are usually packaged with meat, vegetable, dessert, and other items in compartments —similar to frozen TV dinners. This style of service may become monotonous unless the staff makes plans and special efforts to provide variety through table arrangements, variety of placemats, napkins, and table decorations.

Some catering services provide the food in large containers. The center staff or cook then places the food in serving dishes, thus providing opportunities for a variety of table services. This type of catering, however, may be expensive in terms of staff time and use of serving dishes. Warming equipment may be needed in the kitchen if the food is served cafeteria style. Someone has to wash the dishes too!

In making the decision to use either kitchen preparation or a catering service, keep these considerations in mind:

- What is appropriate in relation to the overall goals of the program?
- What is best for the children in learning concepts about food (color, texture, flavor, form, temperature); developing independence and manipulative skills (helping with preparation, service, cleanup); developing sensory acuity (experiencing aromas of foods during the cooking or warming process, seeing foods in various stages of preparation, tasting and touching foods); improving daily living skills (ability to feed oneself, help with service and cleanup, pass foods to each other, practice table manners, and develop eating habits)?
- What is best in terms of quality of food?
- Is there a significant cost difference?
- What contributes to the efficient use of time, energy, and money?
- What is best in terms of existing and needed kitchen facilities and equipment?

Check with the local catering services to get information about the cost per child for serving meals in the children's center. Find out what facilities and equipment must be provided by the center to make the catering operation work effectively. Request consultation from health department nutrition specialists or the public school lunch supervisors for cost per serving of kitchen-prepared foods. Remember to take into account the number of children in your center compared with the number served by the school.

Laundry and Diaper Service

Decisions about laundry and diaper service are influenced by such factors as the number of children in a center, ages of children, length of time the center is open, space for laundry facilities, staff available to assume laundry responsibilities, and availability of dependable and satisfactory laundry and diaper service vendors. The alternatives for securing services are usually limited to: (1) doing the laundry in the center; (2) purchasing laundry service from a commercial supplier; or (3) contracting with an individual in the community who provides laundry services on a private basis.

Consider advantages of each alternative in relation to the needs of the center. An infant program serving several babies requires many diapers day after day, whereas a program serving four- and five-year-olds for afternoons only will require much less laundry service per child. The type of food service will also influence laundry needs. If food is catered, there is a minimal need for dishcloths and kitchen linens, but if food is prepared in the center, the number of laundry items will be much greater. Answer these questions before deciding on the type of laundry service for a center:

- How much staff time will be required to manage laundry service if provided in the center, handled commercially, or managed on a contract basis?
- What is the approximate amount of laundry per day or week in units of standard washer loads?
- What amount of clean linen, diapers, and clothing must be kept on hand while laundry is processed?
- What amount of linen, diapers, and clothing are presently on hand?

Ch. 20: Managing Center Operations

- On a yearly basis, can laundry service be purchased commercially for less than it can be done in the center? (Take into consideration the cost of equipment and operations—washer, dryer, repairs, electricity, gas, detergent, time, and space.)
- Is commercial or contracted laundry service approved for meeting sanitation and health requirements?
- Are the delivery services dependable?
- Are delivery dates appropriate to meet needs of the center's operation?
- In cities or towns diaper service is usually available on a commercial basis. Will quality service be provided?

Diapers must be sanitary to protect the health of infants. They must also be appropriate for the facilities. Consider environmental factors such as pollution of sewer lines with disposable diapers which may not disintegrate when dumped into sewer outlets. Burning disposable diapers as trash is prohibited in most areas, as it adds to air pollution. Some states and local areas prohibit or discourage centers from using disposable diapers for these reasons.

Although an advantage of hanging laundry outside to dry is the sunlight and fresh air, many areas are not exposed to much sunlight because of surrounding buildings or long winter seasons. Fresh air is not always plentiful, especially in heavily populated urban or industrial areas. Moreover, zoning regulations must be considered. In some commercial areas, hanging laundry outdoors is not permitted. Even if you have clotheslines, sunshine, fresh air, and you do the laundry in the center, it may not be possible to hang the laundry outside to dry.

Part V: Working In Children's Centers

Chapter Highlights

- Efficient operation of a center depends upon the director's management skills and the cooperation and support of each employee.
- A most important task in operating a center is to secure and maintain quality personnel.
- A written job description should be on file for each position in the center, explaining tasks and responsibilities of the employee.
- Policies, the conditions under which each employee works, should be reviewed at least once each year to be sure they meet legal requirements and current employment practices.
- Every potential employee should fill out an application form.
- An interview should be complete enough to secure the necessary information about an applicant in order to make fair and sound decisions about employment.
- References should be checked to secure information about the applicant's quality of performance.
- Wages (hourly pay) and salaries (monthly pay) are usually established on an individual center basis but in keeping with national and state trends.
- Staff members should be given special assistance and leadership for updating and improving their effectiveness as employees.
- It is better to have a smaller program which is adequate for the children than to try to stretch the budget at the expense of quality child care.
- After a budget plan has been made, some flexibility is needed, but you should not exceed ten percent when moving money from one category to another.
- A child care center should have financial, personnel, and children's records.
- Two keys to purchasing know-how include (1) knowledge of each component of the center and what is required to carry out its function and (2) knowledge of suppliers of services and goods within the general vicinity.
- The cost of staff time is usually one of the most expensive budget items.
- Children should be taught where the traffic lanes are leading *in* and *out* of the center.
- When transportation is provided by the center, adequate provisions must be made for meeting legal and safety requirements.
- Items of correspondence, such as business letters, newsletters to parents, and bulletins containing center information, bring attention to the quality of a center's management.
- Some children's centers provide professional services such as health and medical service; educational, testing, and consulting services; guidance and counseling; and welfare and social services (including caseworkers).
- Food is an expensive budget item, yet meals and snacks must be carefully planned to meet the nutritional needs of children as efficiently as possible.
- Food may be prepared by a cook in the kitchen of the center or it may be catered by a professional catering service. There are advantages and limitations to each of these plans.
- The alternatives for securing laundry services usually include doing the laundry at the center, purchasing laundry service from a commercial supplier, or contracting with an individual in the community who provides laundry services on a private basis.

Ch. 20: Managing Center Operations

Thinking It Over

1. What do you think is the most interesting facet in managing a child care center? Which is the least interesting to you? Give reasons for your choices.
2. How are the employees of a children's center responsible for the success of the center?
3. Do you think it is important to be given a job description when you are hired as a child care worker? Give reasons. Can any job description ever cover all a child care worker will do? What should it cover?
4. What is the value in sitting down with other staff members and leaders and evaluating your effectiveness as a team in relation to the center's purposes?
5. What problems might come from poor record-keeping concerning personnel?
6. What could result if the information in a child's folder is not kept confidential?
7. How can a current inventory of equipment and supplies be of value in a children's center?
8. Have you ever driven with children in the car? Were the doors locked? Were the children secured in their seats? If not, did this have any effect on your driving? How can children's safety during travel be promoted?

Things To Do

1. Prepare a sample budget for a child care center serving fifty children.
2. Make a detailed list of the materials and equipment to be purchased for a child care center serving fifty children.
3. Interview each other for positions in a child care center. Prepare and present a resumé and a folder of information.
4. Write a position description for one job in a child care center.
5. Make a list of nearby suppliers of services and goods needed by a child care center. Post the list in the classroom.
6. Invite a bookkeeper or an accountant to speak to the class about purchase orders and bookkeeping concepts useful to the child care worker.
7. Working in groups of three or four students, inquire about the traffic codes, safety regulations, insurance, and driver's license requirements for local child care centers. Report this information to the class. Design *safety first* cards which can be given to parents of a children's center. Include information on how parents can help children develop concepts of safety for traveling in automobiles and on buses.
8. Demonstrate how to answer the telephone in a center and give reasons for your choice of method.
9. Create a short newsletter about a children's center which can be sent to parents of children in the center.

Recommended Reading

Can I Love This Place? Washington, D.C.: Educational Systems Corporation, 1969.
How to Operate Your Day Care Program. Wyomissing, Pennsylvania: Ryan Jones Associates, Inc., 1970.
Preschool Guide. Denver, Colorado: Colorado Association of Future Homemakers of America, 1968.

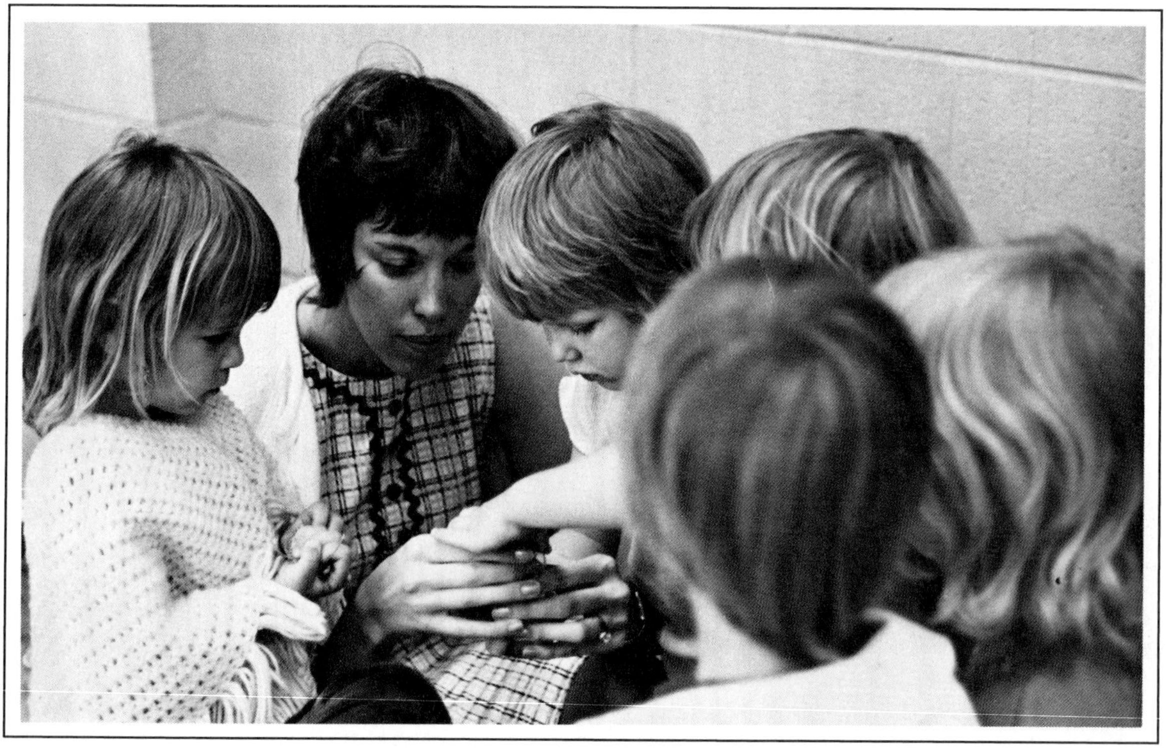

PART VI
Planning a Children's Program

Chapter 21.
Program Models

Chapter 22.
Goals and Objectives

Chapter 23.
Teaching and Learning Strategies

Chapter 24.
Activities for Children

Chapter 25.
Sample Developmental Units

Chapter 21.

Program Models

Your Challenge

This chapter will enable you to ....

- *Define program model (framework).*
- *Describe the two basic types of models.*
- *List and explain some elements of a program.*
- *Explain the value of a program model.*
- *Describe some specific program models.*

DEFINING FRAMEWORK

The philosophy by which a center operates is directly related to the operation of its program. In fact, you might say a program is the philosophy put into action. A program model is a specific plan for setting up and operating a children's program. A model is often developed for use as an example for others to follow. Another term used to refer to a program model is *framework*.

A framework may be thought of as a guide for operating a program. Compare a framework to a set of guidelines for playing football, baseball, or basketball. Each game has a specific set of guidelines. With each game there are certain rules to follow. The field or court has identified boundary lines, and each has certain markers and signals used to keep the players informed of their limits. The framework helps players know where they are, where they need to go, and what they can do to get there.

The framework of a children's program is similar. It keeps the children and adults in line with the program goals and objectives. It helps them know where they are, where they are headed, what to do to get there, and what the limits are.

The key words are *where, what, why* and *how*. Developing a plan helps the staff and parents identify *where* the children are in their development, *what* a program is supposed to do for the children, and *why*. The plan also serves as a guide for *how* the activities will be carried out.

TWO BASIC MODELS

Although new models or frameworks are continuously developing, two general types are basic to many early childhood programs. These are the *instructional* and *discovery* approaches. Whether for child care, nursery school, kindergarten, Head Start, or other types of children's centers, one of

University of Oklahoma Health Sciences Center
Using the instructional approach in an early childhood program, the adult initiates the action and the children respond. These children are enjoying musical instruments along with the record. The teacher demonstrates and then the children play their own instruments.

these approaches is usually basic to the program.

The instructional approach places greater emphasis on the adult initiating action, with the children responding. The discovery approach emphasizes the children initiating activities, with adults responding.

Compare these:

Instructional

Adult begins activity and children respond by participating. Adult decides what materials to use and what experiences to have, and children follow suggestions or directions. Adult may show children how to do a task. Many models are provided for children to follow.

Discovery

Children begin an activity, and adult responds by assisting when needed. Children decide what activities to participate in, and adult helps supply materials and helps children when necessary or when the children ask for help. Children explore until they discover how to do a task, receiving minimal help.

There are advantages and disadvantages to each approach. Can you suggest some in addition to the following?

Instructional

Advantages: Adults guide children toward appropriate goals. Adults have greater control of the activities and can

Part VI: Planning a Children's Program

University of Oklahoma Institute of Child Development
If the discovery approach is used as the basis for a program, the children will initiate activities and the adults will respond. This little girl chose an art activity. The child care worker will help if needed.

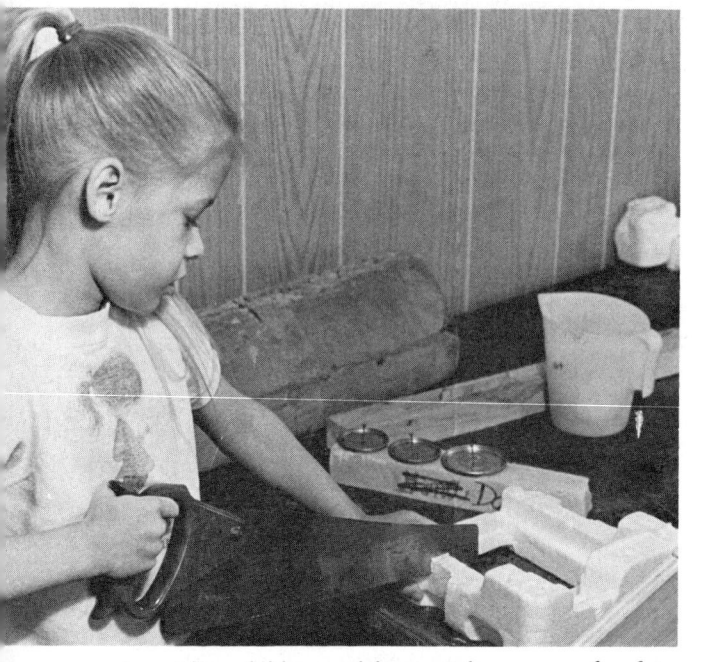

In guiding children, adults must be aware of safety precautions. Here, an adult must be ready to help Darby protect her fingers and thumb while she is learning to enjoy carpentry activities.

plan for specific experiences with use of certain materials and equipment.

Children learn to cooperate and follow instructions; learn to be dependable; know limits; know what to expect and what is expected.

Disadvantages: Children have less opportunity to develop independence and participate in decision-making experiences.

Adults have less opportunity to observe children's abilities in decision-making and initiating their own activities.

Children have less opportunity to learn by spontaneous involvement.

Discovery

Advantages: Children learn to direct themselves and their action.

Children have greater control over decisions and activities; they develop independence and a sense of self in a natural way.

Adults can readily observe each child's ability to make decisions and carry them

Ch. 21: Program Models

out. Adults can see strengths and areas of need.

Children learn primarily through spontaneous experiences within a given environment.

Disadvantages: Adults must have a flexible plan which allows for a variety of children's experiences and many opportunities for making decisions. The environment must be carefully planned to assure appropriate choices of activities by each child in order to avoid aimless wandering and meaningless involvement.

Adults must find ways, without controlling, to help children direct or redirect their own actions toward achieving appropriate goals.

Children may miss valuable experiences because of special interests in a few self-selected activities.

In either the instructional or discovery approach, the adults must provide an appropriate and organized environment. Even when children initiate activities, these should be within a suitable setting for their stage and level of development. Although the discovery approach appears to offer greater freedom for the children, each child must still be responsible for his behavior and show respect for self, others, and property. Although the instructional approach may lend itself to greater control by adults, children must be provided with freedom and a warm, relaxed atmosphere in which to learn responsibility and respect in a natural and meaningful way. In either approach, the adults must be responsible for providing situations in which children are happy and motivated toward further development.

Consider the examples shown here in chart form of the two approaches as they relate to specific activities. Keep in mind that these examples are related to only one

Oklahoma City Christian Church Day Care Center

If children have some control over activities, they develop independence and a sense of self in a natural way. Sturdy equipment that children can use, like this record player, allows them to be more independent.

area of the child's development. Which approach do you favor? Why? Is there another approach you could use for achieving the same goal and objective?

A program may strive to have a balance between the instructional and discovery approaches whereby the adult and child are about equal in initiating activities and about equal in responding.

COMPONENTS OF A MODEL

Dr. Bernard Spodek, educator and child psychologist, introduced the concept of elements in a model or program framework. The following elements are some that will help you become familiar with what comprises a program. These elements may be subtly communicated by what goes on

Part VI: Planning a Children's Program

Central State University Child Study Center

In either the instructional or discovery approach, the adults must provide an appropriate and organized environment. How many learning opportunities do you see in this part of a center?

INSTRUCTIONAL APPROACH

Goal	Objective	Activities	Strategies
Concept formation: classification of objects.	The child will be able to classify objects by placing those that are alike in groups and removing those that are different without assistance.	Playing with objects, some of which are alike and some different. Objects include empty juice cans, some with labels of apples, some with oranges, and some with grapes; a variety of empty food cartons; a ball; and a doll.	Adult initiates classification activities and shows child what materials and equipment to use and where to use them. Adult asks questions about the objects and makes suggestions to help the child start separating objects into groups. Adult then provides games or planned procedures so the child will respond to activities for classifying objects without assistance.

Ch. 21: Program Models

DISCOVERY APPROACH

Goal	Objective	Activities	Strategies
Concept formation: classification of objects.	The child will be able to classify objects by placing those that are alike in groups and removing those that are different without assistance.	Separating and grouping items according to alike and unlike properties in a spontaneous manner. The house area contains empty grocery containers such as juice cans, milk cartons, cereal boxes, and egg cartons. The manipulative area contains boxes of shapes—such as squares, circles, triangles, and rectangles—in various colors. The carpentry area contains tools such as wrenches, spools, nails, hammers, and saws.	Child decides in which area of the room to play. Available materials and equipment make it possible for the child to play with objects which can be classified. Adult observes and assists child by providing opportunities and by responding to child's questions or comments about the objects. Eventually the child is allowed to classify the objects without assistance. If errors occur, the adult will wait until the child again chooses to classify and subtly offer assistance.

with the children in a program or explicitly communicated by a written description.

Assumptions

The assumptions, underlying ideas that are accepted as fact about children and how they develop, are the bases for any program. Assumptions vary from one program to another depending on the philosophy of those in charge. Here are examples of assumptions for a *developmental* program using a *discovery* approach:

- All children benefit from an enriched environment.
- Children can initiate meaningful activities in an environment planned and structured according to the stages of development and expected ability ranges of children.
- Adults can best serve children by responding to their inquiries and requests and by making sure meaningful experiences are provided.
- Children learn from each other and by interacting with the environment.
- Children can make decisions about their activities and can assume responsibilities for following through with their decisions.

Can you list the assumptions for an *instructional* program model?

Goals and Objectives

A program, whether instructional or discovery, is implemented to achieve specified goals (broadly stated desires and expectations for children) and objectives (specific tasks and skills expected of each child). The importance of goals and objectives cannot be overemphasized, for they are the targets at which all efforts of the center should be aimed. Here are a few examples of goals and objectives.

Goals

- To help each child develop to his fullest potential in motor coordination, sensory

373

Part VI: Planning a Children's Program

The idea that all children are stimulated by an enriched environment is almost totally accepted. What could be more fun—and rewarding—than these activities?

perception and acuity, language skills, concept formation and problem solving, and daily living skills.
- To help each child become a productive, healthy, and self-motivated individual who is happy and secure, with a positive self-image and feelings of belonging and recognition as a worthy person.

Objectives (four-year-olds)
- To demonstrate the control of body movements in order to walk on a balance beam four inches above the floor's surface. (Motor)
- To identify rough, slick, and fluffy surface textures by handling, naming, and describing how samples of fabric feel. (Sensory)
- To classify objects by manipulating the objects and talking about their properties that are alike. (Concepts)
- To communicate, verbally, concepts about the size of objects, such as "bigger than," "smaller than," and "the same as." (Language)
- To manipulate fasteners on clothing while putting on garments which have snaps, hooks, zippers, and buttons. (Motor and living skills)

Strategies

Strategies refer to the plans for how the adults (teachers, assistants, parents) will help the children carry out their activities. Strategies include the *curriculum,* organization of activities; the *methods,* the way things are done; and the *style* of teaching, the personal manner in which each adult carries out the methods.

Curriculum

The curriculum is a plan of activities for the children. Assumptions, goals, and objectives are considered as the plan is made.

Ch. 21: Program Models

University of Oklahoma Institute of Child Development
For the child's total development, space and equipment for outdoor activities must be provided.

Efficient use must be made of staff, time, space, equipment, and materials in the plan. As part of the curriculum plan, rooms are arranged to fit uses, and an amount of time is allowed for each activity. Outdoor as well as indoor space must be included in planning.

Methods

How the activities are carried out depends on the *methods* employed. As you know, in a *discovery* approach the method would likely be to allow each child as much freedom as possible to decide where he wants to play and what he wants to do. The areas of the room include furnishings and equipment planned to meet the developmental levels of the children. Each child is allowed and encouraged to initiate action, with the adult responding only when help is requested or when needed for the safety and well-being of the children.

Teaching Style

The teaching style is the particular way in which each adult responds to and interacts with children. For example, some adults are very soft-spoken and somewhat reserved, while others are more outgoing. Children quickly recognize the types of adults around them. Surprising though it may seem, the children's responses are often in keeping with the styles used by adults. Have you been in a class with a teacher who was rather loud and outspoken? Did you see the students responding much the same way? As the teacher raises his or her voice, so do the students in many situations. Think about this in relation to a group of young children.

Keep in mind that it is possible to use new methods for carrying out activities with children, but it is seldom possible, or advisable, to try to change an individual's teaching style. The style, after all, is what makes each person a unique individual.

Evaluation

The task of evaluating is an on-going one, beginning with the early stages of a program. Periodically, the staff must get together and assess their accomplishment of goals and objectives. They must decide whether or not the program design is still suitable for the children. Sometimes what works for some children will not work for others, and changes have to be made to meet the needs of children.

A word of caution about evaluation: As you evaluate the quality of a program for children, you must be sure to evaluate it on the basis of what the program is designed to do and not on what *you* personally think it should be doing. People often have a tendency to make judgments based on their own convictions, but this is not appropriate, regardless of how excellent one's ideas are. A program should be looked at and evaluated on the basis of what it sets out to do for the children. If a program's focus is only on language skills and motor coordination, then its effectiveness should be assessed only in those two areas. To what extent has the program accomplished the desired goals in language and motor skills with the children? Can you see that in a program with these two goals it would be unfair and in error to evaluate the areas of sharing and cooperation because this is not a focus or goal for the children—even though you may consider it a most important dimension?

Of course, when parents are looking for a center in which to enroll their children, they evaluate the program based on what they as parents want for their children. They make judgments based on what their goals, as parents, are and choose a center that most closely meets their expectations. This is different from evaluating a program for its effectiveness in terms of what it sets out to do for children. Do you see the difference?

Consider the case of the Moores. They are looking for a center in which they can enroll their three-year-old daughter, Karen. Their main interest is to have Karen enjoy the companionship of other children her age for a couple of hours each day. What is their goal for Karen? It is socialization—getting along with and enjoying others, extending friendships. Naturally, the Moores will choose a center with a program that will fulfill their goal. In which center do you think they might enroll Karen?

- Developmental Day Care Center—focus on total development; ten-hour per day program.
- Community Preschool—focus on motor coordination; two hours each morning.
- Neighborhood Center—focus on motor, sensory, language, and thinking skills; four hours each morning.
- Nursery School—focus on social skills; two hours each morning, three days per week.

Looking at these same centers, how would you evaluate them in terms of program effectiveness? Will you use the same basis as the Moores? No, because the Moores are concerned only about extending Karen's social skills. You would be assessing the centers on the basis of what they claim to do for children. If the design is to enhance the child's total development, you would judge the effectiveness of that program on how successful it was in actually providing meaningful experiences for the total development of children. In

Ch. 21: Program Models

the community preschool above, which focuses on motor coordination for two hours each day, you would determine the effectiveness of the program based on how well it accomplishes activities and experiences for the improvement of children's motor skills—and that is all. You would look at the kind of materials and equipment used, the activities, the room arrangement, and the ability of the staff to help children with motor coordination.

What would you look for in evaluating the effectiveness of the other programs listed above? Why?

THE VALUE OF A MODEL

Are models or frameworks really necessary? Most evidence indicates they are. Programs without a framework often result in a type of baby-sitting or custodial care which, as you know, simply offers a place for children to play with some variety of materials. Centers without a framework may also lack concern for specific aspects of development which help children increase strengths and overcome weaknesses.

Children learn in a custodial setting, but learning is *incidental* because it *just happens* from time to time as a child reacts and acts within the environment. The teachers and assistants in many nursery school and day care settings are not held accountable for seeing that children learn and develop. Instead, they see their roles as providing an opportunity for children to play together with courtesy and respect, share toys, and cooperate in keeping order. These are essential but are not enough. Following a program model provides guidelines to help adults plan activities which will enrich and improve the daily living of children now and in the future.

Without a model or framework, can you see how a program might fall short of providing children with needed experiences?

Early childhood specialists caution, however, that having a model does not necessarily insure an adequate program. Other factors may cause the model to be ineffective. One reason for this is often the child care worker's lack of knowledge and understanding about children. A second reason is the lack of background in planning, organizing, and managing the program. Furthermore, adults who work in some centers may be insecure even though they are interested in their work with young children. In addition, a staff may not be committed to following the model used by the center. Any of these may contribute to the ineffectiveness of a program model.

Some programs have been heavily criticized, not so much for what they do but for *what they do not do*. When you consider the amount of time children are present in many centers, you can see that a large portion of the children's daytime living occurs there. This presents a challenge to the child care worker. Ideally, every minute should be beneficial, whether it is time for snacks, games, stories, resting, freely exploring, or special activities like field trips. Goals that are successfully met will not provoke criticism, but goals that are not met will. A program model that makes good use of the child's time will be the most successful.

Some specific program models have names which identify them. A name is sometimes derived from the person who designed the model or from the place where the model was developed. The name may also represent the type of program used. The following are some models you may have studied or wish to learn more about:

Part VI: Planning a Children's Program

Learning takes place spontaneously as children play. Here, Darby sees her image often. This helps Darby develop concepts about herself.

Tucson Early Education Model (TEEM)

This program provides children with educational experiences designed to promote the social and academic abilities required to function effectively and confidently in society. The emphasis is in several areas. Developing each child's ability to think is stressed. The child also increases skills for effective social interaction and communication. Attitudes and behavioral patterns that will help the child in his particular situation are developed. Academic skills, such as the ability to make decisions and determine values, are advanced.

This program has been used primarily with children in early elementary grades. Learning experiences take place in small groups of three to six children organized into interest centers planned to stimulate the development of academic skills and self-discovery. Social reinforcement includes praise, attention, and affection. The core of the curriculum is designed around activities in which the children are involved through participation.

The Englemann-Becker Model (The University of Oregon)

This program model is designed to help children build the academic skills needed in a school setting. A major premise of this program is that basic learning skills be achieved at a faster than normal rate of mastery. The materials and activities are programmed for carefully controlled sequencing of tasks. The tasks promote each child's level of competency. There is an emphasis on learning to think logically and on developing intelligent behavior through the use of programmed materials and behavior modification principles. Unproductive and antisocial behavior is usually ignored. There are many verbal responses in the form of questions which have been programmed for the teachers. The teachers and aides work with groups of five or six children, rotating them through each planned activity for the day.

The Bank Street Model

The Bank Street model operates on the premise that children learn most effectively through active participation with adults who allow and support each child's autonomy. It focuses on satisfying the child's goals for cognitive and affective development.

The classroom environment emphasizes learning through actual experiences of probing, discovering, and problem solving. Content is directly related to the child's own world. The model encourages communication which is self-initiated, creative, and expressive. In the early elementary grades the model emphasizes a mastery of language and symbolic processes for reading and writing and the understanding of the practical application of numerical concepts and skills. Emphasis is not only on the acquisition of language but also on the mastery of how to learn. The limits of behavior in the classroom are well defined, giving children full freedom of expression within the limits.

The Responsive Educational Model

This model has a major focus on the development of a healthy self-concept, which is considered important for the child. With this focus, the child can appreciate his culture more fully, estimate his own ability and limitations, and develop confidence in his own capacity to succeed. It is assumed that children learn best in an environment where they are allowed to develop independence, self-direction, and internal motivation. Learning how to learn is more important than learning specific content. Children are allowed to pursue their interests in whatever they are doing. Problem solving is considered a major element of learning; therefore, the environment presents problems and encourages the discovery of solutions.

The staff responds to each individual child's needs. Importance is placed on the use of experiences, materials, games, manipulative toys, and audio-visual equipment. Children receive immediate feedback from teachers, peers, and from materials. This feedback helps children develop problem-solving skills. The classroom is organized in such a way that each child is likely to make a series of related discoveries about the physical environment and social world. The approach is individualized so that each child is free to choose between a variety of activities, explore his environment, and set his own learning pace.

The Florida Parent Education Model

A premise of the Florida model is that learning and personality are formed largely by the child's early home environment. Parents are considered to be a key factor in the emotional and intellectual development of their children. The model promotes the idea that the home should be as academically stimulating as the school. Parents are trained to supervise their children's learning experiences in the home in order to increase their intellectual and social competencies.

The teaching patterns and activities in the center programs are flexible enough to be applied easily in the home. The program objectives are to improve the child's school achievements through work on tasks at home, to expand the child's learning environment beyond the school, to educate parents to participate directly in the education of their children, to motivate parents to develop a home environment that stimulates the growth and development of their children, and to promote a home-school partnership in all activities.

The Cognitive Curriculum Model

This model emphasizes the development of the child's thinking, reasoning, and communication skills. The program encourages children to become actively in-

Part VI: Planning a Children's Program

Oklahoma Child and Family Institute
A listening corner provides pleasant experiences for cognitive development.

volved in learning. It is assumed that children learn, not by being told, but by planning, experimenting, exploring, and by talking about what they are doing. The focus of the curriculum is on levels of representation, areas of physical and logical relations, and learning through the children's involvement in action and language.

Objectives include the ability to make decisions, to express oneself, to understand others, to work with other children and adults, to develop self-discipline, and to develop a spirit of inquiry and openness to knowledge and others' points of view.

An open classroom provides interest areas which include settings for art; housekeeping; woodworking and carpentry; block and large toy play; and such quiet activities as manipulative games, stories, and individualized learning experiences.

The Behavior Analysis Model

This model operates on the premise that children learn best when they receive praise and approval for progress in developing academic and behavioral skills. Motivation is achieved with tokens which provide concrete evidence of approval of the child's behavior and progress. The token system establishes a noncompetitive way for each child to achieve maximum results. Criticism and pressure are considered harmful to the learning process.

The children work in small groups at their own pace. They move from one instructor to another. The teachers award tokens, along with verbal and physical praise, to reinforce the appropriate behavioral skill of each child. Teachers give attention to each child and reinforce each according to the individual's progress.

Ch. 21: Program Models

Chapter Highlights

- The philosophy of a children's center is portrayed by what goes on in the program.
- A program model, sometimes referred to as a framework, is a specific plan for setting up and operating a children's program.
- A framework helps adults and children at a center know where they are, where they are headed, and what is expected.
- The *instructional* and *discovery* models are basic approaches used in many early childhood programs.
- The *instructional* approach places emphasis on the adult initiating action, with the children responding.
- The *discovery* approach emphasizes the children initiating activities, with adults responding.
- In both the instructional and discovery approaches the adults must provide an appropriate and organized environment.
- A program model is made up of elements, including *assumptions*—underlying ideas that are the bases for the program; *goals and objectives*—the purpose of the program for the children; *strategies*—plans for how the adults will help the children carry out their activities, including methods, teaching styles, and organization; *curriculum*—the activities for the children; and *evaluation*—assessment of the accomplishment of goals and objectives.
- Evidence indicates that a model provides guidelines that make working with the children more effective and more enjoyable.
- Having a model does not necessarily insure an adequate program unless the entire staff understands and uses the model.
- A program model generally gets its name from the person who designed the model, from the place where the model was developed, or from a theory which prevails in the program.

Thinking It Over

1. How is a children's program related to the philosophy of those in charge of the center?
2. Define program model.
3. How does a program model keep the adults and children in a center on the same wavelength?
4. Describe the two types of models basic to many early childhood programs.
5. Do you think a children's program can be a combination of these two models? Explain your answer.
6. Which basic program model do you think you would prefer to carry out? Why?
7. Why are definite goals and objectives important components of a children's program? In what way do they place added responsibility on the center staff?
8. What does the term *teaching style* refer to in a children's program?
9. What should be evaluated in a children's program?
10. Are models really necessary to a center? Explain.

Part VI: Planning a Children's Program

Things To Do

1. Have a class debate on this topic: "A children's center should use a discovery model for program effectiveness."
2. Working in groups of three or four students, develop sample activities and strategies that could be used to meet one goal and three or four objectives for the children. Use both the instructional and discovery approaches. Each student should have a different objective. Discuss these in class.
3. Review the philosophy written in chapter 18 and relate it to the program models discussed in this chapter.
4. Working in groups, develop evaluation check sheets to be used in evaluating a children's center. Each group may choose to devise an evaluation check sheet for a different part or element of a program. Bring these together in a class discussion and integrate them into one overall evaluation devise.
5. Have a panel of teachers with quite different teaching styles discuss their philosophies concerning some area of teaching. Discuss differences in styles of teaching and similarities in philosophies.
6. Show the filmstrip, with cassette tapes, entitled "Early Childhood Information Unit." (Eight Program Models Filmstrip, Educational Products Information Exchange Institute, 463 West Street, New York, N.Y. 10014.) *May also be secured from the State Head Start Training Office.* Discuss the major components of each model.

Recommended Reading

Cherian, Edward J. and Associates, Inc. *A Guide to Follow Through.* Washington, D.C.: U.S. Office of Education, 1973.

Spodek, Bernard. *Teaching in the Early Years.* Englewood Cliffs, New Jersey: Prentice-Hall, Inc., 1972.

Stanley, Julian C. *Preschool Programs for the Disadvantaged.* Baltimore: The Johns Hopkins University Press, 1972.

Weber, Evelyn. *Early Childhood Education: Perspectives on Change.* Worthington, Ohio: Charles A. Jones Publishing Co., 1970.

Chapter 22.

Goals and Objectives

Your Challenge

This chapter will enable you to . . . .

- *Define goals and objectives.*
- *Explain some considerations that deal with planning goals and objectives.*
- *Tell why children's needs and interests are important when setting up goals.*
- *Explain why parents should be included in planning.*

COMPARING GOALS AND OBJECTIVES

To be effective, every children's program should be based on goals and objectives, one of the main components of a program model, which you read about in the previous chapter. As a child care worker or parent, you can help children extend their capacities for living and learning through carefully planned goals and objectives.

A *goal* is the general target to be accomplished. Goals may be very simple or very complex. They may cover a single aspect or a large area of development. For example, the development of living skills is a broad goal for preschool children. A single aspect of this area of development is the ability of children to feed themselves.

Objectives are observable tasks to be achieved and are more specific than goals. For the late infant period, an example of an objective is acquiring the skill to drink liquid from a cup without assistance. An objective for the three-year-old is to pour milk from a pitcher into a small glass with success most of the time. These specific objectives are associated with a broad goal of self-feeding.

From an earlier discussion on developmental tasks, you learned that an objective can best be accomplished at the critical period—the point of readiness—when the child is willing, eager, and mature enough to accomplish a certain task. One objective above was to hold and manage a cup by coordinating and controlling eye, arm, and hand muscles. The child must be ready physically (adequate muscle development and control) as well as socially (family and others expect this achievement) and psychologically ("I want to do it; I think I can do it").

PLANNING GOALS AND OBJECTIVES

Setting up the goals and objectives for a center is not easy. You have read about many of the tasks of childhood. Can you expect to cover all of these in your goals and objectives? Probably not, but you can

Ch. 22: Goals and Objectives

David Michels

A common goal for all children in the development of a positive self-concept. An objective in this area is for children to see themselves as significant and unique individuals.

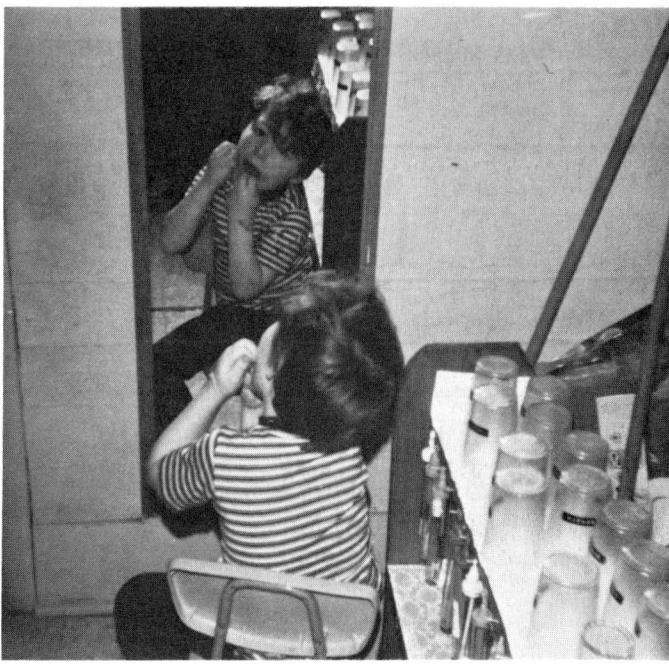

Arkoma Head Start Center

The child who is willing and eager, as well as physically ready, generally accomplishes a task or skill with success. Here a four-year-old practices flossing.

provide a program with a range of goals and objectives. Such a program will contribute much to the learning of all children in the center.

A specific set of goals and objectives cannot be prescribed for all centers. The reasons why are obvious. In the first place, centers are not physically alike in size and facilities. One center may be equipped to handle some objectives more easily than others. Secondly, the length of the program may be limiting. You cannot hope to accomplish the same number of objectives in half a day that another center has in a full-day session. Finally, the children's needs, abilities, and developmental levels will not be the same. Can you imagine the difficulty—even the uselessness—in having a child draw a picture of a farm with animals when he has never seen one? How can a child build a house of blocks if he doesn't even know what blocks are for? Certainly, objectives must be suited to the children in the center.

In planning a program, you will want to set up certain realistic goals. Even though a center may not accomplish all of its goals, those which are most appropriate for the children it serves can be selected. The following broad goals for early childhood development are suggested but may be altered according to need:

Part VI: Planning a Children's Program

Central State University Child Study Center
Socialization occurs as children interact, play, and learn together.

- Positive self-concept.
- Sensory perception and acuity.
- Motor coordination.
- Language skills.
- Concept formation and problem solving.
- Socialization and living skills.

Often a single objective contributes to the achievement of more than one goal. For example, in learning to drink from a cup without help, the child progresses toward the main goal of self-feeding. Besides this, the child develops coordination that will also help him with self-dressing, another goal. Moreover, success in handling the cup promotes a positive self-concept in the child, still another goal. Consequently, one objective has influenced three goals. Can you think of other goals that might be promoted with this same objective?

Additional goals may be achieved as by-products of a program. Optimum *physical development,* good *health,* and proper *nutrition* result when children are in a safe and healthy center with nutritious meals and snacks and plenty of indoor and outdoor space for exercise. Motivation, a vital concern for every child, should occur as the result of appropriately planned activities, even when the primary goal is something other than motivation. To a great degree, *socialization* is achieved as children interact, play, and learn together. Many activities promote socialization—not just those designed for that purpose. When children and adults are engaged in meaningful activities in a well-planned setting, they learn to get along, cooperate, enjoy each other, and make contributions to the group. They develop socialization skills.

Children's Needs and Interests

Recognition of children's needs and interests, together with knowledge of developmental levels, helps determine what goals should be included in a program.

Some children, for a variety of reasons, have not had an adequate home environment with opportunities for optimal development. These children may be from very poor homes, some without one or both parents, and some from neighborhoods where poor health conditions prevail. These children are often called disadvantaged because they have not had the same opportunities for growing and living as most children in this country. Other children may be considered disadvantaged because they speak Spanish instead of English or because they cannot speak the standard language well for their age. Some children are bilingual—they can speak two languages—however, they have only learned a special, local "street" language. You are probably familiar with disadvantaged children in your own community or in nearby areas. What goals do you think are important for these children? Can you think of important areas other than economic in which children may be disadvantaged?

Keep in mind the major difference between disadvantaged and nondisadvantaged children in respect to learning. Generally, disadvantaged children do not have less potential for learning; they do not have less ability; they are not less responsive to motivation. Perhaps the most significant difference is that disadvantaged children have a *lag in learning* because of a lack of opportunity, limited experiences, and a less stimulating environment.

As you formulate goals for the children, remember, a lag in the learning level of disadvantaged children requires special attention. A program of only a few hours a day has little hope of accumulating the necessary experiences for disadvantaged children that will allow them to catch up with the nondisadvantaged children. As the disadvantaged children progress, so do the nondisadvantaged. How, then, can the gap that separates these children's levels of achievement be closed?

Look carefully at what disadvantaged children must achieve to live fully and happily and to catch up in their development. What are the highest priorities for disadvantaged children—in what areas do they need the most help? Parents, teachers, child development specialists, and other professionals must work together to determine the most appropriate goals for these children in a program—or in a home setting for that matter. Goals and objectives can then be identified to form the basis for meaningful experiences.

Of course, there are also accelerated children who have had a variety of experiences at home, enabling them to do more than is generally expected of their age group or stage of development. For example, some four- and five-year-olds are ready to read; some have broad vocabularies and can speak very well; others naturally excel in learning tasks and living skills.

Many children, even in adequate home and neighborhood environments, have two working parents and must attend a child care center until one parent returns from work. Some families take advantage of preschool enrichment programs to expand their children's experiences and provide opportunities for being with others their own age. Can you see how goals for these children might vary?

Including Parents in Planning

Parents should be included in planning and implementing goals and objectives as much as possible. Sharing information makes planning more meaningful. Some programs have weekly or monthly sessions to bring parents and teachers together concerning the center's activities and the chil-

Oklahoma VoTech (Stillwater Head Start)
Children who have had a variety of experiences at home are generally ready for more challenging activities in the child care center.

dren's developmental progress. Parents make suggestions which can often be incorporated in the plans for the center. Some parents make excellent volunteers for helping in the center if they have the time and if they understand the program's goals and objectives.

In order for parents and the center staff to work cooperatively in strengthening each child's total development, both parties need to be kept up to date on the children's activities. Parents should be well acquainted with what is going on in the center, what the goals are for their children, what activities are included each week, and how their children are progressing. Knowing what the center does may give parents ideas for enriching the child's home environment.

For example, three-year-old Trevino needed help with language skills. In talking with the center staff, Trevino's mother learned several methods she could use at home to help. For one thing, she made it a point to spend at least a few minutes each day talking with her son about something that interested him. In addition, they read simple stories together and talked about a puzzle Trevino had put together successfully. At mealtime she talked about the foods served. Finally, she made a puppet and used it to practice language skills

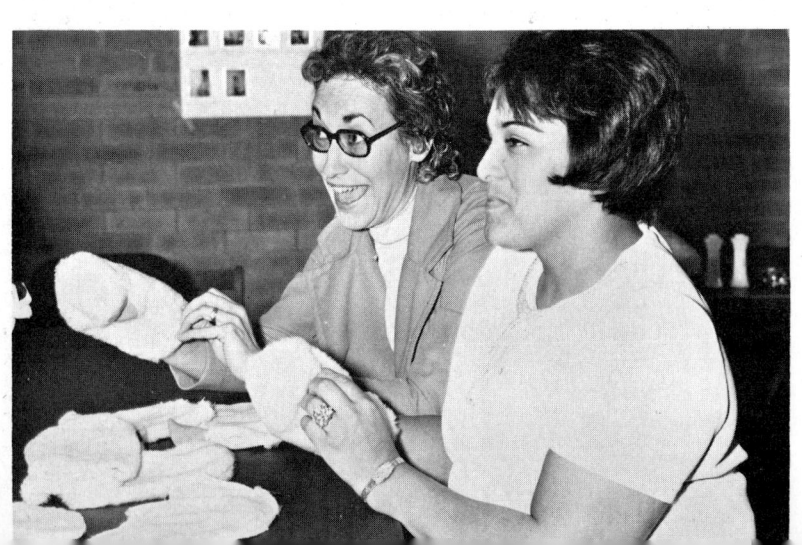

Beggs Project
Parents, as well as teachers, enjoy planning and working together to meet goals and objectives for children. These adults are making hand puppets for use at story time and for creative play.

388

Ch. 22: Goals and Objectives

Kentucky Youth Research Center, Inc.
When parents know what the children do in the center, they can provide supportive activities at home. Making gelatin in the center could be followed by other kitchen experiences at home.

with Trevino. As a result of her efforts, combined with those of the center staff, Trevino made considerable progress with language skills.

Four-year-old Arch was having no difficulties at the center. Still his aunt and uncle, with whom he lived, wanted home experiences to complement those in the center. Therefore, knowing that the center was working on sensory activities, they took Arch for a walk in the evening and let him find rocks, leaves, pieces of wood, and other objects with contrasting textures. They talked about the items and felt them along the way. When the center worked on developing a positive self-image, Arch's uncle had him lie on the floor on a large piece of paper and drew around him with a crayon. Then Arch drew in his face, body parts, clothing, and other details. This coordinated approach to learning was good for Arch, as it would be for any child.

Everything that goes on in the center should be planned around goals and objectives. The child care worker has a responsibility to help define appropriate goals for children and then to develop specific objectives or expected behaviors to be accomplished by the children. From time to time, of course, the goals and objectives should be re-evaluated in light of children's changing needs and developmental progress. Perhaps some goals and objec-

Part VI: Planning a Children's Program

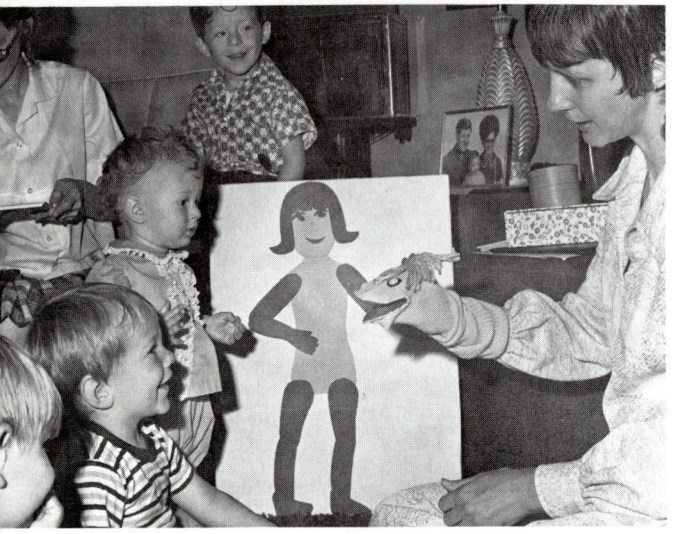

Oklahoma VoTech

Whether in a family day care home or a child care center, adults must understand the purposes of the children's activities. The adult here should have a goal in mind as she encourages the children to talk to the puppet. Can you think of goals that might be met through such an activity?

tives will need to be changed, some deleted, and others added.

An excellent way to let parents, visitors, and volunteers know what the targets are for the children is to post a list of goals in the center. As people view these, they will know what the priorities are for the program and for the children. Obviously, a program cannot do everything for every child. Those which try to reach too many goals often wind up with a little of everything and not much of anything. The program directors and child care workers—hopefully with parents—have the task of clearly defining what goals for the children will be emphasized. Then specific objectives may be defined for each goal.

Teacher, aides, and volunteers must each clearly understand what the program is designed to do for the children. This knowledge serves as a foundation for planning appropriate activities and strategies for implementing them.

Chapter Highlights

- A *goal* is a general target to be accomplished.
- *Objectives* are specific tasks we expect children to achieve.
- A common set of goals and objectives cannot be prescribed for all centers.
- Examples of broad goals for early childhood development include a positive self-concept, sensory perception and acuity, motor coordination, language skills, concept formation and problem solving, and socialization and living skills.
- Recognition of children's needs and interests helps determine the goals to include in a program.
- A most significant difference in disadvantaged and nondisadvantaged children is that disadvantaged children have a *lag in learning* because of a lack of opportunity, limited experiences, and a less stimulating environment.
- The *lag in learning* in disadvantaged children requires special attention in order to help them live meaningful lives.
- In order for parents and the center staff to work cooperatively in strengthening each child's total development, both parties need to be kept up to date on the children's activities.
- Parents should be included in planning and implementing goals and objectives in a children's center.

Ch. 22: Goals and Objectives

- Everything that goes on in a center should be planned around goals and objectives for the children.
- An excellent way to let parents, visitors, and volunteers know what the targets are for the children is to post a *list of goals* in the center.
- Clearly defined and understood goals and objectives serve as a foundation for planning appropriate activities and strategies for implementing them.

Thinking It Over

1. How does a goal differ from an objective?
2. Why are goals and objectives important in children's centers?
3. Why can't a common list of goals and objectives, developed by child development specialists, be handed to all children's center directors for use in their respective programs?
4. How can goals for early childhood development be used as a basis for planning? How does a center decide on a set of goals for its children?
5. How can the accomplishment of a single objective contribute to the achievement of more than one goal?
6. What is the major difference between disadvantaged and nondisadvantaged children with respect to learning?
7. How would you include parents in planning and implementing the goals and objectives of a children's center?
8. Do the goals and objectives of a children's center ever have to be changed? Why?

Things To Do

1. Divide into groups. Each group take one of the goals for child development as identified in this chapter. Write specific objectives for the particular goal assigned. Bring these before the class and discuss them. Invite parents of young children to class to help the groups develop objectives for the goals.
2. List objectives developed by the groups and display them in the classroom.
3. Have child care workers associated with Head Start or Home Start programs present a panel discussion on the *lag in learning* which disadvantaged children may experience.
4. Visit a children's center and interview the director. Inquire about the goals for the children. Observe the activities of the program and identify ways in which the goals are accomplished.

Recommended Reading

Spodek, Bernard. *Teaching in the Early Years.* Englewood Cliffs, New Jersey: Prentice-Hall, Inc., 1972.

Weber, Evelyn. *Early Childhood Education: Perspectives on Change.* Worthington, Ohio: Charles A. Jones Publishing Co., 1970.

Chapter 23.

Teaching and Learning Strategies

Your Challenge

This chapter will enable you to . . . .

- Define and explain *curriculum* and *theme*.
- Distinguish between a structured and unstructured setting, relating this to an open setting.
- Explain how a routine is useful in the child care center.
- Describe the use of a schedule in the center.
- Explain the need for both individual and group activities.
- Explain how equipment, materials, and supplies should be stored and used in the center.
- Describe how space is best used in the center.

CHILDREN IN ACTION

An active child becomes bored unless interesting things are provided to stimulate excitement and enthusiasm. Children need freedom and space to be themselves and to explore naturally, but they also need to be provided with games, toys, materials, and activity programs which encourage them to develop their interests and pursue their curiosity. They need a bright and colorful world which presents challenges and excitement for them.

How can such an environment be provided for children in a center? What strategies, or planned ways to meet goals, can be used to make the program effective? This chapter will help you answer these questions. You have already read about goals and objectives, the first part of a program model. Strategies make up the second major part of a program model.

The curriculum is a planned set of experiences for children. The purpose is to carry out the goals of the program. Along with the curriculum, concern must be given to the setting; routines and schedules; individual and group activities; equipment, materials, and supplies; and room arrangement and use of space. Different strategies, which you will read about in this chapter, can be used to make each of these a meaningful part of the child care program.

Ch. 23: Teaching and Learning Strategies

University of Oklahoma Institute of Child Development
Children's learning is enhanced when the environment stimulates them to explore and express ideas.

Kickapoo Head Start Center
Each center must develop a teaching strategy to meet the range of needs, interests, and abilities in their children. These children are obviously interested in what they are doing.

CURRICULUM

You might think of a curriculum as a map which leads to a treasure. Even though you may have to take some detours, if you stay on the general route, you will surely reach the destination. There are many ways to design and carry out a curriculum for young children. The suggestions here serve only as guidelines. Each center must develop a teaching strategy for its children, taking into consideration their range of needs, interests, and abilities.

A theme, or topic of special interest, is often helpful in carrying out the curriculum. Children usually identify with a particular concept or subject when it is presented in a framework which they can understand. A theme is used to build a fence around an area of interest. It helps to focus the energies and attention of both children and staff. Consider these and many more themes listed in the Appendix for use in planning a curriculum.

- Families
- Homes
- Community life
- Community services (hospitals, fire stations, police department, water filtration plants)
- Clothing
- City/rural
- Transportation (land, water, air, space)
- Stores/shopping centers
- Farms/ranches
- Weather
- Animals (fish, birds, mammals, wild animals, domestic pets)
- Industry (factories, construction, mills, refineries, chemical plants, dairies)

Part VI: Planning a Children's Program

Kickapoo Head Start Center

To help children achieve goals and objectives, staff members must understand and be comfortable with the methods for working with children center's.

- Plants (trees, flowers, vegetables, fruit, tropical, desert)
- Food (plant, animal, processed, natural, vegetable, fruit, sweet, sour, salty)
- Accidents
- Health

Some themes may last from a few days to a week, yet others may last only one day. The children often get so excited about a certain topic that they want to extend it with their own suggestions. This may call for an extra day, which also calls for flexibility in the schedule and adaptation by the adults. Although the theme should be used as a vehicle, or a tool, to provide interesting and exciting experiences for the children, it must not become the goal. It is simply a framework to organize the activities in order to achieve the goals. A theme helps to maintain continuity throughout the day, but it does not have to be incorporated into every activity. Sometimes, teachers become so concerned about a theme they lose sight of the focus on the children's development.

Implementing the curriculum calls for a knowledge of *how* to work with the children. This is often called the *methodology* of teaching. There are hundreds of methods, varying from those with little organization to those with precise instructions for carrying out children's activities. To achieve the goals for the children, staff members must have a thorough understanding of the method they are using and must feel comfortable with it.

SETTING

Recently *open settings* for children's activities have become popular. The term *open*, however, has been broadly interpreted. These interpretations are of two general types. (1) To some, it means a completely free setting, with no particular purposes or limitations. Baby-sitting, or custodial care, can be placed in this category. (2) To others, open refers to a planned environment. Through planning and preparation, adults provide children with the freedom to make choices, move about, express themselves, use materials and equipment, and relate to each other. Definite goals and objectives underlie the program. Which use of the term *open* do you think is the best?

You can easily see the problems connected with the first usage of open. Flexibility and openness will be ineffective in a situation which has not been carefully planned in advance. Simply calling a program open or free does not mean it is offering the children freedom to learn. It could actually mean that children wander aimlessly, doing only what they can within a

Ch. 23: Teaching and Learning Strategies

limited environment. Just because children are allowed to choose does not mean they will learn to choose wisely, especially if there are few appropriate alternatives.

Sometimes open may refer to only one aspect of a program—the type of space, equipment and furnishings, activities, teacher-child relationships, groupings of children, curriculum design. Other times it means the total program. Be wary, however, of identifying an open setting with just any use of the term *open*. An open space, for example, does not necessarily mean an open program. An activity area may be literally open, without partitions or rooms, and still not contain an open setting. If the schedule is rigid, the materials and equipment limited, and the activities highly regimented, the program is not open regardless of the room arrangement.

A common misconception sometimes occurs in the early childhood field with regard to *structured* and *nonstructured* settings for children. Do you know what is meant by these terms? A structured setting has a type of form, or framework, so that activities will take place according to an overall plan. A nonstructured setting has little form, or framework, so that activities take place at will. Many people mistakenly think that open programs are nonstructured and that this is good. Therefore they think that programs which are structured are poor. To them a lack of structure represents freedom, and structure represents rigidity. This is not necessarily true. Actually, open programs have structure and must in order to work.

Naturally, there are different degrees of structure. Some programs are vague and undefined. Others are rigid and inflexible. Think of the classroom with children seated at desks in rows and the teacher in a ruling position at a large desk at the front of the room. This traditional setting is not necessarily bad, but it often leads to a severely structured environment if the adult in charge is not creative enough to overcome the limits imposed by the physical setting. Do you see the extremes here? Just as structure can give strength to the program, it can also be very restricting. Those who find the word *structure* unpleasant probably think first of a strict, formal setting. Instead they should realize that it can also mean an organized framework in which children are allowed controlled choice of alternatives. This kind of structure is an important part of an open setting if it is to be effective.

ROUTINE AND DAILY SCHEDULE

Although related, the terms *routine* and *schedule* are not used synonymously here. A *routine* is a *pattern of behavior* that children and adults can look forward to on a daily basis. It is closely connected to the events and activities of the day. The *schedule* is a *plan of activities* that provide experiences which lead to the achievement of goals and objectives for the children.

Routines

Routines refer to expected behaviors like these:

- Hanging coats and storing personal items in their designated places such as cubbies (small storage places) or tote trays.
- Toileting before and after snack and mealtimes. (Although toileting may occur one by one, in small groups, by taking turns, or as need demands during activity periods, it is still a part of the routine.)
- Putting away materials and equipment.
- Getting one's own mat for napping or resting and putting it away.

Part VI: Planning a Children's Program

Oklahoma VoTech (Stillwater Head Start)
Cleaning up after an activity is part of the daily routine.

- Preparing to go home at the end of the day.

A routine provides guidelines which help each child and adult assume responsibilities and meet expectations. This is of great value. Children generally like routines because they learn what to expect. They are often eager to remind each other and adults about these expectations. Remember that children are easily influenced, and a rigid routine imposed upon a group can make a children's center look perfect because everyone is following the routine precisely and with loyalty. Just because the children are behaving according to a prescribed pattern, however, does not necessarily mean they are learning in a meaningful way. As you know by now, children need to feel a sense of freedom. Routines should not restrict. Instead they should help each child become secure, comfortable, and responsible as an individual and as a group member.

Occasionally, people who work with children adopt some rather confining routines. They line the children up in rows to go to the bathroom, lunchroom, or outdoors. They ask children to raise their hands for permission to move or speak. They seat children in the same place every day, with desks or tables and chairs always arranged the same way. None of these fit the concept of routine presented here. Do you agree that these procedures can create problems? Can you support your opinion with some reasons?

A routine can usually be established in a few days to a couple of weeks after the program starts if the pattern is consistent. Children learn quickly to recognize inconsistent child and adult behavior. Chaos may result unless adults are kind but firm and respectful while establishing a routine. Of course, once a routine is well established, the total program functions in an orderly way, making the entire situation pleasant and less frustrating for everyone.

Even though children can and should help establish the routine, they cannot be expected to devise their own. They need help in developing patterns for starting and carrying out activities. Those who are very young and inexperienced need adult help in setting limitations on daily activities. Children depend on the sound judgment of adults to set the stage for creating an environment which will help them become independent, respectful, and cooperative individuals.

Schedules

The schedule usually consists of a sequence of events. For example:

- Arrival.
- Self-selected activities.
- Large-group activities.
- Developmental/learning unit—individualized activities and/or small groups.
- Snack time.
- Outdoor activities.
- Developmental/learning unit—individualized activities and/or small groups.
- Lunch.
- Rest or self-selected quiet activities.
- Self-selected activities.
- Preparation to go home.
- Departure.

Again, details of the schedule depend on the type of program design. If you visit children's centers, you will probably see many types of schedules. You may see rigidly timed programs of specified activities or completely free settings with no limitations other than snack time and lunch time.

Flexibility, the quality of being able to change, is the key to an effective schedule. Planning ahead for a variety of activities that can be used throughout the day and week makes changes easier. Adults can often detect whether some or all of the children are interested in certain activities or whether a change is in order. Some children remain enthusiastic about an experience for a long time, yet others are ready after several minutes to move to other adventures. For young children, short periods of ten to twenty minutes for planned large and small group activity have been found quite successful. A flexible schedule is one which can be altered to meet the needs and interests of the children without disrupting the curriculum or losing its effectiveness.

Time influences schedules. Obviously, a day care center that is open for twelve hours each day will have a different type of schedule from that of a half-day program. However, the all-day program cannot simply be an extension of the short schedule by making each activity last longer. This is a mistake often made in children's centers.

The daily schedule is a significant part of organization and management and should be planned to meet the needs of the children. Thoughts to keep in mind when planning a schedule are:

- Goals and objectives for the children.
- Appropriate activities for the particular ages of children and their developmental stages.
- Children's own interests, abilities, and special needs.
- Time plan—how much time will be used for each activity.
- Room arrangement to accommodate the activities.
- Maintaining a general routine.
- Flexibility.
- Children's interest spans.
- Individual variations.
- Motivations.
- Materials and supplies needed to carry out the activities.
- Furnishings and equipment needed and the placement of these in a given space.
- Adult responsibilities for implementing the program.
- Planning far enough in advance to facilitate preparation of materials and activity areas.

Part VI: Planning a Children's Program

- Including the children in some of the planning to help them become involved in decision-making about activities which concern them.

To give you some ideas about daily schedules, a sample is presented and notes are added to provide suggestions and explanations. See the Appendix for additional sample schedules. As you study the one presented here, identify ways in which the activities help accomplish the goals and objectives. Notice how often a theme can be used. How long are the time periods? How can flexibility occur with this schedule? What could you do differently and still maintain a good plan?

SAMPLE SCHEDULE

Goals:	To promote language development; self-concept; motor development; sensory perception; and concept formation.
Theme:	Food from plants.
8:30–8:45:	*Arrival.* (Children place personal items in lockers or cubbies and hang wraps on hooks or hangers.)
	Greet children. (Each adult is responsible for certain children to assure that every child is greeted individually by name.)
	Health check. (An adult checks each child for signs of illness.)
	Self-selected activities. (Planned alternatives are provided, such as block building, playing house, and large toy and table activities.)
8:45–9:00:	*Large group session.* (Informal but quiet gathering of all children.)
	Identify children present. (The ways may vary—song, roll-call game, show and tell.)
	Discuss reasons why a child is absent when appropriate.
	Introduce theme or review week's topic and activities.
	Identify hour, day of week, month, year, weather, room coolness or warmth.
	Recognize birthdays of children and approaching holidays.
9:00–9:15:	Nutritious foods which are appropriate for children are served early to compensate those who have had little or no breakfast at home. This does not interfere with lunch appetites. Children will concentrate better on the morning's activities with the snack behind them.
	Children can help with the snack by setting small pitchers or cans of juice at tables or counting out napkins, cups, glasses, etc.
	Talk about the food served (cereal, fruit, other foods from plants).
	A short story may be used to calm children until they become familiar with snack routine.
	Informal conversation should eventually develop without need for a story during snack time.
	Through snack experiences children develop:
	Motor coordination (pouring, passing, handling).

Ch. 23: Teaching and Learning Strategies

                Concept formation (counting; learning color, texture, shapes).
                Sensory perception (see, touch, taste, smell).
                Daily living skills (manners, conversation, helping tasks).

9:15–9:40:   *Indoor activity session.* (Organized and flexible.)
                Small group activities with supervision and assistance but not strictly or rigidly controlled.
                Plan in keeping with goals and theme.
                Purposes of activity period will vary with goals. For example, the purpose might be to promote responsibility, enjoyment of work, cooperation, independence, dependability, motivation, learning concepts, perception, or motor development.
                A few sample activities:
                    Puzzles (individual and cooperative types): Include those which relate to foods from plants; adults help with descriptions, conversations, explanation, concept formation, and language development.
                    Matching games: Sizes, shapes, quantity, and color of objects; pictures of foods; cards with cutouts and pictures; and posters.
                    Small block manipulation: Mosaic block designs; models for block formations. Promotes eye-to-hand coordination, thinking, and use of the senses; usually an individualized activity.

9:40–10:05:   *Outdoor activities.* (These should be planned for achieving goals or objectives. Using the theme may be helpful here too.)
                Walks for listening and looking (sensory perception, exploring, inquiring).
                Activities with large-muscle toys and equipment. (Swimming, wading, including guided activities and using large balls, rolling toys, and climbing apparatus.)
                Short field trips in relation to the theme.

10:05–10:30:   *Independent or self-selected activity.* (Planned possibilities.)
                Housekeeping, store, or shopping center.
                Large and small block play; assembling materials.
                Science (plants watered, fish fed, animals fed).
                Table activities of short duration (play dough, puzzles, and other individualized activities).
                Toileting and washing can take place with adults assisting a few children at a time as necessary.

10:30–11:00:   *Activity session.* (Small groups with supervision or adult help when needed.)
                Creative and manipulative media (painting, clay, dough).
                Individual reading and listening (pictures, books, listening sets).
                Number concept activities (games, puzzles).

Part VI: Planning a Children's Program

University of Oklahoma Institute of Child Development

A wide range of indoor activities provides children with alternatives for individual and group involvement. How many of us would think of playing in the sand as an indoor activity?

JoAnne Michels

Some activities aid children in understanding cause and effect relationships.

At times, children enjoy working independently even though alongside their playmates.

Kickapoo Head Start Center

Children enjoy the freedom of outdoor space to explore large motor activities.

Ch. 23: Teaching and Learning Strategies

	Sequences (pictures, numbers, objects, stories). Music (record player, songs, musical instruments). Art (painting, drawing, modeling). Story time (small groups in quiet circle with books, pictures, objects, slides, or film-showing).
11:00–11:30:	*Self-selected activity period.* (Planned possibilities with use of theme when possible.)

11:30–12:00:	*Lunch.*
	Some examples of learning during lunch:
	  Cleanliness.
	  Preparing table (arranging dishes, silver, napkins, with help from adults).
	  Talking about foods from plants (excellent opportunity for achieving goals and carrying out theme).
	  Eating skills (holding fork, spoon; manipulation).
	  Drinking milk and other liquids with success from glasses or cups.
	  Formulating appropriate eating habits.
	  Learning delayed gratification (waiting for others; dessert).
	  Pleasant experience (relaxed atmosphere).
	  General conversation (enlightening; where food comes from; how prepared; cold or hot; color; texture; sweet or sour).
	  Review activities of the day.
	  Learning concepts such as counting plates, napkins; matching correct side for fork, spoon; left and right sides; shapes and sizes. Forming small groups during eating time accommodates this type of learning.
	  Cleanup (cooperation, independence, contributions).

12:00–12:20:	*Cleanup and rest period.* Wash hands and face, toileting, brush teeth, using individual washcloths and toothbrushes and toothpaste. Learning opportunities: brushing teeth up and down; recognizing color of own toothbrush and color of own washcloth; handling slippery soap; flushing water. Rest—flexible in way this is handled. (Some children require sleep, others only quiet rest.)
12:20–12:30:	*Children prepare to go home.* Review experiences of the day. Gather materials to take home—art work; messages to parents. (Try various ways—newsletters, notes in envelopes pinned to back of child's garment, information sheets.) Put on clothing to be worn home. Greet parents. Adults assist children in leaving and getting into cars or buses.

Part VI: Planning a Children's Program

Although preparing to go home is the last activity of the day's routine, it is a very significant experience.

Kentucky Youth Research Center, Inc.
Working with children in small groups is a good idea.

One-to-one contact between adult and child is important but not necessary all the time.
Oklahoma Child and Family Institute

How routines and schedules are developed and carried out for your center will, of course, depend upon the type of curriculum design you have and the philosophy underlying your program. The previous discussion of routines and schedules was presented with the hope that you will apply the principles to your particular situation.

INDIVIDUAL AND GROUP ACTIVITIES

Young children need as much individualized attention as possible. Although a one-to-one contact between adult and child is not necessary throughout the entire day's activities, each child should experience some. This is possible with small groups, a suitable adult-child ratio, and a program design which allows children to have opportunities for playing and working alone as well as with others.

Ch. 23: Teaching and Learning Strategies

In groups of less than eight children—preferably five or six—with each adult, each child can express himself, participate, and be recognized. Children need many opportunities for developing self-concepts, learning to communicate, and getting along with others. Development in these areas is usually quite effective in small groups. Language development, sensory perception, and concept formation, on the other hand, require work with individuals or a few children at a time.

There are, of course, many opportunities for large-group activities such as all-together sessions at the beginning of the day, games, music, and some story activities.

Both large- and small-group activities require coordination and advanced planning by adults. Each worker should be so well acquainted with the activities for a large or small group that he or she can take over at any time with any group if necessary. Usually in a team setup, each adult assists with certain activities during the day's program. Even so, each should be able to float throughout the center when needed, especially during periods of self-selected indoor and outdoor activities and small group experiences.

Children are often capable of working in small groups with little help from adults. Activities concerned with language development, concept formation, and sensory perception, of course, may require adult participation. After children are acquainted with a routine, they can often participate independently in an activity which has been introduced to them. Examples are table activities with manipulative games or materials, creative media, listening experiences (head sets, record players, tape recorders), and dramatic play. Obviously, the self-selected activities—especially when children use the house, shopping, and block areas—require little direct help. Children do quite well for themselves. Of course, adults should be on hand at all times for emergencies and to encourage conversation and exploration as well as help when needed.

EQUIPMENT, MATERIALS, AND SUPPLIES

Equipment can be used over and over again. Toys, listening sets, tape recorders, record players, blocks, puzzles, games, housekeeping items, books, pictures, and scissors are all examples of equipment. *Materials* and *supplies* are expendable (eventually used up). Paper, play dough, clay, paint, crayons, marking pens, and paste are such items. Both the equipment and materials should be selected and used to help children accomplish their objectives. The Appendix contains listings of equipment and materials appropriate for various activities.

Equipment, materials, and supplies should be organized and placed conveniently in or near their places of use, depending on whether they are fixed or movable. Extras should be labeled and stored safely and neatly in a storage area where children cannot reach them. Children will usually tell you when the supplies are depleted—paper towels, paint, paste, soap. Items in the activity areas can be labeled with words or coded with pictures, shapes, or colors which match those on the storage shelves. This helps children identify the words or pictures with the items even though they cannot spell or read the words. Shelves can be coded for storage of some equipment, like blocks, manipulative toys, games, and puzzles, by painting the shape or drawing the outline of the item on the shelf. Children learn to identify shapes,

403

Part VI: Planning a Children's Program

Kickapoo Head Start Center
Equipment should be sturdy, safe, and in proper working condition.

sizes, and colors as they put things away. Some equipment is designed to fit together in a particular way, such as nesting containers. Some block sets are as much fun and as challenging to put away as they are to play with—especially those which fit together by a pattern. These serve as incentives and add interest for the children as they help put things away after use. The children can make contributions and be independent at the same time.

Can you think of other ways to promote independence? One way is to let children help get the materials out before an activity begins and organize things at the end of an activity. When shelves and storage units are at low levels and within easy reach and sight, children can establish good work habits and patterns of orderliness. They often welcome the cleanup activities, especially when there is time for additional experiences such as using a damp sponge or wet paper towel. They enjoy the tactile stimulation and fun involved while developing a feeling of importance, all of which enhances the self-image.

Only safe, appropriate, sturdy, and well-designed equipment should be included in a center. All electrical and mechanical equipment should be checked often to insure safety and proper functioning for daily use. Items should be well constructed, with durable, nontoxic coverings or paint.

Using Equipment and Materials

A child's life is not enriched so greatly by how much equipment and how many materials are available as it is by how these are used. It is better to have a limited amount of appropriate equipment and materials which are used meaningfully than to provide an endless number of things, some of which are inappropriate and misused—or never used.

Perhaps the greatest responsibility in this area for adults is to learn what equipment and materials are appropriate for the various stages of development and how to use these with the children. Here are some points to remember in selecting equipment and materials:

- For what purpose are they to be used?
- Do they coincide with the child's ability and interest ranges?
- Are they well constructed, safe, and free from unnecessary parts or devices?
- Are the colors of items appropriate —clear, bright, and attractive?
- Can items be stored adequately and arranged for easy access to children?

The more appropriate a piece of equipment is for children, the greater freedom they can have in exploring its use. Equipment that is too complicated can be confusing and frustrating for a child. Something that is too simple for a particular stage of development may leave the child bored and disinterested.

ROOM ARRANGEMENT AND USE OF SPACE

The amount of space available for children's activities varies from center to center. With the goals and objectives well in mind, maximum use of space must be planned to accommodate appropriate activities and experiences for children. Good management of space is necessary to provide:

- An organized environment with orderliness and an even flow of activities.
- Ease in children's moving about throughout the day.
- Planned space for children to have a variety of activities—quiet, boisterous, problem-solving, manipulative, listening, music, and creative play.
- Storage for children's personal items.
- Storage for equipment, materials, and supplies.
- Work areas for preparation of materials.
- Food service.
- Office and reception areas.
- Restrooms with toilets and washing facilities for children.
- Restrooms for adults.
- Room for janitorial equipment and supplies.

Many centers have spaces already defined by the construction of the building. For example, a large house which has been converted into a child care center may have rooms which must be used to provide the above areas unless money is available for renovation and remodeling.

Some centers are located in church basements with one or two large areas which are used during the week by a child care program. On the weekends, all equipment and materials must be stored in order for the church to use the same space for its program.

Community centers often have large open spaces which can be arranged to meet plans for a children's program. There are also commercial child care centers built for specific programs. Each area is designed for a purpose. Family day care homes must be used as they are for one to five children. As a child care worker, you might work in any or all of these situations. Therefore it will help you to know some basic principles of room arrangement, or *space utilization*.

Flexibility is important. This is the ability to change space to meet several purposes. You can see that a large open space would offer greater flexibility than a building with solid walls dividing the space into rooms. Why is this true?

Flexible space can be divided into interest areas by the use of movable partitions, dividers, pieces of furniture, or floor coverings. It isn't necessary to divide the children into separate rooms for separate activities. They are able to adapt very well to different activities occurring at the same time—even without dividers to block their view of the sounds of other children. Some partitioning may be helpful, however, in separating areas which serve as storage for supplies, for displays, or for activities that use such things as a peg-board wall with pots and pans for the house area.

Activity Areas

Activity areas are needed in a children's center. They make the setting work for both the children and adults. Well-planned areas will do much to stimulate children and help them develop. On the next few

Part VI: Planning a Children's Program

*University of Oklahoma
Institute of Child Development*
This listening area provides records, tapes, and books for a variety of listening activities.

pages, you will read about areas that can be included in a child care setting. Of course, every center will not have all the areas listed. Some large centers, however, may have more than one of the same area. Even though the areas are described separately, some can be combined in centers which have limited space. For example, the creative media area and manipulative table area could occupy the same space. Equipment and materials are mentioned to give you a better idea about the use of these areas. *The areas which are starred should be included in a center. The others are recommended.*

Reading, Library, Story, and Music Area*

A carpet or large rug serves as a learning surface. A soft and resilient (able to return to its original shape) covering cuts down on noise while adding comfort. Book shelves display each book separately at the child's eye level. Child-size tables and chairs are needed. A rocking chair or large easy chair is also recommended. The rug or floor space should be large enough for a group of about eight to ten children to sit together while listening to stories and music or participating in these activities. This space is often called the listening area.

Block and Large Toy Area*

Children need enough room to move about with ease while building with blocks and while playing with large toys like trucks, wagons, or boats. The paths that children use as they do other things should not interfere with this area. Unobstructed space is needed for building and tearing down structures. Some space where constructions can be kept for awhile is also needed. Carpeting in this area helps reduce noise. Open shelves, coded for stacking blocks and toys, are useful. They also encourage children to replace items.

Ch. 23: Teaching and Learning Strategies

Central State University Child Study Center

The block and large toy area provides for activities which enhance motor development and thinking skills as well as the ability to get along with others.

University of Oklahoma Institute of Child Development

The family living area provides for activities that both boys and girls can enjoy.

Dramatic Play or House Area*

Corner space is ideal for this interest area. It can easily be divided with child-size furniture, such as a stove, sink, counter top, refrigerator, open closet for dress-up clothes (for both girls and boys), ironing board, table and chairs, baby crib, and shelves for baby things and household items. A full length mirror is an item which must be included to make this area complete. Storage cabinets or movable shelf stands may serve as partitions to make the activities in the house area somewhat private. The arrangement of furniture in this space should be as realistic as possible—homelike, of course.

Shopping Center or Store Area

Children enjoy having an area where they can play grocery store or shopping center. They want this area to be next to the house area so that the children playing mother, father, and other family members can go easily from home to store and back. A counter top with a cash register, surrounded by shelves of groceries with empty containers of all sorts, is a natural divider for this area. This space can be small, since only one or two clerks and customers occupy it at the same time.

Creative Media Area*

Types of materials for this area include play dough, scissors, paste, paints, brushes, crayons, and paper. This area should have an easy-to-clean floor covering. Enough space is needed for one or two child-size tables, several chairs, and one or two easels. The area should be well lighted, since children will be engaged in eye-to-hand activities requiring good visibility. Shelves which hold materials and supplies where children can reach them make it easier for them to get materials out and put them away. A display rack or bulletin board for artwork can also serve as a divider in this space. Some centers use a clothesline.

Part VI: Planning a Children's Program

Kickapoo Head Start Center

Number concepts and classification and social skills are learned in the store area.

Kickapoo Head Start Center

Tables can be improvised with a large door or piece of wood. Children need plenty of space on which to work and explore their ideas.

In an area arranged for creative activities children develop many concepts and motor skills while expressing their thoughts and feelings.

University of Oklahoma Institute of Child Development

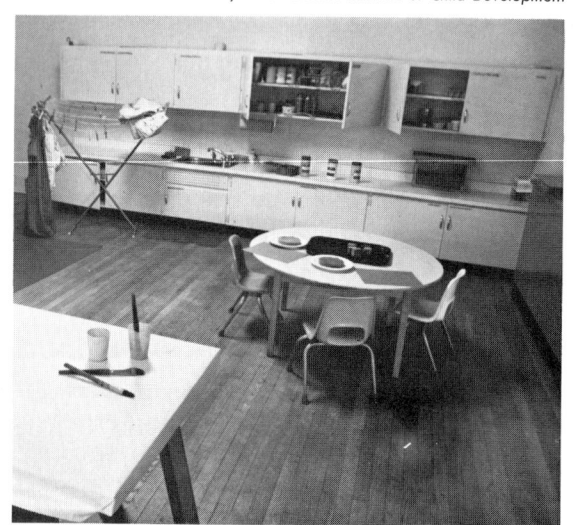

The science area is a favorite place to experiment with foods, plants, and animals, as well as weights and measures.

University of Oklahoma Institute of Child Development

Table Area for Manipulative Activities*

In the manipulative area, toys or objects are operated with the hands. Lottos, puzzles, and matching games, for example, are used at child-size tables. Working with play dough and sensory materials like clay can also occur in this area. One or two tables and several chairs in a space away from the block area are needed for this interest area. Stored nearby should be equipment such as lottos, color and number bingo, puzzles, pegs and boards, word and picture games, nesting toys, and sorting sets.

Science Area

An easy-to-clean floor with counters or tables is needed here. Pet cages, aquariums, terrariums, plants, rock displays, magnets, clocks, gears, counting trays, latches, and scales can provide many exciting learning experiences for children. If at all possible, this area should be close to the outdoors for easy cleaning of equipment, especially cages. It should also be near faucets for watering plants and animals. Shelves for holding buckets and utensils for measuring, planting, and doing science experiments should also be located in this area.

Carpentry Area*

Workbenches with tools for cutting and building need to be safely arranged in this interest area. The floor should be easy to clean, with a hard surface that will resist nicks and mars from the youthful carpenters' work. This area should be in a space which offers full view for the adult who must supervise carpentry activities at all times. Table or work surfaces must be sturdy, well stabilized, and safe.

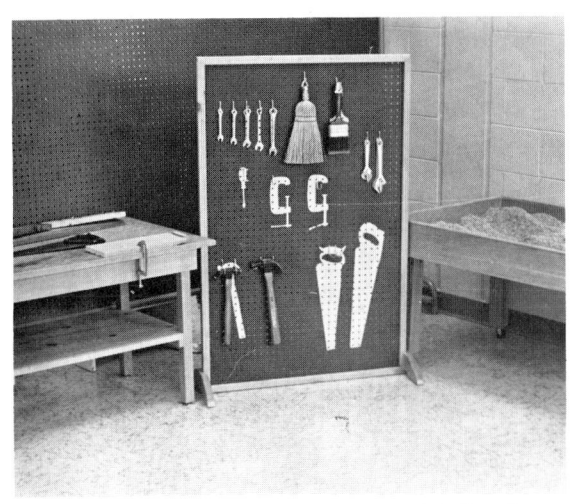

University of Oklahoma Institute of Child Development

The carpentry, or woodworking, area should provide safe and durable equipment on an easy-to-clean floor surface.

Service Areas

The following areas are not interest centers for children's activities, but they serve a purpose in the daily program. Again, some of these areas may be combined where space is limited.

Receiving Area

A space is needed where children can be greeted daily and given a quick health check. This can take place in the activity room if no other space is available. Any area designated for this purpose should be near the entrance of the building to accommodate children and parents as they enter and leave the center.

Personal Storage Area

Children need a place for coats, boots, sweaters, extra clothing, and other personal things. This area serves its purpose best when located near the entrance or

Part VI: Planning a Children's Program

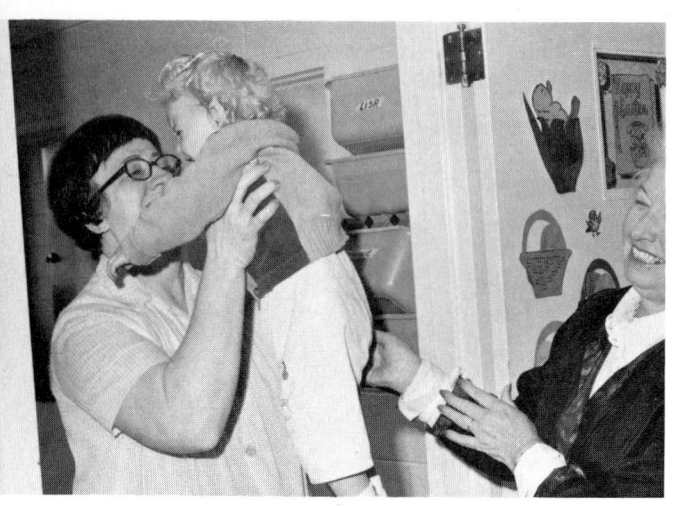

Oklahoma City Christian Day Care Center
A receiving area provides a place where children can be greeted and given a health check.

University of Oklahoma Institute of Child Development
Children need storage spaces, such as these cubbies, for their personal items.

receiving area. Each child's storage place should be labeled by name. Children learn to identify their own names and the places for their things if they each have a cubbie, tray, or locker in which to place these items. This arrangement also helps a child build his self-concept because he can identify his own items and enjoy having a special place to keep them.

Restrooms

Toilets and washing facilities should be child-size, with wash basins and paper towel dispensers within easy reach. Hot and cold water faucets should be labeled. This helps with language development, concept formation, and safety. Children should each have a toothbrush identified by name. Children quickly learn which items belong to them. By marking items with names or some other means of identification, children are more likely to enjoy using the items. Thus, they are encouraged to develop good health habits.

Toilet stalls are safest without doors. Little fingers are easily squeezed while opening and closing doors and heads are bumped with swinging doors. More adequate supervision is possible when doors within the bathroom are eliminated. Help is easier to give with clothing and with toilet routines. Children are naturally curious and often get answers to healthy questions about sex in a situation where supervision can occur easily. Activity in an open toilet area is easier to guide and control than it would be behind closed doors.

Eating Area

Some centers provide a special area for eating although others use the main activity room. Whichever is available, if children are seated in small groups, they can relax and enjoy pleasant conversations at meal and snack times. The area must be spotlessly clean, with easy-to-care-for equipment and a washable floor. Washable tables and chairs should be child-size be-

Ch. 23: Teaching and Learning Strategies

Kickapoo Head Start Center
The eating area should provide a comfortable and relaxed setting.

Central State University Child Study Center
Children like to see their work displayed.

cause children need to be comfortable while eating.

Display Area

Displays of children's work, announcements, pictures, and other items of special interest can be located throughout the center. If space is available for a separate display area, there are many advantages to using it as a *gallery*. A few examples of things to be displayed here include pictures of children with names of each, snapshots of children's activities, pictures reflecting the theme or topic for the day or week, information about the community, and children's work—pictures, collages, sculptures, finger paintings.

Office and Work Space

For the director and other adults, space for office work and preparation of materials will depend on the size of each center and the number of staff members. Adults also need a place for personal items such as wraps, handbags, hats, and umbrellas.

Outdoor Areas

The outdoor activities are no less important than the indoor ones for achieving specific goals and objectives while enriching children's lives. The same principles of management and organization apply to both indoor and outdoor activities. Working with children in small groups, for example, is important outdoors as well as indoors.

The outdoor environment should provide fresh air, sunlight, shade, and a variety of natural settings for children's enjoyment and development. Spaces may be large open areas or quiet, secluded ones. A range of surfaces provides texture and tactile stimulation. These may include natural and artificial grass or turf, cement, gravel, sand, dirt, stone, rubber, and asphalt.

Part VI: Planning a Children's Program

Kickapoo Head Start Center
Outdoor play requires safe areas with appropriate equipment.

Stationary equipment should be stable and securely anchored.

Places are needed for water play, digging, rolling, climbing, running, and sliding. Children enjoy less active experiences outdoors too. Some include story time, fingerplay, painting, and dramatic play.

Children must be free to move with ease from one area to another. The terrain or surface contour need not be level. It can vary from flat to mounded and terraced areas. Children enjoy running up, down, and around grades and jumping from one level to another—if safe, of course.

Outdoor Equipment

Equipment used outdoors should be durable and simple in design. Children can expand their imaginations when using abstract, or less defined, equipment. For example, a smooth block of wood containing a few simple curves and rounded on the ends may be used as a doll, a truck, an animal, or whatever the child chooses. Mounds and large abstract structures, such as climbing gyms, intrigue children. They like to climb and romp. Children enjoy crawling through tunnels, using them as imaginary hide-a-ways, roads, subway routes, and secret passages. Swings, merry-go-rounds and slides can become monotonous and often boring because they leave little for a child's imagination.

Stationary outdoor equipment should be stable and securely anchored. Many movable pieces of equipment will need to be stored in an outdoor facility or in the building, preferably with easy access to the outdoor play area. Children learn within a few days where things belong, how to get them, and how to put them away. Limitations should be made clear to help children know what they can and cannot do in using equipment. Outdoor equipment includes items like these: sand and digging toys and equipment; large boxes and tiles; rocking boats; jungle gyms; climbing equipment; balls, bean bags, and other hand toys; large boats, trucks, planes, trains, and cars; store and housekeeping equipment; push and pull toys; and science equipment.

Outdoor Safety

You read about safety in an earlier chapter. A quick review of outdoor safety, however, will be helpful here.

The first rule of outdoor safety is that adults must be able to see all areas where children play.

Surfaces under climbing and sliding areas where children are likely to fall should be resilient. Mats, sand, or soft stone pebbles are good in such areas.

Fences should be high enough to safeguard children, preventing them from wandering out of the play areas. If possible, however, fences that do not exclude a view of the outside are desirable because children enjoy watching the world around them. Of course, in some areas it may be necessary to have solid fences for protection from traffic or construction. Fences must also discourage persons on the outside from climbing over and suffering injury and from removing items of equipment.

The entire outdoor area should have good drainage and should be in good general condition. Child care workers must check the outdoor areas each day to be certain they are ready for children's use and are free from dangerous objects and litter. Equipment should be checked to see that everything is in working condition and free from broken parts.

Chapter Highlights

- The curriculum of a children's center is a planned process designed to meet goals and objectives for the children.
- A set of goals provides the guidelines around which a curriculum is developed.
- A theme or topic of special interest is often helpful in carrying out the curriculum.
- A theme must never become the goal; it is simply a means of reaching the goal.
- The term *open setting* carries a variety of meanings, from a completely free and unstructured setting with no purposes or limitations to a planned environment which provides many alternatives and great flexibility for achieving the identifiable goals and objectives.
- A *routine* is a *pattern of behavior*, related to *events* and *activities*, that children and adults can look forward to on a daily basis.
- The *schedule* is a *plan of activities* to provide experiences which lead to the achievement of goals and objectives for the children.
- A routine provides guidelines which help each child and adult assume responsibilities and meet expectations.
- Children depend on adults to set the stage for an environment which will help them become independent, respectful, and cooperative individuals.
- A flexible schedule is one which can be altered to meet the varying needs and interests of the children without disrupting the curriculum or losing its effectiveness.
- Young children need much individualized attention which may be achieved through small-group participation. Large-group activities are needed too.

Part VI: Planning a Children's Program

- Only safe, appropriate, sturdy, and well-designed equipment should be included in a center.
- A child's life is not enriched so greatly by how much equipment and how many materials are provided as it is by how those available are used.
- Flexible spaces may be used as interest areas by the grouping of equipment, the use of movable partitions, dividers, pieces of furniture, or various types of floor coverings.

Thinking It Over

1. How can a theme be used effectively in developing a curriculum in a children's center?
2. What does the term *open setting* mean?
3. Describe structured and nonstructured settings for children.
4. Discriminate between a routine and a schedule. How can these concepts help you develop an orderly environment aimed at accomplishing established goals and objectives?
5. What do you think is the greatest value received from establishing routines in a children's center?
6. What determines the type of schedule a children's center will develop?
7. How can individualized attention, a special need of young children, be provided in a center?
8. What guidelines enable a center to choose equipment that will enrich a child's life?
9. Describe an appropriate piece of equipment for children, giving the reason for your choice.
10. Choose three important activity areas that might be found in a center and explain their use.
11. What measures should be taken in a children's center to help insure outdoor safety?

Things To Do

1. Brainstorm with class members to list themes useful in carrying out children's activities.
2. Choose one theme and develop it with activities to meet a goal and several objectives.
3. During observation in a child care center identify the routine activities from those that make up the schedule. Discuss these in class.
4. Develop a schedule for a children's center. Identify the number of children involved, number of staff members, size and type of center, and hours per day in operation.
5. Make a floor plan and divide it into interest areas. Identify equipment and materials for each area.
6. Visit a department store or use a catalog to identify equipment and prices. Working in groups, plan a list of indoor and outdoor equipment for a day care center with twenty-five children.
7. Develop a check sheet for evaluating the areas of a children's center. This should include durability of equipment, provisions for developmental experiences, safety, schedule of activities, routines, etc.

Ch. 23: Teaching and Learning Strategies

Recommended Reading

Arbuthnot, May Hill. *Children and Books.* Glenview, Illinois: Scott Foresman and Co., 1964.

Becker, Wesley C. *Parents Are Teachers: A Child Management Program.* Champaign, Illinois: Research Press, 1971.

Carmichael, Viola S. *Curriculum Ideas for Young Children.* Los Angeles, California: Southern California Association for the Education of Young Children, 1972.

Christianson, Helen M., and others. *The Nursery School, Adventure in Living and Learning.* Boston: Houghton Mifflin Co., 1961.

Environmental Criteria, Preschool Day Care Facilities. College Station, Texas: Research Center, Texas A&M University.

Gundiff, Ruby E. *Storytelling For You.* Yellow Springs, Ohio: Antioch Press, 1957.

Karnes, Merle. *Helping Young Children Develop Language Skills.* Arlington, Virginia: The Council for Exceptional Children.

Kritchevsky, Sybil; Prescott, Elizabeth; and Wailing, Lee. *Planning Environments for Young Children: Physical Space.* Washington, D.C. 20009: National Association for the Education of Young Children, Publications Department, 1969.

Larrick, Nancy. *A Parent's Guide to Children's Education.* New York: Trident Press, 1963.

Lorton, Mary Baratta. *Workjobs.* Menlo Park, California: Addison-Wesley Publishing Co., 1972.

Meyers, Elizabeth; Ball, Helen H.; and Crutchfield, Marjorie. *The Kindergarten Teacher's Handbook.* Los Angeles, California: Gramercy Press, 1973.

Phillips, John L. *The Origins of Intellect: Piaget's Theory.* San Francisco: W. H. Freeman and Co., 1969.

Pitcher, Evelyn Goodenough; Lasher, Miriam G.; Feinburg, Sylvia; and Hammond, Nancy C. *Helping Young Children Learn.* Columbus, Ohio: Charles E. Merrill Publishing Co., 1966.

Rogers, Sarah F., and Simpson, Claire E. *Pathways: Parents as Teachers at Home Working to Aid Youngsters Succeed.* 2324 Nineteenth Street, N.W., Washington, D.C., 1972.

Schwebel, Milton, and Ralph, Jane. *Piaget in the Classroom.* New York: Basic Books, Inc., 1973.

Spodek, Bernard. *Teaching in the Early Years.* Englewood Cliffs, New Jersey: Prentice-Hall, Inc., 1972.

Taylor, Barbara. *A Child Goes Forth (A Curriculum Guide for Teachers of Preschool Children).* Provo, Utah: Brigham Young University Press, 1964.

Weber, Evelyn. *Early Childhood Education: Perspectives on Change.* Worthington, Ohio: Charles A. Jones Publishing Co., 1970.

Weikart, David P., et al. *The Cognitively Oriented Curriculum.* Washington, D.C.: National Association for the Education of Young Children, May, 1970.

White; Spodek; Andrews; Lee; and Riley. *Black Curriculum for Early Childhood Teaching Units.* Urbana, Illinois: University of Illinois Curriculum Lab.

Chapter 24.

Activities for Children

Your Challenge

This chapter will enable you to . . . .

- *Explain concept formation.*
- *Describe how play equipment should be selected and used in the center.*
- *Explain and give examples of the different kinds of creative and manipulative activities.*
- *Describe dramatic and imaginative play.*
- *Explain the use of music and creative movements.*
- *Select appropriate books and stories for children and read them aloud effectively.*
- *List science activities that children enjoy.*

PLANNING AHEAD

Planning activities for children is not an easy task. You must think ahead, be creative, and make sure you have the necessary materials and equipment. What advantages are there to planning ahead?

- Eliminates confusion about who will do what.
- Gives a total picture of what the children and staff will be doing.
- Avoids conflict between staff members and between staff and children.
- Eliminates most potential behavior problems of children because the program of activities is planned to meet children's interests and needs.
- Insures development of children at appropriate levels of skill.
- Provides assurance for smooth operations—if a staff member is absent, another can assume his responsibilities.

In addition to planning ahead, you must keep in mind the developmental levels so that children can enjoy success. Finally, you need to know a variety of appropriate activities so that you can plan an interesting set of daily experiences for children in the center. The following pages will offer you some ideas about activities that young children like and need.

CONCEPT FORMATION

Hoping to get the five children in her group thinking about their environment, a Head Start teacher asked this question: "Where does water come from?" The chil-

Play experiences, such as pouring, provide children with simple ways to learn concepts.

Kentucky Youth Research Center, Inc.

dren responded right away. The first answer was the *bathroom*. The next was the *kitchen*. After some discussion, the children were able to identify lakes, oceans, rivers, and rain as additional sources of water. Which response would you have expected? Can you see why the children responded as they did?

Sometimes the way children see things is surprising to adults. Often we forget that children have so much to learn. How can we help them learn about all of those things that we take for granted? This chapter has some answers.

Concept formation is a large part of the learning process. A concept is an understanding about something that is reached by putting together other bits of knowledge and experience. For example, a small child may not know what *round* means. From time to time the child sees, feels, and hears about the roundness of balls, circles on paper, lollipops, and many other objects. Eventually, he grasps the idea of what *round* really means.

Children form concepts more easily when the ideas are presented regularly. Actual play experiences with objects of various colors, shapes, sizes, and textures offer ways to develop concepts of classification. Children develop concepts of spatial (space) relationships as they move about during play and as they fit things together and take things apart. Of course, all of these experiences are helped by verbal communications. Talking with children helps them develop meaningful vocabularies along with concept formation.

Even as children encounter simple things around them, they are dependent on adults for help. Children need to talk about daily happenings and be encouraged. As children become familiar with what is going on around them, they become more sensitive to their environment. For example, sounds from clocks, radios, rain, and wind

Part VI: Planning a Children's Program

Toys are used as tools for learning and as aids for developing muscles and bodies.

take on greater meaning when children have many firsthand experiences. Children soon recognize the sounds of flowing water from a faucet, crying from the baby's room, humming from the refrigerator motor, and chirping from the birds outdoors. Naturally, there are thousands of other listening concepts that children need to learn. Through activities children learn these concepts and improve their thinking ability.

As you know, activities make up a third major part of a child care program. You have already read about (1) goals and objectives and (2) strategies. These, combined with the proper activities, will make a complete and useful program for children.

PLAY EQUIPMENT

Activities for children will often require some materials for learning, usually equipment and games. When selecting play equipment for children keep these points in mind:

- Play equipment should be selected to meet the needs of the children in helping them grow and learn.
- A toy should suit the child's capabilities for the level of his development.
- Toys are used as tools for learning and as aids for developing muscles and bodies.
- A child should be given only enough toys to fulfill his needs—not too many.
- Some toys can be made or supplied at home.
- Toys should help a child use his imagination as well as develop muscle coordination.
- Toys should be durable and constructed well so they will last a long time.
- Toys should be easy to clean.
- The colors of toys should be in good taste to help children develop an appreciation for art and beauty.
- Play should help children learn to get along with others with opportunities to share and cooperate.
- Language and word-building should be aided by play equipment.
- The child should be able to express feelings and thoughts through play.

In addition to being fun, wisely chosen toys and games can motivate children toward furthering the learning process. Examples are sorting and nesting sets, puzzles, matching games, picture dictionaries, alphabet books, play money, cards, bingo, checkers, and dominoes. Activities which involve body movements, singing, and talking also aid concept formation. In fact, any meaningful activity helps children learn to think.

Play need not be restricted to conventional toys and games designed especially for children. There are other exciting things in the world around them. The typewriter, for example, has become a useful

Ch. 24: Activities for Children

and interesting piece of equipment for young children. Their interest is often in the mechanism itself and its production of symbols rather than its production of words. The shift key for capital letters is an intriguing feature. As conversion from lower case to capitals occurs, a child can watch just how the change takes place. The dollar sign, parenthesis, question mark, asterisk, and other symbols are also eye-catching. Children do not learn to type, but they do become acquainted with symbols while developing eye-to-hand coordination. A *primary* typewriter is an excellent machine because the typed symbols are larger and easier for children to see than those on a regular typewriter. (A primary typewriter is designed mainly for stencil work, but many child care centers are finding other uses for them with children.) Can you name other objects which might be useful in developing children's thinking even though they are not designed as toys for children?

CREATIVE AND MANIPULATIVE ACTIVITIES

For these activities children must use their minds and hands. By thinking with as much imagination as possible, the children learn *creativity*. By using their hands to put their thoughts into a visible form, the children learn *manipulative skills*.

Included in manipulative activities are the use of play dough, modeling sawdust, modeling clay, and papier maché. Cutting paper and cloth, pasting, taping, sticking, and plastering activities offer delightful ways for young children to increase their sensory abilities, motor coordination, and concept formation. These activities provide opportunities for children to work independently as well as with others. Materials that children handle provide concrete ways for them to become acquainted with their environment.

Sensory abilities are expanded as children use materials such as clay, paint, wood, paper, paste, cloth, felt, plastic, fabric, and wire. Children can actively explore physical properties—textures, colors, patterns, shapes, and sizes.

Through these activities, children express themselves. They expand their imaginations. Motor coordination is improved. Thought processes become more complex. As children face more difficult problems in

Beggs Project

Common objects like cans of different sizes may be used in developing concepts of classification and seriation.

Part VI: Planning a Children's Program

Stringing beads offers a delightful way to develop manipulative skills.

the future, they will be better equipped to deal with them. All of these are benefits which come with creative and manipulative activities.

Perhaps the greatest value, however, in creative and manipulative activities occurs in the *process* of the experience—through active participation. The child's development and pleasure is more important than the production of a finished product. For example, five-year-old Leo watched his paintbrush, which had been dipped in brilliant colors of tempera, form lines and patterns on his paper. He was seeing and creating spatial relationships. Leo's eyes sparkled with excitement as he told Josh and Tina about an imaginary trip in space as portrayed by his brush strokes across the large piece of newsprint.

It isn't as important for a child to finish a collage (artwork made from an assortment of cutouts, prints, etc.) as it is for him to develop eye-to-hand coordination; perception of texture and color; concepts of composition; and, most of all, a feeling of enjoyment. The language development and socialization that go on with others while engaged in artwork is also more important than completing a product. The opportunity to express ideas and feelings while working is far more valuable than the product itself.

You can see that there are many good things to be derived from creative and manipulative experiences. A child care program needs many of these activities. Artwork, table games and crafts, and woodworking and carpentry are three areas of interest that give children opportunities to use both their hands and their minds.

Art

Art is more than self-expression. Art offers a way for children to enjoy learning while having fun. Children enjoy art activities because they can bring something into reality—whether a feeling, a thought, or a concept. Art experiences should be carried out with freedom in a relaxed atmosphere. Children should not be rushed. Each should be allowed to work at his own pace. This will help eliminate frustration. Corrections and demonstrations on how to do art should be minimal. Children need encouragement to do it their own way even if it is different from the others. Moreover, young children should not be forced to perform art in a given manner. They may become discouraged and dissatisfied if they do not meet specified standards set by adults. Keeping this in mind, evaluate the use of coloring books, copying a model, and tracing as art activities.

Children may be encouraged, but not expected, to talk about their artwork. For

Ch. 24: Activities for Children

Active participation in creative and manipulative activities helps children express themselves and expand their imaginations.

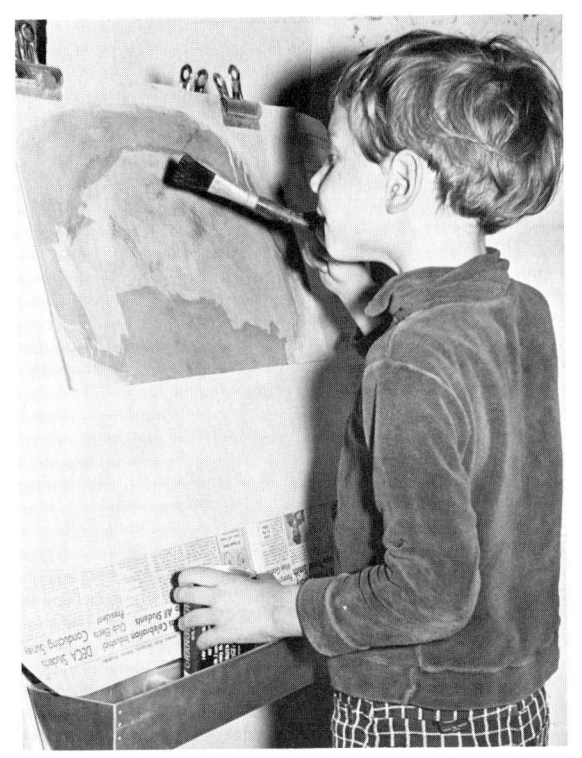

Art experiences carried out with freedom in a relaxed atmosphere combine learning with fun.

example, you may ask a child if he would like to tell you about his drawing or sculpture, but you should not ask him to tell you what it is. Why? The child may know what the work represents and he would probably expect you to know also without asking. If you ask what it is, he may think that what he has done is not adequate because you do not recognize it. If, however, you ask if he wants to tell you about it, he has the choice of sharing his thoughts or keeping them private. On the other hand, maybe the product doesn't represent anything. Maybe the child was just rolling the clay to see how it feels or to learn how to manipulate it. Perhaps the child was just trying the brush out in the paint or seeing what happens when one color is put next to another. What happens if you ask her, "What is that, Cheryl?" You have communicated that she is supposed to be making something even though she has not.

Children need to feel secure about their creativity. Adult support is needed to give them assurance and a positive attitude. Children gain self-confidence as adults reinforce their efforts through positive statements about their work. As each child becomes confident and comfortable, freedom of expression and creativity naturally increase.

Periodic displays of professional artwork help children develop appreciation for the beauty of art. Of course, they

421

Part VI: Planning a Children's Program

University of Oklahoma Institute of Child Development

Painting with tempera helps children become more sensitive to their environment as well as develop eye-to-hand coordination. An extra bonus is the pride that comes when adults display and admire the work.

should be told that there is no single, or right, way to produce art, but that many ways result from the ideas of different people. Encourage children to talk about their responses when viewing works of art.

Perhaps the best help you can give children with art is instruction in the use of materials. For example, you can demonstrate how to use a brush so that it does not get too full of paint or show children what paper may be used with chalk, paint, and paste.

Equipment should be in good condition. All scissors should be sharp enough to cut with ease but should have blunt tips. Art materials and supplies should be selected on the basis of the ability ranges of the children, the goals for their development, and the time available for the activity. (See the chart in the Appendix which lists basic art supplies.)

Scribbling, Drawing, and Painting

Scribbling with chalk, painting with tempera, water coloring, making cloth drawings, crayon coloring, and similar activities help children:

- Develop appreciation for self and one's efforts.
- Develop eye-to-hand coordination.
- Become more sensitive to the environment.
- Clarify and use ideas and thoughts; formulate concepts.
- Learn to think imaginatively.
- Learn that it is alright for individuals to think and feel differently about the same things.

Children go through several stages before trying to make pictures look real by the use of perspective, color, and design. From covering entire surfaces with scrib-

Ch. 24: Activities for Children

bles, or even solid colors, they gradually progress to making pictures which show how they see things. Finally, by about age nine or ten, they are skillfully able to make pictures resemble the real thing. The following sequence usually occurs as children learn to draw: scribblings, line drawings, circular motions, random drawings, partial representations, complete representations.

Scribbling is a nonverbal manner of expression as well as a way to practice eye-to-hand coordination. Between the ages of about two and four years, most children scribble a great deal and some scribble even after beginning to draw. Scribbling should not be discouraged. Instead, large paper and crayons, chalk, charcoal sticks, marking pencils, and finger paints should be provided for funfilled scribbling experiences. Many children enjoy making up stories about their scribbled pictures. It is a mistake to lead a child to think that scribbling indicates babyish behavior.

Between the ages of about four and six years, most children begin to see the relationship between the marks on the surface of the paper and the thoughts in their minds. This is sometimes called the *representational stage*. Representation refers to the meaning of the work, or what the drawing or picture portrays from the child's viewpoint. The child begins by drawing what he thinks and feels and not by what something actually looks like. The distortions, including smallness or largeness of drawn objects, often indicates their degree of importance to the child.

Adult standards of right and wrong ways to draw should not be imposed on children, particularly during this stage. They need freedom to create symbols without restriction. A child usually thinks about his drawings carefully. The work often shows

Scribbling is often a picture of what a child thinks and feels rather than what he sees.

insight about the child's ideas. In addition to being beautiful, children's art may portray humor, joy, excitement, sadness, anger, and hostility.

Sculpture

Working in three dimensions with materials like clay, plaster, and pasted paper is exciting and fun for children. While getting acquainted with new materials, they learn manipulative skills and control of the media.

A wide range of materials is needed to go along with changes in levels of interests and abilities. Twisting, squeezing, squashing, rolling, pulling, pounding, or just dabbling with soft and pliable materials enables children to make objects that have meaning for them—a horse, doll, truck, cake, banana, person.

In addition to soft, pliable media, materials such as wire, soap, styrofoam, wood,

Part VI: Planning a Children's Program

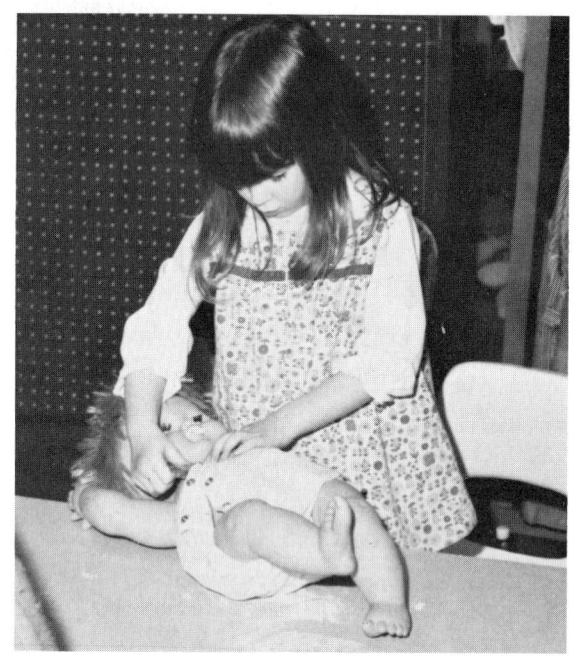

University of Oklahoma Institute of Child Development
Dressing and undressing a doll helps children develop skills they need in dressing and undressing themselves.

and plastic can be sculptured into many forms. Again, children should be given basic instructions for the use of materials but should not be told how to create.

Collages

Closely related to sculpturing are collage activities which provide visual and tactile (touch) experiences. Pasting scraps or cut-outs of paper, fabric, plastic, or wood on boxes, posterboard, or wood and paper surfaces provides activities which delight the imagination of children while increasing their skills. Smooth, crinkly, scratchy, rough, hard, fluffy, and slick textures are examples of materials to use. Can you imagine all the concepts children learn as they manipulate these materials? Combining pictures, textures, and colors leads to creative expression of ideas and eye-to-hand skills. Talking about how things look and feel while working helps develop language abilities and gives children opportunities to express themselves.

Table Games and Crafts

Puzzles, pegs-in-boards, lottos, matching games, and color bingo are popular table games. These are usually quiet activities that can be pursued independently or in small groups at tables or on the floor. These games not only delight but also challenge young children. As soon as they master one level of manipulation, such as a large peg in a large hole or a few large pieces which complete a simple puzzle, they are ready to go on to more complex tasks—small pegs in small holes and small puzzle pieces.

Simple manual skills are increased through craftlike activities. These may begin with stringing large colored beads or spools on thick yarn or cord. Later a child tries more intricate skills—smaller beads, buttons, or macaroni on thin string. Exploration of materials sometimes occurs at random and sometimes with a purpose, according to the child's idea at the moment. Some children delight in simply handling and examining rocks, stones, buttons, and plastic trinkets. Others enjoy making designs with dried corn, beans, rice, and seeds.

Dolls and puzzles provide ways to develop skills for managing zippers, shoestrings, snaps, buttons, and hooks. Can you see how daily living skills begin through play? Children have fun playing with learning toys. Stuffed dolls with zippers and boards with canvas flaps containing buttons, snaps, and frames for lacing are good learning toys. Soon children are ready to use these skills in dressing and undressing themselves. Can you see how independence and self-confidence develops along with motor skills? Concepts are learned too, zipping *up* and *down,* lacing *in* and *out,* and snapping to *close* and *open* a jacket?

While having fun, children learn about fitting things together, taking things apart, up and down directions, and right and left sides. Objects of different shapes, sizes, colors, and textures help develop these concepts. As children manipulate objects, they see how one object relates to another and how these objects fit into space around them—stacking small blocks, fitting cubes together to form a construction, slipping marbles through slots, and sorting objects.

Remember, children work with one concept at a time. Sorting by shape usually precedes sorting by color. Sorting objects according to size usually follows these. Do not expect children to handle all three concepts—shape, color, and size—at the same time.

Woodworking and Carpentry

Woodworking and carpentry activities introduce children to new materials while providing practice for coordinating eye-to-hand muscles. Working with wood and handling carpentry tools helps children understand spatial relationships—how boards fit together; how one board becomes two boards.

Children enjoy working and actually making something they can use or take home. Keep in mind, however, that woodworking is like other creative activities. The process is more important than the finished product.

Skills developed through working with wood have life-long values—cutting, sawing, nailing, sanding, and painting. Measuring concepts come with handling and comparing boards—*long* and *short;* wide and narrow; thick and thin. Children, also develop appreciation for wood materials and learn to recognize properties of wood as they work. They learn safety and responsibility when using tools.

Children and adults alike must follow certain rules for the use of tools and for working in the carpentry area. Children learn safety through the firm but kind enforcement of these rules:

- An adult must be present during the carpentry activities.

University of Oklahoma Health Sciences Center

Artwork provides opportunities to develop creativity and fine motor skills and to learn responsibility for care of the equipment.

- Children must learn to use tools correctly. They need to understand that tools must be used only for carpentry—not for general play. Children may have to pay the consequence of losing carpentry privileges for the day if this rule is violated.
- A sturdy, well-built, solid-surface carpentry table built at a level for use by children is important. Pounding and sawing require a sturdy surface.
- C-clamps or vises must be used to hold wood securely in place for sawing.
- Saws must be sharp. Dull ones are dangerous.
- All tools must be in excellent working condition. These must be kept in specific places when not in use.

As you might expect, carpentry skills depend on the abilities of individual children. Hammering pegs with wooden or rubber hammers is an experience for two- and three-year-olds that should come before they use real tools. Girls and boys as young as three and four enjoy pounding nails into boards, gluing wood scraps together, and nailing lids to wooden surfaces. A favorite activity for many beginners in the carpentry area is nailing bottle tops to wood bases. For some these become cars, airplanes, and musical instruments; for others it is simply a thrill to watch the tops swirl when nailed loosely to a piece of wood.

By age six most children are ready and eager for carpentry experiences. Some five- and six-year-olds, however, still need lots of practice with banging nails, sawing boards, and fastening one piece of wood to another with glue and then nails. Of course, just using a real saw can be exciting for the youngsters of five or six as they develop muscle control and eye-to-hand coordination—under the watchful eye of an adult.

DRAMATIC AND IMAGINATIVE PLAY

Large Blocks and Toys

Would it surprise you to know that many little ones who come to a child care center do not even know what to do with blocks? Though it doesn't seem possible, this is true, especially if the children come from a disadvantaged situation. Children who have had little experience with blocks may need a careful introduction to them. Adults can explain and demonstrate possible ways of handling blocks without interfering with the child's imaginative work. Children, of course, benefit from an adult's occasional positive comment about their achievements and progress during a block-building session.

The tower of blocks to be ultimately pushed over is the delight of most two- and three-year-olds, and even the four-year-olds still enjoy doing this. It gives them a sense of power and may offer tension release for some. Stacking blocks also helps children see how the objects relate to each other and to the space they occupy. Children also develop ideas about their own body shapes in relation to the toys and large blocks. You can observe them climbing over or huddling within a structure they have created. They grasp ideas about the location of one block in relation to another and to the space in which they are used. In addition, playing with large blocks and toys increases social skills, self-expression, concept formation, and large-muscle development. Children need time to discover the idea of weight as related to different block sizes. With much experimenting, they gradually develop the ability

Ch. 24: Activities for Children

University of Oklahoma Institute of Child Development

While building with blocks and playing with large toys, a child's imagination is delightfully stimulated as his mind and body are developed.

to manage the blocks themselves—moving, carrying, stacking, and constructing.

By about age four or five children will often play in groups of three or four. They enjoy building houses, forts, farms, stores, castles, fire trucks, airplanes, and space ships. Some will play independently, but they usually prefer to play alongside others until about age four or five. Then they enjoy playing alone only once in awhile. As a child approaches six years, block building takes on broader meaning. Projects may turn into communities, tunnels, bridges, highways, and outer space travel. Objects such as trucks, cars, boats, and people may be added to the block activities to expand learning through play.

As children begin to use their imaginations more vividly, objects of abstract shapes are usually more stimulating, offering greater usefulness for play than realistic objects. For example, a child can use a block to represent a real object. A block of smooth wood can be an animal, car, truck, or other familiar object. In contrast, a toy car can only represent a car.

Playing House

Playing house is one of the most exciting activities enjoyed by boys and girls during their early years. Pretending and role-playing take on special meaning for each child. One child may take on the roles of mother, baby brother, mailman, and grandmother—all within fifteen minutes. Children express their thoughts and feelings about family members as they act out roles. You can often learn a great deal about a child during role-play.

Dress up is a favorite activity as children adorn themselves with coats, pants, dresses, boots, shoes, hats, purses, lunch

427

Part VI: Planning a Children's Program

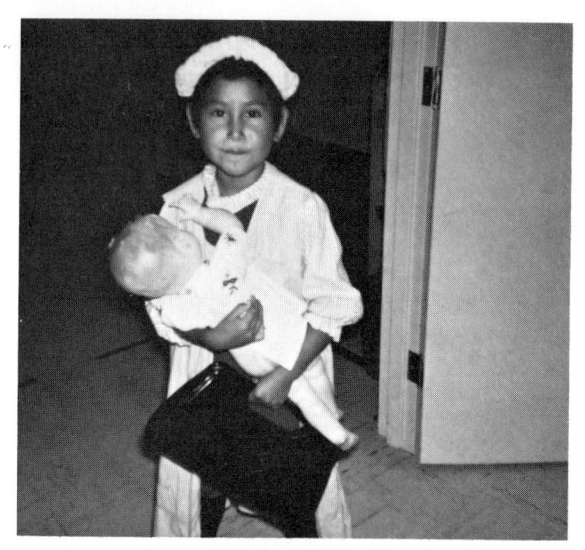

A favorite activity of children is dressing up and role-playing the part.

baskets, briefcases, or other items which help depict the person they are portraying. Children enjoy seeing themselves in a mirror. Not only do they have fun trying on clothes, combing hair, and making up faces, but they increase self-awareness every time they see themselves in a mirror—especially a full-length one.

Concepts of spatial relationships begin to form as children place chairs around a table, chill baby bottles in the refrigerator, stack dishes in the cabinets, hang clothes on racks, and line up pots and pans on the wall. As children handle these objects, they learn to classify. You will find them organizing items and returning toys to their places, especially if shelves are coded for storage. Separating dishes and kitchen utensils and grouping them according to properties that are alike can be challenging and fun while playing house.

When children set the table in their make-believe house, think of the concepts they are forming. By placing dishes, forks, spoons, knives, napkins, glasses, and cups on placemats, children learn spatial relationships and how to classify objects in a realistic setting. They grasp concepts of shape. Cups, glasses, and plates are round or circular. Placemats may be oval or rectangular. Knives are long and thin. Dishes are short or tall, small or large, heavy or lightweight.

Seriation (placing objects in a logical series) begins with such tasks as lining up measuring cups on a pegboard with hooks and outlines of each cup. Manipulating nesting sets or mixing bowls in the kitchen are extensions of seriation experiences.

Children increase eye-to-hand coordination as they use objects in their house—kitchen equipment such as egg beaters and measuring cups. Mixing, stirring, kneading dough (real or play dough), making candy (real or imagined with play dough), and ironing also improve eye-to-hand coordination.

Children should play house the way they want to. They should be free to dramatize and express themselves in ways that are natural for them. They also need to play house in an organized environment. Too many items are overwhelming and distracting. Playing with a few things at a time is generally less frustrating for children.

Playing house offers opportunities for interaction. It is a time when role-playing and identification are at their best. The child care worker can serve as a model in helping the children learn courtesy and respect. Values concerning family life, sharing, responsibility, and helping with household chores can be encouraged. Like block play, of course, children also enjoy playing house alone. There should be some time for private role-playing without interference.

Ch. 24: Activities for Children

Spreading frosting on cookies develops manipulative skills and concept formations.

Kickapoo Head Start Center

Music and rhythmic activities enrich a child's life and provide opportunities to learn new concepts.

Closely related to playing house is playing store or shopping. Children like to go shopping and then hurry home to prepare a meal or have a party.

The store setting may simply consist of a few shelves or a table with empty grocery cartons, cans, and plastic replicas of fresh fruits and vegetables. Children can be seen sorting and classifying objects according to pictures on labels and sizes and shapes of boxes and cans. While playing store, children also increase their knowledge about how foods are packaged. They learn that some foods are available in several forms—fresh, canned, and frozen.

MUSIC AND CREATIVE MOVEMENTS

Children enjoy music and rhythmic activities. They are eager to express themselves through singing and body movements. They like to hear repetition in words and musical tones.

Every community has resources to enrich children's experiences with music. Children learn quickly from those whom they admire. Often a guitarist or folk singing teenager is eager to volunteer some time with children for singing and music-making. Mothers, fathers, and grandparents have talents with the piano, other instruments, or singing. These volunteers are excellent leaders in musical activities when scheduled in advance, and when they are included in the planning.

The autoharp, melody bells, and guitar are excellent accompaniments to songs for children. These instruments add interest to musical activities while broadening children's experiences. Creative expression can be accomplished through music with body movements, finger plays, and vocal expressions. Tunes from different countries and cultures and in other languages present further learning opportunities. Musical activities help children increase listening skills. Group and individual use of tape recorders and record players offers self-directed experiences.

Tension may be released by some children when soothing music is played or songs are sung. Children quickly learn to recognize tunes played regularly as a reminder to change from one activity to another during the daily routine.

Creative movement is a musical activity which is useful in developing body coordination and sensitivity to rhythm and sound. Dramatic and imaginative expression fills this time with delight for young children as they move about to interpret musical sounds. Concepts of body awareness and spatial relationships are also learned through creative movement. As children move about, hold hands, and play musical games, they gain understandings about themselves in relation to their environment and their playmates.

Active song-game experiences offer children another means for developing motor coordination, language skills, and socialization. Large-muscle development becomes a part of musical activities when children are free to flop their arms, hop to the music, and try out body movements. Most children respond gleefully to rhythmic beats with uninhibited actions. Acting out the words and phrases in songs is a delight.

Pantomiming, funny songs, and chants are all useful as well as enjoyable musical experiences. Children need opportunities to sing aloud to themselves and with others. This may occur spontaneously during the day's activities or it may be planned. Many children create their own original tunes and some even make up stories and poems to sing to each other.

Songs, whether sung by adults or the children, should be sung slowly and distinctly enough to pronounce words and sounds clearly. Listening skills and vocal control develop faster for some children than others; therefore patience and planning are needed for successful musical activities. Drill is not necessary or even helpful for most young children. They do need encouragement to sing, even if off key. This experience is important if children are to build self-confidence, develop vocal cords, and feel free to express themselves.

A favorite activity is singing songs which use the children's names and bring attention to them individually. Can you see how this activity would help develop a positive self-image?

Musical activities are usually best accomplished with small groups of five to eight children in areas which offer enough space for moving about with ease. Larger groups will work if there is enough room. The area should be free of toys or objects which may attract a child's attention or get in the way of the active children. The room itself should not be too warm, as children will be somewhat active. Children should be relatively rested and ready for this type of activity. A balance of singing, listening, and movement within a ten to twenty minute period is often adequate, although some children may want to go on for longer periods. Even though music is a creative activity, it should be planned in advance with flexibility in mind in order to meet children's interests and needs. Talented children should neither be constantly used by the teacher nor allowed to dominate the group. These children, however, may be some of the most effective teachers with their peers.

Musical Instruments

Instruments help develop the children's sensitivity to sounds, variation in tones, rhythm, tempo, and harmony. A standard

Ch. 24: Activities for Children

instrument for musical activities is the autoharp. Very little practice is needed for an adult to be able to use this instrument to accompany singing. The autoharp is especially useful in the development of harmony. Children enjoy strumming across the strings with the felt plectrum (or pick) while the adult presses the selector bars. Children also enjoy experimenting with sounds and tones by pressing the selector bars themselves.

Some simple instruments for children's use can be made easily:

- Drums (for dramatic play, marching, and rhythmic dancing)—covered wooden box; nail keg with tightly stretched rubber band attached across the opening; strong balloon secured over the open end of cylinder-shaped box such as an oatmeal, cornmeal, or salt box.
- Cymbals—lightweight cooking utensil lids with knobs or handles in the center for easy grasping.
- Tambourines—plastic lids with four or five small bells (Christmas type) attached; an old pie pan with layers of soft-drink bottle tops wired around the edges.
- Rhythm blocks—wooden blocks covered with sandpaper.
- Rhythm sticks—smooth sticks about eight inches long and one inch in diameter.
- Rattles—cylinder-type boxes, cans, or plastic containers partially filled with rice, beans, seeds, or corn.

BOOKS AND STORIES FOR CHILDREN

Children enjoy snuggling quietly in the lap of a parent to listen to a story at home. They also like to join a circle of playmates for story time in the children's center. They delight in poring over a book that has been

Kickapoo Head Start Center

Most children like to have an adult read to them. When children have books at their level to enjoy, they often develop a love for books and reading that may last a lifetime.

read to them often. It is not unusual to find a child "reading" a book alone.

A child will usually express a desire to have an adult read to him when he is interested. Without forcing children, you should encourage them to explore books, thus enhancing their appreciation of books and their desire to use them. Children soon learn that books are sources of both information and pleasure. Through daily use of books, children learn how to handle them.

If books are not available or if a change is desired, adults can make up stories about people, animals, or objects from colorful and easy-to-identify pictures. Poems can be read, using pictures or body motions to help children understand the poem. Children enjoy making up stories about pictures too. Perhaps some of them would like to tell about pictures completed during art activities.

Parents can help their children develop an appreciation of books at home. Simply

Part VI: Planning a Children's Program

reading a short story or making one up is not only fun and exciting for children but this also increases their language skills while providing a closer relationship with parents. Fathers or mothers who work all day and are busy when they get home can usually manage five to ten minutes each evening for reading a story together.

Children's interest in books can be stimulated by quoting from stories familiar to them. They like to make associations between their own experiences and those of characters in favorite books. Children enjoy imitating sounds and pantomiming gestures of animals and people in stories. Take time to allow children freedom to express themselves and their ideas during story time.

Selecting Books and Stories

How can stories help children? The following list will enable you to recognize the value of stories in the lives of young children. A story can:

- Provide new information.
- Help children develop listening skills.
- Provide appropriate patterns of speech.
- Help children learn to follow a sequence of events.
- Present new words.
- Help children use their imaginations and increase their appreciation of beauty and nature.
- Give children a better understanding of people, animals, and things about them.
- Show appropriate behavior and satisfactory living habits.
- Arouse and stimulate a desire to learn to read.

Selecting books for children requires consideration of the child's interest and abilities rather than what appeals to adults. For example, short stories with clear colors and simple illustrations are more appropriate than busy designs, abstractions, grotesque illustrations, or pop art. Stories should be written and illustrated in an orderly manner, ending with a satisfactory conclusion. Stories should have some action and surprise but should not frighten children.

The following criteria will help you choose books for children:

Construction and Physical Concerns

- The paper should be substantial and difficult to tear.
- Pages should be well bound with a stitched binding.
- The cover should be sturdy.
- The material the book is made of should be easy to clean.
- A book should be strong but not too heavy.
- The size of the book should be neither too large nor too small for the child to handle with ease.
- Pages should be large enough to convey sizes and shapes of pictured animals, people, or objects.
- Type should be large enough to attract the child's eye (14 to 18 point type; *Little Toot,* a well-known child's book, for example, is 18 point).

Artwork

- The colors and pictures in the book should be realistic, simple, and in a logical order so the children will not become confused.
- Pictures and artwork should have spatial balance and harmony of color.

Content

- The theme and plot should be built around the concerns of children.

Ch. 24: Activities for Children

- Themes and plots should be free from prejudice.
- When appropriate, people of different races and religions should be portrayed.
- Characters should be memorable and unique, not stereotypes.
- The style should provide an easy-to-read text.
- The heroes of the stories should display model behavior.
- Something should be happening all the time.
- There should be some familiar characters and happenings and some new ones.
- The story should appeal to the senses of touch, taste, hearing, and sight if there are pictures involved.
- The story should have a strong beginning and ending.

What Children Like

Remember that toddlers, rompers, and kindergartners have different characteristics. Review these things about children when choosing stories for them.

Toddlers

- Like to learn *new words* if they are not too difficult.
- Are interested in *themselves* and like pictures of children, mother, and father.
- Enjoy stories about *familiar* things, such as animals and people.
- Like animal books with many *colorful pictures* which are easy to understand.
- Like to hear the *same stories* more than once.
- Enjoy *rhythmic sounds* and *repetition* of sounds.
- Usually listen quietly and with interest for about six to ten minutes.
- Like to have books of their own.

Rompers

- Like new words.
- Can sit and listen longer than toddlers, about ten to fifteen minutes.
- Want to know what is happening and *why*.
- Are interested in *real* live things that move and have activity.
- Still like *realistic stories* about children, not fairy tales.
- Like stories and poems with *rhythmic sounds*.
- Like stories with a *plot* and lots of *imagination*, such as animals talking and acting like humans.
- Like to make up stories and *act them out*.

Kindergartners

- Stories should stir the imagination and help children think beyond themselves and the immediate surroundings.
- The child is learning and experimenting with creativity—astronaut on a trip to the moon or king of the elephants in the enchanted forest.
- The world of make-believe provides interesting story subjects for kindergartners.
- Can usually listen for fifteen to twenty minutes at one time.

The Art of Storytelling

Telling stories to young children can be as enjoyable for you as for the children. You can develop the art of storytelling by practicing and by applying some principles that contribute to success with this task.

There should be an area in the room with enough space for children to be seated in a circle or a semicircle, facing the storyteller. They should be close enough to hear and see clearly. The storyteller and the children should be seated on the same

Part VI: Planning a Children's Program

level for best results. The floor is a good place, especially on a rug or carpet. Some centers that don't have these floor coverings use mats or throw-pillows.

When you tell a story, put your heart into it! Show your enthusiasm about the story. Talk to the children loudly enough so they can all hear. You should know the story well enough so that you don't have to read it word for word. Tell the story slowly enough to enable the children to keep up with what is happening.

Pause frequently and use motions in telling the story to make it more vivid and to help illustrate shapes of objects and characters. Remember to call attention to the important things in the story, but don't drag the story out by making it too long or by talking about it too much after it is over.

Don't hesitate to use the same stories more than one time. Children enjoy hearing the same story several times. They like the sounds of certain words. As you read earlier, children enjoy rhythmic sounds and simple patterns of repetition.

Change your voice and facial expressions to make the story more appealing and to help the children understand the characters and actions more clearly. When characters speak, you can add so much to the reality of the story by giving the characters very special voices. What can be more thrilling to a child than a big bear with a deep, throaty voice or a tiny mouse with a high-pitched, squeaky one? As you watch the children's eyes get wider and the interest mount, you will know the good feeling that comes with telling a story the best way you know how.

SCIENCE ACTIVITIES

Because children have a natural desire to explore, they enjoy inquiry, observation, and manipulation. You have no doubt seen curious children investigate plants, worms, insects, and other interesting creatures and objects. Scientific principles surround the child who eagerly reaches out to unlock the mysteries. This eagerness can be used to advantage by providing ways to extend children's curiosity and deepen their desire for experimentation in safe and meaningful ways. Through science activities children will be able to grasp the concepts and solve the problems that puzzle them. At the same time they will increase their sensory and perceptive skills.

Children need freedom to explore and discover things for themselves. At times adults have a tendency to exert too much control or to structure science experiences rigidly and then answer questions before children have a chance to explore and search themselves. Adult help is necessary but in a nonrestricting way. Still, opportunities should be structured enough to provide more than incidental learning.

Both natural and man-made aspects of the environment can be used as resources for science experiences. Changes in seasons of the year; pets, wildlife, plants, and flowers; refineries, construction sites, and factories; zoos, museums and parks; and communication and transportation systems all provide exciting adventures for children. Field trips and excursions, when planned in advance, add meaning to children's daily living.

Cooking, carpentry, and gardening are excellent activities for developing science concepts. Tools and equipment used in science activities help children develop life-long skills and knowledge—measuring, observing physical changes, recognizing properties and characteristics of things in the environment. Adults can supply equipment and materials and encourage exploration without stifling the child's enthusiasm.

Many mothers report their greatest problem at home is what to do with children who are always underfoot in the kitchen. One mother said she could hardly tolerate having her toddler around while she prepared meals or cleaned. After she learned about the many things children enjoy doing, however, her whole attitude changed. For example, she was amazed that her son Todd experimented with trays of ice cubes on a bath towel on the kitchen floor for an hour while she defrosted the refrigerator. He first experienced eye-to-hand coordination as he manipulated the handles on the cube separators. Then he enjoyed the sensory experience of simply picking up and dropping the cold cubes in and out of the trays. He would get so excited, saying, "Ice, cold, cold!" Todd continued his learning through play by watching the solid ice cubes *melt* into liquid. He dipped his fingers into the ice cold water and giggled with glee. This is just one example of how adults can help children enjoy themselves as they learn about the world around them. Use your imagination for a moment. How can the kitchen become one of the most exciting and meaningful learning centers in the home? How can these same ideas be used in a children's center?

Kitchen equipment—measuring cups and spoons, mixing bowls and spoons, sifters, funnels, egg beaters, and cooking and baking equipment—provide learning tools for manipulation skills and concept formation. Foods and chemicals—eggs, sugar, salt, flour, vinegar, baking powder, and baking soda are available in most centers as well as in homes. Activities are possible for learning to organize, measure, count, mix, stir, beat, shake, cook, bake,

Kickapoo Head Start Center

Dozens of science activities can be provided to help children learn about the world around them. This little girl is experimenting with weights.

taste, and clean up—all of which add to the child's information about his world. Baking, freezing, thawing, and other processes help the child learn physical concepts. Chemical and physical reactions become familiar as children have firsthand experiences with boiling, steaming, and using leavening agents like baking powder, yeast, or eggs.

Making butter by shaking a jar of cream is an exciting, yet simple, experiment. Children actually see the change from a liquid to a solid, even though they do not understand the principles involved.

Washing potatoes, wrapping them in foil, and baking them helps children see the difference between raw and cooked potatoes and experience the concept of changing texture by use of heat—hard to soft. Of

Part VI: Planning a Children's Program

Children enjoy activities and learn best in an organized environment. Note how the kitchen utensils can be placed correctly by matching the objects to the painted shapes on the pegboard.

course, using their own homemade butter on the potatoes at lunch is the perfect finishing touch.

Making and eating cookies is another interesting—and delicious—project. Can you name some things you think a child might learn while making cookies? Recipes in the form of pictures make cooking a problem-solving activity that children enjoy. Don't you agree that the most meaningful way for children to learn is for them to be actively involved?

Have you ever thought of an egg as a learning tool? It can be one. Breaking the shell of raw eggs, separating yolks from whites, beating air into whites, and scrambling the yolks are experiences that help children become familiar with properties of eggs. Cooking eggs to show the difference between a raw and a cooked egg is a basic experiment. Children actually see what happens when heat is applied. Cutting a hard-cooked (boiled) egg in half helps them see the difference in texture between a raw and a cooked egg as well as the location of the yolk. Can you list the concepts children can learn in these experiences with eggs?

Words like sweet, sour, salty, and strong have meaning when children apply them to foods. Tasting games can be fun and educational.

Children enjoy using their sense of smell in experiments with foods. They learn to identify familiar aromas of foods through simple experiences with them. One center uses clear plastic bottles or vials for such samples of food as peanut butter, honey, and mustard. Soon the children can sniff the contents blindfolded and name the food by its smell.

Household and mechanical gadgets and equipment—light bulbs, kitchen and garage tools, magnets, scales, and prisms—help children find answers to questions while increasing sensory and manipulative skills. When children experiment with everyday things around them, they begin to understand how things work and why.

Observing living creatures is another fascinating experience for children. Children, especially those who live in rural areas, learn about their environment by observing polliwogs, frogs, fish, insects, gerbils, rabbits, birds, and domestic pets. A children's center can have some pets in

Ch. 24: Activities for Children

cages. Be sure to check local and state health requirements and take precautions for protecting children's health when selecting animals for the center.

Seed planting, followed by watering, feeding, and cultivating the growing plants, mystifies children and also reveals some of the secrets surrounding plant life and growth processes. Transplanting is fun and offers both sensory experiences and concept formation—feeling the dirt, handling delicate plants, and observing the plant's growth. Grasping basic ideas about root systems and photosynthesis (the taking in of light to form carbohydrates) results from simple yet meaningful activities.

Water and sand play are delightful sensory activities. Many kitchen utensils can be used to learn about floating, sinking, bubbling, dipping, and pouring.

Collections of such outdoor objects as rocks, leaves, and pebbles give children a sense of importance and ownership. They can study the textures, colors, shapes, and sizes of objects found outdoors. Some develop hobby interests at an early age when exposed to the possibilities for collecting.

Through science activities, children also learn responsibility. Plants and animals must be fed and cared for, cooking must be attended to, and clean up follows all activities. You can see that there are many learning opportunities in the science-related areas. If you are interested and concerned, you can guide children to all sorts of discoveries.

Chapter Highlights

- Play is one of the most significant activities in the child's life from infancy through the early childhood years.
- Play helps children build both physical and mental abilities.
- In addition to being fun, wisely chosen toys and games motivate children toward further learning.
- Art is more than self-expression; art offers a way for children to enjoy learning while having fun.
- Creative and manipulative experiences for young children should be personal and individual, not competitive with other children.
- The greatest value in art activities occurs in the *process* of the art experience, through active participation.
- The child's development and the pleasure gained from artwork is more important than producing a finished product.
- Play with large blocks and toys increases concept formation, social skills, and self-expression as well as large-muscle development.
- Playing house is one of the most exciting activities enjoyed by boys and girls during their early years. It provides many opportunities for developing thinking skills as well as skills in socialization.
- Music activities help children develop sensitivity to sounds and variations in tone, rhythm, tempo, and harmony.
- Active song-game experiences offer children another means for developing motor coordination, language development, concept formation, and socialization skills.
- A child will usually express the desire to have an adult read to him when he is interested.

Part VI: Planning a Children's Program

- Parents can help their children develop a joy in the use of books at home through simple daily story-time activities.
- Selecting books for children requires consideration of the child's interest and abilities rather than what appeals to adults.
- Stories should be written and illustrated in an orderly manner, ending with a satisfactory conclusion.
- Both natural and man-made aspects of the environment can be used as resources for science experiences.
- Cooking, carpentry, and gardening are excellent activities for developing science concepts with young children.
- Children need freedom to explore and discover things for themselves.

Thinking It Over

1. Describe what is meant by *concept formation* and list some concepts that children must learn.
2. Why is play important to children? Relate your favorite play activities as a child to skills you were developing.
3. Do you like to touch and feel objects as well as look at them? How important is this experience for children?
4. How can you help children become more aware of sounds?
5. List the skills a child may learn while playing house.
6. What are the sequential learning steps which lead to the development of the concept of time?
7. What does the term *seriation* mean?
8. What are the sequential stages through which a child proceeds in order to draw pictures that look real?
9. What is the real value of art activities for children? What happens when an adult does not appreciate a child's artistic efforts?
10. What are some values received from block building?
11. Which is more important, the process or the product? Why?
12. Does music affect your moods? Do you think it has a similar effect on children? How?
13. Name some simple musical instruments children could use.
14. What are some important criteria to consider when choosing books for children?
15. When books are not available, how can story time for children be handled?
16. Why are science experiences enjoyed so much by children?

Things To Do

1. Visit a toy department to find puzzles for different age groups. Make cardboard or wooden puzzles which are appropriate to use with young children.
2. Make colored squares, circles, and triangles to use for concept development in young children. Make these in different sizes as well as different colors.

(Continued on page 439)

Things To Do Continued

3. Make color bingo sets for children to use during play. List the concepts children may formulate with this activity.
4. Make play dough and finger paints which can be used by class members to demonstrate manipulative activities for the children. Discuss how these products feel.
5. Make a touch box from a large ice cream carton or a large can. Put several different objects in the box to stimulate the sense of touch. Use it with several young children.
6. Collect drawings done by children of different ages and compare with the sequential steps of children's development from scribbling to pictures.
7. Make simple musical instruments listed in the chapter and share these with a children's program.
8. Write and illustrate a storybook for a young child. Share this with a child.
9. Work out the strategies for carrying out a science experience. Try these with children and report your results to the class.

Recommended Reading

Arbuthnot, May Hill. *Children and Books.* Glenview, Illinois: Scott Foresman and Co., 1964.

Carmichael, Viola S. *Curriculum Ideas for Young Children.* Los Angeles, California: Southern California Association for the Education of Young Children, 1972.

Cooper, Elizabeth K. *Science in Your Own Back Yard.* New York: Harcourt, Brace and World, 1958.

Gundiff, Ruby E. *Storytelling For You.* Yellow Springs, Ohio: Antioch Press, 1957.

Hartley, Ruth E., and Goldenson, Robert M. *The Complete Book of Children's Play.* New York: Thomas Y. Crowell, 1963.

Karnes, Merle. *Helping Young Children Develop Language Skills.* Arlington, Virginia: The Council for Exceptional Children, 1973.

Larrick, Nancy. *A Parent's Guide to Children's Education.* New York: Trident Press, 1963.

Lorton, Mary Baratta. *Workjobs.* Menlo Park, California: Addison-Wesley Publishing Co., 1972.

Meyers, Elizabeth S.; Ball, Helen H.; and Crutchfield, Marjorie. *The Kindergarten Teacher's Handbook.* Los Angeles, California: Gramercy Press, 1973.

Pitcher, Evelyn Goodenough; Lasher, Miriam G.; Feinburg, Sylvia; and Hammond, Nancy C. *Helping Young Children Learn.* Columbus, Ohio: Charles E. Merrill Publishing Co., 1966.

Rogers, Sarah F., and Simpson, Claire E. *Pathways: Parents as Teachers at Home Working to Aid Youngsters Succeed.* 2324 Nineteenth Street, N.W., Washington, D.C., 1972.

Taylor, Barbara. *A Child Goes Forth (A Curriculum Guide for Teachers of Preschool Children).* Provo, Utah: Brigham Young University Press, 1964.

Weikart, David P., et al. *The Cognitively Oriented Curriculum.* Washington, D.C.: National Association for the Education of Young Children, May, 1970.

Chapter 25.

Sample Developmental Units

Your Challenge

This chapter will enable you to . . . .
- Select activities that are designed to help children progress toward appropriate goals and objectives.
- Organize specific activities with children from infant to kindergarten stage.
- List ideas of your own for activities that will help children's development.

This chapter is designed to provide a sample of activities for young children. The activities are organized into *developmental units*. Each developmental unit contains suggested materials and activities for use with children at a given stage of development. Each unit is planned to achieve certain goals and objectives. Suggestions are also included for evaluating children's progress toward achieving the goals and objectives.

The units contain suggestions for helping children develop in the areas of six goals: sensory, motor, language, concept formation, self-concept, and daily living skills. There are two sample units for each of these areas. Units are presented in each stage of development: infant, toddler, romper, and kindergartner.

Some units contain several activities and use a variety of materials to achieve one or two objectives. Therefore, one unit may be used for several days. Other units have a few activities and may be completed in a single period. Some units can be repeated from time to time with the same children, depending on their interests and levels of ability.

The activities in the sample units should be carried out in a very natural and spontaneous way through children's play. They are not designed to be presented to the children as lessons. Each activity should be a pleasant and exciting experience for the children.

Perhaps you can try some of the units and add your own ideas to achieve specific objectives for the children in your care. These samples may be used in preparing additional units to meet the developmental needs of the children with whom you work.

Ch. 25: Sample Developmental Units

Infant

GOAL: **SENSORY DEVELOPMENT—TOUCH, SIGHT, AND HEARING**
OBJECTIVE: The child will be able to explore and manipulate objects that make noise, are colorful, and of varying textures.
MATERIALS: Rattle, squeaking toys, pull toy (with 10- to 12-inch string attached), plastic jar with seeds and tightly closed lid, textured balls and blocks.
ACTIVITIES:
1. Provide the baby with one or two of the above toys and objects at a time.
2. Place rattle in child's sight. If necessary, place it in the child's hand.
3. Squeeze a squeaky toy and then place it in reach or close enough for the child to try to get it. Assist the child as necessary to squeeze the toy.
4. Pull a toy by its string; encourage the child to imitate.
5. Talk about the objects. (Do not expect the infant to respond.)

EVALUATION:
1. Describe evidence that the child can hear, grasp, and manipulate objects.
2. Record the responses of the child to sounds.
3. What evidence is present that the child is learning through hearing, seeing, and touching?
4. What does the child do with the blocks?

GOAL: **SENSORY DEVELOPMENT—FEELING AND TOUCHING**
OBJECTIVE: The child will be able to play with and/or manipulate objects of varying textures.
MATERIALS: Blocks made of sponge rubber and covered with cloth in a variety of textures (fuzzy, fluffy, smooth, slick); plastic blocks in sizes from about 2 to 8 inches—squares or rectangles; "feel" ball covered in sections with textured fabrics, such as flannel, satin, terry cloth, napped, or fur-like material.
ACTIVITIES:
1. Child plays at will with blocks and "feel" ball.
2. Hand objects to child. Describe the texture. For example, say "Squeeze the soft ball" or "Touch the fuzzy ball."

EVALUATION:
1. Does the child explore through the sense of touch? How?
2. What does the child do with blocks?
3. What does the child do with the "feel" ball?

GOAL: **MOTOR DEVELOPMENT—ENHANCE GROSS MOTOR SKILLS**
OBJECTIVE: The child will be able to use his or her large muscles.
MATERIALS: A box large enough for the child to sit in with ease; a large 3- or 4-inch ring (from a jar lid or plastic bracelet); a string or ribbon 18 inches long.

Part VI: Planning a Children's Program

ACTIVITIES:
1. Place the child on his stomach for 10 to 15 minutes at a time during the waking hours.
2. For a few minutes each day, hold the child erect and support his back with the palm of your hand.
3. Allow the child to kick and play without clothes after a bath or while dressing.
4. Give the child help in pulling up.
5. For a few minutes two or three times a day, place the child in a box large enough to sit in with ease. Let the baby watch you while you are nearby. (This is helpful in getting ready for sitting.)
6. Call the baby's name, rattle a toy, or jingle a bell to get the baby's attention and exercise eye and neck muscles.
7. Dangle a ring on a string in front of the baby. Swing the ring back and forth by the string. Encourage the baby to take the ring and hold and feel it.
8. Give the child the ring on a string to hold a few minutes. Then put it out of reach. Point the string toward the baby. Show the baby how to pull the string and make the ring come toward him.

EVALUATION:
1. What responses or actions does the baby have while in the box?
2. Describe the baby's actions with the ring and string activities.
3. How long does the baby stay in one place during a five-minute period?

GOAL: **MOTOR DEVELOPMENT—ENHANCE FINE MOTOR SKILLS**
OBJECTIVE: The child will be able to use fine motor parts of his body.
MATERIALS: Colorful mobile for baby's room, paper windmill, small toys the baby can hold (some that make noise when squeezed or handled; some that are soft and spongy).

ACTIVITIES:
1. Place the mobile over baby's bed or hang it in an area where the baby can track it (follow it with the eyes) during the waking hours.
2. Place the paper windmill near baby. Touch it to cause it to turn and encourage the baby to touch it too. (Baby may simply follow the movement with his eyes or also touch it.)
3. Place small toys (such as rattles, squeeze-type objects, sponge or rubber balls and blocks) within the child's reach.
4. You may have to place an object in the baby's hand and help shake or squeeze it. Allow the baby to play with these as long as interest lasts.

EVALUATION:
1. Describe the responses the child makes to the mobile.
2. Record the baby's reaction to the windmill.
3. Does the child reach for small toys when they are placed in his view?
4. What does the child do with the various toys?
5. What does the child do when a toy nearby makes a noise?

Ch. 25: Sample Developmental Units

GOAL: **LANGUAGE DEVELOPMENT—LISTENING SKILLS**
OBJECTIVE: The child will be able to listen to examples of verbal language.
MATERIALS: Story books, toys.
ACTIVITIES:
1. While playing with the infant, name simple toys and objects. Talk about each item. Give simple information without expectations of a response. Give one-word sentences followed by a simple statement. Examples:
   Toys: "Ball—See the blue ball."
   "Doll—This is a doll. This is a baby doll."
   Objects: "Pillow—The pillow is soft." (Squeeze it; let the child squeeze it.)
2. Read simple stories with one- to three-word sentences:
   "Dog—This is a dog."(Point to the picture of a dog.)
   "Ears—The dog has ears." (Point to each ear.)
   "Nose—This is the dog's nose." (Point to the nose.)

EVALUATION:
1. List the one-word sentences used while reading and playing.
2. List objects to which the child gave attention.
3. Which words did the infant associate with objects? Give examples.

GOAL: **LANGUAGE—VERBAL STIMULATION (FIRST 9 TO 12 MONTHS)**
OBJECTIVE: The child will be able to respond, by action, to verbal language from an adult.
MATERIALS: Baby bottle, infant toys, infant clothing.
ACTIVITIES:
1. Talk to the infant during feeding time.
2. While bathing the infant, talk and recite nursery rhymes and sing simple songs.
3. Talk while dressing the infant.
4. While playing with the infant, talk about him and the toys or objects used.
(You will not expect to teach the infant specific words. Talking provides an experience in language that will take on meaning later.)

EVALUATION:
1. Give examples of statements made by the adult to the child while feeding, dressing, and playing.
2. Record the infant's response to the songs and rhymes that were used while bathing the infant.
3. Which of the above activities caused the greatest response in the infant's attention?

GOAL: **CONCEPT FORMATION—SQUARE AND CIRCULAR OBJECTS**
OBJECTIVE: The child will be able to explore and manipulate square and circular objects.
MATERIALS: Sponge rubber blocks (square in shape), each covered with a different texture, such as flannel, plastic, and fuzzy fabric; ball about 4 or 5

443

Part VI: Planning a Children's Program

	inches in diameter; ball about 3 inches in diameter; small wooden blocks about 2 or 3 inches high.
ACTIVITIES:	1. Provide the above objects for the child to play with at will.
2. Sit on the floor with the infant facing you. Roll the ball to the child. Encourage the child to push the ball around.
3. As the child begins to crawl and walk, encourage him to go after the ball and roll or push it to you.
4. Stack two, and then three, foam blocks in front of the child. Encourage the child to carry the blocks and to play with them.
5. Place 2-inch blocks near the child. Play with the child and talk about the blocks. (Do not expect the child to respond.)
EVALUATION:	1. Does the child appear to enjoy playing with blocks and balls?
2. What does the child do with each of the above items?
3. Describe evidence that indicates the child is becoming familiar with circles and squares.
GOAL:
OBJECTIVES:	**CONCEPT FORMATION—SHAPE AND COLOR**
1. The child will be able to explore and manipulate colorful objects such as squares, triangles, and circles.
2. The child will be able to play with familiar toys.
3. The child will evidence some understanding of object permanence by repetitious use of familiar toys and by looking for toys where they were last used.
MATERIALS:	Shapes (squares, triangles, circles) made of wood, plastic, foam, pasteboard, or other sturdy material; set of shapes in colors of yellow, blue, and red; familiar toys, such as balls, blocks, rattles, rubber or plastic rings (3 inches in diameter).
ACTIVITIES:	1. Provide shapes for the infant during waking hours.
2. Present rattle and rings to the child to explore at will. Place these items near the infant. Place them in the infant's hand until he begins to grasp them at will.
3. Place familiar toys near the infant's play area.
4. Talk about familiar toys as the child plays. Point to characteristics of toys and describe them.
Example: "The Teddy bear has a red nose." (Do not expect the child to respond.)
5. Name the toys and familiar objects each time you are near when the child picks up one or manipulates and plays with one.
6. Help the child feel pointed edges of squares and triangles and rounded edges of circular objects.
EVALUATION:	1. Record the level of interest the child shows in playing with objects and toys.
2. List objects and toys which are most often used by the child.

Ch. 25: Sample Developmental Units

    3. Record what the child does with the shapes—squares, circles, triangles.
    4. What evidence do you observe that indicates the child has an understanding of object permanence?

GOAL: **SELF-CONCEPT—SELF-IMAGE**
OBJECTIVE: The child will be able to identify his own image in a mirror.
MATERIALS: Full-length mirror.
ACTIVITIES:
1. Place the child in front of a mirror. Name the child. Talk about the child's hands and feet and name the body parts. ("This is baby's foot;" "See baby's hand;" etc.)
2. Place a mirror in the area where the child plays.

EVALUATION:
1. Record the child's response in the above activities.
2. What evidence does the child give that he recognizes the image in the mirror to be himself?

GOAL: **SELF-CONCEPT—BODY PARTS**
OBJECTIVE: The child will be able to identify parts of his body by touching parts of the face and body when each is named by an adult.
MATERIALS: None.
ACTIVITIES:
1. On the floor, place the child seated in front of you and facing you. Identify the child's nose, eyes, and mouth. Touch the child's nose and say, "This is baby Tara's nose." Touch your nose and say, "This is mommy's (teacher's, etc.) nose." Do the same with mouth and eyes.
2. Repeat with hands, feet, legs, and arms.
3. Name the body parts for the child but do not expect the child to be able to find them yet. Point to the child's body part, such as hand, foot, knee, and head.

EVALUATION: What evidence does the child show that he is familiar with parts of his face and body?

GOAL: **LIVING SKILLS—SELF-FEEDING**
OBJECTIVES:
1. The child will be able to hold a bottle while feeding.
2. The child will be able to drink from a cup with little assistance.

MATERIALS: Baby bottle, infant cup.
ACTIVITIES:
1. Place the bottle in the child's hands while feeding.
2. During play, place an empty cup in the child's hands.
3. As the child is able to hold the cup securely, place a small amount of milk or juice in the cup at feeding time. Assist the child in learning to drink from a cup.

EVALUATION:
1. Describe the child's response to holding the bottle.
2. Can the child hold a bottle with both hands and drink unaided?
3. At what age does a child usually begin to drink from a cup?

Part VI: Planning a Children's Program

GOAL: **LIVING SKILLS—SELF-FEEDING**
OBJECTIVES:
1. The child will be able to use a spoon with some assistance while eating.
2. The child will be able to eat some foods by finger feeding.

MATERIALS: Spoon (child-size).

ACTIVITIES:
1. Place a spoon within the child's reach at mealtime. When the child begins to grasp the spoon, put a small amount of food on it. Help the child feel comfortable in trying to use the spoon. (The child will be messy and food will be on the child's face and around the bowl.)
2. Provide many opportunities for the child to attempt to feed himself with a spoon.
3. Provide foods such as crackers, cooked meat, and vegetables that can be manipulated with the fingers. Encourage the child to feed himself with his fingers.

EVALUATION:
1. Record the age at which a child can be expected to begin to try to feed himself with a spoon.
2. Describe the procedure the child goes through in learning to eat with a spoon.
3. Rate the level of success the child is able to achieve in using a spoon to feed himself.

Toddler

GOAL: **SENSORY DEVELOPMENT—SHAPES**
OBJECTIVE: The child will be able to pick up and manipulate objects which are square, circular, triangular, and rectangular.

MATERIALS: Set of touch cards containing the above shapes—2- by 4-inch cards with felt and/or sandpaper cutouts glued on to represent the above shapes (set should contain about 4 or 5 cards of each shape); flannel board; a square of felt cloth about 18 by 18 inches; set of felt cutouts of shapes graduated in size from 1 inch to about 3 inches with 4 cutouts of each shape; shape sorter (toy containing 6 or 8 of each of the above shapes that can be sorted into slots).

ACTIVITIES:
1. Children play at will with set of touch cards.
2. Match touch cards by sorting according to shape.
3. Talk about shapes with children.
4. Children play at will with flannel board and/or felt cloth cutouts.
5. Children play at will with shape sorter.

EVALUATION:
1. List evidence that the child is able to differentiate between the various shapes.
2. List evidence that the child is able to sort shapes when playing alone or with others.

        3. List evidence that the child is able to keep cutouts on felt square of flannel board.
        4. Describe how the child sorts shapes in sorter.

GOAL: **SENSORY DEVELOPMENT—SOFT AND HARD TEXTURES**
OBJECTIVE: The child will select soft and hard objects by handling them during play.
MATERIALS: A touch box or bag to hold soft and hard objects; hard objects such as wooden blocks, hard plastic toy objects, crayon, golf ball, buttons, stones, rocks; soft objects such as stuffed animals, cotton balls, small pillow, soft rubber ball, sponge blocks.
ACTIVITIES:
1. Play with and manipulate soft and hard objects.
2. Help children select soft objects and hard objects from several toys such as those listed above. As the child manipulates the objects, talk about how they feel—hard or soft.
3. Place several soft and hard objects in one group. Ask the child to pick out an object that is soft, then one that is hard. Talk about them.
4. Place a few small soft and hard objects, such as a sponge, small rubber ball, spoon, cotton ball, and crayon, in a touch box or bag. Have the child feel one object at a time inside the box and say if it is hard or soft; then pull it out and look at it to be sure.
5. For variation, with more experienced toddlers, place two pairs of objects in the touch box or bag (two soft and two hard) and have the child pull out the two which feel about the same. Talk about the objects. Change the items in the box periodically. Allow the child to put things in the box that are soft and hard.

EVALUATION:
1. List evidence that the child can manipulate soft and hard objects.
2. Describe the child's actions in selecting from a group of objects that are soft and hard.

GOAL: **MOTOR DEVELOPMENT—LARGE MUSCLE COORDINATION**
OBJECTIVES:
1. The child will be able to walk on the floor between two straight lines 6 inches apart with some help from an adult in balancing.
2. The child will be able to walk forward on a 2- by 4-inch board placed flat on floor.
3. The child will be able to control body movements by rolling on a floor mat or tumbling mat.
4. The child will be able to climb up and down a climbing gym (3 or 4 steps).
5. The child will be able to crawl through large barrels and boxes open at each end.
6. The child will be able to push and move small barrels and other round objects.

Part VI: Planning a Children's Program

MATERIALS: Masking tape (1 inch wide); 2- by 4-inch board, 6 feet long; floor mat, tumbling pad, or large foam pillows or mattress; climbing gym; slide; large barrels and boxes with both ends open; round objects for pushing, such as 18-inch high wooden spools (originally used to hold electrical wire).

ACTIVITIES:
1. Assist the child in walking forward on the floor between two lines made with masking tape 6 inches apart.
2. Assist the child in walking on the board placed flat on the floor. Hold the child's hand if necessary to achieve balance.
3. Encourage the child to roll and tumble at will on a mat or pad on the floor.
4. Encourage the child to walk up the steps of a climbing gym and slide down in a sitting or outstretched position on the slide.
5. Encourage the child to crawl in and out of boxes and barrels.
6. Provide the child with barrels and round objects to push with the entire body.

EVALUATION:
1. Describe the child's success in balancing on walking boards.
2. List evidence that the child shows signs of enjoying or not enjoying tumbling.
3. Describe the level of success the child has in climbing up and sliding down.
4. Does the child crawl through barrels and boxes? What does this achieve in the area of large muscle control?

GOAL: **MOTOR DEVELOPMENT—EYE-TO-HAND COORDINATION**

OBJECTIVES:
1. The child will be able to pour substances through a funnel into such containers as jars and bowls.
2. The child will be able to transfer substances from one container to another by use of a hand shovel, scooper, or large kitchen spoon.
3. The child will be able to string large beads, spools, buttons, macaroni, and other such objects.
4. The child will be able to manipulate small objects to paste them on a flat surface.

MATERIALS: Tray or large cake pan; 1 cup of corn meal; plastic bowl, jar, measuring cups; funnel; large kitchen spoon; hand shovel or scooper; wide, flat metal spatula; small containers; sandbox; beads; buttons; empty thread spools; macaroni; seeds; beans; small rocks; fabric scraps; plastic scraps; yarn; bodkin needle, paste, cardboard.

ACTIVITIES:
1. Provide the child with a tray containing a plastic bowl, jar, measuring cup, funnel, cup of cornmeal, and a large kitchen spoon or metal spatula. Demonstrate how to dip or scoop cornmeal and put it into a funnel to transfer it to another container. Pour meal on the tray and scoop with a spoon or spatula. Pour meal from one container to another. Encourage the child to play at will with the

Ch. 25: Sample Developmental Units

corn-meal and utensils. (At completion of the activity, save meal in labeled container for use again in similar experiences.)
2. Using small containers, scoopers, and hand shovel, let the child play in a sandbox. Talk about moving, digging, lifting, and pouring sand.
3. Provide the child with yarn threaded in a bodkin needle. Show the child how to string beads, buttons, macaroni, and scraps of fabric and plastic.
4. Show the child how to dip objects in paste or how to put paste on cardboard. Let the child paste items to form a collage of his own design. Display the child's product and ask if the child wants to tell about it.

EVALUATION:
1. Describe the child's ability to transfer and pour cornmeal.
2. Describe the child's ability to manipulate containers and sand during sand play.
3. Can the child string beads on yarn with a bodkin needle? Give other examples of the child's eye-to-hand coordination.
4. Describe the child's ability to paste objects on a flat surface. How does the child manipulate objects, secure paste, and paste items on a surface?

GOAL: **LANGUAGE DEVELOPMENT—IDENTIFYING THE MEANING OF WORDS**

OBJECTIVE: The child will verbally name and imitate the facial expressions, mad, sad, and glad, after experience with adult models and pictures.

MATERIALS: Three or four pictures of each of these facial expressions: mad, sad, and glad.
Three puppets, each having an expression: mad, sad, and glad.

ACTIVITIES:
1. Make facial expressions of mad, sad, glad during play. Talk about these. With the child, use a mirror to look at your own faces. Ask the child to make faces. Name these. Ask the child to name these.
2. Talk about pictures of mad, sad, and glad. Play games such as match the faces that are alike in these expressions. Mix all the pictures and have the child sort out the respective expressions. Use one picture at a time and have the child imitate facial expressions and name them.
3. Using puppets, make up stories that can be illustrated by mad, sad, and glad facial expressions such as, "Happy Sam," "The Sad Magician Who Made Everyone Laugh," "The Mad Monkey," etc.
4. Encourage the children to play with puppets, using them to express mad, sad, and glad feelings through imaginary play and role-playing.
5. Encourage the child to make up stories with one or more puppets. Ask the child to name the expression on the face of each puppet.

Part VI: Planning a Children's Program

EVALUATION:
1. Which expressions can children identify by imitation? By naming?
2. Which activities are most effective in helping children learn meanings and labels of facial expressions of mad, sad, and glad?

GOAL: **LANGUAGE DEVELOPMENT—RECALL AND USE OF SIMPLE WORDS**

OBJECTIVES:
1. The child will give evidence of listening to sounds and understanding what he hears.
2. The child will demonstrate understanding of a word by giving a concept of a word and a response to a question or direction related to the word.

MATERIALS: Appropriate children's stories and poems, which are short, about things familiar to the children, and have simple plots and large, clear pictures. A red, a green, and a yellow sign to represent traffic lights.

ACTIVITIES:
1. Read or tell simple stories about familiar things. These should be short and have simple plots and many large, clear pictures. Use books and flannel-board stories to introduce new objects and words to the children.
2. After the children have had some experience with listening to stories, at the conclusion of a story, ask two or three very simple questions about the story. If the questions are asked in the order they appeared in the story, this will help the child to think logically. As an alternative, one child at a time could retell the story. If there are pictures available which illustrate the story, one child at a time could put these on a flannel board in the order that they appeared in the story.
3. Give the children simple one-part directions, such as touch your nose, make a happy face, stand up and stretch, etc. Make up a list appropriate for toddlers; do a few each time this activity is used.
4. Make up a list of two-part directions, such as touch your toes to your nose, lie on your back and raise your legs up in the air, etc. Use a few of these at one time.
5. Play the game, traffic policeman, using the terms red light, green light, and yellow light. When red light is said, the child must stop; on green light he runs; and on yellow light he walks. This can be made into a game with several children as they try to reach an established boundary. It will be easier, especially for younger children, if the policeman has three different signs of red, yellow, and green to hold up with each signal change.
6. At intervals during the day, ask the children to stop and see how many things they can hear. Then have one at a time name something he hears. For variation, go for a walk and see how many different sounds the children can hear. Encourage them to note all sounds,

Ch. 25: Sample Developmental Units

such as walking on leaves, an animal making noise in the background, etc.
7. Help children to differentiate among various sounds in the environment by calling attention to one at a time. Then help them evaluate each sound by asking questions about it. Is the car going fast or slowly? Is the airplane flying to us or away?

EVALUATION:
1. What evidence does the child give that he is able to understand the sounds he hears?
2. List examples of words or objects the child can identify.

GOAL: **CONCEPT FORMATION—BECOME AWARE OF SHAPE DIFFERENCES**

OBJECTIVES:
1. The child will be able to sort objects by shape.
2. The child will be able to identify squares, triangles, and circles by sorting and matching.

MATERIALS: Commercial form box or shape sorter; three-piece wooden inlay puzzles; three-piece form board with a circle, square, and triangle; geometric shapes of felt, construction paper, or wood (two of each shape); flannel board; objects that are circular; objects that are square.

ACTIVITIES:
1. Provide commercial form boxes or shape sorters. These help children perceive the form of an object as they place the forms in their corresponding slots.
2. Show a three-piece wooden inlay puzzle and allow the child to explore it at will. Turn the puzzle to remove the pieces. Encourage the child to put it back together.
3. Cut geometric shapes from felt or construction paper or use commercial shapes. Show the child one shape and ask him to find one just like it from a choice of two shapes. When he can do this successfully, do it with three shapes. Felt shapes can be used with a flannel board.
4. Point out to the child aspects of the environment which are in the form of shapes—books that are square, a ball which is circular, etc.
5. Make a display of objects which are the same shape, such as a circle. Include such items as a ball, a doorknob, a cookie, a colorful bracelet. Talk about how these objects are all circles. They could be arranged on a circular background. Do the same with squares.
6. Make geometric shapes from felt. Encourage the child to play with these by placing them on a flannel board. Talk about the circles, squares, and triangles.
7. Provide a form board with three holes for circular, square, and triangular cutouts.
8. Place three objects, two of which are the same, before the child. Ask him to find the two which are the same. Any objects would be appropriate.

Part VI: Planning a Children's Program

9. Place a number of paired objects together in a box. Allow the children to explore and play with these objects. After a child has played with these for some time, ask him to group the ones that are alike.

EVALUATION: What evidence does the child show that he is aware of the shape differences of squares, triangles, and circles?

GOAL: **CONCEPT FORMATION—COLOR DIFFERENCES**

OBJECTIVES:
1. The child will be able to match correctly at least three of these four colors: *red, yellow, blue,* and *green.*
2. The child will be able to label three of four colors after becoming familiar with red, yellow, blue, and green objects.
3. The child will be able to classify objects according to color.

MATERIALS: Various colored art materials for the child's use—crayons, paints, colored pencils; colored blocks, pegs, marbles, felt cutouts, buttons, paper shapes, fabric swatches, etc.; items found in the home or center which are a well-defined color; large circles of color—one each of red, yellow, blue, and green—about 2 or 3 inches in diameter; various colors of wooden or plastic chips; geometric shapes made of felt and sponge material in the above colors; a flannel board; several objects which can be sorted by color, such as blocks and colored, construction-paper cutouts; a shape sorter containing colored geometric shapes.

ACTIVITIES:
1. Start with learning one color. Make marks of this color with crayon or paint. Point out this color in books, toys, items in the house or center, and the child's clothes. Name the color frequently when the child uses objects of this color.
2. Place a large circle of color on the wall. When the child goes to it or asks about it, identify its color. Leave each color up for about a week at a time.
3. Encourage the child to find the posted color in his environment—in the house or center, on walks, on trips, while playing, etc.
4. Encourage, but do not instruct or pressure, the child to sort things by color. This can be done with socks, blocks, colored pegs, marbles, colored scraps of cloth, and pieces of paper or felt cut in interesting shapes.
5. Talk about the color of objects when the child appears to be interested.
6. Place two chips of different colors in front of a child. Then give him another which is identical to one of the two and ask him to put it with the one just like it. When the child can do this well, add a third color. Label the colors for the child each time by saying something like, "Yes, that one is *red.*" Allow the child to identify the colors when he can but do not pressure him to memorize them.

Ch. 25: Sample Developmental Units

7. Make a flannel or sponge covered board and cut a number of shapes of different colors from felt or sponge material. Show the child how these will stay on the board. Put up a red shape on the board and ask the child to put up one like it. Again, name the colors while doing the activity.
8. Provide a number of objects which can be sorted by color, such as blocks, chips, and shapes. Place one object of each color on a sheet of construction paper of the same color. Encourage the child to put all items of each color together. Talk with the child about the colors.
9. Code several areas of the room by use of a different color. Refer children to each area by its color. For example, say, "You may now go to the blue area for story time."

EVALUATION:
1. Which of the above colors can the child correctly match?
2. Which colors can the child name?
3. Describe how the child classifies objects according to color.

GOAL: **SELF CONCEPT—BODY IMAGE**
OBJECTIVE: The child will be able to identify his arms, legs, hands, and feet by pointing to each upon request.
MATERIALS: Full-length, unbreakable mirror; large, rubber baby doll and equipment to care for it; paper and crayon or magic marker; magazine pictures of full-length human figures; tagboard and clear contact paper; square of opaque fabric.
ACTIVITIES:
1. Provide a full-length mirror in which the child can view himself as often as he wishes.
2. As you help dress, bathe, and/or diaper the child, talk to him about the action that is taking place with his arms, legs, hands, and feet. "Now we will wash John's leg." "Now we put the arm in the sleeve."
3. Provide the child with a square of cloth and show him how to hide and then find parts of his body. "Where did Sherri's feet go? There they are!"
4. The adult points to one of the parts of his body and asks the child to imitate his action. "This is my foot. Touch your foot."
5. Provide the child with a large, rubber baby doll and equipment to care for the baby. Talk about the doll's limbs, hands, and feet while playing. On occasion, ask the child to point to the doll's legs, hands, etc. Do this in a natural, spontaneous way when the child is interested.
6. Draw around the child's hands and feet with a crayon or magic marker, talking about the action occurring. See if the child can then place his hands and feet on the outline so they match.

Part VI: Planning a Children's Program

	7. Cut large, full-size magazine pictures which are mounted on tagboard and covered with clear construction paper into two or three pieces to form a puzzle of a person for the child to complete.
EVALUATION:	1. List the body parts the child can identify by pointing.
	2. List the body parts the child can identify verbally.
	3. Can the child match his hands and feet with outlined patterns of these on paper?
GOAL:	**SELF CONCEPT—DEVELOPING A SELF-IMAGE**
OBJECTIVES:	1. The child will be able to identify himself by name.
	2. The child will be able to talk about, or refer by actions, to himself during play.
	3. The child will be able to identify products of his work.
MATERIALS:	Art materials, dress-up clothes, puppets, dolls.
ACTIVITIES:	1. Call the child by name often.
	2. During activities refer to the child's work by name. ("This is Tracy's picture." "Tracy, you may hang your picture on the board." "Tracy, would you like to tell me about your picture?")
	3. Encourage the child to talk about himself. Play games that provide opportunities for self identification.
	4. Place a photograph of the child in the child's play area. Print his name under the picture. Refer to the photograph by using the child's name.
	5. Using hand puppets, talk with the child, calling him by name. Encourage the child to talk about himself through the puppet.
	6. When the child has made something with art materials, display it with the child's name on it. Talk about the item and encourage the child to talk about what he has done.
	7. Provide the child with dress-up clothes, dolls, and puppets for dramatic play.
EVALUATION:	1. What evidence indicates that the child knows himself by name?
	2. Give examples of ways the child talks about or refers to himself during play.
	3. Describe the child's response to items he has made with art materials.
	4. How does the child reflect his self-image through dramatic play with dolls, dress-up clothes, and puppets?
GOAL:	**LIVING SKILLS—SELF-DRESSING**
OBJECTIVES:	1. The child will be able to put on a hat and shoes.
	2. The child will be able to remove a coat and a dress or shirt.
	3. The child will be able to put on a coat and a dress or shirt.
	4. The child will be able to pull down clothes for toileting.

Ch. 25: Sample Developmental Units

MATERIALS: Child's clothing and dress-up play clothes; doll with clothes that snap and button easily.
ACTIVITIES:
1. Encourage the child to remove a coat, dress or shirt, and other simple items of clothing.
2. Encourage the child to put on simple items of clothing.
3. Encourage the child to put on a hat and shoes.
4. Encourage the child to pull down clothes for toileting.
5. During dramatic play, encourage the child to put on and take off dress-up clothes with little assistance.
6. Encourage the child to try to snap and button doll clothes during play. Give assistance when necessary but allow the child to practice manipulative skills.

EVALUATION:
1. Describe the child's efforts in putting on a hat and shoes.
2. Can the child remove a coat and a dress or shirt? At what age?
3. Describe the child's need for assistance in putting on dress-up clothes during dramatic play.
4. At about what age can the child pull down clothes for toileting?

GOAL: **LIVING SKILLS—SELF-FEEDING**
OBJECTIVES:
1. The child will be able to drink from a cup or glass with little spilling.
2. The child will be able to hold a spoon and get food on it and to the mouth without spilling.
3. The child will be able to ask for food and drink.
4. The child will be able to unwrap crackers.
5. The child will be able to eat with a fork.
6. The child will be able to get a drink of water unassisted.
7. The child will be able to dry his hands after washing.

MATERIALS: Regular eating utensils, towel for hands, small packet of crackers.
ACTIVITIES:
1. Allow the child to hold a cup or glass while drinking. Give encouragement without warning about spilling.
2. Encourage the child to hold a spoon and eat with it.
3. Provide crackers in individual packages to give the child practice in manipulating the wrappers.
4. When the child succeeds in eating with a spoon, encourage him to try using a fork.
5. Allow the child to get a drink of water with a disposable paper cup or his drinking glass. Assist as needed with turning faucets on and off.
6. Encourage the child to dry his hands after washing.

EVALUATION:
1. Describe the child's ability to eat with a spoon and fork.
2. What is the child's response to success in unwrapping a package of crackers?
3. Describe the child's ability to drink from a cup or glass.

Part VI: Planning a Children's Program

Romper

GOAL: **SENSORY DEVELOPMENT—SURFACE TEXTURES**

OBJECTIVES:
1. The child will be able, upon request, to select objects which are smooth, rough, fluffy, and slick.
2. The child will be able to distinguish between smooth and rough textures and fluffy and slick textures by verbally describing each and by manipulating objects with these surface textures.

MATERIALS: A *touch* board (2 feet long and 4 inches wide) covered with four textured materials, such as rough sandpaper next to a smooth piece of plastic, hard block of wood next to a soft sponge, or a fur-like fabric next to a piece of satin cloth; several objects or toys that represent the above textures; a "feely" bag containing two objects of each of the above textures (two smooth stones, two cotton balls or sponges, two sandpaper blocks, two plastic squares, etc.).

ACTIVITIES:
1. The child may walk on the touch board barefoot and/or touch it with his hands. Encourage the child to talk about how the surface areas feel. Have the child close his eyes or blindfold them and feel the surface areas; describe each.
2. Play with objects and toys at will. When the child is interested, talk about the objects in terms of feeling them and identifying textures. Compare objects:
   slick compared with rough; soft compared with hard, and similar comparisons.
Talk about how they look different and how they feel different.
3. Using the "feely" bag, place two objects of different textures inside. Have the child reach in, feel each object, and describe them; then take them out and look at them. Do the same with four items at a time, two of each texture.

EVALUATION:
1. What evidence indicates that the child knows the differences in how textures feel?
2. Which textures can the child label?
3. Which textures can the child describe?
4. How does the child recognize differences of textures when comparisons are made?
5. How does the child describe the feel of an object?
6. Does the child talk about how an object *does not* feel?

GOAL: **SENSORY DEVELOPMENT—VISUAL MEMORY**

OBJECTIVES:
1. The child will be able to recall an image after observing it a few minutes.

Ch. 25: Sample Developmental Units

2. The child will be able to recall, in correct sequence, the happenings of a simple and familiar story immediately after it has been read to him (with pictures).

MATERIALS: Small familiar objects (such as a toy car, animal, doll, ball, etc.) and a felt square (14 by 14 inches) on which to arrange them; a young children's book with one large picture of an object on each page; a simple storybook with words and pictures; flannel board and pictures that tell a story.

ACTIVITIES:
1. The child looks out the window for about a minute and then relates as many things as he can remember seeing. Encourage him by asking leading questions regarding his responses.
2. Arrange two or three familiar items in a row on a felt square and have the child name each item. Ask him to close his eyes. Remove one item and have the child tell which has been removed. Repeat this several times, using a variety of familiar objects.
3. Arrange two familiar objects on a felt square. Ask the child to close his eyes. Add a third item. Then ask him what has been added.
4. Use a book which has one large picture of an object on each page. Have the child look at the picture for a while. Then close the book and ask him to name the object. Look at the picture again to help him check his response. Ask questions, such as the name of the pictured object, its color, and what it does, to help increase the child's understanding and memory.
5. Play the circle game with a small group of five or six children or one adult and one child. Hand each child, in turn, two familiar items. Ask him to hand them back to you the same way you gave them to him.
6. Make two simple motions such as clapping your hands and then rubbing your head. Encourage the child to imitate these motions in the same order.
7. Read a simple story (familiar book with pictures). Ask the child to recall the sequence of events.
8. Using a flannel board and pictures, tell a story. Let the child recall the events, replacing the pictures on the flannel board.

EVALUATION:
1. Is the child able to recall an image after viewing it a few minutes?
2. Can the child recall more than one image after viewing several? How many? Explain what he does.
3. Can the child recall a sequence of events in a story read to him with pictures illustrating happenings? Describe the child's ability to do this.

GOAL:
OBJECTIVES:

MOTOR DEVELOPMENT—EYE-TO-HAND COORDINATION
1. The child will be able to toss a bean bag at a target 6 to 12 feet away.

Part VI: Planning a Children's Program

	2. The child will be able to drop a small object into small, medium, and large containers by standing in an upright position and dropping the object from waist to shoulder height.
MATERIALS:	Six bean bags; three cans (No. 2 vegetable can, 3-pound coffee can, No. 10 fruit can—or equivalent sizes of boxes); one dozen clothespins; one cardboard box about 12 by 18 inches; one circle of cardboard 18 inches in diameter; masking tape.
ACTIVITIES:	1. Demonstrate how to throw bean bags at the box and at the circular target on the wall. Encourage the child to begin by pitching bean bags, one at a time, into a 12 by 18 inch box about 3 feet from where the child is standing. As the child succeeds, move the box further away.
	2. Encourage the child to stand about 3 feet away from a circular target on the wall or a square target outlined with masking tape. As the child succeeds, have him move further away from the target.
	3. Show the child how to line up three cans or boxes on the floor. Have him stand above these and drop the clothespins into each. As the child plays, begin at the largest can first. Encourage the child to gradually raise his arm and hand until success is achieved from shoulder height.
	4. Place numbers (1, 2, 3) on the cans. Ask the child to identify the one in which the clothespins will be dropped.
EVALUATION:	1. List the necessary steps for the child to achieve success at hitting the target with the bean bags.
	2. Describe the child's level of ability in dropping clothespins into buckets.
GOAL:	**MOTOR DEVELOPMENT—MANIPULATIVE SKILLS**
OBJECTIVES:	1. The child will be able to dip fingers into fingerpaint and create designs on slick paper.
	2. The child will be able to manipulate brushes and paint on newsprint to create a drawing or picture.
	3. The child will be able to manipulate small, 2-inch, square sponges by holding them with clothespins and dipping them into tempera paint and making designs on paper placed on a table top or on the floor.
MATERIALS:	Finger paint; tempera paint; thin paper; newsprint; six clothespins, six or eight 2-inch sponge squares; easel or place to secure paper while painting (can be taped to a wall).
ACTIVITIES:	1. Provide finger paint (or liquid starch with food coloring added) and slick paper for the child. Demonstrate dipping fingers into paint and smearing on paper. Encourage the child to finger paint at will. Hang products to dry and display for a few days or until another is made.

Ch. 25: Sample Developmental Units

2. Provide paper, such as newsprint, tempera paint in three or four bright colors, sponges, and clothespins. Demonstrate how to pick up a sponge with a clothespin, dip it in paint, and make a print on paper. Encourage the child to make designs at will. Display designs.
3. Provide an easel or place to secure newsprint. Show the child how to dip brushes into jars of paint, keeping colors separated. Allow the child to create designs and pictures at will. Ask if the child wants to tell about his picture. Display the artwork.

EVALUATION:
1. Describe the child's response to finger painting.
2. Describe the child's ability to manipulate paint brushes while drawing.
3. How does the child use the sponges for sponge painting?

GOAL:
OBJECTIVE:

LANGUAGE DEVELOPMENT—SPEAKING
The child will be able verbally to express his thoughts and feelings effectively.

MATERIALS: Stories and nursery rhymes appropriate for three- and four-year-old children; tape recorder, pencil, and paper for taking children's dictation; various kinds of puppets which can be purchased or constructed; a large box with a hole cut out for a puppet stage; props for the children to engage in dramatic play; equipment and space for some of the following play situations; barber and beauty shop, doctor or nurse, postman, eating in a restaurant; doll house with furniture and dolls to represent different family members; a housekeeping area with child-size furniture, dolls, equipment, dress-up clothes.

ACTIVITIES:
1. Read stories and simple nursery rhymes to the children daily. Encourage the children to talk about the stories. Encourage the children to repeat rhyming sounds.
2. In group activities sing songs with repetitive verses and rhyming words which are easy to remember. Encourage the children to participate and to express themselves freely.
3. Use fingerplays and action rhymes which are simple enough for the children to learn quickly. Do the same ones many times to give the children practice in speaking and expressing themselves. Encourage the children to act out rhymes as they recite them.
4. Use many opportunities for children to dictate stories which can be written by an adult or recorded on tape. Accept the stories as they are without making corrections. When reading the story back to the child, use correct grammar. Some ways to begin the use of this kind of activity include:
   a. Take a colored snapshot of a child. Have the child dictate a story about himself as he looks at the picture.
   b. Provide discarded magazines and encourage the child to cut out pictures and then dictate a story about the pictures.

Part VI: Planning a Children's Program

      c. When the child has drawn a picture with tempera paint or crayons, give him an opportunity to dictate a story about it.

      d. Use tapes or records of classic children's stories. One child or several can listen to these at one time. Encourage the children to tell the story again after they have listened.

5. Have a story time in which the adult begins a story. Stop relating the story at an exciting point, and let a child make up the next part. If the story is familiar, emphasize that the ending is to be a surprise one. In a group, let the children take turns until an ending is reached.

6. Provide puppets for general play. Encourage the children to use the puppets to retell or act out a familiar story or engage in conversations between puppets. (This is often an effective way to help children who do not talk much to have language experiences.)

7. Act out a story which is familiar to all the children. State who the characters are and then encourage the children to play these characters with their props (hats, dress-up clothes, dolls, tools, toys, etc.). The story can be read by an adult with the children acting out the story, or the children can both act out and verbalize their parts.

8. Simulate a TV set with a large cardboard box with a portion cut out for the screen. While one child talks or sings before the group, the other children can be the audience. Provide dress-up clothes for the children to wear as they perform.

9. Have a housekeeping area with child-size furniture, such as a sink, stove, desk, and bed. There should be clothes for playing different roles, telephones, cooking and eating utensils, large dolls, etc. Allow for a wide variety of dramatic play that may include imitating a dentist, teacher, fireman, truck driver, astronaut, and policeman.

EVALUATION:
1. What evidence do you observe that the child feels comfortable when talking with other children or adults?
2. How does the child express himself when talking before a group of children such as when playing TV or with puppets?
3. What improvement has occurred in the ability of the child to express thoughts and feelings through talking?
4. Describe four examples of how the child verbally expresses thoughts and feelings effectively.

GOAL: **LANGUAGE DEVELOPMENT—RECEPTIVE AND EXPRESSIVE LANGUAGE (SINGULAR AND PLURAL WORDS)**

OBJECTIVE: After experience with objects and pictures of objects, the child will be able to identify and distinguish the single items and plural items by pointing and naming.

MATERIALS: Flannel board with felt cutouts and pictures of single and plural objects—tree, shoe, hat, ball, cat, baby; objects and toys that can be

Ch. 25: Sample Developmental Units

ACTIVITIES:

presented as single objects or combined into groups of more than one object—dishes, cars, fruit, dolls, balls, blocks, cans, boxes.

1. Arrange objects on a flannel board in two columns. Place one object in the left column and two or more objects in the right column directly opposite; one apple on left, three apples on right; one shoe on left, two shoes on right; one ball on left, three balls on right; etc. Talk about each object and name the singular form:

    "This is one shoe; these are two shoes."

    Encourage the child to identify and name single and plural objects.

2. During random play, identify single and plural objects for the child. Encourage the child to identify each form. "I see you are playing with *many* blocks. This is *one* block." (Hold one up.)

3. Present objects to the child in a game to experience what is one and more than one object. Hold up a single object and ask the child to identify it by name. Help the child become familiar with the singular word form. Hold up more than one object and ask the child to identify these by name, using the correct plural word form.

4. Place objects in two locations, one containing a single object, the other containing more than one of the same object—one hat on your left, three hats on your right. Then give the child an object and ask him to place it with the single object or with the objects that are more than one. Talk about these in terms of singular and plural word forms.

EVALUATION:

1. Which activities promote the greatest competency in singular and plural word forms?
2. List the objects which the child can identify and label correctly in the singular or plural word form.
3. Describe ways in which the child learns singular and plural labels of objects.

GOAL:
OBJECTIVES:

CONCEPT FORMATION—SPATIAL RELATIONS

1. The child will be able to identify, by words and actions, the position of objects in space around him.
2. The child will be able to demonstrate his concept of spatial relationships by movement of his body in relation to other persons and objects.

MATERIALS:

Such toys as stacking blocks, nesting toys, beads for stringing, puzzles, form boards, and other manipulative objects; dolls or stuffed animals; two wooden blocks about 3 by 3 inches and three strips of $\frac{1}{2}$-inch board of different lengths (12, 8, and 6 inches); pictures which show different spatial concepts, such as near, far, beside, over, under; a large piece of paper or posterboard; play dough or play goop (see Appendix for recipes); finger paint; tempera; newsprint; butcher paper.

Part VI: Planning a Children's Program

ACTIVITIES:
1. Use daily activities to help the child develop spatial concepts of position. The activities might include getting materials ready for use, using materials, and putting materials away. For example, the adult might say:
    "Put the book *on* the shelf." "Place the toy car *above* the trucks."
2. Talk about the spatial position of objects and people in the room. "Janie is standing *near* you (*next to* me; *close* to her brother)."
3. Play guessing games as a group activity. As the leader, the adult begins: "I am thinking of something square which is *far away* from me on the wall." "I am thinking of someone *near* and she has brown hair tied with a red ribbon." The child who answers correctly can have a turn as leader.
4. After children are familiar with the position of the home or center in relation to the neighborhood, talk about the relative distance of such locations as the ice cream store, fire station, park, car wash, grocery store, church, and school.
5. Provide manipulative toys for the child to play with, such as blocks, puzzles, beads for stringing, and nesting and stacking toys.
6. Take a toy doll or stuffed animal and move it in relation to a table such as over it, on it, under it, beside it, etc. (the doll *in* the doll bed; the teddy bear *at* the table). Ask the child to describe the position of each toy. Then let the child move a toy in relation to the table or other object and ask the other children to describe its position.
7. Place two wooden blocks (3 by 3 inches square) on the floor about 10 inches apart. Place three strips of $\frac{1}{2}$-inch board (12, 8, and 6 inches long) on the floor near these. Two of the strips will be shorter than the distance between the two blocks. One will span the distance between the two blocks and can be placed to rest on each. Ask the child to look at the distance between the two blocks and the lengths of the three strips of board and guess which will make a bridge across the blocks. Allow the child to explore, arranging and playing with the objects.
8. Arrange displays of pictures which can be used to show spatial concepts. Encourage the child to look at these from time to time. Later, initiate discussions about the spatial concepts demonstrated in the pictures (the book *in* the child's lap; the boy *on* the steps of the porch; the snow falling *down* to the ground; the bird *on* top of the tree; etc.)
9. Draw a horizontal line across a chalkboard or on a large piece of posterboard. Take a strip or circle of colored paper or felt and place it in different spatial positions in relation to the line such as over it, on it, across it, below it, at one end of it, etc. Ask the child to describe the position of the strip or circle.

Ch. 25: Sample Developmental Units

                                10. Provide creative art materials, such as crayons, paint, and paper, for the child to use to increase understanding of movement through space by seeing spatial relations of lines in drawings.

                                11. Provide opportunities for both indoor and outdoor activities in which the child can move in and out of, under, around, through, and on top of objects. Climbing, running, rolling, and tumbling activities should be encouraged.

EVALUATION:
1. Describe several examples of ways the child recognizes positions of objects around him.
2. List activities in which the child demonstrates awareness of spatial relations by words and gestures.
3. What words related to spatial relations can the child use or understand (such as on, under, over, etc.)?
4. Describe ways the child demonstrates an understanding of his body in relation to other people or objects.

GOAL: **CONCEPT FORMATION—SERIATION (PLACING OBJECTS IN ORDER ACCORDING TO SIZE)**

OBJECTIVES:
1. The child will be able to arrange a group of objects in order by size.
2. The child will be able to line up objects according to size from shortest to tallest and from smallest to largest.
3. The child will be able to nest objects of graduated sizes.
4. The child will be able to identify the largest and smallest objects in a group of three graduated sizes by pointing to and verbally labeling them.

MATERIALS: Items which can be ordered in sequence according to size, such as plastic or metal bowls, measuring cups and spoons, nested plastic toys, graduated-size hair rollers; a cupcake tin or ice tray and a number of small items such as beads, buttons, and pegs; a group of tin cans of graduated sizes; two identical books of familiar stories, such as *The Three Bears*; a flannel board and flannel scraps; pegboard, hooks, and felt marking pen; a board with drilled holes of graduated sizes and bolts or pegs to correspond to each hole size; a form board with at least three circles, three squares, and three triangles of graduated sizes; a dowel pin (wooden rod about $\frac{1}{2}$ inch in diameter and 6 to 8 inches long) mounted on a 3 by 3 inch square of wood; plastic rings or wooden spools graduated in size to fit on the pin in a tower formation.

ACTIVITIES:
1. Use the ordering activities regularly as an opportunity to talk about comparisons such as large-small, tallest-shortest, more-less, many-few, first-last, first-second.
2. Provide three objects which can be arranged in order by graduated sizes. Talk about which is largest and smallest; which is first, second, and last; which is in the middle; which is between.

463

Part VI: Planning a Children's Program

3. Provide materials for the child to explore and order according to size such as measuring cups and spoons, nested plastic toys, and graduated sizes of hair rollers. As the child orders these objects, talk about the placement as in the preceding activity.
4. Using two objects which are different in size, talk about and play with items to help the child become aware of differences in size. For example, provide two balls for the child to play with at will. Later, ask which is the larger and which is the smaller. Use everyday experiences to reinforce these concepts; i.e., as food is being prepared, ask which of two potatoes is the larger or smaller.
5. Provide the child with objects of graduated sizes which can be nested. Allow the child to explore and play with these at will.
6. Provide a dowel pin and objects graduated in size to fit on it. Also provide objects that do not fit on the dowel pin but have holes in them. Allow the child to explore freely. Demonstrate, if necessary, the way to stack the objects on the pin but do not pressure or drill the child to do the same.
7. Arrange a series of objects, such as measuring cups or spoons, which are designed to hang on a pegboard. Outline these on the pegboard with a magic marker. Provide the child with the board, objects and hooks. Demonstrate how to place hooks and hang objects but do not direct the child as to the order in which to place them; allow him to discover this by matching the outlines on the pegboard.
8. Provide a board containing holes of varying sizes from small to large. Provide pegs or bolts which fit correctly into each hole. (Each object must correctly fit into only one hole.) Allow the child to explore and play with these items.
9. Provide a form board in which there are graduated sizes of circles, squares, and triangles which allow each piece to be correctly placed in only one slot. If the child shows interest, talk with him about small, bigger, biggest, etc., while he is working on this puzzle.
10. Place in the family living or housekeeping area a set of plastic or metal mixing bowls and a set of measuring spoons or cups which can be nested. Allow the child to play with these at will.
11. When the child is dressing, talk about putting socks on first, then shoes; underwear on first, then clothes, then coat. (These experiences help the child grasp the concept of seriation.)

EVALUATION:
1. In what ways (such as pointing) does the child identify the first, second, and last of a series of three objects of graduated size?
2. Describe how the child arranges nesting objects in a graduated-size sequence of smallest to largest, or vice versa.
3. When presented with a series of objects of graduated sizes, such

Ch. 25: Sample Developmental Units

as cans, boxes, or bowls, is the child able to nest these? What procedure is used by the child?
4. Is the child able to indicate correctly and verbally which is the larger of two objects of different sizes; the largest of graduated sizes?

GOAL:
OBJECTIVES:

SELF-CONCEPT—THE BODY AND BODY PARTS
1. The child will be able to recognize himself in a full-length mirror.
2. The child will be able to identify, by name, the different body parts and their relationship to one another.

MATERIALS: Scale and weight chart; height chart; a large piece of paper, tempera paint and brush or felt marking pen or crayons; scrapbook with pictures and mementos of early childhood; lightweight paper, pencil, paste; felt face with cutouts of individual facial features (eyes, nose, mouth, ears); large realistic doll with movable parts and materials for feeding, bathing, and dressing the doll; large pictures of people mounted on cardboard and cut into three to five pieces; disassembled puppet made of cardboard or lightweight wood and brads; chalk and chalkboard; full-length mirror.

ACTIVITIES:
1. Weigh the child and record his weight on a chart every two or three months. Post the weight chart where the child will be able to see how his weight increases.
2. Measure the height of the child monthly. Keep his height recorded on a wall chart so he can see how the pattern of his height increases.
3. Have the child lie on a large piece of wrapping paper with his arms and legs outstretched. Draw around the child with a felt pen or crayon. Let him draw in facial features and clothing. Display this drawing and let the child add details at will. The child may enjoy lying on the outline after a month or two to get an indication of how much growth has occurred by comparing the first outline with a second.
4. Make a scrapbook with the child including pictures at various stages of development. Also include a biographical sketch of the child which can be added to gradually, with the child supplying such information as:
My name is _____. I am _____ years old. I live in _____. This should be available for the child to look at when desired.
5. Place the child between a wall and a light shining on that wall in a darkened room. Draw a silhouette of the child's head, cut it out, and mount it on contrasting paper. Label it with the child's name.

Part VI: Planning a Children's Program

6. Make up simple riddles which are concerned with the parts of the face and their functions. ("You have two of these and they allow you to see your friends.")
7. Let the child trace around his own hands and feet to make prints. Encourage the child to fill such details as fingernails and toenails.
8. Provide opportunities for the child to engage in self-directed play with a doll. Provide materials for such make-believe play as feeding, bathing, and dressing activities. Ask the child to name the doll's body parts as the adult points to them.
9. Encourage the child to assemble puzzles made of magazine pictures mounted on cardboard and cut into three to five large pieces so that a picture of a person is formed.
10. Use the game, Simon Says, to help the child move body parts. ("Simon says:
    Kick your leg; wave your hand.")
    Use the game to give directions for touching body parts to each other. ("Simon says:
    Touch your elbow to your knee.")
11. Sing the song, *If You're Happy,* using large body movements. ("If you're happy, shake your arms.")
12. Ask the child to lie on the floor blindfolded and touch each body part as it is named. This may be done by singing to the tune of *Around the Mulberry Bush.* ("This is the way I touch my head, touch my head, touch my head . . .")
13. Encourage the child to name the parts of a disassembled cardboard puppet and assist in determining the order in which it is to be fastened together at the joints so it is movable.
14. Use the cardboard puppet as a guide for making body formations. For example, hang the puppet on the wall with one arm outstretched and the other hanging down. Have the child imitate with his own body.

EVALUATION:
1. What evidence indicates the child is able to follow simple directions involving his body? Can he do this in relation to objects surrounding him?
2. Is the child able to reconstruct simple puzzles of a human figure and face correctly? What does he do?
3. Give examples of the child's ability to name body parts by playing games and answering riddles.
4. Describe activities in which the child dramatizes or portrays himself.

GOAL:
OBJECTIVE:

SELF-CONCEPT—EXPRESSION OF SELF-CONCEPT
The child will be able to express thoughts and feelings about himself through a variety of activities.

Ch. 25: Sample Developmental Units

MATERIALS: Paint brushes, newsprint, drawing paper, crayons, tempera, play dough, wood scraps, finger paint, hand puppets.

ACTIVITIES:
1. Provide art materials for the child to use at will. Display the product and print the child's name on it. Call attention to the results of the child's work.
2. Provide newsprint, tempera, and paint brushes. Encourage the child to paint a picture of himself. Later, encourage the child to paint a picture of himself and parents. Still later, encourage the child to paint a picture of himself and other family members and/or friends. Display the pictures. Place the name of the child under his picture.
3. Encourage the child to tell you a story about himself or something he did. Write the story and let the child draw several pictures on 8½ by 11-inch paper about the story. Always label the child where he appears in the pictures. Make a scrapbook of the pictures and story and let the child add other pictures as he chooses. Place a photograph of the child on the cover with the child's name in large letters.
4. As the child completes artwork, such as sculpture or wood pasting activities, display the work to remind the child of his accomplishments.
5. Encourage the child to talk about himself through the use of puppets.

EVALUATION:
1. Describe the child's reaction to seeing his artwork displayed.
2. Give examples of the child's thoughts and feelings about himself as he makes up stories and as he draws pictures.
3. What evidence is observed that the child is developing a positive self-concept?
4. Describe the child's use of puppets.

GOAL: **LIVING SKILLS—DEVELOP HELPING SKILLS WITH FOOD PREPARATION**

OBJECTIVES:
1. The child will be able to mix frozen orange juice by following pictorial instructions.
2. The child will be able to make open-face sandwiches.
3. The child will be able to pour juice or milk from a small pitcher into cups or glasses.
4. The child will be able to fold napkins and place them on the table.

MATERIALS: Bread, cheese spread, table knife, cookie cutters, frozen orange juice, water, pitcher (four-cup capacity), small glasses or cups, paper napkins.

ACTIVITIES:
1. Demonstrate with the use of a series of simple pictures how to prepare frozen orange juice by adding water and mixing with a spoon. Give the child the ingredients and equipment and encourage him to repeat the process. (Pictorial instructions: Step 1—one can of juice being poured into an empty pitcher; Step 2—three cans of

Part VI: Planning a Children's Program

water added to frozen juice in pitcher; Step 3—stir with a spoon until frozen juice is mixed thoroughly with water.)

2. Assist the child in pouring juice (or milk) from a small pitcher into individual cups or small glasses. The child may place these on the table for service at snack time or mealtime.
3. Provide slices of white and brown bread and encourage the child to cut out shapes with cookie cutters. (You may need to demonstrate.)
4. Provide softened cheese spread and a table knife and show the child how to spread cheese on bread for open-face sandwiches. Let the child complete the task and place sandwiches on a plate to be served for snacks or lunch. Talk about the shapes of the bread and the texture of the spread.
5. Show the child how to fold napkins to form triangles or rectangles. Let the child do this and place napkins on the table for snack or mealtime.

EVALUATION:
1. Describe the child's ability to follow directions in preparing frozen orange juice.
2. Describe the child's progress in using cookie cutters on bread slices.
3. What type of difficulty, if any, did the child have in spreading cheese on bread?
4. In what shape(s) did the child fold napkins?

GOAL:
OBJECTIVES:

LIVING SKILLS—DEVELOP SELF-DRESSING SKILLS
1. Child will be able to put on clothes, manipulating easy-to-reach zippers, hooks, snaps, and/or buttons.
2. The child will be able to put on shoes and lace them or buckle them correctly.
3. The child will be able to buckle belts.

MATERIALS: Dressing frames or manipulative dolls designed for zipping, buttoning, snapping, lacing, and tying; cards with holes and a bodkin needle threaded with yarn or a shoestring; two paper plates with holes punched for lacing together with yarn or heavy string; small objects to place between plates to make noise (seeds, beans, rice); macaroni, 12-inch square of burlap, and plastic needle with string.

ACTIVITIES:
1. Demonstrate how to use a bodkin needle and yarn or string. Provide the child with cards containing holes. Encourage the child to lace or "sew" from one hole to the next.
2. Demonstrate how to use a plastic needle and a string for "sewing" on a burlap square. Let the child "sew" at will with these items.
3. Provide two paper plates with holes punched around the edges. Give the child a shoestring or yarn to lace the plates together. Let the child put objects between the plates that make noise when shaken. Secure the lacing.

Ch. 25: Sample Developmental Units

4. Give the child a bodkin needle and string and let him string macaroni.
5. Encourage the child to manipulate dressing frames at will.
6. Encourage the child to play with doll clothes designed for zipping, buttoning, and snapping. This may occur as a game or while playing house.
7. Encourage the child to practice lacing his own shoes or shoes for playing dress up. Help the child tie laces. (Do not expect rompers to tie a bow.) Encourage the child to buckle shoes.
8. Encourage the child to put on his own clothes with minimum assistance. Provide simple clothing with easy-to-reach and easy-to-manipulate fasteners, such as large buttons, zippers, and snaps.
9. Encourage the child to practice buckling belts both as a game and when dressing.

EVALUATION:
1. Identify the step-by-step process the child goes through to put on clothes and shoes.
2. Describe the child's ability to lace shoes and to buckle belts.
3. What relationship do you observe between the child's play with dress-up dolls and with his own clothing?

Kindergartner

GOAL:
OBJECTIVE:

SENSORY DEVELOPMENT—VISUAL MEMORY
The child will be able to recall images of shapes and patterns by reciting or manually reproducing them from memory.

MATERIALS: Felt pen, crayon, newsprint, drawing paper; geometric shapes (squares, circles, diamonds, rectangles, triangles); square of 18 by 18-inch felt or a felt board; pegboard and pegs; pictures of familiar objects; picture storybook.

ACTIVITIES:
1. Draw a symbol of a cross with the child watching; then cover it and ask the child to draw what he saw. Repeat with squares and other simple symbols, such as T, X, and V.
2. Arrange geometric shapes to form a simple design with the child watching. Cover it and ask the child to reproduce the design from memory. (Should the child have difficulty, encourage him to practice by looking at the model design and repeating it with another set of shapes.)
3. Prepare a very simple pegboard design, such as a cross or a square, and ask the child to look at it carefully and repeat it.
4. Draw two simple designs, such as a cross and a circle. Have the child reproduce these after viewing carefully.

Part VI: Planning a Children's Program

5. Show the child a series of three or four pictures of familiar objects. Then give the pictures to the child and ask him to arrange them in the order they were presented.
6. Tell a simple story with a picture book. Ask questions afterwards that encourage the child to recall the pictures.

EVALUATION:
1. Which symbols can the child reproduce from memory?
2. In which experiences can the child reproduce the pattern or pictures in the same order he viewed them?
3. Describe the child's ability to recall, verbally, events in a simple picture story.

GOAL:
OBJECTIVES:

SENSORY DEVELOPMENT—LISTENING SKILLS

1. The child will be able to listen to sounds and recall what he hears.
2. The child will be able to give correct responses to questions or directions.

MATERIALS: Squares of colored paper (2 by 3 inches); storybooks; record player or tape recorder-player; geometric shapes made of felt; a flannel board or magnetized shapes and a magnetic board.

ACTIVITIES:
1. Play the game, "Just now," with the adult as the first leader. Say, "Listen very carefully while I give you some directions. You are to do what you hear, but wait until I say *just now* before you start." Example:
   "Nod your head—just now!" "Clap your hands two times—just now!"
2. Give each child a square of colored paper. The adult then reads or tells a story in which many colors are mentioned. Each time a color is mentioned the child having this color holds it up for the others to see. The stories which are regularly used can be read but with color adjectives added whenever possible to make the game more fun.
3. Establish a *secret word* with the children. Then narrate a familiar story which has the secret word in it several times. Each time a child hears the word he can hold up his hand or make a mark on a paper which he counts at the end of the story. For variation, prerecord the story on tape and have children listen to it and respond the same way.
4. Read a story or poem, inserting every few lines a command for the child to follow, such as *clap your hands* or *nod your head*. Call the child's name and tell him what to do. Stop the story as the activity is performed; then continue the story. In a group, rotate the children who get to perform each time this activity is done, as all children probably will not get a turn during one session.
5. Give the child directions in placing geometric shapes so that a familiar object, such as a house, wagon, or man, is formed. This

Ch. 25: Sample Developmental Units

can be done with a flannel board, magnetic board, or on a large felt square.

EVALUATION:
1. What evidence do you see that the child is able to understand what he hears well enough to respond by answering questions or by following directions?
2. Describe examples of how the child's response indicates that he has heard words and statements correctly.

GOAL: **MOTOR DEVELOPMENT—LARGE AND SMALL MUSCLE CONTROL**

OBJECTIVES:
1. The child will be able to control body movements while listening to music.
2. The child will be able to control eye-hand coordination while painting and manipulating pliable materials.

MATERIALS: Piano, record player or tape player; records or cassette tapes; tempera paint; brushes; newsprint; easels; finger paint; smooth finish paper; play dough; clay.

ACTIVITIES:
1. Encourage the child to engage in creative movements while music is playing.
2. Play *freeze*. Encourage the child to move about freely, making formations with his body while music is playing. When the music stops, the child is to stop immediately—or freeze—remaining in the same position until the music starts again. The child again moves at will while the music is playing. Repeat several times. The child may wish to pretend he is a bird, a skater, a dancer, or other character or animal. The objective is to control the body by stopping with the music and maintaining a position for a minute or two without losing control of the body.
3. Allow the child to finger paint at will. Display the work.
4. Provide paper, paint, and brushes for the child to paint at will. Display the work and place the child's name on it.
5. Provide play dough and clay for the child to manipulate. Encourage the formation of balls and other simple shapes to help the child develop eye-hand coordination. Allow the child to form designs of his choice for the most part.

EVALUATION:
1. Describe the child's ability to maintain a body position during the game, *freeze*.
2. What observations indicate the child has gross motor control?
3. Describe the extent of the child's eye-hand coordination while painting.
4. Describe the child's control of small muscles while working with play dough or clay.

Part VI: Planning a Children's Program

GOAL: **MOTOR DEVELOPMENT—RIGHT AND LEFT DIRECTIONS AND MIDPOINT POSITION**

OBJECTIVES:
1. The child will be able to hit a suspended ball with his fist or palm.
2. The child will be able to hit a suspended ball, alternating his left, and right hands.
3. With hands clasped behind his body, the child will be able to hit a suspended ball with elbows, alternately.
4. The child will be able to roll a cylinder by pushing it alternately with right and left hands.
5. The child will be able to identify the midpoint between left and right by actively responding to adult suggestions.

MATERIALS: Lightweight rubber ball, long cord or string with a hook on each end, plastic bat, rolling pin with a red strip around the center.

ACTIVITIES:
1. Insert a hook into a rubber ball and secure a cord or string long enough to hang the ball from the ceiling or rafter so that the ball is about chest high to the child. Encourage the child to hit the ball with his fist or palm. Encourage the child to hit the ball, alternating hands. Say, "Left hand, right hand, left hand," etc., during the action.
2. When the child has achieved the above tasks successfully, have him clasp his hands behind his body and hit the suspended ball with his elbows, alternately, swinging his body from the waist. Say, "With your left elbow, Sally; with your right elbow, Sally."
3. Stand behind the child, both facing in the same direction. Hold a rolling pin by the handles in the air in front of the child and let him cause the pin to roll forward by pushing the pin with his left hand, then with his right hand. Cause the pin to roll backward and forward, alternately, by the child hitting the midpoint or center line of the pin.
4. Talk about the center line of the body with left arm and leg on one side and right arm and leg on the other side. Ask the child to point to the center line of his body; to shake his left arm and then leg; his right.
5. Trace around the child's hands and feet, talking about which one is *right* and which one is *left*. Help the child get acquainted with these two words through daily conversation, songs, and rhymes which include body gestures for left and right hands, arms, and legs.
6. Let the child trace around his own hands and feet on butcher or wrapping paper.
7. The child may color outlines of his hands and feet, drawing in fingers and toes at will. These may be cut out and hung up with labels to indicate *right* and *left*. On the floor place cutouts of feet. The child can stand on his cutouts, identifying *right* and *left*.

Ch. 25: Sample Developmental Units

8. Sing songs about right and left hands, arms, legs, and feet. Children may act out the words of the song. Example—Circle game and song:
   "I put my *right* arm in (each waves right arm toward center of circle),
   I pull my *right* arm out,
   I put my *right* arm in and shake it all about."
   (Repeat with other parts of the body.) Emphasize the *right* and *left* body parts by saying those words louder.
9. Have the children stand and make circles in the air with arms and fingers, first with *right* ones, then with *left* ones.
10. Have the children lie on the floor and make circles in the air with right and left arms and then with right and left feet.
11. At snack and mealtimes talk about napkins to the *left* of the plate and spoon to the *right*. Repeat with other items. (Be consistent in placing items in the same place day after day.)
12. Draw a line down the center of a chalkboard or sheet of newsprint to divide right and left sides. Let the children practice scribbling and making circular motions to either side of the center line with chalk (on chalkboard) or crayon (on newsprint). Talk with the children about circular motions and directions of right and left. Allow the children to practice at will until interest changes.
13. Have the children finger paint at an easel or on the table or floor. Emphasize right and left sides with a vertical line through the center of the paper, drawn with paint or crayon or marked with a strip of tape.
14. Paint a line 1 inch wide in the center of a rolling pin. Paint the area on each side a different color. Have the child stand in front of the adult, with both facing in the same direction. The adult holds the rolling pin by handles and instructs the child to turn it by pushing forward or backward, first with the right hand and then with the left hand. ("Turn it on the right side with your right hand [left side with left hand; repeat]. Turn it in the middle by rolling with either hand. Tell me which hand you will use, right or left.")
15. Act out activities with right and left hands, such as shaking hands, saluting the flag, saluting a soldier, waving pom-poms.
16. Help children identify right and left on other children and adults—right and left hands, knees, ears, and shoulders.
17. Have the children stand in the middle of the play area, then walk or run to their right and back to the middle; to left and back; repeat. Children or adults may give instructions as to which direction to go.
18. Let the children practice cutting with scissors on sheets of newspaper or scrap paper. Make several observations to determine handedness of individual children.

Part VI: Planning a Children's Program

EVALUATION:
1. Is the child able to demonstrate the concept of right and left handedness; right and left direction? Give examples of evidence that the child has grasped the idea of these concepts.
2. Describe the action which reflects the child's understanding of right and left directions in relation to other persons; to objects in the room; to movements from a given point between right and left.
3. Describe the child's ability to hit the suspended ball with the left hand and the right hand alternately.
4. How many times, in succession, can the child hit the suspended ball with his elbows?
5. Describe the child's activity with the rolling pin.
6. What evidence indicates that the child is developing the ability to control his body with right and left positions? With the midpoint?

GOAL: **LANGUAGE DEVELOPMENT—LEARNING SINGLE WORD LABELS**

OBJECTIVES:
1. The child will be able to recognize his or her own name in print.
2. The child will be able, orally, to complete a sentence with an appropriate word.

MATERIALS: Felt pen; name cards (3 by 8 inches); simple and familiar objects, such as crayons, pencils, books, chairs, tables.

ACTIVITIES:
1. Print each child's name on a card. Use the cards to call the child's name. (This can be done as roll call in a center or as a game with one child). Hold up the card, say the child's name, and ask the child to take the card and place it on a display board.
2. After a child begins to recognize his own name on a card, call his name and ask the child to take his card from the display board and bring it to you.
3. Place the name card above the child's cubie or other area where personal items are stored.
4. Label familiar objects in the room. On the bookshelf place a card with the printed word *BOOKS;* on supplies that children use daily, label such items as *CRAYONS, PENCILS,* etc.
5. Present simple but incomplete sentences to the child and encourage him to finish the sentence with one word.
   This ball is _____ (round, big, small, red, soft, hard).
   This book is _____ (open, closed, big, small, blue).
   This box is _____ (big, open, closed, square, heavy, tiny).

EVALUATION:
1. In which of the above activities does the child most often recognize his own name?
2. What evidence can you see that a child associates the label of an object with the name of the object?
3. Give examples of words used by the child to complete sentences.

Ch. 25: **Sample Developmental Units**

GOAL: **LANGUAGE DEVELOPMENT—AUDITORY SKILLS (RHYMING)**

OBJECTIVES:
1. The child will demonstrate recognition that some words sound alike by orally supplying words that rhyme when pictures or objects are used as cues.
2. The child will be able to rhyme a word with one that he hears.

MATERIALS: Familiar objects (toys, clothes, food, etc.) which can be paired because their labels sound alike; pictures of familiar objects which can be paired because their labels rhyme.

ACTIVITIES:
1. Provide the child with many experiences of listening to and saying nursery rhymes and jingles which contain words that sound alike.
2. While telling stories and saying rhymes or naming objects, emphasize the similarities in big words such as baseball/caseball. Say each slowly; then ask the child to say each one after you. Talk about the fact that these words sound alike and that this is called *rhyming*. Make up your own words; use some nonsense words; then say one of the words used before. For example, go back to *baseball* and say another word which obviously doesn't rhyme, such as *car,* and ask the child whether these rhyme. Give the child a number of examples of pairs of words that do and do not rhyme and let him show you, by choosing the words that do rhyme, that he can tell the difference.
3. Show a pair of familiar objects, such as a block and a book. Encourage the child to say the name of each object as you point to it. Say that you are thinking of one of the objects and ask the child to guess which one by clues that will be given. Then say a series of words to rhyme with one of the objects until the children can say the name of the object. For example, if the object is book, say *hook, took, look, nook,* etc., until the children can tell that you are thinking about *book*. Move on to another pair of objects as each word is correctly guessed (rather than do the other word in the pair).
4. Place several pairs of objects together which the child has used often enough to know the labels. Ask the child to say the name of each object as you point to it. Present objects, one pair at a time, and ask the child whether the names for these objects rhyme.
5. Place several objects in a box and ask the child to select and place together those that have names that rhyme. Before doing this, have the child say the name of each object to be sure he knows it.
6. Arrange sets of three objects, one at a time, in full view of the child. Ask which two objects out of the three rhyme (block, clock, and doll; nail, pail, and hammer).
7. Arrange pairs of pictures on a bulletin board or flannel board. Point to each pair and ask the child whether the names of the items in the two pictures rhyme. Do this with each pair. Present four or five pairs of pictures and encourage the child to place the two pictures

475

Part VI: Planning a Children's Program

                              together that have names of objects that rhyme (tree and bee; hat and bat; log and dog).

        8. Begin a series of words by saying a word such as *at*. The child then says a word which rhymes, taking turns with you or with other children until no one can think of another rhyming word. (The child may repeat words that have been said before; if so, accept it.)

        9. Play the game, "Which word doesn't belong?" Say three words, two of which rhyme and one which does not. Let the child choose which word does not belong.

EVALUATION:
1. List familiar objects which the child identifies as having a label that rhymes with one or more other words.
2. Describe the child's ability to rhyme a word with one he hears.
3. How does the child respond to cues in pictures or objects that reflect rhyming words?

GOAL:
OBJECTIVE: **CONCEPT FORMATION—CLASSIFYING GEOMETRIC SHAPES**
The child will be able to classify geometric shapes (square, circle, triangle, rectangle, hexagon) by sorting, verbal labeling, or grouping.

MATERIALS: Set of "feel" cards or set of "shape" cards (2- by 4-inch cards with shapes painted or outlined, one on each card—about 24 or 36 cards in a set with several of each shape); shape sorter set containing wood or plastic shapes of squares, circles, triangles, rectangles; large flash cards (5 by 8 inches) containing the above shapes, one on each card.

ACTIVITIES:
1. Play the card game, *I Match,* by dealing out cards at random among two, three, or four children or between one adult and one child. Each, in turn, places a card on the table (or floor) and the next child tries to match the shape with one of his cards. If the card matches, the child has to call out the name of the shape, saying, "Square—I match." The child then picks up the cards that matched and keeps them in his stack. The object of the game is to get the most cards in your own stack.
2. Hold up a flash card for the child to identify by labeling the shape (square, circle, triangle, rectangle, hexagon).
3. Give the child a master card for each of the above geometric shapes and let him place his cards in stacks in front of him to match the master cards.
4. Give the child a set of master cards containing the above geometric shapes. Hold up two flash cards at a time. Let the child select one card at a time and place it in front of him to match the master card. As you continue to hold up two cards each time, the child will place the cards in their respective groups. Encourage the child to say the name of the shape each time.

EVALUATION:
1. How does the child identify and label shapes?
2. Describe the child's method of identifying and classifying shapes.

Ch. 25: Sample Developmental Units

GOAL:
OBJECTIVES: **CONCEPT FORMATION—DEVELOPING CONCEPTS OF TIME**
1. The child will be able to demonstrate an understanding of the relationship of the passage of time to events by participating in sequenced activities.
2. The child will be able to apply concepts of time by participating in time-related activities.

MATERIALS: Two sets of cards, each containing a day of the week; four identical glasses; pictures of a baby, young child, teenager, adult, and older person; a number of pictures which represent happenings in a familiar story; seeds; a sweet potato; a large clock.

ACTIVITIES:
1. Develop for the child a daily schedule which is followed quite regularly to provide a foundation for forming time concepts.
2. Talk with the child about the daily routine to help develop the concept of the passage of time. For instance, talk about what we do *after* juice time, what we do *after* play time, what we do *before* bed time, what happens *after* school, when Dad comes home, etc. Use this technique daily as part of the routine. Decide upon a specific signal to be used when changing from one activity to another, such as a particular tune on a record player, a flashing light, a bell, or a whistle. Use the same signal when it is time to change activities.
3. Talk about events that happened yesterday, today, and those that may happen tomorrow. In talking about yesterday, recall an event important enough that the child will remember it.
4. Display cards with the names of the week on them in sequence. Each day have the child match the day's card with a duplicate. Refer to which day of the week today is; then say what yesterday was and what tomorrow will be.
5. When talking with children, encourage them to sequence events in order. For instance, when a child is telling a story or relating a happening, ask simple questions like these: "What happened then?" "Then what did you do?" Make simple statements to indicate the sequence of events, such as: "Johnny went to the garden. *After* he got there he looked for a carrot. *Finally* he found a good carrot. *Then* he washed the carrot. *At last*, he ate the carrot."
6. Play games involving the sequencing of events. Start by saying, "I get up when my mother calls me." Then the child tells what one does next, such as:
   "Then I take a bath."
   Another child says what would happen next, and so on. Do this with events that occur when the children get home from school or after a trip.
7. Place four water glasses in a row on the table. Leave one empty. Add water to make one about one-third full, another two-thirds

Part VI: Planning a Children's Program

        full, and fill one. Ask the child to arrange these in order. Let the child empty the glasses and refill them with a small pitcher of water. (Color the water with food coloring for variety.) Ask the child which glass took the longest to fill.

8. Use pictures of a baby, child, teenager, adult, and an older person. Ask the child which would come first, then next, etc. Talk about years of age.
9. Give the child large pictures which represent events in a familiar story. Encourage the child to arrange these in the same order as the events in the story. Repeat this activity with a flannel board and pictures backed with flannel.
10. Plant seeds which grow quickly. Place a sweet potato in a jar of water and allow it to sprout. Check the growth of the plants daily. Record the height once a week to see how much growth occurs.
11. Acquaint the child with a clock and talk about the use of it. For example, "It is now 10:00 and time for our juice" or "It is now 12:00 and time to eat lunch," etc. (Even though the child may learn the labels of numbers on the face of the clock and can tell what time it is, do not expect him to understand the passage of time by use of the clock.)
12. When an important holiday, such as Christmas, is approaching, make a calendar to help the children understand the passage of time until the event. Make individual empty squares for each day and a card for each day, which contains the name of the day and the date. Arrange these lined up in sequence and explain that each card means the passing of one day. At the beginning or end of each day, the child may count the number of days until the event by counting the empty squares. This could also be done each week or each month to show the passage of time. (Simply line up the squares on the wall or a display board. Do not duplicate the regular calendar because the child does not understand the uneven number of days in beginning and ending weeks of a month.)

EVALUATION:
1. What is the child's response to the daily routine?
2. Describe the child's ability to place each part of an event in its right place so that the whole is correct.
3. How does the child use a clock?
4. Give three examples which indicate the child's concept of time.

GOAL: **SELF-CONCEPT—DEVELOPING CONCEPTS OF CHARACTERISTICS OF ONE'S OWN BODY**

OBJECTIVES:
1. On a drawing which outlines his body, the child will be able to draw in such details as eyes, nose, mouth, and hair.
2. The child will be able to draw such details of clothing as buttons, skirt, pants, sleeves, and pockets on an outline of his body shape.

Ch. 25: Sample Developmental Units

3. The child will be able to visualize his own body size by comparing himself with the measured height marker and with a life-size drawing of his body.

MATERIALS: Brown or white paper large enough for child to lie on; crayon or felt marking pen; strip of cardboard or poster paper 5 feet long and 6 inches wide, with feet and inches indicated.

ACTIVITIES:
1. Place a large sheet of paper on the floor. Let the child lie on his back on the paper. Trace around him to form the outline of the child's body.
2. Give the outline to the child to draw in details. Help by asking such questions as, "Where will you put your nose?" Encourage the child to draw in other details when he is interested (shoes, buttons, pockets).
3. Place the body shape on the wall and allow the child to draw in other details when he is interested. After about six or eight weeks, repeat this experience and notice additional details the child may draw.
4. Measure the child's height against a marker on the wall made of cardboard or posterboard. Draw a heavy line and write the child's name and the date beside it to indicate the child's height. Repeat every three or four months.

EVALUATION:
1. What facial features does the child draw on the outline?
2. What body parts are made more specific by the child's art work?
3. What details of clothing does the child include?
4. Is there a noticeable change or more detail in the child's concept of self after six or eight weeks?

GOAL: **SELF-CONCEPT—BODY IMAGE**

OBJECTIVES:
1. The child will demonstrate correct use of the limbs, hands, feet, and head.
2. The child will be able to identify the limbs, hands, feet, and head by touching and naming each on his own body and on a simulated human figure.

MATERIALS: Full-length felt or posterboard body figure cut apart at the limbs, hands, feet, and head; cardboard puppet attached at joints with brads; long sheet of butcher paper (about 4 to 6 feet); a dishpan with $\frac{1}{4}$ inch tempera paint; a dishpan with soapy water; towel; large pictures of hands, feet, arms, and legs.

ACTIVITIES:
1. Put together the body parts of the flannel board or posterboard figure so that the body is incorrect in some way. (These could be gross, such as an arm extending from the head, or subtle, such as the legs and feet on the wrong sides.) Leave this puzzle arranged on the flannel board. Encourage the child to notice errors and then change them.

479

Part VI: Planning a Children's Program

    2. Arrange a long sheet of butcher paper on the floor between two child-sized chairs. Beside one chair place a dishpan with ¼ inch tempera paint and by the other a pan of soapy water and a towel (for washing afterwards). Let the child step, one foot at a time, in the paint and then walk across the paper. Label the prints with the child's name. The next day ask the child to retrace his steps by walking on the footprints. Label the left and right foot. Talk about the left and right foot. Encourage the child to count the number of steps taken with the left foot; with the right foot.

    3. Make up a list of sentences which correspond to the use of the limbs, hands, feet, and head for the child to complete.
        "I clap with my _____."
        "I step with my _____."
        "I draw with my _____."
        "I think with my _____."
        "I see with my _____."

    4. Find large pictures of hands, feet, legs, arms, etc. Show these, one at a time, and ask the child to imitate the action with that body part, then a different action with the same body part. Continue as long as the child thinks of new movements.

EVALUATION:
1. Give examples of how the child is able to identify the function of his limbs, hands, feet, and head.
2. To what extent can the child label the parts of his body?
3. To what extent can the child identify the use of body parts?

GOAL: **LIVING SKILLS—TABLE SETTING AND CLEANING TASKS**

OBJECTIVES:
1. The child will be able to set the table for a simple meal.
2. The child will be able to clean his plate by scraping it with a spatula at the completion of a meal.
3. The child will be able to clean the surface of the table after a meal.

MATERIALS: Sponge, dishpan, soapy water, clean water, dry cloth, plates, forks, spoons, glasses, napkins, paper placemat, felt tip pen or crayon.

ACTIVITIES:
1. Assist the child in setting the table for a simple meal by giving him unbreakable plates to place on the table.
2. Draw an outline of a place setting on a paper placemat with a marking pen or crayon. Use the placemat as a guide for the child when learning to set the table. If necessary, demonstrate how to use the coded placemat as a guide for placing the plate, fork, spoon, and glass.
3. Sort forks, spoons, and napkins in separate groups. Encourage the child to place spoons, forks, and napkins on the table.
4. Encourage the child to repeat the table setting experience while playing house.

EVALUATION:	5. Encourage the child to wipe the table after a meal, using a wet, soapy sponge. Then he can rinse the sponge in clean water and wipe the table again. Have him follow this with a clean dry cloth. (You may have to demonstrate this procedure the first time.) 1. Describe the child's use of the coded placemat in setting the table. 2. What evidence indicates the child's ability to clean the table successfully?
GOAL:	**LIVING SKILLS—HELPING WITH SIMPLE FOOD PREPARATION**
OBJECTIVES:	1. The child will be able to make a simple gelatin mixture to be served as a salad. 2. The child will be able to slice bananas and add them to a gelatin mixture.
MATERIALS:	Table knife, bananas, gelatin mixture, large mixing spoon, cutting board, mixing bowl, hot and cold water, one-cup measure.
ACTIVITIES:	1. Provide a bowl for stirring the gelatin mixture, spoon, package of flavored gelatin mix, hot and cold water, and a one-cup measure. Encourage the child to open the package and pour the mix into the empty bowl. Using the hot water, demonstrate how to measure the water in a measuring cup and pour it into the gelatin mix. Let the child stir the mixture with a spoon until the gelatin is dissolved. Let the child measure the cold water and add it to the mixture and stir. Show the child where the bowl of gelatin is placed in the refrigerator to chill. While the mixture is chilling, do the following: 2. Provide a cutting board, table knife, and two bananas. Arrange the items on a table where the child can work comfortably (sitting with feet flat on floor or standing). Demonstrate how to peel bananas. Let the child peel the bananas. Demonstrate how to slice bananas with a table knife on a cutting board. Let the child slice the bananas. Let the child add banana slices to the partially chilled gelatin mixture. When the gelatin salad is ready to serve, let the child spoon it onto lettuce leaves on each plate.
EVALUATION:	1. Describe the child's response while making the gelatin salad. What did the child say? What did the child do? 2. Describe the child's ability to peel and slice bananas. 3. What is the child's response to the finished product?

Recommended Reading

Aaron, David, with Winawer, Bonnie P. *Child's Play*. New York: Harper and Row, 1965.

Braley, William, et al. *Daily Sensorimotor Training Activities*. Freeport, Long Island, New York: Educational Activities, Inc., 1968.

Caldwell, Bettye M. *Home Teaching Activities*. 814 Sherman, Little Rock, Arkansas.

Part VI: Planning a Children's Program

Carmichael, Viola S. *Curriculum Ideas for Young Children.* Los Angeles, California: Southern California Association for the Education of Young Children, 1972.
Preschool Guide. Denver, Colorado: Colorado Association of Future Homemakers of America, 1968.
Croft, J., and Hess, R. D. *An Activities Handbook for Teachers of Young Children.* Boston: Houghton-Mifflin.
Hartley, Ruth E., and Goldenson, Robert M. *The Complete Book of Children's Play.* New York: Thomas Y. Crowell, 1963.
Lorton, Mary Baratta. *Workjobs.* Menlo Park, California: Addison-Wesley Publishing Co., 1972.
Pitcher, E. G.; Lasher, M. G.; and Feinburg, Sylvia. *Helping Young Children Learn.* Columbus, Ohio: Charles E. Merrill Publishing Co., 1966.
Rogers, Sarah F., and Simpson, Claire E. *Pathways: Parents as Teachers at Home Working to Aid Youngsters Succeed.* 2324 Nineteenth Street, N.W., Washington, D.C., 1972.
——— *The Scrap Book.* Ann Arbor, Michigan: Perry Nursery School, 1972.
Taylor, Barbara. *A Child Goes Forth (A Curriculum Guide for Teachers of Preschool Children).* Provo, Utah: Brigham Young University Press, 1964.
Taylor, Frank D.; Artuso, Alfred A.; and Hewett, Frank M. *Creative Art Tasks for Children.* Denver, Colorado: Love Publishing Co., 1970.
Upchurch, Beverly. *Easy-to-do-Toys and Activities for Infants and Toddlers.* Greensboro, North Carolina: Infant Care Project, University of North Carolina, 1971.

APPENDIX A

Meal Planning and Food Services

EXAMPLES OF CHILD-SIZE PORTIONS OF COMMON FOODS FOR ONE MEAL

FOOD	AGE Three to Five Years
Milk	6 oz.
Meat, fish, poultry, liver	2–3 Tbsp.
Egg	½
Fruits	2 Tbsp. (½ cup for ages four and five)
Vegetables	2–3 Tbsp.
Cereal	⅓ cup
Bread	½ slice
Butter or fortified margarine	1 tsp.
Desserts	¼ cup (½ cup for ages four and five)

These are portions of initial servings; seconds should be available.

Appendix A

MENUS
A Six-weeks Cycle

These menus with breakfast snack, lunch, and afternoon snack have been developed for young children.

Meal	Monday	Tuesday	Wednesday	Thursday	Friday
Breakfast Snack	Canned biscuits Honey Orange juice	½ boiled egg ½ piece wheat toast and butter Apple juice	Oatmeal Buttered toast Milk	Melted cheese on toast Apple slice	Dry cereal Raisins Milk
Lunch	Fish sticks Corn on cob Frozen spinach Spiced apple rings Bread and butter Milk Chocolate pudding—whipped topping*	Meat loaf Mashed potatoes Green peas Sliced tomato Whole wheat bread and butter Milk Baked apple*	Liver fingers Buttered rice Broccoli Red jello with applesauce Bread and butter Milk Quick apple crisp*	Ham and potato casserole Green beans Slaw Bread and butter Milk Strawberry whip and chill	Spaghetti and meatball or sauce Carrot stick Asparagus Hot roll and butter Sherbet
Afternoon Snack	Graham cracker with peanut butter Orange juice	½ boiled egg Whole wheat bread and butter Apple juice	Milk Peanut butter cookie*	Orange juice over sliced bananas in bowl	Cinnamon crisp crackers Fortified grape drink
Breakfast Snack	Toast and Honey Orange juice Raisins	Dry cereal Milk Apple slice	Cinnamon toast Orange juice	Cream of Wheat ½ toast Milk	Orange juice over bananas
Lunch	Scrambled eggs Spam sticks Green beans Toast strips Apple wedge Milk Decorated yellow cake	Chicken and egg noodles Frozen spinach Sliced tomato Hot roll and butter Milk Quick fruit cobbler*	Beans and ham Broccoli Celery with cheese Cornbread and butter Ambrosia*	Oven fried chicken Mashed potatoes Green peas Lettuce and tomato salad Milk Lemon pudding	Beef pot roast cooked with carrots (onions) Hot rolls and butter Milk Ice cream delight*
Afternoon Snack	Cheese nips Orange juice	Fortified grape juice Oatmeal cookies	Celery stuffed with peanut butter Fortified fruit punch	Cheerios Fortified fruit punch	Orange juice over bananas
Breakfast Snack	Canned biscuits Butter and honey Orange juice	½ boiled egg ½ toast Tomato juice	Frozen waffles Apple butter Orange juice	Cooked cereal Milk Raisins	Dry cereal Milk
Lunch	Hamburger patties Creamed corn Brussel sprouts Cottage cheese with pineapple chunks Bread and butter Milk Yellow cake with glaze	Wieners and cheese with bacon Creamed potatoes Green beans Carrot sticks Fruit cocktail Milk	Creamed chipped beef* Buttered noodles Frozen peas and carrots Spiced apple ring Hot rolls/butter Milk Banana pudding	Liver patties* Tater tots Yellow squash Lime jello with crushed pineapple Muffins and butter Milk Quick apple crisp*	Baked ham Yam patties Frozen mixed vegetables Slaw Hot rolls and butter Milk Sherbet

484

Appendix A

Afternoon Snack	Cheese and crackers Orange juice	Tomato juice Cheese nips	½ peanut butter sandwich Orange juice	Lemon cookies Grape juice	Whole wheat bread and butter sandwich (½) Pink lemonade
Breakfast	Vienna sausages wrapped in biscuits Orange juice	Oatmeal Milk	Toast and honey Tang	½ boiled egg Apple juice	Dry cereal Milk
Lunch	Beef potato casserole* Cottage cheese and peach Cornbread/butter Milk Oatmeal-raisin cookies*	Oven fried chicken Mashed potatoes Green beans Carrot and raisin salad* Biscuits and butter Milk Peach turnovers	Pork roast New parsley potatoes Green peas Unpeeled apple wedge Bread and butter Milk Chocolate no-bake cookies*	Goulash (macaroni and cheese, ground beef) Broccoli Berry jello square Muffin and butter Milk Cinnamon pears*	Slim Jim burgers* Baked beans with molasses Lettuce and tomato Milk Plums and sugar cookies
Afternoon Snack	Ritz crackers and peanut butter Orange juice	No-bake crispies* Fortified cherry juice	Bread, butter, and honey Fortified orange juice	½ boiled egg Apple juice	Dry finger cereal Milk
Breakfast	Cinnamon toast Fortified grape juice	½ boiled egg Orange juice	Cheese toast Orange juice	Oatmeal ½ toast Milk	Toasted raisin bread Apple juice
Lunch	Ham balls* Sweet potatoes Cauliflower with cheese sauce Green pepper strip Whole wheat bread and butter Red applesauce	Tuna croquettes* Corn Glazed carrots Green jello square Corn bread Milk Baked apple*	Chicken and rice Spinach Spiced apple ring Bread and butter Banana pudding Milk	Pork chops Black-eyed peas Yellow squash Carrot stick Bread and butter Milk Strawberry whip and chill	Liver and crisp bacon* Broccoli Apple wedge Bread and butter Milk Ice cream and chocolate syrup
Afternoon Snack	½ peanut butter and honey sandwich Fortified grape juice	Applesauce Raisin cookies Milk	Cheese nips Orange juice	Whole grain cereal Milk	Raisin bread and butter Apple juice
Breakfast	Biscuits, honey, or jelly Fortified fruit punch	Cinnamon toast Apple juice	Tang Peanut butter, honey sandwich	Orange juice Blueberry muffins (mix)	Cream of Wheat ½ piece toast Milk
Lunch	Scrambled eggs Spam sticks Green beans Tomato slice Toast strip Milk Fruit cocktail	Hamburger noodle casserole* Green peas Orange slice Bread and butter Milk Gingerbread*	Fish sticks Scalloped potatoes* Spinach Carrot sticks Corn bread/butter Milk Fruit jello with dream whip	Vegetable soup ¼ cheese salad sandwich Green jello with pears Milk Peanut butter cookies	Meatballs with cream of mushroom gravy Baked potatoes Asparagus Slaw with carrots Bread and butter Milk
Afternoon Snack	Bread, butter and molasses Fortified fruit punch	Cheese and Ritz crackers Apple juice	Peanut butter and honey sandwich Fortified orange juice	Blueberry muffins Orange juice	Dry cereal Milk

* Recipe is included in Appendix A.

Kaye Sears, Oklahoma State Dept. of Health

Appendix A

RECIPES FOR CHILDREN
(Serve 20–25 Young Children)
COOKIES

GINGERBREAD

2 eggs	½ tsp. soda
1 cup sugar	2 tsp. baking powder
1 cup milk	1 tsp. cinnamon
1¼ cup molasses	½ tsp. ginger
3 cups flour—sifted	3 Tbsp. margarine or bacon fat

Beat eggs, add sugar, and mix well. Add milk and molasses. Sift together flour, soda, baking powder, cinnamon, and ginger, and mix in gradually. Add melted margarine. Mix well. Put into greased pans and bake in a moderate oven, 325° F., 40–45 minutes.

CHOCOLATE NO-BAKE COOKIES

2 cups sugar	3 cups oatmeal
½ cup cocoa	½ cup crunchy peanut butter
½ cup milk	1 tsp. vanilla

Boil sugar, cocoa, and milk for one minute. Add oatmeal, peanut butter, and vanilla. Beat until all are mixed together. Drop by spoonfuls on waxed paper.

NO-BAKE CRISPIES

Combine: ½ cup Karo syrup with ½ cup peanut butter. Stir in 3 cups of Rice Krispies. Shape into balls.

OATMEAL RAISIN COOKIES

1 cup raisins	¼ tsp. soda
1 cup sugar	⅔ cup margarine
2 cups flour—sifted	2 eggs
1½ tsp. baking powder	⅓ cup water
¼ tsp. salt	1⅓ cups rolled oats, raw

Pick raisins over carefully to remove stems. Mix with 1 Tbsp. flour. Sift remaining flour, baking powder, soda, and salt. Melt fat, add sugar, and mix well. Add beaten egg and water. Stir in flour mixture and rolled oats. Stir in raisins and drop by teaspoonfuls on greased pan. Bake in a moderate oven, 325° F., 20 minutes.

PEANUT BUTTER COOKIES

½ cup margarine or bacon fat	1 egg
½ cup peanut butter	1½ cups flour—sifted
½ cup sugar, white	½ tsp. salt
½ cup sugar, brown	½ tsp. soda

Appendix A

Cream peanut butter and fat; add white and brown sugar; cream well. Add eggs. Mix well. Sift flour, salt, and soda and work in well. Shape into balls the size of a walnut. Place on a greased pan and press out with a fork. Bake in a moderate oven, 325° F., about 8 minutes.

DESSERTS

BAKED APPLES

6 pounds apples   ¾ cup sugar, brown or white

Wash and core apples. Put in a baking dish. Add sugar to cavity in each apple. Cover bottom of dish with water and bake in a moderate oven, 350° F., until tender, basting frequently. Cut apples and skins into small pieces before serving. If desired, ¾ cup of strained honey may be substituted for each ½ cup of sugar. Raisins may be added as filling for apples.

CINNAMON PEARS

Lay pear half cut side down. Sprinkle with red or green jello, combined with cinnamon and sugar.

ICE CREAM DELIGHT

3 pkg. gelatin mix (strawberry or cherry)
3 cups hot water
3 cups cold water
3 pints ice cream, vanilla

Dissolve gelatin in hot water. Add cold water and chill until begins to thicken. Soften ice cream and fold into gelatin. Pour into individual dishes and chill.

NON-FAT DRY MILK WHIPPED TOPPING

½ cup cold water
½ cup non-fat dry milk
2 Tbsp. lemon juice
2-4 Tbsp. sugar

Sprinkle dry milk on water. Beat until stiff enough to stand in soft peaks. Add lemon juice. Continue beating until stiff. Beat in sugar.

QUICK APPLE CRISP

Turn 6 cups canned or frozen applesauce into a greased shallow casserole or pie pans (2). Crumble 12 graham crackers into ½ cup melted butter, stir in 6 Tbsp. brown or white sugar, cinnamon. Sprinkle over applesauce. Bake in a moderate oven 35-40 min. or put 5 inches under broiler for about 10 minutes.

QUICK FRUIT COBBLER

Place 2 cans of any kind of fruit pie filling in a large baking dish. Sprinkle 1 box dry yellow cake mix over the surface, and dot well with 1 cube of butter. Bake 350° F. for 45 minutes-1 hour, or until cake mix is browned well.

Appendix A

MAIN DISHES

BEEF-POTATO CASSEROLE

1½ lb. ground beef
3 cups shredded raw potatoes
½ cup chopped onion
12 slices American cheese
Stuffed olives and parsley to garnish, if desired.

½ cup chopped green pepper
4 Tbsp. Worcestershire sauce
2 Tbsp. salt
2 cans tomato sauce

Mix beef, potatoes, onion, pepper, Worcestershire sauce, and salt. Put ½ mixture into a 3-quart casserole. Pour 1 can of tomato sauce over it. Cover with 6 slices of the cheese. Add rest of meat; top with remaining sauce. Bake at 350° F. for one hour. When done, cut rest of cheese diagonally. Arrange it diagonally on the top. Garnish with sliced olives and parsley.

CREAMED CHIPPED BEEF

1 lb. chipped beef
2 quarts milk
1 cup flour

1 cup butter
pimentos and green peppers

Make medium white sauce in top of double boiler by melting butter, adding flour and then milk. Do not salt as the beef is salty. When thickened, add beef cut with scissors into very small pieces. If desired, add 1 can pimentos and 1 green pepper chopped fine. They may be omitted. This recipe can be prepared early and left over hot water until ready to serve. Serve in 3-inch patty shells.

HAM BALLS

1 lb. cured ham (ground)
1½ lb. fresh ham (ground)
1 cup bread crumbs
   (toasted and ground)

1 cup sweet milk
2 eggs (beaten)
salt

Combine ingredients and shape into ball or loaf. Place in roaster and cover with the following sauce:

1 cup brown sugar
½ cup vinegar

½ cup water
1 tsp. mustard

Place in oven and bake at 325° F. about 2 hours. Baste every 30 minutes. Delicious cold.

HAMBURGER-NOODLE CASSEROLE

2 pkgs. noodles, cooked according to directions
2 lbs. ground beef
2 #2 cans tomatoes or tomato juice
2 small cans tomato paste
2 medium-sized onions

6 Tbsp. parsley
1 lb. grated cheese
salt and pepper

Brown meat and onions (chopped fine) in skillet. Add noodles that have been cooked, tomato juice, paste, parsley and put cheese on the top. Cover and let simmer about 30 minutes.

LIVER AND CRISP BACON

Brown floured liver fingers on both sides and cook until tender, about 8 minutes. Serve with crisp, crumbled bacon.

LIVER PATTIES

1½ lbs. beef liver
   ground together with
1 lb. ground beef
Cracker crumbs or rolled oats, as filler

5 slices bacon
4 eggs
1 tsp. salt

Combine all ingredients and make into small patties. Bake in oven 325° F. for 30 minutes. For variety, these can be covered with cream of mushroom soup or served with tomato sauce as meatballs.

PORCUPINE MEATBALLS

2 lbs. ground beef
½ tsp. salt
½ tsp. pepper

1 cup uncooked rice
½ cup chopped onion
Dash of thyme

Sauce: Two cans cream of tomato soup diluted with equal water plus 1 Tbsp. vinegar.
Mix the above ingredients together. Brown in 4 Tbsp. shortening. Simmer in sauce 50 minutes.

SLIM JIM BURGERS

2 lbs. ground beef
2 eggs, beaten
1 cup dry bread crumbs
1 cup milk
16 frankfurter buns

½ tsp. pepper
⅔ cup onion, minced
1 tsp. Worcestershire sauce
16 slices cheese, cut into strips
  3½ × ¼ × ¼"

Heat oven to 400° F. (moderately hot). Combine all ingredients except cheese and buns. Divide meat into equal portions; mold each portion around a cheese stick. Place on lightly greased baking pan with sides. Bake about 20 minutes. Serve in warm split frankfurter buns. Top with catsup.
Note: Serve ½ Slim Jim to small children; allow a whole one for large eaters.

TUNA CROQUETTES

3 cans grated tuna
1 can cream of celery or
  mushroom soup
2 eggs, beaten

Bread crumbs or cracker crumbs,
  to hold together

Shape into patties or croquettes. Roll in a mixture of flour and cornmeal, and place in hot oil. Cook until brown on all sides. Serve with catsup.
Oven method: Place croquettes on lightly greased cookie pan, brush lightly with oil or butter, and place in hot oven, 400° F., until brown.

Appendix A

SIDE DISHES

AMBROSIA

2 cups each of three fruits (raisins, oranges, bananas, etc.). Mix with coconut.

CARROT AND RAISIN SALAD

2 lbs. carrots, shredded
1 lb. raisins

Custard salad dressing

Prepare custard salad dressing:

3 eggs, beaten
2 Tbsp. sugar
¾ tsp. salt

1 cup milk
3 Tbsp. lemon juice

Mix beaten eggs, sugar, salt, and milk and cook in a double boiler, stirring until mixture thickens. Add lemon juice. Cool and beat with egg beater until smooth. (Set aside.)

Toss all ingredients together lightly. (If raisins are dry, cover with boiling water and let stand a few minutes until they become soft and plump.) Drain well and cool before using in salad. Add salad dressing.

SCALLOPED POTATOES

6 medium-sized potatoes
4 Tbsp. butter or margarine
4 Tbsp. all-purpose flour

3 tsp. salt
4 cups milk

Peel potatoes and slice medium thin. Place in a baking dish. Melt butter or margarine in a sauce pan over medium heat. Add flour. Stir until smooth. Add salt and milk, stirring constantly until thickened. Remove from heat and pour over potatoes. Bake in uncovered dish for 1 hour in preheated oven at 375° F. For variation, 1½ cups cheese may be added to white sauce shortly before removing from heat.

VEGETABLES

BUTTERED VEGETABLES

Allow 2 Tbsp. of butter or margarine for 1 quart of cooked vegetables.

CREAMED VEGETABLES

Allow 2 cups of medium white sauce to about 1 quart of cooked vegetables.

ESCALLOPED VEGETABLES

Allow 2 quarts of medium white sauce to 1 quart of vegetables. Combine cooked vegetables with white sauce in alternate layers in a buttered baking dish. Top with buttered crumbs. Bake 15 to 25 minutes in a moderate oven, 325° F., until crumbs are browned.

Appendix A

CANNED VEGETABLES

Drain liquid into a saucepan and boil down to ⅓ of the original amount. Add vegetable and heat for a few minutes only.

FROZEN VEGETABLES

Put small amount of salted water in a saucepan. Bring to a boil, add frozen vegetable, and when boiling starts again, cover pan tightly. After 2 or 3 minutes, break melting mass of vegetables apart with a fork so heat will reach all parts evenly, and cook uncovered until tender but not soft.

SAFETY AND SANITATION WITH FOOD SERVICE

Sanitation means: clean water, clean food, proper storage, suitable and clean equipment, and good food handling practices by personnel.

FOOD SANITATION

Examine food when it is delivered to make sure it is not spoiled or dirty and that no insects are present.

Store food at proper temperatures at all times.

Keep perishable food either refrigerated or hot. Some foods such as custards made from milk and eggs spoil quickly and may cause illness if not handled properly.

Protect food from insects and rodents by storing in tight containers. Label all containers.

Use oldest supplies first.

Clean up spilled food immediately.

Check food supplies before using—when in doubt . . . *throw out!*

Throw out portions of food served but not eaten.

Provide for garbage or trash disposal in compliance with local regulating authorities.

Keep garbage containers clean and tightly covered.

EQUIPMENT SANITATION

Keep equipment, dishes, utensils, floors, and walls clean and in good repair. Remember to clean can opener.

Have good light and ventilation in food preparation area.

Avoid the use of cracked or chipped utensils and dishes. (Enamelware chips easily.)

Use only dish washing equipment that meets local health agency regulations.

STEPS IN WASHING AND SANITIZING DISHES

1. Scrape food and scraps from dishes into garbage can.
2. Wash in a good detergent in warm water.
3. Rinse dishes in warm, clear water.
4. To sanitize: Immerse dishes in 170-degree water for 2 minutes. Or: Immerse for 2 minutes in a solution of a suitable chemical sanitizer. (Check with your county health department for approved chemical compounds.)

PERSONNEL SANITATION

All kitchen personnel should have periodic health examinations.

Provide toilet facilities that include a lavatory, hot and cold water, soap, and clean towels. Put up a sign to remind employees to wash hands before returning to kitchen.

Additional hand washing facilities and towels should be easily accessible in the kitchen.

Wash hands with soap and water before starting work, after handling dirty dishes, after using a handkerchief, and after toileting.

Protect food from coughs and sneezes.

Hair nets or head covering should be worn when working with food.

Appendix A

Do not handle food when suffering from a cold or when there are cuts and sores on the hands.

Use appropriate utensils when handling food. Avoid use of fingers.

STORAGE OF POISON AND TOXIC MATERIALS

All toxic and poisonous materials and compounds such as insecticides, rodenticides, polishes, bleaches, and petroleum products should be kept in sealed containers in a locked cabinet in a room away from all food products. These should always be *labeled*. They should never be put in a container (can or bottle) that food originally came in.

SANITATION HINTS

Disease can be passed from person to person. As a child care worker, your health affects you and your work and also the health of the children.

Safe, sanitary food cannot be prepared, stored, or served using unsanitary facilities. Only quality products properly prepared and handled in a clean environment can be depended on to produce a safe meal or snack.

Food cannot be kept clean and safe if it comes in contact with utensils and equipment which have not been properly cleaned and sanitized. Eating and drinking utensils may be responsible for spreading contagious diseases. Germs may be coughed or sneezed on food, dishes, and utensils; they may be left on utensils which come in contact with the mouth.

The rule is pre-wash—wash—rinse—sanitize. Give special attention to tines of forks and bowls of spoons. It has been shown that disease organisms can be transferred from infected persons to eating utensils and that disease germs may survive poor dish washing methods.

Properly cleaned utensils and equipment will become contaminated unless properly stored and handled.

Lack of adequate refrigeration can be responsible for the spread of food infection and food poisoning outbreaks.

All garbage and refuse are potential breeding places of disease producing germs and disease bearing insects and serve as a food supply for rodents.

The kitchen and food storage areas should be free of all pests, particularly flies, roaches, ants, mice, or rats. The reason for preventing and eliminating rodents and insects is that they spread disease. They walk and feed on all kinds of filth, picking up germs on their feet and bodies, then depositing them on any food and utensils they touch.

Food poisoning is a general term, not exact in itself, but often used to describe any type of disease or illness caused by taking into the body spoiled, contaminated, or adulterated food or drink. (Mistakenly, it has many times been referred to as "ptomaine poisoning.")

Clean people make clean places—Dirty people make dirty places—It is not the place that makes the people—It is the people who make the place!

APPENDIX B

Schedules and Routines for Children's Activities

SAMPLE OF A DAILY ROUTINE

Arrival

Adults greet each child by name as they arrive. One adult makes a health check of each child to detect symptoms or signs of illness.

Children take off coats, jackets, hats, or other garments and place them in cubbies or lockers.

Each child picks up his name tag and hangs it around his neck.

Self-selected activities

Each child goes to the interest area of his choice. Materials and equipment are available for playing in centers such as: house, store, large block and toy, art, manipulative, story-library, science. Children will generally move to the area which attracts their interest. Children's interest spans are short, and they are often eager to move to another area. However, if a child continually goes to the same area day after day, the adults may want to encourage him to try something new. Perhaps the new activity could be related to the child's interest but with different materials and equipment.

Changing activities

When the children hear the tune on the record player or another designated sound, they begin putting things away and then move to the next activity.

Large group

All children come together in a large group. One of the adults assists the children in songs and/or large group activities. For example, the first large group session may include a song which names each child while he or she stands up. Following the song, another staff member may introduce the theme for the day and talk briefly about some of the day's activities. This not only helps the children get an idea of what is ahead, but it also stimulates interest and adds to each child's enthusiasm. A few minutes are devoted to an exchange of thoughts and ideas children may wish to express.

Snack time

Children divide into small groups of about five or six in each as they move to the small tables in the activity area for snack time. The children go, a group at a time, to the bathroom and wash their hands before beginning their snacks. While the other groups of children are waiting to use the bathroom, they sing finger-play songs or engage in a simple, short activity. During snack time the following activities may occur:

A child counts out the napkins. Depending on the child's level of ability, he may count them out in order, 1, 2, 3, 4, 5, or simply say something like, "One for you, one for you," repeating this five times and placing the napkins in front of each child or handing them out.

Another child pours the juice from a can, or a small enough pitcher to manage, into each of five cups. He or another child may pass the cups of juice, or each child may reach for his own.

Children may make their own cheese sandwiches. Materials placed on each table include: two kitchen trays; a plastic mixing bowl; a wooden mixing spoon; one cup of softened cheese; one small jar of chopped pimento; two tablespoons of mayonnaise; cookie cutters (circles and triangles); several slices of bread (some white, some brown); five table knives for spread-

Appendix B

ing cheese at each table. Children mix the cheese, mayonnaise, and chopped pimento in the mixing bowl and stir with the wooden spoon. The other children use cookie cutters to cut bread slices into circles and triangles. Each child may spread the cheese on his bread. Sandwiches may be open-faced or with two slices of bread, depending on the child's preference.

During this activity, the adult talks with children about what is going on. For example, the following words and terms may apply to this snack time—mix, stir, cut, spread, circle, triangle, soft, pour, orange, red, white, brown.

To help children develop concepts, some of the following ideas may be emphasized: The cheese is spread *on* the bread. The cheese is *between* two pieces of bread. There are *two* slices of bread used for this sandwich. Which sandwich has *more* bread? This one or this one? (Show open-faced and closed sandwiches.) This piece of bread is in the shape of a *circle*. This piece of bread is in the shape of a *triangle*. This sandwich is a *triangle;* a *circle.* Which sandwich is *round?* Which sandwich is *not round?* Is the cheese *soft?* Is the cheese *hard?*

When children have finished snack time, they help clean up. Napkins go into the waste basket; knives, juice cups or glasses, mixing bowl and spoon, on one tray; food items on another tray. If the trays are not too heavy, children enjoy carrying them to the kitchen. Children can also wipe the tables with wet, soapy sponges. Then they can rinse the tables and wipe them with dry towels. Children will need to wash their hands after this activity.

Developmental or learning units—small groups

Children are seated in about four small groups of four to eight children in various areas of the room such as in the manipulative area, the floor of the block area, and the story/quiet area. An adult works with each group. If there are not enough adults, one or two will have to float from one group of children to another.

Outdoor activities

Children may select a playground area and activities to engage in during outdoor play, or planned interest areas may be identified. Adults should be on hand to talk with the children, answer questions, encourage children, and insure safety of children.

Lunch

Children wash hands prior to lunch. They may help set the tables if easy tasks are planned ahead such as placing napkins, plates, spoons, glasses, and other items on the tables.

Sample *concepts* that may occur during lunch: shapes and spacial relationships, colors and textures of food, and names of food. To enhance the child's mealtime experience, simple ideas can be introduced. For example, this was one way a center promoted the concepts of *shapes* and *spacial relationships.*

White butcher paper was cut into 18 × 14 inch placemats for each child. A wide-tip felt pen was used to draw the outlines of the dishes and flatware to be used for this meal.

Each child's task was to place the items on his mat correctly by matching the shapes of the dishes with the outlines on the placemats—another form of a puzzle for learning spatial relationships. The children not only experienced activities related to classifying objects according to shape, but they also experienced the relationship of an object to the space on the placemat and of one object to another.

Appendix B

SAMPLE SCHEDULE
All-Day Care

7:30–7:45	Arrival	12:15–1:00	Rest/nap/quiet activities
7:30–8:00	Self-selected activities	1:00–1:30	Self-selected activities
8:00–8:10	Large group activities	1:30–2:15	Outdoor activities
8:10–8:30	Snack time	2:15–2:30	Large group activities
8:30–8:50	Developmental or learning activities—small groups	2:30–3:15	Developmental or learning activities—small group and individual
8:50–9:20	Outdoor activities	3:15–3:30	Snack time
9:20–9:45	Developmental or learning activities—individual and small groups	3:30–4:00	Large group activities—story/music/creative movements
9:45–10:00	Large group activities	4:00–4:45	Self-selected activities
10:00–10:20	Self-selected activities—quiet individual type	4:45–5:00	Preparation to go home
10:20–10:50	Small group activities	or	
10:50–11:15	Outdoor play	4:45–5:30	Outdoor play
11:15–11:30	Large group activities	5:30–6:00	Self-selected activities/prepare to go home
11:30–12:15	Lunch		

SAMPLE SCHEDULE
Half-Day Programs

Morning Program

8:30–8:40	Greeting and arrival/name tags
8:40–9:00	Large group activities
9:00–9:45	Self-selected activities
9:45–10:00	Small groups—evaluation time
10:00–10:15	Snack time
10:15–10:45	Outdoor activities
10:45–11:20	Small group activities
11:20–11:30	Preparation to go home

Afternoon Program

12:30–12:40	Greeting/lockers/name tags
12:40–1:00	Large group activities
1:00–1:50	Self-selected activities
1:50–2:00	Small groups—evaluation time
2:00–2:30	Outdoor activities
2:30–3:00	Snack and cleanup time
3:00–3:20	Small groups
3:20–3:30	Preparation to go home

SAMPLE SCHEDULE
"Open" Classroom

8:00–8:30	Arrival, health check, individualized activities	10:45–11:45	Story/music/creative movements (or self-selected activities)
8:30–8:45	Planning time for children	11:45–12:30	Lunch
8:45–9:45	Self-selected activities (children work in small groups or independently)	12:30–12:50	Individualized quiet activities
		12:50–2:00	Self-selected activities
9:45–10:15	Outdoor activities	2:00–2:30	Outdoor activities
10:15–10:45	Snack time	2:30–3:00	Snack time
		3:00–3:15	Prepare to go home

APPENDIX C
Sample Room Arrangements for Children's Activities

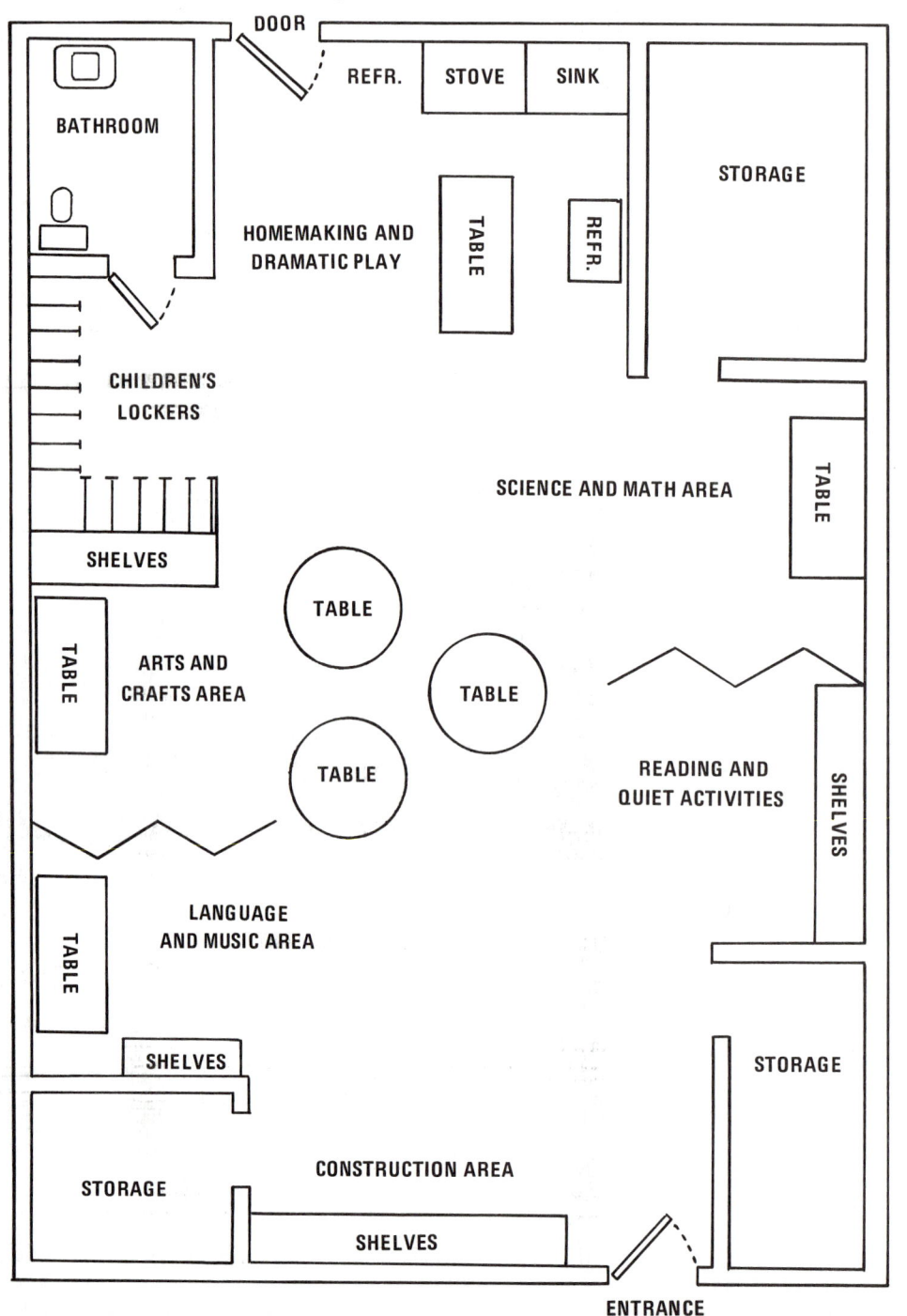

Appendix C

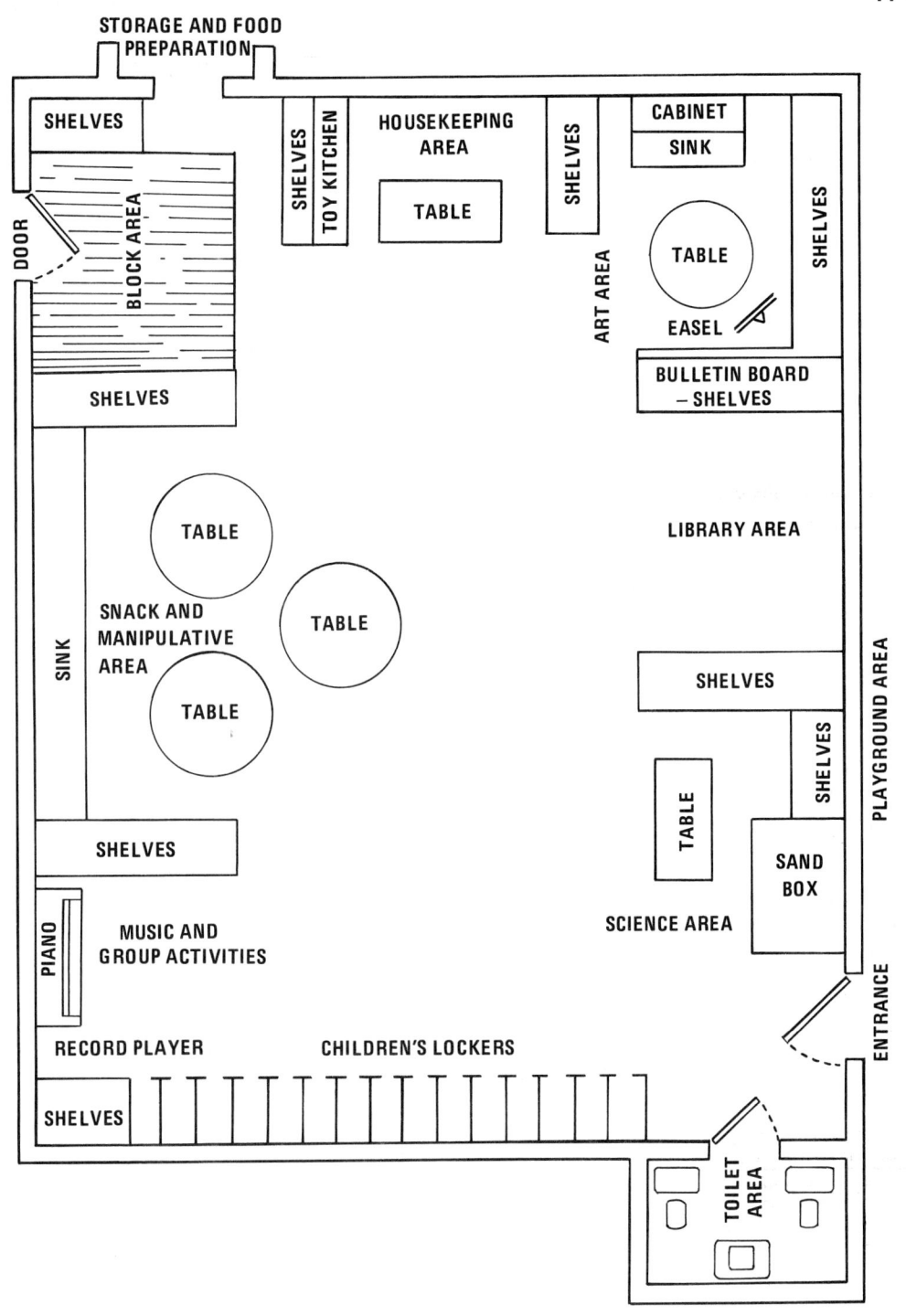

Appendix C

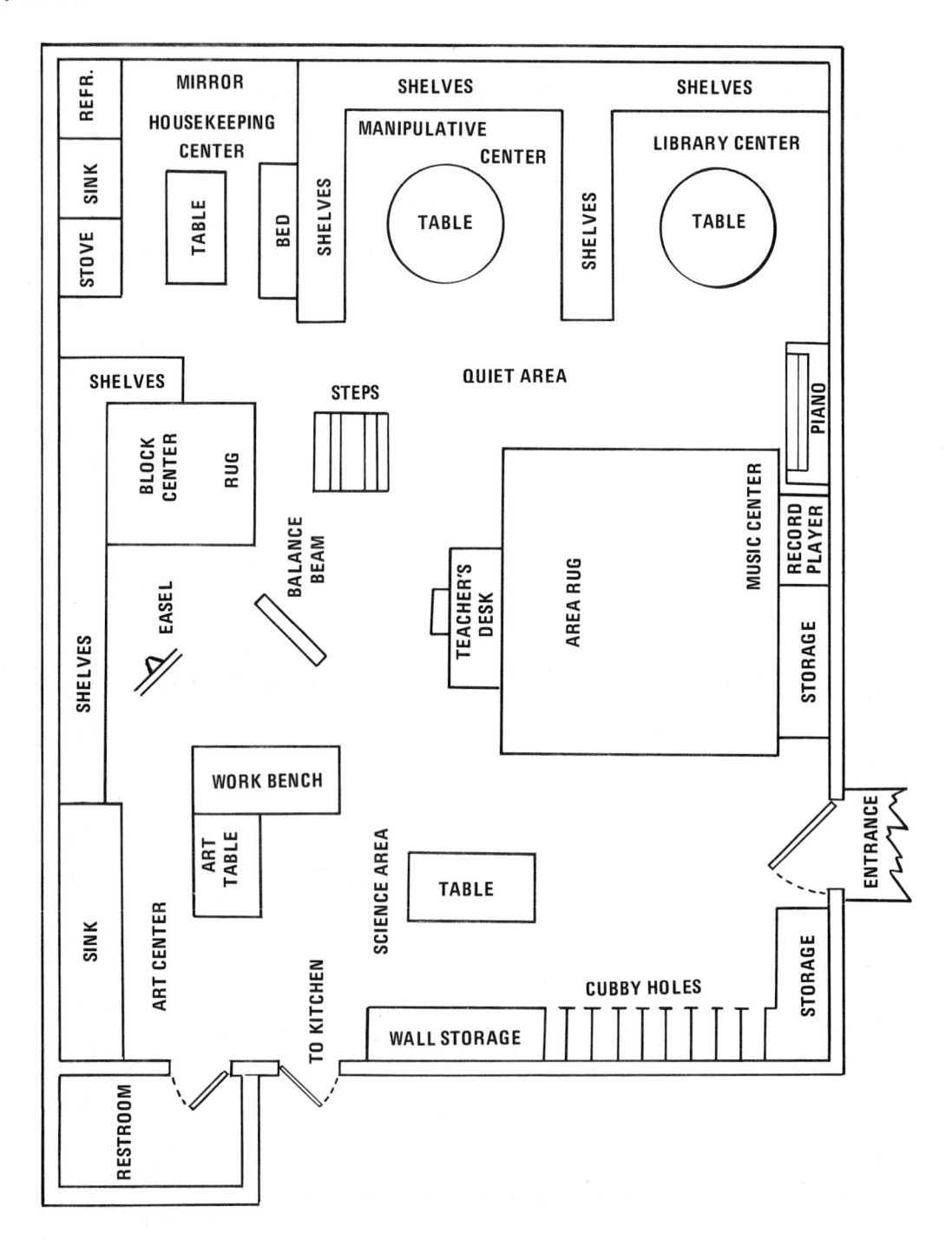

Appendix C

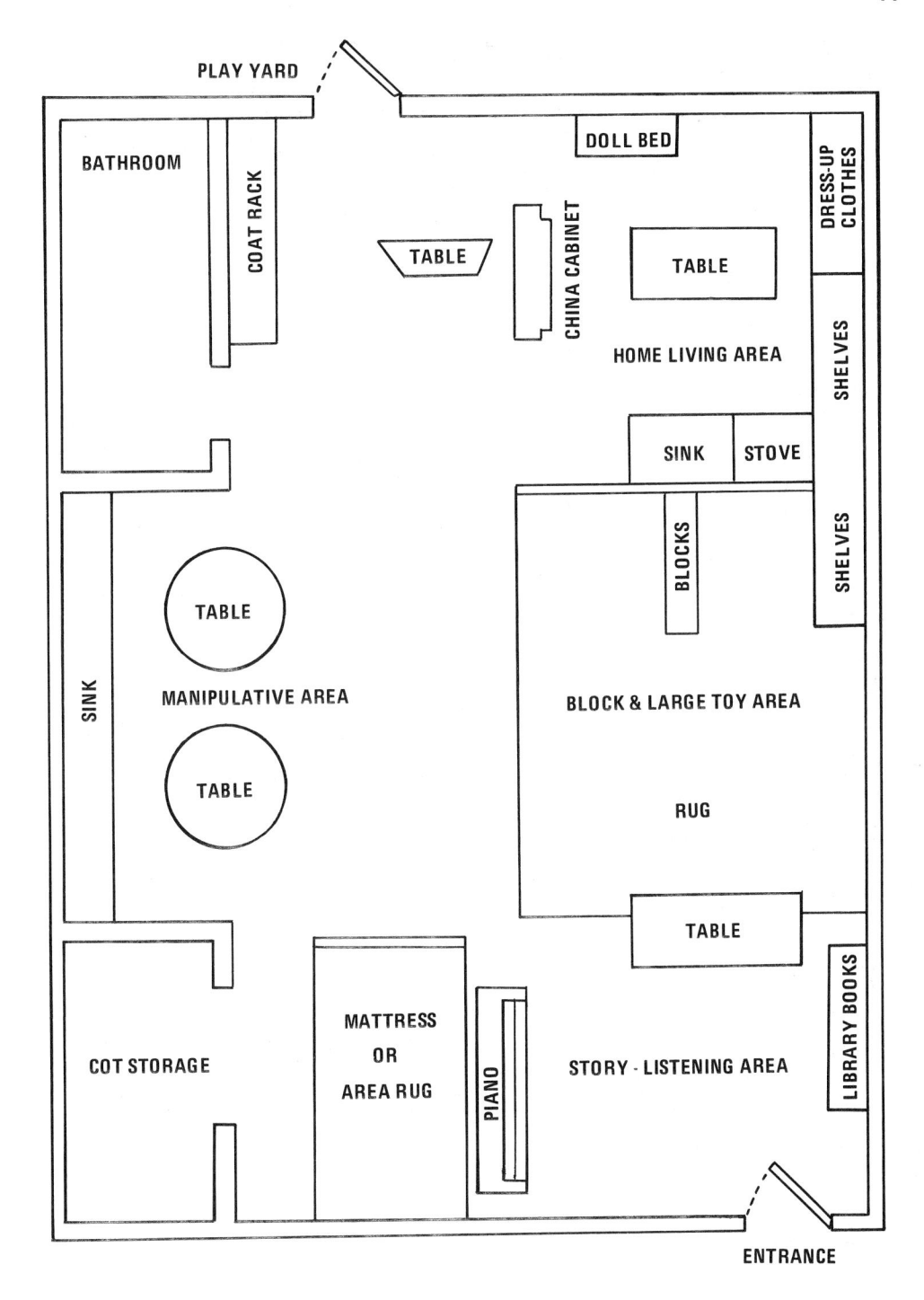

- PLAY YARD
- BATHROOM
- COAT RACK
- DOLL BED
- TABLE
- CHINA CABINET
- TABLE
- DRESS-UP CLOTHES
- HOME LIVING AREA
- SHELVES
- SINK
- STOVE
- SHELVES
- BLOCKS
- SINK
- TABLE
- TABLE
- MANIPULATIVE AREA
- BLOCK & LARGE TOY AREA
- RUG
- TABLE
- LIBRARY BOOKS
- COT STORAGE
- MATTRESS OR AREA RUG
- PIANO
- STORY - LISTENING AREA
- ENTRANCE

APPENDIX D

Suggested Equipment, Materials, and Supplies for a Children's Program

Carpentry
    Scrap pieces of soft wood
    Yarn in variety of colors
    Bottle caps
    Rubber bands
    Large-headed hammers
    Roofing nails (large heads)
    Cross-cut saws
    Large nuts, bolts, screws
    Workbench with vise and clamps
    Storage boxes or bins
    Pegboard coded for hanging tools

Gardening
    Small flower pots
    Paper cups and empty egg cartons
    Gardener's tools: rake, hoe, shovel, trowel, claw (child's size)
    Seeds (flower, vegetable)
    Water bucket or pitcher

Sand Play
    Sand pile or sand table
    Sturdy small shovels
    Large smooth-rim tin cans, old pots and pans
    Small buckets
    Large wooden buckets
    Measuring cups
    Scoops or large spoons
    Funnels
    Wooden tool set—short handle (shovel, rake, hoe)
    Small spades
    Sand box or boxes (preferably large—protected from sun)
    Sifting screens
    Collection of cars, boats, trucks, to stimulate dramatic play (3 to 5 each)

Kitchen Utensils
    Large wooden spoons
    Set plastic forks and spoons
    Plastic dustpan
    Rolling pins (wooden)
    Large spoons
    Mashers
    Strainers (large and small)
    Meat mallet
    Plastic measuring cups
    Jelly molds
    Sifters

Water Play
    Hose, with turn-off valve, permitting only a small stream of water (25′)
    A second hose (50′)
    Garden sprinkler
    Sprinkling cans (plastic)
    Water table
    Wide, not deep, plastic buckets
    Variety of objects that float
    Variety of bath toys—including squeeze toys
    Flutter ball (floats)
    Sand and water mill

Music and Rhythm (Larger, expensive items optional)
    Piano
    Music books for teacher
    Stereo portable record player (with rolling stand)
    Records for music appreciation, holidays, singing, rhythm, games, stories
    Storage cabinet
    Autoharp

Appendix D

Rhythm instruments:
  Triangles (2)
  Drum (1)
  Cymbal (1 pair)
  Wrist bells (2)
  Maracas (2)
  Sand blocks (4 pair)
  Tambourine (1)
  Sleigh bell (1)
  Rhythm sticks (1 pair per child)
  Castanets on wooden handle (2)
  Tom-tom (1)
Area rug
Cassette tape recorder (twelve cassette tapes)
Rhythm bells
Step bells
Melody bells
Music cabinet—built-in (Optional)

Art
  Large equipment:
    Double easels
    Rectangular tables
    Stack chairs (14″)
    Magnetic chalkboard (green)—portable
    Chalkboard combination—portable
    Sand table (indoor)
    Sand table (outdoor)
    Clayboards, hard surface tops
  Small equipment:
    Easel brushes
    Paste brushes
    Outdoor paintbrushes
    Medium water pail
    Spatter paint boxes
    Toothbrushes (spatter paint)
    Spatter ink (eight color pack)
    Pipe cleaners (200—assorted colors)
    Wooden beads, colored
    Flannel board and scraps
    Modeling clay
    Charcoal
    Regular dustless chalk
    Colored dustless chalk

Erasers
Crayons
Tempera powder, 6 colors
Paste
Butcher paper
Drawing paper
Newsprint
Construction paper
Sand box toys (small pots, pans, spoons, egg beaters, lids, etc.)
Scissors (blunt points)
Scissors rack
Scissors (adult size)
Waterproof aprons or smocks
Box assorted buttons
Pins, domestic
½″ cellophane tape
½″ masking tape
Thumbtacks (200 ct.)
Clothespins
Stapler
Staples
Hole punch
Pencil sharpener
Twine
Cellulose sponges
Sandpaper
Pencils, regular size
Pencils, large
Mixing bowls
Rectangular pan
Large mixing spoons
Flour
Salt
Wesson oil
Starch (Argo lump)
Soap flakes
Sawdust
Sand
Plastic straws
Small jars and plastic containers
Empty spools (assorted)
Paper towels
Ivory soap

Appendix D

Miscellaneous:
  1 Polaroid camera
  Corrugated paper (assorted)

Home-Family and Community
Kitchen (child size):
  Sink, stove (set of four)
  Refrigerator, cupboard
  Dress-up clothes (variety for role play)
  Table with two chairs
  Ironing board
  Iron
  Cookware set
  2 cutlery sets
  Wooden laundry set
  Broom and dustpan
  Washtub
  Clothesline and pins
  Telephone set
  Pegboard coded with hooks for hanging equipment
Bedroom:
  Child-size bed(s)
  Dresser
  Mirror—full-length floor model
  Dolls
  Doll clothes

Block and Large-Muscle
Gym step-platform slide
Triangle set
Punching bag
Trampoline
Rocking boat
Child rockers
Small wooden boxes nailed shut, painted (use cigar boxes)
Collection of assorted blocks, sanded and painted
Large wooden boxes for storage (apple boxes)
Dramatic play set (3 boxes, 3 boards, 3 steering wheels, 4 casters)
Storage shelves and/or shelf units
Hollow blocks, set of 6 each
Assorted blocks
Cart for above
Small transportation set
Large wooden transportation set:
  Trucks—wrecker, van, dump, plan transfer
  Bulldozer
  Boat
  Tractor and trailer
  Power shovel or derrick
  Hardwood train—riding size, floor train, child guidance railroad
  Gas station pumps

Language Activities
Sturdy, hard-covered picture books about transportation, animals, and everyday experiences of children
Simple wooden puzzles
Wooden capital letters
Shelves for books, or racks like those in public libraries
Racks to hold puzzles
Hand puppets (family, animals, story characters)
Finger puppets
Puppet stage (made of large box or crate)
Large attractive paintings hung at child's eye level
Table and chairs with chair pads, small rugs, or bean bag cushions to sit on
Flannel board and storytelling material

Science Activities
Table and/or low shelves to display plants and science activities
Magnifying glass (large)
Horseshoe magnets (large)
Large indoor thermometer
Large outdoor thermometer
Aquarium
Prisms
Ant farm
Trowel
Cultivator, small hand-type
Watering cans

Appendix D

Plant beds (low wooden boxes)—seeds and bulbs
Plastic refrigerator dishes
Hot plate
Animal cage for visiting pets
Measuring cups and spoons
Pouring utensils

Numerical and Quantitative Concepts
Scales
Measuring cups
Yardsticks
Time-learning kit
Rulers
Puzzles involving numbers
Felt numbers and shapes on felt board
Books which mention numbers of things
Wooden number and math symbols
Number sorter
Pegboards and accessories
Play money
Pint bottle
Quart bottle
Picture/number dominoes

Dramatic Play
Small Stage
Material (square yard of colorful fabric)
Wooden trucks
Wooden boats
Wooden train
Dolls
Family puppets
Doll house with accessories
Hats and handbags
Dress-up clothes
Lunch kits
Beauty shop supplies and equipment
Office area:
    Typewriter
    Adding machine
    Pens and pencils
    Paper and notebook
    Telephone
    Desk
    Swivel chair
    Wastebasket
Store area:
    Empty food cartons and containers
    Paper bags
    Play money
    Basket
    Cash register or adding machine
    Shelf or table for counter

Manipulative Activities
Puzzles
Nesting blocks
Pegboards and pegs
Bead stringing
Button stringing
Table blocks
Matching games
Play dough
Lacing cards
Lotto games
Paper
Pens and pencils
Slate
Chalk
Bingo games
Dominoes (picture, color, shape)
Art materials and supplies

Outdoor Equipment
Large wooden crates
Wooden crates, boxes
Wooden ladders with cleats
Lightweight planks with cleats
Push toys:
    Barrels
    Wheelbarrows
    Walker
    Tricycles (16" front wheels)
    Metal wagons with solid rubber tires
    Large wooden spools
Large inflated utility balls—6", 8½", punching bag
Low jungle gym (5' high)
Low slide of hardwood (6' high)

Appendix D

Sawhorses (pairs ranging from 12" to 24" in height)
Nail kegs
Swings with canvas seats (8' frame)—6 swings
Barrel with both ends out; screwed or nailed on platform
Rocking boats
Large train
Large fire engine
Large bus
Car body (stripped)
Boat—small (real)
Scooters
Footballs
Basketballs
Hoops
Stilts
Farm tractor and trailer
Large cardboard boxes to hide in, crawl through, etc.
Metal climbing gym

General Supplies

Cots or mats (for all-day program)
Locker units
Extra set of clothes for each child
First aid kit
Blankets
Flashlight

APPENDIX E
Suggested Resources for Equipment, Materials, and Supplies for a Children's Program

ABC School Supply Co.
  437 Armor Circle, N.E.
  Atlanta, Georgia 30324
American Desk Manufacturing Company
  Educational Materials and Equipment
  Division
  P. O. Box 429
  Temple, Texas 76501
American Guidance Service, Inc.
  Publisher's Building
  Circle Pines, Minnesota 55014
Beloved Toys, Inc.
  1601 Bellfountain
  Kansas City, Missouri 64127
Bernstein Max and Son
  906 Broadway
  Kansas City, Missouri 64105
Childcraft Education Corporation
  964 Third Avenue
  New York, New York 10022
Child Guidance
  1055 Bronx River Avenue
  Bronx, New York 10472
Constructive Playthings
  1040 East 85th Street
  Kansas City, Missouri 64131
Creative Playthings
  Princeton, New Jersey 08540
The Early Learning Division of General
  Learning Corporation
  Heffernan Supply Company
  926 Fredericksburg Road
  San Antonio, Texas 78201
Farha Toys and Hobbies
  4605 North Stiles
  Oklahoma City, Oklahoma 73105

Fischer-Price Toys
  East Aurora
  Erie County, New Jersey 14052
Helen Gallagher-Foster House
  P. O. Box 1711
  Peoria, Illinois 61601
Holbrook-Patterson, Inc.
  Coldwater, Michigan 49036
Hoover's
  Educational Equipment and Materials
  Division
  2930 Canton Street
  Dallas, Texas 75226
House of Lloyd, Inc.
  4417 East 119th Street
  Grandview, Missouri 64030
Kansas City Carnival Supply Company, Inc.
  820 Broadway
  Kansas City, Missouri 64105
Lyons
  430 Wrightwood Avenue
  Elmhurst, Illinois 60126
Maid of Scandinavia Company
  3245 Raleigh Avenue
  Minneapolis, Minnesota 55416
Maple Wood Products Company, Inc.
  Peabody, Massachusetts 01960
Mead Educational Services
  245 N. Highland Avenue, N.E.
  Atlanta, Georgia 30307
Mead Educational Services
  5522 Willowbend Boulevard
  Houston, Texas 77035
Miles Kimball Company
  41 West Eighth Avenue
  Oshkosh, Wisconsin 54901

Appendix E

Milton Bradley Company
　Springfield, Massachusetts 01101

Miracle Equipment Company
　Grinnell, Iowa 50112

Montessori Toys
　Division DAC Toy Makers
　15 Central Drive
　Farmingdale, New York 10010

Playskool
　3720 North Kedzie Avenue
　Chicago, Illinois 60618

Practical Drawing Company
　2205 Cockrell Avenue
　Dallas, Texas 75222

Rand-McNally Books
　P. O. Box 7600
　Chicago, Illinois 60680

Regional Curriculum Center
　CCM: Standard School, Inc.
　200 West First Street
　Austin, Texas 78701

Schwarz
　745 Fifth Avenue at 58th Street
　New York, New York 10022

Spencer Gifts
　360 Spencer Building
　Atlantic City, New Jersey 08404

Sunset House
　167 Sunset Building
　Beverly Hills, California 90213

Teacher Catalog
　Ideal School Supply Company
　Oak Lawn, Illinois 60453

Threshold Learning
　Heffernan Supply Company
　926 Fredericksburg Road
　San Antonio, Texas 78201

APPENDIX F
Recipes for Art and Manipulative Supplies

Cooked Play Dough

1 cup flour
½ cup salt
1 Tbsp. oil
1 tsp. cream of tartar
1 cup water
food coloring (desired amount)

Method: Mix together all ingredients. Cook mixture over low heat until thickened. Store in airtight container when not in use.

Note: This cooked play dough is a better quality than the uncooked play dough.

Uncooked Play Dough

1 cup flour
½ cup salt
1 tsp. oil
1 tsp. cream of tartar
Food coloring
Enough water to make dough good handling consistency

Method: Mix all ingredients except water. Add water slowly in small amounts until dough is easy to handle. Store in airtight container when not in use.

Note: Children enjoy helping make this type of play dough.

Finger Paint #1

1 cup liquid starch
6 cups lukewarm water
½ cup Ivory soap flakes

Method: Mix starch into the soap flakes. Add lukewarm water. Stir. Pour into small individual containers. Add pigment to each container of finger paint mixture.

Finger Paint #2

½ cup Linit Laundry Starch
1 cup cold water
1 quart water
1 cup soap flakes

Method: Dissolve starch into one cup of cold water. Add one quart of cold water to this mixture. Place over low heat. Cook until thick. Stir constantly. Remove from heat. Add soap flakes. Stir until well blended. Add tempera paint or food coloring to mixture. Let cool. Store in covered container.

Finger Paint Variations

1 cup of salt may be added to finger paint mixture, as children enjoy the different touch sensation.

1 cup sawdust may be added to above recipes, making a consistency of soft putty. This can be shaped, dried, and painted. Then shellac.

Wood Stain #1

Method: Mix 2 Tbsp. powder tempera paint with turpentine or liquid starch to make a thick paste. Add varnish until mixture is smooth.

Wood Stain #2

Method: Rub crayons with the grain of the wood. Then rub the wood vigorously with a cloth saturated in linseed oil.

Silly Puddy

Method: Mix equal parts of Elmer's glue and liquid starch for a few minutes until smooth. Do not cook. Store covered.

Oil Paint

Method: Add a few drops of glycerine and powder tempera to raw linseed oil to make a thick, creamy consistency.

Appendix F

Enamel Paint

Add clear shellac or varnish to the powder tempera paint until a desired brushing consistency is reached.

Goop Dough

1 cup cornstarch
2 cups salt
½ cup water
⅔ cup water

Method: Mix 2 cups salt and ⅔ cup water in a small pan and heat over low flame for 3 to 4 minutes. Remove from heat. Mix 1 cup of cornstarch and ½ cup of tap water. Blend well. Add cornstarch mixture *quickly* to the hot salt mixture, stirring constantly. This mixture should form a stiff dough. If it fails to thicken, return to heat. Stir constantly.

Mixture may be colored with tempera paint or food coloring. Stiff dough lends to modeling objects, which may be painted, dried, and coated with clear lacquer. Store mixture in air-tight container when not in use.

Note: Children enjoy goop dough for modeling objects to decorate the Christmas tree.

Homemade Paste

1 cup sugar
1 cup flour
1 tsp. alum
1 quart water
Oil of cloves

Method: Mix dry ingredients; add water. Cook until thick, stirring constantly. Cool. Add several drops of oil of cloves. Store in covered jars.

Flour Paste

½ cup flour
Water

Method: Add enough water to make a thin paste. Boil 5 minutes over a slow fire, stirring constantly. Cool and thin with water. Add a few drops of wintergreen or peppermint to keep it from spoiling. Keep in covered jar. Use in any projects requiring large quantities of paste.

Cornstarch Paste

2 Tbsp. cornstarch
Water

Method: Add enough cold water to make a smooth paste. Add boiling water until the mixture turns clear. Cook until it thickens, and remove from the fire. This paste becomes thicker as it cools. It may be thinned with water.

Use cornstarch paste on tissue paper or thin cloth, since it is less likely to show than flour paste.

Powder Paint #1

5 Tbsp. powder tempera paint
5 Tbsp. water

Method: Put powder paint and water in an empty milk carton. Press the lid down firmly and shake the carton until the paint is thoroughly mixed. To make the paint keep better and go on more smoothly, add enough liquid starch or detergent to make it the consistency of cream or of show-card colors.

Powder Paint #2

8 Tbsp. powder tempera paint
1 tsp. white library paste
2 Tbsp. liquid starch

Method: Add enough water to give the mixture a consistency of cream or of show-card colors. To prevent a sour smell, add a little oil of cloves, wintergreen, or peppermint.

Powder Paint Watercolors

Transparent watercolor: Add sufficient water to the powder paint to obtain a runny consistency.

Opaque watercolor: Add enough water or liquid starch to the powder paint to make a creamy consistency.

Mixing certain colors:

1. For bright powder paint, add a small amount of glycerine or evaporated milk to make the powder paint glossy.

Appendix F

2. Darker colors can be made by adding black, blue, brown, or purple.

3. With pastel colors start with white and gradually add more color until the desired tint is reached. This will save paint. For example, white with a small amount of red added will give a tint of pink.

4. Red, orange, and violet are difficult pigments to mix with water. A few drops of alcohol will speed the mixing.

Suggestion for mixing:

Buttermilk paint—use buttermilk instead of water when mixing powdered tempera paint. The result will be a chalklike effect which will not rub off.

APPENDIX G

Songs, Action Rhymes, and Finger Plays

If You're Happy

Sing to the tune of "She'll Be Comin' Round the Mountain When She Comes."
1) If you're happy and you know it, clap your hands;
2) If you're happy and you know it, clap your hands;
3) If you're happy and you know it,
4) Then you really ought to show it;
5) If you're happy and you know it, clap your hands.
(1), (2), (5) (clap, clap)
Variations:

Sitting

Open your mouth.
Raise your eyebrows.
Touch your ear.

Wink your eye.
Bow your head.
Wave good-bye.

Standing

Turn around.
Swing your leg.
Jump up high.

Squat down low.
Raise your knee.
Touch your toes.

Hands and Shoulders

Left, right, left, right a marching to and fro,
Left, right, left, right a marching we will go;
Left, right, left, right marching with a friend,
Left, right, left, right we stop and face our friend;
We shake hands with our right hand; our left stays at our side.
Left, right, left, right a marching to and fro,
Left, right, left, right a marching we will go.
(This is to be done in a line formation, each child with a partner.)

Miss Polly

Miss Polly had a dolly that was sick, sick, sick;
She called for the Doctor to come quick, quick, quick!
The Doctor came with his bag and his hat,
And he knocked on the door with a rat-atat-tat!

He looked at the dolly and he shook his head;
He said, "Miss Polly, put her straight to bed!"
He wrote on his pad for a pill, pill, pill,
And he said, "I'll be back tomorrow with my bill, bill, bill!"

Appendix G

Ironing Out the Wiggles

All may stand up straight and tall;
Don't touch anything at all;
Hands on hips, hands on knees,
Put them behind you, if you please;
Touch your ears, and now your toes;
Raise your arms high up in the air,
Down at your sides, now touch your hair;
Raise your hands, high as before;
Now you may clap, one, two, three, four;
Nod your head; stand up tall and thin;
Touch your ears, then your chin;
Now sit down, hands folded once more,
Eyes to the front, feet on the floor.

I Have Ten Little Fingers

I have ten little fingers, ten little toes,
Two little arms and one little nose,
One little mouth and two little ears,
Two little eyes, for smiles and tears.

Hands

My hands upon my head I place,
Upon my shoulders, upon my face;
At my waist and by my side,
And then behind me they will hide;
Then I raise them way up high,
And let my fingers swiftly fly;
Then clap, one, two, three,
And see how quiet they can be.

Me and My Body

My head nods;
My elbows bend;
My eyes move
For hours on end.

My waist twists;
My hands clap;
Or just stay still
Upon my lap.

My legs stretch;
My arms do, too;
I curl my toes
Inside my shoes.

What My Body Can Do

My hands can clap;
  (Clap three times.)
My feet can tap;
  (Tap feet three times.)
My eyes can brightly shine;
  (Blink eyes.)
My ears can hear;
  (Cup hand to ear.)
My nose can smell;
  (Sniff.)
My mouth can speak a rhyme.
  (Cup hands to mouth.)

Right Hand, Left Hand

This is my right hand;
I'll raise it high;
This is my left hand;
I'll touch the sky.

Right hand, left hand,
  (Extend them.)
Twirl them round;
Right hand, left hand,
Pound, pound, pound.

A Rest Exercise

Turn to the right and stand if you please;
Touch your elbows, and now your knees;
Touch both heels, now your nose;
Hands on your hips, and now on your toes;
Hands on shoulders, and on your shoes;
Turn to the left and read the news;
Hands on heads, also on hair;
Hands on hips, now in the air;
Touch your face, now your feet;
Clap your hands and take your seat.

Appendix G

See What I Can Do

These are my ears, and I have two;
These are my eyes, and I see you;
This is my chin, that moves to talk,
And I use my legs to take a walk;
See how I breathe through my nose;
I have to bend to touch my toes;
Shoulders and chest, arms and head,
And with all of them jump into bed!

Looby Loo

Form a circle; hold hands and walk while singing the chorus; do actions suggested by the words of the song in the verses.

CHORUS:
    Here we dance Looby Loo;
    Here we dance Looby Light;
    Here we dance Looby Loo;
    All on a Saturday night.

VERSES:
1. I put my right hand in,
   I take my right hand out,
   I give my right hand a shake, shake, shake,
   And turn myself about.

2. I put my left hand in, etc.
3. I put my right foot in, etc.
4. I put my left foot in, etc.
5. I put my head right in, etc.
6. I put my whole self in, etc.

Hands on Shoulders

Hands on shoulders, hands on knees,
Hands behind you if you please;
Touch your shoulders, now your nose,
Now your hair, and now your toes;
Hands up high in the air,
Down at your sides, and touch your hair;
Hands up high as before;
Now clap your hands,
One-two-three-four.

All About Me

Here are my ears, and here is my nose,
Here are my fingers, and here are my toes;
Here are my eyes, both open wide,
Here is my mouth with my white teeth inside;
And my busy tongue that helps me speak;
Here is my chin, and here are my cheeks,
Here are my hands that help me play,
And my feet that run about all day.
(Touch each part of the person as names
   are mentioned.)

We'll All Walk a Mile

Sing the following verse to the tune of "The Farmer in the Dell."

We'll all walk a mile; we'll all walk a mile;
We'll walk awhile and rest awhile;
We're *one* mile from home.

We'll all walk a mile; we'll all walk a mile;
We'll walk awhile and rest awhile;
We're *two* miles from home.

Repeat the above verse for about 5 or 6 times (miles) as the children walk around the room in a line formation. Reverse the line at then end of 5 or 6 miles and walk back, letting the children fill in how many miles are left to be walked. Continue until the last verse:

We'll all walk a mile; we'll all walk a mile;
We'll walk awhile and rest awhile;
We're all back home.

Relaxing

I'm just a rag doll, so limpety limp,
My body is made without bones;
My head, my arms, my legs, my feet,
Are heavy, as heavy as stones;
I'm just a rag doll, so limpety limp,
So limpety—limpety—limp.

What the Animals Do

We'll hop, hop, hop like a bunny,
And run, run, run like a dog;
We'll walk, walk, walk like an elephant,
And jump, jump, jump like a frog;
We'll swim, swim, swim like a goldfish,
And fly, fly, fly like a bird;
We'll sit right down and fold our hands, and say not a single word.
(Words suggest actions.)

Exercise Fun

Two little feet go tap, tap, tap,
Two little hands go clap, clap, clap;
A quick little leap up from the chair,
Two little arms reach high in the air;
Two little feet go jump, jump, jump,
Two little hands go thump, thump, thump;
One little body goes round and round,
One little child sits quietly down.

Reach high, touch the sky,
See the birds go flying by;
Bend low, touch your toes,
Wobble, as the old duck goes.

Teddy Bear

(Materials: jumping rope. If jumping rope is too difficult for the child, just lay the rope on the floor and let the child jump over it while he says the rhyme. Different parts of the body can be used instead of the knee.)

Teddy bear, teddy bear, turn around;
Teddy bear, teddy bear, touch the ground;
Teddy bear, teddy bear, touch your knee;
Teddy bear, teddy bear, run out for me.

I Am a Seed

I am a seed in the earth below;
(Crouch to the floor.)
Down comes the rain and makes me grow.
(Rise slowly.)

A Fence

A fence is tall;
(Raise arms.)
A fence is wide;
(Extend arms.)
It helps to keep
My pets inside.
(Hug body.)

Stretching

I stretch my arms out far and wide,
And whirl them 'round and 'round;
Then once more shake
My hands and feet,
And tumble to the ground.
(Words suggest actions.)

Hands and Feet

One little hand reaches out so wide,
One little hand is down by my side;
I bring my hands together to clap, clap, clap;
One and one are two hands now resting in my lap.

One little foot goes thump, thump, thump,
But one and one are two feet that jump, jump, jump;
One little body turns 'round and 'round;
Then one little me sits quietly down.

The Elephant

The elephant is so big;
He has no hands;
He has no toes;
But, oh my goodness,
What a nose!
(Use arms for elephant. Point to hands and toes. Make trunk with hands.)

Appendix G

My Family

This is my father;
   (Point to thumb.)
This is my mother;
   (Point to index finger.)
This is my brother tall;
   (Point to middle finger.)
This is my sister;
   (Point to ring finger.)
This is the baby;
   (Point to little finger.)
Oh! How we love them all!
   (Clasp hands.)

The Bunny

Here's a little bunny,
   (Hold up two fingers.)
Who hops so funny;
   (Two fingers in hopping motion.)
Here's his hole in the ground;
   (Make circle of thumb and first finger of opposite hand.)
When he hears a little noise,
He pricks up his ears,
And hops in the hole in the ground.
   (Two fingers disappear in circle.)

Little Green Frog

Aaaagung! went the little green frog one day,
Aaaagung! went the little green frog;
Aaaagung! went the little green frog one day,
And his eyes went a-a-a-a-a gung!!

Rainbow Song

Red and yellow and green and blue,
Purple and orange too;
I can sing a rainbow,
Sing a rainbow;
You can sing a rainbow, too!

Animal Fair

I went to the animal fair;
The birds and the bees were there;
The big baboon, by the light of the moon,
Was combing his auburn hair;
The monkey turned, *Kerplunk!*
And he climbed up the elephant's trunk;
The elephant sneezed!!
And fell to his knees,
And there goes the *monkedy monkedy monk.*

Three Fat Puppies

Three fat puppies were playing in the sun;
This one saw a rabbit and he began to run;
This one saw a kitten and he began to chase;
This one saw a butterfly and he began to race;
Three fat puppies chased their tails,
And they went round and round;
   (Roll hands.)
Three fat puppies went to sleep and never made a sound.
   (Palms together beside face.)

Six Little Ducks

Six little ducks that I once knew,
Fat ones, skinny ones, there were two.

Chorus:
But the one little duck
   with the feathers on his back,
He drew the others with a quack, quack, quack!

Rain

This is the sun, high up in the sky;
   (Raise arms to form sun.)
A dark cloud suddenly comes sailing by;
   (Hands move through air in parallel motion.)
These are the raindrops pitter-pattering down,
   (Bring arms down, shaking fingers.)
Watering the flowers growing in the ground.
   (Cup hands to form flower.)

Appendix G

Ball for Baby

Here's a ball for baby, big and soft and round;
   (Make a ball with both hands.)
Here is baby's hammer; Oh, how he can pound!
   (Make fists and pound together.)
Here's the baby's music, clapping, clapping, so;
Here are the baby's soldiers standing in a row;
   (Fingers upright as soldiers.)
Here's a big umbrella to keep the baby dry;
   (Forefinger of one hand in palm of other hand.)
Here's the baby's cradle, rock-a-by.
   (Rock arms as if holding baby.)

The Wheels on the Bus

The wheels on the bus go round and round,
Round and round, round and round;
The wheels on the bus go round and round,
All over town.

Variations:
1. The children on the bus wave to their friends.
2. The people on the bus go up and down.
3. The babies on the bus go wa-a, wa-a, wa-a.
4. The mommies on the bus go sh, sh, sh.
5. The daddies on the bus just read their paper.
6. The horn on the bus goes toot, toot, toot.

Houses

This is a nest for the bluebird;
   (Cup hands, palms up.)
This is a hive for the bee;
   (Fists together palm to palm.)
This is a hole for the bunny rabbit;
   (Fingers make a hole.)
And this is a house for me.
   (Fingertips together to make a peak.)

I Wish I Were

I wish I were a rabbit, a rabbit, a rabbit;
I wish I were a rabbit and I'd hop around;
I'd hop and hop; I'd hop and hop;
I wish I were a rabbit and I'd hop around.

Variation: Choose a fish to swim or
             a frog to leap.

Astronaut

Down by the launching pad
Early in the morning;
See all the rockets
Standing in a row;
See how the astronauts
Push all the buttons;
5, 4, 3, 2, 1, 0, Lift off!
There it goes! ! ! !

Helicopter Song

Tiptoe up, tiptoe down;
Start the motor and turn around;
Raise your arms to the sky;
Twist and turn for a helicopter ride.

Sleepy Kitten

The kitten stretches
   (Stretch.)
And makes herself long;
Then she makes a soft little purring song;
   (Purr.)
She yawns a big yawn,
   (Children yawn.)
And stretches some more,
   (Stretch.)
And then she falls fast asleep on the floor.
   (Children close eyes.)

APPENDIX H

Sample Recipes for Children's Food Experiences

MINI PIZZA

1. can of biscuits

2. open

3. flatten

4. pour on tomato sauce

5. sprinkle with cheese

6. heat

7. EAT!

Appendix H

HOT COCOA

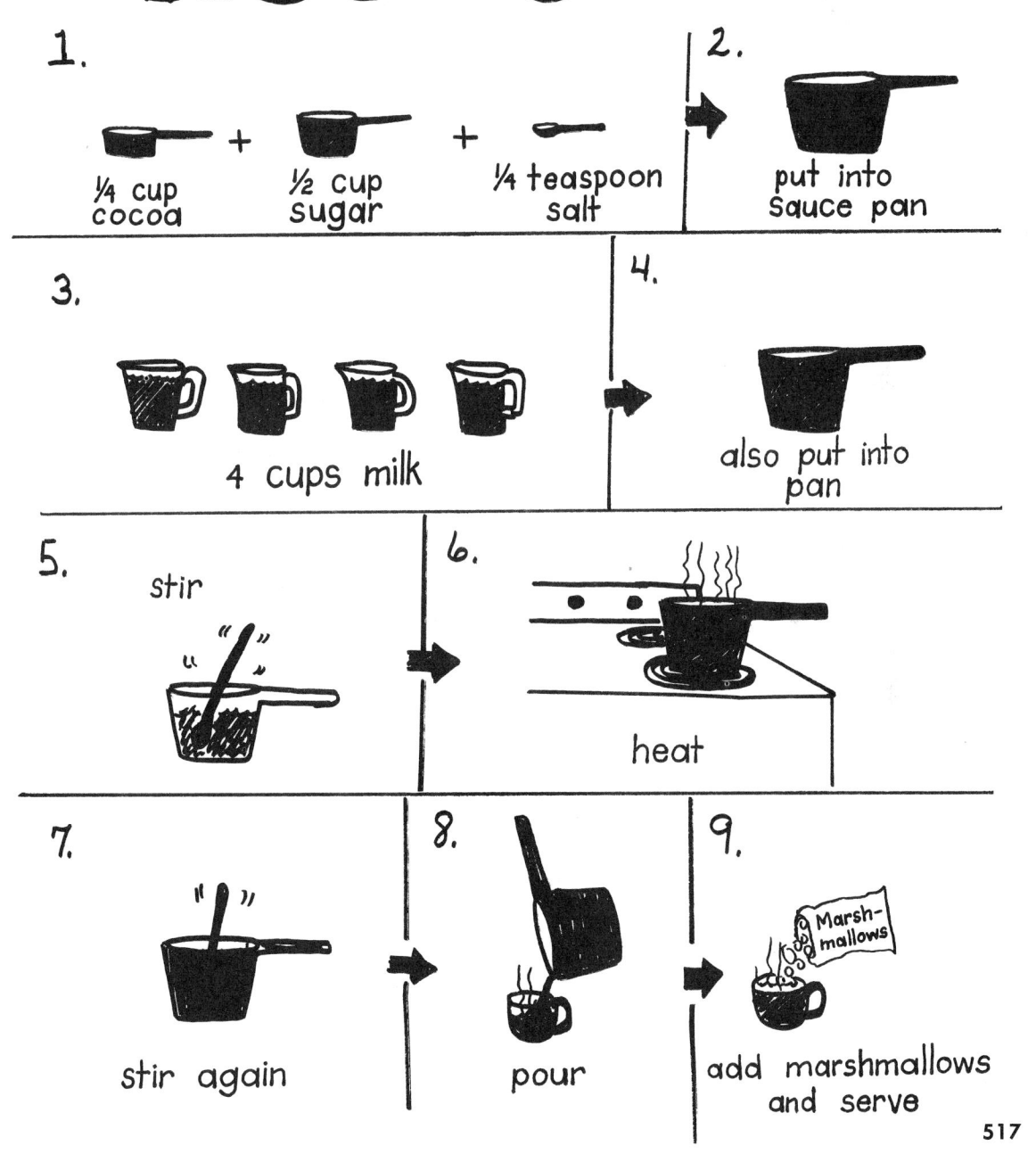

1. ¼ cup cocoa + ½ cup sugar + ¼ teaspoon salt
2. put into sauce pan
3. 4 cups milk
4. also put into pan
5. stir
6. heat
7. stir again
8. pour
9. add marshmallows and serve

517

Appendix H

LEMONADE

1. SUGAR ½ — LEMON JUICE ¼ cup

2.

3.

4. COLD WATER

5. ADD ICE — STIR

6. POUR AND SERVE

Appendix H

LEMONADE

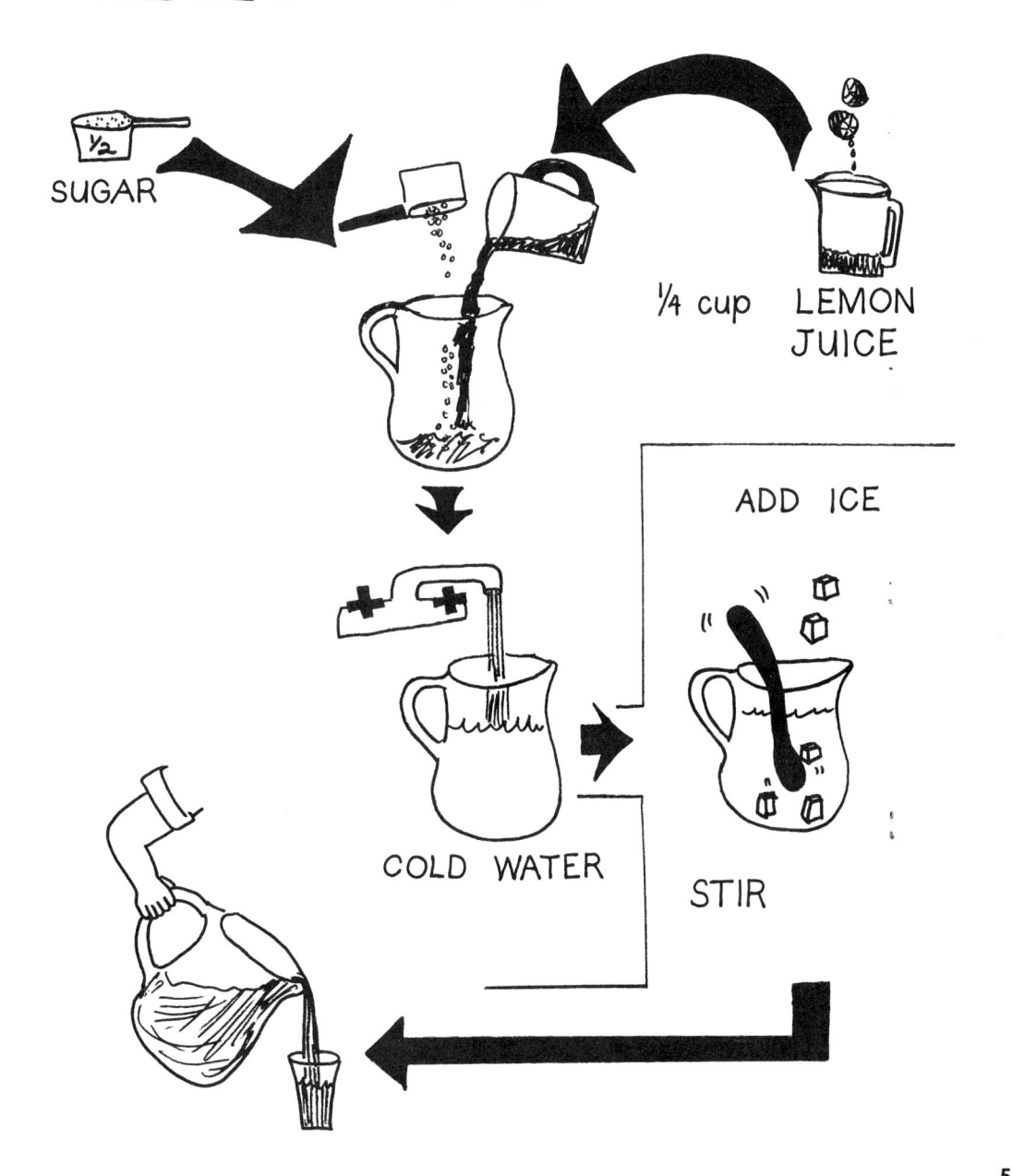

½ SUGAR

¼ cup LEMON JUICE

COLD WATER

ADD ICE

STIR

Appendix H

BUTTER

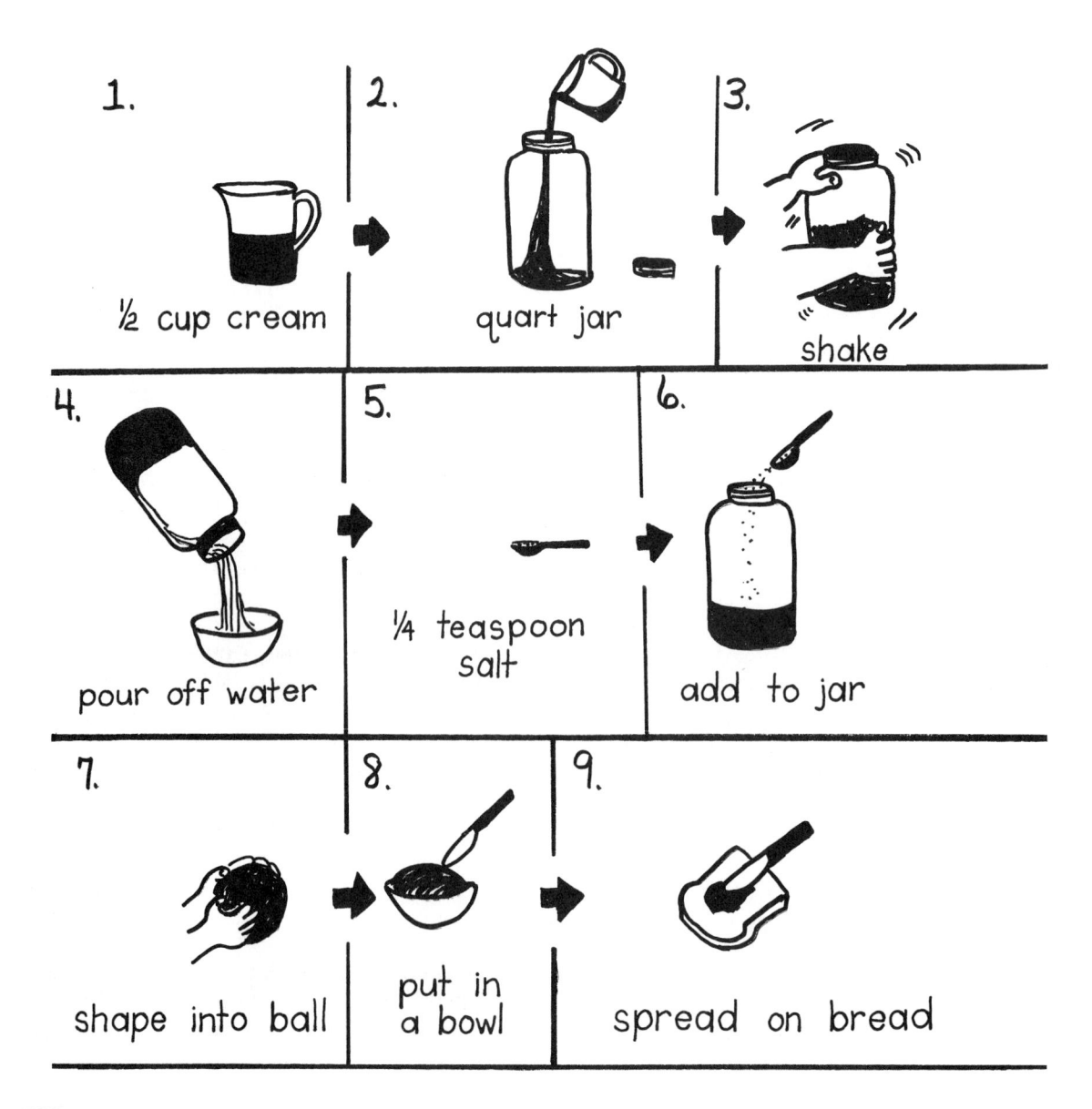

1. ½ cup cream
2. quart jar
3. shake
4. pour off water
5. ¼ teaspoon salt
6. add to jar
7. shape into ball
8. put in a bowl
9. spread on bread

APPENDIX I
Annotated Bibliography of Books for Children

A B C's

Alexander, Anne. *ABC of Cars and Trucks*. New York: Doubleday and Company, Inc., 1956. A favorite, especially with children who enjoy looking at the cars and trucks.

Bond, Susan. *Ride With Me, Through ABC*. New York: Scroll Press, Inc., 1968.

Duvoisin, Roger. *A For the Ark*. New York: Lothrop, Lee, and Shepard Company. Delightfully illustrated story of Noah as he goes through the alphabet to be sure he gets two of each kind of animal.

Ga-g, Wanda. *ABC Bunny*. New York: Coward-McCann, Inc. A simple ABC book giving a continuing story of a rabbit's adventures.

Lear, Edmond. *A Nonsense Alphabet*. Garden City, New York: Doubleday and Company, Inc., 1962. A read aloud book of delightful nonsense verse such as: "I was once an apple pie,
Pidy
Widy
Tidy
Nice insidsy,
Apple pie."

Munan, Bruno. *ABC*. New York: The World Publishing Company, 1960. Clear, bright, simple, and large illustrations.

Turlay, Clare Newberry. *The Kittens ABC*. New York: Harper and Row, Publishers, 1965. Reissue of a favorite large book with illustrations of kittens on each page.

Wildsmith, Brian. *Brian Wildsmith's ABC*. New York: Franklin Watts, Inc., 1962. Large, modern, colorful illustrations, each accompanied by a word in upper-case and lower-case letters.

ABOUT ME

Hall, Marie, Ets. *Just Me*. New York: The Viking Press, 1965. Illustrations were done by author. All done in black and white. Story of a small boy on a farm who imitates the farm animals. He imitates the mannerisms of all the animals. When he sees his father, he runs to him, running like nobody else at all—Just Me!

Hall, Marie, Ets. *Play With Me*. New York: The Viking Press, 1965. A story suitable for quiet times—tells about a little girl who gets her wish to have the woodland creatures come and play with her when she sits quietly.

Field, Rachel. *Prayer For a Child*. New York: Macmillan Company. Pictures by Elizabeth Orton Jones, possessing real warmth. Shows everyday things that children are familiar with. This prayer is for a small child. Thanks are given for familiar things, the love of family and friends, and the protection of God. Pictures show each thing the child is thankful for.

Flack, Marjorie, and Wiese, Kurt. *The Story About Ping*. New York: The Viking Press. An old favorite about a little duck who lives on a boat on the Yangtze River and his adventures when he hides from his master in order to avoid getting a spank on the back. Children identify easily with not wanting to get a spanking.

Freeman, Don. *Mop Top*. New York: The Viking Press. Cute story of Moppy, a little boy who goes to get a haircut. Good for self-concept.

Gipson, Morrell. *Hello, Peter*. New York: Doubleday and Company. About Peter who is two years old and the things he does everyday.

Green, Mary McBurney. *Is It Hard? Is It Easy?* New York: Young Scott Books, 1950. Silhouette-type photographs of children doing such things as skipping, tying shoes. Good for visual perception.

Joslin, Sesyle. *What Do You Say, Dear?* New York: William R. Scott, Inc., 1966. This is a book of manners for all occasions. Unique presentation.

Appendix I

Krasilovsky, Phyllis. *The Very Little Girl*. New York: Doubleday and Company, 1953. Self-concept story of little girl growing up.

Krasilovsky, Phyllis. *The Very Little Boy*. New York: Doubleday and Company, 1962. Self-concept story of a little boy growing up.

Perkins, Al. *Hand, Hand, Fingers, Thumb*. New York: Random House, 1969. Illustrated with cute monkey characters and written in verse. Good for body awareness for hand, fingers, and thumb.

Zolotow, Charlotte. *Sleepy Book*. New York: Lothrop, Lee, and Shepard Company, 1958. How everybody sleeps, even children. Illustrated in quiet, restful colors.

ANIMALS

Anderson, C. W. *Billy and Blaze*. New York: Macmillan Company, 1966. The story of Billy, who loves horses and on his birthday gets a beautiful pony.

Brown, Marcia. *Once a Mouse*. New York: Charles Scribner's Sons, 1961. Illustrations bring out the native setting of India. Story tells of a tiger's fall from grace and of a hermit who thought about big and small. The hermit changes his mouse into a tiger and back to a mouse.

Davis, Alice. *Timothy Turtle*. New York: Harcourt, Brace and World, Inc. Story of Timothy turtle who gets stuck in the mud and all the animals help him.

DeRegniers, Beatrice S. *May I Bring a Friend?* New York: Antheneum, 1965. Beautifully illustrated by Beni Montresor and recipient of the 1964 Caldecott Award for outstanding illustrations. A little boy brings an amazing series of his animal friends to call on the king and queen.

Elliott, Gilbert. *A Cat Story*. New York: Holt Publishing Company, 1963. This is literally a picture book (no text) about a mother cat and her four kittens who meet a mouse, bird, and a dog.

Flack, Marjorie. *Angus and the Cat*. New York: Doubleday and Company, Inc. Story of a Scottie puppy whose curiosity gets him in trouble.

Flack, Marjorie. *Ask Mr. Bear*. New York: Macmillan Company, 1966. Story of Danny, who asks the animals what to give his mother for her birthday.

Ga-g, Wanda. *Millions of Cats*. New York: Coward-McCann, Inc. A classic about an old man and woman who wanted a cat and got "millions and billions and trillions of cats."

Hader, Elmer and Berta. *Lost in the Zoo*. New York: Macmillan Company, 1959. This is the story of John Henry William and his adventure in the zoo with his sister Karen. Delightful adventure story.

Keats, Ezra Jack, and Cherr, Pat. *My Dog Is Lost!* New York: Thomas Y. Crowell Company, 1960. Jaunito, who speaks only Spanish, has just arrived in New York from Puerto Rico and is sad because he lost his dog. His search takes him to Park Avenue, Chinatown, and Harlem where he meets friends who help him find his dog. Some simple Spanish phrases are introduced.

Lipkind, William, and Mordivinoff, Nicolas. *Finders Keepers*. New York: Harcourt, Brace, and Company, 1951. The story of two dogs who argue over a bone until a big dog takes it from them. Then they retrieve the bone together and are friends.

McCloskey, Robert. *Make Way For Ducklings*. New York: The Viking Press, 1961. The story of a duck family in Boston and their adventures while moving through the busy streets of Boston. A kindly policeman makes their trip possible and safe.

Parsons, Virginia. *Homes*. New York: Garden City Books, 1958. Inexpensive and colorful book, showing various animals and their homes in full-page and double-page illustrations.

Petersham, Maud and Miska. *The Box with Red Wheels*. New York: Macmillan Company. This is a story of curious barnyard animals who peek into a baby's cart.

Slobodkin, Louis. *The Friendly Animals.* New York: The Vanguard Press. A picture book designed to promote better understanding of familiar animals of hoof and horn among their admirers. Includes the cat, dog, bear, duck, rabbit, pig, and others. Ages 2 to 3½.

Steiner, Charlotte. *A Surprise for Mrs. Bunny.* New York: Grosset and Dunlap (Wonder Books). It's Mrs. Bunny's birthday and all her little bunnies want to give her a surprise. The bunny who overslept finally has the biggest surprise of all.

Ward, Lynd. *The Biggest Bear.* Boston: Houghton Mifflin Company, 1952. Story of Johnny who went on a bear hunt and came home with a baby bear that grew into the "biggest bear."

CONCEPTS OF COLOR

Borten, Helen. *Do You See What I See?* London: Abelard Schuman, 1959. This colorful book introduces art concepts of shape, line, and color.

Bright, Robert. *I Like Red.* Garden City, New York: Doubleday and Company, 1955. This is the story of a little girl who did not like her hair because it was red. Good for color perception.

Brown, Margaret Wise. *Color Kittens.* New York: Simon and Schuster. How the kittens named Bruch and Hush learn to mix new colors.

Duvoisin, Roger. *The House of Four Seasons.* New York: Lothrop, Lee and Shepard Company, 1956. Brilliant book about color and a family who chose them all in painting their house. Introduction to color mixing.

Freeman, Don. *A Rainbow of My Own.* New York: The Viking Press, 1966. A child sees a rainbow and runs to catch it for his own. Good for color perception.

Hoffman, Beth Greiner. *Red Is For Apples.* New York: Random House, 1966. A book in rhyme calling attention to familiar objects and their colors.

Lionni, Leo. *Little Blue and Little Yellow.* New York: Astor-Honor, Inc., 1959. Torn paper illustrations showing how two colors can make a third. Good for adapting for use on the flannel board with cellophane or tissue paper mounted on flannel or sandpaper frames.

Martin, Janet. *Red and Blue.* New York: Platt and Munk. Beautifully illustrated story of colors.

O'Neill, Mary. *Hailstones and Halibut Bones.* New York: Doubleday and Company, Inc., 1961. A book of verses about color, sensitively illustrated by Leonard Weisgard.

CONCEPTS OF NUMBERS AND COUNTING

Berenstain, Stan and Jan. *Bears on Wheels.* New York: Random House, 1969. Counting book of 1 to 10. Tells about bears on wheels.

Elkin, Benjamin. *Six Foolish Fishermen.* New York: Children's Press, 1961. An amusing folk tale about six brothers who had trouble counting.

Friskey, Margaret. *Chicken Little, Count To Ten.* New York: Children's Press, 1964. In this counting book, a little chick accidentally finds the right way for him to drink water, but first he tries to follow the suggestions of other animals he meets.

McLeod, Emile. *One Snail and Me.* Boston: Little, Brown and Company, 1961. A good book to use with one child or small group, so children can look for the snail on each page.

Oxenbury, Helen. *Numbers of Things.* New York: Franklin Watts, Inc., 1968. The child can count the number of colorful illustrations on each page, such as two cars, four mice. Good for one child with adult. The illustrations encourage putting finger on each object while the child counts.

Seignobose, Francoise. *Jeanne-Marie Counts Her Sheep.* New York: Charles Scribner's Sons, 1957. A number book about a little girl and her pet sheep, Patapan.

Appendix I

Sendok, Maurice. *One Was Johnny*. New York: Harper and Row, 1962. A little counting book whose absurd rhymes will delight young children.

Slobodkin, Louis. *Millions and Millions and Millions!* New York: The Vanguard Press, 1955. Large, colorfully illustrated book calling attention to the fact that there are millions of stars and millions of cars, millions of other common things, but there is only one you and one me.

Steiner, Charlotte. *Ten In a Family*. New York: Alfred A. Knopf, 1960. This teaches adding and subtracting as well as counting from one to ten. Can be adapted for use with a flannel board.

Tudor, Tasha. *1 is One*. New York: Oxford Press, 1956. Tasha Tudor uses her soft pastel colors to illustrate a counting book in verse.

Ungerer, Tomi. *One, Two, Where's My Shoe?* New York: Harper and Row, 1964. The artist disguises drawings of all kinds of shoes in his illustrations and the child must go on a pictorial search through the pages. Good for use with one or two children.

Ungerer, Tomi. *Snail, Where Are You?* New York: Harper and Row, 1962. Same format as above except the snail is hidden in illustrations.

Wildsmith, Brian. *Brian Wildsmith's 1, 2, 3's*. New York: Franklin Watts, Inc., 1965. Numbers are illustrated with bright shapes, such as one colorful circle, five different size triangles, etc. The combinations of numbers, shapes, and forms may be confusing for the beginner.

Ziner, Feenie. *Counting Carnival*. New York: Coward, 1962. A counting book in verse about children includes two Negro children and an Oriental child.

CONCEPTS OF SHAPE

Atwood, Ann. *The Little Circle*. New York: Charles Scribner's Sons, 1967. This is the story of a little circle who becomes many circle-shaped objects. Good for visual perception, form constancy.

Budney, Blossom. *A Kiss is Round*. New York: Lothrop, Lee and Shepard Company, Inc., 1954. Colorful illustrations of common objects which are round—a ring, balloon, pie, doughnut, money, clock, etc.

Craig, M. Jean. *Boxes*. New York: W. W. Norton and Company, 1964. All shapes and sizes of boxes, what they are made of, their uses, and what you can do with them.

Feltser, Eleanor B. *The Sesame Street Book of Shapes*. New York: Time-Life Books, 1970. Photographs and illustrations developed from material provided by the Sesame Street series. Good for visual perception.

Hoban, Tana. *Shapes and Things*. New York: Macmillan Company, 1970. Common articles such as comb, brush, hammer. Letters in white on black background without words.

Lerner, Sharon. *Square is a Shape*. Minneapolis, Minnesota: Lerner Publications Company, 1970. Different shapes done in torn colored paper.

Marino, Dorothy. *Edward and the Boxes*. Philadelphia: J. B. Lippincott Company, 1957. Adventure with boxes.

Matthiesen, Thomas. *Things To See: A Child's World of Familiar Objects*. New York: Platt and Monk Company, 1966. Lovely color photography of familiar objects.

Schlein, Mariam. *Shapes*. New York: William R. Scott, Inc., 1952. Roundness, squareness, and lines are explored in this book about shapes.

Shapur, Fredun. *Round and Round and Square*. London: Abelard Schuman Limited, 1965. Circles and squares illustrated in primary colors showing how different shapes can be made from parts of the basic shapes. A square can be cut into triangles and parts of triangles, and circles can make houses, kites, etc.

EMOTIONS

Anglund, Joan Walsh. *A Friend is Someone Who Likes You*. New York: Harcourt, Brace and

Appendix I

World, Inc., 1958. This tells about feelings. The illustrations have Hummell-like figures and pictures. A good book to help develop feelings.

Anglund, Joan Walsh. *Love Is A Special Way of Feeling*. New York: Harcourt, Brace and World, Inc., 1960. This book beautifully defines love. The book is beautifully illustrated. Good for affective development.

Baker, Betty (Arnold Lobel, illustrator). *Little Runner*. New York: Harper and Row, 1962. Little Runner is envious of his older brother who is allowed to participate in the Iroquois New Year's ceremonies. Young children will be able to identify with his persistence in trying to convince his mother that he is not too young. He finally persuades her to give him a bowl of maple sugar.

Borack, Barbara. *Someone Small*. New York: Harper and Row, 1969. A child's daily experiences with a new baby in the house and with her bird that dies.

Felt, Sue. *Hello–Good-bye*. New York: Doubleday and Company, Inc., 1960. Candace and her baby sister have to move because their daddy has been transferred. Candace is unhappy about leaving. Illustrations show the routine of moving and how the girls make new friends after they move.

Flack, Marjorie. *Wait For William*. Boston: Houghton Mifflin Company. A little boy gets left behind by his older brother and sister on their way to see a circus parade because he had to stop to tie his shoe. Good for affective development.

Hittie, Kathryn. *Boy, Was I Mad!* New York: Parents' Magazine Press, 1969. A little boy is so mad he decides to run away from home, but he sees so many interesting things when he goes out that he forgets he is running away.

Hobart, Lois. *What Is a Whispery Secret?* New York: Parents' Magazine Press, 1968. A delicately illustrated book about quiet things like leaves whispering in the breeze and kittens and frogs making soft sounds, and holding someone close and whispering "I love you." A good lap book.

Hoban, Russell. *A Baby Sister For Frances*. New York: Harper and Row, 1964. This is one of several books about a badger named Frances. When a new baby comes to the house Frances is unhappy because she does not get enough attention.

Keats, Ezra Jack. *Peter's Chair*. New York: Harper and Row, 1967. Peter's old cradle, high chair, and crib are all painted pink for his new baby sister. He is so unhappy that he decides to take his little blue chair and run away from home.

Langstaff, Nancy. *A Tiny Baby For You*. New York: Harcourt, Brace and Company, 1955. A boy learns to accept a new baby in the house. Good photography by Suzanne Szasz.

Mayer, Mercer. *There's a Nightmare In My Closet*. New York: Dial Press, Inc., 1968. A child has nightmares about monsters in his closet until he finally decides to invite them into bed with him.

Schick, Eleanor. *Peggy's New Brother*. New York: Macmillan Company, 1970. Peggy tries to be helpful with her new baby brother, but everything she does goes wrong.

Schlein, Miriam. *Laurie's New Brother*. London: Abelard Schuman, 1961. Laurie is accustomed to having mommy and daddy all to herself, so she resents her new baby brother because he takes so much of their time. She gradually becomes adjusted to his presence.

Steptoe, John. *Stevie*. New York: Harper and Row, 1969. Robert, a black child, is jealous when his mother takes care of a younger child, Stevie, in their home. The text is written as if Robert is telling the story. He learns about his sensitive feelings for Stevie when his mother no longer has to baby-sit.

Viorst, Judith. *I'll Fix Anthony*. New York: Harper and Row, 1969. Younger children can relate to this humorously written story about little brother who is planning all kinds of revenge on big brother Anthony.

Appendix I

Books For Children About Death

Brown, Margaret Wise. *The Dead Bird.* New York: Scott Books, 1965. A simple story touchingly illustrated by Remy Charlip about some children who find a dead bird and bury it in the woods. The description of death is factual and handles the subject in a way that a child can understand and accept.

Freschet, Burneice. *The Old Bullfrog.* New York: Charles Scribner's Sons, 1968. A beautifully written book about the understanding of survival.

Harris, Audrey. *Why Did He Die?* Minneapolis, Minnesota: Lerner Publications Company, 1965. A mother's poem explaining to her child about the death of his friend's grandfather. Good for use with young children. Unusual because the story deals with the death of a human being.

Books For Children About Divorce

Goff, Beth. *Where Is Daddy?* Boston: Beacon Press, 1969. Very few stories are written for the preschooler about divorce. This one was written by a psychiatric social worker to help a child cope with the complexities and adjustments found by a family when a divorce occurs.

FAMILIES AND HOMES

Buckley, Helen E. *Grandfather and I.* New York: Lothrop, Lee, and Shepard Co., 1959. Appropriate for ages 3 to 6 because it talks about an everyday happening that every young child has experienced. Namely, a walk with grandfather. The child can identify with this.

Eastman, Philip. *Are You My Mother?* New York: Random House, 1960. A story about a baby bird looking for his mother. He asks everyone he meets, even an old car, "Are You My Mother?"

Felt, Sue. *Hello, Good-bye.* New York: Doubleday, 1960. This book pictures and tells about a five-member family's experience in moving, from the packing to the important making of new friends.

Green, Mary McBurney. *Everybody Has a House.* New York: Young Scott Books, 1954. About houses with a simple text. "The house of a mouse is a wee little hole."

McCloskey, Robert. *Blueberries For Sal.* New York: The Viking Press. Story of a little girl who goes out to pick blueberries with her mother, and a little bear who goes out to eat blueberries with his mother. The babies get mixed up to the surprise of both mothers.

Newman, Paul. *The Birthday Party.* New York: Grosset and Dunlap, 1954. Tom and Janey make a birthday surprise for their mother and even Father doesn't know about it. Also, a beginning reader.

Sauer, Julia L. *Mike's House.* New York: The Viking Press, 1954. A story of a four-year-old boy, Robert, and his dilemma as he gets lost on the way to the library.

Scott, Ann Herbert (Symeon Shimin, illustrator). *Sam.* New York: McGraw-Hill Book Company, 1967. Everyone in the family is too busy to pay any attention to Sam until he finally begins to cry. Then they find a job for him which is just right.

Sonneborn, Ruth A. *Friday Night Is Papa Night.* New York: The Viking Press, 1970. The tender story of a black family looking forward to having Papa come home on Friday night.

Wright, Ethel. *Saturday Walk.* Eau Claire, Wisconsin: E. M. Hale and Company, 1954. Story of a boy and his daddy who take a walk on a Saturday.

FARMS AND FARM ANIMALS

Brown, Margaret Wise. *The Little Farmer.* Eau Claire, Wisconsin: E. M. Hale and Company, 1958. Story of a big farmer and a little farmer who lived side by side. Everything on the big farm was big and everything on the little farm was little. When the farmers took a nap, the big farmer dreamed he was little and the little farmer that he was big. The printing is done to correspond with each, big and bold for the big farmer and little for the little farmer.

Tresselt, Alvin. *Wake Up Farm!* New York: Lothrop, Lee, and Shepard Co., Inc., 1955. Another day is beginning and one by one, the farm animals come back from the fields to sleep.

Williams, Garth. *Baby Farm Animals.* New York: Simon and Schuster, Inc. Baby farm animals play and frisk about in this enchantingly illustrated book.

HEALTH

Berger, Knute; Tidwell, Robert A.; and Haseltine, Margaret. *A Visit To the Doctor.* New York: Grosset and Dunlap, 1960. A detailed discussion about a child going to the doctor for a physical examination, with illustrations of the little boy getting his height, weight, temperature, and pulse recorded. The doctor listens to his chest with a stethoscope and he gets a booster injection. The text is factual and written for the young child, but there may be too many explanations for the three-year-old. Good to use as a basis for discussion.

Chase, Francine. *A Visit To the Hospital.* New York: Grosset and Dunlap, 1957. This is a well-written and accurately illustrated book about a boy who goes to the hospital to have his tonsils removed. A shorter version of the same book is published under the same title by Wonder Books, 1958.

Collier, James Lincoln. *Danny Goes To the Hospital.* New York: W. W. Norton and Company, Inc., 1970. Actual photographs of a little boy who goes to the hospital to have an operation to repair a damaged eye muscle. Pictures show different people and parts of the hospital as well as the things that happen to Danny.

Garn, Bernard J. *A Visit To the Dentist.* New York: Grosset and Dunlap, 1959. Illustrations and text of a little boy who goes to the dentist for a regular checkup. Many details and factual information. If this book is too wordy, the same publisher has a shorter version in its Wonder Book series (1959) under the same title and author.

Paulin, Ellen. *No More Tonsils!* Boston: Beacon Press, 1958. Good photography of a little girl going to the hospital to have her tonsils taken out.

Shay, Arthur. *What Happens When You Go To the Hospital.* Chicago; Reilly and Lee, 1969. Photographs of a black girl named Karen who goes to the hospital for two days to have her tonsils removed. Details show routine procedures of taking temperature, blood test, x-rays, etc., and finally the operating room and recovery.

Showers, Paul. *How Many Teeth?* New York: Thomas Y. Crowell Company, 1962. Well-written book on learning about the teeth and their care.

Tamburine, Jean. *I Think I will Go To the Hospital.* New York: Abingdon Press, 1965. Susy doesn't want to go to the hospital to have her tonsils out. She plays hospital with her pets and visits friends who have been hospitalized and soon realizes that the hospital is a good place to be when you are sick.

MOTOR DEVELOPMENT

Hall, Marie, Ets. *Just Me.* New York: The Viking Press, 1965. Story of a boy on a farm who imitates the farm animals. Good for children because it encourages movements.

Hall, Marie, Ets. *Talking Without Words.* New York: The Viking Press, 1968. Animals make their wishes known without words. Good for manual expression.

Woodcock, Louise. *This Is the Way the Animals Walk.* New York: William R. Scott Publishers. Pictures of various animals and how they walk. Suggestions are given on how children can imitate these walks.

MULTI-ETHNIC

Beim, Lorraine and Jerrold. *Two Is a Team.* New York: Harcourt, Brace and Company, 1954.

Appendix I

Two boys find they can work together. The illustrations show one a Negro and the other Caucasian. Printed in large 24-point type.

Hall, Marie, Ets. *Nine Days to Christmas*. New York: The Viking Press, 1960. Caldecott Medal Award winner in 1960. Story of Ceci who chooses a star pinata and stays up for her first posada.

Jaynes, Ruth. *Friends! Friends! Friends!* Glendale, California: Bowmar Publishing Corporation, 1967. This book of photographs is one of the Bowmar Early Childhood Series showing mixed racial groups. Check other titles in the series.

Liang, Yen. *Tommy and Dee-Dee*. New York: Henry Z. Walck, Inc., 1953. A simply written story illustrating how two boys living in different parts of the world are alike in many ways. Tommy is an American and Dee-Dee is Chinese.

Martin, William I., and Martin, Bernard H. *The Brave Little Indian*. Kansas City, Missouri: Tell-Well Press, 1951. A little Navajo is the brave little Indian who goes out to hunt a grizzly bear. Illustrations and caligraphy by Charlene Bisch.

Politi, Leo. *Rosa*. New York: Charles Scribner's Sons, 1963. Rosa is a little girl who lives in San Felipe, Mexico. Her wish for a doll comes true in a special way when a baby sister is born on Christmas eve. This book is also available in Spanish.

Politi, Leo. *Moy Moy*. New York: Charles Scribner's Sons, 1960. Authentic story of a little Chinese-American girl who celebrates Chinese New Year in Los Angeles. Includes some Chinese phrases.

Radlauer, Ed and Ruth. *Father Is Big*. Glendale, California: Bowmar Publishing Corporation, 1967. Close-up photographs by Harvey Mandlin show how a black child looks up to his father.

Robbins, Ruth. *Baboushka and the Three Kings*. Berkeley, California: Parnassus Publishing, 1960. Nicolas Sidjakov richly illustrated this 1961 Caldecott Medal Award winner. A Russian tale of Baboushka, the counterpart of our Santa Claus.

Showers, Paul. *Your Skin and Mine*. New York: Thomas Y. Crowell Company, 1965. This book shows three boys, Oriental, Negro, and Caucasian, examining and finding out about skin—how it protects you, different colors of skin, etc. This book is good for use with a small group of children in order to allow each one to share in the discussion. Illustrated by Paul Galdone.

MUSIC

Coleman, Satis N., and Thorn, Alice G. *Singing Time*. New York: John Day Company. Songs about everything children enjoy: boats, cars, animals, children, Christmas, and other holidays.

Coleman, Satis N., and Thorn, Alice G. *Another Singing Time*. New York: John Day Company. More songs like those in *Singing Time*.

Coleman, Satis N., and Thorn, Alice G. *The Little Singing Time*. New York: John Day Company. Short, simple songs of one sentence or more for two-year-olds. Attractively illustrated.

Hunt, Evelyn. *Music Time*. New York: The Viking Press. A collection of action songs for nursery, kindergarten, and primary children.

Landeck, Beatrice. *More Songs to Grow On*. New York: William Sloane Associates, 1954. Contains some of the simpler and more childlike folk songs in classified form.

McCall, Adeline. *This Is Music For Kindergarten and Nursery School*. Belmont, California: Allyn and Bacon, 1966. A well-organized collection of music and songs for activities—holidays, seasons, etc.

Seeger, Ruth Crawford. *American Folk Songs For Children*. New York: Doubleday Doran. A charming collection of American folk songs suitable for children of all ages. The kinds of songs that children like to sing over and over again.

Appendix I

Suggested Phonograph Records

A good resource for children's records and musical instruments is Children's Music Center, 5373 West Pico Boulevard, Los Angeles, California 90010. Catalog on request.

Bowmar Records
BOL53—*Pictures and Patterns*
CL7—*Imagination and Insight*
B118—*Songs For Children With Special Needs, Album No. 1*

Children's Record Guild
1001—*Train to the Zoo*
1011—*Train to the Farm*
1018—*Daddy Comes Home*

Columbia
MJV-1—*Animal Fair*

Decca
16322—*Mother Goose Sleepytime Songs*
87995—*Charity Bailey Sings*
88103—*French Folk Songs for Children*

Educational Series—Phoebe James
1. Combined Free Rhythms
2. Animal Rhythms
3. Drum Beats

Folkcraft
1192—*Skip To My Lou, etc.*

Folkway
FC7054—*Children's Songs and Games*

High Fidelity Recording
Cal 1003—*Lullabies For Sleepy Heads*
  Shirele—*Israel Folk Songs*, Imane Foundation, New York

Kay Ortman Productions
Basic Rhythms

Musical Sound Books
MSB78303—*Soldier's March, The Wild Rider,* and others
MSB78037—*The Snow Is Dancing* and others
MSB78311—*Country Gardens, Greensleeves,* and others
MSB78312—*Lullaby (Brahms)* and others
MSB78202—*Dear Dance* and others
MSB78110—*Hungarian Dance*
MSB78115—*Cielito Lindo, La Golondrina*

RCA Victor
45-6180—*Pop Goes The Weasel*
LM1761—*Carnival of The Animals, Peter and The Wolf*

Rhythms Productions
A102—*Activity Songs,* Marcia Berman

Young People's Record Series
603—*Muffin In The Country*
615—*The Little Fireman*
620—*Little Indian Drum*
711—*Building a City*
716—*The Little Cowboy*
725—*When I Grow Up*
737—*The Men Who Came To Our House*
805—*Little Old Car*
804—*A Walk In the Forest*
10012—*My Playful Scarf* and others

NATURE AND SCIENCE

Bendick, Jeanne. *All Around You.* New York: McGraw-Hill Book Company. A science book that answers how and why questions about the sun, wind, rain, and others.

Braniey, Franklyn M., and Vaughn, Eleanor. *Mickey's Magnet.* New York: Thomas Y. Crowell Company, 1956. Mickey gets help and a lesson in magnetism when his father shows him how to pick up the pins he has spilled.

Downer, Mary. *The Flower.* New York: Young Scott Publishing Company, 1955. Tells the beautiful cycle of seed to flower to seed again.

Appendix I

Green, Mary McBurney. *Everybody Eats.* New York: William R. Scott, Inc., 1961. An "early science concept book" describing the foods that different animals eat.

Huntington, Harriet. *Let's Go Outdoors.* New York: Doubleday and Company. About little creatures who live outdoors. Excellent photographs and text about common things like snails, spiders, and ladybugs.

Krauss, Ruth. *Carrot Seed.* New York: Harper and Row, Publishers. A little boy plants a carrot seed and it does come up, to his family's surprise.

Lionni, Leo. *Inch By Inch.* Stanford, Connecticut: Astor Books, 1960. In this beautifully illustrated book, we follow an inch worm who is demonstrating his usefulness in measurement, and thus saves his life from a hungry robin.

Schwartz, Julius. *Through the Magnifying Glass.* New York: McGraw-Hill Book Company, 1954. This book, illustrated by Jeanne Bendick, opens a new world through the use of a magnifying glass.

Stevens, Carla. *Catch a Cricket.* New York: Young Scott Books. Excellent photographs by Martin Ingar.

Udry, Janice May. *A Tree Is Nice.* New York: Harper and Brothers, 1956. The story of how nice trees can be. Good nature book.

Webber, Irma. *Up Above and Down Below.* New York: William R. Scott, Inc., 1953. Gives simple introduction to plants above and below the earth.

Yashima, Taro. *Umbrella.* New York: The Viking Press, 1958. Sweet story of a little girl's expectations and excitement as she looks forward to the rain because she has a new umbrella.

Zion, Gene. *All Falling Down.* New York: Harper and Brothers. Pictures and text tell of leaves, nuts, flower petals, rain—all falling down.

SEASONS AND HOLIDAY STORIES

Keats, Ezra Jack. *The Snowy Day.* New York: The Viking Press, 1962. Cute story of little Peter who loves to play in the snow and decides to save a snowball in his pocket.

Geisel, Theodor (Dr. Seuss). *How The Grinch Stole Christmas.* New York: Random House, 1957. The story of the Grinch's attempt to stop Christmas. Seasonal.

Tresselt, Alvin. *White Snow, Bright Snow.* New York: Lothrop, Lee, and Shepard Company. Story of what happens to the postman, policeman, farmer, and children when the snow falls. Tells what our community helpers do when it snows, and what children can do in the snow.

SENSORY

Aliki. *My Five Senses.* New York: Thomas Y. Crowell Company, 1962. Discovering through sound, smell, sight, and touch.

Aliki. *My Hands.* New York: Thomas Y. Crowell Company, 1962. This gaily illustrated book explores the use of hands and fingers in touching, work, and play.

Borten, Helen. *Do You Hear What I Hear?* London: Abelard-Schuman, 1960. A book that focuses on sound. Varied art techniques illustrate the material.

Brown, Margaret Wise. *Country Noisy Book.* New York: Harper and Row. In this book illustrated by Leonard Weisgard, little Muffin hears noises of the country such as the sounds made by different farm animals.

Brown, Margaret Wise. *Indoor Noisy Book.* New York: Harper and Row. A little black dog named Muffin hears the sounds which are usually heard in the home, such as the telephone, a fly, etc.

Brown, Margaret Wise. *Seashore Noisy Book.* New York: Harper and Row. A terrier called Muffin hears the sounds at the seashore.

Brown, Margaret Wise. *The Noisy Book.* New York: Harper and Row. The story is about the noises that a little dog named Muffin hears as he walks about the city. Good for association and sequencing.

Brown, Margaret Wise. *Shh, Bang*. New York: Harper and Row. Story of a little boy who came to a town where everyone whispers. Written for spoken and whispered voice indicated by size of print.

Brown, Margaret Wise. *The Summer Noisy Book*. New York: Harper and Row, 1951. Story about Muffin, a little dog, who hears many noises as he sleeps in the backseat of a car: birds, cow bells, frogs, kittens, sheep, and at the end, a summer storm. Good for children to try to recognize the sounds.

Clure, Beth, and Rumsey, Helen. *How Does It Feel?* Glendale, California: Bowmar Publishing Company, 1968. Visual, auditory, and tactile sensory development are achieved through the skillful use of this book.

Gibson, Myra Tomback. *What Is Your Favorite Smell, My Dear?* New York: Grosset and Dunlap, 1964. A book of rhymes and colored pictures recalling favorite smells.

Gibson, Myra Tomback. *What Is Your Favorite Thing to Touch?* New York: Grosset and Dunlap, 1965. Familiar things like water and marshmallows are explored through the sense of touch, in rhyme.

Keats, Ezra Jack. *Whistle For Willie*. New York: The Viking Press, 1966. This is a story about a little boy who wants to learn how to whistle.

Klein, Leonore. *Can You Guess?* New York: Grosset and Dunlap (Wonder Books), 1953. A little book about touching and feeling common things around us.

Lowery, Lawrence F. *Sounds Are High, Sounds Are Low*. New York: Holt, Rinehart and Winston, Inc., 1969. Sounds can be very different, and this rhyming book calls attention to sounds that are familiar to the young child. Good for rhyming and verbal concept development.

Seuss, Dr. *Mr. Brown Can Moo! Can You?* New York: Random House, 1970. A book of wonderful noises like: Moo Moo, Pop Pop, Eek Eek, Splatt Splatt. Good sensory story.

Showers, Paul. *Find Out By Touching*. New York: Thomas Y. Crowell Company, 1961. "Your fingers tell you the right answer." A beginning science book with simple text.

Showers, Paul. *Follow Your Nose*. New York: Thomas Y. Crowell Company, 1963. A book about smells and the information they give us.

Showers, Paul. *The Listening Walk*. New York: Thomas Y. Crowell Company, 1961. Things to hear on a walk and the need to listen so they may be heard.

Tinkleman, Murray. *Who Says Hoo?* New York: Golden Press, 1963. Animal sounds are introduced and children answer the questions asked about the various sounds on each page.

Witte, Pat and Eve. *The Touch Me Book*. New York: Golden Press, 1961. A little book which children will enjoy touching.

SOCIALIZATION

Bemelmans, Ludwig. *Madeline*. New York: The Viking Press. This is the story of twelve little girls living in a French boarding school. Madeline has to have her appendix removed. This story is written in rhythmetical form. It emphasizes that the attention given one child was wanted by the others also.

Bryant, Bernice. *Let's Be Friends!* Chicago: Children's Press, 1954. This is the story of Butch and his first day at kindergarten.

SPECIAL LANGUAGE DEVELOPMENT

Clure, Beth, and Rumsey, Helen. *A Cowboy Can*. Glendale, California: Bowmar Publishing Company, 1969. The authors develop the verbal concepts of in-out, on-off, over-under, up-down, and come-go in this well-illustrated book.

Geisel, Theodor (Dr. Seuss). *Horton Hatches The Egg*. New York: Random House. This book is about Horton, the faithful elephant. Good for listening and the development of rhyming skills.

Geisel, Theodor (Dr. Seuss). *One Fish, Two Fish, Red Fish, Blue Fish*. New York: Random House,

Appendix I

1960. A book of rhymes with ending words that children will easily supply.

Milne, A. A. *Now We Are Six*. New York: E. P. Dutton and Company, Inc., 1955. Poetry. Good for rhyming.

TRANSPORTATION AND TRAVEL

Gramatky, Hardie. *Little Toot*. Eau Claire, Wisconsin: E. M. Hale and Company. The story of Little Toot, a tugboat, who lived on a busy river. Appealing to children who love transportation stories.

Green, Graham. *The Little Red Fire Engine*. New York: Lothrop, Lee, and Shepard Company. The adventures of Old Sam Trolley, the one-time sailor, and his remarkable fire engine in the town of Little Snoring.

Kessler, Leonard and Ethel. *Big Red Bus*. Garden City, New York: Doubleday and Company, 1957. This story is the sensation of a bus ride.

Lenski, Lois. *The Little Auto*. New York: Oxford University Press. Tells the details of Mr. Small's ride in his auto from the time he gets it ready for driving, through traffic, and back to his garage.

Lenski, Lois. *The Little Train*. New York: Oxford University Press. A little book about Engineer Small and his train with vocabulary about trains, stations, and railway workers.

Schlein, Miriam. *How Do You Travel?* New York: Abingdon Press, 1954. Story of fascinating ways to travel; has action and humor.

WATER AND SAND

Foster, Joanna. *Pete's Puddle*. Boston: Houghton Mifflin Company, 1950. The story of a boy named Pete who experiences many creative ideas when he finds a puddle all his own to play in. Walks in it, sees his face in it, makes mudpies, builds a dam. Suggests creative experiences and sensory pleasures.

Martin, Dick. *The Sand Pail Book*. New York: Golden Press, 1964. Colorful illustrations of varied kinds of containers may be used to begin discussion on putting things in provided areas.

Myrus, Donald, and Squillace, Albert. *Story In the Sand*. New York: Macmillan Company, 1963. Aesthetic photographs of beach and sand.

THE WORLD ABOUT LIFE AND US

Burton, Virginia Lee. *The Little House*. Boston: Houghton Mifflin Company, 1955. The story is about a little house that watches the countryside turn into a city. Children will enjoy this book because they will associate with the little house in their desire to explore and see something new.

Keats, Ezra Jack. *Goggles!* Toronto: Macmillan Company, Collier-Macmillan Canada, Ltd., 1969. Two black children find a pair of motorcycle goggles but have to outsmart a gang of "big guys" in order to keep them. The author is well known for his excellent stories and illustrations.

Kessler, Ethel and Leonard. *Crunch, Crunch*. New York: Doubleday, 1955. A story of a little boy's trip to a supermarket with his mother.

Lenski, Lois. *Policeman Small*. New York: Walck, 1962. Little picture book story about Policeman Small and his duties as a community helper.

Moncure, Jane Belk. *Pinney's Day At Playschool*. New York: Lothrop, Lee and Shepard, 1955. Photographs picture the activities that make up a day in the nursery school.

Schneider, Nina. *While Susie Sleeps*. New York: William R. Scott, Inc. This is a picture book of what goes on at home, in the garden, field, and town while Susie sleeps.

Scott, Ann Herbert. *Big Cowboy Western*. New York: Lothrop, Lee and Shepard, 1965. Warm story of Martin and his family who live in an urban housing development. A Negro family is pictured.

Witte, Pat and Eve. *Who Lives Here?* New York: Golden Press, 1961. Lift the flaps on each page to find out who lives here.

APPENDIX J

Suggested Pamphlets for Child Care Workers and Parents

National Association for the Education of Young Children
1629 21st Street, N.W., Washington, D.C. 20009
Catalog of listings on request

Do Nursery School Children Have More Colds? Isabelle Diehl.
Do They Need to Be Bored in Kindergarten? Sister Mary de Lourdes.
The Essentials of Nursery Education.
How Can Nursery School Be Expected to Benefit a Child? Barbara Biber.
Let's Play Outdoors. Katherine Read.
Living Music with Children. Mary Barrett.
Teaching the Disadvantaged Young Child. Compilation of selected articles.
What Does the Nursery School Teacher Teach? Elizabeth Doak Tarnay.
Why Have Nursery Schools? James L. Hymes, Jr.
NAEYC publishes the periodical *Young Children* bi-monthly.

Association for Childhood Education International
3615 Wisconsin Avenue, N.W. Washington, D.C. 20016

All Children Have Gifts.
Children's View of Themsleves.
Nursery School Portfolio. Helpful to teachers and students.
Readings from Childhood Education—Articles of Lasting Value, 1966. $3.75.

Public Affairs Pamphlets
381 Park Avenue South New York: 10016

Building Your Marriage. Evelyn Millis Duval.
Enjoy Your Child: Ages 1, 2, and 3. James L. Hymes, Jr.
How to Be a Good Mother-in-Law and Grandmother. Edith G. Neisser.
How to Tell Your Child about Sex. James L. Hymes, Jr.
Making the Grade as a Dad. Walter and Edith Neisser.
The Modern Mother's Dilemma. Sidonie M. Gruenberg and Hild S. Krech.
Three to Six: Your Child Starts to School. James L. Hymes, Jr.
When You Lose a Loved One. Ernest Osborne.
You and Your Adopted Child. Eda Le Shan.
Your Child's Emotional Health. Anna M. Wolf.
Your Child's Safety. Harry F. Dietrich, M.D., and Sidonie M. Gruenberg.

Child Study Association
9 East 89th Street New York 10028

Aggressiveness in Children. Edith Lesser Atkin and Child Study Assoc. Staff.
How to Protect Children Against Prejudice. Kenneth B. Clark.
When Children Need Special Help with Emotional Problems. Greta Mayer and Mary Hoover.
You Don't Have to Be Perfect (even if you are a parent). Jean Schick Grossman.

Better Living Booklets Science Research Association
259 East Erie Street Chicago, Illinois

Building Self-Confidence in Children. Nina Ridenour.

Appendix J

Developing Responsibility in Children. Constance J. Foster.
Helping Brothers and Sisters Get Along. Helen W. Puner.
Self-Understanding. William C. Menninger, M.D.
When Children Face Crises. George J. Mohr, M.D.
Why Children Misbehave. Charles W. Leonard.

Other Pamphlets

A Healthy Personality for Your Child (No. 337). Government Printing Office, Washington, D.C.
Being a Good Parent. James L. Hymes, Jr. Teachers College, Columbia University.
Brief Encounters in Family Living. Jean Schick Grossman. The Play Schools Association, New York.
Discipline. James L. Hymes, Jr. Teachers College, Columbia University.
Packets for Parents. Bank Street College of Education, 69 Bank Street, New York. Fifteen leaflets on subjects that are of concern to all parents.
Primer for Parents. Anti-Defamation League, Madison Avenue, New York.
Some Special Problems of Children, Aged 2–5. Nina Ridenour, Ph.D., and Isabel Johnson. National Association for Mental Health, 1790 Broadway, New York. Includes: When a Child Hurts Other Children, When a Child is Destructive, When a Child Uses Bad Language, When a Child Won't Share, When a Child Still Sucks His Thumb, When a Child Wets, and When a Child Has Fears.
Understanding Children's Behavior. Fritz Redl. Teachers College, Columbia University.
Values in Early Childhood Education. Evangeline Burgess. National Education Association, 1201 Sixteenth Street, N.W., Washington, D.C. 20036.

APPENDIX K

Themes for Young Children's Activities and Samples of Ways to Develop Them

NOTE: Children should have as many firsthand experiences as possible with real objects. Children need to be actively involved in exploring and experimenting with items in each theme area.

- **Animals**

    Name, talk about, and illustrate ten adult and five young animals.

    Name five male and five female animals.

    Name and classify coverings of various animals: shell, fur, scales, wool.

    Differentiate between animals: wild, circus, and farm animals; verbalize how these animals are alike and how they are different in color, sound, and shape.

    Identify animals from pictures of footprints: claws, hooves, paws, etc.

- **Birds**

    Name and illustrate various birds: humming bird, eagle, crow, flamingo, etc.

    Talk about the colors of birds and differences in colors.

    Imitate sounds of various birds.

    Discuss differences in nests: in water, on land, in trees, etc.

    Explain how they help man: sounds, eating insects, beauty.

    Use pictures of different kinds of eggs they lay: size, color, etc.

    Describe similarities and differences in birds.

- **Growing Things**

    Name and identify common plants: flowers, trees, bushes, vines.

    Describe differences in where plants grow such as: stones, sand, water, soil, air.

    Note differences in flowers: some are large, some are small, some yellow, some blue.

    Name and illustrate fruit grown on trees; vines (watermelon); plants (strawberries).

    Discuss what grows on top of soil and what grows down in the soil (tubers and bulbs).

- **Sizes and Shapes**

    Identify straight lines, curves, and corners.

    Name shapes: circle, square, triangle, trapezoid, rectangle, oval, diamond.

    Identify shapes of objects in rooms in our daily lives.

    Experiment with how one shape can make another; 2 triangles make a square, etc.; reproduce shapes with string or with toothpicks in fingerpaint; model shapes with clay; draw shapes with crayons.

    Play with shapes of various colors and textures such as felt, sandpaper, wood, plastic, and cloth.

- **Color**

    Match colors. (Can you find a color the same as this red?)

    Select a designated color from a group of other colors. (Can you find red?)

    Identify color when it is held up. Verbalize: "That's red."

    Classify two or more colors.

    Discuss uses of colors: red for stop; green for go.

- **Health and Cleanliness**

    Demonstrate and describe how we clean various parts of our bodies (ears, hands, face, etc.).

Appendix K

Name and illustrate the professional people who help us: dentists, manicurists, pedicurists, hair stylists, etc.

Name and illustrate reasons for keeping clean: we smell good, look good, and feel well.

Verbalize how persons can be helped by picking up clothes and putting clothes away after bathing.

- **Insects and Reptiles**

Name and illustrate different kinds of insects.

Describe how they mature: caterpillar to moth; egg to tadpole to frog.

Discuss how they are alike; how different.

Talk about how they help us (make honey, fabric, food, help plants grow, clean our ponds).

Describe what they do to protect themselves (hide in shell, sting).

- **Clothing—Pattern—Design**

Name five garments: pants, shirt, coat, skirt, blouse, dress.

Picture seasons for wearing certain garments: swimsuit in summer; coat and gloves in winter.

Demonstrate sequence for dressing one's self; socks then shoes.

Talk about clothing children are wearing (color, lines, fabric, etc.).

Demonstrate use of clothing (warmth, movement, protection, beauty).

- **Materials**

Identify different building materials visually and tactilly: brick, wood, fiberglass, cement, steel, metal, paper.

Describe textures: wet—dry; hard—soft; rough—smooth; etc.

Classify paper, wood, glass, cloth, leather, rubber, foil, wire.

For language development describe how materials are different and alike by naming properties such as texture, color, shape, size.

- **Science**

Identify and use magnets.

Name, manipulate, and demonstrate appropriately: measuring tape, ruler, yardstick, cupfuls, filling a pan, spoonfuls, filling one cup.

Describe how heat changes things (cooking, drying, melting).

Describe and experiment with shadows, silhouettes, and their relation to light.

Review and demonstrate liquids, solids, gases.

Measure and pour substances such as water, cornmeal, flour, sand, sawdust.

- **Families**

Name immediate family members: mother, father, sister and name, brother and name, baby and name.

Name where they live—near or far.

Describe what family activities may be done together: sleep, eat, wash clothes, wash dishes, take trips, play, work.

Describe different jobs and responsibilities of family members: mowing lawn; cooking; making beds; emptying trash. What is child's job? How do they help?

Identify family names and addresses and phone numbers.

- **Homes**

Child will describe where he or she lives, town or city and street; mother's and dad's names; what their house looks like—inside and out.

Name the rooms in the house.

Name the furniture in different rooms.

Tell who lives in the house.

Identify address and phone number.

Name different kinds of homes: apartments, one floor, two floors, mobile homes.

Visit a house or apartment being built and/or finished.

Appendix K

- **The Community and Community Helpers**

  Name and describe: parks, highways, streets, roads, kinds of buildings and businesses, clothing store, movies, hardware store, florist, nursery, pet store, shoe store, beauty shop, barber shop.

  Describe what takes place inside these places.

  Name objects from stores that can be worn on specific parts of body: ring—finger, bracelet—wrist, hat—head, shoe—foot.

  Name and describe community helpers, their places of work, activities and services such as, policeman, fireman, postman, doctor, nurse, dentist, milkman, baker, mayor, saleslady, secretary.

  Have community helpers visit children's program to demonstrate what they do.

- **Weather**

  Identify different types of precipitation: rain, snow, sleet, hail.

  Describe lightning and thunder and their function.

  Talk about migration and hibernation.

  Describe wind.

  Demonstrate water being repelled and absorbed in sponges and cloth versus plastic and raincoats and rainboots.

  Talk about today's weather.

- **Seasons**

  Name the seasons.

  Describe characteristics of each.

  Name what people wear during different seasons.

  Discuss activities during different seasons.

  Describe family customs for different holidays.

  Discuss present season.

- **Transportation**

  Name and illustrate different kinds of transportation.

  Match boat with water, plane with air, car with street, train with track.

  Describe what each type of vehicle carries and how it feels to ride in one.

  Experiment with wheels and gears.

  Experiment with things that sink and things that float.

- **Space Travel**

  Name space vehicles: module, capsule, rocket.

  Identify space clothing.

  Taste and name space foods.

  Define and name some astronauts.

  Describe splashdown including those people and various types of transportation that helps.

- **Safety**

  Describe times and places where we practice safety precautions, such as holding an adult's hand when crossing street; looking both ways before crossing street; fastening seat belts and reminding mom or dad to fasten theirs when driving in a car; being sure the other person knows when you are going to get off the see-saw; going to an adult for help when someone is hurt; calling parent or adult when you want to plug something into an electrical outlet; calling parent or adult when you need to light a match.

- **Machines**

  Identify machines for the home (electrical appliances—small and large).

  Describe how they work and how we use such things as a refrigerator, sewing machine, mixer, car.

  Discuss and illustrate machines for industry, such as crane, trucks, threshing machine, bottling machine, cement mixer.

  Demonstrate use of such small machines as a pencil sharpener, stapler, hole puncher, paper dispenser, slide projecter.

Appendix K

- **Position and Location**

    Demonstrate and name such concepts as: in—on—off, over—under, behind—in front of, beside—behind, around—through, inside—outside, next to—near and far.

- **Music and Rhythms**

    Sing three different songs with gusto.
    Name two favorite records used in the program.
    Describe or imitate various sounds.
    Describe and respond to how different kinds of music makes you feel.
    Participate in musical activities.
    Listen to records, tape recordings, other listening devices.

- **Sound**

    Identify sounds of everyday life.
    Identify direction of sound.
    Differentiate between loud and soft.
    Recognize various familiar sounds.
    Make simple musical instruments.

- **Food**

    Name and illustrate various kinds of food.
    Taste various kinds of food.
    Differentiate between sweet and sour, salty and bitter, hot and cold.
    Name different parts of the plant we eat such as corn—seed; cauliflower—flower; bulb—carrot and sweet potato.
    Verbalize differences in things that look alike and taste different.

- **Sports**

    Name kinds of sports such as football, baseball, basketball, bowling, skiing, skating, wrestling.
    Describe summer sports—swimming, golfing—and winter sports—skiing, hockey, ice skating.
    Name three pieces of equipment used in each: football, baseball, basketball.

APPENDIX L
Steps for Licensing

The steps for licensing are reprinted from the following source: *State and Local Day Care Licensing Requirements,* Prepared by Social and Administrative Services and Systems Association in conjunction with Consulting Services Corporation, For The Office of Child Development, Department of Health, Education, and Welfare, Washington, D.C., 1971.

SEQUENTIAL FLOW OF LICENSING PROCEDURES—FAMILY DAY CARE HOMES

1. The applicant contacts the licensing agency either in person or by telephone. The area licensing worker is assigned to investigate the request and makes an appointment to visit the home. At the same time, the licensing worker provides review materials which usually consist of an application form, a copy of standards and requirements, and resource materials.
2. The licensing worker visits the home for consultation and screening. The licensing worker normally questions the applicant's motives for wanting a family day care home.
3. The applicant is instructed to check with local zoning for a permit. Often an applicant will need to obtain a "special" or "conditional use" permit for zoning, which will usually require a public hearing.
4. The applicant submits floor and building plans to the licensing worker and the local building.
5. If required, the applicant obtains a building inspection in order to meet local building, electrical, and plumbing requirements.
6. Where required, the licensing worker requests a fire safety inspection from the local fire department.
7. Where required, the licensing worker requests a health and sanitation inspection from the local health authorities. The applicant must obtain a water supply approval for a private system.
8. The applicant submits a list of three character references. The agency requests the persons named as references to complete and return the reference forms.
9. The applicant submits physical examination certificates from an M.D. for all staff or members of the household, including TB X-ray reports.
10. The applicant submits formal application to the state licensing agency and pays a fee, if applicable. The application form includes or requires submittal of the following information:
    a. Staff qualification and job descriptions, age, education, and training.
    b. Names of all household members.
    c. Program plans and daily schedules.
    d. Verification of financial stability.
    e. A description of the facility and equipment.
    f. Proof that local requirements have been met.
11. The licensing worker makes a visit to evaluate the home and lists any discrepancies and remarks in his report, which is sent to the state licensing agency headquarters.
12. The applicant makes any necessary corrections and changes to meet any final requirements.

Appendix L

13. After all forms and reports have been submitted to the state licensing agency headquarters and they meet the department's regulations and requirements, the department issues a license to the applicant.
14. A provisional license will be issued when discrepancies exist, with a full license issued only when all discrepancies are corrected.

NOTE: The licensing flow may end here if a full license is issued. However, if the license is provisional, the home is further observed, and consultations are given generally for not longer than six months, during which period a full license may be issued after requirements have been met and the licensing agency is satisfied with the facility's operation.

SEQUENTIAL FLOW FOR RENEWAL OF DAY CARE HOME LICENSE

1. The licensing agency notifies the facility its license will expire within a short period, and encloses a renewal application.
2. The operator fills out the application and sends it back with a renewal fee if required.
3. The licensing worker visits and evaluates the facility, and requests an inspection by either the health or fire departments if necessary.
4. After all materials required by the licensing agency, including any fire or health clearances, have been received and approved, the applicant is issued a new license.

The preceding steps in the licensing process exclude the many clerical steps and professional judgments made by the state licensing agency in the processing of an application.

SEQUENTIAL FLOW OF LICENSING PROCEDURES—DAY CARE CENTERS

1. The applicant contacts the state licensing agency by phone or by letter for information concerning a license to operate a day care center.
2. The applicant is placed in contact with an area licensing worker. The licensing worker determines if the applicant is experienced in day care by discussing the applicant's potential program and preliminary plans for the facility during the initial conversation.
3. Review materials are sent to the applicant from the licensing agency. These usually consist of an application form and a copy of standards and requirements.
4. The applicant contacts the licensing worker and an appointment is made to visit the site of the proposed day care center.
5. The licensing worker makes an evaluation of the facility and:

   a. Suggests that the applicant contact the local zoning and building departments. Often the applicant will need to obtain a "special" or "conditional use" permit for zoning which usually will require a public hearing. The requirements of the building department will vary, depending on whether a facility is new or remodeled.

   b. The licensing worker discusses available funds as well as the applicant's motives for opening a center.

   c. The licensing worker discusses state day care licensing regulations.

6. The applicant submits floor and building plans for a new or remodeled facility to the licensing agency as well as to health, fire, zoning, and building departments for approval.

Appendix L

7. The applicant obtains a building permit for a new or remodeled center.
8. The applicant obtains clearances after the local and/or state building, health, and fire department inspections are accomplished. The requests for inspections are made by the licensing agency and/or the applicant, depending on the licensing agency's procedures.
9. During the time of planning and construction, there are frequent consultations between the licensing worker and the applicant.
10. The licensing worker visits the completed facility to ascertain readiness and check equipment.
11. The application and accompanying material is submitted to the state licensing agency by the applicant. For a new center, materials filed with initial application are:
    a. A statement detailing the ownership and organization of the center, together with other information showing who is responsible for policy-making, administration, and operation.
    b. A copy of the articles of incorporation if the center is incorporated.
    c. A copy of the constitution and by-laws, if any.
    d. A list of board members and committees, if any.
    e. A list of qualifications of the staff. (A form is provided by the department of welfare.)
    f. Physical examination certificates from an M.D. for all staff members, including TB X-ray reports.
    g. References of the director or operator.
    h. Samples of all forms used by the center.
    i. Verification of financial stability.
    j. Insurance (fire, liability, transportation).
    k. Proposed budget.
    l. A draft of policies and procedures.
    m. Program plans and daily schedules.
    n. A description of the facilities and equipment.
    o. A typical weekly menu.
    p. Proof that local requirements have been met.
12. The licensing worker visits the center for final inspection and prepares recommendations which are sent to the licensing agency headquarters.
13. The licensing agency reviews recommendations and supporting documents. If approved, a license is issued to the applicant.
14. The applicant makes any necessary corrections and changes to meet final requirements of the state licensing agency.
15. Verification of the new license is sent to the center, the licensing worker, the local fire department and local health department.
16. Control cards are made to cross-reference the facility with all interested departments.

NOTE: The licensing flow may end here if a full license is issued. A provisional license will be issued when discrepancies exist, with a full license issued only when all discrepancies are corrected. If the license is provisional, the center is further observed and consultations are given generally for not longer than six months, during which period a full license may be issued after requirements have been met and the licensing agency is satisfied with the facility.

Appendix L

SEQUENTIAL FLOW FOR RENEWAL OF DAY CARE CENTER LICENSE

1. The licensing agency notifies the facility its license will expire within a short period, and encloses a renewal application.
2. The operator fills out the application and sends it back with a renewal fee, if required.
3. The licensing agency notifies the fire and health departments, requesting inspection of the facility for a renewal license.
4. The licensing worker visits and evaluates the facility.
5. After all materials required by the licensing agency, including fire or health clearances, have been approved, the applicant is issued a new license.

NOTE: If the number of children utilizing a facility increases beyond the licensed capacity, application for a new license is required. The licensing worker visits the facility to see that regulations related to the changes are complied with in order for a new license to be issued.

The preceding steps in the licensing process exclude the many clerical steps and procedures utilized by the state licensing agency in the processing of an application.

APPENDIX M
Sample Children's Records

All forms except for "Recruitment of Children" are from the following source: *How to Operate Your Day Care Program,* Ryan Jones Associates, Inc., 906 Penn Avenue, Wyomissing, Pa. 19610, 1970.

REQUEST FOR SERVICE FORM

RECRUITMENT OF CHILDREN

Date _____

1. Child's Name

_____
    Last   First   Middle

2. Address   Telephone Number

_____

3. Date of Birth _____ / _____ / _____ Age Last Birthday _____ Sex _____
4.   Name of Parents or Person Requesting Service:

_____
    Last   First   Middle Initial

5. Address   Telephone Number

_____

6. Reasons Child Care is Needed _____

_____

7. Hours of Care Requested: From _____ To _____

8. Special Needs of Child (if any) _____

_____

_____   _____
Name of Person Receiving Request   Date

_____   _____
Date of Action or Request   Authorization Signature

Appendix M

NUMBER OF CHILDREN ENROLLED IN THE DAY CARE PROGRAM

Less Than 3 Years of Age		3 to 4 Years of Age		4 to 5 Years of Age		5 to 6 Years of Age		Over 6 Years of Age		Total Enrolled For Month: ___	
M	F	M	F	M	F	M	F	M	F	M	F

EMERGENCY INFORMATION RECORD

Child's Name _____

Parent's Name _____ Phone: Home _____

Address _____ Business _____

_____
Name of Person to Contact if Parents are Unavailable

Address _____ Phone _____

_____ Phone _____
Name of Family Physician

_____
Name of Hospital Where Child is Taken in Event of Serious Injury

_____
Hospital Preferred by Family

_____
Signature of Parent or Guardian

544

CENTER _____   DATE _____

INFANT AND PRESCHOOL HEALTH RECORD

NAME LAST FIRST MIDDLE	SEX ☐ M ☐ F BIRTHDATE PHONE
ADDRESS	FATHER'S NAME LAST FIRST MIDDLE AGE
CITY STATE ZIP	MOTHER'S NAME LAST FIRST MIDDLE AGE
FATHER'S OCCUPATION	FAMILY PHYSICIAN PHONE
CHILD LIVES WITH	CHIEF CARE BY (SPECIFY) REFERRED BY

FAMILY HISTORY: NOTE: DIABETES, ALLERGIES, CONVULSIONS, RHEUMATIC FEVER, MENTAL ILLNESS, BLEEDING DISEASES OR ANEMIA, TUBERCULOSIS, SYPHILIS, ETC. GIVE DATES AND FAMILY RELATIONSHIP.

PRENATAL AND NEONATAL HISTORY / FEEDING HISTORY

PRENATAL AND NEONATAL HISTORY		FEEDING HISTORY	
MONTH PRENATAL CARE BEGAN:	NO. PRENATAL VISITS: BORN AT MO.	BREAST FED UNTIL (AGE) MOS.	BOTTLE FED FROM (AGE) WEANED AT AGE
MOTHER'S HEALTH DURING PREGNANCY		AGE SOLID FOODS BEGAN	VITAMINS
DIFFICULTIES IN LABOR AND DELIVERY		PRESENT DIET	
	BIRTH- WEIGHT LB. OZ.	IMMUNIZATIONS AND TESTS	
CONDITION OF CHILD AT BIRTH:	(NOTE CYANOSIS, CONVULSIONS, JAUNDICE, BLEEDING, INJURIES, ETC.)		

IMMUNIZATIONS AND TESTS

PRIMARY

	DATE	DATE	DATE	DATE
DPT				
DT				
POLIO (TRI-VALENT)				
MEASLES				
GERMAN MEASLES				
OTHER				

MEDICAL HISTORY (Enter Age and Type)

HANDICAPPING CONDITIONS (CONGENITAL OR ACQUIRED)	
OPERATIONS	

BOOSTERS

	DATE	DATE	DATE
DPT			
DT			
POLIO (TRI-VALENT)			
OTHER			

ALLERGY	
TONSILLITIS (FREQUENCY) OTITIS (FREQUENCY)	
ACCIDENTS	

KEEP CURRENT ON PROGRESS NOTES

SMALLPOX	DATE	RESULT	DATE	RESULT
TUBERCULIN TEST	DATE	RESULT	DATE	RESULT
	DATE	RESULT	DATE	RESULT
HEMOGLOBIN	DATE	RESULT	DATE	RESULT
P.K.U.	DATE	RESULT	DATE	RESULT

CONTAGIOUS DISEASES

DISEASES	DATE	DISEASES	DATE

REQUEST FOR IMMUNIZATION: I HEREBY REQUEST MY CHILD BE GIVEN ANY OR ALL OF THE IMMUNIZATIONS, VACCINATIONS OR TESTS DEEMED NECESSARY BY THE PHYSICIAN.

DATE _____   SIGNED _____   RELATIONSHIP _____

545

DEVELOPMENT AND ANTICIPATORY GUIDANCE

EXPECTED AGE	DEVELOPMENT	AGE ATTAINED	ANTICIPATORY GUIDANCE
1 THRU 3 MONTHS	STRONG GRASP REFLEX		CONSISTENCY IN LOVE AND CARE
	HOLDS CHIN UP FROM PRONE POSITION		CHARACTERISTICS—SPITTING UP, SNEEZING,
	EYES FOLLOW MOVING OBJECTS		CRYING, INDIVIDUAL DIFFERENCES
	HOLDS HEAD ERECT		FIRST SOLID FOODS
4 THRU 8 MONTHS	REACHES FOR A RATTLE		SAFETY—FALLING, PUTTING OBJECTS IN MOUTH
	FIRST TOOTH ERUPTS		EARLY WEIGHT BEARING (BOW-LEGS)
	ROLLS OVER		TEETHING
	SITS ALONE		PERIODS OF STRANGENESS
9 THRU 12 MONTHS	CREEPS AND PULLS SELF TO FEET		CHOPPED FOODS, WEANED TO CUP, SELF-FEEDING
	WALKS WITH SUPPORT		DECREASED APPETITE, SLOWER WEIGHT GAIN
	PLAYS "PAT-A-CAKE"		SLEEPING PROBLEMS
13 THRU 18 MONTHS	ATTEMPTS SELF-FEEDING		DECREASED NAP PERIODS
	STANDS AND WALKS ALONE		SAFETY—POISONS, PICA (PAINT), BURNS, FALLS
	NAMES OBJECTS—FAMILIAR PICTURES		PHYSIOLOGICAL ANOREXIA
	ANTERIOR FONTANEL CLOSES		PHYSICAL AND VERBAL RESTRAINT
	HURLS OBJECTS IN PLAY OR ANGER		BOWEL AND BLADDER CONTROL
18 THRU 24 MONTHS	USES SHORT SENTENCES		NEGATIVISM, ENCOURAGE INDEPENDENCE
	OBEYS SIMPLE COMMANDS		HELP WITH SPEECH (TEMPORARY STAMMERING)
	CLIMBS ON FURNITURE—JUMPS		USE OF TOOTHBRUSH
	DEVELOPS BOWEL CONTROL		SAFETY—ELECTRIC OUTLETS, STOVES, FIRE
2ND AND 3RD YEARS	16-20 TEETH ERUPTED		ADULT IMITATION
	ASKS MANY QUESTIONS (WHY STAGE)		BEDTIME RITUALS AND FEARS
	DAY AND NIGHT BLADDER CONTROL		INTRODUCTION TO DENTIST
	DRESSES SELF WITH HELP		CONFORMITY AND COOPERATIVE PLAY
4TH AND 5TH YEARS	KNOWS FULL NAME AND ADDRESS		EMOTIONAL STORMS
	WALKS DOWNSTAIRS ALTERNATING FEET		NEED FOR PARENTAL LOVE AND UNDERSTANDING
	RUNS ERRANDS IN NEIGHBORHOOD		SAFETY—TRAFFIC, DOG BITES
	TIES SHOE LACES		SCHOOL READINESS

PHYSICAL EXAMINATION: RECORD INITIAL EXAMINATION AND MONTHLY 1ST 6 MONTHS; BIMONTHLY 2ND 6 MONTHS; EVERY 3 MONTHS 2ND YEAR; EVERY 6 MONTHS 2-6 YEARS

DATE	AGE IN MONTHS	HEIGHT	WEIGHT	HEAD CIRC.	GENERAL APPEARANCE	SKIN	GLANDS	EYES	EARS	MOUTH TEETH	NASO-PHARYNX	HEART	CHEST LUNGS	ABDOMEN	GENITALIA	SKELETAL	FEET	NEURO-LOGICAL

Code: X-needs attention   R-Referred for care

PHYSICAL FINDINGS AND RECOMMENDATIONS

DATE	INCLUDE ABNORMAL FINDINGS, DIET, VITAMINS (KIND AND AMOUNT), PROBLEMS IN THE FAMILY, COUNSELING, GUIDANCE AND SEVERE REACTION TO ANY IMMUNIZATION PROCEDURE.	M.D. OR R.N.

Appendix M

INTAKE MEDICAL HISTORY: NUMBER OF KNOWN, MAJOR MEDICAL CONDITIONS

MEDICAL CONDITION:	Total For Mo.	Total For Yr.	MEDICAL CONDITION:	Total For Mo.	Total For Yr.	MEDICAL CONDITION:	Total For Mo.	Total For Yr.
Eye			Gastrointestinal			Neurological		
ENT			Genitourinary			Hematological		
Respiratory			Orthopedic			Emotional		
Cardiac			Skin			Other		

Total: _____

CHILD'S DENTAL RECORD

Name of Child　　Last　　First　　Middle	Age Nearest Birthday	
Home Address		Sex　M　F

The Above Information Should Be Filled In Before The Examination Or Screening

Date	Recommendations For Preventive Services (Complete Referral Record Below)					
	Prophylaxis	Topical F Application	Toothbrush Instruction	Nutrition Counseling	Space Maintainer	Remarks

Appendix M

CHILD'S DENTAL RECORD

Patient Referral Record

Date	Referred By	Referred To	Remarks on Follow-Up

MEDICAL/DENTAL EXAMINATIONS

	MEDICAL/DENTAL Care Received From:	Funded by the Child Care Program — Total for Month	Funded by the Child Care Program — Total for Year	Not Funded by the Child Care Program — Total for Month	Not Funded by the Child Care Program — Total for Year
Medical	Child Care Program Physician				
Medical	Child's Family Physician				
Medical	Public Clinic — Hospital				
Medical	Public Clinic — Health Dept.				
Medical	Other (specify)				
Dental	Child Care Program Dentist				
Dental	Child's Family Dentist				
Dental	Public Clinic				
Dental	Other (specify)				

549

Appendix M

MEDICAL/DENTAL EXAMINATIONS

DEFECT:	Referred		Referral Completed	
	Total for Month	Total for Year	Total for Month	Total for Year
EYE				
ENT				
RESPIRATORY				
CARDIAC				
GASTROINTESTINAL				
GENITOURINARY				
ORTHOPEDIC				
SKIN				
NEUROLOGICAL				
HEMATOLOGICAL				
EMOTIONAL				
DENTAL				
OTHER				

IMMUNIZATION RECORD

Completed Immunization Series Prior To Enrollment:						Total: Month	Total: Year
Smallpox	DPT	Polio	Measles	Rubella	Mumps		
Completed Immunization Series During The Month:							
Smallpox	DPT	Polio	Measles	Rubella	Mumps		

Appendix M

CUMULATIVE (Monthly-Yearly) STATISTICAL REPORT

	CHILDREN:	Total for Month	Total for Year
MEDICAL:	found to be normal		
	found to have defects		
	found to have conditions already under treatment		
	found to have conditions not amenable to Rx & therefore not referred		
	referred to a source of medical care for further services		
DENTAL:	screened and classified by a dental hygienist		
	dental cleaning		
	dental prophylaxis: Topical Fluoride		
	receiving corrective dental services funded by the program		
	receiving dental prophylaxis: Oral Fluoride		

SCREENING EXAMINATIONS

SCREENING TEST	Screened		Failed		Referred		Referral Completed	
	Total For Mo.	Total For Yr.	Total For Mo.	Total For Yr.	Total For Mo.	Total For Yr.	Total For Mo.	Total For Yr.
Physical Growth Assessment								
Vision								
Hearing								
Tuberculin								
Anemia								
Urinalysis								
Speech								
Other—Identify								

551

APPENDIX N

Interview Sheet

INTERVIEW SHEET FOR A CHILDREN'S CENTER

Name of Interviewer _____ Date _____

Name of Center _____

Address _____

Type of Program:
- _____ Day Care Center
- _____ Family Day Care Home
- _____ Nursery School
- _____ Preschool
- _____ Head Start
- _____ Other (Name)

Location:
- _____ Rural
- _____ City
- _____ Small Town

Type of Setting:
- _____ Custom Built Center
- _____ School Building
- _____ Converted House
- _____ Residence

Length of Program:
    Time: _____ to _____
    Days per week: M T W Th F S S

Number of Children _____

Number of Square Feet per Child: _____ indoors _____ outdoors

Age Range of Children: _____ to _____

Number of Adults on Staff _____

Positions include:
- _____ Director
- _____ Teacher
- _____ Teacher Assistant
- _____ Volunteer
- _____ Aide
- _____ Cook
- _____ Custodian
- _____ Other

Does the center serve a cross section of cultural groups?

Is the center licensed?

What areas of child development are emphasized?

Do parents participate in the program? How?

Do staff members have special training for working with children? (Give examples)

How long has the center been operating?

INDEX

A

Abdominal pain, first aid for, 201
Accidents
  general discussion of, 177-179
  prevention of, 179-191
  reports of, 195, 196
  with poisons, 182-186
Activities for children
  areas for, 405-409
  general discussion of, 416-419
  in programs, 402, 403
  skill development, 440-481
  themes for, 535-538
  types of, 419-437
Acuity, 135
Adler, Alfred, 98
Affection, 104-107
Age
  chronological, 48
  factor in pregnancy, 28, 29
  in relationship to child's development, 48, 49, 56
Aide, in child care, 18, 19
Ambidextrous, 129, 130
American Medical Association, 182
Anger, expressing, 282, 293, 294
Animal bites, first aid for, 200
Anxiety of children in hospital, 164, 165
Appetite, 206, 207
Application, job, 304-310, 338
Art
  as activity for children, 420-424
  supplies, how to make, 507-509
Artificial insemination, 29
Artificial respiration, 202
Aspirin, 182, 183
Attention, as goal of misbehavior, 255, 256
Autoharp, 429, 431

B

Baby. *See* Infant
Baby-sitting, 303
Balance beam, 142, 143
Ball throwing and catching, 134
Bank Street model child care program, 378, 379
Bathing of infants, 238-241

Behavior
  definition of, 45
  individual, 98, 99
  influences on, 252, 253
  learning patterns in, 258-262, 272, 273
  responsible, general discussion of, 266-277
  types of, 250, 251
  understanding of, 253-258
Behavior analysis model child care program, 380
Binet, Alfred, 75
Birth
  defects, 25-29, 49-51
  premature, 29
  weight, 28
Bites, first aid for, 200, 201
Bleeding, first aid for, 198
Blocks, as toys, 134, 426, 427
Books for children
  bibliography of, 521-532
  selection of, 431-433
Bottles for feeding infants, 233-236
Bowel movement, in illness, 161
Bread, in nutrition, 212
Breast feeding, 233, 234
Broken bones and dislocations, first aid for, 197, 198
Bronfenbrenner, Dr. Urie, 32
Bruises, first aid for, 198
Bruner, Jerome S., 81, 82
Budgets for child care center, 339-344
Burns, first aid for, 198
Burping of infants, 236

C

Calories, 215
Carbohydrates, 211, 213, 215
Careers in child care, 18-21, 302-321
Carpentry, 425, 426
Car seat, 188, 189
Catering service, 361, 362
Cell
  differentiation, 28
  specialization, 30
Centimetre (cm), 61
Chamber of Commerce, 332

553

Index

Charge accounts, 350
Charts
  Absence from work request (form), 349
  Automobile restraint systems for children, 189
  Budget for child care center, 342–344
  Children's records (forms), 543–551
  Common poisonous plants/trees, 184–186
  Communicable childhood diseases, 154–157
  Discovery and instructional approach (child care programs), 372, 373
  Job application forms, 308, 309
  Menus, 484, 485
  Motivation, 260
  Motor development, 68–70
  Nutritional value of cow's milk and human milk, 232
  Organizational, flow of staff responsibility, 337
  Personnel information record (form), 346
  Petty cash record (form), 352
  Piaget's levels of representation, 90
  Prenatal development, 28
  Recommended daily dietary allowances, 214
  Requisition/purchase order (form), 351
  Resumé, 307
  Stages and ages of development, 49
  Stages of development according to Muller, 117
  Stages of personality development according to Erikson, 119
  Telephone message (form), 356
  Time sheets (forms), 347, 348
  Weight and height, birth to 6 years, 57–60
  Working mothers, 16
Chicken pox, 154
Child and Family Resource Project (CFRP), 327
Child care
  developmental activities, 138–143
  services, 16–18
  types of, 324, 325
  workers, 302–321
Child care centers, 18–20, 35
  behavior patterns in, 251, 256–262, 273
  caring for ill children in, 153, 160–163
  clothing for children in, 227, 228
  emergencies in, 195, 196
  establishment of, 331–333
  evaluation of, 330, 331
  health and medical facilities in, 158, 159
  infant's care in, 230, 235
  management of, 336–364
  pets in, 186
  planning meals and snacks for, 215–217
  programs of, 368–390
  rules of safety in, 190, 191
  safety (accident prevention) in, 179–188
  social development in, 100, 101
  types of, 324–330
  workers in, 302–321
Child development
  associate (CDA), 20
  emotional, 104–111
  general discussion of, 42–46
  individual differences in, 47, 48
  influences on, 49–51
  intellectual, 74–91
  motor, 62–71
  physical, 54–61
  socialization in, 94–102
  specialist, 19
  stages of, 48, 49
  tasks and skills, 114–144
Child-parent relationships, 12–14, 31–34, 42–44
Child Protection and Toy Safety Act, 181
Children's Hospital Medical Center (Boston), 177, 178
Child-resistant packaging, 183
Choking, first aid for, 201
Chronological age, 48
Clothing
  children's, 220–228
  infant's, 241–244
Cognitive curriculum model child care program, 379, 380
Cognitive development, 81, 82
Cold, common, 154
Collage, 420, 424
Communication
  developing skills of, 125–127
  with children, 266–268
Comprehensive child care, 325
Concept formation, 417
Conjunctivitis. See Pinkeye

Index

Conscience, development of a, 127
Conservation, concept of, 85
Contagious, 152
Convulsions, 163
Cook, cook aide, in child care, 19
Cook, Dr. Robert, 327
Coordination, motor, 62-66
Counseling, genetic, 26
Crafts, 424, 425
Credentials, job, 305
Crises in family, 35
Cup feeding, 234
Curriculum, in child care programs, 374, 375, 392-394
Custodial child care, 324
Cutaneous feeling, 79
Cuts, first aid for, 198
Cystic fibrosis, 26

D

Day care center, 325, 326. See also Child care center
Developmental
   child care, 325, 327
   disorders and problems, 50, 54, 55
   tasks and skills, 114-144
Development, stages of, according to Piaget, 82-86
Diaper, 241-243
   rash, 243
   service, 362, 363
Dietitian, 19
Dinkmeyer, Dr. Don, 95
Diphtheria, 151, 154
Director of child care program, 18
Disability, as goal of misbehavior, 257, 258
Disadvantaged children, 387
Discipline, 280-297
Discovery approach in child care programs, 368-371, 373, 375
Diseases, 150-157
Down's Syndrome, 29
DPT, immunization injection, 151, 152
Drawing, 132, 133, 423
Dreikurs, Dr. Rudolph, 255
Dressing, skill development in young children, 130, 131
Drugs, effects on pregnancy, 27, 28

Dysentery, 154

E

Ear
   first aid for, 199
   parts of, 79, 80
Early childhood specialists, 19, 20
Eating habits, 206-208, 237, 238
Educational requirements in child care work, 19, 20
Egocentricity, 84
Electrical shock, first aid for, 201, 202
Embryo, embryonic stage, 30
Emergencies, handling of, 194-203
Emotional development, 104-111
Encephalitis, 152
Encouragement for children, 270, 271
Englemann-Becker model child care program (University of Oregon), 378
Equipment for child care programs, 403-405, 412, 413, 500-506
Erikson, Erik, 118, 119
Exceptional behavior, 250, 251
Eye
   first aid for, 199
   safety, 189, 190
   -to-hand coordination, 131-133, 448, 449, 457, 458

F

Fainting, first aid for, 202
Fallopian tube, 29, 30
Family
   day care homes, 326
   mobility, 14
   size, 35
   social experiences, 99, 100
Fats, in nutrition, 211, 213, 215
FDA. See U.S. Food and Drug Administration
Feeding infants, 231-237
Feeling, as a sense, 79, 80
Fertilization of egg in human, 29, 30
Fetus, 28, 30, 62
Fine (small) muscle control, 65
Fire-resistant fabrics, 223
Fireworks, 186
First aid
   courses, 195
   kit, 203

555

Index

procedures, 197-202
Fleas, treatment if infected by, 201
Florida parent education model child care program, 379
Food
  groups, four basic, 211, 212
  "jags," 207, 208
  service at child care center, 358-362
Formula for feeding infants, 234, 235
Framework of operating program, 368, 371, 377, 395
Frostbite, first aid for, 201
Fruit, in nutrition, 211, 212

G

Games, 424, 425
Gamma globulin, 154, 155
Genetics, 26, 51
Genotype disorder, 51
German measles. See Rubella
Gesell, Dr. Arnold, 134
Ginott, Dr. Haim, 96, 97, 271, 294, 296
Glandular function, 49, 50
Goals of child care program, 384-390
Grains, in nutrition, 212
Gram (g), 61
Grooming, 131
Gross (large) muscle control, 65
Group
  day care home, 326
  interaction, 100
Growth, 45, 55, 56
Gustatory receptor (in mouth), 80

H

Handedness, 129, 130
Handwriting, 132, 133
Harvard Center for Cognitive Studies, 81
Havighurst, Robert J., 116
Head Start program, 16, 17, 19, 20, 303, 327, 328, 357
Health care
  general discussion of, 150-160
  in illness, 160-167
  standards of child care center, 159, 160
Hearing abilities, 79
Height, at various ages, 56-61
Hemophilia, 26
Hepatitis, 154

Heredity, 26, 51
Home
  for child care, 326
  influence on child, 31-35
  Start program, 328, 329
Hospitalization, preparing children for, 164-167
Human bites, first aid for, 201

I

Identification, in behavior, 258, 259
Illness occurring in child care center, 160-163
Imagination, 426, 427
Imitation, in behavior, 258, 272, 273
Immunization, 151, 152
Impetigo, 155
Incubation period (I.P.) of diseases, 154-157
Industrial revolution, 14
Infant
  bathing, 238-241
  caring for, 230, 244, 245
  clothing for, 241-244
  communication skills of, 125
  expression of affection by, 106
  feeding of, 231-237
  learning by senses, 135, 136
  safety precautions for, 173, 174, 244
  skill development activities for, 441-446
  toilet training of, 124, 125
  weaning and self-feeding of, 121, 122
Infantile paralysis. See Polio
Influenza, 155
Insect bites, first aid for, 200
In-service training for child care worker, 310, 311
Insight, 261, 273
Instructional model program in child care, 368-370, 372
Insurance for child care center, 332
Integrated motor movements, 64
Intelligence
  development of, 74-91
  quotient (IQ), 75, 76
  tests, 75, 76
Internal Revenue Service, 352
Interview, job, 306, 310, 338, 552
Intrauterine environment, 27

J

"Jag," food, 207, 208
Job training for child care worker, 310, 311

Index

K

Kilogram (kg), 61
Kindergarten, 326, 327
Kindergartner, as an age
  play activities of, 137
  safety precautions for, 177
  skill development activities for, 469-481
  stories for, 433
Kinesthetic feeling, 79, 80
Kitchen equipment in children's play, 435, 436

L

Labyrinthine receptors (in ear), 80
Lag in learning, 387
Language
  skill development by
    infant, 443
    kindergartener, 474-476
    romper, 459-461
    toddler, 449-451
Laterality, 133
Laundry service at child care center, 362, 363
Learning
  definition of, 46
  developmental tasks and skills, 114, 115
  disability, 74
  mastery of skills, 134-138
  through clothing and dressing skills, 225-227
  to eat, 237, 238
Left-handed, 129, 130
Lice, first aid treatment for, 201. *See also* Pediculosis
Licensing for child care facilities, 332, 333, 539-542
Lies, telling of, 294, 295
Locomotor behavior, 83
Love, general discussion of, 108-110

M

Malnutrition, 27, 28, 210, 211
Management of child care center, 336-364
Mass, in metric measurement, 61
Matches, hazards of playing with, 181, 182
Maturation, 45
Meals, mealtime, 208, 209, 215, 216
Mean, in measurement, 56
Measles, 28, 151, 152, 155, 156
Meat, as food group, 212
Medical records, 151, 158, 160
Medicine, proper storage of, 183
Meningitis, 155
Men's role in child care, 21, 22, 128
Mental age, 48
Menus, 358-360, 484, 485
Metric measurement, 61
Milk, 211, 231, 232
Millimetre (mm), 61
Minerals, in nutrition, 211, 213
Misbehavior, 255-258, 274, 275
Miscarriage, 30
Mongolism, 29
Mother
  care of in pregnancy, 27-29
  working, 14-16
Motivation, in behavior, 253, 260
Motor development, 62-71, 134
Muller, Philippe, 117, 118
Mumps, 155
Muscle, control of, 64, 65
Music, musical instruments, in children's activity, 429-431, 510-515
Mutilation anxiety, 165

N

National Highway Traffic Safety Administration, 189
National Society for the Prevention of Blindness, Inc., 189
Negative
  behavior, 250, 251, 255
  emotions, 110, 111
Nosebleed, first aid for, 198, 199
Nursery, 176, 177, 326. *See also* Child care center
Nutrition, 209-215
  of child in development, 49
  of mother in pregnancy, 27, 28
Nutritionist, 19

O

Objectives of child care program, 384-390
Olfactory nerve, 80
Open setting for children's activities, 394, 395
Outdoor equipment, 412, 413
Ovum, 29-31

Index

P

Packaging of medicine for safety, 183
Painting, 422
Para-professional, in child care work, 19
Parathyroid glands, 50
Parent
   and Child Centers, 329
   -child relationship, 12-14, 31-34, 42-44
   working in child care center, 387-390
Peace Corps, 19
Pediculosis (lice), 153, 156
Permissiveness, 281
Personality development, 119
Personnel of child care center
   policies, 336-339
   records, 345-347
Pertussis. *See* Whooping cough
Pets, 186, 187
Philosophy of child care, 317-321
Physical
   development, 54-61
   fitness, 63, 64
   punishment, 293, 294
Piaget, Jean, 82
   theories on
      levels of representation, 89-91
      relational concepts, 86-89
      stages of development, 82-86
Pinkeye (conjunctivitis), 156
Pitch (of sound), 79
Play
   as aid in learning, 136, 137
   equipment, 418, 419
Playground equipment, 180, 181
Playing house, store, as children's activity, 427-429
Poison, 182-186
   control center, 199
   first aid for, 199, 200
Polio (infantile paralysis), 151, 156
Positive behavior, 250
Positive response, 271, 272
Power, as goal of misbehavior, 256, 257
Pregnancy
   care in, 27, 28
   rubella in, 152
Prejudice, 99, 100
Premature birth, 29

Prenatal
   development, 28-31
   environment, 27
Pre-professional, in child care work, 19
Pre-service training for child care worker, 310, 311
Primary motor movement, 64
Professional
   definition of, 313
   services, 357
Programs of child care
   development and models of, 368-380
   goals and objectives of, 384-390
   teaching strategies of, 392-413
Proteins, 211-213, 215
Punishment of children, 13, 293, 294
Purchasing for child care center, 349-352

R

Rabies, 200
Recipes
   for food, 486-491, 516-520
   for art supplies, 507-509
Records kept by child care center, 344-349
Red Cross, 195
Red measles (rubeola), 151, 152, 155
Reinforcement, 259, 260, 273
Responsible behavior, 266-277
Responsive education model child care program, 379
Resumé, 305-307
Revenge, as goal of misbehavior, 257
Right-handed, 129, 130
Ringworm, 156
Rompers, as an age group
   play activities for, 137
   skill development activities for, 456-469
   stories for, 433
Room arrangement in child care programs, 405-413, 496-499
Routines, daily, 395-397, 493, 494
Rubella (German measles), 28, 151, 152, 156
Rubeola. *See* Red measles

S

Safety
   and development, 173-177
   factors of clothing, 223, 224
   general discussion of, 170-173

Index

in child's environment, 179–191
in transporting children, 353, 354
outdoor, 413
Salaries in child care centers, 338, 339
Salmonella infections, 186, 187
Sanitation in food service, 491, 492
Scabies, 157
Scarlet fever, 157
Schedules
   feeding, for infants, 232, 233, 235, 236
   in child care programs, 397–402, 495
School, as social situation, 101. See also Child care center
Science activities for children, 434–437
Scissors, mastering use of, 139–142
Scribbling, as children's activity, 132, 133, 422, 423
Sculpture, 423, 424
Secondary motor movements, 64
Seeing, as a sense, 78, 79
Self-concept (self-image), 95–98, 127
Self-control, 281, 287, 288
Self-dressing, 130, 131, 454, 455, 468, 469
Self-feeding, 121, 122, 445, 446, 455
Self-motivation, 78
Senses, development of in relation to learning, 135, 136
Sensory
   abilities, 64, 78–81
   perception, 76, 80, 135
Separation anxiety, 164
Seriation, 86, 87, 428, 463–465
Sex information for children, 127–129
Shampooing infants, 241
Shock, first aid for, 202
Shoes, 224, 225
Sibling relationships, 34, 50, 51, 105, 106
Sickle cell anemia, 26
Sick room in child care center, 160
Small Business Association (SBA), 332
Smallpox vaccination, 152
Smell, as a sense, 80
Smocks, 227
"Smother love," 106
Snacks, 216, 217
Snake bites, first aid for, 200, 201
Socialization, 35, 94–102, 386
Social Security, 341, 358

Sore throat, 157
Spatial relations, 87–89, 461–463
Speech, development of, 125–127
Splinters, first aid for, 199
Spodek, Dr. Bernard, 371
Standards
   health and safety, 159, 160
   required to license, 333
Stanford-Binet intelligence scale, 75
Stealing, 296
Sterilizing infant's formula, 234
Storage and distribution in child care center, 352, 353
Stories, story time, 431–434
Street and vehicle safety, 187–189
Streptococcal infections, 157
Swallowed objects, first aid for, 201

T

Taste, as a sense, 80, 81
Tay-Sachs disease, 26
Teacher, teacher's assistant, 18
Teaching
   strategies of, in child care programs, 392–413
   team approach in, 328
Teeth, 131, 132
Temperature, methods of taking, 161, 162
Tetanus, 151
   booster shot, 200
Thumb sucking, 236, 237
Thyroid glands, 50
Thyroxin, 50
Timbre (of sound), 79
Time, developing concepts of, 477, 478
Toddlers, as age group,
   play activities for, 137
   safety precautions for, 174, 175
   skill development activities for, 446–455
   stories for, 433
Toilet training, 124, 125
Toxoplasmosis, 28
Toys, 181, 426, 427
Training, job, for child care worker, 310, 311
Transportation to child care center, 353, 354
Tuberculosis (TB), 152, 153, 157
Tucson Early Education Model (TEEM) child care program, 378

Index

U

Unconsciousness, first aid for, 202
"Universal Antidote," 200
U.S. Department of Health, Education, and Welfare, Office of Child Development, 20, 327, 328
U.S. Department of Labor, Bureau of Labor Statistics, 15, 16
U.S. Food and Drug Administration (FDA)
  Bureau of Product Safety, 180, 181
  packaging safety, 183
  Toy Review Committee, 181
Uterus, 27, 29, 30

V

Vaccines, 152
Vegetables, in nutrition, 211, 212
Vendor, 350, 351, 363
VISTA, 19
Visual abilities, 78, 79
Vitamins, 211–214, 232
Volume (of sound), 79
Volunteer work in child care, 20, 21

W

Wages in child care center, 20, 338, 339
Walking, 122–124
Weaning, 121
Weight, at various ages, 57–61
Whooping cough (pertussis), 151, 157
Woodworking, 425, 426
Working mothers, 14–16

X, Y, Z

Zygote, 29, 30